Local and Family History in South Carolina: A Bibliography

by

Richard N. Côté

Charleston, South Carolina:
The South Carolina Historical Society
1981

This volume was compiled and printed with partial funding from the South Carolina Committee for the Humanities, an agent for the National Endowment for the Humanities.

300 copies printed for free distribution to South Carolina libraries, historical and genealogical societies by the South Carolina Historical Society.

Additional copies may be purchased from: Southern Historical Press, P.O. Box 738, Easley, S.C. 29640.

ISBN: 0-89308-200-7

TABLE OF CONTENTS

INTRODUCTION AND USE

In the Spring of 1980, the South Carolina Historical Society sponsored a project entitled "Genealogy, Community and Identity: Finding Local Roots", which was partially funded through a grant from the South Carolina Committee for the Humanities, an agent of the National Endowment for the Humanities. The project was designed to make South Carolinians more aware of their local and family history through a series of ten regional conferences, a television program, and the compilation and publication of a "...comprehensive guide to the large masses of little-known local and family history resources in major and local libraries, archives, and society collections, most of which have never been described...". This volume is that guide.

This bibliography was compiled from the holdings reported by over eighty South Carolina libraries, archives, historical and genealogical societies, as an aid to researchers interested in local and family history in South Carolina. It is divided into thirteen subject sections, a section of appendices, an addenda section, and an index to proper names. It covers collections of material in published, typed and mimeographed form, and some collections of manuscript church and other records. It does not attempt either to be a union list or to deal with the vast quantity of manuscript and primary source records, many of which are described in a number of published manuscript guides.

Materials listed here are available for reference use at the listed library, society or archive. Due to differences in researching, reporting and cataloging, much material available in various libraries and archives is not listed here. The main objectives when compiling this volume were to locate materials available in these subject areas: local history (Section 7), church history (Section 8), family history (Section 13), and compiled lists of information (Section 6). These sections comprise the body of this bibliography. The other sections were compiled from holdings reported by libraries in addition to the information which was specifically requested. As a result, these sections should not be considered comprehensive, and are presented only as a convenience to researchers.

Researchers wishing to find information on a particular family, such as the Robinson family; a particular church, such as the White Oak Baptist Church; a particular city, such as Rock Hill, South Carolina; or a particular institution, such as the Winyah Indigo Society should turn directly to the proper name index, which begins on page 420. All proper, personal, place and institutional names are indexed. Due to funding limitations, subject indexing ("Reconstruction", Afro-Americans", "Trade and Commerce") was impossible.

Researchers wishing to find information on broad subject areas, such as the Methodist Church in South Carolina, for example, should turn directly to the major section of the bibliography relating to their area of interest. In this example, it would be Section 8: Church, denominational and religious histories. The contents of each section are detailed on pages v-vi.

In most libraries and archives, the reference material does not circulate. Virtually all of the material listed in this volume is considered reference material, and much of it is also rare or scarce. Researchers wishing to obtain copies of this material will need to contact the institution holding the material to determine copying restrictions. In this volume there is no distinction made between original publications or records and copies of the publications or records, be they found in the form of photocopies (Xerox or equivalent), republications, transcripts or microform.

Many abbreviations have been used for words and phrases which occurred frequently, such as "A.M.E." for African Methodist Episcopal, "W.P.A." for Work Projects Administration, etc. In addition, a three or four letter code has been used to show the location(s) of materials which were found to be rare or scarce, i.e., held by three or fewer institutions. These abbreviations and library location codes are found on pages viii - x.

One symbol needs further explanation, however. It is the symbol "[SpC]", which designates a "Special Collection" of materials. It is used whenever material was reported which did not meet the bibliographic format, but was considered to be of value to researchers. Many libraries and archives have special files and collections of materials which fit this description. Some libraries, such as the South Carolina Historical Society and the South Caroliniana Library have well-ordered and readily available files like these which contain material from different and varied sources: correspondence, photocopies of articles, clippings, photographs and the like. Though difficult to catalog, these files frequently contain valuable information not readily available elsewhere, and have been included whenever the libraries reported them. Researchers should note that these files are seldom indexed, and few libraries will be able to tell them by mail or telephone exactly what a file contains. Personal, on-the-spot research will usually be necessary.

SECTION CONTENTS

1. Bibliographies: printed materials. Includes bibliographies of southern and South Carolina materials, lists of South Carolina imprints, collections of printed materials, library collections, library resources and reading lists.

2. Guides: manuscript collections. Lists the availability of guides to unpublished (manuscript) materials in various archives and libraries.

3. Periodicals and periodical indexes. Lists a number of quarterlies and other serials (but not newspapers) which contain significant amounts of information of use to local and family historians. Lists of the specific contents from some of the more important periodicals may be found in Section 14: Appendices.

4. Census schedules and indexes. Lists printed versions, abstracts of or guides or indexes to the federal population census schedules, and also to a number of locally compiled censuses. The federal schedules have been microfilmed by the National Archives, and may usually be obtained on inter-library loan.

5. Immigration, naturalization and passenger lists. Gives lists of persons entering South Carolina at various periods.

6. Lists of names. Consists of sources of information on, and lists of persons, places, organizations, officers, soldiers and sailors in rosters, directories, rolls, records and indexes of churches, cemeteries, organizations, military units, state records, local records and private records.

7. Local, regional and state histories. Lists histories and historical sketches of South Carolina, regions of the state, towns, villages, counties, districts, settlements, organizations, institutions, schools, businesses, societies and groups.

8. Church, denominational and religious histories. Lists histories and historical sketches of South Carolina religious bodies, such as synods, presbyteries, conferences and other religious jurisdictions; thousands of individual congregations, and church-affiliated societies and institutions. The manuscript records and registers of churches which are held by reporting libraries and archives are found in Section 6: Lists of names.

9. Published state records. Lists printed versions of the numerous state records compiled and published by the South Carolina Department of Archives and History, its predecessors, and by private organizations and individuals.

10. Indians and Afro-Americans. Lists some sources of information on the ethnic history of South Carolina and the roles played by these two groups. Many other materials in other sections of this bibliography also apply to these groups, of course.

11. Collective biography. Lists many materials containing two or more biographies. Those wishing to locate a particular biography will wish to consult the many collections of individual biographies in the various libraries.

12. Genealogy handbooks. Lists "how-to-do-it" books for those seeking information on the methods used to trace family histories.

13. Genealogies and family histories. In addition to the books, pamphlets, typescripts and mimeographed histories presented here, the section lists the family names which may be found in a number of major manuscript and typescript genealogical collections at the South Caroliniana Library, The South Carolina Historical Society and other institutions.

14. Appendices. Lists the contents of selected periodicals and also the contents of some special collections of material of interest to local and family historians, such as church records inventories, cemetery transcripts, and other information.

15. Addenda. Lists additions received after the publishing deadline, or which were not included in sections 1-14 due to time or other factors.

16. Index. Contains approximately 18,000 personal, place and institutional names, and the numbers of the pages on which they may be found.

ABBREVIATIONS AND LIBRARY LOCATION CODES

GENERAL ABBREVIATIONS & TERMS

A.A.U.W. American Association of University Women

A.F.W.B. African Free Will Baptist Church

A.M.E. African Methodist Episcopal Church

A.R.P. Associate Reformed Presbyterian Church

c. Circa, about

C.M.E. Colored Methodist Episcopal Church

Chstn Charleston, SC

Cola Columbia, SC

COMMON Item may be found in four or more libraries

D.A.R. Daughters of the American Revolution

DEALER Information found in book dealer catalog

DIST Information found in distributor's notice

EAST Listed in J.H. Easterby's Guide to the Study & Reading of SC History

G.P.O. Government Printing Office

M.E. Methodist Episcopal Church

M.E.S. Methodist Episcopal Church, South

mimeo Mimeographed

N.B.C. National Baptist Convention

nd No date listed

NP No place of publication reported

NPub No publisher reported

N.S.D.A.R National Society, Daughters of the American Revolution

P.E. Protestant Episcopal Church

PUBL Information obtained from publisher

RLB R.L. Bryan Co., Columbia

R.M.U.E. Reformed Methodist Union Episcopal Church

rp Reprinted

RPC Reprint Company, Publishers, Spartanburg

S.B.C. Southern Baptist Convention

SHP Southern Historical Press, Easley SC

SCDAR South Carolina Society, Daughters of the American Revolution

SCHM South Carolina Historical Magazine

SCH&GM South Carolina Historical & Genealogical Magazine

SCHS South Carolina Historical Society

SCMAR South Carolina Magazine of Ancestral Research

[SpC] Special collection of materials

Trans. Translation or translator

U.D.C. United Daughters of the Confederacy

UNC University of North Carolina, Chapel Hill NC

USC University of South Carolina, Columbia SC

W,E&C Walker, Evans & Cogswell Co., Charleston SC

LIBRARY LOCATION CODES

ABPL   Abbeville Public Library, Abbeville 29620
ACOL   Anderson College Library, Anderson 29621
AHJR   Allendale-Hampton-Jasper Regional Library, Allendale 29810
AICL   Aiken County Library, Aiken 29801
ANCL   Anderson County Library, Anderson 29621
BACL   Bamberg County Library, Bamberg 29003
BKCL   Berkeley County Library, Moncks Corner 29461
BRCL   Barnwell County Library, Barnwell 29812
BUCL   Beaufort County Library, Beaufort 29902
BUHH   Hilton Head Island Branch Library, Hilton Head Island 29928
BUHS   Beaufort County Historical Society, Beaufort 29902
CACL   Calhoun County Library, St. Matthews 29135
CDIO   Catholic Diocese of Charleston, Charleston 29401
CHBC   Rivers Library, Baptist College at Charleston, Charleston 29411
CHCA   City of Charleston Dept. of Archives & Records, Charleston 29401
CHCL   Charleston County Library, Charleston 29403
CHCO   Small Library, College of Charleston, Charleston 29401
CHLS   Charleston Library Society, Charleston 29401
CLBC   Columbia Bible College Library, Columbia 29230
CLCC   Edens Library, Columbia College, Columbia 29203
CLEM   Cooper Library, Clemson University, Clemson 29631

COKL   Coker College Library, Hartsville 29550
COML   Colleton County Memorial Library, Walterboro 29488
CRCL   Cherokee County Library Gaffney 29340
CSCL   Chester County Library Chester 29706
CTCL   Chesterfield County Library, Chesterfield 29709
DACL   Darlington County Library, Darlington 29532
DAHC   Darlington County Historical Commission, Court House, Darlington 29532
DHML   Hartsville Branch Library, Hartsville 29550
DICL   Dillon County Library, Latta 29565
DIDU   Dunbar Memorial Library, Dillon 29536
DOCL   Dorchester County Library, St. George 29477
DOTM   Timrod Library, Summerville 29483
EDTO   Edgefield County Library Edgefield 29824
EPDI   Episcopal Diocese of South Carolina, Charleston 29402
FACL   Fairfield County Library, Winnsboro 29180
FACM   Fairfield County Museum, Winnsboro 29180
FLCL   Florence County Library, Florence 29501
FLMC   Rogers Library, Francis Marion College, Florence 29501
FURM   Baptist Special Collections, Furman University Greenville 29613
GNCL   Greenwood County Library Greenwood SC 29646
GNLN   Lander College Library, Greenwood 29646
GRCL   Greenville County Library, Greenville 29601
GWPL   Greenwood Public Library Greenwood 29646

GSGN Greenwood Chapter, S.C.
      Genealogical Society,
      Greenwood 29646
GTML Georgetown County Memor-
      ial Library, Georgetown
HOCL Horry County Library,
      Conway 29526
HUGS Huguenot Society of S.C.
      Charleston 29401
KECA Camden Archives, Camden
      29020
KECL Kershaw County Library,
      Camden 29020
LECL Lee County Library,
      Bishopville 29010
LNCL Lancaster County Library
      Lancaster 29720
LRCL Laurens County Library,
      Laurens 29360
LTSS Lineberger Library, Lu-
      theran Theological
      Southern Seminary, Co-
      lumbia 29203
LXCL Lexington County Library
      Batesburg 29006
LXMU Lexington County Museum,
      Lexington 29072
MACL Marion County Library,
      Marion 29571
MONT Historical Foundation of
      the Presbyterian Church
      Montreat N.C. 28757
MRCL Marlboro County Library,
      Bennetsville 29512
NABL North Augusta Branch
      Library, North Augusta
      29841
NAHS North Augusta Histori-
      cal Society, North
      Augusta 29841
NWNC Wessels Library, New-
      berry College, New-
      berry 29108
NWRL Newberry-Saluda Reg-
      ional Library, New-
      berry 29108
OCCL Oconee County Library,
      Walhalla 29691
ORCC Manning Library, Claf-
      lin College, Orange-
      burg 29115

ORCL Orangeburg County Li-
      brary, Orangeburg
      29115
PICL Pickens County Library,
      Easley 29640
PIPD Pendleton District
      Historical & Recrea-
      tional Commission,
      Pendleton 29670
SCDAH S.C. Department of Ar-
      chives & History, Co-
      lumbia 29211
SCHS S. C. Historical So-
      ciety, Charleston
      29401
SCL   South Caroliniana Li-
      brary, U.S.C., Colum-
      bia 29208
SCLB S.C. State Library,
      Columbia 29201
SMCL Sumter County Library,
      Sumter 29150
SPCL Spartanburg County Li-
      brary, Spartanburg
      29304
UMBOD University Microfilms
      Books-On-Demand Ser-
      vice, Ann Arbor MI
UNCL Union County Library,
      Union 29379
USAI U.S.C.-Aiken Campus Li-
      brary, Aiken 29801
USBU U.S.C.-Beaufort Campus
      Library, Beaufort
      29902
USSA U.S.C.-Salkehatchie
      Campus, Allendale
      29810
VCOL Wilkinson Library, Vor-
      hees College, Denmark
      29042
WMCL Williamsburg County Li-
      brary, Kingstree 29556
WMTR Three Rivers Historical
      Society, Hemingway
      29554
WOFF Teszler Library, Wof-
      ford College, Spartan-
      burg 29302

WOMA	Methodist Archives, Wofford College, Spartanburg 29302	OR	Oregon
		PA	Pennsylvania
		PR	Puerto Rico
YOCL	York County Library, Rock Hill 29730	RI	Rhode Island
		SC	South Carolina
YOWC	Winthrop College Archives, Rock Hill 29733	SD	South Dakota
		TN	Tennessee
		TX	Texas
		UT	Utah
		VT	Vermont

STATE ABBREVIATIONS

		VA	Virginia
		VI	Virgin Islands
		WA	Washington
AL	Alabama	WV	West Virginia
AK	Alaska	WI	Wisconsin
AZ	Arizona	WY	Wyoming
AR	Arkansas		
CA	California		
CO	Colorado		
CT	Connecticut		
DE	Delaware		
DC	District of Columbia		
FL	Florida		
GA	Georgia		
GU	Guam		
HI	Hawaii		
ID	Idaho		
IL	Illinois		
IN	Indiana		
IA	Iowa		
KS	Kansas		
KY	Kentucky		
LA	Louisiana		
ME	Maine		
MD	Maryland		
MA	Massachusetts		
MI	Michigan		
MN	Minnesota		
MS	Mississippi		
MO	Missouri		
MT	Montana		
NE	Nebraska		
NV	Nevada		
NH	New Hampshire		
NJ	New Jersey		
NM	New Mexico		
NY	New York		
NC	North Carolina		
ND	North Dakota		
OH	Ohio		
OK	Oklahoma		

HOW THIS VOLUME WAS COMPILED

This bibliography concentrates on printed, typed or mimeographed materials which support the study of local, family and church history in South Carolina. It was designed to pay special attention to the small collections of locally produced materials in the county, historical and genealogical society libraries, as these libraries hold valuable collections of material which is not widely known outside the local areas of the libraries. In addition, the special collections of the various denominational libraries were to be included. The four main areas of this book, which are entitled "Lists of Names", "Local, Regional and State Histories", "Church, Denominational and Religious Histories", and "Genealogies and Family Histories" are the core of this volume, and have received the greatest attention.

These sections were originally to have been the entire scope of the bibliography, but it became apparent that a substantial amount of other information not originally planned for would be helpful to the local, family or church historian. It should be stressed that, except for the four sections noted above, this bibliography should not be considered comprehensive. In particular, the holdings of the South Caroliniana Library, which were used as the basis for the four main sections, were not heavily used to compile the rest of the sections, because of time and funding limitations. Researchers interested in finding materials outside the four main sections of this bibliography should make detailed searches in the South Caroliniana and other research libraries before concluding that a particular title is or is not available.

Though this bibliography was to have referred only to printed materials, the collections of church records and registers were felt to be both little known and of substantial use to local, family and church historians, and these were included for those reasons.

Each South Carolina library known to have a collection of materials in the four areas noted above was asked to make copies of their shelf list cards in these areas, and submit the copies to the editor, Richard N. Côté. This request was made in March of 1980, with a submission deadline of June 30, 1980. The extent to which the libraries were able to comply varied greatly, as the degree of their cataloging, availability of staff time and availability of photocopy facilities varied greatly. The editor undertook the gathering of information from a number of the special collections himself, and various volunteer groups and organizations assisted in making copies of the cards from other libraries where staff time was not available.

The accuracy and completeness of the main title entries varies considerably. Many of the titles are from collections which had never before been cataloged at all, and some titles are from rough lists compiled by hand by non-professional catalogers. In most cases, the libraries and societies reporting their holdings were not research libraries, and their cataloging was not precise enough to distinguish between various editions or versions of publications, or, sometimes, to completely identify the title or author. Many titles were very incomplete when received, and had to be referred back to the holding libraries for additional information. A total of about 2,700 such requests were made in all.

By June of 1980, over 19,000 card copies had been received, but it was evident that many more would be forthcoming if the original deadline was extended. This was done, and by September 30, the total number of submissions had reached 39,000. As the card copies came in, they were annotated with the library location code, cut apart, and filed alphabetically by author's name. As a great number of titles came in as handwritten lists instead of card copies, each title had to be manually carded in order to interfile it. This resulted in approximately 3,700 additional cards.

The next step was to make a master card (or annotate an existing card), containing the bibliographical information in as complete form as possible, and carrying the location codes of the libraries holding copies. As the cataloging from library to library varied greatly, it was not possible at all times to identify duplicate titles which were cataloged or identified differently. For that reason, some titles may appear twice, described in various ways.

Next, the cards were sorted into the thirteen subject catagories, and once again alphabetized. All the while, small collections were being received, and they were added to the master files as they came in. The preparation of the camera-ready typescript copy began in December of 1980, and was completed in April of 1981. The index of proper names started as a 32,000 card file, which took two months and approximately 600 man-hours to compile, alphabetize and type.

The volume was partially funded through a grant to the South Carolina Historical Society by the South Carolina Committee for the Humanities; through the donation of approximately $17,000 of time, services and facilities by South Carolina's libraries and volunteer workers, and by the donation of 1,100 hours of time and $2,500 by the editor. In all, over 110 different institutions aided in the completion of the project.

ACKNOWLEDGEMENTS

This bibliography represents the combined efforts of over 150 librarians, archivists, genealogists, historians and community volunteers from 112 organizations, who collectively donated in excess of $27,000 of their funds, facilities, time and materials to this project. The amount of information presented here is due to their unflagging help and support. The county librarians of South Carolina have been especially helpful, and the large amount of hitherto unknown information here is heavily from their collections.

The volume was made possible through partial funding by the South Carolina Committee for the Humanities, an agent of the National Endowment for the Humanities. The project, entitled "Genealogy, Community and Identity: Finding Local Roots", was sponsored by the South Carolina Historical Society, and directed by Richard N. Côté. In addition to the Committee's financial report, the Committee's staff, directed by Dr. Leland H. Cox, was particularly helpful and understanding when the project grew beyond its original size and scope.

Of all the historical collections in the state, those of the South Caroliniana Library at the University of South Carolina, Columbia, are pre-eminent. Without the active support and constructive criticism of Mr. E. L. Inabinett, Director; Mrs. Eleanor Richardson, Reference Librarian; and Dr. Alan Stokes, Manuscripts Curator, this volume would not have been possible. At the South Carolina Department of Archives and History, Mrs. Alexia Helsley gave timely assistance with information on Archives publications.

Particular thanks are due to the members of the editorial review board, which consisted of Kate W. Hood, Director, Georgetown County Memorial Library; Beverly S. Shuler, C.G.R.S., of Mt. Pleasant; Ronald Chepesiuk, Archivist, Winthrop College in Rock Hill; and Dr. Lowry P. Ware of the History Department, Erskine College in Due West. Among the many advisors on aspects of compiling and organizing the book were Marie F. Hollings, Archivist, City of Charleston Department of Archives and Records; Gene Waddell, Director, South Carolina Historical Society, Charleston; and David Moltke-Hansen and Mrs. Camille G. Alexander, also of the Society. A great deal of the monumental job of sorting the 49,000+ titles and 30,000+ index entries was done by Nancy B. Evans. Much of the checking of entries against the South Caroliniana's holdings was capably and cheerfully done by Alex Moore of the University of South Carolina. Ann C. Kruger assisted with many of the corrections to the typescript and with alphabetizing the index, and Pearl M. Baker typed much of the index.

In addition to the scores of volunteers throughout the state who helped furnish information for the body of the text, there were others who helped with the heavy load of sorting, filing and compiling the index. Special thanks are due to these volunteers: Randolph W. Berretta, Diane M. Brandes, Sally J. Côté, Wanda J. Schuster, Anna U.B. Watts and Patricia H. Williams.

The final judgements on style, policy and practice have been made by me, and I of course assume full responsibility for the results. It is my hope that this bibliography will make research life a little easier for South Carolina's local, family and church historians.

Charleston, South Carolina
May 11, 1981

Richard N. Côté

Anderson, Frank J. Carlisle-Smith pamphlet collection. Spartanburg: Wofford College Library Press, 1971. 34 p.   COMMON
Bibliographic guide to black studies: 1976. NY: The Research
Libraries of the NY Public Library, 1976. 340 p.
Brigham, Clarence S. History & bibliography of American newspapers: 1690-1820. Worcester MA: American Antiquarian Society
1947. 2 vol.   COMMON
Bristol, Roger P. Supplement to Charles Evans' American Biblio-
graphy. Charlottesville VA: Bibliographical Society of Amer-
ica, 1970-71. 2 vol.   COMMON
Brown, Julie. A checklist of SC imprints for the years 1873,
1874, 1875 & 1876. With a historical introduction. Washing-
ton DC: Catholic University of America, 1967. 65 p. SCL, SCHS
Catalogue of the library of the Rev. James Warley Miles. Chstn:
Dalcho Historical Society, 1955. 33 p.   EPDI, SCHS
Catalogue of the Old Slave Mart museum & library. Boston MA:
G. K. Hall, 1977. 2 vol.   SCL
Charleston Library Society. Catalogue of books belonging to the
Charleston Library Society. Chstn: A. E. Miller, 1826.
375 p.   COMMON
Charleston Library Society. Catalogue of the portraits, books,
pamphlets, maps & manuscripts presented to the Charleston
Library Society, May 12, 1906, by Wm. Ashmead Courtenay.
Cola: State Co., 1908. 148 p.   SCHS, CHLS
The Citadel. Memorial Military Museum. Early maps from the
collection of Paul Stevens, October, 1962. Chstn: 1962.
7 p.   SCHS
College of Charleston. Robert Scott Small Library. A research
guide to Charleston libraries. Chstn: Robert Scott Small
Library, 1979. 32 p.   COMMON
Conlan, Ann A. A preliminary checklist of imprints, Charleston,
SC, 1858-1864. With a historical introduction. Washington
DC: Catholic University of America, 1958. 179 p.   SCL, SCHS
Cumming, William P. British maps of colonial America. Chicago
IL: Newberry Library, 1974. 114 p.   SCL, SCHS
Cumming, William P. The southeast in early maps... Chapel Hill
NC: UNC Press, 1958. 284 p.   COMMON
Dunn, Barbara B. Checklist of Charleston, SC, imprints for the
years 1826-1830. With a historical introduction. Washington
DC: Catholic University of America, 1967.131 p. SCL,UMBOD,SCHS
Easterby, James H. & Noel Polk. Guide to the study & reading of
SC history. With a supplement: a selected list of books...
published since 1950. With supplement, 1975. Spartanburg:
RPC, 1975. 344 p.   COMMON
English, Thomas H. Roads to research: distinguished library
collections of the southeast. Athens GA: University of Geor-
gia Press, 1968. 116 p.   SCL, SCHS

Evans, Charles. American bibliography: a chronological diction-
ary of all books, pamphlets and periodical publications printed in the United States...1639-1820. NY: Smith, 1941-1967.
14 vol.   COMMON
Eastham, Lucy. A preliminary checklist of imprints: Charleston,
SC, 1800-1810. With a historical introduction. Washington
DC: Catholic University of America, 1961. 89 p.   SCL, SCHS
Filby, P. William. American & British genealogy & heraldry: a
selected list of books. 2nd ed. Baltimore MD: GPC, 1975. SCL
Filby, P. William. Bibliography of ship passenger lists, 1538-
1900. Detroit: Gale Research Co., 1980. 160 p.   PUBL
First (Scots) Presbyterian Church, Charleston. Catalogue of
books for older scholars: Sunday school library. Chstn: Kahrs
Stolze & Welch, 1887. 19 p.   SCHS
Francis Marion College. The Arundel room of the James A. Rogers
library: a select list of the present & forthcoming holdings.
Florence: Francis Marion College, 1976. 49 p.SCL, FLMC, SCHS
Francis Marion College. Some resources for the study of the Pee
Dee region of SC. A partial bibliography of materials in the
James A. Rogers library, Francis Marion College. Florence:
Francis Marion College, 1974. 30 p.   SCL, FLMC, SCHS
Fritz, William R. The library of the SC Theological Seminary at
Lexington, SC, 1834-1852. A collection of 17th, 18th & 19th
century books gathered in SC and GA settlements for the use of
the seminary of the Lutheran Synod of SC, together with other
selected older works to be found in the Lineberger Memorial
Library. Cola: Lutheran Theological Southern Seminary, 1978.
170 p.   LTSS, SCHS
Geimer, Alfred F. Check-list of Columbia, SC, imprints from
1861 through 1865: with a historical introduction. Washington
DC: Catholic University of America, 1958. 92 p.   SCL, SCHS
Gilmer, Gertrude C. Checklist of southern periodicals to 1861.
Boston MA: Gregg Press, 1972. 128 p.   SCL, SCHS
Greenville County Library. South Carolina bicentennial: a
bibliography. Greenville: the library, 1970. 24 p.   COMMON
Holley, Edward C. Resources of SC libraries. Cola: SC Commis-
sion on Higher Education, 1976. 126 p.   SCL, CRCL
Inabinett, E. L. A dissertation bibliography: SC. Ann Arbor
MI: University Microfilms International, 1980. 18 p.   COMMON
Jackson, Ronald V. & others. Encyclopedia of local history &
genealogy: U.S. counties. Bountiful UT: Accelerated Index-
ing Systems, Inc., 1977. 292 p.   PIPD
Jones, Lewis P. Books & articles on SC history: a list for
laymen. Cola: Tricentennial Commission, 1970. 104 p. COMMON
Kaminkow, Marion J. Genealogies in the Library of Congress.
Baltimore MD: Magna Charta Book Co., 1972. 2 vol.   SCL
Kaminkow, Marion J. Genealogies in the Library of Congress...
supplement, 1972-1976. Baltimore MD: GBC, 1977. 285 p.   SCL
Karpinski, Louis C. Early maps of Carolina & adjoining regions.
From the collection of Henry P. Kendall. 2nd ed. Charleston:
Carolina Art Assn., 1937. 67 p.   SCL, YOCL, SCHS

Kirkham, E. Kay. A survey of American church records. 4th ed.
Logan UT: Everton Publishers, 1978. 344 p. COMMON
Koenig, M. Odelia. A check list of Charleston, SC, imprints for
the years 1819-1825, with a historical introduction. Washing-
ton DC: Catholic University of America, 1969. 106 p. SCL,SCHS
Konrad, J. A directory of genealogical periodicals. Monroe
Falls OH: Summit Publications, 1975. 61 p. SCL
Lancour, Harold. A bibliography of ship passenger lists: 1538-
1825. Being a guide to published lists of early immigrants to
North America. 3rd ed. NY: NY Public Library, 1966. 137 p.
COMMON
Lander College Library. Catalogue of the SC Society, Daughters
of the American Revolution state library. January 15, 1972.
NP: typescript, 17 p. SCHS
Libraries & information resources of northwest SC. Greenville:
Greenville County Library, 1975. COMMON
Martin, Neal A. The library of James McBride Dabbs: an inven-
tory. Florence: Francis Marion College, 1980. 201 p. FLMC
Melnick, Ralph. Wendell Mitchell Levi library and archives; a
catalog of its holdings. Chstn: College of Charleston Library
Associates, 1979. 70 p. COMMON
Meriwether, James B. A catalog of the South Caroliniana Col-
lection of J. Rion McKissick. Spartanburg: RPC for the Southern Studies Program, USC, 1977. 455 p. COMMON
Morgan, Richard P. A preliminary bibliography of SC imprints,
1731-1800. Clemson: Clemson University, 1966. 87 p. COMMON
Morrison, Hugh A. Preliminary checklist of American almanacs,
1639-1800. Washington DC: Government Printing Office, 1907.
160 p. SCL, SCHS
Mosimann, Jeanne D. A check list of Charleston, SC, imprints
from 1731 to 1799. With a historical introduction. Washington DC: Catholic University of America, 1959. 240 p.SCL, SCHS
Oliphant, Mary C. The works of A. S. Salley; a descriptive bibliography... Greenville: author, 1949. 49 p. COMMON
Peterson, Clarence S. Consolidated bibliography of county
histories in the 50 states. 1961, rp Baltimore MD: GBC, 1973.
186 p. COMMON
Ragsdale, Betty M. Check list of Columbia, SC, imprints for the
years 1866-1870. With a historical introduction. Washington
DC: Catholic University of America, 1967. 63 p. SCL, SCHS
Ridge, Davy-Jo S. Rare book collection in the McKissick Memor-
ial Library. NY: Vogue Press, 1966. 396 p. COMMON
Rose, James M. & Alice Eichholz. Black genesis: an annotated
bibliography for black genealogical research. Detroit MI:
Gale Research Co., 1978. 326 p. PUBL
Sabin, Elizabeth. Biography. Spartanburg: Wofford Library
Press, 1970. 40 p. WOFF, SCHS
Salley, Alexander S. Catalog of the Salley collection of the
works of William Gilmore Simms. Cola: State Co., 1943.
121 p. COMMON
Second Presbyterian Church, Charleston. Catalogue, Sunday

school library. Chstn: the church, 1874.   SCHS
Schreiner-Yantis, Netti. Genealogical & local history books in
   print. 3rd ed. Springfield VA: Genealogical Books in Print,
   1981. 1000 pp.   COMMON
Smith, Priscilla. Early maps of Carolina & adjoining regions,
   together with early prints of Charleston. Cola: USC, 1930.
   46 p.   COMMON
Snowden, Yates. War-time publications (1861-1865), from the
   press of Walker, Evans & Cogswell, Charleston, SC. An adden-
   dum to "One hundred years of WECCO". Chstn: W,E&C, 1922.
   30 p.   SCL, SCHS
Society Hill Library Society. Catalogue of books belonging to
   the Society Hill Library Society, July 11, 1840. Chstn: Miller, 1840. 23 p.   SCL, SCHS
Some resources for the study of the Pee Dee region of SC. A
   partial bibliography of the materials in the James A. Rogers
   Library, Francis Marion College. Florence: Francis Marion
   College, 1978. 45 p.   COMMON
South Carolina Department of Archives & History. An annotated
   checklist of publications of the SCDAH. Cola: USC Press,
   1970. 15 p.   COMMON
South Caroliniana Library, U.S.C. [List of] card file of W.P.A.
   copied cemetery records in the South Caroliniana Library,
   Columbia, SC. NP: typescript, 1936. 6 p. [Note: see Appendix
   VIII of this volume for a transcript of these cemetery lists.]
                                                           SCL, SCHS
Sweet, James S. Genealogy & local history: an archival & bibli-
   ographical guide.   MACL
Turnbull, Robert J. Bibliography of SC, 1563-1950. Charlottes-
   ville VA: University of Virginia Press, 1956. 5 vol.   COMMON
U.S. Library of Congress. American & English genealogies in the
   Library of Congress. Preliminary catalog... Washington DC:
   GPO, 1910. 805 p.   COMMON
U.S. Library of Congress. American & English Genealogies in the
   Library of Congress. 2nd ed. Washington DC: GPO, 1919.
   1332 p.   COMMON
U.S. Library of Congress. United States Local History in the
   Library of Congress: a bibliography. 4 vol. Baltimore MD:
   Magna Carta Book Co., 1975.   COMMON
Wescott, Mary. A checklist of the U.S. newspapers (and weeklies
   before 1900) in the general library [of Duke University].
   Durham NC: Duke University, 1932-37. 6 vol.   SCHS
Witty, Francis J. A checklist of SC imprints: 1811-1818. NP:
   NPub, nd. Thesis. 83 p.   SCHS
Woodham, Martha A. A historical survey of newspapers published
   in Bishopville, SC. NP: typescript, 1978. 17 p.   LECL
Woody, Robert H. Republican newspapers of SC. Charlottesville
   VA: Historical Publishing Co., 1936.   SCL, SCHS
W.P.A. Historical Records Survey. Checklist of historical
   records survey publications. 1943, rp Baltimore MD: GPC,
   1969.   PUBL

Blosser, Susan S. The southern historical collection: a guide
to manuscripts. Chapel Hill NC: UNC Library, 1970. 1 vol.
COMMON
Chandler, Marion C. & Earl W. Wade. The South Carolina Archives
a temporary summary guide. 2nd ed. Cola: SCDAH, 1976.
161 p.   COMMON
Chepesiuk, Ron. Guide to the manuscript & oral history collect-
ions in the Winthrop College archives & special collections.
Rock Hill: Dacus Library of Winthrop College, 1978. 39 p.
COMMON
Chepesiuk, Ron. The Winthrop College archives & special col-
lections: a guide to the records relating to Winthrop College.
Rock Hill: Archives Dept. of Dacus Library, Winthrop College,
1979. 41 p.   COMMON
Chepesiuk, Ron & Ann Yarborough. Winthrop College & Special
Collections: an inventory of the records of the York County
multiethnic heritage project. Rock Hill: Archives Department
of Dacus Library, Winthrop College, 1978. 16 p.   COMMON
Childs, Arney R. Calendar: Kincaid-Anderson papers, 1767-1900.
Cola: South Caroliniana Society & Library, 1958. 66 p. COMMON
Côte, Richard N. Inventory of the records and historical docu-
ments of Trinity United Methodist Church, Charleston, SC.
Chstn: typescript, 1978. 20 p.   SCL, CHLS, SCHS
Graham, Lannae. Finding aid for the papers of Westminster
Presbyterian Church, Charleston, SC. Montreat NC: The Histor-
ical Foundation of the Presbyterian Church, 1979. 3 p.
MONT, SCHS
Hollings, Marie F. Descriptive inventory of the City of
Charleston Division of Archives & Records. Chstn: Division of
Archives & Records, 1979. 93 p.   SCL, SCHS, CHCA
Melnick, Ralph. "College of Charleston special collections: a
guide to its holdings", in SCHM 81: 131-153.
Moltke-Hansen, David & Sallie Doscher. South Carolina Histori-
cal Society manuscript guide. Chstn: SCHS, 1979. 154 p.
COMMON
Moore, John H. Research materials in SC: a guide. Cola: USC
Press for the SC State Library Board, 1967. 346 p.   COMMON
Old Slave Mart Museum, Charleston. Catalog of the Old Slave
Mart museum & library, Charleston, SC. Boston MA: G. K. Hall,
1978. 2 vol.   SCL, GRCL
Rosen, Barry H. The University of South Carolina archives; a
preliminary guide. Cola: USC, 1977. 23 p.   COMMON
U.S. Library of Congress. The national union catalog of manu-
script collections. Washington DC: COMMON
University of North Carolina. Guide to the microfilm edition of
the Penn School papers, 1862-1976. Chapel Hill NC: UNC
Library, 1977. 42 p.   SCHS
Work Projects Administration. Inventory of the county archives

of SC (Abbeville, Aiken, Allendale, Anderson, Cherokee, Dillon, Florence, Jasper, Lee, McCormick, Oconee, Pickens, Richland & Saluda counties). Cola: Historical Records Survey,
  WPA, 1937-1941. 14 vol.   SCL, CHCL, SCHS
Work Projects Administration. Inventory of federal archives in
  the states. (Series IV. The Dept. of War. No. 39. SC) Cola:
  Historical Records Survey, WPA, 1942. 31 p.   SCL, SCHS
Winyah Indigo Society, Georgetown. Inventory of books and
  manuscripts [preliminary], 1978.   GTML, SCHS

PERIODICALS

The following periodicals have information of substantial use
to local and family historians. Most are in print and may be
fairly easily located.

Lists of the articles pertaining to South Carolina have been
compiled for a number of these periodicals, and may be found in
the appendices to this volume. The periodicals for which lists
have been compiled are marked with an asterisk [*].

The abbreviations for frequency of publication are given
below:

A - Annually   T - Three times per year
I - Irregularly   S - Semi-annually
M - Monthly   W - Weekly
Q - Quarterly   (1966-) Year first published

Bulletin (Q, 1978-). Chester County Genealogical Society,
    Chester.
Bulletin (I, 193_-). Darlington County Historical Society,
    Darlington.
Bulletin (S, 1970-). Newberry County Genealogical Society,
    Newberry.
Bulletin for Genealogists (I, 1975-). Charleston County Library
    Charleston.
Carolina Herald (Q, 1972-). South Carolina Genealogical Society
    Columbia.
*Carolina Genealogist (Q, 1970-). Heritage Papers, Danielsville
    GA. For list of articles, see Appendix VI.
Carolinas Genealogical Society Bulletin (T, 1969-). Carolinas
    Genealogical Society, Monroe NC.
Clingstone (T, 1974-). Piedmont Heritage Fund, Greer. Covers
    Greer area history.
Directory of SC Local Historical Organizations (A). Cola:
    SCDAH. Lists most historical, genealogical, & preservation
    organizations by county. Gives current addresses.
Family Puzzlers (W, 1964-). Heritage Papers, Danielsville GA.
*Georgia Genealogical Magazine (Q, 1961-). Easley: Southern
    Historical Press. Contains SC material. For list of SC
    articles, see Appendix X.
Georgia Genealogical Magazine. Master index to Nos. 1-46,
    1961-1972. Easley: SHP, 1973. 888 p.
Georgia Genealogist (Q, 1969-). Heritage Papers, Danielsville
    GA.
Independent Republic Quarterly (Q, 1967-). Horry County Histor-
    ical Society, Conway.
Journal of the South Carolina Baptist Historical Society (A,
    1975-). SC Baptist Historical Society, Furman University
    Library, Greenville.

7

Minutes (A,   ). Sumter County Historical Society, Sumter.
Names in South Carolina (A, 1954-). Columbia: U.S.C.
News for SC Local Historical Societies (Q, 1964-). Columbia:
   SCDAH.
News from the Marlborough Historical Society (Q, 1975-). Ben-
   netsville: Marlborough Historical Society.
Newsletter (S, 1965-). Pendleton: Foundation for Historic
   Restoration in the Pendleton Area.
Old Mill Stream (A, 1975-). Clover: Clover Printing Co.
Orangeburg Historical & Genealogical Record (Q, 1969-). Orange-
   burg: Orangeburg County Historical & Genealogical Society.
Orangeburg Papers (I, 1970-). Orangeburg: Orangeburg County
   Historical & Genealogical Society.
*Papers (I, 197?-). Beaufort County Historical Society, Beaufort
   For listing, see Appendix IX.
Pee Dee Que (M, 1977-). Pee Dee Chapter, SCGS, Marion.
*Proceedings (A, 1931-). South Carolina Historical Association,
   Columbia. For listing, see Appendix IV.
Proceedings & Papers (A, 1962-). Greenville: Greenville County
   Historical Society.
Sandlapper (Q, 1968-). Columbia: Sandlapper Press, Inc.
South Carolina Genealogical Register (Q, 1963-). Eppes, AL.

*South Carolina Historical (& Genealogical) Magazine (Q, 1900-).
   (SCH & GM 1900-1940, SCHM from 1941-). Charleston: SCHS.
   Contains extensive amounts of primary & secondary materials
   for state, local & family history. For complete list of art-
   icles, see Appendix II.
South Carolina Historical Magazine Index I-XL, 1900-1939, with
   subject index, I-LXI, 1900-1960. 737 p.
South Carolina Historical Magazine Index XLI-LXXI, 1940-1970.
   474 p.
*South Carolina Historical Society Collections (I, 1857-1919)
   5 vol. For listing, see Appendix III.
South Carolina History Illustrated (Q, 1970-). Columbia: Sand-
   lapper Press, Inc.
South Carolina Magazine (,   ). Columbia: South Carolina
   Magazine, Inc.
*South Carolina Magazine of Ancestral Research (Q, 1973-).
   Greenville: A Press, Inc. For listing, see Appendix VII.
Southern Echoes (Q, 1979-). Augusta GA: Augusta Genealogical
   Society. Has much SC border material.
Sperry, Kip. Index to genealogical periodical literature,
   1960-1977. Detroit: Gale Research Co., 1979. 166 p.   PUBL
Sperry, Kip. Survey of American genealogical periodicals &
   periodical indexes. Detroit: Gale Research Co., 1978.   PUBL
*Transactions (A, 1889-). Charleston: Huguenot Society of SC.
   Has extensive genealogy & Huguenot history. For listing, see
   Appendix V. Index in progress.
Transactions (A, 1971-). McCormick: McCormick County Historical
   Society.

*<u>Yearbook</u> (A, 1880-1951). Charleston: City of Charleston.
   Out of print. To be available in 1981 as a SCHS microfiche
   publication. Historical appendices contain much Charleston
   local history, also obituaries. For list, see Appendix I.

American Council of Learned Societies. Surnames in the census
of 1790. 1909, rp Baltimore: GPC, 1971. 441 p.   COMMON
Bronson, Patricia. An index to the U.S. census of 1850, Pickens
District, SC. Schedule 1. Wye Mills MD: author, 1973.
124 p.   SCL, SCHS
Calhoun County Historical Commission. Heads of families at the
first census of the U.S....1790: SC, Orangeburg District
(north part). St. Matthews: Calhoun County Historical Commission, 1954. Typescript, nd. unp.   ORCL
Charleston City Council. Census of the city of Charleston, SC,
for the year 1848. Chstn: J. B. Nixon, 1849. 262 p.   COMMON
Charleston City Council. Census of the city of Charleston, SC,
for the year 1861. Chstn: Evans & Cogswell, 1861. 271 p.
                                                         COMMON
Donne, Carmen R. Federal census schedules, 1850-1880; primary
sources for historical research. Washington DC: National Ar-
chives & Records Service, 1973. 29 p.   SCHS
Elliott, Irene D. The second federal census, 1800: Chesterfield
County, SC. Cola: USC, 1959.   YOCL
Elliott, Irene D. The second federal census, 1800: Edgefield
County, SC. Cola: USC, 1959.   YOCL
Elliott, Irene D. The second federal census, 1800: Laurens
County, SC. Cola: USC, 1959.   SCL, GWPL, YOCL
Emory, Mary M. & Lorene B. Ambrose. 1860 census, Spartanburg
County, SC, vol. I. NP: typescript, 1974. 104 p.   COMMON
Franklin, W. Neil. Federal population & mortality census sched-
ules, 1790-1890, in the National Archives & the states. Out-
line of a lecture on their availability, content & use. Wash-
ington DC, 1971. 89 p.   SCHS
Hart, Joseph E. Yorkville: heads of households listed in the
census of 1900... NP: typescript, 1978.   YOCL
Hazelwood, Jean P. Index to the 1830 census, SC. Fort Worth
TX: Gen Re Put, 197? 433 p.   SCL
Holcomb, Brent. Index to the 1800 census of SC. Baltimore MD:
GPC, 1980. 264 p.   SCL, FACL
Holcomb, Brent. Index to the 1850 federal census mortality
schedules [SC]. Easley: SHP, 1980. 48 p.   SCL
Hollingsworth, Leon S. ...U.S. census of 1800, Laurens District
SC. 1955.   LRCL
Horry County Historical Society. 1880 census of Horry County,
SC. Conway: Horry County Historical Society, 1970. 165 p.
                                                         COMMON
Jackson, Ronald V. SC 1800 census index. Bountiful UT: Accel-
erated Indexing Systems, 1973.   p.   COMMON
Jackson, Ronald V. SC 1810 census index. Bountiful UT: Accel-
erated Indexing Systems, 1976. 97 p.   COMMON
Jackson, Ronald V. SC 1820 census index. Bountiful UT: Accel-
erated Indexing Systems, 1976. 156 p.   COMMON
Jackson, Ronald V. SC 1830 census index. Bountiful UT: Accel-

erated Indexing Systems, 1976. 115 p.   COMMON
Jackson, Ronald V. SC 1840 census index. Bountiful UT: Accel-
erated Indexing Systems, 1976.   COMMON
Jackson, Ronald V. SC 1850 census index. Bountiful UT: Accel-
erated Indexing Systems, 1976. 174 p.   COMMON
Kershaw County Historical Society. The second federal census,
1800, Kershaw County. Camden: the Society, 1970. 24 p.COMMON
Kershaw County Historical Society. The third federal census,
1810, Kershaw County. Camden: the Society, 1972. 27 p.COMMON
Kershaw County Historical Society. The fourth federal census,
1820, Kershaw County. Camden: the Society, 1973. 32 p.COMMON
King, Walter. The second federal census, 1800, Chesterfield
County. Cola: author, 1959. v.p.   SCL, CHCO
McClendon, Carlee T. 1790-1800 federal census of Edgefield
County, SC. Edgefield: the Hive Press, 1959. 46 p.   COMMON
Platt, Gwendolyn B. SC index to the U.S. census of 1820. Tus-
tin CA: G.A.M. Publications, 1972. 426 p.   SCL, CLEM
Reid, Mary R. Williamsburg County censuses, 1790-1840. NP:
typescript, nd. 6 vol.   SCL, WMTR
Reid, Mary R. 1850 census of Williamsburg County, SC. Kings-
tree: author, 1975. 90 p.   COMMON
Reid, Mary R. Williamsburg County censuses, 1860-1880. NP:
typescript, nd. 3 vol.   SCL, WMTR
Stemmons, John D. The U.S. census compendium. Logan UT:
Everton Publishers, 1973. 144 p.   PUBL
Stewart, William C. 1800 census, Pendleton District, SC.
Washington DC: National Genealogical Society. 178 p.   COMMON
Thomas, Elizabeth W. 1820 census, Chesterfield County, SC.
Pass Christian MS: Willo Institute, 1967. 24 p.   SCL, LNCL
Thomas, Elizabeth W. 1820 census, Union County, SC. Pass
Christian MS: Willo Institute, 1966.   SCL, YOCL
Three Rivers Historical Society. 1850 census, Georgetown Coun-
ty. Typescript, 1977.   SCL, WMTR
Three Rivers Historical Society. 1850 census, Marion County.
Typescript, 1978.   WMTR
U.S. Census Bureau. A census of pensioners...1840, for revolu-
tionary war or military service, bound with a general index.
1841 & 1965, rp (2 vol. in 1) Baltimore MD: GPC, 1974. COMMON
U.S. Census Bureau. A century of population growth, from the
first census to the twelfth, 1790-1900. 1909, rp Baltimore
MD: GPC, 1967. 303 p.   COMMON
U.S. Census Bureau. Heads of families at the first census of
the U.S. taken in the year 1790: SC. 1908, rp Spartanburg:
RPC, 1961. 150 p.   COMMON
U.S. National Archives. Federal population censuses, 1790-1890.
A catalog of microfilm copies of the schedules. Washington
DC: National Archives, 1974. 90 p.   COMMON
U.S. National Archives. 1900 federal population census. A cat-
alog of microfilm copies of the schedules. Washington DC:
National Archives, 1978. 84 p.   COMMON
Ward, Carolyn P. & others. 1850 census of Marion County, SC.

NP: NPub, 1978 229 p.   SCL, MACL
Woodard, Janet H. 1850 census of Horry County, SC. Greenville:
   A Press, 1980. 132 p.   COMMON

Baldwin, Agnes L. First settlers of SC, 1670-1680. Cola: USC
 Press, 1969. 82 p.   COMMON
Bolton, Charles K. The founders: portraits of persons born
 abroad who came to the colonies in North America before 1701.
 1919, rp Baltimore: GPC, 1976. 2 vol.   KECA, SCL
Bolton, Charles K. Scotch Irish pioneers in Ulster & America.
 1910, rp Baltimore MD: GBC, 1977. 398 p.   SCL
Boyer, Carl. Ship passenger lists: national & New England
 (1600-1825). Newhall CA: author, 1977. 270 p.   SCL
Boyer, Carl. Ship passenger lists: the south (1538-1825). Newhall CA: author, 1979. 314 p.   SCL, SCHS
Bromwell, William J. History of immigration to the U.S., exhib-
 iting the number, age, sex, occupation and country of birth
 of passengers arriving...by September 30, 1819, to December
 31, 1855. NY: Redfield, 1856. 225 p.   SCL, CHCO
Cameron, Viola R. Emigrants from Scotland to America, 1774-
 1775. 1930, rp Baltimore MD: GPC, 1976.   SCL, GWPL, SCHS
Faust, Albert B. Lists of Swiss emigrants in the eighteenth
 century to the American colonies. 1925, rp. Baltimore MD:
 GPC, 1976. 377 p.   COMMON
Filby, P. William. Passenger & immigration lists index. Detroit MI: Gale Research Co., 1980. 3 vol.   PUBL
Fothergill, Gerald. Emigrants from England, 1773-1776. 1913,
 rp Baltimore MD: GPC, 1976. 206 p.   SCL, GWPL
Fothergill, Gerald. A list of emigrant ministers to America,
 1690-1811. 1904, rp Baltimore MD: GPC, 1965. 65 p.   COMMON
Ghirelli, Michael. List of emigrants from England to America,
 1682-1692. Baltimore MD: Magna Charta Book Co., 1968. 106
 p.   SCL, SCHS
Giuseppi, Montague. Naturalization of foreign protestants in
 the American & West Indian colonies. 1921, rp Baltimore: GPC,
 1969. 196 p.   COMMON
Hotten, John C. The original lists of persons of quality. Emigrants; religious exiles; political rebels...and others who
 went from Great Britain to the American plantations, 1600-
 1700. 1874, rp Baltimore MD: GPC, 1980. 580 p.   COMMON
Hotten, John C. Our early emigrant ancestors. 2nd ed., 1880 ;
 rp Baltimore MD: GPC, 1962. 580 p.   CHLS
Howe, George. The Scotch-Irish, and their first settlements on
 the Tyger River and other neighboring precincts in SC... Cola
 Southern Guardian Steam Power Press, 1861. 31 p.   MONT
                                             SCL, UMBOD, SPCL
Kaminkow, Jack & Marion Kaminkow. A list of emigrants from
 England to America, 1718-1759. Baltimore MD: Magna Charta
 Book Co., 1966. 288 p.   SCL, SCHS
Kaminkow, Jack & Marion Kaminkow. Original lists of emigrants
 in bondage from London to the American colonies, 1719-1744.
 Baltimore MD: Magna Charta Book Co., 1967.   SCL, SCHS
Kohn, August. ...A review of the immigration movement in SC

inasmuch as it pertains to the incoming of Jewish settlers...
April 14th, 1907. Chstn: NPub, nd. 20 p.   SCL
Marshall, William F. Ulster sails west. 1950, rp Baltimore MD:
GBC, 1977. 79 p.   SCL
Names of persons who took the oath of citizenship in Lancaster
County, SC...1800-1825. Typescript, 1958. unp.   YOCL
Nicholson, Cregoe S. Some early emigrants to America. Also,
early emigrants to America from Liverpool. Baltimore MD: GPC,
1965. 110 p.   SCL, SCHS
Pettus, Mildred L. European immigration to SC, 1881-1908. M.A.
thesis, U.S.C., 1954. 62 p.   SCL
Pitts, Annie. Emigration from SC from 1820-1850. NP: type-
script, nd. 68 p.   COKL
Pruitt, Jayne C. Migrations of South Carolinians on Natchez
Trace. NP: NPub, nd. 128 p. [Fairfax, Va.,1949] SCL,MRCL
Report of the special committee...on the subject of encouraging
european immigration... Chstn: Joseph Walker, 1866.   CHCO
Revill, Janie. A compilation of the original lists of protest-
ant immigrants to SC, 1763-1773. 1939, rp Baltimore MD: GPC,
1974. 163 p.   COMMON
Stephenson, Jean. Scotch-Irish migration to SC, 1772. Stras-
burg VA: Shenandoah Publishing House, 1971. 137 p.   COMMON
Tepper, Michael. New world immigrants: a consolidation of ship
passenger lists...from periodical literature. Baltimore MD:
GPC, 1980. 2 vol.   SCL, CRCL
Tepper, Michael. Passengers to America: a consolidation of ship
passenger lists from the New England Historical & Genealogical
Register, 1847-1961. Baltimore MD: GBC, 1978. 554 p.SCL,KECA
U.S. Department of State. Passenger arrivals, 1819-1820; a
transcript of the list of passengers who arrived in the U.S.
from the 1st October, 1819, to the 30th September, 1820. With
an added index. Baltimore MD: GPC, 1971. 342 p.   SCL
U.S. Department of State. Passengers who arrived in the U.S.
September 1821-December 1823. From transcripts made by the
State Department. Baltimore MD: Magna Charta Book Co., 1969.
427 p.   SCL
Virkus, Frederick A. Immigrant ancestors. A list of 2,500 immigrants to America before 1750. 1942, rp Baltimore MD: GPC,
1980. 75 p.   COMMON
York County Clerk of Court. Applications for citizenship, York
District, 1806... NP: typescript, nd. unp.   YOCL

LISTS OF NAMES

Includes lists, rosters, rolls, records & indexes of churches,
cemeteries, juries, taxpayers, local records, military service,
Bibles, directories, pensioners, and families.

Abbeville County family history. Clinton: Inter-collegiate
  Press, 1980. 199 p.   COMMON
Abbeville County land grants. Records from [the] Abbeville
  courthouse... NP: typescript, 1940? 2 vol.   GWPL
Abstracts of all deeds, etc. Laurens County deed book "B", of-
  fice of the Clerk of Court, Laurens, SC.   LRCL
Account of plats for lands granted before the late war with
  Great Britain, which are now in the Surveyor General's office;
  but were never recorded. Cola: Young & Faust, 1796. Typed
  copy.   SCL, SCHS
Agee, Jeanne C. & others. Old Catholic Presbyterian church,
  Chester, SC. Cemetery inscriptions. NP: typescript, 1977.
  32 p.   SCL, CSCL, LNCL, FACM
Agee, Jeanne C. Union Cemetery records, Chester, SC. Type-
  script.   CSCL
Aldredge, Robert C. Charleston directory for 1735. Chstn:
  typescript, 1938. 50 p.   SCL, SCHS
Alexander, Virginia & Colleen M. Elliott. Pendleton District
  & Anderson County, SC, wills, 1793-1880; probate records, es-
  tates, inventories & tax returns, 1835-1861. Easley: SHP,
  1978. 430 p.   COMMON
Allendale Baptist Church. Records 1868-1902.   SCL
Allison Creek Presbyterian Church. Minutes of the session of
  the Presbyterian church: Allison Creek, Bethel Presbytery,
  1835-1953. 3 vol.   YOCL
Anderson burying ground [SpC]   CSCL
Anderson Memorial Association. William Anderson & Rebecca Den-
  ny & their descendants, 1706-1914 [incl. Old Antioch church
  cemetery & Nazareth church cemetery in Spartanburg County].
  Cola: RLB, 1914. 287 p.   SPCL
Andrea, Leonardo. SC colonial soldiers & patriots... Cola: RLB
  1952. 40 p.   COMMON
Anson County, NC: abstracts of early records. NP: NPub, 1950.
  180 p. (Also Baltimore MD: GPC, 1978)   SCL, MACL
Antioch Baptist Church, Kershaw County. Marriage records 1852-
  1884.   SCL
Antioch Presbyterian Church, Spartanburg. Sessions records
  1843-1929.   MONT
Association of Citadel Men. Centennial register. Chstn: NPub,
  1952. 144 p.   SCL, SCHS, GTML
Aveleigh Presbyterian Church, Newberry County. Sessions records
  1879-1904.   MONT
Bailey, James D. Commanders at King's Mountain. 1926, rp
  Greenville: A Press, 1979. 431 p.   SCL, WOFF, CRCL, SPCL
Baker Presbyterian Church, Mayesville. Sessions records 1931-

15

1938.   MONT
Barbot, Louis J. Alphabetical index to all conveyances,
    leases, mortgages, etc., executed by and to the City Council
    of Charleston, 1783-1877. Chstn: News & Courier, 1877.   CHCA
Barnwell Baptist Church. Records 1803-1912.   SCL
Barnwell Presbyterian Church. Records 1866-1961.   MONT
Baskins, Jenkins D. Cypress cemetery records, Lee County, SC.
    NP: typescript, 1961. 10 p.   SCL
Beaufort Presbyterian Church, Beaufort. Sessions records 1883-
    1897, 1912-1935; registers 1912-1948.   MONT
Beaulah Baptist Church. Records 1883-1904.   SCL
Beaver Creek Presbyterian Church, Kershaw. Records 1845-1908.
                                                              MONT
Beaver Dam Primitive Baptist Church, Kershaw County. Records
    1844-1882.   SCL
Beech Branch Baptist Church. Records 1814-1918.   SCL
Bell, Landon C. Address at Johnson's Island in memory of the
    Confederate soldiers who, while prisoners, died and are buried
    on the island. NP: NPub, 1929. 22 p.   SCHS
Belton (formerly Broadway) Presbyterian Church, Belton. Histo-
    ries, 1857 & 1909; sessions records 1851-1882, 1912-1957. MONT
Bethabara Baptist Church, Laurens County. Minutes & roll of
    Bethabara Baptist church, 1801-1881... NP: typescript, 1936.
    unp.   SCL, LRCL
Bethea, Mary B. Ancestral key to the Pee Dee. Latta: Manning &
    Shine, 1979. 782 p.   COMMON
Bethel Baptist church cemetery survey. NP: typescript, nd.
    9 p.   PIPD
Bethel Baptist Church, Newberry County. Records 1841-1910. SCL
Bethel church cemetery survey. NP: typescript, 1967. 12 p.PIPD
Bethel Presbyterian church cemetery list [SpC]   YOWC
Bethel Presbyterian Church. Cemetery roster...   YOCL
Bethel Presbyterian Church, Walhalla. Sessions records 1855-
    1923, register 1859-1922.   MONT
Bethel Presbyterian Church, Walterboro. Sessions records 1841-
    1857.   MONT
Bethesda Baptist Church, Kershaw County. Records 1823-1905. SCL
Bethesda Presbyterian Church. Sessions records, 1834-1871
    (photocopy) [SpC]   YOCL
Bethesda Presbyterian Church, Camden. Sessions records 1806-
    1935.   SCL, MONT
Bethesda Presbyterian Church, McConnels. Sessions records &
    register, 1840-1856.   MONT
Big Creek Baptist Church, Anderson County. Records 1801-1936.
                                                               SCL
Black Creek Baptist Church, Beaufort County. Records 1828-1922.
                                                               SCL
Blacksburg Presbyterian Church, Blacksburg. Sessions records &
    register, 1885-1918.   MONT
Blackville birth-marriage-death register, 1895-1919.   SCL
Blakeney, Jane. Heroes, U.S. Marine Corps 1861-1955... Wash-

ington DC: Guthrie Litho. Co., 1957.   UNCL
Boddie, William W. [General Francis] Marion's men: a list of
    twenty-five hundred. Chstn: Heisser Printing Co., 1938.
    24 p.   COMMON
Bolt, Mrs. James Leland. Laurens County cemetery epitaphs. NP:
    typescript.   SCHS
Book of the proceeding[s] of the elders of the Protestant Dutch
    Church [Lexington County] for the year 1797 [members & finan-
    cial records, 1797-1812].   LTSS
Bounetheau, G. M. Town & country almanac for Carolina & GA, for
    the year of our Lord, 1805... 2nd ed. Chstn: 1804.   SCHS
Brewington Presbyterian Church, Manning. Sessions records 1839-
    1926.   MONT
Brown, Richard L. Bible records of Spartanburg & Greenwood, SC.
    Maplewood NJ: typescript, 1964. 23 p.   SPCL
Bryan, Evelyn M. Cemeteries of upper Colleton County, SC.
    Jacksonville FL: Florentine Press, 1974. 642 p.   COMMON
Bull, Elias B. Founders & pew renters of the Unitarian church
    in Charleston, SC, 1817-1874. 47 p.   SCL, SCHS
Bullock Creek Cemetery Assn. Roster of the cemetery and histor-
    ical sketch of Bullock Creek church. NP: author, 1962. 27 p.
                                                       SCL, SCHS, CSCL
Bullock's Creek Presbyterian Church, Sharon SC. Sessions rec-
    ords 1872-1916; register (nd).   MONT
Burns, Annie W. ...Index to pension list of the War of 1812.
    9 vol.   SCL, SCHS
Burns, Annie W. Revolutionary war soldiers, and other patriotic
    records of Abbeville County, SC. Washington DC: NPub, 1947?
    53 p.   COMMON
Burns, Annie W. SC pension abstracts of the Revolutionary war,
    war of 1812, and indian wars. Washington DC: author, 1960?
    5 vol.   COMMON
Bush River Baptist Church, Newberry County. Records 1792-1923.
                                                                   SCL
Bushy Creek Baptist Church, Greenville County. Records 1794-
    1927.   SCL
Bynum, Curtis. Marriage bonds of Tryon & Lincoln counties, NC.
    Newton NC: Catawba County Historical Assn., 1962.   SCL, CRCL
                                                            MACL, LNCL
Callahan, Anna. Monumental inscriptions of Little River Baptist
    Church cemetery, Abbeville County, SC. Charlotte NC: NPub,
    1969. 15 p.   SCL, ANCL, GWPL
Canaan Baptist Church, Orangeburg County. Records 1823-1910.SCL
Carlisle, James H. & James H. Bryce. Miller's planters' and
    merchants' almanac for Spartanburg, SC,...1878. Chstn: W,E&C,
    1875. 77 p.   WOFF
Carmel Presbyterian Church, Liberty. Sessions records 1832-
    1852, 1860-1895; registers 1860-?   MONT
The Carolina Club. Constitution & by-laws...with a list of of-
    ficers & members. Chstn: Courier Job Presses, 1870. 11 p.
                                                                  SCHS

Carolina Plantation Society, Charleston. List of members and
    constitution. Chstn: NPub, 1940. 27 p.   GRCL
Carter, Emilie L. Inscriptions. St. Paul Methodist cemetery,
    St. Matthews, SC. NP: typescript, 1974. 13 p.   SCL
Carter, Emilie L. Inscriptions. West End Cemetery, St. Matt-
    hews, SC. NP: typescript, 1965. 19 p.   SCL
Catalog of regular & honorary members of the Clariosophic Soci-
    ety of the South Carolina College. Cola: Steam Power Press,
    1853. 59 p.   SCL, WOFF
Catalogue of the officers & pupils of the Yorkville Female Col-
    lege...for the year 1858. Yorkville: Enquirer Office, 1859.
    SCL has 1855, 1856.   YOCL
Catholic gravestones [SpC]   CSCL
Catholic Presbyterian Church, Chester County. Sessions records
    1840-1959. 2 vol.   YOCL, CSCL
Catholic Presbyterian Church & the Hemphill family [SpC]   CSCL
Cemeteries in Dillon County & upper Marion County. Ann Fulmer
    Chapter, U.D.C., nd. unp.   COMMON
Central Methodist Church, Spartanburg. Minutes, 1850-1935, min-
    utes of the board of stewards, 1908-1917.   WOMA
Charles Town register. 1735. Compiled from contemporaneous
    documents by Robert Croom Aldredge...   SCHS
Charleston Assessor. List of the taxpayers of the city of
    Charleston for 1859. Chstn: Walker, Evans & Co., 1860.
    407 p.   SCHS
Charleston Assessor. List of the taxpayers of the city of
    Charleston for 1858. Chstn: Walker, Evans & Co., 1859.   CHCA
Charleston Assessor. Statement of receipts and expenditures...
    from the 1st September, 1850 to the 1st September 1851. With
    a list of the tax paying citizens. Chstn: Miller, 1851. 192+
    51 p.   SCHS
Charleston Chamber of Commerce. ...Roll of officers...during
    the first century of its corporate life, 1784-1884. Chstn:
    W,E&C, 1887. 16 p.   SCL, SCHS, SPCL
Charleston city directory for 1867-1868. Chstn: Jno. Orrin Lea
    & Co., 1867. 190 p.   SCL, WOFF
The Charleston Directory, containing the names of the inhabi-
    tants... Chstn: Walker, Evans & Co., 1859. 277 p.   WOFF
Charleston Free Library. Index to wills of Charleston County,
    SC: 1671-1868. Baltimore MD: GPC, 1974. 324 p.   COMMON
Charleston guide & business directory for 1885-1886. Chstn: Lu-
    cas & Richardson, 1885. 287 p.   SCL, CHCO
Charleston Museum. The streets of Charleston [information on
    the formation of Charleston streets and their names, also in-
    cludes a list of surveyors]. Chstn: typescript, nd.   SCHS
The Charlestown directory for 1782 and the Charleston directory
    for 1785... Chstn: Historical Commission of Charleston, 1951.
    24 p.   COMMON
Cheek, John C. Selected tombstone inscriptions from AL, SC, &
    other southern states. NP: NPub, 1970. 136 p.   SCL
Chester A.R.P. Church, Chester. Sessions records 1857-1939.MONT
                                                             SCL

18

Chester County history of the confederate war...men who served
in the confederate army [SpC]   CSCL
Chester District Circuit, M.E. Church. Register, nd.   WOMA
Chestnut Ridge Baptist Church, Laurens County. Records 1816-
1939.   SCL
Church of the Holy Apostles [Episcopal]. Parish register, 1848-
1957.   SCL, BRCL
Church of the Redeemer [Episcopal], Orangeburg. Register, 1739-
1885.   SCL, SCDAH
Church register, El Bethel, East Chester Circuit [Methodist],
1882-1893. 75 p.   YOCL
Church register of the Richburg M.E. church, South. Typescript,
nd.   YOCL
Clariosophic Society, South Carolina College. Catalogue of the
regular & honorary members...[1806-1847]. Cola: NPub, 1847.
                                                 SCL, EDTO
Clark, Marguerite. A new index to Abstracts of old 96 District
and Abbeville, SC , by Pauline Young. Easley: SHP, 1977.
214 p.   COMMON
Clemens, William M. NC & SC marriage records: from the earliest
colonial days to the Civil War. 1927, rp Baltimore MD: GPC,
1975. 295 p.   COMMON
Clover Presbyterian Church, Clover. Sessions records 1881-1908,
1920-1974.   MONT
Clute, Robert F. The annals & parish register of St. Thomas &
St. Dennis parish in SC, from 1680-1884. 1884, rp Baltimore
MD: GPC, 1974. 111 p.   COMMON
Cohen, Hennig. A name index to the South Carolina Gazette,
1732-1738.   SCHS
Cokesbury Presbyterian Church (extinct). Sessions records 1886-
1901, 1920-1921.   MONT
College of Charleston. Names of the graduates...from the year
1825 to 1870, inclusive. Chstn: W,E&C, 1870. 15 p. SCL, SCHS
The Columbia city directory & business guide for 1885. Cola:
Theo I. Robbins, 1885. 197 p.   CLEM
Columbia Theological Seminary. Catalogue of the officers &
students...for the year 1860-1861. Cola: Stokes, 1861. 29 p.
                                                 SCL, SCHS
The complete church register, Chester District, SC conference,
M.E. church, south. NP: typescript, nd.   YOCL
Complete roll of Company "F", Twenty-fourth Regiment, SC Volun-
teers. 11 p.   PIPD
Concord Presbyterian Church, Harmony Presbytery. Sessions rec-
ords, 1853-1941.   MONT
Cooke, Howard & Co. Pocket map & business guide of Charleston,
SC. Baltimore: Howard Cooke & Co., 1887? 130 p.   SCHS
Corinth Presbyterian Church, Harmony Presbytery. Sessions rec-
ords, 1886-1911.   MONT
Coronaca Presbyterian Church (extinct). Records 1895-1904,
1913-1928.   MONT
Craig, Eloise. Shiloh A.R.P. church, Lancaster County, SC. Cem-

etery inscriptions. NP: NPub, 1979. 32 p.   LNCL, YOCL
Crockett, Nancy. Old Waxhaw graveyard. Lancaster: mimeo, 1965.
    unp.   COMMON
Crockett, Nancy & Mamie G. Davis. Old Waxhaw cemetery inscrip-
    tions. Route 4, Lancaster SC.   SCL, SCHS
Crowder, Louise K. Tombstone records of Chester County, SC, &
    vicinity. Chester: author, 1970. 146 p.   COMMON
Crozier, William A. Key to southern pedigrees: being a compre-
    hensive guide to colonial ancestors of families in the states
    of VA, MD, GA, NC, SC, KY, TN, WV & AL. NP: Southern Book Co.
    1953. 80 p.   MACL, DICL
Curtis, Mary B. Church minutes of Clear Springs Baptist church
    [Simpsonville], 1806-1888. Fort Worth TX: American Reference
    Publishers, 1969. 11 p.   SCL, GRCL
Dandridge, Danske. American prisoners of the Revolution. Bal-
    timore MD: GPC, 1967. 504 p.   SCL, KECA
Darlington County. Record of wills... NP: mimeo, nd. 2 vol.
                                                                 DACL
Darlington Court House. List of converts at the Methodist meet-
    ing, 1832.   WOMA
Darlington Presbyterian Church, Darlington. Records 1827-1966.
                                                           SCL, MONT
D.A.R. [Daughters of the American Revolution]. Index of the
    rolls of honor (ancestor's index) in the lineage books of the
    N.S.D.A.R., volumes 1-160. 1916-1940, rp Baltimore MD: GPC,
    1972. 2 vol.   COMMON
D.A.R. Lineage books. Washington: N.S.D.A.R. 166+ vols. COMMON
D.A.R. Errata for the lineage books. Washington: N.S.D.A.R.
                                                                 CRCL
D.A.R. Patriot index. Washington: N.S.D.A.R., 1967. 771 p.
                                          SCL, CRCL, DICL, SPCL
D.A.R. Patriot index...first supplement. Washington: N.S.D.A.
    R., 1969. 85 p.   SCL, GWPL
D.A.R. Patriot index...second supplement. Washington: N.S.D.A.
    R., 1973. 95 p.   SCL, GWPL
D.A.R. Ann Pamela Cunningham Chapter. SC bible records. Cola:
    author, 1962. 2 vol.   SCHS, YOCL
D.A.R. Old Cheraws Chapter. A guide to the markers of Old St.
    David's [Episcopal] cemetery, Cheraw, SC. Cheraw: author,
    1976. 24 p.   FLMC, CTCL
D.A.R. South Carolina. Roster & ancestral roll, S.C.D.A.R.
    Cola: NPub, 1954. 156 p.   SCL
D.A.R. Star Fort Chapter. Cemetery records: Belle Meade ceme-
    tery, Andrew Chapel Methodist churchyard [Greenwood County].
    NP: typescript, nd. v.p.   GWPL
D.A.R. Star Fort Chapter. Cemetery records: Bush River Baptist
    church cemetery [Newberry County]. NP: typescript, nd. v.p.
                                                                 GWPL
D.A.R. Star Fort Chapter. Cemetery records: Liberty Springs
    Presbyterian Church, Smyrna [Laurens County]. NP: typescript,
    nd. 138 p.   GWPL

D.A.R. Sullivan-Dunklin Chapter. Bible records of Laurens
County [SpC]   LRCL
D.A.R. Sullivan-Dunklin chapter. Union Baptist church cemetery
(old Quaker cemetery). Laurens: typescript, 1956. 9 p. LRCL
Davis, Thomas W. Cemetery records. [epitaphs from 128 cemeter-
ies in Greenwood, Laurens, Union, Newberry, Lexington & other
SC counties.] [SpC]   GWPL
Davis, William Hervey. Marriage records of Rev. William Hervey
Davis...1837-1880...Abbeville District... NP: typescript,
1962. 10 p.   GWPL
DeLano, J.W. The Charleston city guide. Chstn: J.W. DeLano,
1872. 106 p.   SCHS
Delwyn Associates. Abstracts of wills, Edgefield County, SC.
Albany GA: Delwyn Associates, 1973. 139 p.   COMMON
Delwyn Associates. Wills of Marlboro County, SC. Albany GA:
Delwyn Associates, 1976. 123 p.   SCL, CLEM, MRCL, MACL
Denmark Presbyterian Church, Denmark. Sessions records 1895-
1939; register, nd.   MONT
DeSaussure, Wilmot G. The names...of the officers who served in
the SC regiments on the continental establishment; of the of-
ficers who served in the militia; of what troops were upon the
continental establishment... 1886, rp Chstn: NPub, 1894.
34 p.   COMMON
Donalds Presbyterian Church, Donalds. Sessions records 1902-
1965; register, 1902-?   MONT
Dorrah Presbyterian Church [Gray Court, SC?]. Sessions records
1908-1949; register, nd.   MONT
Dowling, Daniel J. Dowling's Charleston directory...for 1837 &
1838... Chstn: A. J. Dowling, 1837. unp.   YOCL
Drake, Elizabeth C. Cemetery records of Marlboro County, SC.
NP: author, 1970. 263 p.   COMMON
Drehr, Godfrey. The journal of the Rev. Godfrey Drehr, 1819-
1851. Easley: SHP, 1978. 104 p.   COMMON
Drennan, Thomas. Pay bill for Captain Thomas Drennan's company
of Catawba indians under the command of General Thomas Sumter
in the State of SC servise for the year 1780...& 1781-1782.
NP: NPub, nd. unp.   YOCL
Duncan Memorial Methodist Church, Georgetown. Register of Dun-
can Memorial Methodist Church, Georgetown, SC [marriages &
baptisms, 1811-1846] NP: typescript, nd. 19 p.   SCL, WOMA
Eaddy, Elaine Y. A survey of the cemeteries of lower Florence
County, SC. Hemingway: Three Rivers Historical Society, 1977-
1978. 4 vol.   SCL, SMCL, FLMC
Eaddy, Elaine Y. Williamsburg County probate record abstracts
[SpC]   WMTR
Eaddy, Elaine Y. & Nell G. Morris. Funeral home records [of]
Morris Funeral Home, Hemingway, and Brockington Funeral Home,
Lake City [Williamsburg County]. [SpC]   WMTR
Easley Presbyterian Church [SpC]   MONT
Ebenezer Baptist Church, Darlington County. Records, 1823-1908.
                                                           SCL

Ebenezer Presbyterian Church, Rock Hill. Records 1785-?   YOWC
Ebenezer Presbyterian Church, York County. Minutes of the sessions...1854-1945. NP: typescript, nd. 4 vol.   YOCL
Edisto Island Presbyterian Church, Edisto Island. Sessions rec-
   ords 1837-1861, 1866-1947; register 1821-1871, corporation
   records 1780-1924, financial records 1871-1965.   MONT
Elim Baptist Church, Effingham. Records 1836-1927.   SCL
Elliott, Colleen M. Early Anderson County, SC, newspapers, mar-
   riages & obituaries, 1841-1882. Easley: SHP, 1978. 252 p.
                                                            COMMON
Elliott, Colleen M. Marriage & death notices from the Keowee
   Courier, 1849-1871 & 1878-1883. Easley: SHP, 1978. 186 p.
                                                            COMMON
Ellis, George H.? Records of the First [Congregational] Church
   at Dorchester [Massachusetts] in New England: 1636-1734 [from
   which the Independent or Congregational Church, St. George's
   Parish, SC, was formed]. Boston, 1891. 270 p.   SCHS
Elon Presbyterian Church, Harmony Presbytery. Sessions records
   1856-1885.   MONT
Elzas, Barnett A. The Jewish cemeteries of SC: an index to the
   inscriptions on their tombstones. Chstn, 1911.   CHLS, SCHS
Elzas, Barnett A. Jewish marriage notices from the newspaper
   press of Charleston, SC, 1775-1906. NY: Bloch, 1917. 64 p.
                                                      SCL, CHLS, SCHS
Elzas, Barnett A. Old Jewish cemeteries at Charleston, SC; a
   transcript of the inscriptions on their tombstones, 1762-1903.
   Chstn: Daggett Printing Co., 1903. 121 p.   SCL, CHCO, SCHS
Enon Christian Church, Hampton. Records 1875-1911.   SCL
Enoree Presbyterian Church, Enoree. Sessions records 1872-1921.
                                                            MONT
Episcopal Church Home for Children, York. Records 1866-1967.
                                                            YOWC
Episcopal Church of Our Savior, Rock Hill. Parish registers
   [Ms] 1869-1961. 4 vol.   YOCL
Episcopal Diocese of South Carolina. Manuscript church records
   on deposit at the South Carolina Historical Society, Charles-
   ton [for details of specific records holdings, contact the
   SCHS]: Chapel of the Holy Cross, Moultrieville [Sullivan's
   Island]; Christ Church Parish; Christ Church, Wilton's Bluff;
   Church of the Messiah, North Santee; All Saint's Parish; Com-
   bahee Church or Church of the Ascension, Edmundsbury; Church
   of the Redeemer, Orangeburg; Holy Cross, Claremont; Prince
   Frederick, Winyah; Prince George, Winyah (Georgetown); St.
   Andrew's Parish Church; St. Helena's, Beaufort; St. Bartholo-
   mew's; St. James', Santee; St. John's, Berkeley; St. John's,
   Colleton; St. Luke's, Charleston; St. Paul's, Stono; St.
   John's, John's Island; St. Peter's, Charleston; St. Stephen's,
   Charleston; St. Philip's, Bradford Springs; St. Stephen's &
   St. John's Parish, Craven County, SC; St. Thomas & St. Denis'
   Parish; St. Stephen's Chapel, Charleston; Society for the Re-
   lief of the Widows & Orphans of the Clergy of the Protestant

Episcopal Church in SC. Also uncataloged pamphlets, church
histories, and periodicals of the Diocese.
Ervin, Sara S. Marriage records of old Ninety-Six District, SC.
Abstracted mostly from the Sullivan-Ervin collection... Ware
Shoals: typescript, 1951. 9 p. LRCL
Ervin, Sara S. South Carolinians in the Revolution, with ser-
vice records and misc. data, also abstracts of wills, Laurens
County (Ninety-Six District), 1775-1855...with added chapter
on the Sullivan family. 1949, rp Baltimore MD: GPC, 1976.
217 p. COMMON
Esker, Katie-Prince W. South Carolina Memorials, Vol. I, 1731-
1776. Abstracts of selected land records...in the SCDAH.
Cottonport LA: Polyanthos, 1973. 140 p. COMMON
Esker, Katie-Prince W. South Carolina Memorials, Vol. II,
Cottonport LA: Polyanthos, 1977. 222 p. SCL
Euhaw Baptist Church, Beaufort County. Records 1831-1908. SCL
Fairforest Baptist Church, Union County. Records 1820-1899. SCL
Fairforest Presbyterian Church, Jonesville. Records of sessions
1791-1803, 1809-1827, 1829-1848; deacon's records 1857-? MONT
Fair Hope Presbyterian Church, Lamar. Sessions records 1953-
1964; register, nd. MONT
Fant, Sandy. [Inscriptions from] U.S. National Cemetery, Beau-
fort. NP: typescript, nd. 7 p. SCL
First Baptist Church, Columbia. Records 1809-1840. SCL
First Presbyterian Church, Anderson. Sessions records 1837-1855
1837-1867, 1867-1927; register 1837-?. MONT
First Presbyterian Church, Cheraw. Sessions records 1828-1879,
1901-1959. MONT
First Presbyterian Church, Columbia. Financial records 1848-
1853; Temporal affairs committee records 1827-1845. SCL, MONT
First Presbyterian Church, Dillon. Records (copies) 1899-1975.
MONT
First Presbyterian Church, Lancaster. Sessions records 1835-
1968. MONT
First Presbyterian Church, Union. Sessions records 1842-1912;
register 1840-1912. MONT
First (Scots) Presbyterian Church, Charleston. [SpC] MONT
First (Scots) Presbyterian Church, Charleston. Misc. records
1967-1970. MONT
Fishing Creek Presbyterian Church. Early records of Fishing
Creek Presbyterian Church, Chester County, SC. Greenville SC:
A Press, 1980. 191 p. SCL
Fishing Creek Presbyterian Church. Roster...as of October, 1960
NP: typescript. YOCL
Fishing Creek Presbyterian Church, Chester District. Sessions
records 1799-1825; register, nd. SCL, MONT
Fishing Creek Presbyterian Church, Chester District. Records,
1799-1839 [SpC] SCL, YOWC
Fishing Creek Presbyterian church records, 1799-1859, copied by

Mary W. Strange, Feb. 1936 [SpC]   CSCL
Flint Hill Baptist Church, York District. Records 1792-1899
   [SpC]   SCL, YOCL
Florence Moore Presbyterian Church, Wellford. Sessions records
   1884-1953.   MONT
Floyd, J. W. Historical roster & itinerary of SC volunteer
   troops who served in the late war between the U.S. & Spain,
   1898. Cola: R.L. Bryan, 1901. 286 p.   COMMON
Forest Lake Presbyterian Church, Columbia. Sessions records
   1957-1966.   MONT
Fowler, Andrew. Confirmations on Edisto Island. In the state
   of SC, in the years 1813 & 1814. NP: Hopkins, 1814? 16 p.SCL
Foxworth, Mrs. G. Duncan. Roster & ancestral roll of the SC
   Daughters of the American Revolution. Cola: RLB, 1954.
   156 p.   SCL, ANCL, KECA, MRCL
Francis, Elisabeth W. Lost links; new recordings of old data
   from many states. 1947, rp Baltimore MD: GPC, 1975. 562 p.
                                                     COMMON
Gamewell, J. A. & D. D. Wallace. The Richland almanac, 1904.
   Spartanburg: W. F. Barnes, 1904? 48 p.   SCL, WOFF
Georgetown Presbyterian Church, Georgetown. Sessions records
   1897-1953.   SCL, MONT
Gilman, Caroline. Record of inscriptions in the cemetery &
   Building of the Unitarian, formerly denominated the Indepen-
   dent Church, Archdale Street, Charleston, from 1777-1860.
   Chstn: W,E&C, 1860. 190 p.   COMMON
Gilmer, Georgia M. American Revolution roster, Fort Sullivan
   (later Fort Moultrie), 1776-1780; battle of Fort Sullivan:
   events leading to the first decisive victory. Chstn: Fort
   Sullivan Chapter, D.A.R., 1976. 311 p.   COMMON
Glebe Street Presbyterian Church, Charleston. Baptismal regis-
   ter 1847-1862; corporation records 1850-?.   MONT
Glenn Springs Presbyterian Church, Glenn Springs. Sessions
   records, 1893-1930.   MONT
Glover, Beulah. In memory of; inscriptions from early cemeteries [of Colleton County]. Walterboro: Press & Standard, 1972.
   58 p.   COMMON
Goldsmith, Morris. Directory & stranger's guide for the city of
   Charleston... Chstn: Office of the Irishman, 1831. 191 p.
                                                  SCL, SCHS
Gravestones of Hoods & Whites in Pleasant Grove Presbyterian
   churchyard, 1947 [SpC]   CSCL
Great Saltketcher Baptist Church, Barnwell County. Records
   1858-1879.   SCL
Green, Ralph T. Rembert [M.E.] church & cemetery... NP: type-
   script, 1973. 10 p.   SCL
Greenville Chapter, SCGS. Greenville County cemeteries, vol. I.
   Greenville: A Press, 1977. 430 p.   COMMON
Greenville Chapter, SCGS. Greenville County cemeteries, vol. II
   Greenville: A Press, 1979.   COMMON
Greenville Chapter, SCGS. Lineage charts. Greenville: author,

1978-. 2 vol.   LNCL
Greenville Female College. Forty-third annual register & an-
   nouncement...register 1895-96. Announcement 1896-97. Green-
   ville: NPub, 1896. 53 p.   SCHS
Greenville Presbyterian Church, Due West. Sessions records
   1846-1956; register 1846-?; treasurer's records 1836-1877.MONT
Greenwood cemetery & Magnolia cemetery [inscriptions, Greenwood
   County] [SpC]   GSGN
Gum Branch Baptist Church, Lower fork of the Lynches River,
   Chester County. Records 1796-1887.   SCL
Harley, Lillian H. Cemetery inscriptions of Dorchester County,
   SC, vol. I. St. George: Dorchester Eagle-Record, 1979. 128
   p.   COMMON
Harley, Lillian H. Cemetery inscriptions of Dorchester County,
   SC, vol. II. St. George: Dorchester Eagle-Record, 1980. 159
   p.   COMMON
Harmony Presbyterian Church, Crocketville. Sessions records
   1870-1956; register 1870-1956.   MONT
Hart, Joseph E. Jr. Marriage & death notices from the Yorkville
   Enquirer, 1855-1889; Yorkville Miscellany, 1851-1854; Remedy,
   1853; Yorkville Compiler, 1840-1841; Encyclopedia, 1825-1826,
   Yorkville Pioneer, 1823-1824. NP: typescript, 1971. 2 vol.
                                                                 YOCL
Hartsville Presbyterian Church, Hartsville. Sessions records,
   1868-1948; register, nd.   MONT
Hebron Methodist Church, Bucksville. Misc. records, including
   membership, 1806-1866; conference minutes, 1866-1880.   WOMA
Hemphill, Mrs. James C. Martin-Aiken family burying ground,
   Fairfield County. NP: typescript, nd. 1 p.   SCL
Hendrix, Ge L. Edgefield County, SC, abstracts of deed books
   1, 2 & 3 [1786-1789]. Greenville: author, 1979.80 p. SCL,GSGN
Hendrix, Ge L. Edgefield County, SC, abstracts of deed books
   4, 5 & 6 [1790-1792]. Greenville: author, 1980.   SCL, GSGN
Hendrix, Ge L. Indexes of Edgefield County, SC, vol. I: probate
   records. Greenville: author, 1979. 160 p.   COMMON
Hendrix, Ge L. Pendleton County deed books, vol. "A": 1790-1792
   & vol. "B": 1791-1795. Greenville: author, 1980. 150 p. SCHS
Hendrix, Ge L. & Morn M. Lindsay. The jury lists of SC, 1778-
   1779. Greenville: authors, 1975. 136 p.   COMMON
Herd, E. Don & Ann B. Herd. Marriage & death notices from the
   Abbeville Banner, 1846-1860. NP: authors, 1980.   SCL,GSGN
Hicklin, Mrs. Frank. List of those buried at Fishing Creek
   Presbyterian churchyard, Chester County... NP: typescript,
   nd.   YOCL
Highland Presbyterian Church, Greenville. Sessions records
   1926-1961; register, nd.   MONT
Hill's Anderson (city & county) city directory...1934. Richmond
   VA: Hill's Directory Co., 1934.   CLEM
Hinshaw, William W. Encyclopedia of Quaker genealogy, vol. I:
   NC [includes SC]. 1936 & 1948, rp Baltimore MD: GPC, 1978.
   1185 p.   SCL, KECA, GWPL

Historical list of the officers & members of the Presbyterian
   Church of Abbeville, SC, organized April 22, 1868. NP: NPub,
   188?. 9 p.   MONT
Holcomb, Brent. Anson County, NC, deed abstracts, 1749-1766;
   abstracts of wills & estates, 1749-1795. Baltimore MD: GPC,
   1980. 170 p. [combined from the two following books]   PUBL
Holcomb, Brent. Anson County, NC, deed abstracts, vol. I: 1749-
   1757. Clinton: author, 1974. 57 p.   COMMON
Holcomb, Brent. Anson County, NC, deed abstracts, vol. II:1757-
   1766. Clinton: author, 1975. 65 p.   COMMON
Holcomb, Brent. Anson County, NC, wills & estates, 1749-1795.
   Clinton: author, 1975. 29 p.   COMMON
Holcomb, Brent. Chester County, SC, minutes of the county court
   1785-1799. Easley: SHP, 1979. 433 p.   COMMON
Holcomb, Brent. Deed abstracts of Tryon, Lincoln & Rutherford
   Counties, NC, 1769-1786, & Tryon County, NC, wills & estates.
   Easley: SHP, 1977. 224 p.   SCL, ANCL, CRCL, SCHS
Holcomb, Brent. Early records of Fishing Creek Presbyterian
   Church, Chester County, SC, 1799-1859. Greenville: A Press,
   1980. 164 p.   SCL, PUBL
Holcomb, Brent. Edgefield County, SC, minutes of the county
   court, 1785-1799. Easley: SHP, 1979. 220 p.   COMMON
Holcomb, Brent. 1800 census of Lexington County, SC. Clinton:
   author, 1974. 17 p.   SCL, PUBL
Holcomb, Brent. Index to the 1800 census of SC. Baltimore MD:
   GPC, 1980. 264 p.   SCL, FACL
Holcomb, Brent. Index to the 1850 [federal census] mortality
   schedules. Easley: SHP, 1980. 100 p.   SCL, PUBL
Holcomb, Brent. Journal of the Rev. Godfrey Drehr, 1819-1851.
   Easley: SHP, 1978. 104 p.   COMMON
Holcomb, Brent. Lancaster County, SC, deed abstracts, 1787-1820
   Easley: SHP, 1980. 200 p.   PUBL
Holcomb, Brent. Marriage & death notices from Camden, SC, news-
   papers, 1816-1865. Easley: SHP, 1978. 166 p.   COMMON
Holcomb, Brent. Marriage & death notices from the Charleston
   Observer, 1827-1845. Greenville: A Press, 1980. 283 p.   SCL
Holcomb, Brent. Marriage & death notices from the Charleston
   Times. 1800-1821. Baltimore MD: GPC, 1979. 374 p.   SCL
Holcomb, Brent. Marriage, death & estate notices from George-
   town, SC, newspapers, 1791-1861. Easley: SHP, 1979. 208 p.
                                                          COMMON
Holcomb, Brent. Marriage & death notices from the Lutheran Ob-
   server, 1831-1861, and the Southern Lutheran, 1861-1865.
   Easley: SHP, 1979. 250 p.   COMMON
Holcomb, Brent. Marriage & death notices from the Pendleton
   Messenger, 1807-1851. Easley: SHP, 1977. 123 p.   COMMON
Holcomb, Brent. Marriage & death notices from the Southern
   Christian Advocate, 1837-1860, vol. I. Easley: SHP, 1979.
   727 p.   COMMON
Holcomb, Brent. Marriage & death notices from the Southern
   Christian Advocate, 1861-1867. Vol. II. Easley: SHP, 1980.

227 p.   PUBL

Holcomb, Brent. Marriage & death notices from upper SC newspapers, 1843-1865. Easley: SHP, 1977. 168 p.   COMMON
Holcomb, Brent. Mecklenburg NC abstracts of early wills, 1763-
1790 (1749-1790). Greenville: A Press, 1979. 101 p. SCL,PUBL
Holcomb, Brent. Mecklenburg County, NC, deed abstracts, books
1-9, 1763-1779. Easley: SHP, 1979. 350 p.   COMMON
Holcomb, Brent. Memorialized records of Lexington District, SC,
1814-1825. Easley: SHP, 1978. 176 p.   COMMON
Holcomb, Brent. Newberry County, SC, minutes of the county
court, 1785-1798. Easley: SHP, 1977. 332 p.   COMMON
Holcomb, Brent. Ninety-Six District, SC: journal of the court
of ordinary, inventory book, will book 1781-1786. Easley:
SHP, 1978. 61 p.   COMMON
Holcomb, Brent. NC land grants in SC, 1745-1773. Greenville:
A Press, 1980. 161 p. [combined volume of the two following
volumes]   SCL, PUBL
Holcomb, Brent. NC land grants in SC, vol. I: Tryon County, NC,
1768-1773. Clinton: author, 1975. 36 p.   SCL, PUBL
Holcomb, Brent. NC land grants in SC, vol. II: Anson & Mecklen-
burg Counties, NC, 1749-1770. Clinton: author, 1976. 89 p.
                                                      SCL, PUBL
Holcomb, Brent. Old Camden District, SC, wills & administra-
tions, 1781-1787. Easley: SHP, 120 p.   COMMON
Holcomb, Brent. Probate records of SC, vol. I: an index to in-
ventories, 1746-1784. Easley: SHP, 1977. 71 p.   COMMON
Holcomb, Brent. Probate records of SC, vol. II: journal of the
Court of Ordinary, 1771-1775; letters of administration for
SC & Charleston District, 1775-1821. Easley: SHP, 1978.
336 p.   COMMON
Holcomb, Brent. Probate records of SC, vol. III: journal of the
court of ordinary, 1764-1771. Easley: SHP, 1979. 153 p.
                                                        COMMON
Holcomb, Brent. St. David's Parish, SC: minutes of the vestry,
1768-1832, and parish register, 1819-1923. Easley: SHP, 1979.
149 p.   COMMON
Holcomb, Brent. SC marriages, 1688-1799. Baltimore MD: GPC,
1980. 349 p.   COMMON
Holcomb, Brent. Spartanburg County, SC, minutes of the county
court, 1785-1799. Easley: SHP, 1980. 325 p.   COMMON
Holcomb, Brent. Two 1787 tax lists from Ninety-Six District,
SC. Clinton: author, 1974. 21 p.   SCL, PUBL
Holcomb, Brent. Union County, SC, minutes of the county court,
1785-1799. Easley: SHP, 1979. 523 p.   COMMON
Holcomb, Brent. Upper SC marriage & death notices, 1843-1865.
Easley: SHP, 1977. 176 p.   COMMON
Holcomb, Brent. Winton County (Barnwell County),SC, minutes of
the county court & will book I, 1785-1791. Easley: SHP, 1978.
184 p.   COMMON
Holcomb, Brent & Silas Emmett Lucas, Jr. Some SC county records
vol. I. Easley: SHP, 1976. 162 p.   COMMON

Holcomb, Brent & Silas Emmett Lucas, Jr. Some SC county records
vol. II. Easley: SHP, 1981.   COMMON
Holcomb, Brent & Elmer O. Parker. Camden District, SC, wills &
administrations, 1781-1787 (1770-1796). Easley: SHP, 1978.
111 p.   COMMON
Holleman, Joseph T. Old White Church [Independent or Congregational Church of St. George's Parish] cemetery, [near] Summerville, SC. 5 p.   SCHS
Honea Path Presbyterian Church, Honea Path. Sessions records,
1860-1886, 1860-1926; register, nd.   MONT
Hopewell A.R.P. Church, Chester County. Records 1832-1939. SCL
Hopewell Baptist Church, Chester County. Records 1871-1895. SCL
Hopewell Presbyterian Church, Florence County. Sessions records
1896-1934.   MONT
Hopewell Presbyterian Church, McCormick (extinct). Sessions
records 1839-1947; register 1839-1847.   MONT
Hopewell Presbyterian Church, Pendleton. Sessions records 1832-
1893.   MONT
Hopkins Presbyterian Church, Congaree Presbytery. Sessions
records 1916-1949.   MONT
Horlbeck, Mrs. Frederick H. Register of National Society of
Colonial Dames of XVII century in the state of SC. NP: Waver-
ly Press, 1945. 176 p.   MRCL
Horn's Creek Baptist Church, Edgefield County. Records 1824-
1859.   SCL
Horry County epitaphs, vol. I: Baker's Chapel cemetery, Bayboro
Baptist churchyard, Bethlehem Baptist churchyard. Typescript
1969. 86 p.   SCL
Horry County epitaphs, vol. II: Branton cemetery, Reaves cemetery, Tilly Swamp Baptist church cemetery, Brown Swamp Methodist church cemetery, Campground cemetery, Centenary Methodist
church cemetery, Singleton family cemetery, Cochean Town
(Greenhole) cemetery, Cool Springs Methodist cemetery. Type-
script, 1969. 70 p.   SCL
Horry County epitaphs, vol. III: Cushion Swamp cemetery, Dew
cemetery, Singleton cemetery, First Methodist Church cemetery,
Graham cemetery, High Point Church cemetery. Typescript, nd.
43 p.   SCL
Horry County epitaphs, vol. IV: Hillcrest cemetery, Conway.
Typescript, nd. 97 p.   SCL
Horry County epitaphs, vol. V: Juniper Bay Baptist church ceme-
tery, Kirton cemetery, Red Hill cemetery, Bunker cemetery,
Lakeside cemetery. Typescript, 1969. 111 p.   SCL
Horry County epitaphs, vol. VI: Lakeside cemetery, McCracken
cemetery, Rehobeth Methodist cemetery, Mt. Herman Baptist
Church cemetery, Patterson cemetery. Typescript, 1969.
75 p.   SCL
Horry County epitaphs, vol. VII: Pawley Swamp Baptist church
cemetery, Pisgah Methodist cemetery, Poplar Methodist church
cemetery. Typescript, nd. 100 p.   SCL
Horry County epitaphs, vol. VIII: Sharon Baptist Church cemete-

ry, Socastee Methodist Church cemetery. Typescript, nd.
64 p. SCL
Horry County epitaphs, vol. IX: State cemetery, Union Methodist
cemetery, United Baptist church cemetery, Waller & McCracken
graveyards. Typescript, nd. 67 p. SCL
Horry County Library. Abstracts of birth, marriage & death in-
formation from local newspapers [SpC] HOCL
Hough, Mrs. Ben C. & others. Kershaw County cemetery inscrip-
tions: Hammond family cemetery, Boykin family cemetery, Ker-
shaw family cemetery, Ancrum family cemetery in Camden, Len-
oir/Blanchard family cemetery in Boykin, Quaker cemetery in
Camden, Chesnut family cemetery at Knight's Hill, Ranging Rock
Church cemetery. Typescript, nd. 14 p. SCL
Houston, Martha L. Indexes to the county wills of SC. 1939, rp
Baltimore MD: GPC, 1964. 261 p. COMMON
Howe, Mrs. C.G. Minutes of St. Michael's [Episcopal] church of
Charleston, SC, 1758-1797. Cola: Colonial Dames, nd. 214
p. COMMON
Huntsville Baptist Church, Laurens County. Records 1838-1871.
SCL
Immanuel Episcopal Church, Chester County. Register, 1843-?YOCL
Independent Presbyterian Church, Stoney Creek. Covenant & reg-
ister, 1743-1760; minutes & accounts records, 1773-1823; con-
gregational records, 1823-1874; financial records, 1823-1902;
register, 1825-1910; sessions records 1855-1910; misc. rec-
ords 1743-1910. SCL, MONT
Independent or Congregational Church of Dorchester & Beech Hill,
St. George's Parish. Minutes, 1794-1856. MONT
Independent or Congregational Church of Dorchester & Beech Hill,
St. George's Parish. Minutes, 1794-1858, 1838-1851, 1803-
1823 [SCHS micropublications #50-87, 50-88, 50-89] MONT, SCHS
Index of..records of the clerk of court, Laurens County, SC,
1789-1803. NP: 1952. LRCL
Indiantown Presbyterian Church, Hemingway. Records 1819-1899;
sessions records 1947-1966. MONT
Indiantown Presbyterian church account book kept by Captain John
James, trustee, with John Wilson...Williamsburg County...1793.
[copy of Ms. & typescript, 7 p.] WMTR
Inscriptions from old cemeteries in Lancaster, SC. Lancaster:
Lancaster County Historical Commission, 1974. 112 p. LNCL
YOCL
Inscriptions on gravestones in cemeteries in Beaufort County:
Evergreen cemetery, First Baptist Church cemetery, First Tab-
ernacle Baptist Church cemetery, Jewish cemetery, Old Sheldon
[Episcopal] Church cemetery, St. Peter's Catholic Church cem-
etery, various small cemeteries [SpC] SCL, BUCL
Inscriptions: tombstones in Tirzah Presbyterian churchyard, in
Lancaster County...& Union County. NP: Tirzah Cemetery Assn.,
1948. SCL, LNCL
Jackson, Mabel. Directory of Ebenezer Presbyterian church ceme-
tery, Town of Ebenezer, York County, SC. Typescript, 1955.

37 p.   LNCL, SCL, YOCL
James Island Exchange Club. Program dedicating the roll of hon-
   or erected by the Exchange Club of James Island in honor of
   James Islanders serving in the armed forces. nd. 16 p. SCL
James Island Presbyterian Church, James Island. Sessions rec-
   ords 1853-1872, corporation minutes, 1847-1909; receipt book,
   1847-1909; register, 1833-1845.   SCL, MONT
Jervey, Clare. Inscriptions on tablets & gravestones in St.
   Michael's [Episcopal] Church... Cola: State Co., 1906.
   334 p.   COMMON
John's Island Presbyterian Church, John's Island. John's Island
   & Wadmalaw Island Presbyterian church records: sessions rec-
   ords 1856-1946; register, 1833-1845.   SCL, MONT
Johnson, Louise R. Inscriptions from the churchyard of Prince
   George, Winyah [Episcopal church], Georgetown, SC. SCL, GTML
Johnston Presbyterian Church, Johnston. Records 1891-1919,
   1923-1953.   MONT
Keesee, Sarah W. & Martha W. Agner. Flint Hill Baptist church
   cemetery inscriptions, York County. NP: mimeo, 1969. 66 p.
                                                       YOCL SCL
Kennedy, Robert M. De mortuis; concerning those that lie in the
   old burial grounds in and about Camden, SC. Cola: State Co.,
   1935. 23 p.   COMMON
Kershaw Presbyterian Church, Kershaw. Sessions records 1892-
   1919.   MONT
Kingston Presbyterian Church, Conway. Records, 1858-1930. MONT
Kingstree Baptist Church, Williamsburg County. Records 1858-
   1894.   SCL
Knox Presbyterian Church, Charleston (extinct). Sessions records 1914-1925.   MONT
Ladies' Memorial Association, Charleston. A brief history...
   From its organization in 1865 to April 1, 1880. Together with
   a roster of the Confederate dead interred at Magnolia [cemete-
   ry]and the various city church yards. Chstn: Cooke, 1880.
   42 p.   SCL, SCHS
Lancaster County Historical Commission. Inscriptions from old
   cemeteries in Lancaster, SC. Lancaster: Tri-county Publishing
   Co., 1974. 112 p.   SCL, CRCL
Landmark Lodge, Charleston. By-laws & roster of members. Chstn
   Daggett, 1913. 59 p.   SCHS
Laurens County cemetery. Epitaphs... Typescript, nd.   SCHS
Laurens M.E. Circuit. Register of churches on Laurens circuit,
   including Smyrna, Laurens Court House, Trinity, Patterson
   Chapel, & New Zion Methodist churches. Includes baptisms,
   1881-1884; marriages 1883.   WOMA
Laurens City directories, 1917-1979 (passim.)   LRCL
Laurensville Female College. Catalogue of the officers & stud-
   ents...1858-1871: LRCL. SCL has 1859.
Lebanon Presbyterian Church, Abbeville. Sessions records & reg-
   ister, 1918-1956.   MONT
Legette, Gladys. Beaver Dam cemetery, McColl. Typescript, nd.

7 p.   SCL
Legette, Gladys. Fletcher's cemetery, McColl, SC. Typescript,
  nd. 5 p.   SCL
Letter from the Secretary of War transmitting a list of every
  person placed on the pension list, on pursuance of the Act of
  the 18th March, 1818, &c; January 20, 1820... 1820, rp Balti-
  more MD: Southern Book Co., 1955. 672 p.   SCL, ORCL, LNCL
Liberty Spring Presbyterian Church, Cross Hill. Sessions rec-
  ords, 1837-1933.   MONT
Limestone Presbyterian Church, Gaffney. Sessions records & reg-
  ister, 1877-1937.   MONT
List of mayors & aldermen of Charleston, SC. Typescript.   SCHS
List of members at Fishing Creek Presbyterian Church, Chester
  County [1799-1858, also baptisms 1799-1814]. Typescript, nd.
  5 p.   SCL, MONT
Little Pee Dee Baptist Church, Pauley's Creek. Records 1868-
  1887.   SCL
Little Rock Presbyterian Church, Little Rock. Sessions records
  1886-?   MONT
Lower Long Cane A.R.P. & Cedar Springs A.R.P. church cemetery
  records [SpC]   GSGN
Lucas, Silas E. Abbeville District, SC, marriages, 1777-1852.
  Easley: SHP, 1979. 69 p.   SCHS
Lucas, Silas E. Wills & administrations, Camden District, 1781-
  1787. Easley: SHP, . 76 p.   FACM, SCHS
Lucas, Silas E. & Brent Holcomb. An index to the deeds of the
  province & state of SC, 1719-1785, & Charleston District,
  1785-1800. Easley: SHP, 1977. 848 p.   COMMON
Lucas, Silas E. Old Ninety-Six & Abbeville District, SC, marriages, 1777-1852. Easley: SHP, 1979. 80 p.   CLEM, SCHS
Maddox, Joseph T. & Mary Carter. SC Revolutionary soldiers,
  patriots, sailors & descendants. NP: Georgia Pioneers Publishing Co., 1976. 191 p.   ORCL
Marceil, Elizabeth. Bethany cemetery, section 2, & German Artillery memorial association. Typescript, nd. 20 p.   SCL
Marceil, Elizabeth C. Tombstone inscriptions from Charleston
  churchyards. Typescript, 1936.   SCHS
Marion Presbyterian Church, Marion. Sessions records 1852-1951.
                                                                    MONT
Marlboro County cemetery records [SpC]   MRCL
Mauldin, Joe L. Muster roll of the Gist Rifles, Col. Hampton's
  legion, Gary's cavalry brigade, 1861-1865. NP: 1883. 8 p.
                                                                    SCL
Mayesville Presbyterian Church, Mayesville. Sessions records
  1881-1930; congregational records, 1881-1906; financial rec-
  ords, 1907-?   MONT
McBryde, Sarah C. Old Lebanon Presbyterian church cemetery,
  Jackson Creek [Fairfield County]. Typescript, nd. 10 p. SCL
McCain, Berta. Sunnyside cemetery, Orangeburg, SC, 1971. Or-
  angeburg SC: Moultrie Chapter, D.A.R., 1973. unp.   ORCL
McCall, James. Copy of the original index book showing the Rev-

olutionary claims filed in SC between August 20, 1783 & August 31, 1786... Baltimore MD: GPC, 1969. 387 p.   SCLB
McClendon, Carlee T. Edgefield death notices & cemetery records. Edgefield: Hive Press, 1977. 300 p.   COMMON
McClendon, Carlee T. Edgefield marriage records, from the late 18th century through 1870. Edgefield: Hive Press, 1970. 234 p.   COMMON
McCollum, Mrs. L.T. Some cemetery inscriptions [from] old Marion District, SC. Latta: Lord Craven Chapter, D.A.R., 1953. 2 vol.   MACL
McGill Memorial Presbyterian Church, Harmony Presbytery. Sessions records, 1909-1929.   MONT
Mechanicsville Baptist Church, Darlington County. Records 1803-1867.   SCL
Midway Presbyterian Church, Midway. Records 1856-1895.   MONT
Miles, William P. Oration...delivered before the alumni of the College of Charleston...with the constitution and list of members of the alumni. Chstn: W,E&C, 1893. 24 p.   SCL, SCHS
Milford Baptist Church, Greenville County. Records 1832-1869.
                    SCL
Miller's planter's and merchants' almanac for 1825-1894 (various years)...   SCL, SCHS
Milligan, Jacob. The Charleston directory and revenue system... Chstn, 1790. 56 p.   SCHS
Mineral Springs Baptist Church, Marlboro County. Records 1867-1905.   SCL
Minutes of the sessions of the Neely's Creek A.R.P. church, 1847-1876. Photocopy of Ms., 42 p. [York County]   YOCL
Miscellaneous Bible & cemetery records, Laurens County area [SpC]   LRCL
Misenhelter, Jane S. St. Stephen's Episcopal church, St. Stephens, SC. Including Church of the Epiphany, in Upper St. John's, Berkeley; and Chapel of Ease, Pineville, SC... Cola: State Co., 1977. 223 p.   COMMON
Mispah Baptist Church, Mars Bluff. Records 1830-1862.   SCL
Moore, Caroline T. Abstracts of the wills of SC, 1670-1740. Cola: RLB, 1960. 346 p.   COMMON
Moore, Caroline T. Abstracts of the wills of SC, 1740-1760. Cola: RLB, 1964. 355 p.   COMMON
Moore, Caroline T. Abstracts of the wills of SC, 1760-1784. Cola: RLB, 1969. 454 p.   COMMON
Moore, Caroline T. Abstracts of the wills of SC, 1783-1800. Cola: RLB, 1974. 526 p.   COMMON
Moore, Caroline T. Records of the secretary of the province of SC, 1692-1721. Cola: RLB, 1978. 457 p.   COMMON
Moore, Caroline T. St. Peter's Episcopal church, Charleston, SC. Register, 1833-1862. Typescript, nd. 78 p.   COMMON
Moses, Herbert A. The early minutes of the Sumter Society of Israelites. Sumter: NPub, 1936. 24 p.   SCL, SCHS
Moss, Maye. Complete record of Mill Creek cemetery... Typescript, 1962. 2 p.   SCL

Moss, Maye. Old Center Church cemetery, York County. Type-
    script, 1962. 1 p.   SCL
Moss, Maye. Wood family cemetery, York County. Typescript,
    1962. 1 p.   SCL
Moss, Maye. Partial record of..Beersheba Presbyterian Church
    cemetery, York County. Typescript, 1962. 2 p.   SCL
Mount Arnon Baptist Church, Allendale. Records 1839-1970
    [SpC]   YOWC
Mount Aron Baptist Church, Allendale County. Records 1839-1937.
                                                               SCL
Mount Carmel Presbyterian Church, Donalds. Sessions records
    1902-1965; register, 1902-?   MONT
Mount Moriah Baptist church cemetery [SpC]   GSGN
Mount Olivet Presbyterian Church, Winnsboro. Sessions records
    & register, 1857-1909.   MONT
Mount Pleasant Exchange Club, Mt. Pleasant. ...Souvenir booklet
    of the unveiling of the honor roll tablet to those in service
    from Mt. Pleasant & Christ Church Parish. Mt. Pleasant:
    author, 1944. 40 p.   SCHS
Mount Pleasant Presbyterian Church, Lowry. Sessions records &
    register, 1882-1942.   MONT
Mount Pleasant Presbyterian Church, Piedmont Presbytery. Ses-
    sions records, 1892-1906.   MONT
Mount Tabor Presbyterian Church, Greer. Sessions records 1841-
    1877.   SCL, MONT
Mount Tabor Presbyterian Church, Union. Sessions records 1879-
    1954.   MONT
Mountain Creek Baptist church cemetery inscriptions. Typescript
    nd. 10 p.   SCL
Mountain Creek Baptist Church, Spartanburg County. Records 1833
    -1854.   SCL
Myrtle Beach Presbyterian Church, Myrtle Beach. Sessions rec-
    ords 1937-1954.   MONT
Nash, Sara M. & Bernice A. George. Miscellaneous Laurens County
    and other records. Laurens: Sullivan Dunklin Chapter, D.A.R.
    1952. 109 p.   LRCL
National Archives & Records Service. Index of Revolutionary War
    pension & bounty land applications in the National Archives.
    Washington DC: National Archives & Records Service, 1977.
    658 p.   PUBL
National Society, Colonial Dames. Register book for the parish
    of Prince Frederick, Winyaw, 1713. Baltimore : Colonial Dames
    1916. 246 p.   SCL, DICL, COKL
Nations, Loye E. Mt. Pisgah Baptist Church, Rt. 2, Jefferson,
    SC...listing of all graves in the cemetery... Typescript,
    1971. 12 p.   SCL
Nazareth Presbyterian Church, Wellford? Sessions records 1854-
    1888; congregational records, 1872-1887; treasurer's records,
    1872-1888.   MONT
Neal's Creek Baptist Church, Anderson County. Records 1832-1901
                                                               SCL

Neely's Creek A.R.P. Church. Minutes of the sessions...1847-
1876.   YOCL
New Allendale Baptist Church, Allendale. Records 1882-1922. SCL
New Harmony Presbyterian Church, Fountain Inn. Sessions records
1853-?   MONT
New Hope Presbyterian Church, Harmony Presbytery (extinct).
Records, 1898-1916.   MONT
Newberry A.R.P. Church, Newberry. Records 1854-1881.   SCL
North Augusta Historical Society. 1918 city directory of North
Augusta, SC. 1918, rp North Augusta: author, 1980. SCL, SCHS
Oakland Avenue Presbyterian Church, Columbia. Sessions records
1952-1967; register, 1952-1967.   MONT
Oakland Avenue Presbyterian Church, Rock Hill. Sessions records
1913-1950; register 1913-1944.   MONT
Obituaries of the 1890's & 1900's..among the papers of Mrs. Cora
Garvin [SpC]   LNCL
Official roster of SC soldiers, sailors & marines in the World
War, 1917-1918. Cola: General Assembly, 1929. 2 vol. COMMON
Official roster of SC servicemen & servicewomen in World War II,
1941-1946. Cola: SC Division of General Services, 1967.
5 vol.   COMMON
Old Fields Presbyterian Church, Ora. Sessions records 1841-1952
                                                               MONT
Old Greenville [Presbyterian] Church cemetery [inscriptions],
near Donalds, SC. Mimeo, nd. 32 p.   MONT
Old Purity [Presbyterian Church] cemetery [inscriptions], Chester, SC. Cola: The Letter Shop, 1939? 40 p.   SCL, MONT
Orangeburg Church. Orangeburg church register of births, mar-
riages & deaths kept by John Ulrich & John Giessendanner, 1727
to 1796.   SCL
Owens, Jean S. & Alma S. Smith. Patent land survey (index of
land acquisitions), 1770-1820 [Index to Commissioners of
Locations books for the northern part of Ninety-Six District].
Greenville: A Press, 1978. 174 p.   SCL, GSGN
Padget's Creek Baptist Church, Union County. Records 1784-1874.
                                                                SCL
Pegram, Ward Sr. Records of some Revolutionary soldiers of
Chester county [SpC]   CSCL
Pinckney, Elise. Register of St. Philip's [Episcopal] church,
Charleston, SC, 1810-1822. Cola: Colonial Dames, 1973.
210 p.   COMMON
Pinson (Jim Pinson) family cemetery, Laurens County [SpC]   GSGN
Pinetree Presbyterian Church, Cassatt. Sessions records & reg-
ister, 1851-1956.   MONT
Pittman, William J. [Some inscriptions from] Scotch cemetery.
Typescript, nd. 4 p.   SCL
Pontotoc County Historical & Genealogical Society. New Hope
Baptist church cemetery & Camp Creek United Methodist church
cemetery, Lancaster County, SC. Ada OK: author, 1970.
19 p.   SCL, LNCL
Poplar Springs Baptist Church, Union County. Records 1794-1937.

(Poplar Springs Baptist Church, continued)   SCL
Port Royal Presbyterian Church, Port Royal. Sessions records
   1881-1895.   MONT
Prentiss, James C. The Charleston city guide. Chstn: J.W.
   Delano, 1872. 106 p.   SCL, SCHS
Presbyterian Church, Enoree.   Sessions records 1872-1921.
                                                             MONT
Presbyterian Church, Georgetown. Sessions records 1897-1953;
   register, nd.   SCL, MONT
Presbyterian Theological Seminary. Catalogue of the officers &
   students...1879-1880. Cola: Presbyterian Publishing House,
   1880. 16 p.   SCHS
Prince George, Winyah [Episcopal] Church, Georgetown. Rectors,
   wardens & vestry; Prince George, Winyah, 1721-1953. NP: NPub,
   1953. 11 p.   SCL, SCHS
Prince William Primitive Baptist Church, Hampton County. Records...1812-1912... Hamilton AL: Vina Chandler Price, 1979.
   126 p.   SCL, SCHS
Prince William's Baptist Church, Hampton County. Records 1812-
   1937.   SCL
Pruitt, Jane C. Revolutionary war pension applicants who served
   from SC. Fairfax County VA: NPub, 1946. 70 p.   COMMON
Purity Presbyterian Church, Chester County. Roster of names of
   persons buried in old Purity Presbyterian church cemetery
   [SpC]   CSCL
Pursley, Larry. 7500 marriages from Ninety-Six and Abbeville
   Districts, SC, 1774-1890. Easley: SHP, 1980. 211 p. SCL,PUBL
Quaker cemetery [tombstone inscriptions, Camden, SC]   KECA
Quattlebaum family cemetery transcript, McCormick County.   GSGN
Rabun Creek Baptist Church, Laurens County. Records 1828-1913.
                                                              SCL
Ravenel, Daniel. Liste des francois et suisses. From an old
   manuscript list of French & Swiss protestants settled in
   Charleston, on the Santee [River] and the Orange Quarter who
   desired naturalization. 1888, rp Baltimore: GPC, 1968. 77 p.
                                                           COMMON
Ravenel, M. Deas. St. Michael's parish register, vol. II: 1862-
   1932. With plan of St. Michael's graveyard. NP: typescript,
   nd.   SCHS
Rebecca Pickens Chapter, D.A.R. Cemeteries in Dillon County &
   upper Marion County. NP: author.   DIDU
Record of Tirzah A.R.P. [church] congregation, 1859-1899. NP:
   typescript, nd.   YOCL
Records of the sessions of Bethesda Presbyterian church, 1840-
   1857. NP: typescript, nd. 220 p.   YOCL
Records of the sessions of Fishing Creek Presbyterian church...
   1799-1859. (copy of originals). 66 p.   SCL, YOCL
Register of Immanuel Episcopal Church, from the beginning of
   that parish...1843. NP: typescript, 1940. 12 p.   YOCL
Register of members in East Chester circuit & Richburg circuit,
   SC conference, M.E. church, south, 1880-1900. NP: typescript,

nd. 100 p.   YOCL
Register of members and probationers in Richburg Circuit, SC
  conference, M.E. church, south. Nashville TN: Stevenson &
  Owen, 1857. 187 p.   YOCL
A regular church book for the congregation of St. Michael's
  [Lutheran] Church... [lists baptisms, members (Lutheran, Re-
  formed & Presbyterian), marriages, deaths, families, communi-
  cants] 1813-c.1841, Lexington County.   LTSS
Reid, Mary R. Civil war pension lists: Williamsburg County.
  NP: typescript, nd. 27 p.   WMTR
Reid, Mary R. Williamsburg County civil war enlistment records.
  NP: typescript, 1980.   WMTR
Reid, Mary R. Williamsburg Presbyterian cemetery, Kingstree.
  Kingstree: typescript, 1977. 84 p.   SCL, WMTR, MRCL
Revill, Janie. Abstract of 128 wills from will book "A", Sumter
  SC, 1777-1815. NP: typescript, nd. 44 p.   SCHS
Revill, Janie. Abstract of marriage & deaths from the Keowee
  Courier, 1852-1871. Cola: typescript, 1935. 44 p.   SCL, CLEM
Revill, Janie. Copy of the original index book showing the
  Revolutionary claims filed in SC between Aug. 20, 1783 & Aug-
  ust 31, 1786. Baltimore MD: GPC, 1969. 387 p.   COMMON
Revolutionary pensioners; a transcript of the pension list of
  the U.S. for 1813. Baltimore MD: Southern Book Co., 1953.
  47 p.   ORCL
Ribble, Hunt & Ribble. Greater Spartanburg directory-guide
  book. Spartanburg: Herald-Journal, various editions. SCL, GRCL
Rich, Peggy B. The old Stone Church cemetery. Clemson: Old
  Stone Church & Cemetery Commission, 1979. 47 p. SCL CLEM, ANCL
Richmond Presbyterian Church, Harmony Presbytery. Sessions
  records 1885-1911.   MONT
Richland School. Catalogue of the officers & students... Cola:
  Times & Gazette, 1830. 10 p.   SCHS
Riley, Mary R. Inscriptions from eight more country churchyards
  of Anderson County [Barker's Creek, Bethany, Dorchester Bap-
  tist Church, Ebenezer Methodist Church, Long Branch Methodist
  Church, Old Hopewell Baptist Church, Rice Church cemeteries].
  NP: Hudson Berry Chapter, D.A.R., 1938.   ANCL, CHCL
Roberts Presbyterian Church, Anderson County. Sessions records
  1839-1885; register, nd.   MONT
Robertson & Garrett family cemetery, Laurens County. [SpC]   GSGN
Robertson, Toliver. An account of the marriages solemnized by
  me, Toliver Robertson [1842-1867]. NP: typescript, nd.
  13 p.   LRCL, GWPL
Rock Presbyterian Church, Greenwood. Sessions records & regis-
  ter, 1823-1906.   MONT
Rockville Presbyterian Church, Rockville. Records 1909-1950.
                                                                        MONT
Rocky River church cemetery, Abbeville County [SpC]   GSGN
Rocky River Presbyterian Church, Rocky River. Records 1818-
  1834; sessions records 1842-1876, 1878-1920.   MONT
Rodman, Ida M. Abstracts of deeds: Lancaster County, SC. NP:

NPub, nd. 3 vol.   LNCL
Roster of the cemetery & historical sketch of Bullock Creek
   church. NP: NPub, 1962. 27 p.   LNCL
St. Andrew's Society, Charleston. Officers & members...1729-
   1929. Chstn: NPub, 1929. 4 p.   SCHS
St. Helena's [Episcopal] Parish, Beaufort. Register (mfm) 1725-
   1824.   SCDAH
St. James [Episcopal] Church, Santee. Register (transcript)
   1758-1788.   CHLS
St. John's [Episcopal] Parish, Berkeley. Vestry minutes 1731-
   1911; register 1872-1944; vestry cash book 1813-1827; misc.
   records 1807-1831 (mfm).   SCL, SCDAH
St. John's [Episcopal] Church, Colleton. Vestry book 1738-1874
   (transcript).   SCL
St. Michael's Episcopal Church, Charleston. The minutes of St.
   Michael's church of Charleston, SC, from 1758-1797. NP:
   Colonial Dames, nd. 197 p.   COMMON
St. Paul's Episcopal Church, Summerville. The epitaphs in St.
   Paul's cemetery, Summerville, SC., 1858-1977. Summerville:
   author, 1977. 160 p.   COMMON
St. Peter's Episcopal Church, Charleston. Register...1833-1862.
   Chstn: typescript, nd. 78 p.   SCHS
St. Philip's Episcopal Church, Charleston. Records...1783-1786,
   1803-1811. Typescript, nd.   SCL, SCHS
St. Stephen & St. John Episcopal church records, 1754-1873.SCDAH,
St. Thaddeus Episcopal Church, Aiken. Records 1842-?:YOWC SCL
Salem Baptist Church, Marlboro County. Records 1797-1930. SCL
Salem Baptist Church, Marlboro County. Membership rolls, 1793-
   1977 [SpC]   MRCL
Salem Baptist Church, Marlboro County. Records 1797-1897; min-
   utes 1885-1930; members 1793-1893. 3 vol. NP: typescript,
   nd. v.p.   SCL, MRCL
Salem Methodist Church, Greenville County. Records of members
   and conference minutes, 1883-1921.   WOMA
Salem Presbyterian Church, Black River. Records 1825-1895;
   congregational minutes 1808-1858.   SCL, MONT
Salem Presbyterian Church, Blair. Sessions records 1831-1925;
   register 1856-1887.   MONT
Salem Presbyterian Church, Union. Minutes of the sessions...
   1840-1876. NP: typescript, nd. 49 p.   YOCL
Salley, Alexander S. Death notices in the South Carolina Ga-
   zette, 1732-1775. 1917, rp Cola: SCAD, 1954. 42 p. COMMON
Salley, Alexander S. Eligibility list of the National Society
   of the Colonial Dames of America in the State of SC. NP:
   NPub, 1962.   COMMON
Salley, Alexander S. Marriage notices in the South Carolina
   Gazette & Country Journal, 1765-1775; and in the Charleston
   Gazette, 1778-1780. Chstn: W,E&C, 1904. 44 p.   COMMON
Salley, Alexander S. Marriage notices in the Charleston Courier
   1803-1808. Cola: HCSC, 1919. 83 p.   COMMON
Salley, Alexander S. Marriage notices in the South-Carolina and

American General Gazette from May 30th, 1766, to February 28, 1781, and in its successor the Royal Gazette (1781-1782)... Cola: HCSC, 1914 & 1954. 52 p. COMMON

Salley, Alexander S. Marriage notices in the South-Carolina Gazette & its successors, 1732-1801... 1902, rp Baltimore MD: GPC, 1976. 174 p. COMMON

Salley, Alexander S. Minutes of the vestry of St. Helena's [Episcopal] parish [Beaufort] SC, 1726-1812. Cola: HCSC, 1919 296 p. COMMON

Salley, Alexander S. Minutes of the vestry of St. Matthew's [Episcopal] parish, SC, 1767-1838. Cola: Colonial Dames, 1939 53 p. COMMON

Salley, Alexander S. Register of St. Philip's [Episcopal] parish, Charles Town, SC, 1720-1758. 1904, rp Cola: USC Press, 1971. 355 p. COMMON

Salley, Alexander S. & D. E. Huger Smith. Register of St. Philip's [Episcopal] Parish...1754-1810. Cola: USC Press, 1971. 505 p. COMMON

Salley, Alexander S. Register of the National Society of the Colonial Dames...in the State of SC...eligibility list... Chstn: Colonial Dames, 1945. 176 p. ORCL

Salley, Alexander S. Tentative roster of the third regiment, SC volunteers, Confederate States Provisional Army. Cola: HCSC, 1908. 129 p. SCL, SCHS

Sally Reed graveyard [SpC] YOWC

Sams, Mrs. J. Hagood. Pay rolls, muster rolls, etc., of SC militia in 1812-1815. NP: U.S. Daughters of 1812, nd. 2 vol. SPCL

Sandy Level Baptist Church, Fairfield County. Records 1817-1908. SCL

Sandy Run Baptist Church, Lexington District. Records 1881-1909. SCL

Sardinia Presbyterian Church, Sardinia. Sessions records & register, 1910-1944. MONT

Schenck, James R. The directory & stranger's guide for the city of Charleston; also, a directory for Charleston Neck...for the year 1822... [incl. directory for the coloured population]. Chstn: Miller, 1822 51 p. SCL, SCHS

Second Baptist Church, Kershaw. Records 1916-1953. YOWC

Second Presbyterian Church, Charleston. Sessions records 1809-1938; registers 1811-1893; extensive records 1809-1954. SCLMONT

Service record book of men & women of Chesterfield & vicinity; World Wars I & II. Chesterfield: American Legion Auxiliary No. 74, nd. 27 p. CTCL

Service record: World War I & II - Marlboro County. Bennetsville: Fletcher Stubb Post #6120, V.F.W., nd. 72 p. SCL, MRCL

Sessions records of Union A.R.P. church, 1875-1939, & other misc. records, 1752-1939. Cola: WPA, nd. 214 p. SCL, YOCL

Shady Grove Presbyterian Church, Clinton. Sessions records & register, 1859-1886. MONT

Sion Presbyterian Church, Winnsboro. Sessions records 1825-

1877; register 1825-?; Bible Society minutes 1818-1888.   MONT
Six Mile Creek Presbyterian Church, Fort Mill.   Records 1893-
1977.   YOWC
Slabtown Presbyterian Church, Slabtown (Piedmont Presbytery)
(extinct).   Records 1887-1915.   MONT
Smith, Bill T.   Directory of Churches of Christ in the Carolinas
vol. 7.   Greenville: Carolina Christian Churches, 1974.   16
p.   PIPD
Smith, D. E. H. & Alexander S. Salley.   Register of St. Philip's
[Episcopal] parish, Charles Town...1754-1810.   1927, rp Cola:
USC Press, 1971.   505 p.   COMMON
Smith, R. M.   Book of the dead...cemeteries of Anderson County.
2nd ed.   Anderson: author, 1967.   447 p.   COMMON
Smith, R. M.   Church deeds of Anderson County, SC.   Anderson:
author, nd.   115 p.   COMMON
Smith, R. M.   Church deeds & cemetery index of Anderson County.
NP: typescript, nd.   422 p.   SCL, SCHS
Smyrna Baptist Church, Hampton County.   Records 1870-1927.   SCL
Smyrna Presbyterian Church, Traveler's Rest.   Sessions records
1837-1857.   MONT
South Carolina College.   Roll of students...1805-1905.   Cola:
1906?   56 p.   SCHS
South Carolina.   College of Agriculture & Mechanics.   A catalog
of the officers & students, 1880-1881.   Cola: Presbyterian
Publishing House, 1881.   42 p.   SCHS
South Carolina and Georgia almanac.   Charlestown directory for
1782 and...1785.   Richmond VA: Historical Commission of
Charleston, 1951.   SCL, SCHS
South Carolina Military Academy.   Official register of the offi-
cers & cadets...Nov. 1850. SCHS has 1850. SCL 1861-1933, pass.
South Carolina Society, D.A.R.   Roster & ancestral roll.   Cola:
RLB, 1954.   156 p.   SCL, EDTO
South Carolina.   University.   Alumni directory.   Cola: USC,
1926.   275 p.   SCL, SCHS
South Carolina Volunteers.   14th Regiment.   Roll of honor of
company "D", 14th regiment, SC volunteers.   Edgefield: Adver-
tiser Office, 1866.   4 p.   SCHS
South Caroliniana Library, U. S. C.   Miscellaneous tombstone inscriptions (typescripts) for the following counties:
Aiken: Hooker cemetery, 1 p.; Evergreen cemetery, 57 p..
Beaufort: Jewish cemetery, 5 p.; Sheldon [Episcopal] church
cemetery, 10 p.; St. Peter's Catholic church cemetery, 8 p.;
Izar-McPherson ["unnamed"] cemetery, 5 p.; First Baptist
church graveyard, Beaufort, unp..
Calhoun: Providence church cemetery, 2 p.; Tabernacle cemete-
ry, 2 p.; Trinity church cemetery, 4 p.; Wesley church ceme-
tery, 3 p.; Limestone cemetery, 4 p.; Andrews Chappel cemete-
ry, 7 p.
Chester: DeGraffinreid family cemetery, 1 p.
Edgefield: Lanham family burials, 1 p.; Bethlehem Baptist/
Asbury Methodist cemetery inscriptions, 2 p.

Greenville: Carter family burying ground, Princeton, 2 p.
Greenwood: Chestnut Hill church cemetery, 3 p.; Red Bank
church cemetery, 8 p.
Lancaster: Tirzah cemetery, 27 p.; cemetery near Hanging Rock,
1 p.; Connors family cemetery, 1 p.
Laurens: Jot Abercrombie cemetery; Abercrombie-Johnson ceme-
tery; Laurens cemetery, sections I & II; Liberty Springs Pres-
byterian church cemetery at Cross Hill.
Lexington: Ebenezer church cemetery, 3 p; Amaker burying
ground, 2 p.
Marlboro: Parker's cemetery near McColl, 2 p.
Orangeburg: Bull Swamp Baptist church cemetery, 3 p.; Hebron
M.E. church cemetery, 6 p.; Houser cemetery plot, 1 p.; Pen.
Branch church cemetery, 4 p.; Riverside cemetery, 5 p.; Salem
Baptist church cemetery, 4 p.; Good Hope cemetery, 15 p.
Sumter: Bloom Hill burying ground, 11 p.
York: Bethel Presbyterian church, 18 p.
Southern Directory & Publishing Co. The Charleston guide & bus-
iness directory for 1885-6. Chstn: Lucas & Richardson, 1885.
                                                    SCL, SCHS
Spartanburg Committee, D.A.R. Cemetery survey. Church yard
[of] Episcopal Church of the Advent... NP: typescript, 1974.
11 p.   SCL
Star Fort Chapter, D.A.R. Cemetery records of Laurens County,
SC. 2 vol. NP: typescript, 1967.   SCL
Star Fort Chapter, D.A.R. Liberty Springs Presbyterian church
cemetery, Cross Hill. Typescript, 1970. 88 p.   SCL
Star Fort Chapter, D.A.R. Smyrna cemetery, Waterloo. Type-
script, 1970. 30 p.   SCL
Star Fort Chapter, D.A.R. Belle Meade cemetery, St. Andrew's
Chapel cemetery inscriptions. Typescripts, 1969. 6 + 16 p.
[Greenwood County]   SCL
Star Fort Chapter, D.A.R. Old Bush River Baptist church & ceme-
tery, Newberry County. Typescript, 1969. 81 p.   SCL
Stoddard, Mrs. David L. Greenville County, SC, cemetery rec-
ords. Pass Christian MS: Willo Institute, 1965.   SCL, YOCL
Stoddard, Mrs. David L. Laurens County, SC, cemetery records.
Pass Christian MS: Willo Institute, 1966 1 vol.   SCL, YOCL
Stoddard, Mrs. David L. Spartanburg County, SC, cemetery rec-
ords. Pass Christian MS: Willo Institute, 1965.   SCL, YOCL
Stoddard, Mrs. David L. Union County, SC, cemetery records.
Pass Christian MS: Willo Institute, 1963. 26 p.SCL,NWRL, YOCL
Stoddard, Mrs. David L. [Union County tombstone inscriptions]
Garner cemetery, Gallman cemetery, Foster Chapel Methodist
church cemetery, Mt. Joy Baptist church cemetery, Sardis Meth-
odist church cemetery, Gillas Baptist church cemetery, Reho-
beth Baptist church cemetery, Mt. Tabor Presbyterian church
cemetery, Taylot burial, Wesley Chapel cemetery, Phillipi
Baptist church cemetery, Boganville Methodist church cemetery,
Putman Baptist church cemetery, Upper Fairforest/Duck Pond
cemetery, Union city cemetery, Hawkins cemetery, New Hope

Methodist Church cemetery, Fair Forest Presbyterian church
cemetery. Typescripts, nd.   SCL
Stoddard, Mary S. Tombstone inscriptions of KY & SC. Pass
Christian MS: Willo Institute, 1965. 1 vol.   LRCL
Stoney Creek Independent Presbyterian Church, Yemassee. Records 1743-1910 (mfm).   SCL, COML
Stoney Creek Independent Presbyterian Church, Yemassee. Ses-
sions records & register, 1910-1964; financial records 1777-
1778.   MONT
Strange, Mary W. The Revolutionary soldiers of Catholic Pres-
byterian Church. NP: York-Clover Printing Co., 1978.
135 p.   COMMON
Summerville Presbyterian Church, Summerville. Sessions records
1859 - 1931.   MONT
Sumter Methodist Church, Sumter. Records, 1820-1838.   WOMA
Sumter Presbyterian Church, Sumter. Membership roll, nd. SCL
Sumter Presbyterian Church, Sumter. Membership roll 1842-1920.
                                                         MONT
Sumter, SC. Municipal officials of Sumter, 1871-1964. NP:
mimeo, 1964.   SMCL
Supplement to memoir #4, vol. 1, of the "Memoirs of the Pendle-
ton Farmers Society" [list of members, 1815-1946].   PIPD
A survey of private cemeteries of old Lexington District.
Batesburg: Lexington County Historical Society, nd.   LXCL
Swift Creek Baptist Church, Kershaw County. Records 1827-1868.
                                                          SCL
Third Presbyterian Church, Charleston. Sessions records 1823-
1881; membership records 1823-?; register 1827-?, misc. min-
utes 1824-1852.   MONT
Thomas, Edward. Copy of the private journal of the Rev. Edward Thomas, 1800-1840... private parochial register for St.
John's [Episcopal] parish, Berkeley [1836-1840]. NP: typescript, nd. 9 p.   EPDI
Thomas, Edward. Copy of the private journal of the Rev. Edward Thomas, 1800-1840 [private register for 1826]. NP:
typescript, nd. 3 p.   EPDI
Thomas, Edward. Edisto Island. 1827. [private journal, reg-
ister, & communicants roll, 1827-1828] Typescript, nd.
21 p.   SCL, EPDI
Thomas, Elizabeth W. Anderson County, SC, will book "A", part
1. Pass Christian MS: Willo Institute, 1967. 24 p. SCL, LNCL
Thomas, Elizabeth W. Chester County, SC: deed book "C", 1786-
1793. Pass Christian MS: Willo Institute, 1966.   SCL, YOCL
Thomas, Elizabeth W. Chester County, SC, will book "A", "B & C"
Pass Christian MS: Willo Institute, 1967.   SCL, LNCL, YOCL
Thomas, Elizabeth W. Fairfield County, SC, wills, 1773-1797.
Pass Christian MS: Willo Institute, 1967.   SCL, LNCL, YOCL
Thomas, Elizabeth W. Laurens County, SC, will books "A, C, D &
E". Pass Christian MS: Willo Institute, 1967. 4 vol.   LNCL
                                                    SCL, GWPL
Thomas, Elizabeth W. SC genealogical records, vol. I: Abbeville

41

District.   Tuscaloosa AL: Willo Publ. Co., 1964.   636 p.   YOCL
Thomas, J. A. W.   Marriage & funeral notices from the daybook of
the Rev. J. A. W. Thomas, 1865-1896.   NP: Dowd Press, 1952.
29 p.   COMMON
Thomas Memorial Baptist Church, Marlboro County.   Records 1832-
1924.   SCL
Thompson, J. Waddy.   Laurens County wills...1766-1853.   Cola:
C.W.A., 1934.   2 vol.   LRCL
Thornwell, James H.   Personal notebooks of Dr. James Henley
Thornwell: Fort Mill & Ebenezer Presbyterian churches [regis-
ters, 1882-1905].   3 vol.   YOCL
Three Rivers Historical Society.   Cemetery surveys of lower
Florence County.   Typescript, 1975-1978.   4 vol.   SCL, WMTR
Three Rivers Historical Society.   Family bible & other genealo-
gical records.   Hemingway: Three Rivers Historical Society,
1979.   102 p.   WMTR, FLMC
Three Rivers Historical Society.   A survey of cemeteries in up-
per Georgetown County.   Hemingway: author, 1978. SCL,WMTR, GTML
Three Rivers Historical Society.   A survey of twenty-two ceme-
teries in the Johnsonville-Hemingway area of old Williamsburg
District...   Hemingway: author, 1977?   2 vol.   WMTR, MACL
Tillman, Mamie N. & Hortense Woodson.   Inscriptions from Edge-
field Village Baptist cemetery including Trinity Episcopal
church section & Willowbrook cemetery.   Edgefield: Edgefield
County Historical Society, 1958.   141 p. SCL,USAI, FURM, MRCL
Tillman, Mamie N.   Edgefield County tombstone inscriptions:
Antioch Baptist church cemetery, Big Stevens Creek Baptist
church cemetery, Norris family cemetery, Red Oak Grove Baptist
church cemetery, Tutt family cemetery, Mims-Tutt cemetery,
Catholic cemetery, Harmony Methodist churchyard.   SCL
Tillman, Mamie N.   Graves in Sweetwater cemetery, Aiken County.
Typescript, nd.   12 p.   SCL
Tirzah A.R.P. Church, Rock Hill.   Sessions records 1849-1947;
register 1831-1868.   MONT
Tirzah Presbyterian Church, Lancaster County.   Index of Tirzah
cemetery.   Typescript.   SCL, YOCL
Tirzah Presbyterian Church, Lancaster County.   Records 1831-
1961.   YOCL
Tobias, Thomas J.   Tombstones that tell a story; Charleston's
historic Coming Street [Jewish] cemetery.   8 p.   SCL, SCHS
Tombstone inscriptions, Oconee County: Bethel cemetery, Walhalla
Choehee cemetery, Tamassee; Nicholson cemetery [SpC]   PICL
Tombstone inscriptions, Pickens County: Day cemetery, Easley;
Mountain Grove cemetery, Pickens; Old Stone Church cemetery,
Clemson; Oolenoy cemetery; Pickens Mill cemetery, Pickens;
Pickens Presbyterian cemetery, Pickens; Secona cemetery, Pick-
ens; Sunrise cemetery, Pickens [SpC]   SCL, PICL
Tombstones of Bethel M.E. church...   Typescript, nd.   17 p. SCL
Townsville Presbyterian Church, Townsville, Piedmont Presbytery.
Sessions records 1883-1899.   MONT
Tranquil United Methodist church cemetery inscriptions, Green-

wood County [SpC]   GSGN
Trapier, Paul. The private register of the Rev. Paul Trapier
   (1830-1864). Chstn: Dalcho Historical Society, 1958. 70 p.
                                              SCL, EPDI, SCHS
Union A.R.P. Church, Chester County. Records 1752-1939.   SCL
Union Baptist church cemetery (old Quaker cemetery). 1956. LRCL
Union Baptist Church, Spartanburg. Records 1804-1843.   SCL
Union County Probate Court. Record of wills, books "A" - "D",
   1777-1900. Typescript, nd. 4 vol.   UNCL
Unity Presbyterian cemetery, York County. Typescript, 2 p. SCL
U.S. Atomic Energy Commission, Savannah River. Record of relo-
   cation of graves in the area [Aiken County]. 1964.   SCL
U.S. Navy Department. Register of officers of the Confederate
   states navy 1861-1865... Washington DC: U.S. Government
   Printing Office, 1931.   SCL, SCHS
U.S. Pension Bureau. Pensioners of the Revolutionary war struck
   off the roll. 1836, rp Baltimore MD: GPC, 1969. 103 p. SCL
U.S. Secretary of War. Letter...transmitting a report of the
   names, rank, & line of every person placed on the pension list
   in pursuance of the Act of the 18th March 1818. Washington
   DC: Gales & Seaton, 1820, rp Baltimore MD: Southern Book Co.,
   1955. 672 p.   SCL, MACL
U.S. Senate. Pensioners on the roll January 1, 1883. 1883, rp
   Baltimore MD: GPC, 1970. 5 vol.   PUBL
U.S. War Department. Pension roll of 1835. 1835, rp Baltimore
   MD: GPC, 1968. 4 vol.   SCL, PUBL
U.S. War Department. Revolutionary pensioners; a transcript of
   the pension lists of the U.S. for 1813. Baltimore MD: South-
   ern Book Co., 1953. 47 p.   MACL
U.S.C. Chapter, D.A.R. St. Stephen's Lutheran church cemetery
   inscriptions to 1920 [incl. Clark, Joyner & Steven family
   burials in a West Columbia cemetery]. Lexington: typescript,
   1967. 16 p.   SCL
Varrenes Presbyterian Church, Starr?. Records 1860-1928.   MONT
Waddel,, Moses. A register of marriages celebrated & solemnized by Moses Waddel in SC & GA, 1795-1836... Danielsville
   GA: Heritage Papers, 1967. 13 p.   SCL, SCHS, CHCO
Walker, Cornelius I. Rolls & historical sketch of the tenth
   regiment, SC volunteers. Chstn: W,E&C, 1881. 138 p.   SCL
                                                    BRCL, MACL
Walnut Grove Baptist church cemetery [SpC]   GSGN
Walsh's Charleston city directory. Chstn: Walsh Directory Co.,
   1887, 1888.   CLEM
Walsh's directory for the city & county of Anderson for 1909-
   1910. Chstn: Walsh Directory Co., 1909. 330 p.   SCL, CLEM
Warren, Mary B. Citizens & immigrants - SC, 1768. Danielsville
   GA: Heritage Papers, 1980. 464 p.   SCL, SCHS, GSGN
Warren, Mary B. South Carolina jury lists, 1718-1783... Dan-
   ielsville GA: Heritage Papers, 1977. 130 p.   COMMON
Warrior's Creek Baptist Church, Laurens County. Records 1843-
   1932.   SCL

                           43

Watson, Samuel. Entries in the Watson Bible [SpC]   YOCL
Watson, Margaret J. Tombstone inscriptions from family grave-
   yards in Greenwood County, SC. Greenwood: Drinkard Printing
   Co., 1972. 98 p.   COMMON
Weis, Frederick L. The colonial clergy of VA, NC & SC. Balti-
   more MD: GPC, 1976. 100 p.   COMMON
Wells family cemetery, Laurens County [SpC]   GSGN
Welsh Neck High School. Catalogue, 1906-1907... Nashville TN:
   Brandon, 1907. 31 p. : SCHS. SCL has 1895-96, 1897.
Westminster Presbyterian Church, Charleston (extinct). Sessions
   records 1921-1926, register 1921-?.   MONT
Westminster Presbyterian Church, Charleston (extinct). Sessions
   records 1900-1931; pew rent records 1875-1889; Sunday school
   records 1823-1933; sessions records 1883-1941; register 1883-
   1898; Ladies Aid Society records 1825-1850, 1853-1880, 1870-
   1920.   MONT
Westminster Presbyterian Church, Westminster (Richland County).
   Sessions records & register, 1833-1947.   MONT
Whaley, Mrs. E.D. Union county cemeteries. Epitaphs... Green-
   ville: A Press, 1976. 362 p.   COMMON
White, William B. Epitaphs in Burnt Meeting House cemetery
   (Lower Fishing Creek Presbyterian Church cemetery)...Chester
   County. Typescript, 1951.   YOCL
Whitmire, Beverly T. Presence of the past: epitaphs of 18th &
   19th century pioneers in Greenville County... Greenville:
   Greenville County Historical Society, 1976. 992 p.   COMMON
Wilkinson, Tom C. Early Anderson County, SC, newspapers, mar-
   riages & obituaries, 1841-1882. Easley: SHP, 1978. 252 p.
                                                           COMMON
Williamsburg Presbyterian Church, Kingstree. Sessions records
   1839-1931; register 1897-1917.   SCL, MONT
Winyaw Indigo Society. Rules... with a short history of the so-
   ciety and a list of living & deceased members, from 1755 to
   1938. Chstn: W,E&C, 1938. 44 p.   SCL, SCHS
Woodrow Memorial Presbyterian Church, Columbia. Sessions rec-
   ords 1909-1923.   MONT
Wooley, James E. A collection of upper SC genealogical & family
   records. Easley: SHP, 1979 & 1981. 3 vol.   COMMON
Work Projects Administration (W.P.A.):
W.P.A. Alphabetical list of the congregation of St. Stephen's
   [Episcopal] chapel, Charleston, SC, 1855 to ... W.P.A. pro-
   ject #165-33-7999. Typescript, 1937. 20 p.   EPDI
W.P.A. Baptisms. St. Stephen's [Episcopal] church. Charleston
   So. Ca 1867-1878. W.P.A. project #165-33-7172. Typescript,
   1937. 16 p.   EPDI
W.P.A. Edmundsbury chapel [Episcopal]. Near Ashepoo ferry -
   history 1854-1856. W.P.A. project # 165-33-7172. Typescript,
   1937. 56 p.   EPDI
W.P.A. Epitaphs. Magnolia cemetery, Spartanburg SC. Spartan-
   burg: W.P.A., 1936. 17 p.   SPCL
W.P.A. Inventory of the church archives of SC: see appendix IX.

of this volume for a complete listing.

W.P.A. Inventory of the county archives of SC: Abbeville County. Typescript, 1937. 106 p.   SCHS, DACL, WOFF, SPCL

W.P.A. Inventory of the county archives...Aiken County. Typescript, 1937. 115 p.   SCHS,DACL, SPCL

W.P.A. Inventory of the county archives...Allendale County. Typescript, 1937. 64 p.   SCHS, DACL, SPCL

W.P.A. Inventory of the county archives...Anderson County. Typescript, 1937. 168 p.   SCHS, DACL, ANCL, SPCL

W.P.A. Inventory of the county archives...Cherokee County. Typescript, 1937. 175 p.   SCHS, DACL, SPCL

W.P.A. Inventory of the county archives...Dillon County. Typescript, 1937.   SCHS, DACL

W.P.A. Inventory of the county archives...Florence County. Typescript, 1937. 105 p.   SCHS, DACL

W.P.A. Inventory of the county archives...Jasper County. Typescript, 1937. 72 p.   SCHS, DACL, SPCL, COML

W.P.A. Inventory of the county archives...Lee County. Typescript, 1937. 46 p.   SCHS, DACL, SPCL

W.P.A. Inventory of the county archives...McCormick County. Typescript, 1937. 135 p.   SCHS, SPCL, DACL

W.P.A. Inventory of the county archives...Oconee County. Typescript, 1937. 133 p.   SCHS, DACL, SPCL

W.P.A. Inventory of the county archives...Pickens County. Typescript, 1937. 256 p.   SCHS, DACL, SPCL

W.P.A. Inventory of the county archives...Richland County. Typescript, 1937. 239 p.   SCHS, DACL, SPCL, COML

W.P.A. Inventory of the county archives...Saluda County. Typescript, 1940. 168 p.   SCHS, EDTO, NWRL, DACL, SPCL

W.P.A. Indexes to the county wills of SC. Cola: USC, 1939.
                                                              COMMON

W.P.A. Memorandum book [& journal of Francis P. DeLavaux] 1818-1847 in St. Michael's, Beaufort, & Flat Rock [NC]. W.P.A. project #165-33-7172. Typescript, 1937. 60 p.   EPDI

W.P.A. Minutes of the Baptist Church of Christ at Horn's Creek, [Edgefield County], 1824-1859. Cola: typescript, 1939. 166 p.   SCL, EDTO

W.P.A. Minutes of the session of the Great Pee Dee Presbyterian church, 1833-1899. Typescript.   MRCL

W.P.A. Minutes of the vestry. St. Matthew's [Episcopal] parish 1767-1838. W.P.A. project #165-33-7172. Typescript, 1937. 35 p.   SCL, EPDI

W.P.A. Orangeburg & Amelia township. Register. 1739-1885. [Register of the Church of the Redeemer, Episcopal] W.P.A. project 2004. Typescript, 1936. 123 p.   SCL, EPDI

W.P.A. Palmetto place names. 1941, rp Spartanburg: RPC, 1975. 158 p.   COMMON

W.P.A. Parochial register of the parishes of St. Thomas & St. Dennis, SC, 1706-1773. W.P.A. project #165-33-7172. Typescript, 1937. 115 p.   SCL, EPDI

W.P.A. Prince George, Winyah [Episcopal church] register. 1813

to 1916. W.P.A. project #165-33-7999. Typescript, nd. 136
p.   SCL, EPDI
W.P.A. Record of burials. St. Stephen's [Episcopal] chapel,
Charleston, So. Ca. 1822 [-1865]. W.P.A. project # 165-33-
7172. Typescript, 1937. 61 p.   SCL, EPDI
W.P.A. Records of the sessions of Fishing Creek Presbyterian
church, 1799-1859. Chester: typescript, 1937.   SCL YOCL
W.P.A. Register. United chapels of St. Stephen's & St. John's,
1828-1844. W.P.A. project # 165-33-7172. Typescript, 1937.
22 p.   SCL, EPDI
W.P.A. Register of St. Stephen's [Episcopal] parish. SC. 1842
to 1936. W.P.A. project #165-33-7172. Typescript, 1937.
113 p.   SCL, EPDI
W.P.A. St. Luke's [Episcopal] Church, Charleston. Minutes of
the vestry. 1866-1886. W.P.A. project #165-33-7172. Typescript, 1937. 116 p.   SCL, EPDI
W.P.A. St. Luke's [Episcopal] Church, Charleston. Minutes of
the vestry, 1886-1905. W.P.A. project #165-33-7172. Typescript, 1937. 58 p.   SCL, EPDI
W.P.A. St. Peter's [Episcopal] Church. Charleston. Signatures
of members, minutes, receipts at re-organization. 1927-1930.
W.P.A. project #165-33-7172. Typescript, 1937. 82 p.SCL,EPDI
W.P.A. St. Stephen's [Episcopal] Church, Charleston. Minute
book. 1866-1880. W.P.A. project #2004. Typescript, 1937.
62 p.   SCL, EPDI
W.P.A. St. Stephen's [Episcopal] Parish & St. John's. Vestry
book, 1754-1873. W.P.A. project #2004. Typescript, 1937.
42 p.   SCL, EPDI
W.P.A. St. Stephen's [Episcopal] chapel, Charleston. Record of
marriages & confirmations, 1822 [-1866]. W.P.A. project #165-
33-7172. Typescript, 1937. 42 p.   EPDI
W.P.A. Sessional records of Union A.R.P. church, 1875-1939, &
other misc. records, 1752-1939. Cola: typescript, 1939.
214 p.   SCL, YOCL
W.P.A. Vestry book. St. Bartholomew's [Episcopal] parish.
1840 [-1854]. W.P.A. project #165-33-7172. Typescript, 1937.
23 p.   SCL, EPDI
W.P.A. Vestry book of St. John's [Episcopal] parish, Colleton.
1738-1817. W.P.A. project #165-33-7172. Typescript, 1937.
92 p.   SCL, EPDI
W.P.A. Vestry book of St. John's [Episcopal] parish, Colleton.
1817-1874. W.P.A. project #165-33-7172. Typescript, 1937.
129 p.   SCL, EPDI
W.P.A. [Vestry book] Prince Frederick [Episcopal church], Winyah. 1713-1778. W.P.A. project #165-33-7172. Typescript,
1937. 34 p.   SCL, EPDI
W.P.A. [Vestry] minute book. Parish of St. John's, Berkeley.
1812-1853. W.P.A. project #165-33-7172. Typescript, 1937.
163 p.   SCL, EPDI
W.P.A. Vestry minutes. St. John's [Episcopal church], John's
Island, SC, 1874-1917. W.P.A. project #165-33-7999. Type-

script, 1937. 75 p. SCL, EPDI
W.P.A. Vestry minutes of St. Philip's [Episcopal] Church, Bradford Springs. 1846-1855. W.P.A. project #165-33-7172. Typescript, 1937. 8 p. SCL, EPDI
York County Clerk of Court. Names of persons drawn for juries
in York District, 1800-1820. Typescript. YOCL
York County Commissioner of Roads. Names of persons to whom
license was granted for keeping inns, publick houses, taverns,
etc... 1806-1852. Typescript. YOCL
York County. Court records: location of Indian lands, 1841-
1879. Typescript. YOCL
Young, Pauline. Abbeville wills & bonds. Typescript, nd.
30 p. SCL, SCHS
Young, Pauline. Abbeville wills & records. Typescript, nd.
40 p. SCL, SCHS
Young, Pauline. Abstracts of old Ninety-Six & Abbeville Dist-
rict, SC, wills & bonds. 1950, rp Easley: SHP, 1977. 797 p.
COMMON
Young, Pauline. A brief history with tombstone inscriptions of
old Little River Church, founded 1791, Abbeville County, SC.
Abbeville: NPub, 1949. 23 p. SCL, CHCL, SCHS
Young, Pauline. "Citizenship Papers" of old Pickens District.
Liberty: author, 1953. 62 p. SCL, PICL, CLEM
Young, Pauline. Equity records of old Ninety-Six and Abbeville
District. Liberty: author, 1957. 100 p. SCL, ANCL
Young, Pauline. A genealogical collection of SC wills & records
vol. I. 1955, rp Easley: SHP, 1969. 266 p. COMMON
Young, Pauline. Historical records of old Pickens District.
Liberty: author, 1952. 31 p. SCL, CLEM, PICL
Young, Pauline. Land plats for 1784, Abbeville District, SC.
Typescript, 1946. 27 p. SCHS
Young, Pauline. Pickens County, SC, wills & bonds. Typescript,
nd. 31 p. MRCL
Young, Pauline. SC historical records: 96 District. SCL, LRCL
Zion Presbyterian Church, Charleston (extinct). Sessions rec-
ords, 1858-1885; white baptism register, 1854-1875; communi-
cants register, 1858-?; marriage register, 1850-1872; Negro
communicants register, 1852-1861. MONT

Abbeville County Historical Society. Abbeville County bicenten-
nial, 1758-1958. Historical souvenir program. NP: NPub, 1958
64 p.   SCL, SCHS
Abbeville, SC Citizens. Souvenir program. Re-enactment of Ab-
beville District meeting, November 22, 1860-November 22, 1960;
Magazine Hill, Abbeville, SC. NP: NPub, 1960. unp. SCL, CLEM
Ackerman, Hugo S. A brief history of Orangeburg. Orangeburg:
Home Federal Savings & Loan, 1972. 12 p.   SCL, ORCL
Ackerman, Hugo S. Orangeburg to 1800: a frontier community.
Typescript, 1953.   ORCL
Ackerman, Robert K. A history of the land policies of proprie-
tary SC. Thesis (M.A.), U.S.C., 1961. 63 p.   SCL
Ackerman, Robert K. SC colonial land policies. Thesis (Ph.D.),
U.S.C., 1965. 204 p.   SCL
Ackerman, Robert K. SC colonial land policies. Cola: USC Press
1977.   SCL, GNCL
Adams, Edward C. Congaree sketches. Chapel Hill NC: UNC Press,
1927.   SCL, KECA
Adams, Georgie L. History of the Orangeburg Free Library...
NP: typescript, 1947. 74 p.   ORCL
Adams, Georgie L. History of the confederate monument, Orange-
burg, SC. NP: typescript, 1956. 68 p.   ORCL
Addy, L. B., Sr. Lexington - 1905 and later. NP: mimeo, 1970.
unp.   LXCL
Aetna Benevolent Association. Constitution & by-laws... Chstn:
News & Courier, 1882. 9 p.   SCHS
After the great earthquake: 9:54 P.M., August 31, 1886. Earth-
quake views, Charleston, SC. Chstn: W,E&C, nd. 24 p.   CLEM
Agricultural Society of SC. Constitution...1833. Chstn: Mil-
ler, 1834. 10 p.   SCHS
Aiken Centennial Commission. A rich heritage of stories on hap-
penings in Aiken County, SC. Aiken: E.N. Braddy, 1955. 36 p.
                                                         SCHS
Aiken, SC, queen of winter resorts. Aiken: Civic League, 1906.
31 p.   SCL, SCHS
Aiken Centennial Commission. Centennial celebration commemorat-
ing the founding of Aiken, SC, April 4-6, 1935. Aiken: author
1935. 48 p.   SCL, CLEM
Aiken, SC. The charter of the town of Aiken with the by-laws &
ordinances...1860. Chstn: A. J. Burke, 1860. 27 p. SCL, SCHS
Aiken, SC, as a health and pleasure resort. Illustrations by
J.A. Palmer. Chstn: W,E&C, 1889. 58 p.   SCL. SCHS
Alderman, Pat. One heroic hour at King's Mountain...battle of
King's Mountain, October 7, 1780. Erwin TN: Erwin Publishing
Co., 1968. 65 p.   SCL
Alexander, W.S. A descriptive sketch of Camden, SC... Chstn:
W,E&C, 1888. 36 p.   FLMC, KECA, SCHS, SCL

48

Alford, Robbie L. Some famous visitors to Georgetown County. Georgetown: Rice Museum, 1975. 4 p.   SCHS
Allan, Susan J. The King's highway (now route 40) through the coastal plantations between Georgetown & Charleston... Chstn: 1930. 13 p.   SCHS
Allen, Clarence B. Centennial history: Dalcho lodge #160, Latta SC, A.F.M., chartered 1870. 1970? 15 p.   SCL, DICL, FLMC
Allen, Hervey & DuBose Heyward. Carolina chansons: legends of the low country. NY: MacMillan, 1922.   SCL, KECA
Allen, Mary M. Origin of names of army & air corps posts, camps & stations in world war II in SC. 15 p.   SCHS
Allen, Mattie M. Central, yesterday & today. Central: Faith Printing Co., 1973. 110 p.   COMMON
Allston, Susan L. Brookgreen, Waccamaw, in the Carolina low country. Chstn: Nelson's Southern Printing, 1956. 38 p.
                                                                    COMMON
Allston, Susan L. Sketches along the PeeDee River. NP: 196? 19 p.   COMMON
Amick, Phyllis W. The frontier tamed. Prepared for the Prosperity bicentennial celebration, Prosperity, SC. A supplement to the history of Prosperity published in 1973. NP: 1978? 12 p.   SCL
Amick, Phyllis W. The history of Prosperity. Prepared for the centennial celebration, 1873-1973. NP: 1973. 54 p.   SCL
And Clover began to grow, 1876-1976. NP: Westmoreland Printers, nd.   YOCL
Anderson County Historical Association. Historic Anderson County, SC. Anderson: NPub, 1959. 4 p.   SCL, CLEM
Anderson County Tricentennial Committee. Anderson County honors the state of SC on her 300th birthday... Anderson: author, 1970. 41 p.   SCL, CLEM
Anderson County Tricentennial Committee. Sketchbook of Anderson County. NP: Droke House, 1969.   SCL, FLCL
Anderson Daily Mail. Fifty years of progress, 1899-1949. Anderson: Anderson Daily Mail, 1949. unp.   ANCL
Anderson, SC. Growth, progress, 1907. Anderson: Anderson Printing Co., 1907. 24 p.   SCL
The Anderson, SC, story. Tampa FL: R.J. Armitage Co, 1967. 59 P.   CLEM
Andrews, Robert W. The life & adventures of Capt. Robert W. Andrews of Sumter, SC... Boston: privately printed, 1887. 87 p.   SCL, FLMC
Andrews, W. J. Sketch of company "K", 23rd SC volunteers, in the civil war from 1862-1865. Sumter: Wilder & Ward, 1909? 33 p.   SCL, KECA
Appalachian Council of Governments. Historic places in the SC Appalachian region. Rev. ed. Greenville: author, 1975. 168 p.   COMMON
Appalachian Council of Governments. Historic preservation plan for Appalachian SC: Greenville County. NP, nd. 170 p. GRCL
Archer, H. P. A historic sketch of public schools in Charleston

49

SC, 1710-1886. Chstn: W,E & C, 1887. 34 p.   SCL, SCHS
Archer, H. P. Local reminiscences. A lecture delivered...be-
fore the Mutual Aid Association, No. 1, of Charleston, SC.
Chstn: Daggett, 1893. 25 p.   SCL, CLEM, SPCL, SCHS
Ariail, Mary G. Weaver of dreams: a history of Parker District.
Cola: RLB, 1977. 128 p.   SCL, ANCL, GRCL
Atkins, Benjamin E. Extracts from the diary of Benjamin Elber-
field Atkins...1848-1909...of Laurens District... Gastonia
NC: privately printed, 1947. 97 p.   SCL
Atlantic Coast Line. A short sketch of Charleston, SC. How it
fared in two wars and an earthquake. 1886. 37p.   SCL, CHCO
Ayer, Hartwell M. ...Co-operation excitement. NP: PeeDee Hist-
orical Society, 1906. 4 p.   SCL
Badders, Hurley E. Broken path: the Cherokee campaign of 1776.
Pendleton: Pendleton District Historical & Recreational Commission, 1976. 60 p.   COMMON
Badders, Hurley E. Pendleton Historic District: a plan. Pendleton: Pendleton District Historical & Recreational Commission, 1973. 31 p.   PIPD
Badders, Hurley E. Pendleton Historic District: a survey. Pendleton: Pendleton District Historical & Recreational Commission, 1973. 72 p.   SCL, PIPD
Bailey, James D. Cowpens; and, Wofford's Iron Works; historical
addresses... Cowpens: NPub, 1908. 28 p.   SCL, SPCL
Bailey, James D. History of Grindal Shoals & some early adjacent families. Gaffney: Ledger Print, 1927. 85 p.   COMMON
Baker, Mary N. The economic history of Abbeville District,
1860-1876. Thesis (M.A.), U.S.C., 1931. 54 p.   SCL
Baker, Steve. A brief history of Florence. Florence: Home
Federal Savings & Loan, 1974. 14 p.   COMMON
Baker, Steven G. Cofitachique: fair province of Carolina. The-
sis (M.A.), U.S.C., 1974. 227 p.   SCL
Baldwin, Dudley. Dudley Baldwin's letters from Hilton Head,
1863-1864... Washington DC: NPub, 1977. 68 p.   BUCL
Ball, William W. The state that forgot; South Carolina's sur-
render to democracy. Indianapolis IN: Bobbs-Merrill, 1932.
COMMON
Bamberg Centennial Corporation. Bamberg through the years, May
9-14, 1955. NPub, 1955. 40 p.   SCL
Bamberg County Committee. Bamberg County celebrating South Car-
olina's tricentennial, 1670-1970. Bamberg: NPub, 1970. 40 p.
SCL, GRCL
Bargar, B. D. Royal SC, 1719-1763. Cola: USC Press, 1970.
74 p.   COMMON
Barnes, Frank. Ft. Sumter National Monument, SC. Washington
DC: GPO, 1952. 48 p.   SCL, SPCL, SCHS
Barnes, Frank. The Greenville story. Greenville: author,
1956.   SCL, CLEM, GRCL
Barnwell, Robert W. The beginnings of the Revolution in the
back country of SC. Thesis (M.A.), U.S.C., 1926. 69 p.   SCL
Barnwell, William H. In Richard's world: the battle of Charles-

50

ton, 1966. Boston: Houghton Mifflin, 1968. 268 p.   COMMON
Barrett, John G. Sherman's march through the Carolinas. Chap-
el Hill NC: UNC Press, 1956. 325 p.   COMMON
Bass, Jack. Porgy comes home: SC after 300 years. Cola: RLB,
1972. 152 p.   SCL, GRCL
Bass, Robert D. Ninety-Six: the struggle for the SC back coun-
try. Lexington: Sandlapper Store, 1978. 456 p.   COMMON
Bateman, John M. A Columbia scrapbook, 1701-1842. Cola: RLB,
1915. 57 p.   SCL
Bates, Steven J. Murrell's Inlet...history, legends, recipes.
NP: SETAB Enterprises, 1977. unp.   HOCL
The battle of Ft. Sumter & first victory of the southern troops,
April 13th, 1861... 1861, rp Chstn: Shaftsbury Press, 1961.
35 p.   SCL
The battle of King's Mountain, October 7, 1780; reprinted from
a rare tract... NP: NPub, nd.   SCL
Bayne, Coy. Lake Murray: legend & leisure. St. Matthews: Wise
Printing Co., 1973. 60 p.   SCL, LXCL, NWRL, PICL
Bearss, Edwin C. The battle of Sullivan's island & the capture
of Ft. Moultrie... Washington DC: National Park Service,
1968. 149 p.   SCL
Bearss, Edwin C. The first two Ft. Moultries... Washington DC:
National Park Service. 86 p.   SCL
Beaty, Ernest A. Lancaster County, economic & social... Cola:
USC, 1923. 115 p.   COMMON
Beaufort, SC. Beaufort County, SC. Rev. ed. Beaufort Chamber
of Commerce, 1953. 35 p.   SCL, SCHS
Beaufort, SC. The lettuce city. Savannah GA: Braid & Hutton,
nd. 12 p.   SCL, SCHS
Beaufort, SC. Prologue to freedom: Ribaut quadricentennial.
Beaufort, 1962. 32 p.   SCL, SCHS
Beaufort County, SC. The shrines, early history & topography.
Augusta GA: Phoenix Printing Co., 1929. 32 p.   COMMON
Beauregard, Pierre G. The defense of Charleston... NP: NPub,
nd. 23 p.   SCL
Bedenbaugh, John H. Centennial history of Newberry College,
1856-1956. 39 p.   SCL, NWNC
Bedenbaugh, J. Holland. A history of Newberry College. Thesis
(M.A.), U.S.C., 1930. 208 p.   SCL, NWNC
Beitzell, Edwin W. Pt. Lookout prison camp for Confederates.
[Washington, D.C.: Kuby Litho Co.,1972] 217p. SCL,KECA
Belton Times. Sketches of Belton, SC. Belton: Belton Times,
1911. 40 p.   SCL
Bennett, Addie O. Orangeburg; 1735... Typescript, 1963. 40 p.
ORCL
Berkeley County, SC. Celebrating 300 years of sovereign state-
hood, 1670-1970. Walterboro: Berkeley County Bicentennial
Committee, 1970. 28 p.   SCL, BKCL
Berkeley County. Rural development economic survey, 1958; cov-
ering location, history, natural resources... Monck's Corner:
Berkeley County, 1958. 251 p.   SCL, BKCL

Berry, Annie M. In the past fifty years, do you remember?
Orangeburg: NPub, 1954. 10 p.   ORCL
Berry, James R. Penn Center, national historic district. Clem-
son: College of Forest & Recreational Resources, 1975. 50 p.
                                                        SCHS
Bilodeau, Francis W. Art in SC, 1670-1970. Cola: SC Tricenten-
nial Commission, 1970. 229 p.   SCL, CRCL, MRCL
Bishopville, Lee County [SpC]   LECL
Black, Clouggeon. Around the clock in Cherokee. Gaffney:
Southern Renaissance Press, 1974. 67 p.   CRCL
Blackman, J. The sea islands of SC: their peaceful & prosperous
condition: a revolution in the system of planting. Chstn:
News & Courier, 1880. 22 p.   SCL, CHCO
Blease, Coleman L. Destruction of property in Columbia, SC,
by Sherman's army. Washington DC: GPO, 1930. 112 p.SCL, COKL
Blue, Kate L. The history of Marion County, SC, & the back-
ground of her present & future development. Typescript, 1933.
8 p.   SCL
Blythewood Garden Club. Blythewood scrapbook. 1976. 69 p.CLCC
Boddie, William W. History of Williamsburg...about 1705 until
1923. Cola: State Co., 1923. 611 p.   COMMON
Bolick, Julian S. A Fairfield sketchbook. Clinton: Jacobs
Brothers, 1963. 330 p.   COMMON
Bolick, Julian S. Georgetown houselore. Clinton: Jacobs Press,
1944. 93 p.   CLEM, SCL, GTML
Bolick, Julian S. Ghosts from the coast; a collection of twelve
stories from Georgetown County, SC. Clinton: Jacobs Brothers,
1966. 158 p.   SCL, SPCL
Bolick, Julian S. A Laurens county sketchbook. Clinton: Jacobs
Press, 1973. 306 p.   COMMON
Bolick, Julian S. The return of the gray man; and, Georgetown
ghosts. Clinton: Jacobs Bros., 1961.   SCL, SPCL
Bolick, Julian S. Waccamaw plantations. Clinton: Jacobs Press,
1946. 130 p.   COMMON
Boling, Katharine. A piece of the fox's hide. Cola: Sandlapper
Press, 1972. 361 p.   SCL, COKL
Bomar, E. E. What happened when "Yankees" came to town in 1870-
1871... Spartanburg: Spartanburg District Office, W.P.A.,
nd. 12 p.   SPCL
Bond, Oliver J. The story of the Citadel. Chstn: Massie, 1936.
242 p.   SCL, KECL, SCHS
Bookhart, Emmie M. Elloree: the home I love. Orangeburg: Ob-
server Print, 1937. 42 p.   SCL, ORCL
Bookhart, Emmie M. Orangeburg County; historical data, sketches
& records... 2 vol.   ORCL
Bowden, David K. The execution of Colonel Isaac Hayne... The-
sis (M.A.), U.S.C., 1974. 101 p.   SCL
Bowden, David K. The execution of Isaac Hayne. Lexington:
Sandlapper Store, 1977. 102 p.   SCL, SPCL
Bowes, Frederick P. The culture of early Charleston. Chapel
Hill: UNC Press, 1942. 156 p.   COMMON

52

Boykin, Edward. Süd-Carolina: dessen Produkte und Vorteile
[trans.: South Carolina: its products & advantages.] NY:
Druck von George F. Nesbitt Co., nd. 15 p.   SCL
Boylston, Raymond P. The battle of Aiken. Cola: NPub, nd.
21 p.   SCL, AICL, GTML
Brabham, Otis. Bamberg & vicinity: the tale of a town...
Bamberg: NPub, 1952. 88 p.   CLEM, SCHS, SCL
Bradley, Francis W. A brief history of the Mt. Zion Society,
founded Jan. 29, 1777. Winnsboro: Fairfield County Chamber of
Commerce, 1949. 7 p.   SCL, SCHS
Brannock, James A. Brookgreen Gardens. Spartanburg: Wofford
Library Press, 1970. 9 p.   SCL
Bratton, Virginia M. History of the SC Daughters of the Ameri-
can Revolution, 1892-1936. NP: S.C.D.A.R., 1937. 162 p.
                                                   COMMON
Bregger, Myra P. Clemson Branch [of the American Association of
University Women] history, 1947-1961. Clemson: A.A.U.W.,
1961. 9 p.   CLEM
Brewster, Lawrence F. Summer migrations & resorts of SC low-
country planters. Durham NC: Duke University Press, 1947.
134 p.   COMMON
Bridwell, Ronald E. Acquisition & conflict: a history of South
Carolina's western lands, 1763-1784. Thesis (M.A.), U. S. C.,
1968. 145 p.   SCL
A brief description of the province of Carolina, on the coasts
of Floreda [sic]. London, 1666; rp Charlottesville VA: Uni-
versity of VA, 1944. 10 p.   SCL, WOFF, COKL
Bristow, Mrs. C. D. Interesting sketch of the early days of
Florence, SC. Florence: Florence Daily Times, 1921.   FLCL
Britton & Britton's Neck [Lee County] [SpC]   LECL
Brookgreen Gardens, Brookgreen, SC. NP: Brookgreen Gardens,
1939, 1954. 30 p.   SCL, SCHS
Brooks, Anna B. Pacolet [Pacolet, SC]. NP: typescript, nd.
8 p.   SPCL
Brooks, Ulysses R. Butler & his cavalry in the war of secession
1861-1865. Cola: State Co., 1909. 591 p.   COMMON
Brooks, Ulysses R. Stories of the confederacy. Cola: State Co.
1912. 410 p.   SCL, EDTO
Brown, Carl H. The reopening of the foreign slave trade in SC,
1803-1807. Thesis (M.A.), U. S. C., 1968. 75 p.   SCL
Brown, Clinton C. Thoughts towards sunset. Greenville: Courier
Printing Co., 1920. 316 p.   SCL, GRCL
Brown, Douglas S. City without cobwebs: a history of Rock Hill,
SC. 1953, rp Spartanburg: RPC, 1973. 334 p.   COMMON
Brown, Frances H. Cokesbury - past & present. Typescript,
1976. 7 p.   GSGN
Brown, Richard M. The SC regulators. Cambridge MA: Belknap
Press of Harvard University Press, 1963. 230 p.   COMMON
Brown, Varina D. A colonel at Gettysburg & Spotsylvania [incl.
South Carolinians at Gettysburg]... Cola: State Co., 1931.
333 p.   SCL

Brumley, Blanche. Diary of a Kiawah [Island] pioneer. Kiawah
    Island: NPub, 1975. 61 p.   SCL, SCHS
Brunson, Eva H. The town of Allendale is located here because
    this train came through July 4, 1872. Allendale: Commercial
    Printing Co., 1970. 16 p.   SCL
Bryan, Irene A. Thine inheritance. Cola: State Co., 1965.
    84 p.   SCL, GRCL
Bryan, Mary L. Proud heritage: a history of the League of Wo-
    men Voters of SC, 1920-1976. Cola: League of Women Voters,
    1978.   SCL, GTML, MRCL, SCHS
Bryan, Wright. Clemson [University]: an informal history...
    1889-1979. Cola: RLB, 1979. 288 p.   SCL, CLEM, PIPD, CRCL
Bryant, Hal. The Cherokee County sketchbook of Hal Bryant.
    Gaffney: Southern Renaissance Press, 1974.unp.SCL,CRCL,GRCL
Bryce, Mrs. Campbell. The personal experiences of Mrs. Campbell
    Bryce during the burning of Columbia, SC, by General W. T.
    Sherman's army, February 17, 1865. Philadelphia PA: Lippin-
    cott, 1899. 23 p.   SCL
Bryson, Iva C. Woman's work in the A.R.P. church. Due West:
    A.R.P. Company, 1940. 256 p.   SCL
Buist, A. J. A history of the Society for the Relief of the
    Families of Deceased and Disabled Indigent Members of the Med-
    ical Profession of the State of South Carolina. NP: NPub, nd.
    8 p.   SCHS
Bull, Elias. Historic preservation inventory, Berkeley County,
    1979. Berkeley-Charleston-Dorchester Council of Governments,
    1979. 54 p.   SCL, SCHS
Bull, Emily L. Eulalie. Aiken: Kalmia Press, 1973. SCL, USAI
Bull, Henry D. Colonial Georgetown. 1935. 14 p.   SCHS
Bunting, Elizabeth B. Out of Wacca Wache. Cola: RLB, 1978.
    71 p.   SCL, HOCL
Burgess, Robert H. Sea, sails & shipwreck: the career of the
    four-master schooner Purnell T. White. NP: Tidewater Press,
    1970. 132 p.   GTML
Burney, Eugenia. Colonial SC. Camden NJ: Thomas Nelson, 1970.
    176 p.   COMMON
The burning of Columbia. Chstn: W,E&C, 1888. 24 p.   SCL
The burning of Columbia, 1865. Cola: State-Columbia Record,
    1965. 80 p.   SCL, CLCC
Burton, E. Milby. Charleston furniture, 1700-1825. Chstn:
    Charleston Museum, 1955.   COMMON
Burton, E. Milby. The siege of Charleston, 1861-1865. Cola:
    USC Press, 1970. 373 p.   COMMON
Bush, C. J. Agnes of Glasgow, a legend still prevalent about a
    tombstone, in Camden, SC. Sumter: Sumter Printing Co., nd.
    16 p.   SPCL
Butler, Harriet J. The black book of Edgeworthstown & other
    Edgeworth memories. London: Faber & Gwyer, 1927. 260 p. SCL
Buzhardt, Beaufort S. [Diary]. 1916. 72 p.   SCL
Bydalek, Bernard. The courthouses at Abbeville. Cola: Southern
    Studies Program, U. S. C., 1980. 16 p.   COMMON

Byrd, Lucille C. My mother told me. NY: Pageant, 1956.
189 p.   SCL, EDTO
Caesar's Head [Greenville County]. NP: NPub, nd. unp.   GRCL
Calcott, W. H. SC: economic & social conditions in 1944. 1945,
rp Spartanburg: RPC, 1975. 239 p.   SCL
Caldwell, James F. The history of a brigade of South Carolin-
ians known first as "Gregg's [brigade]", & subsequently as
"McGowan's brigade." 1866, rp Marietta GA: Continental Book
Co., 1951. 247 p.   COMMON
Calhoun, C. History of Greenwood; some causes of secession,
early battles of the war, sketches of Butler's brigade.
Greenwood: Index Job Print., nd. 119 p.   SCL, CLEM, GWPL
Calhoun, C. M. Liberty dethroned; a concise history of some of
the most startling events before, during, & since the Civil
War [Greenwood County]. NP: NPub, 1903. 385 p.   COMMON
Calhoun County golden jubilee, May 3 through May 10, 1958. NP:
NPub, 1958. 74 p.   SCL, SCHS
Calhoun, Grace W. Long, long ago. Clemson: typescript, 1970.
27 p.   CLEM
Calhoun, Grace W. Tamassee's first decade, 1914-1924 [Tamassee,
SC]. NP: author, nd. 67 p.   SCL, ANCL
Calhoun Land Company, Calhoun. Prospectus. Greenville: Shannon
& Co., 1893. 8 p.   CLEM
Callcott, W. H. SC: economic & social conditions in 1944.
Spartanburg: RPC, 1975. 239 p.   SCHS
Callison, Helen V. Cherokee County's first half-century through
the lens of June H. Carr, photographer. Gaffney: Southern
Renaissance Print, 1975. 75 p.   COMMON
Calvert, Jesse. History of Jonesville. NP: NPub, 1971. 39 p.
                                                    SCL, UNCL
Campbell, J. C. The southern highlander & his homeland.   COKL
Campbell, William H. Reflections: the light & texture of
Charleston. Cola: RLB, 1969. 81 p.   COMMON
Cann, Marvin L. Old Ninety-Six & the SC backcountry, 1700-1775.
Greenwood: Lander College, 1970. 10 p.   CLBC, GNLN, SPCL
Capers, Ellison. Confederate military history, SC. Atlanta GA:
Confederate Publishing Co., 1899.(Vol.5:S.C.)   SCL, YOCL
Capers, Ellison. South Carolina. Atlanta GA: Confederate Pub-
lishing Co., 1899. 931 p.   COKL
Carawan, Guy. Ain't you got a right to the tree of life? The
people of John's Island, SC. NY: Simon & Schuster, 1966.
190 p.   COMMON
Cardozo, Jacob N. Reminiscences of Charleston. Chstn: J. Walk-
er, 1866. 144 p.   COMMON
Carlisle Fitting School, Spartanburg [SpC]   WOMA
Carolina Art Association. Charleston grows: an economic, social
& cultural portrait of an old community in the new south.
Chstn: author, 1949. 353 p.   COMMON
Carolina day; map telling the full story of the battle of Ft.
Moultrie. Chstn: J. McGrady Co., 1926. 4 p.   SCL
Carolina Farm Land Development Co, Andrews. Desirable farm

lands open to homeseekers & farmers... Cola: State Co.,
191?. 23 p.   SCL, CLEM
Carolina Light Infantry. Constitution...adopted 8 June, 1858.
Chstn: Walker & Evans, 1859. 16 p.   SCHS
Carolina Rifle Club, Charleston. Presentation of the battle
flag of the tenth regiment, SC volunteers, Confederate states
army, June 12, 1875. Chstn: W,E&C, 1875.   SCL, SPCL
Carolina Rifle Club, Charleston. Carolina Rifle Club, Charleston, SC, [organized] July 30, 1869. NP: 1905? 78 p. SCL,SCHS
Carroll, Bartholomew R. Historical collections of SC, embracing
many rare & valuable pamphlets & other documents relating to
the history of that state from its first discovery to its independence in the year 1776. NY: Harper & Bros, 1836; rp
Spartanburg: RPC.   2 vol.   COMMON
Carroll, James P. Report of the committee appointed to collect
testimony in relation to the destruction of Columbia, SC, on
the 17th of February, 1865. Cola: RLB, 1893. 20 p.   SCL
Carse, Robert. Department of the South; Hilton Head Island in
the Civil War. Cola: State Co., 1961. 156 p.   COMMON
Carter, Margaret L. History of Lake City, SC. NY: Carlton,
1976. 124 p.   FLCL, GRCL
Carter, R. C. Persons, places & happenings in old Walhalla.
Walhalla: Walhalla Historical Society, 1960. 210 p. SCL, PIPD
Carwile, John B. Reminiscences of Newberry, embracing important
occurrences, brief biographies of prominent citizens, & histo-
rical sketches of prominent churches: to which is appended an
historical account of Newberry College. 1890, rp Cola: RLB,
1970. 313 p.   COMMON
Cash, Ellerbe B. The Cash-Shannon duel. Greenville: Daily News
Job Print., 1881. 48 p.   SCL, USAI
Cassels, Louis. Coontail lagoon: a celebration of life [Aiken
Co.] Philadelphia PA: Westminster Press, 1974. 126 p. COMMON
Cassels, Louise. The unexpected exodus [Ellenton, SC]. Aiken:
Sand Hill Press, 1971. 98 p.   COMMON
Catalogue of the Bamberg Graded School, and history & review of
the town of Bamberg, SC... Bamberg: Herald Job Presses,
1891. 19 p.   WOFF
Catalogue of Columbia Female College, Columbia, SC, for 1894-
1895. Cola: RLB, 1895. 61 p.   WOFF
Catalogue of Newberry College, Newberry, SC, 1898-1899. New-
berry: Elbert H. Aull, 1899. 40 p.   SCL, WOFF
Catawba Male Academy, Rock Hill. Second annual announcement.
Rock Hill, 1904-1905. 36 p.   SCHS
Catawba Regional Planning Council. Historic sites survey,
Chester County. Rock Hill: author, 1976.   SCL, CSCL
Catawba & Wateree Company. Rules & bye laws... Chstn: Young,
1795. 36 p.   SCHS
Catoe, Bernice R. Mt. Pisgah community. NP: privately printed,
1976.   KECA
Caughman, Joseph Ansel. A history of the religious life of
Cedar Grove community and families influencing its culture.

56

Batesburg: Bruner Press, 1952. 215 p.   COMMON
Causey, Beth & Malcolm L. Causey. Ft. Sumter - Ft. Moultrie;
    pictorial story of Charleston's forts... Mt. Pleasant: Hope
    Publ. Co., 1966. 32 p.   COMMON
Causey, Beth G. Ships of the harbor, Charleston, SC. NP: NPub,
    1971. 32 p.   SCL, GTML
Causey, Beth G. SC cities, A - Z. Mt. Pleasant: Hope Publ. Co.
    1969. 64 p.   SCL, GRCL
Causey, Beth G. SC counties. Mt. Pleasant: Hope Publ. Co.,
    1969. 101 p.   COMMON
Causey, Beth G. SC legends. Mt. Pleasant: Hope Publ. Co.,
    1969. 64 p.   SCL, SPCL
Causey, Beth G. SC rivers. Mt. Pleasant: Hope Publ. Co., 1969.
    71 p.   SCL, GRCL, LECL
Cauthen, Charles E. SC goes to war, 1860-1865. Chapel Hill NC:
    UNC Press, 1950. 256 p.   COMMON
Celebration of the thirty-second anniversary of the house of
    George W. Williams & Co., & the inauguration of the Carolina
    Savings Bank of Charleston, SC, May 2, 1874. Chstn: W,E&C,
    1874. 38 p.   WOFF
Centennial celebration of Aiken, 1935.   AICL
Centennial celebration commemorating the founding of Aiken, SC,
    April 4-6, 1935. NP: NPub, 1935. 44 p.   EDTO, CHCO
Centennial celebration of the granting of the charter to the
    South Carolina College, held in Charleston, SC, Dec. 19-20,
    1901. At the S. C. Interstate & West Indian Exposition.
    Chstn: Lucas & Richardson, 1902. 117 p.   SCL, WOFF
Centennial celebration: South Carolina College. Cola: State
    Co., 1905.   SCL, MRCL
The centennial of incorporation [of the city of Charleston.]
    1883. Chstn: News & Courier Presses, 1884. 259 p. SCL, GRCL
Centennial souvenir of the Pendleton Farmers' Society. Anderson
    Oulia Printing & Binding Co., 1916. 87 p.   SCL,WOFF
Central Association for the Relief of South Carolina Soldiers.
    Annual report...1864 (2nd). Cola, 1864.   SCHS
Central midlands historic preservation survey.Cola: Central
    Midlands Regional Planning Council, 1974.323p. SCL, NWRL LXCL
Central Piedmont Regional Planning Commission. Survey of hist-
    oric sites: Chester County. NP: author, 1971.SCL, GRCL, CSCL
Central Piedmont Regional Planning Commission. Survey of hist-
    oric sites: Lancaster County. NP: author, 1971   GRCL, LNCL
Central Piedmont Regional Planning Commission. Survey of hist-
    oric sites: Union County. Rock Hill: author, 1971. 30 p.GRCL
Central Piedmont Regional Planning Commission. Survey of hist-
    oric sites: York County. NP: author, 1971.   GRCL, YOCL
Chadwick, Nancy G. Revised index to Simpson's History of Pen-
    dleton District, SC. Jacksonville FL: author, 1973. 21 p.
                                       SCL, PIPD, GRCL, SCHS
Chambers, Gladys N. The history of Cayce, SC... NP: NPub, 1968
    43 p.   COMMON
Chandler, Helen D. The battle of King's Mountain: "the turning

point of the American Revolution", Oct. 7, 1780.   Gastonia NC:
NPub, nd.   47 p.   SCL
Chapin, George H.   Health resorts of the south [includes Summer-
ville].   Boston, 1893.   277 p.   WOFF, DOTM
Chaplin, Ellen P.   The early schools of Orangeburg County.   Or-
angeburg: typescript, 1972.   16 p.   ORCL
Chaplin, Ellen P.   Orangeburg County schools, SC.   Orangeburg:
Orangeburg County Delegation, 1957.   55 p.   ORCL
Chapman, John A.   History of Edgefield County, from the earliest
settlements to 1897.   1897, rp Easley: SHP, 1976.   521 p.
                                                               COMMON
Chapman, John A.   School history of SC.   Richmond VA: Everett
Waddey Co., 1894 & various eds;   521 p.   COMMON

Charles Towne: birth of a city.   A historical record of the
early years of Charleston.   Chstn: News & Courier, 1970.
48 p.   SCL
Charles, W. E.   Sketch of the Darlington Guards.   NP: mimeo, nd.
7 p.   SCHS
Charleston.   Record of earthquake damages.   Atlanta GA: Winham
& Lester, 1886.   162 p.   SCHS
Charleston and the South Carolina Interstate & West Indian Ex-
position.   An illustrated souvenir...   Chstn, Buffalo NY &
St. Louis: Robert Allen Reid, 1902.   52 p.   SCL, ORCL
Charleston as it is after the earthquake shock of August 31,
1886.   A sketch of the occurrence.   Illustrations of its ef-
fects.   Chstn, 1886.   62 p.   SCL, SCHS
Charleston Chamber of Commerce.   Autographs of the founders
[of the] Charleston Chamber of Commerce, February, 1794.
[Also] Autographs of the Lords Proprietors...   NP: NPub, nd.
12 p.   SCL
Charleston Chamber of Commerce.   Coastal SC.   Chstn: NPub, 1953.
66 p.   SCL, CLEM
Charleston Chamber of Commerce.   Facts about Charleston, America's most historic city.   Chstn: author, nd.   10 p.   SCL
Charleston Chamber of Commerce.   Historic Charleston.   Chstn:
author, 1954.   36 p.   CLEM
Charleston Chamber of Commerce.   A short history & description
of the famous Magnolia Gardens near Charleston, SC.   Chstn,
192?   4 p.   SCHS
Charleston Chamber of Commerce.   Stray leaves garnered [Charles-
ton Chamber of Commerce & St. Andrew's Society, Charleston].
Chstn: Lucas & Richardson, 1900?   11 p.   SCL, SCHS
Charleston Chamber of Commerce.   The trade & commerce of the ci-
ty of Charleston, SC, from September 1, 1865, to September 1,
1872.   Chstn: News Job Presses, 1873.   85 p.   SCL, CLEM
Charleston City Council.   By-laws of the Orphan House of
Charleston, SC, revised...1861.   Chstn: Evans & Cogswell,
1861.   40 p.   SCL, SCHS
Charleston City Council.   The earthquake, 1886.   Exhibits.
Showing the receipts & disbursements...of the Executive Relief

Committee. Chstn: Lucas, Richardson & Co., 1887. 94 p. CHCO
SCHS, SCL
Charleston City Council. The earthquake, 1886. Chstn: Theo. L.
DeVinne & Co., 1887. 15 p. SCHS, SCL, GTML
Charleston City Council. Education in Charleston, SC; the dis-
abilities of the unaided south in public school facilities.
Chstn: News & Courier, 1881. 32 p. SCL, SCHS
Charleston City Council. Memorial of the City Council of
Charleston, SC, praying that a marine hospital be erected...
Washington DC: Gales & Seaton, 1827. 4 p. SCL
Charleston City Council. Report of the committee of the City
Council...upon interments within the city and memorial from
churches & citizens. Chstn: Walker, Evans & Co., 1859. 30 p.
SCL, SCHS
Charleston City Council. Report of the committee...epidemic
yellow fever of 1858. Includes annual report of port physic-
ians of Charleston, containing information on ships, captains,
crews, cargoes, etc., for the year 1858. Chstn: Walker,
Evans & Co., 1859. 68 p. SCL, SCHS
Charleston Civic Services Committee. Charleston grows: an eco-
nomic, social & cultural portrait of an old community in the
new south. Chstn: Carolina Art Assn., 1949. 353 p. SCL, CLEM
Charleston Club. Constitution & by-laws...1881. Reprinted
with amendments...1898. Chstn: W,E&C, 1898. 35 p. SCHS
The Charleston Confederate Centennial Commission, 1960-1965.
Chstn: NPub, 1965. 16 p. SCL
Charleston Confederate Memorial Day. Re-interment of the Caro-
lina dead from Gettysburg; address of Rev. Dr. Girardeau...
Chstn: Mazyck, 1871. 36 p. SCL, SCHS
Charleston County Tricentennial Committee. A pictorial history:
Charles-Towne 1670, Charleston 1970. Chstn: author, 1970.
unp. GRCL
Charleston Exchange Club. Celebration of progress, St. Andrew's
parish: 1670-1943. Chstn, 1943. 40 p. SCL, SCHS
Charleston Female Seminary. [Catalog]. Chstn: W,E&C, 1873.
20 p. SCHS
Charleston Fire Department. Annual report of the chief of the
fire department of the city of Charleston, SC, ending May 21,
1861. Chstn: Harper & Calvo, 1861. 37 p. CHCA
Charleston Fire Department. Rules & regulations concerning the
fire department of Charleston, SC. Chstn: Daggett Printing
Co., 1895. 70 p. CHCA
Charleston Fire Insurance Company. Address of the directors...
to the stockholders... Chstn: J. Hoff, 1812. 55 p. SCHS
Charleston High School. The centennial year book: 1839-1939.
Chstn, 1939. 69 p. SCL, SCHS
Charleston High School. Proceedings upon the occasion of open-
ing the school house, corner Meeting & George streets, Jan. 3,
1881. Chstn: Charleston City Council, 1882? 40 p. SCL, SCHS
Charleston Library Society bicentennial anniversary. June 13,
1948... Chstn: NPub, 1948. 14 p. WOFF, SCL, SCHS

Charleston Light Dragoons. Constitution & by-laws...1733-1892.
  Chstn: Lucas & Richardson, 1892. 18 p.   SCHS
Charleston Light Dragoons Association. Constitution. Chstn:
  W,E&C, 1872. 8 p.   SCHS
Charleston Marine School. Rules of the trustees...adopted 12th
  April, 1859; rev. April 1860. Also the rules & regulations
  of the school. Chstn: W,E&C, 1860. 20 p.   SCHS
Charleston Orphan House. Centennial celebration, 1790-1890.
  Chstn: W,E&C, 1891. 82 p.   SCL, WOFF, SCHS
Charleston Police Department. Official history. Chstn: W,E&C,
  1924? 84 p.   SCHS
Charleston Police Department. Report of the captain of police
  ...showing the number of persons arrested in October & Novem-
  ber, 1864.   CHCA
Charleston Police Department. Rules & regulations...1890.
  Chstn: J.H.E. Stelling, 1890. 43 p.   SCL, CHCA
Charleston Port Society. An historical sketch of the rise &
  progress of religious & moral improvement among seamen in Eng-
  land & the U.S. With a history of the Port Society of
  Charleston, SC... Chstn: Burke, 1851. 22 p.   SCL, SCHS
Charleston Rifle Club. Schutzen Journal. 1941 annual issue.
  Chstn: NPub, 1941. 68 p.   SCL
Charleston, South Carolina-- America's most historic city.
  Milwaukee WI: E. C. Kropp Co., 1930? 30 p.   WOFF
Charleston, South Carolina, 1680-1930, 250 years of honorable
  achievement... Chstn: Mayor & City Council, 1930. 32 p. GRCL
                                                       SPCL, SCL
Charleston, South Carolina in 1883; with heliotypes of the prin-
  cipal objects of interest in & around the city & historical &
  descriptive notices. Boston: Heliotype Printing Co., 1883.
  39 p.   SCL, GRCL
Cheraw Hardware & Supply Co. Historical sketch & vest pocket
  directory of Cheraw, SC. NP: author, 1919? 16 p.   SCL, SCHS
Cherry, William J. A handbook of the city of Rock Hill...
  Charlotte NC: Queen City Printing Co., 1895.   YOCL
Chester News. Spirit of Chester, Chester County, SC. Chester:
  author, 1932. 32 p.   SCL
Chesterfield County Tricentennial Committee. Town of Chester-
  field, 1670-1970. NP: NPub, 1970. 22 p.   SCL
Chichester, C. E. Historical sketch of the Charleston Port So-
  ciety for promoting the gospel among seamen... Chstn: News &
  Courier, 1885. 65 p.   SCL, SCHS
Chidsey, Donald B. The war in the south; the Carolinas & GA in
  the American revolution... NY: Crown, 1969. 176 p.GNCL SPCL
                                                       EDTO, SCL
Childs, St. Julien R. Cavaliers & burghers in the Carolina low
  country. Baltimore: Johns Hopkins Press, 1941. 20 p.   SCHS
Childs, St. Julien R. ...Malaria & colonization in the SC low
  country, 1526-1696. Baltimore: Johns Hopkins Press, 1940.
  292 p.   COMMON
Chiles, James M. A true statement of facts... Edgefield:

Advertiser, 1854. 51 p.   SCL
Christ Church Parish Agricultural Society. Constitution & by-
laws and roll of members...Berkeley County., SC. Chstn:
W,E&C, 1883. 4 p.   SCHS
Christie, Faye & Hortense Woodson. Come out, brave men of
Edgefield! Headlines from the Edgefield Advertiser. Edge-
field: Advertiser Press, 1960. 94 p.   SCL, USAI, EDTO
Christopherson, Merrill G. Biography of an island; General
C. C. Pinckney's sea island plantation. Fennimore WI: West-
burg Associates Publishers, 1976. 120 p. SCL,BUHH, BUCL, SCHS
Church, Henry F. Charleston, SC, 1680-1930. Chstn: J.J. Fur-
long, 1930. 32 p.   SCL
Claremont Theological Scholarship Society. Constitution...
With an address delivered at the formation of the said society
by the Rev. William Barlow. Also, a list of its officers.
Chstn: Sebring, 1826. 16 p.   SCL, SCHS
Clarendon cameos. Manning: Clarendon County Historical Society,
1976. 132 p.   COMMON
Clark, G. Dewey. My south [Manning, SC]. NY: Carleton Press,
1970. 107 p.   SCL, GRCL, CLEM
Clark Hill reservoir & reservation. Augusta GA: Tidwell Print-
ing, Inc., 1953. 99 p.   SCL
Clark, Mary C. Santee stories and other tales. Manning: G.
Dewey Clark, 1962. 68 p.   SCL, CLEM, SPCL
Clark, Thomas D. SC: the grand tour, 1780-1865. Cola: USC
Press, 1973. 342 p.   COMMON
Clark, W. A. History of the State Agriculture Society of SC,
1839-1916. Cola: RLB, 1916.   MRCL
Clark, W. A. History of the banking institutions organized in
SC prior to 1860. Cola: State Co., 1922. 472 p.   COMMON
Clayton, Frederick V. The settlement of Pendleton District,
1777-1800. Thesis (M.A.), U.S.C., 1930. 107p.SCL, PICL, ANCL
Clayton, W.F. A narrative of the Confederate States Navy. Bul-
letin of the Pee Dee Historical Assn, 1910.   SCL, MACL
Clinkscales, John G. On the old plantation; reminiscences of
his childhood. Spartanburg: Band & White, 1916. 142 p. EDTO
                                              SCL, GNLN, FLMC
Clinton Chamber of Commerce. Mary Musgrove, 1776-1783; Revolu-
tionary war period, Laurens, SC.Clinton: author,1975. SCL,LRCL
Clinton Chamber of Commerce. The Revolutionary war period;
battle of Musgrove's Mill & other information, Laurens County,
SC, 1776-1975. Clinton: author, 1975.   LRCL
Clinton, Sir Henry. Memorandums...respecting the unprecedented
treatment which the army have met with respecting plunder
taken after a siege... London: NPub, 1794. 106 p.   SCL
Clowse, Converse D. The Charleston export trade, 1717-1737.
Evanston IL: Northwestern University, 1963. 323 p. SCL, CLEM
Clowse, Converse D. Economic beginnings in colonial SC, 1670-
1730. Cola: USC Press, 1971. 283 p.   COMMON
Cohen, Henning. A Barhamville miscellany: notes & documents
concerning the SC Female Collegiate Institute, 1826-1865.

Cola: USC Press, 1956. 72 p.   SCL, CLCC
Cohen, Hennig. The South Carolina Gazette, 1732-1775. Cola:
USC Press, 1953. 273 p.   COMMON
Cohen, J. Barrett. Judaism & the typical Jew...an address de-
livered...October 26, 1884. Chstn: News & Courier, 1884.
21 p.   SCL
Coker College. The story of Coker College. Hartsville: author,
1945. 10 p.   COKL
Coker, Edwin C. County history; sketch of the early history of
Society Hill... NP: News & Press, 1946. 5 p.   DACL
Coker, Hannah L. A story of the late war. Chstn: W,E&C, 1887.
47 p.   SCL, WOFF, FLMC, SPCL
Coker, James L. Hartsville: its early settlers... NP: Messen-
ger, 1911. 66 p.   COMMON
Coker, James L. History of company "G", ninth SC regiment...
& of company "E", sixth SC regiment, infantry, SC army. 1899,
rp Greenwood: Attic Press, 1979. 210 p.   COMMON
Coker, Lois W. County history. Early history of Hartsville.
NP: News & Press, 1946. 3 p.   DACL
Coker, Robert E. Springville: a summer village of old Darling-
ton District. Chstn: NPub, 1952. 21 p.   SCL
Coker, Thomas H. News & views of Hartsville... Hartsville:
Hartsville Publishing Co., 1909. unp.   COKL
Colcock, Erroll H. Dusky land; gullah poems & sketches of
coastal SC. Clinton: Jacobs Press, 1942. 103 p.   SCL, USAI
Cole, David W. The organization & administration of the SC
militia system, 1670-1783. Thesis (Ph.D.), U.S.C., 1953.
148 p.   SCL
Coleman, Caroline S. Five petticoats on Sunday [Greenville Co.]
Greenville: Hiott Press, 1962. 145 p.   COMMON
Coleman, Caroline S. History of Fountain Inn. Fountain Inn:
Tribune Times, 1966. 105 p.   COMMON
Coleman, J. F. B. Tuskegee to Vorhees. Cola: RLB, 1922.
128 p.   SCL, EPDI
College of Charleston Alumni Association. Fifty years around
the cistern: 1888-1938. Golden jubilee book. Chstn: author,
1938. 108 p.   SCHS
Colleton Artists' Guild. Backward glances. NP: author, 1976.
50 p.   COML
Collins, Charles & others. Happy birthday, Oconee (1868-1968).
NP: NPub, 1968. unp.   PIPD
Columbia City Council. Proceedings of the centennial committee
...the first meeting of the General Assembly of the state of
SC, convened in the city of Columbia in the year 1791, cele-
brated...1891. Cola: NPub, 1891.   SCL
Columbia Public Schools. The story of Columbia... Cola: author
1933. 34 p.   SCL
Columbia Record. The settling of SC. Cola: Columbia Record,
1969.   MRCL
Commissioner of Immigration. SC: a home for the industrious immigrant. Chstn: Joseph Walker, 1867. 48p.   SCL, CHCO

Confederate Home and College. Home for the mothers, widows, &
daughters of Confederate soldiers, Charleston, SC. Constitu-
tion, internal regulations, etc. Chstn: W,E&C, 1869. 12 p.
                                                            SCHS
Confederation of SC Local Historical Societies. Official SC
historical markers: a directory. Cola: SCDAH, 1978. 156 p.
                                                          COMMON
Conrad, August. The destruction of Columbia, SC [translation].
Originally published in Hanover, Germany; rp Cola: Wade
Hampton Chapter, U.D.C., 1926. 32 p.   COMMON
Conway Chamber of Commerce. Conway, SC. Greenville: Peace
Printing Co., 1922. 26 p.   FLMC, SCHS
Cook, George L. Souvenir of the great earthquake at Charleston,
SC, August 31, 1886. Chstn: Southern Directory Co., 1886.
19 p.   SCL
Cook, Harriet H. Fort Hill--John C. Calhoun shrine. 1948.
NP: NPub, 1948. 35 p.   SCL, PIPD
Cook, Harvey T. A historical background of Greenville. Green-
ville: NPub, 1926. 11 p.   SCL
Cook, Harvey T. Rambles in the Pee Dee basin, SC. Cola: State
Co., 1926. 462 p.   COMMON
Cook, Harvey T. Sherman's march through SC in 1865. Greenville
NPub, 1938. 25 p.   SCL, SPCL
Cooley, Rossa B. Homes of the freed. NP: New Republic, 1926.
199 p.   SCL, BUCL
Cooley, Rossa B. School acres: an adventure in rural education.
New Haven CT: Yale University Press, 1930. 166 p. SCL, BUCL
Copeland, D. Graham. Many years after; a bit of history & some
recollections of Bamberg, with an appendix of data concerning
a few Bamberg County families & their connections. NP: typescript, nd. 788 p.   SCL, BACL
Cordle, Charles G. Activities of Beach Island farmer's clubs,
1846-1862. Atlanta GA: Southern Historical Association, 1950.
10 p.   SCL
Corkran, David H. The Carolina indian frontier. Cola: USC
Press, 1970. 71 p.   COMMON
Corkran, David H. The Cherokee frontier; conflict & survival,
1740-1762. Norman OK: University of Oklahoma Press, 1962.
302 p.   SCL, SCHS
Cornelia, William E. Hilton Head Island: a perspective. Hilton
Head Island, 1975. 128 p.   COMMON
Cosgrove, John I. Sketch of the Hibernian Society of Charleston
SC. Chstn: J. Furlong & Sons, 1927. 20 p.   SCL
Cottrell, Joseph E. Reminiscential chitchat...from the Carolina
Spartan, 1885-1890. Spartanburg: Federal Writer's Project,
W.P.A., nd. Typescript, 185 p.   SPCL
Courtenay, William A. Cowpens [battle of] centennial: 1781-
1881. NP: Cowpens Centennial Committee, 1896. 137 p.SCL,MRCL
Courtenay, William A. Earliest voyages to SC...John Ribault,
1562. NY: Francis P. Harper, 1905. 54 p.   SCL
Courtenay, William A. The genesis of SC: 1562-1670. Cola:

State Co., 1907. 177 p. GNLN, SCL, SCHS
Cowpens Centennial Committee. Cowpens centennial, 1781-1881.
  Chstn: NPub, 1881. unp. SCL
Cowpens Centennial Committee. Proceedings at the unveiling of
  the battle monument at Spartanburg, SC, 1881. Chstn: author,
  1896. 137 p. SCL, SPCL
Cox, James R. The history of the Newberry, SC, Opera House,
  1880-1973. Thesis (M.A.), U.S.C., 1974. 108 p. SCL, NWRL
Crane, Verner W. The southern frontier, 1670-1732. 1928, rp
  Ann Arbor MI: University of Michigan Press, 1956. 359 p.
                                              UMBOD, SCL, GNLN
Crane, Verner W. The Tennessee River as the road to Carolina:
  the beginnings of exploration & trade. 18 p. SCL
Craven, Delle M. The neglected thread: a journal from the Cal-
  houn community (by Mary E. Moragne). Cola: USC Press, 1951.
                                              SCL, LNCL
Crawford, Samuel W. The genesis of the Civil War: the story of
  [Ft.] Sumter, 1860-1861. NY: C.L. Webster, 1887. 486 p.GTML
                                              SCL
Crawford, Samuel W. The history of the fall of Ft. Sumter;
  being an inside history of the affairs in SC & Washington,
  1860-1861... NY: Harper, 1896. 486 p. CLCC, SCL, MACL
Crittenden, Stephen S. The Greenville century book, comprising
  an account of the first settlement of the county and the
  founding of the city of Greenville, SC. Greenville: Greenville News, 1903. 162 p. COMMON
Cropper, Mariam D. SC waterways as they appear in Mill's Atlas
  [of South Carolina], including bridges, ferries, & fords.
  Salt Lake City UT: A.I.S. Lightning Press, 1977. 106 p. MRCL
                                              SPCL, SCL
Crouch, C. W. Island taxes: an open letter from a resident to
  the intendant of Moultrieville, SC. NP: NPub, 1878. 9 p.
                                              SCL
Crouch, Katy A. History & traditions: the Ravenel Research Cen-
  ter, Clemson, SC. NP: NPub, 1959. PIPD
Cunningham, Clarence. A history of the Calhoun monument at
  Charleston, SC. Chstn: Lucas & Richardson, 1888. 147 p. WOFF
                                              SCL, GNLN
Dabbs, Edith M. Face of an island. Leigh Richmond Miner's
  photographs of St. Helena Island. Cola: RLB, 1970. 200 p.
                                              COMMON
Dabbs, Edith M. Walking tall: a brief sketch of Penn School...
  Frogmore, SC. Frogmore: Penn Community Services, 1964. 14 p.
                                              SCL, FLMC
Dabney, William M. William Henry Drayton & the American Revolu-
  tion. Albuquerque NM: University of NM Press, 1962. 225 p.
                                              SCL, COKL
Dalcho, Frederick. An Ahiman Rezon, for the use of the Grand
  Lodge of SC, Ancient York-Masons... Wilmington DL: Marchant,
  1807. SCL, BUCL
Daly, Charles P. The settlement of the Jews in North America.

64

NY: Philip Cowen, 1893. 171 p.   SCL
Daniel, Robert N. Furman University, a history. Greenville:
    Hiott, 1951. 289 p.   COMMON
Daniels, Johnathan. The gentlemanly serpent & other columns
    from a newspaperman in paradise [Beaufort County]. Cola:
    USC Press, 1974. 467 p.   COMMON
Darlington County Historical Society. The records & papers of
    the Darlington County Historical Society...1937-...1944.
    NP: author, 1944. 258 p.   DACL
Darlington County Historical Society. History of Darlington
    County. NP: News & Press, 1946. 11 p.   DACL
D.A.R. South Carolina. History of the SC daughters of the
    American Revolution. 2 v.   COMMON
D.A.R. Star Fort Chapter. Early settlements of the up-country:
    Boonesborough Township. Greenwood: typescript, 1950. 11 p.
                                                                GWPL
D.A.R. Star Fort Chapter. Early settlements of the up-country:
    Londonborough Township. Greenwood: typescript, 1950. 14 p.
                                                                GWPL
D.A.R. Star Fort Chapter. Early settlements of the up-country:
    Long Canes. Greenwood: typescript, 1950. 5 p.   GWPL
D.A.R. Star Fort Chapter. Early settlements of the up-country:
    The Waxhaws. Greenwood: typescript, 1949. 9 p.   GWPL
D.A.R. Wizard of Tamaysee Chapter. "The ring fight" that gave
    peace to the Piedmont section and ended indian interference.
    NP: NPub, 1926. 7 p.   SCL
Davidson, Chalmers G. The colonial Scotch-Irish of the Carolina
    Piedmont. Richburg: Chester County Genealogical Society,
    1979? 17 p.   SCL, SCHS
Davidson, Chalmers G. The last foray. The SC planters of 1860.
    Cola: USC Press, 1971. 267 p.   COMMON
Davidson, Chalmers G. Major John Davidson of "Rural Hill",
    Mecklenburg County, NC. Charlotte NC: Lassiter Press, 1943.
    93 p.   LNCL
Davies, Julia E. Colonial SC. Cincinatti OH: Ebbert & Richard-
    son Co., 1925. 57 p.   SCL
Davis, Burke. The Cowpens-Guilford Courthouse campaign. Phila-
    delphia PA: Lippincott, 1962. 208 p.   COMMON
Davis, Evangeline. Charleston houses & gardens. Chstn: Preser-
    vation Society of Charleston, 1975. 80 p.   COMMON
Davis, Nora M. The Cherokee massacre. NP: typescript, nd.
    14 p.   GWPL
Davis, Nora M. Fort Charlotte on the Savannah River & its sig-
    nificance in the American revolution. Greenwood: Star Fort
    Chapter, D.A.R., 1949. 19 p.   COMMON
Davis, Nora M. Military & naval operations in SC, 1860-1865; a
    chronological list, with references... Cola: SCAD, 1959.
    24 p.   SCL, SPCL, EDTO
Davis, Nora M. Public powder magazines at Charleston. Chstn:
    Historical Commission of Charleston, 1944.   SCL, CHCA
Days of Dorchester. NP: Dorchester County Historical Society,

nd.   SCL, DOCL
Deas, Anne S. Dorchester; Ingleside; & St. James, Goose Creek..
  . Summerville: S. P. Driggers, 1905. 19 p.   SCL
Delaplaine, A. Fort Moultrie in the revolution. Spartanburg:
  Wofford Library Press, 1970. 4 p.   SCL
della Torre, Thomas. A sketch of the Charleston Club, with its
  constitution & by-laws & a list of members, 1852-1938. Chstn:
  NPub, 1938. 41 p.   SCL, SCHS
DeLoach, John K. ...Historical outline of Kershaw County, SC...
  Charlotte NC: typescript, 1933. 6 p.   SCL, SCHS
Derrick, Brenda R. The life of Long Branch School, Johnston,
  SC, 1888-1954. NP: typescript, 1975. 19 p.   EDTO
Derrick, Samuel M. Centennial history of the South Carolina
  Railroad. 1930, rp Spartanburg: RPC, 1975. 335 p.   COMMON
DeSaussure, Nancy B. Old plantation days; being recollections
  of southern life before the Civil War. NP: Duffield & Co.,
  1909. 123 p.   SCL, SPCL
DeSaussure, Wilmot G. An account of the siege of Charleston,
  SC, in 1780. Chstn: News & Courier, 1885. 291 p.   SCL
DeTreville, Richard. Sea island lands. St. Helena parish & its
  citizens. A few chapters from a faithful unpublished history
  of the war of secession. NP: NPub, 1870? 16 p.   SCL
Deutsche Schuetzen=Gesellschaft [German Rifle Club], Charleston.
  Golden jubilee of the Deutsche Schuetzen=Gesellschaft...com-
  bined with the May-festival and spring gala week. Schuetzen
  Park, May 8-13, [19]'05. Atlanta GA: Wrigley, nd. 43 p. SCL
DeVorsey, Louis Jr. Indian boundary in the southern colonies:
  1763-1775. Chapel Hill NC: UNC Press, 1966.   SCL, KECA
Dibble, Thomas O. History of Orangeburg: 1884. Orangeburg:
  typescript, 1953. 22 p.   ORCL
Dick, A. W. Lee County: economic & social. Cola: Bulletin of
  the University of SC, 1925. 76 p.   COMMON
Dickert, D. Augustus. History of Kershaw's brigade with complete roll of companies, biographical sketches, incidents...
  1899, rp Dayton OH: Morningside Bookshop, 1973. 583 p. COMMON
Dickson, Frank A. Journeys into the past: the Anderson region's
  heritage. Anderson: author, 1975. 242 p.   COMMON
Dickson, S. H. Address...delivered at the inauguration of the
  public school, fourth of July, 1856. Chstn: Walker, Evans,
  1856. 24 p.   SCL, SCHS
Dillon County Chamber of Commerce. Dillon County, SC. Dillon:
  author, 1957. unp.   CLEM
Doane, Edith R. Saxe-Gotha & Dutch Fork pioneers & their de-
  scendants. NP: typescript, 1956. 3 vol.   LTSS
Doar, David. Rice & rice planting in the SC low country.
  Chstn: Charleston Museum, 1936 & 1970. 70 p. SCL, GTML, SPCL
Doar, David. A sketch of the Agricultural Society of St. James,
  Santee, SC, & an address on the traditions & reminiscences of
  the parish delivered before the society on 4th of July, 1907.
  Chstn: Calder-Fladger Co., 1908.   SCL, CHLS, SCHS, WOFF
Dooley, Elizabeth. Prologue to freedom: Beaufort, SC. souvenir

program. Beaufort: Prologue to Freedom, Inc., 1962 SCL, SCHS
Dorchester in old England. NP: NPub, nd. 27 p.   MONT, SCHS
Dorchester Tricentennial Commission. Days of Dorchester. Sum-
    merville: NPub, 1970. 30 p.   SCL
Doubleday, Abner. Reminiscences of Forts Sumter & Moultrie in
    1860-1861. 1876, rp Spartanburg: RPC, 1976. 184 p.   SCL
Dowling, G. G. Parris Island, from Cusabo to leatherneck.
    Besufort: Peacock Press, 1970. 18 p.   COMMON
Doyle, Mary C. Historic Oconee in SC. Pendleton: Old Pendle-
    ton District Historical Commission, 1967. 69 p.   COMMON
Drake, Jeanie. In old St. Stephen's [Appleton's Town & Country
    Library. Sept. 1, 1892.] NY: Appleton & Co., 1892. 232 p.
                                                         SCL, EPDI
Draper, Lyman C. King's Mountain & its heroes: history of the
    battle of King's Mountain... 1881, rp Spartanburg: RPC, 1973.
    612 p.   COMMON
Drayton, John. Memoirs of the American Revolution...as relating
    to SC... 1821, rp NY: Arno Press, 1969. 2 vol.   COMMON
Drayton, John. A view of SC, as respects her natural & civil
    concerns. 1802, rp Spartanburg: RPC, 1972. 252 p.   COMMON
Driggers, Mary S. Lake City, SC; a comprehensive sketch. Lake
    City: Lake City Chamber of Commerca, 1958? 16 p.   SCHS
DuBose, Henry K. History of company "B", 21st regiment (infan-
    try), SC volunteers, Confederate States Provisional Army.
    Cola: RLB, 1909.   COMMON
DuBose, Samuel. Address delivered at the seventeenth anniversa-
    ry of the Black Oak Agricultural Society, April 27, 1858...to
    which is added, reminiscences of St. Stephen's parish, &
    notices of her old homesteads. Chstn: A.E. Miller, 1858.
    38 p.   SCL, FLMC
DuBose, Samuel & Frederick A. Porcher. A contribution to the
    history of the Huguenots of SC, consisting of pamphlets by
    Samuel DuBose, Esq., of St. John's, Berkeley; & Prof. Freder-
    ick A. Porcher of Charleston. 1887, rp Cola: RLB, 1972.
    234 p.   COMMON
DuBose, Samuel. Reminiscences of St. Stephen's parish, Craven
    County, & notices of her old homesteads. Chstn: A.E. Miller,
    1858. 38 p.   SCL, FLMC, BKCL
Dudley, C. W. History of Bennetsville (1878) [SpC]   MRCL
Dudley, C. W. Personal recollections of Col. C. W. Dudley
    (1899) [SpC]   MRCL
Duffy, John J. A brief history of Beaufort... NP: NPub, 1976?
    11 p.   SCL
Duncan, Magdalen H. Historical data about Pamplico, SC, &
    vicinity. NP: NPub, 1974. 19 p.   FLCL
Duncan, Ruth H. The captain & the submarine C.S.S. H. L. Hunley
    Memphis TN: S. C. Toof & Co., 1965. 109 p.   SCL
Dundas, Francis D. The Calhoun settlement, Abbeville District,
    SC. 2nd ed. Staunton VA: McClure, 1950. 60 p.   COMMON
Dunlop, William S. ...Lee's sharpshooters: or, the forefront
    of battle... Little Rock AR: Tunnah & Pittard. 488 p.   SCL

Dunovant, R. G. M. The Palmetto regiment, SC volunteers, 1846-1848: the battles in the valley of Mexico, 1847-... Chstn: W,E&C, 1897. 26 p. SCL, PRIV

DuPont, Henry A. The story of the Huguenots; as contained in two addresses made before the Huguenot societies of SC & PA. Cambridge ??: Riverside Press, 1920. 62 p. YOCL, SCL

Dutton, Clarence E. The Charleston earthquake. NP: NPub, nd. unp. [Washington: GPO, 1889] 325p. SCL, GTML

Dwight, Henry R. Some historic spots in Berkeley [County]. 1921, rp Chstn: W,E&C, 1944. 48 p. COMMON

Eaddy, Elaine Y. Johnsons [Johnson families] & Johnsonville [SpC] WMTR

Eaddy, Elaine Y. Witherspoon's Ferry, a history. NP: type-script, 1979. 9 p. WMTR

Eaddy, Mrs. Elizabeth W. All in a lifetime; the reminiscences of Judith Crosby Grier Eaddy [concerns Johnsonville-Hemingway area]. NP: typescript, nd. WMTR

Early, Horace H. Bennett School, 1856-1954. Chstn?, 1954? 4 p. SCHS

Easterby, James H. Charleston through two and one half centuries. 1936. 4 p. SCHS

Easterby, James H. A history of the College of Charleston, founded 1770. NY: Scribner Press, 1935. 379 p. COMMON

Easterby, James H. History of St. Andrew's Society of Charleston, SC. 1729-1929. Chstn: St. Andrew's Society, 1929. 154 p. EPDI, SCHS, SCL

Easterby, James H. The SC rice plantations as revealed in the papers of Robert F. W. Allston. Chicago: University of Chicago Press, 1945. 478 p. COMMON

Easterby, James H. Transportation in the ante-bellum period. Cola: HCSC, 1951. 4 p. SCL, COKL

Easterby, James H. Wadboo Barony; its fate as told in the Colleton family papers, 1773-1793. Cola: USC Press, 1952. 29 p. COMMON

Ebaugh, Laura S. Bridging the gap: a guide to early Greenville, SC. Tricentennial ed. Greenville: Greenville County Events-SC Tricentennial, 1970. 98 p. COMMON

Ebaugh, Laura S. A nineteenth century diary of Greenville, SC. ... Greenville: Greenville County Historical Society, 1966. 27 p. SCL, FLCL, GRCL

Edgar, Walter B. The libraries of colonial SC. Thesis (Ph.D.), U.S.C., 1972. 253 p. SCL

Edgefield County Historical Society. Edgefield remembers the Mexican War: honors heroes in the Mexican war centennial. Edgefield: NPub, 1948. 24 p. SCL, EDTO, SCHS

Edisto Island, SC; a brief illustrated history & comprehensive map of the island. Cola: RLB, nd. 31 p.[c.1955] SCL, SCHS

Education in Charleston. 1882. Manual training...physical culture...classical & scientific studies... Chstn: News & Courier, 1882. CHCO

Edwards, Ann D. The governor's mansion of the Palmetto state.

Cola: State Co., 1978. 124 p.   COMMON
Edwards, Sally. Pawley's Island. Charlotte NC: Heritage Printers, 1960. 25p.   SCL, CLEM, GRCL, SPCL
"Elbow Hill"; the annals of a farm [Fairfield County]. 1933.
16 p.   SCL, SCHS
Eleazer, James M. 50 years along the roadside. Anderson: Inde-
pendent Publishing Co., 1968. 192 p.   SCL, GNCL
Ellen, John C., Jr. Political newspapers of the piedmont Caro-
linas in the 1850's. Thesis (Ph.D.), U.S.C., 1959. 364 p.
                                                                  SCL
Eller, Essie M. A grove of hickories [Hickory Grove, York Coun-
ty]. Hickory Grove: Tri-Cities Jaycee-ettes, nd. 28 p. CRCL
Ellerbe, Nellie C. The history of Marion Public Library...
NP: typescript, 1933. 7 p.   SCL
Elliott, William. Address delivered at the commencement of work
on the Port Royal dry dock, Carolina day, 1891... Chstn:
W,E&C, 1891. 17 p.   SCL
Elzas, Barnett A. A century of Judaism in SC. 1800-1900. NP:
NPub, 1904. 19 p.   SCL
Elzas, Barnett A. Documents relative to a proposed settlement
of Jews in SC in 1748. Chstn: Daggett, 1903. 15 p.   SCL
Elzas, Barnett A. The Jews of SC from the earliest times to the
present day. 1905, rp Spartanburg: RPC, 1972. 352 p. COMMON
Elzas, Barnett A. The Jews of SC. Record of the first natural-
ization in the province... NP: NPub, 1903? 4 p.   SCL
Elzas, Barnett A. The Jews of SC; a survey of the records at
present in Charleston. Chstn: Daggett, 1903. 173 p.   SCL
Elzas, Barnett A. Leaves from my historical scrap book. Chstn:
1908. 44 p.   SPCL, SCHS, SCL
Emanuel, Solomon. 1859-1909. An historical sketch of the
Georgetown Rifle Guards, & as company "A" of the tenth regiment, SC volunteers, in the army of the Confederate States.
Georgetown: NPub, 1909. 32 p.   SCL, SCHS, CHCO
Empire Publishing Co. Historical & descriptive review of the
state of SC...manufacturing & mercantile industries of the
cities and counties of Abbeville, Anderson, Greenville, Newberry, Orangeburg, Spartanburg, Sumter, Union, Camden, and
county of Kershaw, and sketches of their leading men & business houses. Chstn: Empire Publishing Co., 1884.   SCL, SPCL
English, Elisabeth D. Richland County, economic & social.
Cola: USC, 1924. 94 p.   COMMON
Ervin, Eliza C. Darlingtoniana. A history of people, places &
events in Darlington County, SC. Cola: RLB, 1964. 502 p.
                                                              COMMON
Erwin, Lane E. Out of great tribulation: early Huguenot settlements in the southern U.S.... Thesis (M. ST.), L.T.S.S., 1968
136 p.   LTSS
Etiwan Lodge, Mt. Pleasant SC. History [100 years]. 1959.
12 p.   SCHS
Evangelical Lutheran Charities Society, Charleston. Charter &
rules: 1896. Chstn: W,E&C, 1896. 18 p.   SCL, SCHS

Evans, Clement A. SC Confederate military history. Secaucus
    NJ: Blue & Grey Press, nd. 931 p.   SCL, DOTM
Evans, James D. The Pee Dee section of SC as a field for in-
    vestment. Florence: PeeDee Printing Co., 1909. 12 p.   SCL
Evans, James & others. Why the proposed new county of Florence
    should be established. Florence: C. H. Prince's Printing
    House, 1888. 6 p.   SCL
Facts about Spartanburg. Spartanburg: Band & White, 1923?
    3 p.   WOFF
Fairey, Robert T. The American Legion in SC. The first thirty
    years. 1953. 232p.   SCL, DHML, DICL, CHBC
[Fairfield County]. Our heritage. [Fairfield? 1949?] SCL, SCHS
Fant, Christie Z. The state house of SC; an illustrated histor-
    ic guide. Cola: RLB, 1970.   COMMON
Farley, M. Foster Newberry County in the American Revolution.
    Newberry: Newberry County Bicentennial Committee, 1975. 30 p.
                                                            COMMON
The Farmer's Mutual Insurance Association of Spartanburg County,
    SC. [brochure] Spartanburg: Fleming & Perry, 1894. 12 p.WOFF
Feaster, William R. A history of Union County, SC. Greenville:
    A Press, 1977. 133 p.   COMMON
Federation of Women's Clubs of Charleston. The Charleston city
    Federation of Women's Clubs, 1899-1924. Chstn: Furlong, 1925?
    58 p.   SCHS
Fellowship Society. Rules...6th ed. Chstn, 1810?   SCHS
Fellowship Society. Rules... Revised 1859. 10th ed. Chstn:
    James & Williams, 1859. 88 p.   SCHS
Fellowship Society. History. Chstn?, 1960? 75 p.   SCHS
Feltham, Curran M. Stop-look-linger in historic Edgefield, SC.
    Edgefield: Advertiser Press, 194? 16 p.   SCL
A few historical facts of interest in & near Cheraw, SC. Cher-
    aw: Chronicle Print, 1922. 6 p.   SCL
Ficken, John F. Colored Orphan Aid Society, with institute
    attached. Chstn, 1894? 3 p.   SCHS
Field, Nora D. The High Falls story. Seneca: Journal Co.,
    1966. 24 p.   COMMON
Field, Nora D. Seneca echoes, Oconee County, SC. Seneca:
    Journal Co., 1954. 42 p.   COMMON
Fifty-first Infantry Division: ready to strike. Fort McClellan
    & Fort Stewart. NP: NPub, 1956. unp.   MACL
Filler, Louis. The removal of the Cherokee nation: manifest
    destiny or national dishonor? Boston: Heath, 1962. 113 p.
                                                            COKL
First Federal Savings & Loan Assn., Charleston. Famous Charles-
    ton firsts. 4th ed. Chstn: W,E&C, [various dates].   COMMON
Fishburne, Anne S. Belvidere, a plantation memory. Cola: USC
    Press, 1950. 113 p.   COMMON
Fleischmann, Glen. The Cherokee Removal, 1838; an entire Indian
    nation is forced out of its homeland. NY: Watts, 1971. 88 p.
                                                            COKL
Floyd, Viola C. Historical notes from Lancaster County. Lan-

caster: Lancaster County Historical Commission, 1977. 366 p.
LNCL, SPCL

Floyd, Viola C. History of the SC Daughters of the American Revolution, vol. III, 1946-1976. NP: S.C.D.A.R., 1976. 152 p.
ANCL, DIDU

Floyd, Viola C. Lancaster County tours. Lancaster: Lancaster County Historical Commission, 1967. 163 p.
COMMON

Flynn, Jean M. A short history of Chick Springs. Taylors: Taylors Garden Club, 1972. 10 p.
GRCL

Foothills folk tales; a collection of family legends, essays & ghost stories, 1800-1900. NP: Piedmont Branch, National League of American Penwomen, 1976. 45 p.
SCL, PICL

Ford, L. M. History of Rocky Mount. 1911 [SpC]
CSCL

Ford, Lacy K. One southern profile: modernization & the development of white terror in York County, 1856-1876 [Ku-Klux Klan]. Thesis (M.A.), U.S.C., 1976. 148 p.
SCL

Fortnightly Club of Sumter. Reflections, a selection of papers on Sumter's people, places & things, 1976. Sumter: author, 1976. 280 p.
SMCL

Fort Sumter Memorial Commission, Charleston. An account of the Fort Sumter memorial, Charleston, SC. Chstn: author, 1933. 37 p.
SCL, CHCO

Foundation for Historic Restoration in the Pendleton Area. A future for the past. Pendleton: author, 1961. 8 p. SCL, CLEM

Fraser, Charles. An address delivered..at the laying of the corner stone of a new college edifice, with masonic ceremonies, on the 12th January, 1828. Chstn: J.S. Burgess, 1828. 24 p.
SCL

Fraser, Charles. A Charleston sketchbook, 1796-1806; forty watercolor drawings of the city & surrounding country, including plantations & parish churches... Chstn: Carolina Art Assn., 1940, 1971. 60 p.
COMMON

Fraser, Charles. Reminiscences of Charleston, lately published in the Charleston Courier, and now rev. & enl. by the author. 1854, rp Chstn: Garnier & Co., 1969.
COMMON

Fraser, Walter J. Patriots, pistols & petticoats. Chstn: Charleston County Bicentennial Committee, 1976. 164 p. COMMON

Fraternal Cemetery Association, Florence. Constitution & by-laws... Florence: Prince & Ayer, 1892. 25 p.
SCL

French, Mrs. A. M. Slavery in SC & the ex-slaves, or, the Port Royal Mission. NY: French, 1862. 312 p.
BUCL

French, Justus Clement. The trip of the steamer Oceanus to Ft. Sumter & Charleston, SC. Comprising the...programme of exercises at the re-raising of the flag over the ruins of Ft. Sumter, April 14th, 1865... Brooklyn NY: "The Union" Steam Printing House, 1865. 172 p.
SCL, SPCL

From indians to industry; an historical spectacle for Orangeburg County's commemoration of SC's 300th anniversary. NP: John B. Rogers, 1970. 74 p.
ORCL

Frost, Donald McKay. Address...on the invitation of the Washington Light Infantry at the celebration of its one hundredth

71

anniversary, Feb. 22, 1907. 26 p.   SCHS
Frost, Mary Pringle. The Miles Brewton house; chronicles & rem-
    iniscences. Chstn: Susan P. & Rebecca M. Frost, 1939.
    168 p.   GRCL
Frost, Susan P. Highlights of the Miles Brewton house, 27 King
    Street, Charleston, SC. Chstn: author, 1944. 76 p. SCL, GRCL
Fuller, Elizabeth B. Anderson County sketches. Anderson: An-
    derson County Tricentennial Committee, 1969. 123 p.   COMMON
Funderburk, Harold W. & James B. Wallace. A history of Kershaw
    Lodge No. 29, Ancient Free Masons, & the affiliated York rite
    bodies of Camden, SC. Camden: NPub, nd. 48 p.   SCL, KECA
Furman, Mary C. SC from the mountains to the sea. Cola: State
    Co., 1964.   SCL, GTML
Fuzzlebug, Fritz. Prison life during the rebellion... 600
    Confederate prisoners sent from Ft. Delaware to Morris' Island
    SC... Singer's Glen VA: J. Funk's Sons, 1869. 48 p.   SPCL
Gadsden, Sam. An oral history of Edisto Island: Sam Gadsden
    tells the story. 2nd ed. Goshen IN: Goshen College, 1975.
    95 p.   SCL
Gaffney, Michael. The journal of Michael Gaffney... Gaffney:
    Gaffney Ledger, 1971. 69 p.   SCL, CRCL
Gaffney Sesquicentennial, 1804-1954. 150th anniversary program,
    containing pictures & short historical sketches... NP: NPub,
    nd. 26 p.   SCL
Gage, Robert J. The Union Library Society. Spartanburg: W.P.A.
    nd. v.p.   SPCL
Gaillard, Leize Palmer. The Rocks plantation in upper St.
    John's parish, Orangeburg County, once Berkeley County, SC:
    a sketch. Eutawville: J. Rutledge Connor, 1962. 24 p. SCHS
                                                                 SCL
Gaillard, Leize P. Springfield plantation, Berkeley County, SC.
    2nd ed. Cola: RLB, 1941. 15 p.   SCL, DOTM
Gandee, Lee R. "The west bank of the Congaree," a speech...
    NP: NPub, nd. 11 p.   LXCL, SCL
Garden, Alexander. Anecdotes of the Revolutionary War in Amer-
    ica, with sketches of character of persons...in the southern
    states... 1822, rp Spartanburg: RPC, 1972. 459 p.   COMMON
Gaston, David A. Chester County, economic & social... Cola:
    USC, 1924. 85 p.   COMMON
Gasque, Lonnie M. History of Clinton Lodge No. 60, A.F.M.,
    Marion SC. Marion: Johnson, Gasque, 1926. 28 p.   FLCL
Geiger, A. F. Scrapbook [Greenville] 1 vol. unp.   GRCL
German Colonization Society, Charleston. German colony protocol
    (minute book). Typescript, 1960.   SCL, ANCL, CLEM
German Friendly Society, Charleston. Rules...9th ed. rev.
    Chstn: W,E&C, 1908. 128 p.   SCL, SCHS
Gettys, James W. Mobilization for secession in Greenville
    District. Thesis (M.A.), U.S.C., 1967. 95 p.   SCL
Gibbes, James G. Who burnt Columbia? Newberry: E.H. Aull,
    1902. 137 p.   COMMON
Gibbes, Robert W. Documentary history of the American revolu-

72

tion...chiefly in South Carolina... 1853-57, rp Spartanburg:
RPC, 1972. 3 vol.   COMMON
Gibert, Anne C. Pierre Gibert, Esq., the devoted Huguenot: a
history of the French settlement of New Bordeaux, SC. NP:
NPub, 1976. 131 p.   CLEM, KECA, SCL
Gilchrist, Robert C. The Confederate defence of Morris Island,
Charleston harbor, by the troops of SC, GA & NC, in the late
war between the states... Chstn: News & Courier,
55 p.   SCL
Gillam, Mrs. Eulalie S. History & records, U.S.D.A.R., Eutaw
Chapter, Orangeburg, SC. NP: typescript, 1942? 44 p.   ORCL
Gilmore, Quincy A. Engineer & artillery operations against the
defences of Charleston harbor in 1863... NY: D. Van Nostrand,
1865. 486 p.   SCL, WOFF
Gilman, Samuel. Semi-centennial sermon delivered...22 Feb.,
1857, before the Washington Light Infantry... Chstn: W,E&C,
1857. 15 p.   SCL, SCHS
Gilmore, Edward C. Famous firsts for SC. Sumter: author, 1969.
12 p.   SPCL, SCL
Gilmore, Leroy H. Holly Hill. A town grows around a tree. NP:
author, 1970. 98 p.   SCL, ORCL
Girardeau, John L. An address on behalf of the Society for the
Relief of superannuated ministers and the indigent families of
deceased ministers of the Synod of SC...delivered at Sumter-
ville, SC, October 29, 1858... Cola: R.W. Gibbes, 1858.
19 p.   SCL
Girardeau, John L. Confederate memorial day at Charleston, SC.
Re-interment of the Carolina dead from Gettysburg. Chstn:
Mazyck, 1871. 36? p.   SCL, SPCL
Gist Rifles Survivors Association. Minutes of the meeting of...
Company "D", Hampton's Legion, C.S.A., at Williamston, SC,
Aug. 15, 1883: and, company muster roll from 1st Manassas to
Appomattox, 1861-1865. NP: NPub, 1883? 12 p.   SCHS
Glen, James. Colonial SC: two contemporary descriptions by
James Glen & George Milligen. Cola: USC Press, 1951. 209 p.
                                                         COMMON
Glenn, Albert Jr. The Pendleton Male Academy. NP: typescript,
1967. 15 p.   CLEM
Glenn, Emily S. Eutawville, SC, in the heart of "Francis Marion
country". NP: NPub, 1969.   ORCL
Glenn Springs, So. Ca. Its location, discovery, history, per-
sonal sketches of its habitues, what it will cure, etc.
Spartanburg: Trimmier's Printing Office, 1888. 32 p. COMMON
Glover, Beulah. The high house Glovers. Walterboro: Press &
Standard, 1978. 10 p.   COML
Glover, Beulah. Historic trails in Colleton County. Walter-
boro: author, 1967. 40 p.   COMMON
Glover, Beulah. Narratives of Colleton County: the land lying
between the Edisto & Combahee rivers. Brunswick GA: author,
1969. 180 p.   COMMON
Glover, Beulah. Winged seed. Brunswick GA: author, 1973.

73

120 p.   SCL, COML, GRCL, SCHS
Glover, J. C. A sketch of Batesburg, SC. Batesburg: Witter &
Cooner, 1903. 14 p.   SCL
Godbold, Sarah E. Marion County, economic & social... Cola:
USC, 1923. 113 p.   COMMON
Golden, Harry L. Jewish roots in the Carolinas... Greensboro
NC: Deal Printing Co., 1955. 72 p.   SCL, YOCL
The Golden Strip Civitan Club. Bicentennial souvenir book -
Mauldin, Simpsonville, Fountain Inn, 1776-1976. Mauldin: NPub
1976. unp.   GRCL
Gongaware, George J. History of the German Friendly Society of
Charleston, SC. Richmond VA: Garrett & Massie, 1935. 226 p.
                                                      COMMON
Goodlett, Emily G. The burning of Columbia by Gen. W. T. Sher-
man... 2nd ed. NP: NPub, 1865. 16 p.   SCL
Goodlett, Mildred W. The history of Traveler's Rest. Travel-
er's Rest?: NPub, 1966. 183 p.   COMMON
Goose Creek Club. By laws of the Goose Creek Club for preserv-
ing game. Chstn: Furlong, nd. 8 p.   SCHS
Gourdin, Peter G. Life along the Santee in Williamsburg County,
SC. Kingstree: County Record Print., 1959. SCL, SCHS, WMCL
Graham, Georgianna. A survey of historic places in the South
Carolina Appalachian region. Greenville: S.C. Appalachian
Council of Governments, 1972. 168 p.   PIPD
Graves, Lawrence B. The beginning of the cotton textile in-
dustry in Newberry County. Thesis (M.A.), U.S.C., 1947.
87 p.   SCL, NWRL
Graydon, Nell S. Eliza of Wappoo: a tale of indigo... Cola:
RLB, 1967. 308 p.   COMMON
Graydon, Nell S. Tales of Beaufort. Cola: RLB, 1963. 156 p.
                                                      COMMON
Graydon, Nell S. Tales of Columbia. Cola: RLB, 1964. 263 p.
                                                      COMMON
Graydon, Nell S. Tales of Edisto. Cola: RLB, 1955. 166 p.
                                                      COMMON
Green, Edwin L. History of Richland County, vol. I: 1732-1805.
1932, rp Baltimore MD: GPC, 1974. 385 p.   COMMON
Green, Edwin L. History of the University of SC. Cola: State
Co., 1916. 475 p.   COMMON
Green, James M. Orangeburg County, economic & social. Cola:
USC, 1923. 110 p.   COMMON
Greene, Jerome A. Ninety-Six: a historical narrative. Historic
resource study & historic structure report. Denver CO: Nat-
ional Park Service, 1978. 294 p.   SCL, SCHS
Greenville Board of Trade. Greenville, SC, "Pearl of the Pied-
mont." Greenville: NPub, nd. 27 p.   SCL, GRCL
Greenville Chamber of Commerce. Greenville, metropolis of the
famed Piedmont section of SC... Greenville: author, 1941?
unp.   GRCL
Greenville Chamber of Commerce. Points of interest about Greenville. Greenville: author, 1927.   GRCL

Greenville Hose Company No. 1. Constitution & rules of order...
Greenville: Daily News, nd. 11 p.   SCHS
Greenville News. Greenville: the gateway to get there, 1911:
commercial, financial, educational. 1911, rp Greenville:
Greenville Print Shop, 1966.   CLEM
Gregg, Alexander. History of the old Cheraws. 1867, 1925; rp
Spartanburg: RPC, 1975. 629 p.   COMMON
Gregg, William. Essays on domestic industry. An inquiry into
the expediency of establishing cotton manufactures in SC...
1845, rp Graniteville: the Greniteville Co., 1941. SCL, USAI
Gregorie, Anne K. History of Sumter County, SC. Sumter: Library
Board of Sumter County, 1954. 553 p.   COMMON
Gregorie, Anne K. Indian trade of Carolina in the seventeenth
century. Thesis (M.A.), U.S.C., 1926. 86 p.   SCL
Griffin, Anne F. Columbia College centennial: an historical
pageant. Cola: Farrell Press, 1956. 89 p.   SCL, WOFF
Griffin, Frank. Main street as it was years ago; fun, facts,
philosophy... Cola: author, 1968. 162 p.   SCL, GNCL, CLEM
Griffin, Willie L. Orangeburg's beginning:... Orangeburg:
Orangeburg County Historical Society, 1970. 6 p.   COMMON
Grimké, John F. The duty of executors & administrators. 1797,
rp Easley: SHP, 1981. 300 p.   SCL, SCHS
Grubbs, Max W. A history of the social, economic & political
development of Belton, SC... Thesis (M.S.), Clemson, 1960.
96 p.   CLEM, ANCL
Guess, William F. SC: annals of pride & protest. NY: Harper,
1960. 337 p.   COMMON
Guide to Charleston, SC. With brief history of the city & map
showing the ward boundaries... Chstn: W,E&C, 192?. 95 p.
                                                                     SCHS
Guide to Charleston, SC, with historical sketch of the city &
directory of historic points. Chstn: W,E&C, 1907. 91 p.
                                         SCL, CLEM, SPCL, SCHS
Gullick, Guy A. Greenville County, economic & social. Cola:
USC, 1921. 89 p.   COMMON
Haggard, Onie K. Stories of the Savannah River valley [incl.
Fort Charlotte, Scott's Ferry] [SpC]   GWPL
Hall, Lindsey G. Things & incidents long ago [Lexington County]
Cola: State Co., 1970. 234 p.   SCL, GRCL, GNCL
Halsey, Ashley. Who fired the first shot? And other untold
stories of the Civil war. NY: Hawthorn Books, 1963. 223 p.
                                                            SCL, SPCL
Hamer, Philip M. The secession movement in SC, 1847-1852.
1918, rp NY: Da Capo Press, 1971. 152 p.   SCL, WOFF
Hammond, John M. Winter journeys in the south...[incl. Aiken,
Camden, Charleston & Summerville]. Philadelphia PA: Lippin-
cott, 1916. 261 p.   SCL, SPCL
Hampton, Ann Fripp. The Charleston County courthouse. Cola:
Southern Studies Program, U.S.C., 1980. 14 p.   COMMON
Hampton, Ann Fripp. History of the Colleton County courthouse.
Cola: Southern Studies Program, U.S.C., 1980. 12 p.   COMMON

Hampton County Tricentennial Commission. Both sides of the
swamp: Hampton County. Cola: RLB, 1970. 187 p.   COMMON
Hampton Legion Survivors. Minutes of the proceedings of the re-
union of the Hampton Legion Survivors..in Columbia, SC, 21
July, 1875. Chstn: W,E&C, 1875. 47 p.   SCL, SCHS
Harris, Herbert R. The confederate war effort in Richland Dist-
rict, SC. Thesis (M.A.), U.S.C., 1976. 90 p.   SCL
Harris, W. A. The record of Fort Sumter, from its occupation by
Major Anderson, to its reduction by SC troops... Cola: South
Carolinian Steam Job Printing Office, 1862. 50 p.   SCL
Harrison, Thomas P. Recollections of Andersonville. Asheville
NC: Stephens Press, 1947. 9 p.   SCL, SCHS
Hartness, George B. By ship, wagon & foot to York County, SC.
Cola: NPub, 1966. 116 p.   COMMON
Hastie, Eleanor L. The story of historic Magnolia Plantation
& gardens; first 300 years. Chstn: NPub, 1975. 16 p.   SCHS
Hastie, Marie C. Magnolia-on-the-Ashley (Magnolia Gardens).
Chstn?, 192?. 14 p.   SCL, SCHS
Hawkins, Benjamin. Benjamin Hawkins's journeys through Oconee
County, SC, in 1796 & 1797... Cola: RLB, 1973. 34 p. COMMON
Hayes, James P. James [Island] & related sea islands. Chstn:
W,E&C, 1978. 140 p.   SCL, SCHS
Hemphill, James C. Charleston looking to the sea. The story of
the Coast Defense Squadron & the cruiser "Charleston". NP:
NPub, nd. 28 p.   SCL
Henderson, Archibald. The conquest of the old southewst. The
romantic story of the early pioneers into VA, the Carolinas,
TN & KY. 1740-1790. 1920, rp Spartanburg: RPC, 1974. 395 p.
SPCL, AICL
Henderson, Peronneau F. A short history of Aiken & Aiken Coun-
ty. Cola: RLB, 1951. 45 p.   COMMON
Hendricks, Peter W. The South Carolinian & his government.
Chapin: author, 1966.   SCL, CHBC
Hendrix, Ge L. A short history of the Greenville Chapter, SC
Genealogical Society. Greenville: Greenville Chapter, S.C.
G.S., 1976. unp.   ANCL
Henning, Helen K. Columbia, capital city of SC, 1786-1936.
Cola: Columbia Sesquicentennial Commission, 1936. 429 p.
COMMON
Henry, Gordon C. Newberry College, Newberry, SC, 1856-1976:
120 years of service to the Lutheran Church & to SC. New-
berry: Newberry College, 1976. 34 p.   SCL,NWNC, CRCL, GTML
Henry, H. M. The police control of the slave in SC... Emory
VA: author, 1914. 216 p.   SCL, WOFF
Henry Wirz & the Andersonville prison. NP: NPub, 1921? 52 p.
SCHS
Herd, Elmer D. Early history of Belton, SC, 1700-1860. Wil-
liamston: NPub, 1959. 15 p.   ANCL
Herd, Elmer D. Early history of Belton, SC, 1700-1860. Rev.
ed. with added materials on later periods. Cola: USC, 1961.
44 p.   ANCL

Herd, Elmer D.   Mount Ariel-Cokesbury, SC: a biography of
an upcountry utopian community. NP: NPub, 1979. 3 vol.COMMON
Herd, Elmer D.   Slave ownership in Belton, Honea Path, William-
ston & surrounding areas of Anderson County, SC, compiled
from the slave census of 1860. 58 p.   ANCL
Hester, Hubert I. They that wait: a history of Anderson College
Anderson: Anderson College, 1969. 204 p.   SCL, ACOL, ANCL
Heyward, DuBose. Fort Sumter, 1861-1865. NY: Farrar & Rinehart
1938. 109 p.   COMMON
Heyward, Duncan S. Seed from Madagascar. 1937, rp Spartanburg:
RPC, 1972. 256 p.   COMMON
Hewatt, Alexander. Historical account of the rise & progress of
the colonies of SC & GA. 1779, rp Spartanburg: RPC, 1962.
2 vol.   COMMON
Hibernian Society of Charleston. Constitution & rules...incor-
porated 19th Decmeber, 1805... Chstn: E. Perry, 1889 [& var.
eds.] 24 p.   SCL, SCHS
Hickok, Julia E. Colonial SC. Cincinatti: Ebbert & Richardson
Co., 1925. 57 p.   SCL
Hilborn, Nat & Sam Hilborn. Battleground of freedom. SC in the
Revolution. Cola: Sandlapper Press, 1970. 239 p.   COMMON
Hilton Head Island Chamber of Commerce. Hilton Head Island; a
guide & history, 1663-1963. Hilton Head Island: author, 1963.
19 p.   SCL, SCHS
Hilton, Mary K. Old homes & churches of Beaufort County, SC.
Cola: State Co., 1970. 88 p.   COMMON
Hilton, William. Voyage to the Carolina coast; Captain William
Hilton's narrative. 1664, rp Hilton Head: Hilton Head Island
Publishing Co., 1967. 34 p.   COMMON
Hirsch, Arthur H. The Huguenots of colonial SC. 1928, rp Ham-
den CT: Archon Books, 1962. 338 p.   COMMON
Historic Beaufort Foundation. A guide to historic Beaufort.
2nd ed. Cola: State Co., 1973. 125 p.   COMMON
Historic Charleston Foundation. Charleston's historic houses.
Chstn: author, 1949. 63 p.   COMMON
Historic Columbia Foundation. ...Guide to historic Columbia.
Cola: author, 1977. 28 p.   COMMON
Historic Sullivan's Island...The Story from original sources.
NP: NPub, nd. 7 p.   SCL
Historical background of Lee County, 1902. NP: typescript, nd.
15 p.   LECL
Historical & descriptive review of the state of SC, including
the manufacturing & mercantile industries of the cities of
Abbeville, Anderson, Greenville, Newberry, Orangeburg, Spar-
tanburg, Sumter, Union, Camden & county of Kershaw, and
sketches of their leading men & business houses. Chstn: Em-
pire Publishing Co., 1884.   WOFF, SCL
Historical sketch & roster of independent battalion, S.C. Volunteer Infantry, U.S.A., Spanish-American War, 1898-1899. Cola:
RLB, 1901. 37 p.   MRCL
Historical & social sketch of Craven County, SC. NP: NPub,

185? 52 p.   SCHS
Historical statements concerning the Battle of Kings Mountain &
   the Battle of Cowpens, SC. Washington DC: GPO, 1928. 77 p.
                                              SCL, MACL, LNCL
History of the Calhoun Monument at Charleston, SC. Chstn: Lu-
   cas & Richardson, 1888.   SCL, KECL
History of Co. "F", 118th Infantry (Hampton Guards), 30th Di-
   vision. Spartanburg: Band & White, 1919. 80 p.   WOFF
History of Prosperity [SC]. NP: NPub, 1973? 54 p.   NWRL
History of St. George [Dorchester County]. NP: typescript, nd.
   5 p.   DOCL
History of the town of North, SC. The North celebration of the
   SC tricentennial, April 19, 1970. 31 p.   SCL, ORCL
Holland, Janice. Pirates, planters & patriots; the story of
   Charleston,SC. NY: Scribner, 1955. 46 p.   COMMON
Holleman, Frances. ...The city of Seneca, SC; the city of op-
   portunity, its centennial, August 11-18, 1973. Greenville:
   Creative Printers Briggs & Associates, 1973. 239 p.   COMMON
Holley, Gerald D. The Darlington riot of 1894. Thesis (M.A.),
   USC, 1970.   FLCL, SCL
Hollis, Daniel W. A brief history of Columbia... Cola: NPub,
   1968. 8 p.   COMMON
Hollis, Daniel W. A brief history of SC. Cola: Home Federal
   Savings & Loan, 1970. 26 p.   COMMON
Hollis, Daniel W. A history of St. Andrews & the Dutch Fork.
   Cola: Home Federal Savings & Loan, 1970? 11 p.   COMMON
Hollis, Daniel W. The University of South Carolina, vol. I:
   South Carolina College. Cola: USC Press, 1951.   COMMON
Hollis, Daniel W. The University of South Carolina, vol. II:
   college to university. Cola: USC Press, 1956.   COMMON
Holmes, Alester G. Pendleton. Clemson: typescript, 193?.
   4 p.   CLEM
Holmes, Ann M. The New York Ladies Southern Relief Association,
   1866-1867: an account of the relief furnished by the citizens
   of New York City... NY: Mary Mildred Sullivan Chapter, UDC,
   1926. 113 p.   SCL, EDTO
Holmgren, Virginia C. Hilton Head, a sea island chronicle.
   Hilton Head Island: Hilton Head Island Publishing Co., 1959.
   140 p.   COMMON
Honea Path Bicentennial Committee. Honea Path milestones...
   Honea Path: Town Council, 1976. 207 p.   COMMON
Hope, Robert M. Union County, economic & social... Cola: USC,
   1923. 108 p.   COMMON
Horne, Erleen. History of the Green Sea [SC] community & high
   school, including graduates 1922-1976. NP: author, nd.
   29 p.   HOCL
Horry County Historical Society. Conway landmarks, late 1800's
   & early 1900's, in commemoration of Horry County's tricenten-
   nial celebration, August 9-15, 1970. Conway: Horry County
   Tricentennial Committee, 1970. 19 p.   HOCL
Horry County Historical Society. The Independent Republic of

Horry. Items from The Independent Republic Quarterly... Con-
way: Horry Printers, 1970. 100 p.   COMMON
Horton, McDavid. St. Helena Island: a Negro community... Cola:
State Co., 1924.   SCL
Hot and Hot Fish Club. Rules & history of the Hot & Hot Fish
Club of All Saints Parish, SC. Chstn: Evans & Cogswell, 1860.
                                                        SCL, SCHS
Hough, Franklin B. The siege of Charleston by the British
fleet and army under the command of Admiral Arbuthnot & Sir
Henry Clinton... 1867, rp Spartanburg: RPC, 1975. 224 p.
                                                            COMMON
Howard, Eugenia W. Purrysburg colony & the Bourquin family.
SCHS micropublication # 50-163.   COMMON
Howard, James A. Dark Corner heritage [Greenville County].
Landrum: author, 1980. 97 p.   COMMON
Howe, George. The Scotch-Irish, & their first settlements on
the Tyger River and other neighboring precincts in SC...
Cola: Southern Guardian Steam Power Press, 1861. 31 p. COMMON
Hoyt, James A. The Palmetto Riflemen. Co. "B", 4th Regiment,
S.C. Volunteers; Co. "C", Palmetto Sharpshooters. Historical
sketch...with a roll of the company... Greenville: Hoyt &
Keys, 1886. 59 p.   SCL
Hoyt, James A. The Phoenix riot, November 8, 1898. Greenwood?
NPub, 1935? 23 p.   FLMC, SCL
Huck's Defeat, Brattonsville, York District, SC, 1780. Pro-
ceedings of the Battle of Huck's Defeat, 1839; and, an account
of the unveiling of monument by the King's Mountain Chapter,
D.A.R., 1903. 23 p.   SPCL, WOFF
Hudson, Joshua H. Sketches & reminiscences [Chester & Marlboro
Counties]. Cola: State Co., 1903. 190 p.   MRCL, SCL
Huger, Mary E. The recollection of a happy childhood... Pen-
dleton, SC. Pendleton: Foundation for Historic Restoration,
1976. 85 p.   COMMON
Hughson, Shirley C. The Carolina pirates & colonial commerce,
1670-1740. 1894, rp Spartanburg: RPC, 1971. 134 p.   COMMON
Huguenot Society of South Carolina. Anniversary celebrating
the two hundred and fiftieth anniversary of the arrival of
the first group of Huguenots at Charles Town, province of
Carolina, April 1680... Programme... NP: NPub, 1930. 2 p.
                                                               SCL
Hull, Edward B. Guide-book of Camden, containing a description
of points of interest, together with an historical sketch...
Camden: author   48 p.   SCL
Hunt, Warren A. A history of the schools & colleges of Anderson
SC. Thesis (M.A.), Furman University. 44 p.   ANCL, FURM
Hunter, Louise G. Historical notes on Pendleton, SC. Pendle-
ton: NPub, 1971. 5 p.   SCL
Hutchins, Carrie. A brief history of Liberty, SC. NP: NPub,
nd. 4 p.   SCL
Hutson, Francis Marion. A brief historical sketch of McPherson-
ville & her two churches. Chstn: NPub, 1932. 27 p.   SCL

Hutson, Francis M. & John R. Todd. Prince William's Parish &
plantations. Richmond VA: Garrett & Massie, 1935. 265 p.
SCL, KECA
Hutson, Mrs. R. W. & Isabel deSaussure. Historical sketch of
the Argyle Louden Campbell Memorial Home for Presbyterian &
Huguenot Women...Charleston, SC. Chstn: Heisser Printing
Co., 192? 6 p. SCHS
Hyde, Joseph B. Union Kilwinning Lodge, No. 4 [Freemasons].
Chstn: NPub, 1930. 56 p. SCL, SCHS
Inabinet, L. Glen. Kershaw County legacy: a commemorative
history. Camden: Kershaw County Bicentennial Commission,
1976. 87 p. COMMON
Inglesby, Charles. Historical sketch of the 1st Regiment, S.C.
Artillery. Chstn: W,E&C, 189? 28 p. SCL, SCHS
Inglesby, Edith. A corner of Carolina: the four seasons in
Hilton Head Island, Beaufort & Bluffton. Cola: State Co.,
1968. 143 p. COMMON
Insh, George P. Scottish colonial schemes, 1620-1686 [incl.
Stuart's Town, SC]. Glasgow, Scotland: Maclehose, Jackson,
1922. 211 p. SCHS
International Paper Company. International Paper Company:
1898-1948, after 50 years. NP: author, 1948. 110 p. SCL,GTML
Introducing Greenville, SC. NP: NPub, nd. 8 p. GRCL
Irby, Hannah B. Woodruff: an historical view. NP: author,
1974. 88 p. COMMON
Irving, John B. A day on the Cooper River...enlarged and edited
by Louisa Cheves Stoney. Reprinted with notes by Samuel Gail-
lard Stoney. 3rd ed. Cola: RLB, 1969. 220 p. COMMON
Irving, John B. Local events & incidents at home. Chstn, 1850.
19 p. SCHS
Irving, John B. The South Carolina Jockey Club. Chstn: Rus-
sell & Jones, 1857. 259 p. COMMON
Iseley, N. Jane & Henry F. Cauthen. Chstn: Preservation Society
of Charleston, 1979. 79 p. COMMON
Iseley, N. Jane. Middleton Place. Chstn: Middleton Place Foun-
dation, 1976. 47 p. COMMON
Iva Bicentennial booklet. NP: typescript, nd. 34 p. ANCL
Ivers, Larry E. Colonial forts of SC, 1670-1775. Cola: Tricen-
tennial Commission, 1970. 77 p. COMMON
Izlar, William V. A sketch of the war record of the Edisto
Rifles, 1861-1865. Cola: State Co., 1914. 168 p. COMMON
Jackson, Melvin H. Privateers in Charleston, 1793-1796. Wash-
ington DC: Smithsonian Institution Press, 1969. 160 p. COMMON
Jacobs, Thornwell. Red lanterns on St. Michael's [Episcopal
church, Charleston]. NY: E.P. Dutton & Co., 1940. 670 p.
COMMON
Jacobs, Thornwell. The story of "The Silk of the Trade". Rion:
Winnsboro Blue Granite, 1952. 30 p. COMMON
Jamison, Alta T. Thirty years of Connie Maxwell [Orphanage]
history. Greenwood: Connie Maxwell Orphanage, 1922. 133 p.
SCL, WOFF

Jamison, Alta T. Forty years of Connie Maxwell [Orphanage]
history. Greenwood: Connie Maxwell Orphanage, 1932. 206 p.
SCL, COKL
Jamison, Elizabeth M. Summerville past & present. NP: NPub,
1939. 42 p. SCHS, DOTM, SCL
Jaynes, Robert T. Brief history of Oconee County... NP: NPub,
1948. 11 p. CLEM, SCL
Jaynes, Robert T. Brief history of Walhalla... Walhalla: NPub,
1950. 47 p. CLEM, SCL
Jaynes, Robert T. The Old Waxhaws; Andrew Jackson, William
Richard Davie, Andrew Pickens, Waxhaw Presbyterian Church,
[Rev.] Francis Asbury, the Methodist church. Cola: RLB, 1939.
23 p. SCL, NWRL, WOFF
Jaynes, Robert T. Some facts of history of old Pickens...
Walhalla: Keowee Courier Press, nd. 23 p. SCL
Jenkins, Sophia S. Rockville [Wadmalaw Island]... NP: mimeo,
1957. 8 p. PICL, SCHS, SCL
Jervey, Susan R. Two diaries from middle St. John's [parish],
Berkeley, SC, February-May, 1865; journals kept by Miss Susan
R. Jervey & Miss Charlotte St. J. Ravenel, at Northhampton &
Pooshee plantations, and reminiscences of Mrs. (Waring) Hen-
agen, with two contemporary reports from federal officials.
Wampee Plantation, SC: St. John's Hunting Club, 1921. 56 p.
SCHS, NWRL, SCL
Jervey, Theodore D. The railroad, the conqueror. Cola: State
Co., 1913. 44 p. SCL, WOFF
Jervey, Theodore D. The slave trade. Cola: State Co., 1925.
344 p. KECL, SCL
Johnson, Elmer D. A brief history of Cherokee County, SC.
Gaffney: Gaffney Chamber of Commerce, 1952. 30 p. COMMON
Johnson, Elmer D. South Carolina. A documentary profile of the
Palmetto state. Cola: USC Press, 1971. 676 p. COMMON
Johnson, Elmer D. The SC story as told by contemporaries. NP:
typescript, 195? SCHS
Johnson, Guion G. A social history of the sea islands, with
special reference to St. Helena's Island, SC. Chapel Hill NC:
UNC Press, 1930. 245 p. COMMON
Johnson, Herbert A. SC legal history. Cola: Southern Studies
Program, USC, 1980. 309 p. COMMON
Johnson, James G. The Spanish period of GA & SC history, 1566-
1709. Athens GA: University of GA Press, 1923. 23 p. SCHS
SCL
Johnson, John. The defense of Charleston harbor, including Ft.
Sumter & the adjacent islands, 1863-1865... Chstn: W,E&C,
1890. 276 p. COMMON
Johnson, John. Historic points of interest in & around Charles-
ton, SC... Chstn: W,E&C, 1896. 48 p. CLEM, SCL
Johnson, John. Views of Ft. Sumter, Charleston SC, showing the
effects of the bombardment, 1863-1865. Chstn: W,E&C, 1899.
30 p. SCHS, SCL
Johnson, Joseph. Traditions & reminiscences, chiefly of the

81

American Revolution in the south. 1851, rp Spartanburg:
RPC, 1972. 592 p. COMMON
Johnson, Kitcy F. The Whitmire area history, Whitmire, SC.
Shawnee Mission KS: Intercollegiate Press, 1980. 128 p. SCL
Johnson, William H. [Colonial church silver in the Episcopal
Diocese of SC]. NP: typescript, nd. 16 p. EPDI
Johnston, Louise. History & homes of Liberty Hill, SC.
[n.p., 1972?] KECL, SCL
Johnston, Louise. History & times of Liberty Hill, SC.
1971. 92 p. SCL, KECL
Johnston, Olin D. Anderson County, economic & social. Cola:
USC Press, 1923. COMMON
Johnston, SC: centennial edition, 1870-1970. NP: NPub, 1970.
100 p. COMMON
Jones, Charles C. Jr. The dead towns of Georgia [incl. informa-
tion on Dorchester, SC]. Savannah GA: Morning News Steam
Printing House, 1878. 263 p. SCL, SCHS
Jones, Eloise. The history of the town of North, SC. NP:
typescript, 1970. 30 p. SCL
Jones, G. N. Bishopville, Lee County [SpC] LECL
Jones, Katharine M. Port Royal under six flags. Indianapolis
IN: Bobbs-Merrill, 1960. 368 p. COMMON
Jones, Lewis P. The SC Civil War of 1775. Cola: Sandlapper
Store, 1975. 86 p. COMMON
Jones, Lewis P. SC: a synoptic history for laymen. Cola: Sand-
lapper Press, 1971. 272 p. COMMON
Julien, Carl. Beneath so kind a sky; the scenic & architectural
beauty of SC. Cola: USC Press, 1958. 89 p. COMMON
Julien, Carl T. Ninety-Six; landmarks of South Carolina's last
frontier region. Cola: USC Press, 1950. 117 p. COMMON
Julien, Carl. PeeDee panorama. Cola: USC Press, 1951. 118 p.
COMMON
Julien, Carl. Sea islands to sand hills. Cola: USC Press,
1954. 119 p. COMMON
Junior League of Charleston. Across the cobblestones [Charles-
ton]. Chstn: Junior League, 1965. 96 p. COMMON
Junior League of Charleston. Historic Charleston guidebook.
Chstn: Junior League, 1968. 107 p. COMMON
Keitt, Lawrence M. Address...on laying the corner-stone of the
fireproof building, at Columbia...1851. Cola:
SCL
Kellogg, Robert H. Life & death in rebel prisons...Anderson-
ville GA & Florence SC. Hartford CT: Stebbins, 1865. 400 p.
SCL, SCHS
Kelly, Margaret M. A short history of Marlboro County, SC,
1600-1979. Baltimore MD: Gateway Press, 1979. 74 p. COMMON
Kennedy, John P. Horseshoe Robinson; a tale of Tory ascend-
ency in SC in 1780. NY: Burt, 1835? 483 p. SCL, KECL, SCHS
Kennedy, Lionel H. & Thomas Parker. An official report of the
trials of sundry Negroes charged with an attempt to raise an
insurrection in the State of SC... NP: Schenck, 1822. SCL

82

Kennedy, Stetson. ...Palmetto country. NY: Duell, Sloan & Pearce, 1942. 340 p. BUCL, SCHS COKL

Kennedy, Walter A. Erskine College before the Civil War. Thesis (M.A.), U.S.C., 1945. 174 p. SCL

The Keowee trail. Program. A historical pageant...1921. Greenville: Peace Printing Co., 1921. 62 p. SCL

Kershaw County Chamber of Commerce. Camden, SC, Kershaw County; scenic-historic, 1732. Camden: NPub, nd. 16 p. SCL, GRCL

Kershaw County Historical Society. Historic, scenic, Camden, SC ... Camden?: Kershaw County Historical Society & Camden-Kershaw Chamber of Commerce, nd. 12 p. SCL

Kershaw County Historical Society. Kirkwood, the story of a neighborhood...2nd ed. Camden: author, 1971. 17 p. COMMON

Kibler, Lillian A. The history of Converse College, 1889-1971. Spartanburg: Converse College, 1973. 547 p. COMMON

Killion, Ronald G. The journal of Michael Gaffney, with an historical introduction & notes... Gaffney: Gaffney Ledger, 1971. 70 p. SCL, SPCL

Kinard, James E. A history of the Summer plantation, Pomaria, with special emphasis on the owners and their lives. Thesis (B.A.), Newberry College, 1942. 32 p. SCL, NWNC

King, Mitchell. Address delivered...before the St. Andrew's Society of the city of Charleston, on their centennial anniversary, the 30th of Nov., 1829. Chstn: Burges, 1829. 58 p. SCHS

King, William L. The newspaper press of Charleston, SC: a chronological & biographical history... Chstn: Perry, 1882. 200 p. SCL, SCHS, COKL

Kirk, Francis Marion. A history of the St. John's Hunting Club. An address delivered...at the sesqui-centennial celebration held April 29, 1950. NP: St. John's Hunting Club, 1950. 21 p. SCL SCHS

Kirk, Francis Marion. The Yemassee War, 1715-1718; a page from South Carolina's colonial history. Mt. Pleasant: Society of Colonial Wars, 1970. 10 p. SCL, SPCL, COKL

Kirkland, Thomas J. & Robert M. Kennedy. Historic Camden, part I: colonial & revolutionary. 1905, rp Cola: State Co., 1964. 423 p. COMMON

Kirkland, Thomas J. & Robert M. Kennedy. Historic Camden, part II: nineteenth century. 1926, rp Cola: State Co., 1965. 485 p. COMMON

Klosky, Beth A. The Pendleton legacy. Cola: Sandlapper Press, 1971. 112 p. COMMON

Kohn, August. The cotton mills of SC. 1907, rp Spartanburg: RPC, 1975. 228 p. COMMON

Kohn, August. A descriptive sketch of Orangeburg, city & county SC... Orangeburg: R. L. Berry, 1888. 48 p. COMMON

Kohn, David. Internal improvements in SC, 1817-1828. Washington DC: author, 1938. 633 p. COMMON

Labaree, Leonard W. Royal instructions to British colonial

governors, 1670-1776. NY: Octagon Books, 1967. 462 p.   KECA
LaBorde, M. History of the South Carolina College from its
    incorporation December 19, 1801, to November 25, 1857, includ-
    ing sketches of its presidents & professors. Cola: Peter B.
    Glass, 1859. 463 p.   COMMON
Lachicotte, Alberta M. Georgetown rice plantations. Cola:
    State Co., 1955. 222 p.   COMMON
Ladies' Auxiliary Christian Association. First annual report...
    May 8, 1858. Chstn: James & Williams, 1858. 11 p.   SCHS
Ladies Benevolent Society, Charleston. Act of incorporation,
    constitution, list of members. Chstn, 1823? 24 p.   SCHS
Ladies Calhoun Monument Association. A history of the Calhoun
    monument of Charleston, SC. Chstn: Lucas & Richardson, 1888.
    147 p.   SCL, SCHS
Land, John E. Charleston; her trade, commerce, & industries,
    1883-1884. Chstn, 1884. 191 p.   SCHS, SCL
Land, Marie M. Clarendon cameos. Manning: Clarendon Art Guild,
    1976. 132 p.   COMMON
Lander, Ernest M. A history of SC, 1865-1960. Chapel Hill NC:
    UNC Press, 1960. 260 p.   COMMON
Lander, Ernest M. Perspectives in SC history, the first 300
    years. Cola: USC Press, 1973. 431 p.   COMMON
Lander, Ernest M. The textile industry in antebellum SC. Baton
    Rouge LA: Louisiana State University Press, 1969. 122 p.
                                              SCL, UNCL, SCHS
Landers, H. L. The battle of Camden, SC, August 16, 1780.
    Washington: GPO, 1929. 65 p.   COMMON
Landmark Lodge, Charleston. The jubilee of Landmark Lodge
    [Freemasons]. Chstn: W,E&C, 1901. 39 p.   SCHS
Landrum, John B. Colonial & revolutionary history of upper SC.
    Embracing for the most part...the original county of Spartan-
    burg... 1897, rp Spartanburg: RPC, 1962.   COMMON
Landrum, John B. History of Spartanburg, SC. 1900, rp Spartan-
    burg: RPC, 1960. 739 p.   COMMON
Lane, Mrs. Joe P. The early beginnings of Dillon County. NP:
    NPub, nd.   DICL
Langley, Mary L. & Albert M. Langley, Jr. The railroad comes
    of age: the historic South Carolina Canal & Railroad, and the
    "Best Friend" of Charleston. Augusta GA, 1970. 26 p. SCL,EDTO
Lanier, J. F. Correspondence with the French Protestant (Hugu-
    enot) Church of Charleston, SC. NP: NPub, 1873? 14 p.   SCHS
Lanier, Sidney. Florida: its scenery, climate, & history. With
    an account of Charleston, Savannah, Augusta & Aiken...
    Philadelphia PA: Lippincott, 1876. 336 p.   SCL, SPCL
Lanneau, Fleetwood. Anniversary oration delivered before the
    Moultrie Guards & their escort, the Palmetto Guards & college
    cadets...June 28, 1852. Chstn: Walker & James, 1853. 19 p.
                                                             SCHS
Lapham, Samuel. Our walled city: Charles Town, province of Car-
    olina. Mt. Pleasant: Society of Colonial Wars, 1970. 11 p.
                                                           COMMON

Larsen, Christian L. Metropolitan Charleston. Cola: USC, 1949.
48 P.   GRCL, SCL
Lathan, Robert. Historical sketch of the Battle of King's Mountain. Yorkville: Yorkville Enquirer, 1880. 18 p. YOCL, SCL
Lathers, Richard. SC. The conditions & the prospects of the
State... Chstn: News & Courier Job Presses, 1874. 18 p. SCL
Latimer, S. L. Almost four score: the story of The State, 1891-
1969, and the Gonzales brothers. Cola: State Co., 1970.
407 P.   SCL, SCHS
Law, Cadet Tom. Citadel cadets; the journal of Tom Law. Clin-
ton: P.C. Press, 1941. 346 p.   COMMON
Lawrence, James W. Shadows of hogback [Landrum SC]. Landrum:
News Leader, 1979. 135 p.   CLEM, SCL
Lawrence, Kay. Heroes, horses & high society; Aiken from 1540.
Cola: RLB, 1971. 151 p.   COMMON
Lawson, Dennis T. Georgetown: the Morgan years. Georgetown:
Rice Museum, 1973. 32 p.   COMMON
Lawson, Dennis T. A goodly heritage. A look at the tangible
past of Georgetown County, SC. Georgetown: Rice Museum, 1972.
unp.   COMMON
Lawson, Dennis T. A guide to historic Georgetown County, SC.
Georgetown: Rice Museum, 1974. 64 p.   COMMON
Lawson, Dennis T. No heir to take its place. The story of rice
in Georgetown County, SC. Georgetown: Rice Museum, 1972.
32 p.   COMMON
Lawson, John. The history of Carolina, containing the exact
description and natural history of that country... 1714, rp
Raleigh NC: Strother & Marcom, 1860. 390 p.   SCL
Lawson, John. A new voyage to Carolina. 17??, rp Chapel Hill
NC: UNC Press, 1967. 305 p.   COMMON
Lawton, Alexania E. Allendale on the Savannah. Bamberg: Bamberg Herald Printers, 1970. 401 p.   COMMON
Lazenby, Mary E. Catawba frontiers, 1775-1781. Memoirs of pen-
sioners.   SCL, GSGN
Lee, A. M. The South Carolina Society: its origin, objects &
historical meaning... Chstn: Lucas & Richardson, 1898.
16 p.   SCL, SCHS
Lee, Benjamin M. Mt. Pleasant. NP: Town Council of Mt. Pleas-
ant, 1935. 40 p.   SCHS
Lee County [SpC]   LECL
Lee County Bicentennial Commission. Lee County, SC. A bicen-
tennial look at its land, people, heritage & future. NP:
author, 1976. unp.   COMMON
Lee, Henry. The campaign of 1781 in the Carolinas. 1824, rp
Spartanburg: RPC, 1975. 511 p.   COMMON
Lee, Henry. Memoirs of the war of the Southern Department of
the U.S. 2 vol. Philadelphia PA: Inkup & Bradford, 1812.
                                                         SCL, EDTO
Lee, Rudolph E. List of old time suburban & rural homes in the
vicinity of Pendleton, SC... Clemson: NPub, 1963. 20 p. CLEM
Lee Steam Fire Engine Co. Constitution & rules of order...

Greenville: Daily News Presses, 1888. 14 p.   SCHS
Legendre, Gertrude S. Medway plantation, 1686-1980. Chstn,
1980. 7 p.   SCHS
Legerton, Clarence W. The South Carolina Society... A sketch
of the charitable & educational activities of the Society in
its early days. Chstn: W,E&C, 1965.   SCHS
Legerton, Clifford L. Historic churches of Charleston, SC.
Chstn: Legerton & Co., 1966. 171 p.   COMMON
Leiding, Harriette K. Charleston, historic & romantic. Phila-
delphia PA: J.B. Lippincott, 1931. 293 p.   COMMON
Leiding, Harriette K. Historic houses of SC. 1921, rp Spartan-
burg: RPC, 1975. 318 p.   COMMON
Leigh, Egerton. The nature of colony constitutions. Cola: USC
Press, 1970. 232 p.   COMMON
LeJau, Francis. Carolina chronicle of Dr. Francis LeJau,1706 -
1717. (Berkeley, Calif.: U.C. Press, 1956)   COMMON
Leland, Jack. 50 famous houses of Charleston SC. Chstn: Even-
ing Post, 1970. 51 p.   GRCL, SCL
Leland, John A. A voice from SC... Chstn: W,E&C, 1879. 231
p.   COMMON
Leland, John S. A history of Kiawah Island. Kiawah Island:
Kiawah Island Co., 1977. 41 p.   COMMON
Lesesne, Joab M. The Bank of the State of SC; a general & poli-
tical history. Cola: USC Press, 1970. 211 p.   COMMON
Lesesne, Joab M. The history of the Bank of the State of SC.
Thesis (Ph.D.), U.S.C., 1948. 205 p.   SCL
Lesesne, Joab M. A hundred years of Erskine College, 1839-1939.
Thesis (Ph.D.), U.S.C., 1967. 316 p.   SCL
Lesesne, Joab M. The reconstruction of Erskine College, 1865-
1890. Thesis (M.A.), U.S.C., 1961. 80 p.   SCL
Lesesne, Thomas P. History of Charleston County, SC; narrative
& biographical. Chstn: A.H. Cawston, 1931. 369 p.   COMMON
Lesesne, Thomas P. Landmarks of Charleston. Richmond VA: Gar-
rett & Massie, 1939. 112 p.   COMMON
Levett, Ella P. Loyalism in Charleston, 1761-1784. Thesis
(M.A.), U.S.C., 1934. 59 p.   SCL
Levkoff, Alice F. & Robert N.S. Whitelaw. Charleston, come hell
or high water. Cola: RLB, 1975. 231 p.   COMMON
Lewis, Elise R. Fort Sumter: the key of Charleston harbor. In
memory of its heroes. Chstn: Lucas & Richardson, nd. 16 p.
                                                               SCL
Lewis, Kenneth E. Camden, a frontier town in eighteenth century
SC. Cola: Institute of Archeology & Anthropology, USC, 1976.
193 p.   COMMON
Linder, Suzanne C. Medicine in Marlboro County, 1736 to 1980.
Bennetsville: Marlborough County Historical Society & Marlboro
County Medical Society, 1980. 206 p.   COMMON
Lindsay, Nick. An oral history of Edisto Island. The life &
times of Bubberson Brown. Goshen IN: Goshen College, 1977.
110 p.   SCHS
Lipscomb, Terry W. South Carolina becomes a state. Cola:

SCDAH, 1976. 36 p. COMMON
Littlejohn, Mary K. Tales of Tigertown; anecdotes of a lifetime
of the Clemson campus. Clemson: author, 1979. 80 p.SCL, PICL
Liverance, Sara V. Anderson County tricentennial souvenir book-
let. NP: Anderson County Tricentennial Commission, 1970.
41 p. ANCL, PIPD, SCL
Lockwood, Greene & Co. Industrial survey of Georgetown, SC.
Atlanta GA: Lockwood, Greene & Co., 1924. v.p. SCL
Lofton, John. Insurrection in SC: the turbulent world of Den-
mark Vesey. Yellow Springs OH: Antioch Press, 1964. SCL, SCHS
Logan, John H. A history of the upper country of SC from the
earliest periods to the close of the war of independence.
Vol. I. 1859, rp Spartanburg: RPC, 1960. 521 p. COMMON
Logan, John H. A history of the upper country of SC, part II.
1910, rp Easley: SHP, 1980. 118 p. SCL
Love, James S. The burning of Columbia. Clover: D.A. Westmore-
land, 1956. 18 p. SCL
Lower Savannah Council of Governments. A survey of historical
sites in the Lower Savannah region. Aiken: author, 1976.
117 p. COMMON
Lucas, Marion B. Sherman & the burning of Columbia. London:
Texas A. & M. University Press, 1976. 188 p. COMMON
Lyman Girl Scouts. History & heritage of Lyman, SC. NP: author
nd. 37 p. SPCL
Lynch, Kenneth M. Medical schooling in SC, 1823-1969. Cola:
RLB, 1970. 153 p. COMMON
Lynn, L. Ross. The story of the Thornwell Orphanage, Clinton,
SC, 1875-1925. NP: Presbyterian Committee of Publication,
1924. 239 p. SCL, GTML
MacArthur, Willaim J. Antebellum politics in an up-country
county...Spartanburg County, SC, 1850-1860. Thesis (M.A.),
U.S.C., 1966. 86 p. CLEM, SCL
Macaulay, Neill W. History of the South Carolina Dental Asso-
ciation. Centennial edition, 1869-1969. Cola: S.C. Dental
Association, 1969. 514 p. SCL, SCHS
MacDowell, Dorothy K. Beech Island, SC: four remarkable centu-
ries & more. NP: First State National Bank, 1968. 12 p.
SCHS, SCL
McColl, D. D. Sketches of old Marlboro. Cola: State Co., 1916.
108 p. SCL, SPCL
McCants, Elliott C. History, stories & legends of SC. Dallas
TX: Southern Publishing Co., 1927. 438 p. COMMON
McChesney, Ralph S. History of education in Dillon County, SC,
1731-1928. NP: NPub, nd. DICL
McClendon, Carlee T. Edgefield, SC in the War of 1812. Edge-
field: Hive Press, 1977. 56 p. COMMON
McClure, Harlan. SC architecture, 1670-1970. Cola: State Co.,
1970. 221 p. SCL, CRCL
McColl, D. D. Sketches of old Marlboro. Cola: State Co., 1916.
108 p. COMMON
McCollough, D. H. Prospectus of the first annual Interstate

87

Farmer's Summer Encampment, to be held at the encampment
grounds, at Spartanburg, SC. Spartanburg: Cofield, Petty &
Co., 1887. 40 p.   WOFF
McCormick, Jo A. The Camden backcountry judicial precinct,
1769-1970. Thesis (M.A.), U.S.C., 127 p.   SCHS, SCL
McCowen, George S. The British occupation of Charleston, 1780-
1782. Cola: USC Press, 1972. 169 p.   COMMON
McCoy, Azile M. A history of Oswego, SC. NP: author, 1975.
unp.   SMCL
McCrady, Edward. A sketch of the history and the rules of the
Ancient Artillery Society... Chstn: W,E&C, 1901. 57 p.
                                                             SCHS
McCrady, Edward. Education in SC prior to and during the Revo-
lution. Chstn: News & Courier, 1883. 54 p.   COMMON
McCrady, Edward. Gregg's Brigade of South Carolinians in the
second battle of Manassas. Richmond VA: Wm. Ellis Jones,
1885. 40 p.   SCL
McCrady, Edward. Heroes of the old Camden District, SC, 1776-
1861; an address to the survivors of Fairfield County...
Richmond VA: Jones, 1888. 35 p.   SCHS, SCL
McCrady, Edward. History of SC under the Proprietary government
1670-1719. 1897, rp NY: Russell & Russell, 1969. 762 p.
                                                           COMMON
McCrady, Edward. History of SC under the royal government,
1719-1776. 1899, rp NY: Russell & Russell, 1969. 847 p.
                                                           COMMON
McCrady, Edward. History of SC in the Revolution, 1775-1780.
1901, rp NY: Russell & Russell, 1969. 899 p.   COMMON
McCrady, Edward. History of SC in the Revolution, 1780-1783.
1901, rp NY: Russell & Russell, 1969. 787 p.   COMMON
McCrady, Edward. Slavery in the province of SC, 1670-1770.
Washington: GPO, 1896. 43 p.   SCL, WOFF
McCravy, John. The history of Easley. 56 p.   PICL
McCue, Margaret C. Lt. Col. James Grant's expedition against
the Cherokee Indians, 1761. Thesis (M.A.), U.S.C., 1967.
135 p.   SCL
McDowell, William L. The SC Revolutionary debt, 1776-1789.
Thesis (M.A.), U.S.C., 1953. 80 p.   SCL
McFall, Pearl S. It happened in Pickens County. Pickens: Sen-
tinel Press, 1959. 216 p.   COMMON
McFall, Pearl S. The Keowee River & Cherokee background. Pick-
ens: author, 1966. 117 p.   COMMON
McFall, Pearl S. So lives the dream; history & story of the old
Pendleton District, SC, & the establishment of Clemson College
NY: Comet Press, 1953. 149 p.   COMMON
McGill, Mrs. H.H. History of the S.C. Daughters of the American
Revolution, 1936-1946. 89 p.   SCL, ANCL
McGill, Samuel D. Narrative of reminiscences in Williamsburg
County. Kingstree: Kingstree Lithographic Co., 1952. 304 p.
                                                           COMMON
McGuinn, Margaret S. The restoration of Magnolia Cemetery; ge-

nealogical history. Spartanburg: Spartanburg Garden Club
Council, 1976. unp. SPCL
McIlvaine, Paul. The dead towns of Sunbury GA & Dorchester SC.
3rd ed. Asheville NC: Groves Printing Co., 1976. 82 p.COMMON
McIvaill, Dwight E. The Georgetown Library Society & the book-
borrowing habits of ten of its antebellum members. Thesis
(M.A.), UNC, 1978. 107 p. SCHS
McIntosh, Beth. Bicentennial history of Dorchester County. NP:
Dorchester County Bicentennial Commission, nd. 26 p. DOCL
McIntosh, David G. Reminiscences of early life in SC. NP:
typescript, 191? 91 p. FLMC
McIver, Petrona R. History of Mt. Pleasant, SC. Mt. Pleasant:
Ashley Printing & Publ. Co., 1960. 135 p. COMMON
McKoy, Henry B. The story of Reedy River [Greenville County].
Greenville: Keys Printing Co., 1969. 74 p. GRCL, CLEM
McLaughlin, Joseph M. Spartanburg 25, 30, 50 years ago. St.
Cloud FL: Double-D Publishing Co., nd. 31 p. SCL, GRCL, SPCL
McLaughlin, Joseph M. A story of Pacolet. NP: mimeo, 1962.
13 p. SPCL
McLaughlin, Sue. Reflections of Graniteville. NP: NPub, 1976.
20 p. SCL
McLure, Harlan. SC architecture, 1670-1970. Cola: S.C. Tricen-
tennial Commission, 1970. 219 p. COMMON
McMaster, Fitz Hugh. History of Fairfield County, SC, from
"before the white man came" to 1942. Cola: State Co., 1946.
220 p. COMMON
McMaster, Fitz Hugh. Soldiers & uniforms: SC military affairs,
1670-1775. Cola: USC Press, 1971. 69 p. COMMON
McMillan, George. Aiken. Aiken: Braddy's, 1960. 15 p. SCHS
McMillan, Montague. A history of Limestone College, 1845-1970.
Cola: RLB, 1970. 428 p. SCL, KECL
McNeill, J. P. Florence County, economic & social. Cola: USC,
1921. 67 p. COMMON
McTeer, James E. Adventure in the woods & waters of the Low-
country. Beaufort: Beaufort Book Co., 1972. 98 p. SCL, SCHS
McTeer, James E. Beaufort, now & then. Beaufort: Beaufort Book
Co., 1971. 143 p. COMMON
Mackey, Albert G. The history of freemasonry in SC from its
origin in the year 1736 to the present time... Cola: S.C.
Steam Power Press, 1861. 584 p. SCHS
Magnolia Cemetery. The proceedings of the dedication of the
grounds... Chstn: Walker & James, 1851. 88 p. SCL, CHCO, SCHS
Manning, Wyndham M. The history of Sumter County, SC... Char-
lotte NC: NPub, 1933. 8 p. SCL
Marion, SC, 1730-1930. Marion: Marion Star, 1930. 12 p. SCL
Marion Fire Engine Company. Consitution... Chstn: Denny & Per-
ry, 1869. 18 p. SCHS
Marion, John Francis. The Charleston story; scenes from a
city's history. Harrisburg PA: Stackpole Books, 1978. 183 p.
COMMON
Marlboro County Bicentennial Committee. Historical tours of

Marlboro County. NP: author, 1976. 38 p.   SCL, SCHS
Marlborough Historical Society. Monuments on the Marlboro Coun-
ty court house square, Bennettsville, SC. Bennettsville:
Marlborough Historical Society, nd. 3 p.   SCL, KECA
Marsh, Blanche. Historic Flat Rock [NC]...a settlement begun in
1827...transplanted from Charleston society... Asheville NC:
Biltmore Press, 1961. 41 p.   SCL, SPCL
Marsh, Blanche. Hitch up the buggy [Greenville County]. Green-
ville: A Press, 1977. 152 p.   COMMON
Marsh, Blanche & Kenneth F. Marsh. The new south: Greenville,
SC. Cola: RLB, 1965. 164 p.   SCL, SPCL, PICL
Marsh, Blanche. Plantation heritage in upcountry SC. Ashe-
ville NC: Biltmore Press, 1962. 189 p.   COMMON
Marshall, J. Q. An address before the survivors of the First
Regiment of Rifles; Orr's Rifles, SC Volunteers. Cola: Pres-
byterian Publishing House, 1885. unp.   SCL, GTML
Martin, C. T. The city of Easley, SC; its beginning & growth
for 54 years. NP: typescript, 1927. 12 p.   GRCL
Martin, Wallace. The Harriott Pinckney Home for Seamen,
Charleston, SC. 1 p.   SCHS
Mather, Rachel C. The storm-swept coast of SC. Woonsocket RI:
C.E. Cook, 1894. 116 p.   SCL, FLMC
May, Eoline E. Harvest of heritage, a synoptic history of Union
County, SC, from about 1749 to 1949... Union: Harvest Festi-
val [Committee?], 1949. 39 p.   UNCL, SCL
May, John A. History & progress of Aiken County. Charlotte
NC: NPub, 1933. 4 p.   SCL
May, John A. Mayfields, Aiken, SC. Aiken: NPub, 1962. 10 p.
                                                          CLEM
May, John A. South Carolina fights. The Palmetto state in the
Confederate war, 1861-1865. NP: NPub, nd. 8 p.   SCL
May, John A. & Joan Reynolds Faunt. South Carolina Secedes...
with biographical sketches of members of South Carolina's
Secession Convention. Cola: USC Press, 1960. 231 p. COMMON
Mazursky, Louise V. Dorchester-on-the-Ashley. Cola: State
Commission of Forestry, Division of State Parks, 1961. 7 p.
                                                          COMMON
Mazyck, Arthur. Charleston, SC, in 1883. With heliotypes of
the principal objects of interest... Boston: Heliotype Print-
ing Co., 1883. 39 p.   SCHS
Mazyck, Arthur. Guide to Charleston, illustrated. Being a
sketch of the history of Charleston, SC, with some account of
its present condition... Chstn: W,E&C, 1875? 215 p. COMMON
Mazyck, William G. The Charleston Museum, its genesis & development... Chstn: W,E&C, 1908.   SCL, CHCO
Memminger High & Normal School, Charleston, SC. [descriptive
pamphlet]. Chstn: W,E&C, 1898? 36 p.   SCL, SCHS
Mendenhall, Samuel B. The history of York County. NP: typescript, nd. unp.   YOCL
Meriwether, Colyer. History of higher education in SC with a
sketch of the free school system. 1889, rp Spartanburg: RPC,

1972. 247 p. COMMON
Meriwether, James B. SC journals & journalists. Cola: RPC for
Southern Studies Program, USC, 1975. 360 p. COMMON
Meriwether, Robert L. The expansion of SC, 1729-1765. Kings-
port TN: Southern Publishers, 1940. 294 p. COMMON
Merrens, H. Roy. The colonial SC scene: contemporary views,
1697-1774. Cola: USC Press, 1977. 295 p. COMMON
Messick, Hank. King's Mountain: the epic of the Blue Ridge
"Mountain Men" in the American Revolution. Boston: Little,
Brown & Co., 1976. 194 p. KECL, SCL
Meyer, Jack Allen. The Mount Sion Society of Charleston &
Winnsboro, SC, 1777-1825. NP: typescript, 1978. 55p. SCL,SCHS
Michaux, André. André Michaux's journeys in Oconee County, SC,
in 1787 & 1788. Cola: RLB, 1976. 67 p. COMMON
Michel, Middleton. Address to the Medical Society... A sketch
of the origin & history of the Medical Society of the state of
SC. Chstn: Perry, 1889. 21 p. SCL, SCHS
Middlebrook, Louis F. The frigate "South Carolina". Salem MA:
Essex Institute, 1929. 38 p. SCL, SPCL, WOFF
Middleton, Alicia H. Life in Carolina & New England during the
nineteenth century. Bristol RI: privately printed, 1929.
233 p. COMMON
Middleton, Margaret S. Affra Harleston & old Charles-Towne in
SC. Cola: RLB, 1971. 54 p. SCL, DOTM, EDTO
Middleton, Margaret S. Live Oak Plantation, Congaree, SC.
Chstn: Nelson, 1956. 30 p. SCL, SCHS
Middleton, N. R. Address delivered before the Chrestomathic So-
ciety of the College of Charleston at its organization, Nov.
24, 1848. Chstn: Burges, 1849. 16 p. SCL, SCHS
Mikell, Isaac J. Rumbling of the chariot wheels [Charleston
County]. Cola: State Co., 1923. 273 p. COMMON
Milam, Jane C. & Malcolm Heller. A dipper of reflections from
Sandy Springs, SC. Sandy Springs: author, 1978. 22 p. ANCL
PIPD
Milbank, Jeremiah & Grace Fox Perry. Turkey Hill Plantation.
NP: privately printed, 1966. 128 p. SCL, GTML, FLCL
Miles, James F. Historic Pendleton needs an angel. Clemson:
NPub, 1959. v.p. CLEM, PIPD, SCHS
Miles, James F. Pickens' family home, Hopewell... Clemson:
NPub, 1960. 5 p. CLEM
Miles, James F. Restoring historic Pendleton. Clemson: NPub,
1956. 17 p. CLEM
Miles, James F. Tour of historic places near Clemson. Clemson:
Clemson Agricultural College, 1961. 9 p. CLEM
Miles, J. W. Annual societies of the South Carolina College.
Chstn: Russell, 1853. 51 p. WOFF
Military Club of Charleston. Rules...1799. Chstn: Freneau &
Paine, 1799. 8 p. SCL
Miller, Samuel H. Official records concerning the Hamburgh, SC,
massacre of 1876, and the parties connected therewith. Wash-
ington DC: NPub, 1882. 16 p. SCL

Milling, Chapman J. Colonial SC: two contemporary descriptions.
Cola: USC Press, 1951. 209 p. COMMON
Milling, Chapman J. Exile without an end. Cola: Bostich &
Thornley, 1943. 88 p. COMMON
Mills, Robert. Mills' atlas of SC. 1825, rp Easley: SHP, 1980.
unp. COMMON
Mills, Robert. Internal improvement of SC, particularly adapted
to the low country... Cola: State Gazette Office, 1822. SCHS
SCL
Mills, Robert. Statistics of SC, including a view of its natu-
ral, civil, and military history. 1826, rp Spartanburg: RPC,
1972. 829 p. COMMON
Mims, Florence Unrecorded history of South Carolina's Woman's
Christian Temperance Union from 1881-1901. Edgefield: author,
1950. 95 p. SCL, EDTO, SCHS
Mims, Julian L. Radical reconstruction in Edgefield County,
1868-1877. Thesis (M.A.), U.S.C., 1969. 95 p. SCL
Mims, Mrs. Matthew Hansford. Edgefield, SC. NP, 1963. 16 p.
SCHS
Mims, Nancy C. Devil in petticoats; or, God's revenge against
husband killing. A tale of eighteenth century Edgefield.
Edgefield, nd. 8 p. SCL, SCHS
Miner, Leigh R. Face of an island [St. Helena's island]. Cola:
RLB, 1970. unp. COMMON
Mitchell, Broadus. The rise of cotton mills in the south. Bal-
timore MD: Johns Hopkins Press, 1921. 281 p. SCL, WOFF
Mitchell, Ethel B. The romance of the Blue Ridge Railroad.
Pendleton: Southern Printing Co., 1972. 18 p. SCL, PIPD
Moerman, Daniel E. Extended family & popular medicine on St.
Helena's Island, SC. Thesis (Ph.D.), University of Michigan,
1974. 289 p. SCL, BUCL
Molloy, Robert. Charleston: a gracious heritage. NY: Appleton-
Century Co., 1947. 311 p. COMMON
Monahan, Sister Mary A. Our Lady of Mercy Welfare Center; the
story of a neighborhood house. Thesis (   ), Catholic Uni-
versity, Washington DC, 1963. 92 p. SCHS
Montgomery, John A. Columbia, SC: history of a city. Woodland
Hills CA: Windsor Publications, 1979. 200 p. SCL, GRCL
Montgomery, Rachel. Camden heritage, yesterday & today. Cola:
RLB, 1971. 145 p. COMMON
Moore, John W. Old Cokesbury in Greenwood County, SC. Green-
wood: Index Printing Co., 1955. 32 p. COMMON
Moore, John W. Photographs & drawings of old Cokesbury & vicin-
ity. NP: NPub, 1960. 55 p. CLEM
Moore, Maurice A. Reminiscences of York. NP: mimeo, 1962.
71 p. YOCL, SCHS, SCL
Moore, W. H. Historical souvenir program of Sumter's sesqui-
centennial, 1800-1950, and tenth annual Iris Festival. Sum-
ter: Osteen-Davis Printing Co., 1950. 52 p. SCL, CLEM
Moragne, Mary E. The neglected thread, a journal from the
Calhoun community, 1836-1842. Cola: USC Press, 1951. 256 p.
SCL, LNCL

Moragne, William C. An address, delivered at New Bordeaux, Ab-
    beville District, SC...on the 90th anniversary of the arrival
    of the French Protestants [Huguenots] at that place. 1857, rp
    McCormick: McCormick County Historical Society, 1972. 48 p.
                                                        GNCL, SCL
Morgan, Elizabeth. Greenville then & now. Greenville: Graphic
    Business Service, 1976. 27 p.   GRCL, SCL
Morris, Samuel C. A tale that is told. Stories ...of Carolina
    life. NP: NPub, 1951. 120 p.   SCL, HOCL, CLEM
Morrison, Andrew. The city of Charleston & state of SC. Chstn:
    George W. Englehardt, nd. 146 p.   SCHS, SCL
Morrison, Gail M. Camden & Kershaw County's courthouses. Cola:
    Southern Studies Program, U.S.C., 1980. 19 p.   COMMON
Moss, Bobby G. Cherokee County's first half-century through the
    lens of June H. Carr, photographer. Gaffney: Southern Renai-
    ssance Press, 1975. 75 p.   SCL, SPCL
Moss, Bobby G. The old Iron District, a study of the develop-
    ment of Cherokee County, 1750-1897. Clinton: Jacobs Press,
    1972. 390 p.   COMMON
Moulton, Brenda S. Sumter County historical vignettes. Sumter:
    Sumter County Tricentennial Commission, 1970. unp.   COMMON
Moultrie, James. Introductory address delivered at the opening
    of the Medical College of the state of SC, Nov. 10, 1834.
    Chstn: Burges, 1834. 32 p.   SCL, SCHS
Moultrie, William. Memoirs of the American Revolution as far as
    it related to the states of NC & SC, & GA. 1802, rp NY: New
    York Times, 1968. 2 vol.   COMMON
Mouzon, Harold A. Privateers of Charleston in the War of 1812.
    Chstn: Historical Commission, 1954. 41 p.   SCL, SCHS, CHCA
Mullen, Harris H. The Cash-Shannon duel, duels around Camden,
    the code of honor. Tampa FL: Trend House, 1963. 42 p. COMMON
Mullins Centennial Commission, Inc. Centennial commemorative
    book about Mullins, 1872-1972. NP: NPub, 1972. unp.MACL, SCL
Murray, Chalmers S. This is our land; the story of the Agri-
    cultural Society of SC... Chstn: Carolina Art Assn., 1949.
    290 p.   SCL, SCHS
Myers, Florence B. Columbia Court House & Post Office: the
    building & its architect, 1870-1874. Thesis (M.A.), U.S.C.,
    1977. 218 p.   SCL
Nafe, Paul O. Middleton Place. Where history was made and
    beauty endures. Cambridge MA: Teknitone Publications, 1942?
    32 p.   SCL, SCHS, CLEM
Nairne, Thomas. A letter from Carolina; giving an account of
    the soil, air, products, trade, government, laws, religion,
    people... London: A. Baldwin, 1710. 63 p. UMBOD, SCHS, SCL
Napier, John M. Historical sketch of the Darlington County Ag-
    ricultural Society, 1846-1946. 27 p.   SCL, COKL
Napier, John M. Society Hill & some of its contributions to
    state & nation. NP: typescript. 15 p.   COMMON
Neely, Lucile B. Hartsville, our community. Cola: RLB, 1965.
    339 p.   COMMON

Nelson, Jack. The Orangeburg massacre. NY: World Publishing
Co., 1970. 272 p. COMMON
Nepveux, Ethel T. George Alfred Trenholm; the company that went
to war, 1861-1865. Chstn: Comprint, 1973. 132 p. COMMON
Neville, Thomas J. Charleston today & yesterday. SC Inter-
State & West Indian Exposition... Chstn: Duffy, 1901. 60 p.
SCL
Newberry County in transition. A series of lectures... New-
berry: Newberry College, 1973? v.p. NWNC
New England Society of Charleston. The New England Society of
Charleston. Chstn: W,E&C, 1967. 23 p. SCL
Newmann, C.L. The Pendleton Farmer's Society. Atlanta GA: Foote
& Davies, 1908. 208 p. SCL, PIPD, MRCL
News & Courier. The burning of Columbia. Chstn: W,E&C, 1888.
24 p. SCL, SCHS
News & Courier. Centennial edition. The record of 100 years,
1803-1903. Cola: News & Courier, 1904. 107 p. WOFF
News & Courier. Charleston, SC, the centennial of incorporation
1883. Chstn: News & Courier, 1884. 259 p. SCL, SCHS, MACL
News & Courier. The Civil War at Charleston... Chstn: News &
Courier, nd. 66 p. SCL
News & Courier. The seaport of the south! a description,
Charleston harbor, and the jetties, to be constructed by the
U.S. government...with a map of the harbor. Chstn, 1878.
14 p. SCL, SCHS
New York State. Chamber of Commerce. Report of the special
committee appointed to obtain relief for the sufferers by the
earthquake at Charleston, SC. NY: author, 1886. 32 p. SCHS
SCL
Nicholes, Cassie. Historical sketches of Sumter County; its
birth & growth. Sumter: Historical Commission, 1975. 546
p. COMMON
Nicholson, S. W. Fairfield County, economic & social. Cola:
USC, 1924. 83 p. SCHS, SPCL, CLCC, SCL
Nicholson, William A. The burning of Columbia. Cola: William
Sloan, 1895. 12 p. SCL
The nineteenth century. Chstn: W,E&C, 1869. 84 p. WOFF
Norment, J. E. A business review of the city of Spartanburg.
Chstn: Lucas & Richardson, 1895. 32 p. CLEM, WOFF
Norris, John. Profitable advice for rich & poor. In a dialogue
or discourse between James Freeman, a Carolina planter...
London: J. How, 1712. 114 p. SCL, UMBOD
Norryce, C. W. A general sketch of the city of Anderson. An-
derson: Roper Printing Co., 1909. 28 p. PIPD, SCL
North Augusta's 50th anniversary. 1906-1956. Augusta GA: NPub,
1956. 126 p. SCL
North Charleston Country Club. History of property & club.
Charleston Heights: NPub, nd. 4 p. SCHS
North, Neeses, Woodford & Livingston Area Bicentennial Committee
Bicentennial book: North, Neeses, Woodford, Livingston. NP:
author, 1976. 75 p. ORCL

Norton, Evan. History of Conway's schools from Conwayboro Acad-
   emy to Burrough's Graded School, from 1856-1910. Conway:
   Field Job Print, nd. 25 p.   HOCL
Norton, James A. The Independent Republic of Horry County.
   Conway: typescript, nd. v.p.   HOCL
Norton, James A. The narrative of Horry County history. Con-
   way: typescript, nd. 141 p.   HOCL
Norton, Julian O. Politics in Horry. Chstn: W,E&C, 1908. 28
   p.   WOFF
Nunnery, Jimmie E. Chester County: 1885-1905; Tillman era.
   Thesis (M.A.), U.S.C., 1975. 104 p.   SCL
Obear, Katharine T. Through the years in old Winnsboro. Cola:
   RLB, 1940. 258 p.   COMMON
Oconee County Library. German Colony protocol; translated by
   B.E. Schaeffer. Walhalla: author, 1960.   SCL, OCCL, SPCL
Oconee County, SC, centennial, 1968. NP: NPub, 1968. 64 p. SCL
Official program of the Spartanburg carnival, October 22-27,
   1900. Spartanburg: W.F. Barnes, 1900. 17 p.   WOFF
Oglethorpe, James E. A new & accurate account of the province
   of SC & GA. London: Worrall, 1732. 76 p.   SCL
Old Star Fort, Ninety-Six. NP: NPub, nd. 12 p.   SPCL
Oliphant, Albert D. The evolution of the penal system of SC
   from 1866-1916. Cola: State Co., 1916. 14 p.   SCL, WOFF
Oliphant, Mary C. Gateway to SC. Cola: State Co., 1947.   GRCL
                                                              SCL
Oliphant, Mary C. The genesis of an up-country town [Greenville]
   NP: NPub, nd. 13 p.   GRCL
Oliphant, Mary C. The history of SC. River Forest IL: Laidlaw
   Bros., 1970. 480 p.   COMMON
Oliphant, Mary C. SC from the mountains to the sea. Cola:
   State Co., 1964. 296 p.   COMMON
O'Neall, John B. The annals of Newberry in two parts; part
   first by John Belton O'Neall; part second by John A. Chapman.
   1859, rp Baltimore MD: GPC, 1974. 816 p.   COMMON
100 years in Aiken County. Aiken: Highway Guides of America,
   1971. 40 p.   AICL
100 years of "WECCO"...a history of Walker, Evans & Cogswell
   Company. Manufacturing stationers. 1821-1921. Chstn: W,E&C,
   1921.   SCL, CHCO
150 years of Orange Lodge, No. 14, A.F.M. [Freemasons]. Its
   by-laws. Its masters. Its members. Chstn, 1939? SCHS, CHCO
Orangeburg County Tricentennial: souvenir program. Orangeburg:
   Quality Printing, 1970. 59 p.   SCL, WOFF
Orange Lodge, No. 14, A.F.M. [Freemasons]. Historical sketch...
   To which is appended the by-laws. Chstn, 1911. 64 p.   SCHS
Orvin, Maxwell C. Historic Berkeley County, SC, 1671-1900.
   Chstn: Comprint, 1973. 239 p.   COMMON
Orvin, Maxwell C. Monck's Corner, Berkeley County, SC. Chstn:
   author, 1950. 59 p.   COMMON
Orvin, Virginia K. History of Clarendon County, 1700-1961.
   Manning: NPub, 1961. 178 p.   COMMON

Ostendorf, Louis F. An historical sketch of the Washington
  Light Infantry, Charleston, SC. Chstn: NPub, 1943. 12 p.
                                                            CHCO
Our forefathers; their homes & their churches. Chstn: W,E&C,
  1860. 172 p.   SCL, WOFF
Our heritage: Fairfield, SC. NP: News & Herald, nd. 71 p. SCL
                                                            FACL
Pace, H. M. Historical & other notes about the utilities of
  Charleston, SC. NP: typescript, 1942. 15 p.   SCHS
Pacolet Manufacturing Co. The picture story of the community
  activities. Pacolet manufacturing Company, Spartanburg, SC.
  1882-1927. Spartanburg: NPub, 1928. 53 p.   WOFF
Palmetto Guards. Report of the chairman of the centennial com-
  mittee to the Palmetto Guard. Chstn: W,E&C, 1876. SCL, SCHS
Parker, Ellen. Historical sketch & catalogue of the Old Powder
  Magazine, Charleston, SC. Chstn: Colonial Dames, 1946. 20 p.
                                                       SCL, SCHS
Parkinson, B. L. A history of the administration of the city
  public schools of Columbia, SC. Cola: USC, 1925. 116 p.
                                                       SCL, SCHS
Parler, Dorothy. Elloree. NP: NPub, 1970. 57 p.   ORCL, SCL
Parler, Dorothy H. Elloree; long ago & now. NP: author, nd.
  19 p.   ORCL
Parler, Josie P. The past blows by on the road to Poinsett
  Park. Sumter: Knight Bros., 1939. 36 p.   CLEM, SCL
Parrish, William S. A history of Coker College. Thesis (M.A.),
  U.S.C., 1938. 122 p.   COKL, SCL
Parsons, Elsie W. Folk-lore of the sea islands, SC. Cambridge
  & NY: American Folk-lore Society, 1923. 219 p. SCL, FLMC, BUCL
Patrons of Husbandry. S.C. State Grange. Darlington County.
  History, description & resources of Darlington County...
  Chstn: News & Courier, 1874. 29 p.   SCL
Patterson, John J. The Hamburgh riots. Washington DC: GPO,
  1876. 47 p.   SPCL
Patterson, William H. "Through the heart of the south", a
  history of the Seaboard Air Line Railroad company, 1832-1950.
  Thesis (Ph.D.), U.S.C., 1951. 510 p.   SCL
Patton, Sadie S. A condensed history of Flat Rock [NC], the
  little Charleston of the mountains. 3rd ed. Asheville NC:
  Church Printing Co., 1961. 73 p.   SCL, SCHS
Pearson, Elizabeth W. Letters from Port Royal, 1862-1868. Bos-
  ton: W.B. Clarke Co., 1906. 345 p.   BUCL, COKL, SCL
PeeDee Regional Planning & Development Council. Historic pres-
  ervation survey & plan. Florence: author, 1972. 87 p. SCHS
Peeples, Robert E. H. Tales of ante bellum island families:
  Hilton Head Island & our family circle. Hilton Head Island:
  author, 1970. 16 p.   SCHS
Peele, C. E. The Dougherty Manual Labor School of the S.C.
  [Methodist] Conference... NP: NPub, 1934. 39 p. SCL, WOMA
Pendergast, Ella W. The charm of Beaufort, SC; where to go to
  meet the Spring. NP: typescript, 1926. 39 p.   BUCL

Pendleton District Historical & Recreational Commission. Pendleton historic district; a survey. Pendleton: author, 1973. 72 p. COMMON

Pendleton District Historical & Recreational Commission. Pendleton historic district; a plan. Pendleton: author, 1973. 31 p. COMMON

Pendleton Farmer's Society. Atlanta GA: Foote & Davies, 1908. 208 p. COMMON

Pendleton Farmer's Society. Centennial souvenir of the Pendleton Farmer's Society. Anderson: NPub, 1916. SLC, ANCL, SCHS

Pendleton Farmer's Society. Old homes in & around Pendleton, SC. Clemson: NPub, 1960. unp. CLEM

Pendleton Sunday School Society. Records of the Pendleton Sunday School Society, 1819-1824. Cola: typescript (W.P.A.), 1936. 50 p. PIPD

Pennington, Edgar L. The Rev. Francis LeJau's work among Indians & Negro slaves. Baton Rouge LA: Franklin Press, 1935? 17 p. SCL

Pennington, Patience. A woman rice planter. Cambridge MA: Harvard University Press, 1961. 446 p. COMMON

The Penn Normal, Industrial & Agricultural School report... St. Helena Island, SC. NP: NPub, 1901. 19 p. SCL, SCHS

Perry, Grace F. Moving finger of Jasper [County]. Golden jubilee ed. Jasper: Jasper County Confederate Centennial Commission, nd. 218 p. COMMON

Peterkin, Julia. Roll, Jordan, Roll. NY: Robert O. Ballou, 1933. COMMON

Petigru, James L. Oration delivered before the Charleston Library Society at its first centennial anniversary, June 13, 1848. Chstn: Nixon, 1848. 19 p. SCL, SCHS

Petit, James R. Freedom's four square miles [Charleston]. Cola: RLB, 1964. 87 p. COMMON

Petit, James R. SC & the sea: day by day toward five centuries, 1492-1976... Chstn: W,E&C, 1976. 2 vol. COMMON

Phoenix Fire Engine Co. Constitution of the Phoenix Fire Engine Co. of Charleston, SC. Chstn: Steam Job Press, 1869. 16 p. SCL

Pickens County Centennial Commission. Pickens County centennial 1868-1968: souvenir program. Pickens: author, 1968. 124 p. CLEM

Pickens County History [SpC] PICL

A pictorial history of Charles-Towne. 1670 - Charleston - 1970. Chstn: Charleston Tricentennial Committee, 1970. 56 p. COMMON

Pinckney, Josephine. Call back yesterday; the first twenty-five years of Ashley Hall. Chstn: Quinn Press, 1934. SCL, SCHS

Pine Forest Inn...Summerville, SC. Summerville, 1914? 20 p. SCL, SCHS

Pinehurst Tea Gardens [description]. Summerville, 1905. 12 p. SCHS

Pipkin, Theron M. A historical sketch of Georgetown Post No. 114. GTML

Pittman, Clyde C. Death of a gold mine...the explosion at Haile
gold mine... Great Falls: NPub, 1972. 83 p.   SCL, KECL
Plowden, Theodosia D. Historical sketch of the Stateburg Lit-
erary & Musical Society, 1885-1949. 15 p.   SCL, SCHS
Pluckette, Clara C. Edisto: a sea island principality. Cleve-
land OH: Seaforth Publ. Co., 1978.   COMMON
Pollitzer, Mabel L. A history of the Charleston County Li-
brary, Charleston, SC. NP: typescript, 1966. 14 p.   SCHS
Pope, Thomas H. History of Newberry County, SC, vol. I: 1749-
1860. Cola: USC Press, 1973. 389 p.   COMMON
Porcher, Frederick A. The history of the Santee Canal. Monck's
Corner: S.C. Public Service Authority, 1950. unp.   COMMON
Porcher, Frederick A. The Ladies' Memorial Association of
Charleston...from 1865 to 1880; together with a roster of the
Confederate dead... Chstn: H.P. Cooke, 1880. 42 p. SCL, SPCL
Porter, Anthony T. Holy Communion Church Institute of Charles-
ton, SC...founded 1867. NY: Appleton, 1875. 63 p.   SPCL
Porter, Anthony T. Led on! Step by step, scenes from clerical,
military, educational, & plantation life in the south, 1828-
1898. ____, rp NY: Arno Press, 1967. 462 p.   COMMON
Potts, John F., Sr. A history of South Carolina State College,
1896-1978. Orangeburg: S.C. State College, 1978. 215 p.
                                                        COMMON
Potwin, Marjorie A. Cotton mill people of the Piedmont. NY:
Columbia University Press, 1927. 166 p.   SCL, SCHS
Powell, William S. The proprietors of Carolina. Raleigh NC:
Carolina Charter Tercentenary Commission, 1963. 70 p.SCL,SCHS
Poyas, Elizabeth A. Days of yore; or, shadows of the past. By
the Ancient Lady of Charleston, SC. Chstn: Mazyck, 1870.
2 parts.   COMMON
Poyas, Elizabeth A. Our forefathers; their homes & their
churches. Chstn: W,E&C, 1860. 172 p.   COMMON
Poyas, Elizabeth A. A peep into the past. Chstn: author, 1853.
238 p.   FLCL
Prevost, Charlotte K. & Effie L. Wilder. Pawley's Island: a
living legend. Cola: State Co., 1972. 72 p.   COMMON
Prince, Julian P. Brief historical sketch of the PeeDee Medical
Association. Florence, 1948. 12 p.   SCHS
Prince, Angie F. Greenville: a portrait of its people. Green-
ville: Keys Printing Co., 1976. 99 p.   SCL, GRCL
Pringle, Elizabeth W. Chronicles of Chicora Wood. NY: Scribner
1922. 366 p.   COMMON
Pringle, Elizabeth W. A woman rice planter. Cambridge: Belknap
Press, 1961. 446 p.   COMMON
Prioleau, Huldah J. Fair View Industrial Home. Cola: NPub, nd.
1 p.   SCHS
Proceedings of the centennial celebration of South Carolina
College. Cola: State Co., 1905. 239 p.   COMMON
Proceedings of the sixty-sixth anniversary of the Orphan House
of Charleston, SC, October 18, 1855. Chstn: A.E. Miller, 1855
68 p.   SCL, SCHS

Ramsay, David. The history of the Revolution in SC, from a British province to an independent state. 1785, rp Spartanburg: RPC, 19 . COMMON
Ramsay, David. History of SC from its first settlement in 1670 to the year 1808. 2 vol. 1858, rp Spartanburg: RPC, 1960. COMMON
Ramsay, David. A sketch of the soil, climate, weather & diseases of SC. Chstn: Young, 1796. 30 p. SCL, SCHS
Ramsey, Ralph H. Sumter County, economic & social. Cola: USC, 1922. 111 p. COMMON
Ramsey, Robert W. Carolina cradle; settlement of the northwest Carolina frontier. Chapel Hill NC: UNC Press, 1964. 252 p. SCL, GNCL, GTML
Randall, Patricia M. A history of the county department of public welfare, Charleston, SC. Chstn?: 1962? 82 p. SCHS
Ravenel, Harriott H. Charleston, the place & the people. NY: Macmillan, 1906. 528 p. SCL, SCHS
Ravenel, Henry W. Anniversary address. Delivered before the Black Oak Agricultural Society, April, 1852. Chstn: Walker & James, 1852. 20 p. SCL, SCHS
Sass, Herbert R. Story of the SC lowcountry. Cola: Hyer Publ. Co., nd. 3 vol. SCL, DICL
Ravenel, Rose P. Piazza tales, a Charleston memoir. Chstn: Shaftsbury Press, 1952. 76 p. COMMON
Ravenel, Mrs. St. Julien. Charleston, the place & the people. 1906, rp Easley: SHP, 1972. 528 p. COMMON
Read, William G. An address delivered before the South Carolina Society on the occasion of opening their Male Academy on the 2d of July, 1827. Chstn: Miller, 1827. 28 p. SCHS
Reception of General Lafayette in Camden, SC...1825.
 SCL
Reece, Bert H. History of Pumpkintown-Oolenoy. Pickens: author, 1970. 61 p. COMMON
Reid, Charles S. Issaquena: a legend of upper Carolina. Walhalla: Steck, 1897. 42 p. SCL, SCHS
Reid, Charles S. Persons, places & happenings in old Walhalla. Walhalla: Walhalla Historical Society, nd. 210 p. COMMON
Reid, J. W. History of the Fourth Regiment of S.C. Volunteers. Greenville: Shannon & Co., 1892. 143 p. COMMON
Rej, M. S. Across the marsh - Pawley's [Island]. Cola: Sandlapper Press, 1965. 31 p. COMMON
Revill, Janie. President Andrew Jackson's birthplace. Cola: author, 1966. 53 p. SCL, KECL, SPCL
Revill, Janie. SC counties, districts or precincts, parishes & townships... Cola: Author, 1969. 14 p. KECL, SCL
Revill, Janie. Sumter District. Cola: State Co., 1968. 39 p. COMMON
Reznikoff, Charles. The Jews of Charleston. Philadelphia PA: Jewish Publication Society of America, 1950. 343 p. COMMON
Rhame, Col. J. A. Battle of Willow Grove & other Revolutionary matters. NP: Jane Campbell Chapter, D.A.R., 1915. 7 p. LECL

Rhett, James M. Charleston then & now. Cola: RLB, 1974. 118
p.   COMMON
Rhett, Robert G. Charleston: an epic of Carolina. Richmond VA:
Garrett & Massie, 1940. 374 p.   COMMON
Rice, James H. Glories of the Carolina coast. Cola: RLB, 1925,
1936. 259 p.   COMMON
Rice, James H. The aftermath of glory. Chstn: W,E&C, 1934.
324 p.   COMMON
Rice, James H. Two addresses: our school system, at dedication
of Courtenay school... With a sketch of Mr. Rice. Cola:
State Co., 1926. 57 p.   SCL, SCHS
A rich heritage of stories on happenings in Aiken County, SC.
NP: privately printed, 1955.   AICL
Richards, J. P. The background of the history of Lancaster
County, SC. NP: NPub, 1933. 8 p.   SCL
Richardson, James M. History of Greenville County, SC, narra-
tive & biographical. Atlanta GA: A.H. Cawston, 1930. 338 p.
                                                          COMMON
Rivers, William J. A chapter in the early history of SC.
Chstn: W,E&C, 1874. 110 p.   COMMON
Rivers, William J. River's account of the raising of troops in
SC. Cola: RLB, 1899. 44 p.   SCL
Rivers, William J. Sketch of the history of SC to the close of
proprietary government by the revolution of 1719. 1856, rp
Spartanburg: RPC, 1972. 470 p.   COMMON
Rivers, William J. Topics in the history of SC. Chstn: Walker
& James, 1853. 60 p.   SCHS, SCL
Robbins, David P. Historical & descriptive sketch of the lead-
ing manufacturing & mercantile enterprises, etc....of Colum-
bia. Cola: Presbyterian Publishing House, 1888. 96 p. COMMON
Roberts, Bruce. The faces of SC. Garden City NJ: Doubleday,
1976. 141 p.   COMMON
Robertson, Ben. Red Hills & Cotton: an upcountry memory. NY:
Knopf, 1942. 296 p.   COMMON
Robertson, Ben. Traveler's Rest. Clemson: Cottonfield Press,
1938. 268 p.   SCL, SCHS
Robinson, Emmett. A guide to the Dock Street Theatre & brief
resume of the theatres in Charleston, SC, from 1730. Chstn:
Footlight Players, 1963. 14 p.   CLEM, SCHS
Robinson, G. O. The character of quality; the story of the
Greenwood Mills... Cola: RLB, 1964. 173 p.   COMMON
Rock Hill Board of Trade. Facts & figures on Rock Hill, SC.
NP: NPub, 1946. 9 p.   SCL
Rock Hill Chamber of Commerce. Centennial celebration...1952.
Rock Hill: NPub, 1952. unp.   CLEM
Rogers, George C. Charleston in the age of the Pinckneys. Nor-
man OK: University of Oklahoma Press, 1969. 187 p.   COMMON
Rogers, George C. Church & state in eighteenth century SC.
Chstn: Dalcho Historical Society, 1959. 46 p.   COMMON
Rogers, George C. The history of Georgetown County, SC. Cola:
USC Press, 1970. 565 p.   COMMON

Rogers, George C. A SC chronology, 1497-1970. Cola: USC Press, 1973. 107 p.   COMMON
Rogers, James A. Theodosia, & other Pee Dee sketches. Cola: RLB, 1978. 269 p.   COMMON
Rogers, James S. The history of Horry County, SC, 1850-1876. Thesis (M.A.), U.S.C., 1972. 122 p.   HOCL, SCL
Rouse, J. K. From Blowing Rock to Georgetown. NP: author, 1975? 101 p.   GTML
Rowell, P. E. Lexington County & its towns. NP: NPub, nd. 64 p.   SCL
Rowell, P. E. Review of Grahams [Denmark], Barnwell County, SC. Cola: J.L. Berg, nd. 25 p.   SCL
Rowland, Lawrence S. The American Revolution & its background in the Port Royal area of SC. Thesis (M.A.), U.S.C., 1971. 99 p.   SCL
Rowland, Lawrence S. Eighteenth century Beaufort: a study of South Carolina's southern parishes to 1800. Thesis (Ph.D.), U.S.C., 1978. 455 p.   SCL
Royall, Francis Martin. East & west. Greenville: Hiott Press, 1952. 164 p.   SCL, GRCL
Rudisill, Horace F. The first one hundred years: Lamar, SC, 1872-1972. NP: NPub, 1972. 88 p.   SCL
Rudisill, Horace F. Historical tours in Darlington County... Darlington: Darlington County Tricentennial Committee, 1970. 51 p.   SCL, COKL
Runnett, Mabel. The early settlement of Beaufort town, 1700-1725. Beaufort: Beaufort County Historical Society, 1978. 17 p.   BUCL
Rush, John D. Brief history of Post No. 28 of the American Legion, 1919-1971, Spartanburg, SC. Spartanburg: NPub, 1971. 16 p.   SCHS
Russell, David H. Historical sketch of old Pendleton District. Anderson: Oulla Printing Co., 1913?   SPCL, CLEM, SCL
Rutledge, Archibald. From the hills to the sea; fact & legend of the Carolinas. Indianapolis IN: Bobbs-Merrill, 1958.
                                                                          COMMON
Rutledge, Archibald H. Home by the river. Cola: Sandlapper, 1970. 167 p.   COMMON
Rutledge, Archibald H. Old plantation days. N.Y.: Frederick A. Stokes [1921]   SCL
Rutledge, Archibald H. Santee paradise. Indianapolis: Bobbs-Merrill, 1956. 232 p.   COMMON
Rutledge, Archibald H. The world around Hampton. Indianapolis IN: Bobbs-Merrill, 1960. 192 p.   COMMON
Rutt, Richard H. Hilton Head Island: a perspective. NP: Cornelia, Rutt, Chapman, Inc. 1975. 128 p.   SCL, BUCL
St. Andrew's Society. The bi-centennial anniversary banquet, St. Andrew's Society, Charleston, SC, November 30, 1929, Ashley Park Pavillion. Chstn?, 1929. 8 p.   SCL
St. Andrew's Society. Bi-centennial service, First (Scots) Presbyterian Church, Charleston, SC. Chstn: Heisser Printing

Co., 1929. 4 p.   SCL
St. Andrew's Society. Rules...from 1729 to 1892; centennial &
other addresses, poems, & historical sketch. Chstn: W,E&C,
1892. 136 p.   SCL, SCHS
St. Cecelia Society. Rules... Charlestown: Robert Wells, 1774.
11 p.   SCHS
St. George's Society. The Saint George's Society of Charleston,
SC. Its establisment...rules..with a list of its present of-
ficers & members. Chstn: W,E&C, 1898. 21 p.   SCL
St. John Hotel. [Brochure]. Chstn: W,E&C, 192? 16 p.   SCHS
Salley, Alexander S. ...the boundary line between NC & SC...
Cola: HCSC, 1929. 38 p.   COMMON
Salley, Alexander S. Col. William Hill's memoirs of the Revo-
lution. Cola: HCSC, 1921. 36 p.   COMMON
Salley, Alexander S. The courthouses of Orangeburg [SpC]   ORCL
Salley, Alexander S. The early English settlers of SC; a paper
read before the Columbia committee of the...Colonial Dames of
America...1945. NP: Colonial Dames, 1946. 19 p.   COMMON
Salley, Alexander S. The flag of the state of SC... Cola:
State Co., 1938, 1957. 14 p.   COMMON
Salley, Alexander S. A guide book & historical sketch of
Charleston, SC. Chstn: Lucas & Richardson, 192?. 41 p.COMMON
Salley, Alexander S. The happy hunting ground. Personal exper-
iences in the low-country. Cola: State Co., 1926. 83 p. GTML
Salley, Alexander S. History of Orangeburg County, from its
first settlement to the close of the Revolutionary War. 1898,
rp Spartanburg: RPC, 1978. 572 p.   COMMON
Salley, Alexander S. How Greenville got its name. Cola: Cary
Printing Co., 1918. 4 p.   SCL
Salley, Alexander S. ...The independent company from SC at
Great Meadows. Cola: HCSC, 1932. 15 p.   COMMON
Salley, Alexander S. ...The introduction of rice culture into
SC. Cola: HCSC, 1919. 23 p.   COMMON
Salley, Alexander S. Narratives of early Carolina, 1650-1708.
1911, rp NY: Barnes & Noble, 1967. 388 p.   COMMON
Salley, Alexander S. An order book of the Third Regiment,
South Carolina Line, Continental Establishment, Dec. 23, 1776-
May 2, 1777. Cola: HCSC, 1942. 44 p.   COMMON
Salley, Alexander S. The origin of South Carolina... Cola:
HCSC, 1926. 22 p.   COMMON
Salley, Alexander S. ...Parris Island, the site of the first
attempt at a settlement of white people within the bounds of
what is now SC... Cola: State Co., 1919. 9 p.   COMMON
Salley, Alexander S. President Washington's tour through SC in
1791. Cola: HCSC, 1932. 30 p.   COMMON
Salley, Alexander S. The seal of the state of SC; 2nd ed.
Cola: State Co., 1906, 1965. 8 p.   COMMON
Salley, Alexander S. South Carolina Gazette of yesterday & today. Incorporating a history of the first newspaper publish-
ed in the province of SC. Cola: HCSC, 193?. 10 p.   SCHS
Salley, Alexander S. The state houses of SC, 1751-1936. Cola:

HCSC, 1936, 1957. 39 p.   COMMON
Salley, Alexander S. The unveiling of the memorial ledger to
Charles Pinckney, St. Philip's churchyard, Charleston, SC,
Dec. 6th, 1949. Atlanta GA: Westminster Publications, 1949.
30 p.   GWPL
Salley, Marion. The Orangeburg papers. Vol. I. Orangeburg:
Orangeburg County Historical & Genealogical Society, 1970.
                                                        SCL, ORCL
Salley, Marion. Two hundred years of Orangeburg; a pageant.
Orangeburg: Observer Publ. Co., 1935. 9 p.   ORCL
Salley, Marion. The writings of Marion Salley. Orangeburg:
Orangeburg County Historical & Genealogical Society, 1970.
77 p.   CLCC
Salley, Olin J. History of Orangeburg Collegiate Institute
(Orangeburg College), 1895-1914. NP: author, 1964. 16 p.
                                                              ORCL
Saluda County Tricentennial Commission. Saluda County in scene
& story. Cola: RLB, 1970. 141 p.   COMMON
Sams, James J. Datha [Island, Beaufort County]. NP: typescript
nd. 22 p.   SCL, SCHS
Santee-Cooper country. Sumter: Osteen Pub. Co., nd. 40 p. GRCL
Santee-Wateree Regional Planning Council. The Santee-Wateree
historic preservation plan & inventory. Cola: SCDAH, 1974.
117 p.   COMMON
Sass, Herbert R. Adventures in green places. NY: Milton, Balch
& Co., 1926. 293 p.   SCL, COKL
Sass, Herbert R. Charleston grows: an economic, social & cul-
tural portrait of an old community in the new south...
Chstn: Carolina Art Assn., 1949. 353 p.   COMMON
Sass, Herbert R. Outspoken: 150 years of the News & Courier.
Cola: USC Press, 1953. 120 p.   COMMON
Sass, Herbert R. The story of the SC low country. West Colum-
bia: J.F. Hyer Publ. Co., 1956. 3 vol.   COMMON
Satterthwaite, Ann. Historic Charleston Foundation: its past,
present & prospects. Washington DC: typescript, 1975. 34
p.   SCHS
Savage, Henry. River of the Carolinas: the Santee. 1956, rp
Chapel Hill NC: UNC Press, 1968. 435 p.   COMMON
Scarborough, Henry L. Some interesting facts in the history of
Sumter County. Sumter: NPub, 1921. 22 p.   SCL, FLMC
Schindler's Antique Shop, Charleston. Come to Charleston & the
low country. Chstn: author, 1950. 81 p.   SCL, GRCL
Scott, Edwin J. Random recollections of a long life [Richland
County]. 1884, rp Cola: RLB, 1969. 210 p.   COMMON
Seaborn, Margaret M. André Michaux's journeys in Oconee County,
SC, in 1787 & 1788. Cola: RLB, 1976. 67 p.   COMMON
Seaborn, Margaret M. Benjamin Hawkin's journeys through Oconee
County, SC, in 1796 & 1797. Cola: RLB, 1973. 34 p.   COMMON
Seaborn, Margaret M. Oconee Station in Oconee County, SC.
Cola: RLB, 1977. 5 p.   SCL, KECA, CLEM
Seabrook, Henrietta & Mrs. H. P. Sitton. Houses of old Pendle-

ton. Clemson: typescript, 1962. 13 p.   CLEM, PIPD
Searson, Louis A. The town of Allendale, a gem of the SC low
     country. Cola: NPub, 1949. 84 p.   COMMON
Seegars, Mary R. Mt. Pisgah community, Kershaw County, SC.
     NP: NPub, 1976. 46 p.   GNLN, KECA, CLEM
Selby, Julian A. Memorabilia & anecdotal reminiscences of
     Columbia, SC, & incidents connected therewith. 1905, rp
     Cola: RLB, 1970. 206 p.   COMMON
Sellers, Leila. Charleston business on the eve of the American
     Revolution. Chapel Hill NC: UNC Press, 1934. 259 p.   COMMON
Sellers, W. W. History of Marion County, SC, from its earliest
     times to the present, 1901. 1902, rp Marion: Marion Public
     Library, 1977. 647 p.   COMMON
Semi-centennial address of Erskine College, delivered at Due
     West, SC, June 26, 1889. Chstn: W,E&C, 1890. 111 p. SCL,WOFF
Semi-centennial of the SC Military Academy. Chstn: W,E&C, 1893.
     63 p.   SCL,CHCO
Seneca centennial, 1873-1973: souvenir program. NP: NPub, 1973?
     28 p.   PIPD, SCL
The settling of SC. Cola: Tricentennial Commission, 1969. COMMON
Shaffer, Edward T. Carolina gardens... NY: Huntington Press,
     1937. 289 p.   SCL, COKL
Shankman, Arnold. Happyville, the forgotten colony. NP: NPub,
     1978? 19 p.   SCL
Shannon, William M. Old times in Camden. (n.p. 1961) SCL, KECL
Shecut, John L. Shecut's medical & philosophical essays...as
     conducing to the formation of a medical history of the state
     of SC. Chstn: A.E. Miller, 1819. 270 p.   SCL, UMBOD
Shepard, Charles U. The Pinehurst Tea-Gardens near Summerville,
     SC. Washington DC: GPO, 1899.   SCL, DOTM
Shepard, Charles U. U.S. Department of Agriculture report No.
     61. Tea culture: the experiment in SC. Washington: GPO,
     1899. 27 p.   SCL, DOTM
Sherer, Palmer G. A partial history of some of the early
     schools & educational movements of York County. Thesis (M.A.)
     U.S.C., 1929. 154 p.   YOCL, SCL
A short history & description of the famous Magnolia Gardens
     near Charleston, SC. (n.p.) 4 p.   SCL, CHCO
A short history of the Winyah Indigo Society of Georgetown, SC,
     1755-1950, with lists of deceased & living members. George-
     town: Winyah Indigo Society, 1950. 44 p.   COMMON
Short sketch of the town of Greers, SC, 1896. Greer: typescript
     1937.   GRCL
Siegling Music House. The hundredth anniversary...1819-1919.
     Chstn, 1919. 8 p.   SCHS
Simkins, Francis B. & Robert H. Woody. SC during reconstruct-
     ion. Chapel Hill NC: UNC Press, 1932. 610 p.   COMMON
Simmons, William E. Charleston County. NP: NPub, 1873? 18 p.
                                                             SCHS
Simms, William G. Charleston: the palmetto city. An essay.
     1857, rp Cola: USC, 1976. 22 p.   SCL, SCHS

Simms, William G. The geography of SC, being a companion to the
history of that state. Chstn: Babcock, 1843. 196 p.   UMBOD
                                                        SCL, GRCL
Simms, William G. The new Simms history of SC, centennial edit-
ion, 1940. Cola: State Co., 1941. 317 p.   COMMON
Simms, William G. Sack & destruction of the city of Columbia,
SC. 2nd ed. Edited, with notes by A.S. Salley. Atlanta GA:
Oglethorp University Press, 1937. 106 p.   COMMON
Simons, Jane K. A guide to Columbia, SC... Cola: Columbia
Chamber of Commerce, 1945. 90 p.   COMMON
Simons, Katherine D. Roads of romance & historic spots near
Summerville, SC. Chstn: Southern Printing & Publ. Co., nd.
37 p.   SCL, SCHS
Simons, Katherine D. Stories from Charleston harbor. Cola:
State Co., 1930. 139 p.   COMMON
Simpson, Ethel. The first fifty years of the Young Women's
Christian Association of Greenville, SC...1917-1967. Green-
ville, 1967. 157 p.   GRCL
Simpson, R. W. History of old Pendleton District & genealogy of
leading families. 1913, rp Easley: SHP, 1978. 264 p.   COMMON
[Simpson, R. W.] Revised index to Simpson's history of Pendleton
District, SC, by Nancy G. Chadwick. Jacksonville FL: author,
1973. 21 p.   SCL, GRCL, GWPL, SCHS
Singer, Charles G. SC in the Confederation. 1962, rp Phila-
delphia PA: Porcupine Press, 1976.   COMMON
Singley, Phoebe S. A survey of education in Newberry County,
prior to 1870. Cola: typescript, 1934. 69 p.   SCL, NWRL
Sirmans, M. Eugene. Colonial SC: a political history, 1663-
1763. Chapel Hill NC: UNC Press, 1966. 394 p.   COMMON
Sitton, Emma A. Some early Pendleton history. Pendleton: auth-
or, 1961. 4 p.   CLEM
Skaggs, Marvin L. NC border disputes involving her southern
line. Chapel Hill NC: UNC Press, 1941. 250 p. SCL,SPCL, PICL
Sloan, Dave U. Fogy days, and now: or, the world has changed.
Atlanta GA: Foote & Davies, 1891. 248 p.   SCL, CLEM
Sloan, Eugene B. SC: a journalist & his state. Cola: Lewis-
Sloan Publ. Co., 1974. 242 p.   COMMON
Smith, Alice R. The dwelling houses of Charleston, SC. Phila-
delphia PA: Lippincott, 1917. 386 p.   COMMON
Smith, Harry W. Life & sport in Aiken & those who made it.
NY: Derrydale Press, 1935. 237 p.   SCL, GRCL, AICL, SCHS
Smith, Henry A. The baronies of SC. Chstn: SCHS, 1931. 193 p.
                                                       SCHS, SCL
Smith, Henry A. The town of Dorchester in SC: a sketch of its
history. Chstn: Daggett, 1905. 33 p.   SCL, SCHS
Smith, Isabel A. Mrs. Isabel A. Smith's school for young ladies
& children. Chstn: W,E&C, 1894-95. 28 p.   SCHS
Smith, Jared M. A history of Lee County... NP: typescript,
1963. 11 p.   LECL
Smith, R. M. Vandiver's history of Anderson County. Anderson:
mimeo, 1970. 304 p.   SCL, ANCL, PIPD

Smith's SC business directory: trade index & shipper's guide to
40 SC towns. Chstn: Marion C. Smith, 1876. 145 p. SCL, SPCL
Smith, Warren B. White servitude in colonial SC. Cola: USC
Press, 1961. 151 p.   COMMON
Smith, William A. Pinehaven Sanatorium: recollections, remini-
scences & reflections of its erstwhile medical director.
Chstn: Nelson's Southern Printing, 1966. 99 p. SCL,CLEM, SCHS
Smith, William R. SC as a royal province, 1719-1776. NY: Mac-
millan, 1903. 441 p.   COMMON
Smoak, W. W. ...Historical outline of Colleton County, SC.
Charlotte NC: typescript, 1933. 8 p.   SCL
Smythe, Augustus T. Centennial address delivered before the
Hibernian Society of Charleston, SC, on its one hundredth
anniversary, 18th March, 1902. Chstn: W,E&C, 1902. 58 p.
                                                        SCHS, SCL
Smyth, William D. A southern odyssey: South Carolinians abroad
in the 1850's. Thesis (M.A.), U.S.C., 1977. 98 p.   SCL
Snowden, Yates. History of the New England Society of Charles-
ton, SC, 1819-1919. Chstn: W,E&C, 1920? 16 p.   SCL
Snowden, Yates. History of SC. NY: Lewis, 1920. 5 vol. COMMON
Snowden, Yates. Notes on labor organizations in SC, 1742-1861.
Cola: USC Press, 1914. 54 p.   SCL, FLMC
Snowden, Yates. The planters of St. John's [parish]: remarks
of professor Yates Snowden...April 13, 1915. Baltimore MD:
Waverly Press, 1915. 15 p.   YOCL, SCL
Société Francaise. 150th anniversary...1816-1966. Chstn:
W,E&C, 1966. 64 p.   SCL, SCHS
Society of the Colonial Dames of America. South Carolina.
Women to remember, 1670-1810. A view of their times...
Chstn: Furlong, 1976. 31 p.   SCHS
Society for the Preservation of Spirituals. The Carolina low-
country. NY: Macmillan, 1931. 342 p.   COMMON
Solomon, Robert S. The "C.S.S. David"; the story of the first
successful torpedo boat. Cola: RLB, 1970. 44 p.   COMMON
Sompayrac, Hewitt A. Society Hill is Welsh Neck, Long Bluff,
old Greenville: a brief history... NP: author, 1976. 36 p.
                                                           COMMON
South Carolina. Agricultural & Mechanical Society. History of
the State Agricultural Society of SC from 1839 to 1845, incl.
...[and] 1855 to 1861, incl...[and] 1869 to 1916, incl.
Cola: RLB, 1916. 306 p.   COKL, SCHS
South Carolina. Agriculture Department. Resources & population
institutions & industries. Chstn: W,E&C, 1883. 726 p. COMMON
South Carolina and the sea: day by day toward five centuries,
1492-1976. Chstn: W,E&C, 1976. 2 vol.   COMMON
South Carolina architecture, 1670-1970. Cola: Tricentennial
Commission, 1970.   COMMON
South Carolina. Archives Department. Guide maps to the devel-
opment of SC parishes, districts & counties. Cola: SCAD,
1964.   COMMON
South Carolina Canal and Railroad Company. By-laws...1828

Chstn: James S. Burges, 1828. 16 p.   SCL, WOFF
South Carolina College. Centennial celebration...held in
Charleston, SC, Dec. 19-20, 1901. Chstn: Lucas & Richardson,
1902. 117 p.   SCHS
South Carolina College. Proceedings of the centennial celebra-
tion of South Carolina College, Jan. 8, 9, & 10, 1905. Cola:
State Co., 1905. 239 p.   SCL, WOFF
South Carolina College. Semi-centennial celebration of the
South Carolina College... Chstn: W,E&C, 1855. 32 p. SCL,SCHS
South Carolina. Confederate War Centennial Commission. South
Carolina fights: the palmetto state in the Confederate War.
NP: author, 1961? 8 p.   SCL
South Carolina. Department of Archives & History. Official SC
historical markers: a directory. Cola: SCDAH, 1978. 156 p.
                                                          COMMON
South Carolina. Department of Archives & History. Preservation
plan & survey, lowcountry region. Cola: SCDAH, 1973. COMMON
South Carolina. Department of Archives & History. Revolution-
ary battles, skirmishes & actions in SC. Cola: American
Revolution Bicentennial Committee, 1976. 16 p.   COMMON
South Carolina. Department of Parks, Recreation & Tourism.
Charles Towne Landing, 1670. The site of the first permanent
settlement of SC. Chstn, author, 1974? 32 p.   COMMON
South Carolina. Department of Parks, Recreation & Tourism.
South Carolina's historic & contemporary house & building
tours. Cola: author, 1970. unp.   COMMON
South Carolina Female Collegiate Institute. A Barhamville misc-
ellany. Notes & documents concerning the SC Female Collegiate
Institute, 1826-1865... Cola: USC Press, 1956. 72 p.SCL,SCHS
South Carolina Genealogical Society. Pedigree charts... 2 vol.
                                                          COMMON
South Carolina. General Assembly. Proceedings of the centen-
nial celebration of the first meeting of the General Assembly
of the state of SC...1791. Celebrated...1891. Cola: Centennial Committee, 1893. 40 p.   SCL, SCHS
South Carolina Historical Society. South Carolina General File:
Localities. The following are file folders of varied information, consisting of typescripts, photographs, newspaper
clippings, etc., on the following locations and subjects:
Abbeville County, Beaufort, Beaufort County, Berkeley County,
Bull's Island in Beaufort County, Calhoun, Charles Towne Land-
ing, Charleston fortifications from 1670-1860, Charleston
social life, Charleston County, Chester County, Childsbury
Town, Clarendon County, Colleton County, Columbia, Craven
County, Dorchester County, Edgefield County, Eutawville, Fair-
field County, Georgetown, Georgetown County, Greenville Coun-
ty, Greenwood County, Horry County, Isle of Palms, Kershaw
County, Lancaster County, Laurens County, Sullivan's Island,
Sullivan's Island architecture, Liberty County, Marlboro
County, Marion, Newberry County, Orangeburg County, Parris
Island, Pendleton, St. John's Parish-Berkeley, Spartanburg

(South Carolina General File: Localities - continued.) Coun-
ty, Sumter County, Union County, Williamsburg County, Winton
County, York County, Pickens County, Folly Beach, Legareville,
Hilton Head Island, John's Island, Walterboro, Morris Island,
Morris Island during the Civil War, Oconee County, Anderson
County, Aiken County, Cherokee County, Darlington County,
Chesterfield County, Barnwell County, Cainhoy on Edisto Island, Richland County, McClellanville, Secessionville, Saluda County, Lexington County, Allendale County, Florence Coun-
ty, Florence, Dillon County, St. Helena's Island, McCormick
County, Adam's Run, Pawley's Island, Bamberg County, Stalls-
ville, Mt. Pleasant, Cool Blow Village, West Columbia, Barn-
well County, Charleston harbor, Dorchester, Indian Fields
Campground in Dorchester County, Charleston Navy Yard, Conway, Myrtle Beach, St. George, Ridgeville, Cypress Campground
in Dorchester County, Rock Hill, Pineville, Aiken, Anderson,
Willtown, New London, Camden, Kiawah Island, Clio, Marlboro
County, Marion County, Mayesville, Spartanburg, Laurens,
Hampton County, Greenville, Darlington, Greenwood, Hartsville,
McColl, Newberry, Orangeburg, Good Hope Camp in Ridgeland,
Riverfalls, Sumter, Westminster, White Rock, Winnsboro, Bel-
ton, Bennettsville, Blackville, Ceasar's Head, Cheraw, Ches-
ter, Chick Springs, Clinton, Goose Creek, Ingleside, Clemson,
Givhans State Park, Granby Ferry, Wadmalaw Island [end].
South Carolina Jockey Club. [History]. Chstn: Russell & Jones,
    1857. 48 p.   SCL, WOFF, SCHS
South Carolina Medical Association. A brief history... To
    which are added short historical sketches of various medical
    institutions & societies of SC. Chstn, 1948. 195 p. SCL,SCHS
South Carolina. Medical University. Sesquicentennial, 1824-
    1974, College of Medicine, Medical University of SC. Chstn:
    author, 1974. 111 p.   SCHS
South Carolina Military Academy. Semi-centennial... 1893.
    Chstn: W,E&C, 1893. 61 p.   SCL, SCHS
South Carolina Monument Association. Origin, history & work;
    with an account of the proceedings at the unveiling of the
    monument to the Confederate dead...1879. Chstn: News & Cour-
    ier, 1879. 70 p.   SCL, SCHS
South Carolina. National Bank. A series of historical sketches
    Chstn, nd. 16 p.   SCHS
South Carolina. Power Company. A century of public service; a
    history & pictorial review of the gas industry in the city
    of Charleston, SC, Dec. 18, 1846-Dec. 18, 1946. Chstn, 1946.
    32 p.   SCHS
South Carolina. Power Company. Seventy seven years of tracks &
    trolleys. Chstn, 1938. 20 p.   SCL, SCHS
South Carolina Public Service Authority. History of the old
    Santee Canal & how this 18th century waterway...lives again
    in the Santee-Cooper hydroelectric & navigation system of
    today. Cola: author, 1945? 1 p.   SCL, SCHS
South Carolina School for the Deaf and the Blind. One hundredth

anniversary: 1849-1949. Spartanburg, 1949. 20 p. SCL, SCHS
South Carolina Society. Bicentennial celebration, March 30,
1937. Chstn, 1938. 30 p.   SCHS
South Carolina Society. The rules of the South Carolina Society
established...1737...containing...a complete roster of officers, members & benefactors and an historical account of the
institution from the date of its foundation to the year 1937,
by J. H. Easterby... 17th ed. Baltimore MD: Waverly Press,
1937. 170 p.   COMMON
South Carolina Tricentennial Commission. Festival of History.
SC tricentennial celebration, 1670-1970. Cola: author, 1967.
20 p.   SCL, SCHS
South Carolina. University. The Clariosophic and Euphradian
Societies of the University of South Carolina, 1806-1931.
Cola: USC, 1931. 64 p.   SCL, SCHS
Southern Studies Program, U.S.C. Figures of the Revolution in
SC, an anthology: Aiken. Cola: author, 1976. 18 p.   COMMON
Southern Studies Program, U.S.C. Figures of the Revolution in
SC, an anthology: Anderson. Cola: author, 1976. 169 p.COMMON
Southern Studies Program, U.S.C. Figures of the Revolution in
SC, an anthology: Beaufort. Cola: author, 1976. 170 p.COMMON
Southern Studies Program, U.S.C. Figures of the Revolution in
SC, an anthology: Florence. Cola: author, 1976. 204 p.COMMON
Southern Studies Program, U.S.C. Figures of the Revolution in
SC, an anthology: Georgetown. Cola: author, 1976. 194 p.
                                                            COMMON
Southern Studies Program, U.S.C. Figures of the Revolution in
SC, an anthology: Spartanburg. Cola: author, 1976. 187 p.
                                                            COMMON
Southern Studies Program, U.S.C. Historic courthouses of SC:
Abbeville. Cola: author, 1980. 16 p.   COMMON
Southern Studies Program, U.S.C. Historic courthouses of SC:
Charleston. Cola: author, 1980. 14 p.   COMMON
Southern Studies Program, U.S.C. Historic courthouses of SC:
Colleton. Cola: author, 1980. 12 p.   COMMON
Southern Studies Program, U.S.C. Historic courthouses of SC:
Kershaw. Cola: author, 1980. 19 p.   COMMON
Southern Studies Program, U.S.C. SC journals & journalists:
proceedings of the Reynolds conference, U.S.C., May 17-18,
1974. Cola: author, 1975. 2 vol.   COMMON
Souvenir, Laurens city schools, 1904-1905. Containing sketches
of the Laurensville Female College, town of Laurens,and or-
ganizations of the city schools... Laurens?: NPub, nd. 75 p.
                                                              LRCL
A souvenir of Aiken. Aiken: King Printing Co., 1975. 32 p.
                                                              AICL
Souvenir of Camp Wadsworth, Spartanburg, SC. Atlanta GA: Byrd
Printing Co., nd. unp.   SPCL
Sparkman, Mary A. Through the turnstile into yesteryear.
Chstn: W,E&C, 1966. 50 p.   COMMON
[Spartanburg] City & county of Spartanburg. Their wonderful

attractions &...advantages as a place of settlement... Spartanburg: Cofield, Petty & Co., 1888. 44 p.   SCL, WOFF, SPCL
Spartanburg, SC: the heart of the Piedmont section of the Carolinas. Spartanburg: Spartanburg Chamber of Commerce, 1920? 27 p.   SCL, WOFF
Spicer, William A. The flag replaced on [Fort] Sumter. Providence RI: Providence Printing Co., 1885. 76 p.   SCL
Springs, Elliott W. The early settlers of Fort Mill township. NP: author, 1938.   YOCL
Sprunt, Alexander Jr. Carolina low country impressions. NY: Devin-Adair, 1964. 191 p.   SCL, MRCL, KECL, PICL
Stanley, Victor B. Historical, biographical, genealogical & economic articles pertaining to the Pee Dee section of SC [SpC]
    MACL
The State, Columbia. College of Charleston... South Carolina's oldest college; its history & its aspirations. Cola: The State Co., nd. 16 p.   SCL, SCHS
The State, Columbia. Sesqui-centennial edition, commemorating the founding of South Carolina's capital city, 1794-1865. Cola: State Co., 1936. v.p.   SCL, CLEM
The State, Columbia. SC in the Revolution. Bicentennial edition. Cola: State Co., 1976. 72 p.   COMMON
The State-The Columbia Record. The burning of Columbia, 1865. Cola: author, 1965. 80 p.   COMMON
Statistics which may be of service to the people of SC. By a Charlestonian. Chstn: Evans & Cogswell, 1860. 10 p.   WOFF
Steedman, Marguerite C. The SC colony. NY: Crowell-Collier, 1970. 134 p.   COMMON
Steele, John C. Charleston then & now. Cola: RLB, 1974. 118 p.   SCL, GTML
Stevens, E. W. Historical outline of Berkeley County, SC. NP: typescript, 1933. 8 p.   SCHS, SCL
Stevenson, Mary. The diary of Clarissa Adger Bowen, Ashtabula plantation, 1865... Pendleton: Pendleton District Historical & Recreational Commission & Foundation for Historic Restoration in the Pendleton Area, 1973. 128 p.   COMMON
Stevenson, Mary. The recollections of a happy childhood. NP: Foundation for Historic Restoration in the Pendleton Area, 1976. 85 p.   SCL, PIPD
Stockman, James E. & D. S. Shull. Lexington County, economic & social. Cola: USC, 1923. 93 p.   COMMON
Stokely, Jim. Constant defender: the story of Fort Moultrie. Washington DC: National Park Service, 1978. 94 p.   GRCL
Stokes, Durward T. The history of Dillon County. Cola: USC Press, 1978. 523 p.   COMMON
Stokes, Thomas L. The Savannah [River]. NY: Rinehart, 1951. 401 p.   COMMON
Stoney, Samuel G. Charleston, azaleas & old brick. Boston: Houghton-Mifflin, 1939. 140 p.   COMMON
Stoney, Samuel G. Colonial church architecture in SC. Chstn: Dalcho Historical Society, 1954. 9 p.   SCL, EPDI

Stoney, Samuel G. Plantations of the Carolina low country.
Chstn: Carolina Art Assn., 1939 (rev. ed., 1964). 247 p.
COMMON
Stoney, Samuel G. SC: appraising a culture. Florence: Florence
Museum, 1970. 30 p.   COMMON
Stoney, Samuel G. The story of South Carolina's senior bank,
the Bank of Charleston, mother of the South Carolina National
Bank of Charleston. Cola: RLB, 1955. 73 p.   COMMON
Stoney, Samuel G. This is Charleston. Chstn: Charleston Civic
Service Committee, 1944. 141 p.   COMMON
Stoney, Mrs. Samuel G. Confederate Home & College. Historical
sketch...1867-1921. Chstn: W,E&C, 1921? 22 p.   SCHS
The story of Aiken, told by citizens. Aiken: NPub, 1956. unp.
GWPL
The story of Lander, 1872-1922. NP: NPub, nd.   GNLN
A story of Spartan puck. The greatest cotton manufacturing
centre of the south. Spartanburg, SC. Chstn: News & Courier,
1890. 70 p.   WOFF
Stribling, J. P. Interesting history of Walnut Hill Farm [incl.
Stribling family]. Walhalla: Keowee Courier, 1937. 3 p. CLEM
Strobel, Philip A. The Salzburgers & their descendants: being
the history of a colony of German (Lutheran) Protestants, who
emigrated to GA in 1734,... Baltimore: T. Newton Kurtz, 1855,
rp Easley: SHP, 1980.   SCL
Stuart, Benjamin P. Magnolia cemetery [Charleston]. An interpretation of some of its monuments & inscriptions, with a rem-
iniscence of Captain James Stuart, a notice of John Allan Stuart, & a tribute to the people of Beaufort. Chstn: Kahrs &
Welch, 1896. 68 p.   SCL, SCHS, CHCO, SCLB
Stubbs, Thomas M. A history of Claremont Lodge No. 64, A.F.M.
[Freemasons], 1854-1949. Together with that of earlier lod-
ges in Sumter County and of the lodges growing out of Clare-
mont Lodge No. 64. Sumter: Osteen-Davis, 1950.131 p.SCL, SCHS
Stubbs, Thomas M. History of the Supreme Court, SC. NP: NPub,
1951? 8 p.   SCL, SCHS
Stuckey, J. F. Early history of Bishopville & vicinity [SpC]
LECL
Sullivan's Island: the sea side resort of SC. Its history...
Chstn: A.M. Cochran, 1884. 84 p.   SCL
Summer, George L, Sr. Folklore of SC, including central & Dutch
Fork sections of the state, and much data on the early Quaker
& Covenanter customs, etc., 1950.   SCL, FACL, NWRL
Summerville, SC, the greatest health resort of the southern
states. NP: NPub, 187? 8 p.   SCHS
Summerville, SC. [Brochure.] 14 p.   SCL, SCHS
Summerville, SC. Charlotte NC: Queen City Printing Co., 191?.
16 p.   SCL, DOTM, SCHS, MONT
[Summerville, SC] Points of interest around Summerville. Sum-
merville: Driggers, 1905. 29 p.   SCHS
Sumner, George L. Newberry County, SC: historical & genealogical annals. 1950, rp Baltimore MD: GPC, 1980. 483 p. COMMON

Sumter Artists' Guild. Sumter County - historical vignettes.
Sumter: Sumter Tricentennial Commission, 1970. unp.   COMMON

Sumter, SC. Encino CA: Windsor Publ., 1970. 48 p.   SCL, GRCL

Sumter Chamber of Commerce. Sumter, SC, the gamecock city.
Sumter: author, 193?.   SCHS

Sumter, SC, sesqui-centennial, 1800-1950. 150 years of progress
& development. NP: NPub, nd. 52 p.   SCL, COKL

Sumter, Thomas S. Stateburg & its people. Some old Stateburg
homes & the Church of the Holy Cross [Episcopal]. 2nd ed.
Sumter: Sumter Printing Co., 1949. 116 p.   COMMON

Survey of historical sites: Chester County. Rock Hill: Central
Piedmont Regional Planning Commission, 1971. 74 p.   COMMON

Swanberg, W. A. First blood: the story of Fort Sumter. NY:
Scribner, 1957. 373 p.   COMMON

Sweet, Ethel W. Camden homes & heritage. Camden: Kershaw County Historical Society, 1978. 80 p.   COMMON

Swindell, Anna T. The burning of Columbia. NP: NPub, nd.
25 p.   SCL

Tarleton, Banastre. A history of the campaigns of 1780 & 1781,
in the southern provinces of North America. London: 1781; rp
Spartanburg: RPC, 1968. 518 p.   COMMON

Taylor, Benjamin F. The Darlington riot. Cola: USC Press, 1910
11 p.   FLMC, SCL

Taylor, John S. 16th S.C. Regiment, C.S.A., from Greenville,
SC. Greenville: author, 1964. 52 p.   COMMON

Taylor, Mary. A history of the Memminger Normal School,
Charleston, SC. Chstn: W,E&C, 1941. 89 p.   SCL, SCHS, CHCO

Taylor, Rosser H. Ante-bellum SC: a social & cultural history.
Chapel Hill NC: UNC Press, 1942. 201 p.   COMMON

Teal, Isom. Chesterfield County, economic & social. Cola: USC,
1922. 88 p.   COMMON

Tennent, Mary A. Light in darkness: the story of William Tennent, Sr., & the log college. Greensboro NC: Greensboro
Printing Co., 1971. 282 p.   SCL, SPCL

Thomas, J. A. W. A history of Marlboro County, with traditions
& sketches of numerous families. 1897, rp Baltimore MD:
Regional Publishing Co., 1971. 325 p.   COMMON

Thomas, John P. The formation of judicial & political sub-
divisions in SC. Cola: RLB, 1890. 26 p.   SCL

Thomas, John P. Historical sketch of the South Carolina Military Academy. Chstn: W,E&C, 1879. 100 p.   SCL, SCHS, WOFF

Thomas, John P. History of the South Carolina Military Academy,
with appendixes. Chstn: W,E&C, 1893. 579 p.   COMMON

Thomas, John P. SC in arms, arts & the industries. NY: Brown &
Warner, 1875. 28 p.   SCL

Thomas, Theodore G. A contribution to the history of the Huguenots of SC, consisting of pamphlets by Samuel DuBose...&
Prof. Frederick A. Porcher... NY: Knickerbocker Press, 1887.
176 p.   COMMON

Tompkins, Daniel A. Company "K", 14th S.C. Volunteers. Charlotte NC: Observer Press, 1897. 36 p.   UMBOD, SCL

Thompson, Edgar T. Dillon County, economic & social. Cola: USC
1922. 84 p.   COMMON
Thompson, Elizabeth C. Chester County's black heritage. Ches-
ter: Chester County Arts Council, 1978. 66 p.   CSCL
Thompson, Henry T. The establishment of the public school sys-
tem of SC. Cola: RLB, 1927. 61 p.   SCL, EDTO
Thompson, Henry T. Historical sketch & roster of the
Battalion, S.C. Volunteer Infantry... Cola: RLB, 1901. 37 p.
                                                              SCL
Thompson, William W. History of Mackey Lodge No. 77, Ancient
Free Masons of Dillon, SC. NP: NPub, 1953. 72 p. DICL, FLMC
Three Rivers Historical Society. Index to McGill's Reminiscen-
ses of Williamsburg County, SC. Hemingway: author, 1979.
23 p.   WMTR, CLEM
Tilley, John S. Facts the historians leave out. NP: Paragon
Press, 1951.   SPCL
Tillman, Benjamin R. MA & SC in the Revolution. Washington:
GPO, 1902. 28 p.   SCL
Tobias, Thomas J. The cemetery we rededicate...Kahal Kadosh
Beth Elohim [Synagogue]. Coming Street Cemetery. 1764-1964...
Chstn, 1964.   SCL, CHCO
Tobias, Thomas J. The Hebrew Benevolent Society of Charleston,
SC, founded 1784. Chstn: Hebrew Benevolent Society, 1965.
62 p.   COMMON
Tobias, Thomas J. The Hebrew Orphan Society of Charleston,
founded 1801; an historical sketch. Chstn: Hebrew Orphan
Society, 1957. 61 p.   COMMON
Todd, John R. Prince William's parish & plantations. Richmond
VA: Garrett & Massie, 1935. 265 p.   COMMON
Tolbert, Joseph W. The story of the old Star Fort at Ninety-
Six, Greenwood County, SC. NP: author, 1921. 16 p.   COKL
Tompkins, Daniel A. Company "K", Fourteenth S.C. Volunteers.
Charlotte NC: UMBOD, SCL
Toole, Casper L. Ninety years in Aiken County. Chstn: W,E&C,
1957? 404 p.   COMMON
Toomer, Joshua W. An oration...at the celebration of the first
centennial anniversary of the South Carolina Society...1837.
Chstn: A.E. Miller, 1837. 94 p.   SCL, FLMC, SCHS
Tower, Roderick. The defense of Fort Sumter. Chstn: W,E&C,
1938. 39 p.   USAI, SCL
Towne, Laura M. Letters & diary of Laura M. Towne; written from
the sea islands of SC, 1862-1884. Cambridge MA: Riverside
Press, 1912. 364 p.   COMMON
Trenholm, William L. The centennial address before the Charles-
ton Chamber of Commerce... Chstn: News & Courier, 1884. 50
p.   CLEM, SCL
Trezevant, Daniel H. The burning of Columbia, SC. Cola: S.C.
Steam Power Press, 1866. 27 p.   COMMON
The Truth Company. Spartanburg County, SC. Spartanburg: The
Truth Co., nd. 23 p.   SCL
The truth about the cotton mills of SC. NP: NPub, 1929. 18 p.
                                                             WOFF

113

Two diaries from middle St. John's [Parish], Berkeley, SC, Feb-
ruary-May, 1865...by Miss Susan R. Jervey & Miss Charlotte
St. J. Ravenel...& reminiscences of Mrs. (Waring) Henagen.
NP: St. John's Hunting Club, 1921.   SCL, CHCO
Uhlendorf, Bernard A. The siege of Charleston. NY: NY Times &
Arno Press, 1968. 445 p.   COMMON
Union County Historical Foundation. A history of Union County,
SC. Union: author, 1971. 133 p.   COMMON
Union County Historical Foundation. Index [to] land grant maps
[covering parts of Chester, Fairfield, Greenville, Laurens,
Newberry, Spartanburg & Union Counties]. Greenville: A Press,
1976. 28 p.   COMMON
U.D.C. A. Manigault Chapter. For love of a rebel. Chstn:
W,E&C, 1964. 212 p.   COMMON
U.D.C. Stephen D. Lee Chapter. Yesteryear in Clinton. NP:
NPub, 1976. 3 vol.   LRCL
U.S. Army War College. The battle of Camden, SC. Washington:
GPO, 1929. 64 p.   USAI, SCL
U.S. Congress. House of Representatives. Navy yard, Charles-
ton. Washington DC: Blair & Rivers, 1836? 46 p.   SCL
U.S. Congress. House of Representatives. Defences of the
harbor of Charleston, and the distribution of arms. Washing-
ton: GPO, 1861. 7 p.   SCL
U.S. Congress. House of Representatives. Georgetown harbor-
Sampit River...Winyah Bay, SC. Washington: GPO, nd. 19 p.SCL
U.S. Congress. House of Representatives. Navy yard - Charles-
ton, SC. Washington: Gales & Seaton, 1834? 40 p.   SCL
U.S. Congress. Senate. Destruction of property in Columbia,
SC, by Sherman's Army. Washington: GPO, 1930. 112 p.SCL,ORCL
U.S. Congress. Senate. Memorial of a number of citizens of
Charleston, SC, praying the establishment of a navy yard at
that place...1837. Np: NPub, nd. 6 p.   SCL
Up to Date Club, Chester. Fond recollections [of Chester].
Chester: author, 1976. 148 p.   SCL, CSCL
Upper Long Cane Society, Abbeville. The constitution & by-laws
...with a short sketch of its organization. Abbeville: Wilson
& Wardlaw, 1881. 23 p.   SCL
VanClayton, Frederick. The settlement of Pendleton District,
1777-1800. Thesis (M.A.), U.S.C., 1930. 123 p.   PIPD, SCL
Vandiver, Louise A. Traditions & history of Anderson County.
Atlanta GA: RURalist Press, 1928. 318 p.   COMMON
Vandiver, Louise A. History of Anderson County. Revised ed.
Anderson: R.M. Smith, 1970. 327 p.   COMMON
Variety Club, Chester. Scrapbook of historical information
about, & recollections of, Chester County schools, 1811-1976.
NP: typescript, 1976? unp.   CSCL
Vaughan, Celina M. Pawley's [Island]-as it was. Cola: State
Co., 1969. 73 p.   COMMON
Vedder, Charles S. The Huguenot Society of SC. NP: NPub, nd.
pp. 217-223 from ?   SCL
VerSteeg, Clarence L. Origins of a southern mosaic. Studies of

early Carolina & GA. Athens GA: University of Georgia Press,
1975. 152 p.   GRCL, SCL
Vexler, Robert I. & William F. Swindler. Chronology & documen-
tary handbook of SC. Dobbs Ferry NY: Oceana Publications,
1979. 147 p.   CRCL, SCL
Views of prominent places in Charleston, SC, the cyclone of 1885
Chstn: A.M. Cochran, 1885.   SCL, SPCL
Vigilant Steam Fire Engine Co. Constitution. Chstn: J.S. Burgess, 1875. 13 p.   SCL
Voigt, Gilbert P. The German & German-Swiss element in SC
[Saxe-Gotha or Congaree section], 1732-1752. Cola: USC, 1922.
60 p.   COMMON
von Kolnitz, Alfred H. The battery in Charleston, SC; a panorama of three centuries of history viewed from Charleston's
famous Battery. Chstn: Historical Commission of Charleston,
1937. 36 p.   COMMON
von Kolnitz, Sarah C. History of the South Carolina Society of
the Colonial Dames in America, 1893-1935. NP: Colonial
Dames, 1935. 26 p.   SCHS
The Waccamaw Club. Sumter: NPub, nd. 8 p.   SCL
Waccamaw Regional Planning & Development Council. An enviorn-
mental, historical & recreation atlas of the Waccamaw region.
Georgetown: author, 1973. 77 p.   SCL, GTML
Waccamaw Regional Planning & Development Council. Horry County
survey of historic places. Rev. ed. Georgetown: author,
1973. 117 p.   SCL, SCHS, HOCL
Waccamaw Regional Planning & Development Commission. Waccamaw:
survey of historic places. Georgetown: author, 1971.   GTML
Walhalla Centennial Committee. Souvenir program: Walhalla cen-
tennial...1950. Walhalla: author, 1950. unp.   SCL, CLEM
Walhalla, Oconee County, SC... Chstn: Perry, 1888? 20 p. SCHS
Walker, Cornelius I. The Carolina Rifle Club. Chstn: NPub,
1904? 78 p.   SCL, FLMC, SCHS
Walker, Cornelius I. Guide to Charleston, SC; with brief his-
tory of the city & map thereof. Chstn: W,E&C, 1919. 126 p.
                                                         SCL, SCHS
Walker, Cornelius I. Historic Charleston; colonial, Revolution-
ary & Confederate. Chstn: Southern Printing Co., 1927. 18 p.
                                                              SCHS
Walker, Cornelius I. History of the Agricultural Society of SC.
Chstn: author, 1919? 168 p.   SCL, ORCL, SCHS
Walker, Cornelius I. The romance of lower Carolina. Chstn:
Art Publishing Co., 1915. 161 p.   COMMON
Walker, Evans & Cogswell. Earthquake views, Charleston, SC.
After the great earthquake, 9:54 P.M., Aug. 31, 1886. Chstn:
W,E&C, 1886.   SCHS
Walker, George E. Exposition of the proceedings of commission -
ers of the new State Capitol, Columbia, SC. Cola: R.M. Stokes
1855. 66 p.   SCL
Walker, George R. Newington plantation & the Summerville Coun-
try Club. NP: typescript, 1940. 11 p.   SCHS

Walker, Legare. Dorchester County, SC, a history... Summerville: typescript, 1941; published Chstn: Walker Family, 1979. 385 p. COMMON
Walker, Legare. General ordinances of the town of Summerville, SC,...a sketch of Summerville; and a partial list of its intendants and mayors and other officers... Summerville: S.P. Driggers, 1912. CHCO
Walker, Legare. Post offices in the village and town of Summerville, SC. Summerville, 1938. 12 p. SCHS, SCL
Walker, Legare. A sketch of the town of Summerville, SC. Summerville, 1910. 27 p. COMMON
Walker, O. K. Historic Edgefield County, 1787-1960. Augusta GA: Commercial Printing Co., 1960. unp. EDTO
Wallace, David D. Civil government of SC. Dallas TX: Southern Publishing Co., 1906. 167 p. COMMON
Wallace, David D. Constitutional history of SC, from 1725 to 1775. Abbeville: Hugh Wilson, 1899. 93 p. COMMON
Wallace, David D. The history of SC. NY: American Historical Society, 1934. 4 vol. COMMON
Wallace, David D. History of the S.C. Teacher's Association. Cola: State Co., 1924. 56 p. SCHS
Wallace, David D. History of Wofford College, 1854-1949. Nashville TN: Vanderbilt University Press, 1951. 287 p.COMMON
Wallace, David D. SC: a short history. Chapel Hill NC: UNC Press, 1951. 753 p. COMMON
Wallace, James B. A history of Kershaw Lodge No. 29, Ancient Free Masons and the affiliated York Rite bodies of Camden, SC. Camden: NPub, 1953. 93 p. SCL, KECA, SCHS
Wallace, John S. Education for girls in colonial SC. Spartanburg: typescript, 1935. 69 p. SCHS
Walsh, Richard. Charleston's sons of liberty: a study of the artisans, 1763-1789. Cola: USC Press, 1959. 166 p. COMMON
Walsh, Richard. Charleston's sons of liberty: a study of the mechanics, 1760-1785. Thesis (Ph.D.), U.S.C., 1954. 204 p.
SCL

Wannamaker, William J. The battle of Eutaw Springs. Orangeburg: Walter D. Berry, nd. 8 p. COMMON
Wannamaker, W. W. Long Island south: stories of Sullivan's Island and the Isle of Palms, two of South Carolina's barrier beaches. Cola: State Co., 1975. 270 p. COMMON
Wansley, Reba. Iva, SC. Bicentennial number. Anderson: Palmetto Publishing Co., 1976. 36 p. CLEM
Waring, Joseph I. Brief history of the S. C. Medical Association. Cola: RLB, 1948. 197 p. COMMON
Waring, Joseph I. The first voyage & settlement at Charles Town: 1670-1680. Cola: Tricentennial Commission, 1970. 59 p. COMMON
Waring, Joseph I. A history of medicine in SC. 1964-67, rp Spartanburg: RPC, 1977. 3 vol. COMMON
Warr, Osta L. Darlington County, economic & social. Cola: USC, 1927. 66 p. SCHS, SCL

116

Warren, J. L. Little pieces on doings in the nineties [Colle-
ton County]. Walterboro: Press & Standard, 1939. SCL, COML
Washington Light Infantry. An account of the revival of the
company... Chstn: W,E&C, 1873? 86 p. SCL, SPCL, SCHS
Washington Light Infantry. Centennial celebration... Chstn:
author, 1907? 57 p. SCHS
Washington Light Infantry. An historical sketch... NY: Apple-
ton, 1875. 10 p. SCL, SCHS
Washington Light Infantry. Proceedings of the centennial cele-
bration... 1907. Chstn?, 1907. 57 p. SCHS
Watkins, Jack. Happy birthday, Oconee, 1868-1968. NP: NPub,
1968. unp. SCL, GRCL
Watkins, Martin G. Facts of Oconee County. Westminster: Wat-
kins, 1962. 10 p. CLEM
Watson, Alan D. The quitrent system in SC. Thesis (Ph.D.),
U.S.C., 1971. 242 p. SCL
Watson, E. J. The textile industry in SC in the mid-year 1910.
Cola: State Co., 1910. 16 p. SCL, WOFF
Watson, H. L. Ninety-Six: landmarks of South Carolina's last
frontier region. Cola: USC Press, 1950. 117 p.SCL,GTML, BRCL
Watson, Harry L. Our old roads. Scrapbook of serialized news-
paper articles. 8 vol. [SpC] GWPL
Watson, Louise M. Old Ninety-Six, Star Fort, & Cambridge.
Greenwood: Greenwood County Historical Society, 1960. 51 p.
COMMON
Watson, Margaret J. Greenwood County sketches; old roads &
early families. Greenwood: Attic Press, 1970. 425 p. COMMON
Watters, Pat. Events at Orangeburg: a report based on study &
interviews in Orangeburg, SC... Atlanta GA: Southern Regional
Council, 1968. 42 p. CLEM, SCL
Way, William. History of the New England Society of Charleston,
SC. Chstn: New England Society, 1920. 307 p. COMMON
Way, William. History of Orange Lodge, No. 14, Ancient Free
Masons, Charleston, SC...during the Civil War period, 1860-
1865. Chstn, nd. 19 p. SCL, SCHS
Way, William. The old Exchange & Custom House... Chstn: Rebec-
ca Motte Chapter, S.C.D.A.R., 1942. 18 p. COMMON
Webb, Edwin Y. The battle of King's Mountain. Washington: GPO,
1930. 14 p. SCL
Webster, Laura J. The operation of the Freedmen's Bureau in SC.
NY: Russell & Russell, 1970. 97 p. COMMON
Wegner, Daniel P. Recollections of life in a southern textile
mill village. Thesis (M.A.), Clemson, 1979. 85 p. PIPD
Weigley, Russell F. The partisan war: the campaign of 1780-
1782. Cola: USC Press, 1970. 77 p. COMMON
Weir, Robert M. A most important epocha: the coming of the
Revolution in SC. Cola: USC Press, 1970. 80 p. COMMON
Welcome to a great town: Bennettsville, SC. NP: NPub, nd.
8 p. KECA
Wells, Edward L. Hampton & his calvary in '64. Richmond VA:
B.F. Johnson, 1899. 429 p. COMMON

117

Wells, Edward L. A sketch of the Charleston Light Dragoons.
  Chstn: Lucas, Richardson & Co., 1888. 97 p.   SCHS, SCL
Wessinger, Harry E. 60 years with American Legion Post No. 7.
  Lexington: American Legion Post # 7, 1978.   LXCL
Weston, Plowden C. Documents connected with the history of SC..
  . London: privately printed, 1856. 227 p.   SCL
Whelese, Roberta M. & Warren Mersereau. A Greenville County
  album. Greenville: Metropolitan Arts Council & the Friends of
  the Greenville County Library, 1977.   SCL, GRCL
Whitaker, Urban G. The world and Ridgeway, SC. Cola: USC Press
  1967. 94 p.   COMMON
White, Henry A. The making of SC. NY: Silver, Burdett & Co.,
  1914. 344 p.   COMMON
White, Mrs. John G. Old homes of Chester, SC. Chester: Tri-
  County Publishing Co., 1948. 16 p.   SCL, CSCL
White, Katherine K. The King's Mountain men; the story of the
  battle, with sketches of the American soldiers who took part.
  Dayton VA: Joseph K. Ruebush Co., 1924. 271 p.   COMMON
White, Laura P. Plantations on the Cooper River. Typescript.
                                                        SCHS
White, Pamela M. "Free & open": the radical University of S.C.,
  1873-1877. Thesis (M.A.), U.S.C., 1975. 66 p.   SCL
White, William B. Jr. A history of the public schools of the
  city of Rock Hill, SC, 1888-1951. Thesis (M.A.), U.S.C.,
  1952. 150 p.   YOCL, SCL
White, William B. Jr. Sixty-five historic spots of York County,
  SC. NP: typescript, 1970.   YOCL
Whitelaw, Robert N. Charleston, come hell or high water. Cola:
  RLB, 1976. 232 p.   COMMON
The Whitmire area history. Clinton: Intercollegiate Press,
  1980. 128 p.   SCL, NWRL
Whitmire Parent-Teacher Association. Program of founder's day
  celebration...honoring...Phoebe Hearst...whose ancestors
  founded Whitmire, SC. Whitmire: NPub, 1936. 8 p.   SCL
Whitney, Edson L. Government of the colony of SC. 1895, rp
  NY: Negro Universities Press, 1969. 121 p.   COMMON
Whitten, Benjamin O. A history of Whitten village. NP: Jacobs
  Press, 1967. 188 p.   COMMON
Who burnt Columbia? Part 1st. Official depositions of Wm. Te-
  cumseh Sherman and Gen. O. O. Howard... Extracts from some
  of the depositions for the claimants... Chstn: W,E&C, 1873.
  121 p.   SCHS, SCL
Wiggins, Archibald L. Hartsville's most creative years, 1889-
  1904. NP: mimeo, 1966.   COKL, SCL
Wiggins, A. Lee The Hartsville community center & the Hartsville Memorial Library, 1933-1966. Hartsville: mimeo, 1966.
  13 p.   COKL
Wiggins, A. Lee. One hundred years of J. L. Coker & Co., 1865-
  1965. Hartsville: author, 1966. 36 p.   SCL, COKL
Wilcox, Arthur M. The Civil War at Charleston. Chstn: Post-
  Courier, 1980. 84 p.   SCL, SCHS

Wilkes, Marion R. History of Laurens County, SC. Part 1: Earliest times to 1840. NP: typescript, 1945. 150 p.   LRCL
Wilkes, Marion R. Rosemont & its famous daughter: the story of
  Rosemont plantation, Laurens County, SC, & Ann Pamela Cunningham... Washington DC, 1947. 36 p.   SCL, CLEM, SCHS
Willcox, Clarke A. Musings of a hermit at three score & ten,
  with historical sketches of places on the Waccamaw Neck. 2nd
  ed. NP: W,E&C, 1967. 153 p.   SCL, HOCL, GRCL
Willet, N.L. Beaufort County, SC; the shrines, early history &
  topography. Revised ed. Beaufort: Chamber of Commerce, 1940.
  32 p.   SCL, SCHS, SPCL
Williams, George W. History of Banking in SC from 1712-1900.
  Chstn: W,E&C, 1900.   SCL, WOFF, CHCO
Williams, Jack K. Vogues in villany: crime & retribution in
  ante-bellum SC. Cola: USC Press, 1959. 191 p.   SCL, SCHS
Williams, James F. Old & new Columbia. Cola: Epworth Orphanage Press, 1929. 157 p.   COMMON
Williams, John G. De ole plantation. Chstn: W,E&C, 1895. 67
  p.   SCL, WOFF
Willis, Eola. The Charleston stage in the eighteenth century.
  Cola: State Co., 1924. 483 p.   COMMON
Williston Tricentennial Committee. History of Williston, SC.
  NP: author, 1970. 28 p.   GNLN, SCL
Wilson, Jane L. Memories of Society Hill. Hartsville: Hartsville Publishing Co., 1910. 87 p.   SCL, COKL
Wilson, Miriam B. Street strolls around Charleston, SC. Chstn:
  NPub, 1946. 124 p.   COMMON
Wilson, Robert. An address delivered before the St. John's
  Hunting Club, at Indianfield plantation, St. John's [Parish],
  Berkeley...together with an historical sketch of the club,
  rules and list of members. Chstn: W,E&C, 1907. 25 p.SCL,SCHS
Wilson, Robert. Half forgotten by-ways of the old south. Cola:
  State Co., 1928. 321 p.   COMMON
Wilson, Winship M. Archdale: a history of the settlement &
  growth of a quiet little village. NP: M.W. Wall, 1912. 34
  p.   CLBC
Winthrop Normal & Industrial College. Anniversary number. Rock
  Hill: NPub, 1912. unp.   WOFF
Winyaw & All Saints Agricultural Society. Constitution...1842.
  Georgetown: Observer Press, 1842? 7 p.   SCHS
Winyah Indigo Society. Rules of the Winyah Indigo Society of
  Georgetown, SC,... & a list of...members from 1755-1938.
  Chstn: W,E&C, 1938.   COMMON
Wise, Clarice J. History of Trenton, SC, 1877-1977. NP: mimeo,
  nd. unp.   EDTO
Wittkowsky, George H. Kershaw County, economic & social. Cola:
  USC, 1923. 89 p.   COMMON
The Woman's Association for the Improvement of Rural Schools in
  SC. Cola: Office of the State Superintendent of Education,
  1906. 24 p.   SCHS
Wood, E. J. Aiken, SC, as a winter resort for invalids, or a

desirable location for permanent residents... Aiken: author,
1871. 47 p.   SCL, CLEM
Woodmason, Charles. The Carolina backcountry on the eve of the
Revolution. Chapel Hill NC: UNC Press, 1953. 305 p.   COMMON
Woodson, Hortense. Come out, brave men of Edgefield! Edgefield
Edgefield Advertiser Press, 1960. 94 p.   EDTO, SCL
Wootten, Bayard M. Charleston; azaleas & old brick. Boston:
Houghton-Mifflin Co., 1937. 24 p.   COMMON
Workman, W. D. Jr. The settling of SC. Cola: State-Columbia
Record, 1969. 130 p.   COMMON
W. P. A. Federal Writer's Project. Beaufort & the sea islands.
Savannah: Review Printing Co., 1938. 47 p.   COMMON
W. P. A. Federal Writer's Project. Our SC, today from yester-
day. Clinton: P.C. Press, 1942. 436 p.   COMMON
W. P. A. Federal Writer's Project. SC: a guide to the Palmetto
state. NY: Oxford University Press, 1941. 514 p.   COMMON
W. P. A. Federal Writer's Project. Spartanburg Unit. Clifton
cotton factory; and, Clifton: what brains, labor & money will
accomplish. Spartanburg: typescript, nd. 16 p.   SPCL
W. P. A. Federal Writer's Project. Spartanburg Unit. College
of the poor: our public schools; Prof. Gamewell on the founding of the Y.M.C.A.; the Kennedy Library; Cannon's Camp Meeting; Dr. Vandiver talks. Spartanburg: typescript, nd. 14
p.   SPCL
W. P. A. Federal Writer's Project. Spartanburg Unit. Glimp-
ses of earlier days & ways in Spartanburg. Spartanburg: typescript, nd. 35 p.   SPCL
W. P. A. Federal Writer's Project. Spartanburg Unit. Grindal
Shoals; old Pinckneyville; Maj. Thomas Young's memoirs; Cane
Creek Church; Jefferies' reminiscences of the Revolution.
Spartanburg: typescript, nd. v.p.   SPCL
W. P. A. Federal Writer's Project. Spartanburg Unit. Historic
views of Spartanburg... Spartanburg: typescript, nd. 38
p.   SPCL
W. P. A. Federal Writer's Project. Spartanburg Unit. The
history of Converse; how it came to have a fine female college... Spartanburg: typescript, nd. 17 p.   SPCL
W. P. A. Federal Writer's Project. Spartanburg Unit. A history of Spartanburg County. Spartanburg: Band & White, 1940.
304 p.   COMMON
W. P. A. Federal Writer's Project. Spartanburg Unit. The
history of the town of Spartanburg, 1785-1900... Spartanburg:
typescript, nd. 27 p.   SPCL
W. P. A. Federal Writer's Project. Spartanburg Unit. Journal
of Captain Michael Gaffney. Spartanburg: typescript, nd.
39 p.   SPCL
W. P. A. Federal Writer's Project. Spartanburg Unit. May day
stories. Spartanburg: typescript, nd. 55 p.   SPCL
W. P. A. Federal Writer's Project. Spartanburg Unit. War
time letters; from a Revolutionary soldier, a Confederate
soldier, a World War I soldier's wife, and a freedman in 1867.
                                                         SPCL

Wright, Louis B.   Barefoot in Arcadia: memories of a more inno-
   cent era.   Cola: USC Press, 1974.   175 p.   COMMON
Wright, Louis B.   SC: a bicentennial history.   NY: Norton, 1976.
   225 p.   COMMON
Wright, Russell.   A preservation plan for the Georgetown historic District.   Georgetown: Waccamaw Regional Planning & Development Council, 1974.   58 p.   SCL, SCHS
Yates, William B.   An historical sketch of the rise & progress
   of religious & moral improvement among seamen, in England &
   the U.S., with a history of the Port Society of Charleston,
   SC...   Chstn: A. J. Burke, 1851.   32 p.   SCL, HOCL
Yeaman's Hall Club, Charleston.   NY: Bartlett Orr Press, 1924?
   31 p.   GRCL
Yonge, Francis.   A narrative of the proceedings of the people of
   SC in the year 1719.   1726, rp Washington: P. Force, 1837.
   39 p.   SCL
York, SC [SpC]   YOWC
Young Men's Christian Association.   Half a century in Charleston
   1854-1904.   Chstn, 1904.   47 p.   SCL, SCHS
Zeigler, John A.   History of Berkeley County.   NP: typescript,
   1960.   7 p.   BKCL
Zeigler, John A.   The swamp fox at Pond Bluff.   NP: typescript,
   1960.   13 p.   SCL, BKCL

Abbott, Sarah R. Rembert's church in the olden times: clippings
from an old scrapbook of Mrs. Sarah Rembert Heriot Abbott.
14 p.   SCL
Aimwell Presbyterian Church [SpC]   FACM
Aimwell Presbyterian Church, Ridgeway [SpC]   MONT
Alexander, Maggie. History of Pine Grove church. Typescript,
nd.   DAHC
Alexander, W. R. First Baptist church, Florence, SC. 1866-
1941. 1941.   DAHC
Alice Drive Baptist church, 1956-1966. NP: mimeo, 1966.   FURM
Allen, Clarence B. A brochure of Catfish Creek Baptist Church
[Latta, SC]. 1970.   SCL, DICL
Allen, Clarence B. History of Antioch Baptist church [Marion
County]. Dillon: Herald Press, 1973. 8 p.   FLMC, SCL
Allen, Clarence B. A history of Catfish Creek Baptist church,
Latta, SC. Dillon: Herald Publ. Co., 1971. 27 p.   SCL, FLMC
                                                            DICL
Allen, Mattie M. The story of Mt. Zion Methodist church [Cen-
tral, SC]. 1967. 85 p.   PIPD
Allen, William. Centennial history, 1861-1961, of the Union
Baptist church. Typescript, 1961. 25 p.   FURM
Allen, William C. History of the Beulah Baptist church, Rich-
land County, SC. Cola: Vogue Press, 1962. 88 p.   SCL, FURM
Allen, William C. A history of the First Baptist church, Colum-
bia, SC. Cola: the church, 1959. 240 p.   COMMON
Allen, William C. History of the Pee Dee Baptist Association,
including sketches of churches, biographical sketches, the
Woman's Missionary Union... Dillon: Pee Dee Baptist Assn.,
1924. 232 p.   COMMON
All Saints Episcopal Church, Clinton. Brief history of All
Saints... Clinton: author, 1976.   LRCL
Allston, Susan L. Early sketch of St. John in the Wilderness
[Episcopal church], and Flat Rock, NC. 1964. 37 p. GTML, SCL
Anderson, Emma B. & Julia R. Reynolds. The Church of the Holy
Comforter [Episcopal]. Sumter, SC. 1857-1959. Sumter: Os-
teen-Davis, 1959. 47 p.   SCL, EPDI, SCHS
Anderson, Mrs. Frank. Dedication: White Oak Baptist church.
Greenville: the church, 1963. 3 p.   FURM
Anderson, Hugh G. Lutheranism in the southeastern states, 1860-
1886. A social history. Paris & the Hague: Mouton, 1969.
276 p.   SCL
Anderson, James S. The history of the Church of England in the
colonies & foreign dependencies of the British empire. 2nd
ed. London: Rivington's, 1856. 3 vol.   SCL
Anderson, W. V & J. H. Anderson. History of Mt. Moriah Baptist
church. Typescript, 1933. 8 p.   FURM
Anderson, Wylina. History of Sardis Baptist church. 1950. DAHC

[Andrew Chapel Methodist Church] Methodist Episcopal Church.
  1853-1953. NP: typescript, 1953? 5 p.   WOMA
Apalache Baptist Church, Spartanburg County [SpC]   FURM
Arrington, Charles A. A brief history of Clemson Baptist Church
  1907-1957. NP: mimeo, 1957. 29 p.   PIPD, FURM
Arsenal Hill Presbyterian Church, Columbia [SpC]   MONT
Asbill, Mrs. L. M. The story of Ridge Spring Baptist Church.
  NP: typescript, 1969. 13 p.   FURM
Asbury, Francis. The journal of the Rev. Francis Asbury, Bishop
  of the Methodist Episcopal Church, from August 7, 1771, to
  December 7, 1815... NY: N. Bangs & T. Mason, 1821. 3 vol.
                                                             SCL
Asbury Methodist Church [Pacolet SC]. ...Commemorative program
  of the bicentennial observance. NP: NPub, nd. unp.   WOMA
Ashley River Baptist Church [Charleston]. History of the Ashley
  River Baptist Church, April 18, 1943-April 21, 1946. NP:
  mimeo, 1946. 17 p.   FURM
Ashley River Baptist Church, Charleston. History of the Ashley
  River Baptist Church...1943-1963. NP: NPub, 1963? 87 p. FURM
Ashmore, Nancy V. The development of the African Methodist
  Episcopal Church in SC, 1865-1965. Thesis (M.A.), U.S.C.,
  1969. 117 p.   SCL
Asplund, John. The annual register of the Baptist denomination
  in North America, to the first of November, 1790. Containing
  an account of the churches & their constitutions, ministers,
  members, associations... NP: NPub, 1792. 70 p.   SCL
Associate Reformed Presbyterian (A.R.P.) Church. The centennial
  history...1803-1903. Chstn: W,E&C, 1905. 750 p.   SCL, SCHS
A.R.P. Church. The sesquicentennial history...1903-1951...
  Clinton: Jacobs Bros., 1951. 701 p.   SCL, SPCL, SCL, YOCL
A.R.P. Church. Studies in church history... Due West: NPub,
  1954. 48 p.   SPCL
A.R.P. Church, Anderson. Year book & directory... Anderson:
  NPub, 1928. 20 p.   SCL, MONT
A.R.P. Church, Chester. History...1869-1959. NP: NPub, 1959.
  23 p.   MONT
A.R.P. Church, Union. Union A.R.P. Church, Chester County [SpC]
                                                           CSCL
Augusta Heights Baptist Church, Greenville. Dedication service.
  Greenville: NPub, 1952. 11 p.   FURM
Augusta Heights Baptist Church, Greenville. Fifth anniversary,
  1950-1955. Greenville: NPub, 1955? 19 p.   FURM
Aull, James L. Historical sketch of the First Baptist Church,
  Newberry, SC, 1831-1931. NP: NPub, 1931. 34 p.   FURM
Austin, Mrs. Robert A. Liberty Springs [Presbyterian] church,
  Cross Hill, SC. Laurens County... NP: NPub, 1926. 14 p.
                                                     SCL, MONT
Baggott, H. L. A history of the Dean Swamp Baptist Church
  [Barnwell County]...1803-1903. NP: typescript, nd. 5 p. FURM
Baggott, Hiram L. History of Sardis Baptist Church, 1804-1904.
  Saluda: Saluda Standard, 1904. 17 p.   FURM

123

Bailey, J. D. A brief history of the Antioch, SC, Baptist
Church... NP: NPub, 1915. 18 p.   FURM
Bailey, J. D. A brief history of Antioch Baptist Church [York
County]...revised for the one hundred and fiftieth anniver-
sary. NP: NPub, 1965. 20 p.   FURM
Bailey, James D. History of Bethesda [Baptist] Church, Broad
River Association. Cowpens: NPub, 1921. 17 p.   FURM
Bailey, James D. Reverends Philip Mulkey & James Fowler. The
story of the first Baptist church planted in upper SC. Gaf-
fney: Ledger Print, 1924. 26 p.   COMMON
Bailey, John C. History of Ebenezer Presbyterian Church... NP:
NPub, 1935. 58 p.   YOCL, MONT, SCL
Bailey, John C & William B. White. The sesquicentennial [histo-
ry] of Hopewell Presbyterian Church, York County, SC, 1808-
1958, containing histories of connected families [Wherry,
Davies, Dunlop, McFadden]. Rock Hill: White Printing Co.,
1958. 59 p.   MONT, SCL
Baker, Robert A. The first southern Baptists. Nashville TN:
Broadman Press, 1966. 80 p.   SCL, FURM
Baldy, Dr. E. V. Historical sketch of the First Baptist Church,
Hartsville. 1915.   DAHC
Ballentine, Arthur W. A history of Macedonia Evangelical Luth-
eran Church...located in Lexington County, SC. 1847-1947.
Prosperity: NPub, 1947. 36 p.   LTSS
Banks, William. Catholic [Presbyterian] Church: a historical
discourse...on the 101st anniversary of the organization of
Catholic church, Chester District, SC... 1876, rp 1967 by the
congregation. 21 p.   COMMON
Baptists. Charleston Association. Baptist church discipline:
a historical introduction to the practices of Baptist churches
... Nashville: Broadman Press, 1962.   SCL, GRCL
Baptists. Charleston Association. A confession of faith...
adopted by the Baptist Association in Charleston... Charlestown: David Bruce, 1774. 88 p.   SCL
Baptists. Charleston Association. A summary of church discipline...by the Baptist Association of Charleston... Richmond
VA: John Dixon, 1794. 30 p.   SCL
Baptists. Charleston Association. A summary of church discipline; shewing the qualifications & duties of the officers &
members of a gospel-church... Chstn: J. Hoff, 1808. 36 p.
                                                          SCL
Baptist Church, Beaufort. Christian fellowship: or the solemn
covenant of the Baptist Church of Christ in Beaufort, SC.
With a summary of church discipline, rules, & a brief history
of the origin of said church...4th ed... Chstn: W. Riley,
1834. 48 p.   FURM
Barnes, William W. The Southern Baptist Convention, 1845-1953.
... Nashville TN: Broadman Press, 1954. 330 p.   SCL, COKL
Barton, Hugh M. Brief history of Douglas Presbyterian Church.
NP: NPub, 1958. 23 p. [Lancaster County]   MONT
Bartram, R. C. The history of the church of St. Thadeus [Epis-

124

copal. Aiken, SC]. Revised edition... September 1842 to July
1966... Aiken: NPub, 1967. 93 p.   SCL, AICL, SCHS
Bass, Mrs. Frances L. History of the Conway Baptist Church.
NP: NPub, nd. 3 p.   SCL
Bates, Mrs. John R. 200th anniversary & homecoming; Lower Fair-
forest Baptist Church, Union, SC. NP: NPub, 1962. 28 p. FURM
Batson, Annie J. Rockville Presbyterian Church, Wadmalaw Island
SC. The early 1700's - 1975. Chstn: W,E&C, 1976. 31 p.
                                                   MONT, SCHS
Batson, William M. History of Reedy River Baptist Church,
Traveler's Rest, SC. Greenville: Poinsett Printing Co., 1959.
49 p.   FURM
Beasley, Joseph S. The South Carolina Conference [, M.E. Church
South] thirty-eight years ago. An address... Cola: State
Co., 1908. 17 p.   SCL
Beaver Creek Presbyterian Church, Kershaw. History of... NP:
typescript, 1971. 5 p.   MONT
Beaverdam Baptist Church, Williamston. Historical sketch of
the Beaverdam Baptist Church, 1852-1952. Williamston: NPub,
1952. 40 p.   FURM
Beaver Hills Baptist Church, Roebuck. My church, Beaver Hills
Baptist, R.F.D., Roebuck, SC. NP: NPub, 1957? 16 p.   FURM
Beazley, G. Fitz. Asbury Memorial United Methodist Church:
historical highlights, 1958-1971. Cola: NPub, 1971. 7 p. SCL
Bedinger, Henry G. Manual. First Presbyterian Church, Harts-
ville SC. NP: NPub, 1926. 24 p.   MONT
Beech Branch Baptist Church, Luray [SpC]   FURM
Beersheba Presbyterian Church, York County. Historical sketch..
NP: typescript, nd. 9 p.   MONT
Beesley, Charles N. Beesley's illustrated guide to St. Mich-
ael's [Episcopal] Church, Charleston. 1898, rp Chstn:
Southern Printing Co., 1939. 78 p.   COMMON
Belcher, Posey. The dedication of the First Baptist Church of
Barnwell, SC. NP: NPub, 1962. 17 p.   FURM
Belcher, Posey. The one hundred seventy-fifth anniversary of
the First Baptist Church of Barnwell, SC. NP: NPub, 1977.
20 p.   FURM
Belin Memorial Methodist Church, Murrell's Inlet [SpC]   WOMA
Bell, Martha & Clarence Smith. Historical facts concerning
Little Stevens Creek Baptist Church. Edgefield. 15 p.   EDTO
Belton Presbyterian Church, Belton. Historical sketch... NP:
typescript, 1950. 5 p.   MONT
Belton Presbyterian Church, Belton. Historical sketch...1770-
1951. NP: NPub, 1951. 9 p.   MONT
Bennetsville Methodist Church, Marlboro County [SpC]   WOMA
Berea Baptist Church, Greenville. Articles of faith...with
historical sketch of the... NP: NPub, 1917. 32 p.   FURM
Bernheim, Gothardt D. History of the German settlements & of
the Lutheran Church in NC & SC. 1872, rp Spartanburg: RPC,
1972.   COMMON
Bethabara Baptist Church, Laurens County. Historical sketch...

1794-1956. NP: mimeo, 1956? 10 p.   FURM
Beth Elohim Synagogue, Charleston. The congregation "Beth Elo-
him" of Charleston, SC, 1750-1883. Chstn: News & Courier,
1884. 18 p.   SCL
Beth Elohim Synagogue, Charleston. Constitution of the Hebrew
congregation of Kahal Kadosh Beth Elohim, or House of God,
Charleston, SC, 1820. Chstn: Daggett, 1904 [reprinted by Dr.
Barnett A. Elzas.] 19 p.   SCL
Beth Elohim Synagogue, Charleston. Rededication...1750-1950.
Chstn: NPub, 1950. 11 p.   SCL
Bethel African Methodist Episcopal Church, Columbia. Centennial
celebration. Cola: the church, 1966. 35 p.   SCL
Bethel A.R.P. Church [SpC]   FACM
Bethel Baptist Church, Colleton County. History...1881-1966.
NP: mimeo, 1966. unp.   FURM
Bethel Baptist Church, Sumter [SpC]   FURM
Bethel Baptist Church, Sumter. History [SpC]   YOWC
Bethel Methodist Church, Pelion, SC, since 1852. Pelion:
author, 1968. 9 p.   LXMU
Bethel United Methodist Church, Spartanburg [SpC]   WOMA
Bethel Methodist Church, Valley Falls. History... NP: type-
script, 196? unp.   WOMA
Bethel United Methodist Church, Columbia. Historical sketch
...1835-1970. NP: typescript, 1970. 3 p.   WOMA
Bethel United Methodist Church, Charleston [SpC]   WOMA
Bethesda Presbyterian Church, Camden. ...Sesquicentennial,
1805-1955. Camden: author, 1955. 34 p.   SCL, MONT, KECA
Bethesda Presbyterian Church, York County. History of... near
McConnellsville, SC, 1760-1938. McConnellsville: typescript,
1938? 97 p.   YOCL
Bethlehem Baptist Church, Roebuck. The history of our church,
1800-1950... Spartanburg: Williams Printing Co., 1950. 16 p.
                                                             FURM
Bethlehem Lutheran Church, Pomaria. A history of...1816-1966.
Revised 1966... NP: NPub, 1966. 30 p.   LTSS
Betts, Albert D. Historical sketch of St. George Methodist
Episcopal Church, South [St. George, SC]... NP: NPub, nd.
29 p.   SCL
Betts, Albert D. History of SC Methodism. Cola: Advocate Press
1952. 544 p.   COMMON
Beulah United Methodist Church, Columbia [SpC]   WOMA
Big Stevens Creek Baptist Church, Edgefield County. Bicenten-
nial...1762-1962. NP: NPub, 1962. 4 p.   FURM
Bishopville Presbyterian Church, Bishopville [SpC]   MONT
Bishopville Presbyterian Church, Bishopville. 75th anniversary
& burning of the mortgage...November 30, 1913. NP: NPub, nd.
unp.   LECL
Black Creek Baptist Church, Dovesville [SpC]   FURM
Black, Sallie M. The chimes of St. Michael's [Episcopal Church,
Charleston]. Cola: RLB, 1903. 4 p.   SCL
Blackman, Harold T. History of St. Michael United Methodist

Church. Bennetsville: NPub, 1968. 30 p.   MRCL
Blackman, J. B. Wesley United Methodist Church. nd.   DAHC
Black Mingo Baptist Church, Williamsburg County [SpC]   FURM
Blackville Methodist Church, Blackville [SpC]   WOMA
Blatt, Solomon. Address delivered to the Hebrew Benevolent
  Society of Charleston... NP: NPub, nd. 15 p.   SCL
Blount, Mrs. Alston W. The Education Society of the Second
  Presbyterian Church, Charleston, SC, 1821-1946. Chstn: NPub,
  1946. 6 p.   MONT
Boddie, William W. Midway Presbyterian Church [history], Wil-
  liamsburg County. NP: NPub, nd. 8 p.   SCL, SCHS
Boggs, Annie L. Early religious effort in old Pendleton Dist-
  rict, 1785-1970. Pendleton: Piedmont Presbytery, 1971. 8 p.
                                                     PIPD, CLEM
Boggs, Annie L. Pendleton Presbyterian Church [Pendleton SC],
  1789-1966. NP: NPub, 1966. 117 p.   PIPD, MONT, ANCL
Boggs, Doyle W. Evangelism & expansion: SC white Protestant-
  ism, 1800-1810. Thesis (M.A.), U.S.C., 1972. 81 p.   SCL
Boice, Lewis. A historical sketch of Orangeburg Lutheran
  Church, Orangeburg SC. NP: privately printed, 1955. 40 p.
                                                            ORCL
Boiling Springs First Baptist Church, Spartanburg County [SpC]
                                                            FURM
Boisvert, Henry P. Church of the Epiphany [Episcopal]; 1845-
  present, Laurens, SC. Laurens: the church, 1977.   LRCL
Boleman, G.N.C. Historical sketch of the Central Presbyterian
  Church of Anderson, SC. NP: NPub, 1922. 8 p.   MONT
Bolin, Maggie. Trinity Methodist Episcopal Church. Home coming
  celebration, Sunday, July 29, 1934. York SC.   5 p.   SCHS
Boucher, Edward Joseph. Vestrymen & churchwardens [of the An-
  glican or Episcopal Church] in SC, 1706-1778. Thesis (M.A.),
  U.S.C., 1948. 57 p.   SCL
Bouknight, Frances L. A sketch of Cypress Methodist Episcopal
  Church, South, & the Cypress cemetery in Lee County, SC.
  NP: NPub, nd. 60 p.   LECL, WOMA, DAHC
Boulware, Marcus. Metropolitan A.M.E. Zion Church, Chester, SC,
  1866-1979. Cola: RLB, 1980.   SCL
Bowden, Haygood S. History of Savannah [GA] Methodism from John
  Wesley to Silas Johnson. Macon GA: J. W. Burke, 1929. 321
  p.   SCL
Boykin Methodist Church, Marlboro County. History... Fayette-
  ville NC: G.H. Thompson, 1905.   WOMA
Brackett, Gilbert R. Manual for the use of the members of the
  Second Presbyterian Church, Charleston SC. Chstn: W,E&C,
  1894.   SCL, GRCL
Brackett, Richard N. The Old Stone Church, Oconee County, SC.
  Cola: RLB, 1950. 223 p.   COMMON
Braddy, Robert A. Main Street Methodist Church, Dillon, SC,
  1892-1963. Chstn: W,E&C, 1963. 147 p.   SCL, FLMC, DIDU
Bradham, Lila M. Highlights of history. First Baptist Church,
  Manning, SC, 1856-1970. Manning: NPub, 1970. 11 p.   SCL

127

Bradley, Delphine A. History of Second Calvary Baptist Church.
Cola: Capitol Printing Co., 1958? 93 p.   SCL

Bragg, George F. History of the Afro-American group of the
Episcopal Church. Baltimore MD: Church Advocate Press, 1922.
319 p.   SCL

Brandenburg, Mabel G. Historical sketch of St. Paul's Methodist
Church, St. Matthews, SC...50th anniversary... NP: mimeo,
1966. 25 p.   SCL

Brearley, Cecil D. History of the First Presbyterian Church,
Myrtle Beach, SC, 1928-1968. NP: Sun Printing Co., 1968.
36 p.   HOCL, MONT

Bridges, Mrs. Louree & others. A history of Siloam Baptist
Church, Powdersville, SC, 1791-1978. NP: NPub, 1978. 28 p.
                                                          PIPD

A brief history of the Presbyterian Church of Edisto Island.
NP: NPub, 1933 & 1963. 15 p.   SCL, MONT

A brief history of the Rock Hill Presbyterian Church...to 1895.
Asheville NC: Hugh Wilson, 1895. 21 p.   MONT

A brief history of the Rowan Presbyterian Church, 1916-1966.
NP: NPub, 1966. 8 p.   MONT

A brief history of Wittenberg Lutheran Church, Leesville...1870-
1970. NP: NPub, 1970. 31 p.   LTSS

Brissie, Margia Lou. A history of Providence Baptist Church of
Hodges, SC, 1794-1972. Greenwood: Drinkard Printing Co.,
1972. 60 p.   SCL, GNCL

Bristow, Mollie. The true history of the First Baptist Church
of Florence...Origin to 1916... NP: NPub, 1966. 6 p.   FURM

Broaddus, Luther. History of Newberry Baptist Church, from its
organization in 1831 to 1881. A memorial discourse... Chstn:
W,E&C, 1882. 25 p.   FURM

Brooks, J. L. Saxon Baptist Church. NP: typescript, nd. 2 p.
                                                          FURM

Browder, Georgia G. History of Piney Forest Baptist Church [An-
drews SC]. 1972. 17 p.   FURM

Brown, Clinton C. History of the First Baptist Church, Sumter,
SC, 1813-1938. Sumter: Sumter Printing Co., 1938. 126 p.
                                               SCL, SMCL, FURM

Brown, C. C. The Swift Creek Church. 1903.   DAHC

Brown Swamp United Methodist Church, Rt. 4, Conway (Marion County) [SpC]   WOMA

Brown Swamp United Methodist Church. History of... NP: NPub,
1975. 4 p.   HOCL

Browne, Henry B. Methodist sunday schools after a hundred
years... NP: NPub, 1911   16 p.   WOMA

Bruce, Winnie J. 75th anniversary & history, First Baptist
Church, Greer, SC. Greer: Charles P. Smith, 1955. 95 p.
                                                   GRCL, FURM

Brunson Baptist Church, Brunson, SC, 1874-1974. NP: NPub, 1974.
32 p.   FURM

Brunson, Mrs. C. N. History of the Graham Baptist Church
[Sumter County]. NP: typescript, 1964. 4 p.   FURM

Brunson, Nolan L.   Beech Branch Baptist Church, 1759-1959...
NP: NPub, 1959? 21 p.   FURM
Brunson, W. A. History of old Ebenezer church. 1909. SCL, DAHC
Brushy Fork Baptist Church, Chester County [SpC]   FURM
Bryan, Thomas R. History of Callie Self Memorial Baptist Church
Clinton: Jacobs Press, 1977. 95 p.   SCL, GNCL, FURM
Buchholz, Mrs. L. E. Peniel Baptist Church [Florence County].
NP: typescript, 1938. 5 p.   FURM
Bull, Henry D. All Saints' [Episcopal Church, Waccamaw. The
parish, the place, & the people, 1739-1968. Georgetown:
Winyah Press, 1968. 107 p.   COMMON
Bulletin-Dedication number. Mt. Calvary Lutheran Church, John-
ston, SC... NP: NPub, 1934. 24 p.   LTSS
Burgess, James M. Chronicles of St. Mark's Parish, Santee cir-
cuit, and Williamsburg township, SC, 1731-1885. 1888, rp
Sumter: Wilder & Ward, 1968. 108 p.   COMMON
Burgess, James M. Index. Chronicles of St. Mark's Parish...
NP: typescript, nd. 16 p.   SCHS
Burgess, Mrs. James. History of Riverside Baptist Church from
1901-1967, including membership list. NP: NPub, 1967. unp.
                                                          PIPD
Burkhead, J. D. Oration...delivered at the centennial celebra-
tion of Carmel Church...1889. Pickens: Sentinel Book & Job
Print., 1889. 34 p.   SCL, MONT
Burns, James C. History of Mt. Olive Baptist Church.   LRCL
Burns, James C. Home-coming service & history. Aug. 26, 1973.
NP: NPub, 1973. 10 p.   FURM
Bush River Baptist Church, Newberry. A potpourri of the Bush
River Baptist Church, 1933-1965. NP: typescript, 1965?
111 p.   FURM
Butt, Winnie J. One hundred years of christian life & service:
St. Matthew's [Lutheran] Church. Chstn, 1940.   SCL, SCHS
Byrd, E. J. C. First Baptist Church of Darlington. 1923. DAHC
Calcote, Claude A. Historical sketches of Aveleigh Presbyterian
Church, Newberry, SC. Newberry: Herald & News, 1935. 20 p.
                                                           SCL
Caldwell, May. History of Carter's Ford Baptist Church [Colle-
ton County]. NP: typescript, 1977. unp.   FURM
Calvary Episcopal Church, Charleston. Report on religious in-
struction of negroes at Calvary Church, 1848. NP: NPub, 1848.
1 p.   SCHS
Calvary Episcopal Church, Glenn Springs, SC. 125th anniversary,
...1850...1975. Glenn Springs: NPub, 1975. 14 p.   SCL
                                                    SPCL, SCHS
Calvary Methodist Church. History... NP: typescript, 1971.
6 p.   LXMU
Camden Baptist Church. Centennial Celebration...1910... Cola:
State Co., 1910. 20 p.   SCL
Campbell, M. Anne. Bishop England's sisterhood, 1829-1929. St.
Louis MS: author, 1968. 330 p.   GRCL
Camp Creek United Methodist Church, Lancaster [SpC]   WOMA

Canaan Baptist Church, Spartanburg County. Canaan: the first 50
years, 1921-1971. NP: Piedmont Press, 1971? 98 p.   FURM
Canady, G. History of the Zion Methodist Church (Dorchester
Circuit). Dorchester: the church, 1961. 12 p.   SCL
Cane Branch Baptist Church, Loris. Directory. 197? unp. HOCL
Cardozo, Isaac N. A discourse, delivered in Charleston on the
21st of November, 1827, before the Reformed Society of Israel-
ites...on their third anniversary. Chstn: Burges, 1827.
18 p.   SCL
Carlisle, Mark L. The presiding eldership, a study. Gaffney:
NPub, 1907. 12 p.   SCL
Carmel Church, Pickens. Oration of the Rev. J. DeWitt Burkhead,
D.D., delivered at the centennial-:- celebration (1789-1889)
of Carmel Church,...and oration of Hon. Jno. S. Verner...on
the life & labors of Rev. J. L. Kennedy. Pickens: Sentinel
Book & Job Print, 1889. 34 p.   SCL
Carter, Margaret L. Let there be light. A history of Lake
City Baptist Church, 1828-1953. NP: NPub, 1953. 84 p. FURM
Carter, Margaret L. Let there be light: a history of Lake City
First Baptist Church, 1828-1978. Greenwood: Connie Maxwell
Press, 1978. 107 p.   FURM
Cason, Mollie T. History of Jackson Grove Methodist Church,
1832-1966. Taylors: Faith Printing Co., 1966. 40 p.   GRCL
Cathedral of St. John the Baptist, Charleston, SC. Chstn: Cal-
der, Fladger & Co., nd. 64 p.   SCL
Cathedral of St. John the Baptist, Charleston SC. Its consecra-
tion & history. NP: NPub, 1907. 64 p.   SCHS, SCL, CDIO
Cathedral of St. John the Baptist, of Charleston... Fiftieth
anniversary of consecration. NP: NPub, 1957. 47 p. SCL, SCHS
Catholic Presbyterian Church, Chester [SpC]   YOWC
The Cayce Church of the Nazarene, 1955-1970. NP: typescript,
1970. 3 p.   LXMU
Cayce Methodist Church, Cayce. Year book & directory [for]
Cayce Methodist Church, Cayce; Pisgah Methodist Church, State
Park; Shiloh Methodist Church, Dixiana. 1937. 34 p.   SCL
Centennial A.R.P. Church, Columbia [SpC]   MONT
Centennial A.R.P. Church, Columbia. A brief history of...
Cola: NPub, 1972. 11 p.   SCL
Centennial of Bethel Presbytery, York County, SC. Beersheba
Church, September 16, 1924.   YOCL
Centennial celebration, 1858-1958. Aiken Presbyterian Church.
NP: NPub, 1958. 12 p.   MONT
Centennial celebration of the dedication of the First Presbyter-
ian Church, Charleston, SC, organized 1732... Chstn: W,E&C,
1915.   SPCL
Centennial celebration of the First Presbyterian Church, Ben-
netsville, SC. NP: NPub, 1955. 7 p.   MONT
Centennial celebration of the dedication of the First Presbyter-
ian Church, Charleston, SC. Chstn: W,E&C, 1915. 156 p.
DACL, SMCL, MONT
Centennial Committee. History of the First Baptist Church. AICL

130

Centennial program & history of Grace Church, Anderson, SC.
NP: NPub, 1951. 26 p.   PIPD
Centennial program & history. St. Luke's Episcopal Church.
1855-1955. Newberry, SC. NP: NPub, 1955. 20 p.   SCL, EPDI
Central Baptist Church, Greenville [SpC]   FURM
Central Baptist Church, Greenville. History...1893-1913.
Greenville: Baptist Courier Job Rooms, 1913. 23 p.   FURM
Central Methodist Church. History of the march of missions. By
the women of Central Methodist Church: 1879-1958. NP: type-
script, nd. 21 p.   SCHS
Central Presbyterian Church, Kingstree [SpC]   MONT
Central United Methodist Church, Spartanburg [SpC]   WOMA
Central United Methodist Church, Newberry. A history of...
Newberry: SC Tricentennial, 1970. 28 p.   NWRL
Chandler, Harry. The people called Methodists. Rock Hill:
Record Printing Co., 1975. 30 p.   SCL
Chandler, Marion C. Church incorporations in SC under the con-
stitution of 1778 (1778-1790). Thesis (M.A.), U.S.C., 1969.
92 p.   SCL
Chaplin, Ellen P. History of Neeses Baptist Church. Orange-
burg: NPub, 1956. 5 p.   ORCL
Chapter "B", Women's Auxiliary. Old St. David's [Episcopal]
Church, Cheraw, SC. 1770-1947. NP: NPub, nd. 50 p.   EPDI
Charles, Allan D. The narrative history of the First Baptist
Church, Union, SC. NP:NPub, 1972. 31 p.   SCL, FURM
Charles, Lois P. Some missionary achievements of Southern
Methodist women. NP: NPub, 1937. 27 p.   SCL, GRCL
Charles, William K. History of Main Street Methodist Church,
Greenwood SC. 1858-1958. Greenwood: NPub, 1958. 59 p.   SCL
Charleston Baptist Association. Minutes...at its one hundredth
anniversary, held with the First Baptist Church, Charleston
SC... Chstn: A.J. Burke, 1851. 70 p.   SCL
Charleston Bible Society. Annual report [various eds.]   SCHS
Charleston Bible Society. The constitution...with amendments.
Chstn: Walker & Evans, 1856. 20 p.   SCHS
Charleston City Council. Church histories. Republished from
the Yearbook of the city of Charleston, 1882. Chstn: News &
Courier, 1883. 56 p.   SCL
Charleston Heights Baptist Church, Charleston [SpC]   FURM
Charleston Jewish Community. Bicentennial celebration of the
Jews of Charleston, 1750-1950. Chstn: NPub, 1950. 8 p. SCHS
Charleston Jewish Community. The souvenir book of the bicenten-
nial; the story of the celebration of the bicentennial of the
Charleston Jewish community... Chstn: NPub, 1951. 159 p. SCL
Charleston Methodist Churches. Wesley bi-centennial celebration
...June 24-28, 1903. Chstn: W, E & C, 1903. 15 p.   SCHS
Cheraw Baptist Church. Manual...1925. Greenville: Provence
Printing Co., 1925. 27 p.   SCHS
Chester A.R.P. Church. History...July 1869-July 1969. Chester:
the church, 1970. 62 p.   LNCL, YOCL
Chestnut Ridge Baptist Church, Laurens County. Centennial cele-

131

bration, July 1, 1921. NP: NPub, 1921. 7 p.   SCL
Chick Springs [Baptist] Church, Taylors. NP: typescript, nd.
    19 p.   FURM
Chreitzberg, Abel M. Early Methodism in the Carolinas. 1897,
    rp Spartanburg: RPC, 1972. 364 p.   COMMON
Christ Church, Greenville. The dedication of Christ Church
    [Episcopal], Greenville, SC... Greenville: NPub, 1968. 19 p.
                                                         SCHS, SCL
Christ Church, Greenville. [History.] Greenville: NPub, 1969?
    4 p.   SCHS
Christ Church, Greenville. One hundredth anniversary of the
    present church building of Christ Church [Episcopal], Green-
    ville, SC. 1854-1954. Greenville: author, 1954. 32 p.
                                                   GRCL, SCHS, SCL
Christ Church, Greenville. Year book & directory. Greenville:
    NPub, 1938.   SCL
Christ Episcopal Church, Charleston. Yearbook & directory.
    Chstn: NPub, 1927.   SCHS
Christian Science Society of Sumter, SC. Sumter: typescript,
    nd. 2 p.   SMCL
Church Committee. A brief history of Platt Spring Methodist
    Church. 1970. 5 p.   LXMU
Church Committee. History of Swansea Methodist Church, Swansea,
    SC, 1896-1966. NP: typescript, 1966. 148 p.   LXMU
Church Committee. Minutes, mileastones & memories of the Wom-
    an's Missionary Union, First Baptist Church, Hartsville, SC.
    NP: NPub, 1974. 57 p.   FURM
Church of the Holy Comforter, Sumter, SC, 1857-1959. Sumter:
    the church, 1959. 47 p.   SMCL, SCL
Church of the Redeemer, Orangeburg. Yearbook, 1924.   SCHS
Church Roll. Sumter Presbyterian Church...August 1, 1925. NP:
    NPub, 1925. 21 p.   MONT
Citadel Square Baptist Church, Charleston. Manual of the Cita-
    del Square Church, Charleston, SC. Organized May 29, A.D.
    1854. Chstn: James & Williams, 1856.   CHCO
Citadel Square Baptist Church, Charleston. Manual...[includes
    history]. Chstn: Lucas & Richardson, 1880. 46 p.   SCL, FURM
Clark, Chovine R. History of the Manning Methodist Church.
    Manning: NPub, 1966. 40 p.   COMMON
Clarke, Erskine. Wrestlin' Jacob: a portrait of religion in the
    old south. Atlanta: John Knox Press, 1979. 207 p.   SCL
Clarke, Philip G., Jr. Anglicanism in SC, 1660-1976. 1976, rp
    Easley: SHP, 1977. 156 p.   COMMON
Clarke, Philip G., Jr. A brief history of the Diocese of Upper
    SC, fiftieth anniversary year, 1922-1972. NP: NPub, 1972.
    16 p.   SCL
Clayton, Glenn. Siloam Baptist Church, Easley. NP: typescript,
    nd. 2 p.   FURM
Clemson Agricultural College. Open-country churches in Anderson
    County. NP: NPub, nd. 13 p.   SCL
Clinton United Methodist Church, Wagener [SpC]   WOMA

132

Clyde, Mrs. E. Effingham Presbyterian Church, Effingham, SC, 1906-1956. Effingham: NPub, 1956. 11 p. MONT, SCL
Cloud's Creek Baptist Church, Edgefield [SpC] FURM
Cobe, M. L. & T. Cook. Welsh Neck Baptist Church. NP: type-script, 1914. 6 p. FURM
Cohh, Alice. History of Riverside Baptist Church [Anderson]. NP: typescript, 1937. 2 p. FURM
Coit, John C. A sermon preached before the Presbyterian Church at Cheraw, SC, January 20, 1839. Philadelphia PA: W.S. Martien, 1839. 11 p. FLMC
Coker, J. L. History of New Providence [Baptist] Church [Darlington County]. NP: typescript, nd. 4 p. FURM
Coker, Leon W. Historical sketch & membership roll - First Baptist Church, Darlington, SC, as of August 15, 1945. NP: NPub, 1945. 31 p. COKL, FURM, DAHC
Colclough, Emma. History of St. Philip's [Episcopal] Church, Bradford Springs [Sumter County]. NP: typescript, 1936. 3 p. SCL, FLMC, SCHS, EPDI
Coleman, Mattie. History of Green Pond Baptist Church [Spartanburg]. Greer: Charles Smith Printing Co., 1955. 30 p. FURM
Colonial Heights Baptist Church, Columbia. 50th anniversary... 1912-1962. NP: NPub, 1962. 12 p. FURM
Commemorating the seventy-fifth anniversary of Wittenberg Ev. Lutheran Church, Leesville, SC...1870-1945. NP: NPub, 1945. 23 p. LTSS
Committee of Chapter B of the Women's Auxiliary of St. David's [Episcopal Church]. Old St. David's [Episcopal] Church, Cheraw, SC, 1770-1947. Cheraw: author, 1947. 50 p.SCL,COKL, SMCL
Committee on History & Records. A history of Chiquola United Methodist Church. Honea Path: NPub, 1974. PIPD
Committee of the Vestry. History of St. Paul's [Episcopal] Church, Radcliffeborough. Chstn: Lucas & Richardson, 1878. 44 p. EPDI
Congregational & Presbyterian Female Association. Report of the directresses... Chstn: Stephens, 1819. 7 p. SCHS
The constitution & by-laws of Stoney Creek Independent Presbyterian Church, adopted August 12, 1854. Chstn: A.J. Burke, 1854. 12 p. MONT
Cooper, James F. An historical sketch of Indiantown Presbyterian Church in Williamsburg County, SC, 1757-1957. Indiantown: Indiantown Bicentennial Committee, 1957. 55 p. COMMON
Corley, B. F. A short history of the resuscitation of the old Fairfield [Baptist] Church. Typescript, nd. 1 p. FURM
Cothran, Lily G & Grange S. Cothran. Second Baptist Church [Laurens], 1948. Laurens: Laurens Advertizer, 1948. 12 p. LRCL, FURM
Covenanters of Rock Creek SC. History, 1886 [SpC] YOWC
Covington & Kinney. History of First Methodist Church, Bennettsville, SC. NP: typescript, 1979. MRCL
Cowpens First Baptist Church, Cowpens [SpC] FURM
Cox, Mrs. L. D. History of Langford Baptist Church [Laurens

County]. NP: typescript, 1947. 2 p.   FURM
Craven, Mrs. H. H. Historical sketch of the First Baptist
  Church of Georgetown, SC. NP: typescript, 1954. 4 p.   FURM
Creswell, Michael D. A history of the Savannah River Baptist
  Association. Ridgeland: Savannah River Baptist Assn., 1977.
  155 p.   SCL
Crittenden, Stephen S. History of Christ Church [Episcopal],
  Greenville SC. Greenville: Greenville News Print., 1901,
  1967.   COMMON
Croft Baptist Church, Spartanburg. History... NP: NPub, 1969.
  21 p.   FURM
Cromer, Willie S. History of West Side Baptist Church, West
  Columbia. NP: typescript, 1970. 1 p.   LXMU
Crooked Run Baptist Church [SpC]   FACM
Cross, J. Russell. A brief history of Friendship United Meth-
  odist Church, Highway 6, Cross, SC. NP: NPub, 1975. 5 p. SCL
Crouch, Katy A. Fort Hill Presbyterian Church, Clemson College,
  SC. NP: NPub, 1957. 2 vol.   COMMON
Crowder, Louise K. The First Baptist Church of Chester, SC.
  Chester: author, 1958. 28 p.   COMMON
Crum, George Milton. Historical data concerning St. Paul's
  Methodist Church in Orangeburg, SC. Orangeburg: the church,
  1956. 41 p.   ORCL, SCL
Cruse, Guy C. A history of Bethel Ev. Lutheran Church, White
  Rock, SC. Cola: Farrell Printing Co., 1962. 27 p. LXMU, LTSS
Culbertson, B. Y. Historical sketch of the First Baptist Church
  Laurens, SC. 1834-1934. NP: NPub, 1934. 29 p. LRCL, FURM, SCL
Culbertson, W. P. How Mountville [Laurens County] was named.
  NP: NPub, nd. 1 p.   FURM
Cumberland [M.E. Church, South] Sunday School Society. Consti-
  tution. Chstn: Walker & James, 1851. 9 p.   SCHS
Cunningham, Mrs. C.D. History of Liberty Hill Presbyterian
  Church, Liberty Hill, SC. NP: NPub, 1952. 13 p.   LNCL, MONT
Cuttino, Marguerite A. History of Calvary Baptist Church, Pine-
  wood, SC, 1769-1954. NP: NPub, 1956. 13 p.   FURM, SCL
Cypress Camp Ground & Methodist Church, Ridgeville [SpC]   WOMA
Dalcho, Frederick. An historical account of the Protestant
  Episcopal church, in SC, from the first settlement of the
  province, to the war of the Revolution... 1820, rp NY: Arno
  Press, 1970. 613 p.   COMMON
Dalcho Historical Society. A short history of the[Episcopal]
  Diocese of SC. Chstn: Dalcho Historical Society, 1953.
  189 p.   SCL, GTML, EPDI, SCHS
Dallas, James M. Historic Greenvale. Old Greenville Church
  from the organization of the church till the close of 1923.
  Abbeville: Banner Publ. Co., 1925. 55 p.   GRCL, MONT, SCL
Dana, William C. A discourse delivered on the seventh anniver-
  sary of the dedication of the Central Presbyterian Church,
  Charleston, February 1, 1857. Chstn: Walker, Evans & Co.,
  1857. 24 p.   SCL
Daniel, J. W. Out from under Caesar's frown... Nashville TN:

Publishing House of the M.E. Church, South, 1891. 284 p. SPCL
                                                       SCL, CSCL
Daniel, Robert N. A century of progress, being the history of
    First Baptist Church, Greenville, SC. Greenville: the church,
    1957. 129 p.   GRCL, FURM
Daugherty, Lawton. Little River-Dominick Presbyterian Church,
    1761-1961 [incl. cemetery inscriptions]. NP: mimeo, 1961.
    22 p.   SCL
Davidson, Elizabeth H. The Presbytery of Pee Dee, a history:
    1889-1977. NP: author, 1978. 80 p.   HOCL
Davis, Mrs. George E. A century of achievement, the First
    Baptist Church, 'the church on the square,' Orangeburg, SC...
    Greenville: Keys Print. Co., 1960. 51 p.   FURM, SCHS
Davis, Henry E. An address...on the occasion of the celebration
    of the 200th anniversary of the founding of the Williamsburg
    Presbyterian Church, October 11, 1936. NP: NPub, nd. 32 p.
                                                         HOCL, SCL
Davis, Henry E. History of the Marion Presbyterian Church, Mar-
    ion SC, 1852-1952. NP: NPub, nd. 10 p.   MONT, SCL
Davis, Henry E. History of the Union Presbyterian Church and
    of the Salters, SC, community in which it is located. Septem-
    ber 29, 1963. NP: NPub, 1963. 35 p.   MONT, FLCL, SCL
Davis, Henry E. & James E. Cousar. The history of the First
    Presbyterian Church, Florence, SC...centennial edition, 1861-
    1961. Florence: NPub, 1962. 48 p.   DAHC, SCL, MONT
Davis, Henry E. The Williamsburg Presbyterian Church, Kings-
    tree, SC. Chstn: W,E&C, 1961. 24 p.   MONT, SCL
Davis, Henry E. The Williamsburg Presbyterian Church, Kings-
    tree, SC. NP: NPub, 1936. 32 p.   MONT
Davis, Nora M. An historical sketch of the Long Cane Associate
    Reformed Presbyterian Church. Greenwood: Index-Journal, 1941.
    18 p.   GWPL, SCL
Davis, Mrs. R. D. History highlights of Rivelon Baptist Church
    [Orangeburg]. NP: typescript, 1969. 3 p.   FURM
Decade of progress; town & country churches, the Evangelical
    Lutheran Synod of SC, 1951-1960. NP: Committee on Rural Work,
    1961.
Dedication. St. Andrews Lutheran Church [includes history].
    Cola: NPub, 1977. unp.   LTSS
Dedication services, Mt. Zion Presbyterian Church, Lee County,
    SC. Sumter: Osteen Publishing Co., 1912. 8 p.   MONT
Denmark Baptist Church, organized 1844. NP: mimeo, 1947. unp.
                                                            FURM
Dial, Emma M. History of Dials Church, 1808-1929. nd. SCL,LRCL
Dickson, E. Meek. Bethel Presbytery; Beersheba Presbyterian
    Church, Route 1, York, SC. York: typescript, 1959. unp. YOCL
Dickson, Harvey R. The centennial history of First Presbyterian
    Church, Anderson, SC. NP: NPub, 1971. 15 p.   PIPD
Dickson, W. A. & others. Historical sketches of South Union
    Baptist Church [Westminster SC]. NP: typescript, 1964.
    12 p.   FURM

Diocese of South Carolina. Report of the committee on the de-
struction of churches, in the [Episcopal] Diocese of SC, dur-
ing the late war...May 1868. Chstn: John Walker, 1868.
16 p.   SCL
Directory. First Presbyterian Church. Anderson, SC, 192? NP:
NPub, nd. 28 p.   MONT
Directory of the First Presbyterian Church of Rock Hill, SC,
October 1, 1903. Rock Hill: London Printery, 1903. unp. YOCL
Directory of the First Presbyterian Church, Spartanburg. Spar-
tanburg: Band & White, 1915. 42 p.   MONT
Directory of Purity Presbyterian Church, Wylie St., Chester, SC.
Richmond VA: Whittet & Shepperson, 1904. 36 p.   MONT
Directory & rules of the Summerville Presbyterian Church of Sum-
merville, SC, 1885. Chstn: Lucas & Richardson, 1885. 20 p.
                                                   MONT, SCHS
Directory of the Westminster Presbyterian Church of Charleston,
SC, for 1885. Chstn: W,E&C, 1885. 24 p.   MONT
Dixon, Brenda. History of Ramah Presbyterian Church [York Coun-
ty], 1879-1966. Lancaster: typescript, 1966. 16 p.   SCHS
Dofy, Annie S. A history of the First Baptist Church [Winnsbo-
ro]. Winnsboro: News & Herald, 1960. 44 p.   FURM
Doherty, John E. History of St. Andrew's [Catholic Church]
Barnwell SC. Chstn: Diocese of Charleston, 1979. 28 p. ORCL
                                             CDIO, SCL, SMCL
Dothan Methodist Church (extinct, Dillon County)[SpC]   WOMA
Doty, Annie S. The centennial history of the First Baptist
Church...Winnsboro, SC. Winnsboro: News & Herald, 1960. 44
p.   SCL, FURM
Douglas, John. Dedication sermon preached at the opening of the
new Presbyterian Church in Chesterville, SC. Chstn: Burke,
1855. 16 p.   SCL, SCHS
Douglas, John. The history of Purity [Presbyterian] Church,
compiled & written by Rev. John Douglas, 1865. Cola: Presby-
terian Publishing House, 1870. 30 p.   SCL, MONT
Dowling, W. H. Church histories from the minutes of Savannah
River Baptist Association. NP: typescript, nd. 43 p.   FURM
Drake, Elise B. A history of Cross Roads Baptist Church of
Seneca, SC. Seneca: Journal Co., 1976. unp.   PIPD, FURM
DuBose, Bell E. History of the Presbyterian Church in Camden,
SC, sesqui-centennial, 1805-1955. NP: Bethesda Sesqui-centen-
nial Committee, 1955. 34 p.   SMCL, SCL
DuBose, Horace M. A history of Methodism, Vol. II. NP: Publ.
House of the M.E. Church, South, 1916. unp.   KECA
Dufford, Mrs. J. Philip. A brief history of the Lutheran Church
of the Resurrection, 1844-1969. NP: NPub, 1969. 8 p.   SCL
Dukes, Peggy. A historical account of the Church of the Redeem-
er [Episcopal], Orangeburg, SC. NP: privately printed, 1961.
8 p.   COMMON
Duncan Memorial Methodist Church, Georgetown [SpC]   WOMA
Duncan Memorial Methodist Church, Georgetown. 175 years of
Methodism in Georgetown, SC, 1785-1960. Georgetown: the

church, 1961? 12 p.   SCL
Duncan, Watson B. The leadership of Methodism. An address...
   at Columbia, SC, November 27, 1906... NP: NPub, nd. 19 p.SCL
Duncan, Watson B. Trials & triumphs of Charleston Methodism.
   An address..at Charleston, SC, December 6, 1910. Cola: State
   Co., 1910. 20 p.   SCL
Dunean Baptist Church, Greenville. 50th anniversary...1912-1962
   ... Greenville: Hiott Press, 1962. unp.   FURM
Dunton United Methodist Church, Gaffney, SC. 1871-1971. Gaff-
   ney: NPub, 1971. 48 p.   CRCL, SCL
Durden, Robert F. The establishment of Calvary Protestant Epis-
   copal Church for Negroes in Charleston... Chstn: Dalcho
   Historical Society, 1965. 22 p.   SCL, EPDI
Duryla, Robert H. & Fred J. Kern. History of St. Andrew's Luth-
   eran Church. Chstn: NPub, 1978. 32 p.   SCHS
Eaddy, Elaine Y. Black Mingo Baptist Church [SpC]   WMTR
Eaddy, Elaine Y. First United Methodist Church, Hemingway, SC,
   & its roots from old Johnsonville, Muddy Creek, Prospect.
   Hemingway: the church, 1977. 60 p.   COMMON
Earle Street Baptist Church, Greenville. Manual & directory...
   Greenville: author, 1922. 4 p.   FURM
Eastminster Presbyterian Church, Columbia [SpC]   MONT
Eastminster Presbyterian Church, Columbia. Early history...
   1948-1968. Cola: the church, 1968. 8 p.   SCL
East Park Baptist Church, Greenville. History...1913-1957.
   Greenville: mimeo, 1957. 29 p.   FURM
Eau Claire Baptist Church, Columbia [SpC]   FURM
Eau Claire Presbyterian Church, Columbia [SpC]   MONT
Eau Claire Presbyterian Church, Eau Claire. Golden anniversary,
   May 1916-May 1966. Np: NPub, 1966. 10 p.   SCL
Ebenezer Lutheran Church, Columbia. Program of the first servi-
   ces...1931. Cola: RLB, 1931. 12 p.   SCL
Ebenezer Methodist Church, Abbeville County [SpC]   GSGN
Ebenezer Presbyterian Church, Rock Hill [SpC]   YOWC
Edgefield County Historical Society. Dr. William Bullein John-
   son and the organization of the Southern Baptist Convention,
   including the pageant, "Publish glad tidings." Edgefield:
   Advertiser Print., 1945. 48 p.   SCL
Edgefield Village Baptist Church, Edgefield. Address...to the
   other churches composing the Edgefield Baptist Association.
   Edgefield: William F. Durisoe, 1853. 23 p.   SCL
Edgefield Village Baptist Church, Edgefield. Supplement to the
   address of the Edgefield Village Baptist Church. Edgefield:
   1854? 8 p.   SCL
Edisto Island Presbyterian Church. A brief history of the Pres-
   byterian church of Edisto Island. Edisto Island: NPub, 1933,
   1963. 15 p.   SCHS, SCL
Edwards, George N. A history of the Independent or Congregational Church of Charleston, SC, commonly known as Circular
   Church. Boston MA: Pilgrim Press, 1947. 160 p.   COMMON
Edwards, Morgan. A history of the Baptists of SC [Euhaw Baptist

137

Church, Jasper County]. NP: typescript, 1925. 6 p.   FURM
1809-1909. Exercises connected with the one hundredth anniversary of the Second Presbyterian Church of Charleston, SC.
Chstn: Daggett, 1910. 106 p.   MONT
1835 - centennial celebration - 1935. Lancaster Presbyterian
Church, Lancaster, SC. NP: NPub, 1935. 31 p.   MONT
1842 - 1942. Centennial. First Presbyterian Church, York, SC.
York: Church Home Press, 1942. 8 p.   MONT
1843-1943. One hundredth anniversary of the First Presbyterian
Church of Spartanburg, SC. Spartanburg: Band & White, 1943.
11 p.   SCL, MONT
1844-1944. One hundredth anniversary of the New Harmony Presbyterian Church, Fountain Inn, SC. NP: NPub, 1944. 10 p. MONT
1853-1953. Centennial commemorating the one hundredth anniversary. Emanuel Lutheran Church...West Columbia, SC. NP: NPub,
1953. 20 p.   LTSS
1855-1955. Manning Presbyterian Church. NP: NPub, 1955. 8 p.
                                                            MONT
1869-1944. Seventy-fifth anniversary...of the First Presbyterian Church of Rock Hill, SC. NP: NPub, 1944. 20 p.   MONT
El Bethel Baptist Church [Greer]. NP: typescript, nd. 2 p.FURM
Elgin, Frank. History of Neals Creek Baptist Church, Anderson,
SC, March, 1972. 12 p.   PIPD
Ellerbe, Napoleon G. ...A brief history of the Church of the
Ascension, Hagood, SC. [parish program]...vol. 4, no. 3,
1936.   SCL
Elzas, Barnett A. A history of the congregation Beth Elohim of
Charleston, SC, 1800-1810. Chstn: Daggett, 1902. 13 p. SCL
Elzas, Barnett A. The organ in the synagogue. An interesting
chapter in the history of Reform Judaism in America. NP:
NPub, nd. 8 p.   SCL
Elzas, Barnett A. The Reformed Society of Israelites of
Charleston, SC...with an appendix: the constitution of the
society. NY: Bloch, 1916. 54 p.   SCL
Emanuel Lutheran Church, West Columbia. A history... NP: NPub,
1953. 20 p.   LXMU
Emerson, Lewis A. The first fifty years. A history of St.
John's Shandon Episcopal Church, Columbia, SC. NP: NPub, 1965
170 p.   SCL
Emfinger, Henry A. Crossroads for the kingdom; a history of the
Hickory Road Baptist Church, Sumter, SC, October 1960-October
1972. NP: privately printed, 1972. 30 p.   SMCL
Emory Methodist Church, Saluda County. A historical sketch of
Emory Methodist Church... Edgefield: Advertiser Press, 1965.
107 p.   SCL, MRCL, GRCL, SMCL
England, John. A brief account of the introduction of the Cath-
olic religion into the states of NC, SC & GA...& of the cre-
ation of the Diocess of Charleston... Dublin, Ireland: T.
O'Flanagan, 1832. 48 p.   SCL
English, Thomas R. Historical address at the centennial cele-
bration of Mt. Zion Church, 1809-1909. Sumter?, typescript,

nd. 19 p.   SCL
Episcopal Churches of Columbia. The Episcopal church in Colum-
bia. NP: NPub, nd. 9 p.   SCL
Episcopal Church of Our Savior, Rock Hill, SC, 1870-1976. Rock
Hill: NPub, 1976? 67 p.   YOCL, SCL
Episcopal Diocese of SC. A memorial of the special services
held May, 1875...in commemoration of the planting of the
Church of England in the province of Carolina. Chstn: W,E&C,
1876. 172 p.   SCHS
Episcopal Diocese of SC. Report of the committee on the de-
struction of churches in the Diocese of SC during the late
war. Chstn: Walker, 1868. 16 p.   SCL, SCHS
Episcopal Diocese of SC. Woman's Auxiliary. Executive Board.
The story of the SC branch of the Woman's Auxiliary, 1885-1935
Sumter: Sumter Printing Co., 1935. 18 p.   SCL
Episcopal Diocese of SC. Woman's Auxiliary. Historical Commit-
tee. Continued story of the Woman's Auxiliary, 1935-1959.
Episcopal Church-women, 1959-1960. NP: NPub, nd. 21 p.   SCL
Ervin, Julia. History of the Darlington Presbyterian Church,
Darlington, SC, 1827-1952. NP: NPub, nd. 42 p.   COMMON
Estes, Frank B. History of Orangeburg Presbyterian Church,
1835-1935. Orangeburg: Observer Publ. Co., 1935? 14 p.
                                                          SCL, SCHS, MONT
Euhaw Baptist Church, Jasper County [SpC]   FURM
Euhaw Baptist Church, Jasper County. Sketch of church history
of the Euhaw Baptist Church. NP: typescript, 1928. 4 p. FURM
Eulonia Baptist Church [Marion County]. NP:typescript, 1936.
1 p.   FURM
Eureka Baptist Church, Anderson County. History & highlights of
Eureka Baptist Church, 1888-1971. NP: NPub, 1971. unp. PIPD
Evangelical Lutheran Synod of SC. History of the Evangelical
Lutheran Synod of SC, 1824-1924. Cola: Farrell Print. Co.,
1924. 318 p.   ORCL, GNCL, SCHS
Evans, E. G. The first one hundred twenty-five years. NP:
typescript, 1968. 8 p.   FURM
Exposition of the causes & character of the difficulties in the
[Methodist Episcopal] church in Charleston, in the year 1833;
up to November 28, of that year. Chstn: J.S. Burges, 1834.
v.p.   WOFF
Faile, J. A. Celebration of the one hundredth anniversary of
the organization of New Hope Baptist Church, Lancaster County,
SC. Kershaw: Kershaw Era, 1932. 18 p.   FURM
Fairview Baptist Church, Greer. A history...1885-1968. NP:
author, 1960? 30 p.   FURM
Fairview [Baptist Church] #2. NP: typescript, 1936. 1 p. FURM
Fairview Baptist Church, Greer. A history... NP: NPub, 1960.
32 p.   FURM
Fairview [Presbyterian] Church [Greenville]. NP: typescript,
nd. 11 p.   MONT
Faith Bible Church, Lynchburg. [History.] NP: typescript, nd.
7 p.   SMCL

Fant, Mrs. George C. A brief sketch of St. John's United Methodist Church. Anderson: author, 1970. 4 p.   PIPD
Felkel, Nancy B. A history of Jericho Methodist Church [Orangeburg County]. NP: mimeo, 1952. 11 p.   ORCL
Fender, Anne. Hunters Chapel Baptist Church [Bamberg County].
History. NP: NPub, 1973. 22 p.   SCL
Fernwood Baptist Church [Spartanburg County]. NP: NPub, 1962.
27 p.   FURM
Finch, J. S. History of Unity [Baptist] Church [Spartanburg].
NP: typescript, nd. 4 p.   FURM
Ficken, John F. St. John's Lutheran Church of Charleston, SC.
An historical address... NP: NPub, 1918. 19 p.   SCHS, SCL
Finklea, Enoch S. Ebenezer Methodist Church, 1792-1969. NP:
typescript, nd. 36 p.   LXMU
Fickling, Susan Marea. Christianization of the Negro in SC,
1830-1860. Thesis (M.A.), U.S.C., 1923. 40 p.   SCL
First Baptist Church [SpC]   FACM
First Baptist Church, Abbeville. Historical sketch & brochure
for building campaign. Abbeville? 1953? 18 p.   FURM
First Baptist Church, Abbeville. History... Abbeville: Banner
Publ. Co., 1939. 14 p.   SCL, FURM
First Baptist Church, Aiken. Centennial...1937. Aiken: Aiken
Standard & Review, 1937. 34 p.   SCL, FURM
First Baptist Church, Aiken. Sesquicentennial celebration,
1805-1955. Aiken: NPub, 1955. 24 p.   FURM
First Baptist Church, Anderson. Covenant, by-laws & directory
... Anderson: the church, 1922. 11 p.   SCL
First Baptist Church, Bamberg. 1872-1972...A century of service
for Christ. NP: NPub, 1972. unp.   FURM
First Baptist Church, Barnwell [SpC]   FURM
First Baptist Church, Barnwell. The one hundred seventy-fifth
anniversary...1977. NP: NPub, 1977. 20 p.   SCL
First Baptist Church, Batesburg. The First Baptist Church,
Batesburg, SC, 1872-1958. NP: NPub, 1972. 24 p.   LXMU
First Baptist Church, Batesburg. A historical sketch of the...
...in Lexington County, SC, 1872-1958. NP: NPub, 1958. 24
p.   LXCL, FURM
First Baptist Church, Camden [SpC]   FURM
First Baptist Church, Camden. Sesqui-centennial celebration...
November 13th, 1960. NP: NPub, nd. 10 p.   KECA, SCL
First Baptist Church, Charleston [SpC]   FURM
First Baptist Church, Chester. 1833-1933. Centennial number.
Bulletin of the First Baptist Church, Chester, SC... Chester:
NPub, 1933. unp.   SCL, FURM
First Baptist Church, Columbia. A decade...the Lord's servant,
with the Lord's message for the Lord's people. 1953-1963.
NP: NPub, 1963. 4 p.   SCL
First Baptist Church, Columbia. Dedication. The First Baptist
Church, Hampton & Sumter streets, Columbia, SC... April 15,
1945. NP: NPub, nd. 20 p.   SCL
First Baptist Church, Columbia. A half century together, 1927-

1977. NP: NPub, 1977. 43 p.   SCL
First Baptist Church, Columbia. Your church yesterday, today,
    tomorrow... NP: NPub, 1960? 16 p.   SCL
First Baptist Church, Conway [SpC]   FURM
First Baptist Church, Conway. After 100 years: the month of
    celebration... 1866-1966. Conway: the church, 1966. unp.
                                                      HOCL, FURM
First Baptist Church, Duncan. 100 years... NP: NPub, 1975.
    unp.   FURM
First Baptist Church, Easley [SpC]   FURM
First Baptist Church, Easley. A century for Christ, 1873-1973..
    Easley: the church, 1973. 10 p.   FURM
First Baptist Church, Edgefield. First Baptist Church, Edge-
    field, SC: organized 1823. One hundred years for Christ.
    Edgefield: the church, 1979.   EDTO
First Baptist Church, Fairfax. The First Baptist Church, Fair-
    fax, SC, constituted 1852... NP: NPub, 1963? 64 p.   FURM
First Baptist Church, Florence. After 100 years: the week of
    celebration: centennial, 1866-1966, Florence SC, June 10,
    1966. Florence: Centennial Committee, 1966? 68 p. DAHC, FURM
First Baptist Church, Florence. Centennial, 1866-1966. Flor-
    ence: the church, 1966. 33 p.   SCL, FLCL, CLCC
First Baptist Church, Florence. The First Baptist Church...
    1866-1941... NP: NPub, 1941. 38 p.   FLCL
First Baptist Church, Gaffney. History... NP: NPub, 1951.
    2 p.   FURM
First Baptist Church, Georgetown. [History, ms.] 1805. 40 p.
                                                            FURM
First Baptist Church, Greenville. Manual... Constituted Novem-
    ber 2d, 1831. Greenville: Keys & Thomas, 1894. 45 p.SCL,SPCL
First Baptist Church, Greer. 75th anniversary & history, 1880-
    1955... Greer: Charles P. Smith Printing Co., 1955. 95 p.
                                                            FURM
First Baptist Church, Hartsville. [History] 1850-1950.   DAHC
First Baptist Church, Hartsville. ...One hundred years of ser-
    vice; 1850-1950. 45 p.   COKL, SCL
First Baptist Church, Hartsville. ...One hundred twenty-five
    years of service. NP: NPub, 1975. 11 p.   DAHC, FURM
First Baptist Church, Hemingway. The first fifty years: a hist-
    ory...1921-1971. NP: NPub, 1971? 52 p.   FURM
First Baptist Church, Inman. Centennial history...1865-1965...
    NP: NPub, 1965. 21 p.   FURM
First Baptist Church, Jackson. [History]...1952-1977. NP:NPub,
    1977. 30 p.   FURM
First Baptist Church, Kershaw. [History.] NP: NPub, 1963. 61
    p.   FURM
First Baptist Church, Lancaster. ...Church library bulletin.
    Anniversary number. July 1943-July 1945. Lancaster: the
    church, 1945. 7 p.   SCL
First Baptist Church, Laurens. Dedication service, May 18,
    1958,... NP: NPub, 1958. 8 p.   SCL

First Baptist Church, Laurens. Historical sketch, 1834-1934,
   read at [the] centennial celebration, Sunday, Oct. 21, 1934.
   Laurens: the church, 1934. 29 p.   SCL, FURM
First Baptist Church, Myrtle Beach. [History.] Myrtle Beach:
   the church, 1950. 3 p.   FURM
First Baptist Church, Myrtle Beach. The First Baptist Church.
   The King's Highway at Fourth Ave., North, Myrtle Beach, SC.
   NP: NPub, 1970. unp.   HOCL
First Baptist Church, North Augusta. A history ...1902-1962.
   North Augusta: Npub, 1962? 35 p.   FURM
First Baptist Church, North Charleston. Dedication week...
   NP: NPub, 1960. 18 p.   FURM
First Baptist Church, Orangeburg. Centennial booklet... One
   hundredth anniversary number, 1860-1960. NP: NPub, nd. 42
   p.   FURM
First Baptist Church, Pamplico. [History.] Pamplico: the
   church, 1971. 7 p.   FURM
First Baptist Church, St. Matthews. 1875-1975: centennial Sun-
   day. St. Matthews: NPub, 1975. 10 p.   SCL
First Baptist Church, Simpsonville. A history... NP: typescript, nd. 5 p.   FURM
First Baptist Church, Spartanburg. Centennial booklet...one
   hundredth anniversary number, 1839-1939. Spartanburg: Wil-
   liams Printing Co., 1939? 69 p.   FURM, SCL
First Baptist Church, Surfside Beach. History... NP: type-
   script, 1964. 2 p.   FURM
First Baptist Church, Timmonsville. A history... Timmonsville:
   Rutledge Printing Co., 1972. 41 p.   FURM
First Baptist Church, Union. A history...centennial year, 1856-
   1956... NP: Delmar Publ. Co., 1956. 126 p.   YOCL, FURM
First Baptist Church, Wagner. Heritage day... NP: typescript,
   nd. 6 p.   FURM
First Baptist Church, Walhalla. History...centennial edition.
   Walhalla: the church, 1967. 51 p.   FURM
First Baptist Church, Warrenville. [History.] NP: typescript,
   1975. 6 p.   FURM
First Baptist Church, Winnsboro. Diamond jubilee, 1860-1935...
   NP: NPub, 1935? 13 p.   SCHS
First Baptist Church, York. A brief history... York: the
   church, 1976. 11 p.   FURM
First Christian Church, Charleston. Directory. NP: NPub, nd.
   24 p.   SCL
First Methodist Church [SpC]   FACM
First Methodist Episcopal Church, South, Cheraw. Historical
   year book & directory...1933. NP: NPub, nd. 20 p.   SCL
First Presbyterian Church, Aiken. Directory [& history], 1980.
   Aiken: the church, 1980. 59 p.   SCL, SCHS
First Presbyterian Church, Anderson. History of the Nell Town-
   send Memorial Chapel, Anderson, SC [SpC]   MONT
First Presbyterian Church, Charleston. Centennial celebration
   of the dedication of the First Presbyterian Church, Charles-

ton, SC. Organized 1732... Chstn: W,E&C, 1915. 156 p.
GRCL, SCL, SCHS
First Presbyterian Church, Charleston. ...Bi-centennial, First
(Scotch) Presbyterian Church...1931. Chstn: NPub, 1931.
20 p.   SCL, SCHS
First Presbyterian Church, Columbia [SpC]   MONT
First Presbyterian Church, Columbia. Manual...1914. Cola: RLB,
1913. 45 p.   MONT
First Presbyterian Church, Columbia. Rules & regulations for
the spiritual & temporal concerns of the...church... Cola:
Morgan's Letter Press, 1844. 12 p.   SCL
First Presbyterian Church, Florence. The history...centennial
edition, 1861-1961. Florence: the church, 1962. 48 p.
SCL, FLMC, COKL, FLCL
First Presbyterian Church, Greenville. Centennial celebration..
. February 26, 29, 1948. NP: NPub, nd. 16 p.   SCL
First Presbyterian Church, Greenwood. The First Presbyterian
Church... 1883-1958. Greenwood: the church, 1959? 88 p.
GWPL, SCL
First Presbyterian Church, Hartsville. Manual... June 15, 1926
NP: NPub, nd. 20 p.   SCL, MONT
First Presbyterian Church, Rock Hill. Centennial Sunday: in
commemoration of the one hundredth anniversary of the organ-
ization of the church, 1869-1969. Rock Hill: the church,
1969. 16 p.   SCL
First Presbyterian Church, Rock Hill. The order of service for
the commemoration of the two hundredth anniversary of the
organization of the Old Waxhaw Presbyterian Church, Lancaster
County, SC. Rock Hill: White Printing Co., 1955. 4 p.   SCL
First Presbyterian Church, Spartanburg. 1843-1943. One hund-
redth anniversary... Spartanburg: Band & White, 1943. 11 p.
SCL, SPCL
First Presbyterian Church, Sumter [SpC]   MONT
First Presbyterian Church, Sumter. History... Organized May
29, 1823... Sumter: Sumter Printing Co., 1973. 22 p. SCL MONT
First Presbyterian Church, Sumter. History... NP: NPub, 1923.
8 p.   MONT
First Presbyterian Church, Woodruff. History... 1877-1977.
NP: NPub, 1977. 17 p.   MONT
First Presbyterian Church, York. Programme of the celebration
of the seventy-fifth anniversary... 1842-1917. Cola: State
Co., nd. 3 p.   SCL
First Presbyterian Church, York. Programme of opening exercises
of McNeil Memorial Sunday school building...1917. NP: NPub,
1917. 2 p.   SCL
First Presbyterian Church, Yorkville. Manual...August 1st,
1903. Yorkville: Enquirer Office, 1903. 8 p.   SCL
First (Scots) Presbyterian Church, Charleston. Documents relative to the controversy in the First Presbyterian Church of
the city of Charleston, SC, which terminated in the resigna-
tion of the pastor. Chstn: Miller, 1817. 37 p.   SCL, SCHS

First (Scots) Presbyterian Church, Charleston. The First Pres-
byterian Church, organized A.D. 1732, Meeting & Tradd Streets,
Charleston, SC. [Bulletin for the service on the occasion of
the 200th anniversary of the St. Andrew's Society.] Chstn:
Heisser Print. Co., 1929. 4 p.   SCL
First United Methodist Church, Cheraw. A history... NP: NPub,
1974. 15 p.   WOMA
Fischer, Susan E. The Tree of Life Temple, 1896-1971. Cola:
Vogue Press, 1972. 140 p.   SCL
Fisher, Mary S. Memorials & gifts to Trinity Church. Cola:
NPub, 1934. 13 p.   SCL
Fishing Creek Presbyterian Church, Chester County. History...
with miscellaneous notes. Rock Hill: typescript, nd. unp.
                                                       YOCL
Fiske, Evlyn. Pine Grove Baptist Church No. 1, Colleton Asso-
ciation [SpC]   FURM
Flat Creek Baptist Church, Lynch Creek. [History.] NP: mimeo,
nd. 2 p.   FURM
Fleming, Ambrose G. The bi-centennial history of Wesley Memor-
ial Methodist Church, formerly Waverly Methodist Episcopal
Church, South, Columbia, SC. Cola: RLB, 1960. 45 p.   SCL
Floyd, Viola. History of Lancaster First Methodist Church,
1833-1961. Lancaster: NPub, 1962. 172 p.   COMMON
Flynn, Jean M. History of the First Baptist Church of Taylors,
SC. Clinton: Jacobs Bros., 1964. 133 p.   SCL, SPCL, GRCL
Formal opening & dedication of the educational building & Skin-
ner Organ. The First Baptist Church, Spartanburg, SC. Spar-
tanburg: Band & White, 1928. 10 p.   WOFF
Fort Hill Presbyterian Church, Clemson. History & mission...
Clemson: NPub, 1952. 8 p.   SCL, MONT
Freeman, J. Earle. History of Mt. Elon Baptist Church.   DAHC
Freeman, J. Earle. Pleasant Grove Baptist Church. A century of
history. Greer: typescript, 1933. 26 p.   FURM
French Protestant [Huguenot] Church, Charleston. Correspondence
with the French Protestant Church of Charleston. NP: NPub,
1873? 14 p.   SCL
French Protestant [Huguenot] Church, Charleston. The French
Protestant (Huguenot) Church in the city of Charleston, SC.
NP: NPub, nd. 23 p.   SPCL, SCL
French Protestant [Huguenot] Church, Charleston. The French
Protestant Church in the city of Charleston, "The Huguenot
church.". A brief history of the church and two addresses
delivered on the two hundred and twenty-fifth anniversary of
the founding of the church, April fourteenth, nineteen hundred
and twelve. Chstn: W,E&C, 1912. 38 p.   SCL, SCHS
French Protestant [Huguenot] Church, Charleston. Celebrating
the 250th anniversary of the arrival of the ship "Richmond"

144

with forty-five Huguenots at Charles Town, province of Carolina, April, 1680. Chstn, 1930. 4 p.   SCHS
French Protestant [Huguenot] Church, Charleston. The French
Protestant (Huguenot) Church in the city of Charleston, SC.
Chstn?, 1898? 12 p.   SCHS
French Protestant [Huguenot] Church, Charleston. The liturgy of
the French Protestant church, translated from the editions of
1737 & 1772, published at Neuchatel, with additional prayers,
carefully selected, and some alterations: arranged for the use
of the congregation in the city of Charleston, SC. Chstn:
James S. Burges, 1836. 128 p. 2nd ed., 226 p.   GRCL, SCL
French Protestant [Huguenot] Church, Charleston. The two hundred and twenty-fifth anniversary of the founding...April 14,
1912. 4 p.   SCHS
Friendship Baptist Church, Spartanburg County. The history of
Friendship Baptist Church, Pauline, SC. NP: NPub, 1965. 2 p.
                                                            FURM
Frierson, John L. History of the Church of the Holy Cross...
given at the celebration of the one hundredth anniversary of
the laying of the cornerstone, September 11, 1850. Stateburg:
NPub, 1950. 27 p.   SMCL, SCL
Fulmer, Verley L. History of St. Peter's Lutheran Church, Piney
Woods. Newberry: NPub, 1944. 36 p.   LTSS, SCL
Furman, James C. An historical discourse delivered before the
Charleston Baptist Association, at its hundredth anniversary,
held in Charleston in November, 1851... Chstn: Southern Bap-
tist Publication Society, 1852. 22 p.   SCL
Furman, W. A history of the Charleston Association of Baptist
Churches. Chstn: J. Hoff, 1811. 238 p.   COKL, FLCL, SCL
Gapway Baptist Church, Mullins. [History.] NP: mimeo, 1936.
3 p.   FURM
Gapway Baptist Church, Mullins. History... NP: NPub, 1975.
1 p.   FURM
Garber, Paul N. The legal & historical aspects of the plan of
union for the unification of the Methodist Protestant Church,
the Methodist Episcopal Church, & the Methodist Episcopal
Church, South. Greensboro NC: Piedmont Press, 1938. 40 p.
                                                            WOFF
Gardner, George W. The history of Bull Swamp Baptist Church, of
Orangeburg County, from its organization, July 6, 1816, to
July 6, 1916. Greenwood: Sheridan Printing Co., 1916. 25 p.
                                                            SCHS
Garrett, T. H. A history of the Saluda Baptist Association, together with historical sketches of the churches composing the
body, biographical sketches of deceased ministers, moderators,
clerks, assistant clerks & treasurers; lists of ministers
raised up in the association; also interesting statistical
tables. Richmond VA: B.F. Johnson Publishing Co., 1896.
350 p.   SCL, ANCL
George, Annie L. Lexington Methodist Church, 1850-1950. Lexington: Lexington Methodist Church, 1950. 15 p.   LXMU

George, Virginia M. History of Friendship Presbyterian Church
   [Laurens County]. NP: NPub, 1970. 22 p.   MONT
Getsinger, Boardman G. Harmony Presbyterian Church [Crocket-
   ville]...1870-1970... NP: NPub, 1970. 17 p.   MONT
Gettys, Ebenezer. Studies in church history of the Associate
   Reformed Presbyterian Church. Due West: Associate Reformed
   Presbyterian Co., 1954. 47 p.   SCL
Gibbes, D. L. Lynchburg Presbyterian Church of Harmony Presby-
   tery. NP: typescript, nd.   DAHC
Gibson, B. M. Berea First Baptist Church [Greenville]. Her
   walk with God for one hundred and twenty-five years. NP:
   typescript, nd. 17 p.   FURM
Gibson, Lewis W. History of Coneross Baptist Church [Oconee
   County], from its beginnings in 1798. NP: NPub, 1971. 103
   p.   PIPD, FURM
Girinni, Bettie W. History & directory. Wesley M.E. Church.
   NP: NPub, 1936.   DAHC
Glenn Springs Presbyterian Church, Glenn Springs [SpC]   MONT
Glover, Beulah. Methodism in Colleton County, 1786-1957. Wal-
   terboro: Press & Standard, 1957. 38 p.   COMMON
Godfrey, W. R. A historical sketch of old St. David's [Episco-
   pal] Church, Cheraw, SC, from 1768 to 1916. Cheraw: NPub,
   1916. 20 p.   COMMON
Goldsmith, William. Clear Spring Baptist Church [history.
   Greenville County]. NP: typescript, 1925. unp.   FURM
Good Hope Baptist Church, Saluda County. A historical sketch...
   Saluda: the church, 1954. 9 p.   FURM
Goodlett, Mildred W. Our heritage; a history of Smyrna Church
   & of the Boozers of Smyrna. Traveler's Rest, 1963. 272 p.
                                          CLEM, SCL, SMCL
Gordon Memorial Methodist Church [SpC]   FACM
Gordon, Will. Historical sketch of Beersheba [Presbyterian]
   Church [York County]. NP: typescript, 1918. 5 p.   MONT
Gore, Mrs. Herman W. History of Loris First Baptist Church
   [1881-1969]. NP: typescript, 1969? unp.   HOCL
Gower, Arthur G. Short story of Presbyterian church life in
   Greenville...75th anniversary of the First Presbyterian Church
   1848-1923. NP: NPub, 1923. 52 p.   GRCL, SCL, MONT
Grace Episcopal Church, Anderson. Program of the centennial
   celebration to commemorate the founding of the Episcopal
   church in Anderson, called Grace Church. In the year of our
   Lord eighteen hundred and fifty-one. NP: NPub, nd. 26 p. SCL
Grace Episcopal Church, Charleston. Charter, constitution & by-
   Laws of Grace Church, Charleston, SC. NP: NPub, nd. 15 p.SCL
Grace Episcopal Church, Charleston. Grace Church & greater
   Charleston. Chstn: the church, 1957. 16 p.   SCL
Graham, L. Clifton. History of Central United Methodist Church,
   Newberry, SC. NP: NPub, 1970. 28 p.   SCL
Grant, Henry M. Historical sketch of the "Circular" Independent
   or Congregational Church of Charleston, SC. NP: NPub, 1890.
   9 p.   SCL, YOCL, SCHS

Grant, Kathleen. Milford Baptist Church, 1832-1972. Greer:
typescript, 1972? 16 p.   GRCL
Gray, Z. L. Historical sketch of the Brownsville Baptist Church
Blenheim, SC. Blenheim?: NPub, 1954. 12 p.   FURM
A great missionary force, 1877-1977: Santee Baptist Association,
SC, 1977: historical supplement. NP: NPub, 1977? 74 p. FURM
Green, Anna. Greer First Baptist Church. NP: typescript, nd.
9 p.   FURM
Green, Leslie. History of Mt. Gallagher [Baptist] Church [Laur-
ens County]. NP: typescript, 1962. 6 p.   FURM
Greenlawn Baptist Church, Columbia. Eighty-one years of service
Cola: the church, 1965. 19 p.   FURM
Green, Mary C. Boiling Springs Baptist Church; where the saints
have trod. Clinton: Jacobs Bros., 1959. 192 p.   FURM, SPCL
                                                          SCHS
Green, Mary L. Augusta Heights Baptist Church; twenty-fifth
anniversary. Greenville: the church, 1975. unp. FURM, GRCL
Green, Samuel M. An historical outline of Greenville Circuit,
SC Conference, Methodist Episcopal Church, South. 15 p. GRCL
Green Sea Baptist Church, Horry County. [History.] NP: mimeo,
1936. 2 p.   FURM
Green Street Baptist Church, Spartanburg. Diamond jubilee
history. Spartanburg: the church, 1966. 12 p.   SPCL, FURM
Greenbriar Methodist Church [SpC]   FACM
Greenwood Presbyterian Church, Greenwood. Manual... Abbeville:
Press & Banner, 1892. 26 p.   MONT
Greer, Carl E. Pathways to glory; a history of Honea Path Bap-
tist Church, 1869-1969. Greenville: Barfield Printing Co.,
1969. 120 p.   FURM, PIPD
Gregg, Bessie A. & Constance A. Gregg. Sketches on the history
of Christ [Episcopal] Church, Florence County, SC. Florence:
Fry's Mimeograph Shop, nd. 42 p.   EPDI, DAHC, SCL
Gregg, Frances W. A brief history of Bethel Presbytery to 1900.
Rock Hill: Winthrop College, 1948. 90 p.   YOCL
Gregorie, Anne K. Christ [Episcopal] Church, 1706-1959; a plan-
tation parish. Chstn: Dalcho Historical Society, 1961. 169
p.   COMMON
Gregory, Ola. History of Monaghan Baptist Church [Greenville].
Greenville: the church, 1970. 16 p.   FURM
Grier, Mrs. Boyce M. The First Presbyterian Church of Green-
wood, SC. 1883-1958. NP: NPub, nd. 88 p.   SCHS, MONT
Griffin, Charles M. The story of SC Baptists, 1683-1933.
Greenwood: Connie Maxwell Orphanage Press, 1934. 113 p. SCHS
                                                     GRCL, SCL
Grigsby, Mrs. Charlotte C. Cloud of Witnesses, 1879-1959. A
history of the Grassy Pond Baptist Church. Gaffney: NPub,
1959? 64 p.   FURM
Gunter, M. B. The Mt. Pisgah Baptist Church [Kershaw County].
NP: typescript, nd. 2 p.   FURM
Gwynn, Andrew K. History of St. Mary Help of Christians Church
& the Aiken missions.   GTML

147

Hallman, S. T.   A history of the Evangelical Lutheran Synod of
   SC, 1824-1924. Cola: Farrell Printing Co., 1924. 318 p.
                                                              COMMON
Hamer, Lewis M.   Historical address...at the dedication of
   Beauty Spot Methodist Church, June 17, 1883, Marlboro County,
   SC. [typescript copy.] 26 p.   MRCL, WOMA
Hamilton, John A.   History of Orangeburg Presbyterian Church...
   1835...1896. Orangeburg: R.L. Berry, 1896. 39 p. MONT, ORCL
Hamlet, Georgia.   A history of the First Baptist Church, Ander-
   son, SC, 1821-1979. Anderson: author, 1979. 109 p.   ANCL
                                              SCL, PIPD, FURM
Hamlet, Georgia.   The Saluda Baptist Association; one hundred
   and seventy-five years of progress, 1803-1978. Anderson:
   Saluda Baptist Assn., 1978. 23 p.   ANCL, PIPD, SCL
Hammett, Pauline.   Fifty fruitful years of Holston Creek Baptist
   Church, 1901-1951. Greer: Smith Printing Co., 1951. 14 p.
                                                              FURM
Hannum, Eleanor C.   The parish in SC, 1706-1868. Thesis (M.A.),
   U.S.C., 1970. 77 p.   SCL
Hardee, Nell.   Historical sketch of the First Baptist Church of
   Florence, 1916-1966. NP: NPub, 1966. 16 p.   FURM
Hardin, Joan.   Fiftieth Anniversary, 1971 [Mayo Baptist Church,
   Mayo]. Mayo: the church, 1971. 34 p.   FURM
Harper, Edwin.   History of the Baptist church at Andrews, SC
   [Georgetown County]. NP: typescript, nd. 7 p.   FURM
Hart, Georgia H.   Trinity Episcopal Church [Columbia]; a
   thoughtful study & pocket guide. Cola, 1965. 111 p.   COMMON
Hart, Joseph E. Jr.   The Church of the Good Shepherd [Episcopal]
   York, SC; a centennial history, 1855-1955. York: NPub, 1955.
   38 p.   COMMON
Hart, Tillie.   A brief history of Enoree Baptist Church [Trav-
   eler's Rest]. NP: typescript, 1952. 8 p.   FURM
Hatcher, Leila N.   History of the Woman's Missionary Union of
   the First Baptist Church, Gaffney, SC. Gaffney: Southland
   Printers, nd. 87 p.   CRCL
Hay, Percy D.   St. Helena's Episcopal Church, Beaufort, SC. Two
   hundredth anniversary, 1712-1912. A short historical sketch
   of the parish from the first English settlement... NP: NPub,
   1912. 6 p.   SCL
Hayne Baptist Church, Spartanburg. Dedication services, 1951.
   Spartanburg? 1951? 12 p.   FURM
Heath Springs Baptist Church, Lancaster County. Parade of
   history... NP: typescript, 1 p.   FURM
Heemsoth, Wilhelm. Gesetze der deutsch-evangelisch-lutherisch-
   en Gemeinde zu Charleston, Süd-Carolina. Baltimore MD: Druck-
   eri von William Raine, 1843. 20 p.   SCL
Hegarty, Thomas J. History of St. Peter's parish, Columbia, SC.
   Cola: State Co., 1914. 27 p.   CDIO, SCL
Heiss, Willard. Quakers in the SC backcountry; Wateree & Bush
   River. NP: Indiana Quaker Records, 1969. 24 p.   SCL, SMCL
Helms, Hal M. The history of Unity Baptist Church, 1900-1950.

148

NP: NPub, 195? 23 p.   FURM
Hemphill, James C. Scotch-Irish Presbyterianism in history.
    Address by J.C. Hemphill... Winnsboro, SC, Saturday, November
    7, 1903. NP: NPub, nd. 11 p.   SCL, YOCL
Henderson, E. F. Reedy Fork Baptist Church [History]. NP:
    typescript, nd. 5 p.   FURM
Henderson, Gertrude. History of Gap Hill Baptist Church [Green-
    ville]. NP: typescript, 1971. 3 p.   FURM
Henderson, Thomas. History of Standing Spring Baptist Church
    [Greenville County]. NP: typescript, 1919. 3 p.   FURM
Hendrix, Mrs. H. B. History of Grace Evangelical Lutheran
    Church, 1859-1959... NP: NPub, 1959. 26 p.   SCL
Hendrix, Marion H. Some items of historical interest...Cedar
    Spring Baptist Church...Organized 1786. NP: mimeo, 1971.
    3 p.   FURM
Henerey, J. T. Washington Baptist Church [Pelzer]. Pelzer:
    the church, nd. 10 p.   FURM
Hennig, Helen K. The tree of life. Fifty years of congrega-
    tional life at the Tree of Life Synagogue, Columbia, SC.
    Cola: Tree of Life Congregation, 1945. 144 p.   SCL
Herbert, Walter I. Fifty wonderful years, 1878-1928. Story of
    missionary work by Methodist women in SC. NP: Jubilee Commit-
    tee, 1928. 283 p.   COMMON
Heyward, Marie H. The [Episcopal] Diocese of SC. Chstn: NPub,
    1938. 52 p.   SCL, SCHS
Hicklin, Mrs. Frank. History of Fishing Creek Presbyterian
    Church [Chester County]. NP: mimeo, 1958. 6 p.   MONT
High Hills of Santee Baptist Church, Sumter County, SC. Sumter:
    Sumter Chamber of Commerce, 1974. 2 p.   FURM
Highland Park Baptist Church. NP: NPub, 1978. 11 p.   FURM
High Point Baptist Church, Lancaster. 50th anniversary, 1911-
    1961. NP: NPub, 1961. 23 p.   FURM
Hilborn, Mrs. R. B., Jr. History of Mt. Olivet Lutheran Church,
    Spring Hill, Chapin, SC. Chapin: the church, 1973. 72 p.LXMU
Hills, Isabel L. A historical sketch of the John's Island
    Presbyterian Church, 1710-1960. NP: mimeo, 1937. 9 p.   SCHS
                                                        SCL, MONT
Hilson, James B. History of the SC Conference of the Wesleyan
    Methodist Church of America; fifty-five years of Wesleyan
    Methodism in SC. Winona Lake IN: Light & Life Press, 1950.
    308 p.   SCL, GRCL, PICL
Historical address and commemorative ode, delivered in the[Pres-
    byterian] Synod of SC...1885 [incl. Scots or First Presbyter-
    ian Church, Charleston; Waxhaw Presbyterian Church, Lancaster
    County; Purity Presbyterian Church, Chester]. Richmond VA:
    Whittet & Shepperson, 1886. 86 p.   SCL, MONT
Historical sketch. High Hill Baptist Church. NP: typescript,
    1940.   DAHC
History of Beaverdam Baptist Church. 1957.   LRCL
A history of Cannon's Camp Ground, United Methodist Church,
    Route 1, Box 166, Spartanburg... NP: NPub, 1976. SCL, WOMA

History of Dunean Baptist Church. Greenville: the church, 1962.
    2 p.   FURM
History of Lebanon Church & community. 1952.   LRCL
History of Walnut Grove Baptist Church, 1826-1976.   GSGN
History of the Marion Methodist Church, one hundred and seventy
    years, 1786-1956 and a pageant from Asbury onward. Marion:
    the church, 1956. 49 p.   SCL, MACL
Hitt, Clara L. The Barnwell Baptist Association. Greenville:
    Baptist Courier Co., 1914. 236 p.   SCL
Holcombe, Lena. Brief history of Harmony Baptist Church of
    Laurens Association. 1845-1945. NP: NPub, 1946. 8 p. LRCL
                                                             FURM
Holiday, Billy. A brief history of Brookland United Methodist
    Church. NP: typescript, 1970. 6 p.   LXMU
Hollis, Daniel W. Development of the Presbyterian church in the
    Carolinas. NP: typescript, 1963. 8 p.   SCL
Hollis, Daniel W. Look to the rock: one hundred ante-bellum
    Presbyterian churches of the south. NP: John Knox Press,
    1961. 142 p.   SCL, GTML, SCHS
Holly Springs Baptist Church, Spartanburg County. History...
    NP: NPub, 1955. 22 p.   FURM
Holmes, A. G. Points of historic interest: the old Stone Church
    [Hopewell Presbyterian Church]. Pendleton & Clemson College.
    NP: NPub, nd. 8 p.   SCHS
Holmes, George S. The parish church of St. Michael in Charles
    Town, in the province of South Carolina. Founded 1752. Cola:
    State Co., 1887. 47 p.   COMMON
Holy Communion Church Institute, Charleston. History... NY:
    D. Appleton & Co., 1875. 63 p.   EPDI
Holy Communion Church Institute, Charleston. History of a work
    of faith & love in Charleston, SC...founded by the Rev. A.
    Toomer Porter...3rd ed. NY: D. Appleton & Co., 1881.
    (SCL has 1st, 2nd & 4th eds.)   SCL, EPDI
Honea Path Presbyterian Church. History... NP: NPub, nd. 4
    p.   MONT
Hood, C. W. Durkin Creek [Baptist Church, Fountain Inn].
    Ms., 1921. 3 p.   FURM
Hopewell Baptist Church, Hampton. Centennial program, 1854-
    1956. NP: NPub, 1956. 8 p.   FURM
Hopewell Church, Chester County. History...[SpC]   CSCL
Hopkins, Laura J. History of St. John's Episcopal church, 1858-
    1958, Congaree, SC. Cola: RLB, 1958. 83 p.   SCL
Horeb Baptist Church, Sumter County. [History.] NP: mimeo,
    1936. 1 p.   FURM
Horn, Edward T. A discourse: embracing a sketch of the history
    of St. John's Lutheran Church, Charleston, SC, from 1734 to
    1861... Chstn: Lucas & Richardson, 1883. 24 p. SCL FLCL, SCHS
Howard, Charles W. Sermon delivered at the reopening & dedica-
    tion of the French Protestant [Huguenot] Church of Charleston,
    SC. Chstn: Burges, 1845. (Copy at the Presbyterian Historical
    Society, Philadelphia.)   SCL

Howard, A. J. Dedication of Tigerville Baptist Church. NP:
   typescript, 1963. 6 p.   FURM
Howard, James A. & Ruth H. Howard. History of Highland Baptist
   Church [Greenville County]. NP: NPub, 1974. 10 p.   FURM
Howe, Mrs. Christopher G. History of St. Philip's Church.
   Chstn: NPub, nd. 4 p.   SCHS
Howe, George. An appeal to the young men of the Presbyterian
   Church in the Synod of South Carolina & Georgia. Cola: NPub,
   1836. 48 p.   SCL, SPCL, GRCL
Howe, George. The early Presbyterian immigration into SC...
   Cola: R. W. Gibbes, 1858. 41 p.   SCL
Howe, George. History of the Presbyterian Church in SC. 1870,
   rp Cola: [Presbyterian] Synod of SC, 1965. 2 vol.   COMMON
Howe, William B. Relations of the [Episcopal] church to the
   colored race. NP: NPub, nd. 7 p.   SCL
Howe, William B. Sermon preached...at the centennial convention
   held in the Church of the Holy Communion, Charleston, on May
   7th, 1890. Chstn: W,E&C, 1890. 24 p.   SCL
Howe, William B. Special services held at St. Philip's Church,
   Charleston, SC, May 12-13, 1875... historical address...by
   J.J. Pringle Smith... Chstn: W,E&C, 1876. 172 p. SCL, SPCL
Huff, Archie V. Tried by fire: Washington Street United Meth-
   odist Church, Columbia. Cola: RLB, 1975. 163 p.

                                                             COMMON
Humphreys, David. An historical account of the incorporated
   Society for the Propagation of the Gospel in Foreign Parts.
   Containing their foundation, proceedings, and the success of
   their missionaries in the British colonies, to the year 1728.
   London: Joseph Downing, 1730; rp NY: Arno Press, 1965. 356
   p.   SCL
Humphreys, Mrs. John D. A brief history, 1926-1967...Inman
   Presbyterian Church, Inman, SC. NP: NPub, nd. 4 p.   MONT
Humphries, Arthur L. Articles about the history of Beulah
   United Methodist Church. NP: typescript, nd. unp.   WOMA
Humphries, Arthur L. Beulah United Methodist Church: the first
   hundred years, 1877-1977. NP: NPub, 1977. 18 p.   KECA
Hunters Chapel Baptist Church, Barnwell County. History...
   NP: typescript, nd. 1 p. (SCL has 1973, 19 p.)   SCL, FURM
Hutto, Nola M. History of the Baptist Church of Christ called
   Reedy Branch, Barnwell County, SC. 1874-1974. Bamberg:
   Kilgus Printing Co., 1973. 127 p.   SCL, FURM
Immanuel Baptist Church, Florence. Golden anniversary...1909-
   1959.   FURM, DAHC
Immanuel Lutheran Church, Greenwood. God with us. 1902-1977...
   NP: NPub, 1977. 18 p.   LTSS
Immanuel Lutheran Church, Greenwood. The history...1902-1962.
   NP: mimeo, 1962. 5 p.   LTSS
Independent or Congregational Church, Charleston. Fundamental
   articles of faith...adopted July 8, 1889... Chstn: W,E&C,
   1889. 30 p.   SCL
Independent or Congregational Church, Charleston. Historical

sketch of the Independent or Congregational (Circular) Church, from its origin to the present time. Boston: T. R. Marvin, 1887. 7 p.   SCL

Independent or Congregational Church, Charleston. Manual... Chstn: W,E&C, 1870. 68 p.   SCL, SCHS

Independent Presbyterian Church. Constitution & form of government...in the U.S.A., as adopted by the churches in convention held at Salem Church in Union District, SC, A.D. 1838... Cola: South Carolinian Print, 1839.   SCL, SPCL

Indiantown Presbyterian Church, Williamsburg County. An historical sketch...1757-1957. NP: NPub, 1957. 55 p.   COMMON

Ivey, Robert A. A history of the First Baptist Church of Woodruff, SC...published June 20, 1962 on the occasion of its 175th anniversary celebration... NP: NPub, 1962. 58 p. FURM

Ivey, Robert A. A history of the Pacolet Mills Baptist Church, 1884-1966. NP: NPub, 1966? 53 p.   FURM

Jackson Creek Baptist Church, Richland County. Centennial observance... NP: NPub, 1956. 10 p.   FURM

Jackson, Pearl. History of Stiefeltown Baptist Church [Warrenville]. NP: typescript, 1968. 6 p.   FURM

Jackson, Virginia. A short history of Bethel Presbyterian Church. Term paper, Winthrop College, 1949. 43 p.   YOCL

Jackson, William N. & others. Clover Presbyterian Church... fiftieth anniversary...1931. NP: NPub, 1931. 15 p. SCL, MONT

Jacobs, Thornwell. The generation of the silver bell... [First Presbyterian Church, Clinton]. Atlanta: Westminster Publishers, 1946? 23 p.   SCL, CLEM

Jacobs, William P. The history of the Presbyterian Church, Clinton, SC. Clinton: Thornwell Orphanage Press, 1901. 16 p.   SCL

James Island Presbyterian Church, Charleston County. History... [250th anniversary, 1956]. NP: NPub, 1956. 19 p. MONT, GRCL

Jarrott, C. E. History of St. John's Episcopal Church. 1920.
                                                        DAHC

Jaynes, Robert T. Homecoming held at old Center Methodist Church [Oconee County]... NP: NPub, 1944. 7 p.   SCL

Jaynes, Robert T. Methodism yesterday, today & tomorrow; an address... Cola: Epworth Orphanage Press, 1936. 24 p.   SCL
                                                        WOFF

Jaynes, Robert T. Three churches (Bethel Presbyterian Church, old Stone Presbyterian Church, Waxhaw Presbyterian Church.) NP: NPub, 1941. 34 p.   COMMON

Jenkins, Sophia S. ...Commemorative history of St. John's Parish, John's Island & Wadmalaw Island, SC... Chstn: W,E&C, 1970. 50 p.   COMMON

Jenkins, Warren M. Steps along the way...the origin & development of the SC Conference of the Central Jurisdiction of the Methodist Church. Cola: State Co., 1967. 87 p.   SCL

Jennings, Marie E. The story of an old church; in scrapbook form. Orangeburg, 1970. 34 p.   ORCL

Jeter, Edwin R. A history of Oakland Avenue Presbyterian Church

Rock Hill, SC, 1913-1963. NP: NPub, 1963? 20 p.   YOCL
                                                    MONT, SCL
John's Island Presbyterian Church...1710-1960. NP: NPub, 1960.
  9 p.   SCL, MONT
Jalmson, Callie. Organization & history of North Baptist
  Church [North, SC]. NP: typescript, 1962. 17 p.   FURM
Johnson, Elizabeth S. 176 years of service & love. Philadel-
  phia Baptist Church [Spartanburg County]. NP: typescript,
  1979. 17 p.   FURM
Johnson, Grant F. First Associate Reformed Presbyterian Church,
  Lancaster, SC, organized 1887. Lancaster: NPub, 1971. unp.
                                                             LNCL
Johnson, J. The first five years: history of the Woodfields
  Baptist Church, Greenwood, SC, 1959-1964. Greenwood: Drinkard
  Printing Co., 1964. 61 p.   FURM
Johnson, J. Albert & Mary N. Johnson. The first fifteen years:
  history of the Woodfields Baptist Church, Greenwood, SC, 1959-
  1974. NP: NPub, 1974. 118 p.   FURM
Johnson, O. E. The Summerville Presbyterian Church: a sketch of
  its origin & history. NP: NPub, 1894. 4 p.   SCL
Johnson, William B. Reply to the address of Edgefield Village
  Baptist Church, to the other churches composing the Edgefield
  Baptist Association. Abbeville: T. Moore Knox, 1854. 29 p.
                                                             SCL
Johnston Charge, M.E. Church, South. Directory...Columbia Dist-
  rict, Upper SC Conference. Composed of three churches: John-
  ston, Harmony & Spann. Johnston: NPub, 1926. 55 p.   SCL
Johnston, Coy K. Two centuries of Lawtonville Baptists, 1775-
  1975: an account of the founding & people of Lawtonville Bap-
  tist Church, originally known as the Savannah River, Carolina,
  Church, and after 1786 and for ninety-eight years as the Pipe
  Creek Church of Regular Baptists. Estill: Historical Committee of Lawtonville Baptist Church, 1975. 227 p.   SCHS
                                                    SCL, FURM
Jones, Allene S. The history of Rocky Creek Baptist Church,
  1834-1954. Greenville?: NPub, nd. 31 p.   GRCL
Jones, Charles C. Address delivered at Midway Meeting House in
  Liberty County, GA...1889...in honor of the founders of Mid-
  way Church & congregation. Augusta GA: Chronicle Publishing
  Co., 1889. 20 p.   SCL, SCHS
Jones, Dudley. A history of Liberty Springs Presbyterian Church
  Cross Hill, SC, 1787-1937. Clinton: Jacobs Graphic Arts Co.,
  1937. 34 p.   LRCL, MONT
Jones, Frank D & W. H. Mills. History of the Presbyterian
  Church in SC since 1850. Cola: RLB, 1926. 1094 p.   COMMON
Jones, Frank D. History of Purity Presbyterian Church of Ches-
  ter, SC, 1787-1937. Charlotte NC: Standard Printing Co.,
  1938. 186 p.   COMMON
Jones, G. Troy. Historical sketch, Mt. Pleasant Baptist Church,
  Laurens County, SC, 1767-1949. NP: NPub, nd. 12 p.LRCL, GWPL
Jones, G. Troy. Historical sketch. Mt. Pleasant Baptist

Church. Laurens County, SC. NP: typescript, nd. 12 p. FURM
Jones, G. Troy. History of Beaverdam Baptist Church, Laurens
County, SC...150th anniversary... NP: mimeo, 1957. 11 p.GWPL
FURM
Jones, G. Troy. Mount Pleasant Baptist Church [Laurens County].
Clerk's record, 1860-1943. NP: NPub, 1944. LRCL
Jones, Hazel P. The history of Sand Hill Baptist Church. Ker-
shaw Baptist Association, 1814-1955. Clinton: Jacobs Broth-
ers, 1956. 48 p. COMMON
Jones, Marie P. History of the Longtown Baptist Church [Fair-
field County]. NP: typescript, nd. 5 p. FURM
Jones, Troy. Mt. Gallagher [Baptist] Church. [History.] LRCL
Josey, R. M. History of Mt. Elon Baptist Church [Darlington
County]. Past & present. Cola: Cary Printing Co., nd. 7 p.
FURM
Joslin, Allen W. Church of the Resurrection, Greenwood, SC...
Historical sketch... NP: NPub, 1952. 16 p. SCL
Kahal Kadosh Beth Elohim [Synagogue, Charleston]. Since 1749;
the story of K. K. Beth Elohim of Charleston, SC. Chstn,
196? 4 p. SCHS
Keisler, Efird B. A history of St. Paul's Evangelical Lutheran
Church, Gilbert, SC. Gilbert: the church, 1978. 150 p. LXCL
SCL
Kelly, Ann M. Sparrow Swamp Baptist Church, 1891-1953. DAHC
Kenner, Helen C. Historical records of Trinity Episcopal Church
Edisto Island, SC. Rockingham NC: Dorsett Printing Co., 1975.
144 p. SCL, SCHS
Kentyre Presbyterian Church, Dillon County. A history...1871-
1963. NP: NPub, 1963. 8 p. MONT
Kershaw, John. History of the parish & the church of Saint
Michael. Chstn: W,E&C, 1915. 98 p. COMMON
Ketchen, Jane G. The history of Union Associate Reformed Pres-
byterian Church. 1745-1967. Richburg, Chester County, SC.
NP: NPub, 1967. 93 p. SCL
King, Mrs. Levis. History of the First Westminister Baptist
Church [Oconee County]. NP: typescript, nd. 5 p. FURM
King, Joe M. A history of SC Baptists. Cola: RLB, 1964. 494
p. COMMON
King, P. A. Roper Mountain Baptist [Church, Greenville County].
NP: typescript, nd. 6 p. FURM
King, Ray A. A history of the Associate Reformed Presbyterian
Church. Charlotte NC: Board of Christian Education of the
A.R.P. Church, 1966. 132 p. SCL
Kings Creek Cemetery Association. History of Kings Creek A.R.P.
Church & cemetery association., Newberry County, SC. 1767-
1980. NP: NPub, 1980. SCL
Kirkland, Lewis M. ...Moriah Baptist Association. Lancaster
County, SC, 1815-1965. 150th anniversary. NP: NPub, 1965.
82 p. SCL
Kirkpatrick, G. F. Historical sketch, Blenheim Presbyterian
Church, Blenheim SC...1833-1950. NP: NPub, 1950. 15 p. MONT

Kirkpatrick, G. F.   Sixtieth anniversary of Dunbar Presbyterian
Church...1890-1950. NP: NPub, 1950. 7 p.   MONT
Kirkpatrick, M. R.   Centennial of Concord Presbyterian Church,
Bethel Presbytery, SC...1896. Statesville NC: Landmark Job
Presses, 1896. 38 p.   MONT
Kitchens, Jane G.   History of Union A.R.P. Church, 1745-1967;
Richburg, Chester County, SC. 2nd ed. NP: mimeo, 1969.
93 p.   SCL, YOCL, GWPL
Klauber, Mrs. E. H. & others.   Historical sketch of the Memorial
Baptist Church [St. George, Dorchester County]. St. George:
the church, 1966. 12 p.   FURM
Klauber, Emily H.   Historical sketch of the Memorial Baptist
Church of St. George, SC. 1941.   DOCL
Kolb, Mrs. L. L.   History of the Pinewood Baptist Church [Pine-
wood]. NP: typescript, 1955. 3 p.   FURM
Konopa, Leola W.   Philadelphia Methodist Episcopal Church. NP:
typescript, nd.   DAHC
Lake City Baptist Church...history... NP: NPub, 1938. 12 p.
                                                        SCL, FURM
Lake View Baptist Church.   A brief history in commemoration of
the 25th anniversary... 1970.   DAHC
Lakeview Baptist Church, Darlington County.   A history...1944-
1978. NP: NPub, 1978. 25 p.   FURM
Lamb, Bessie P.   The history of Cedar Shoals Baptist Church,
1804-1951. Enoree: NPub, 1951. 21 p.   FURM
Landrum, J. B.   History of Mt. Zion [Baptist] Church & her peo-
ple [Spartanburg County]. NP: Trimmers Printing Office, 1885.
12 p.   FURM
Larisey, Mary Maxine.   The Unitarian Church in Charleston, SC.
A brief history. Rev. ed. Chstn: NPub, 1967. 8 p.   SCHS
Lathan, R.   A historical sketch of Union A.R.P. Church, Chester
County, SC. NP: A.R.P. Printing Co., 1888. 88 p.   SCL, MONT
Lathan, R.   History of the A.R.P. Synod of the South. Harris-
burg PA: author, 1882. 418 p.   COMMON
Lathan, Robert.   History of Hopewell A.R.P. Church, Chester
County, SC, together with biographical sketches of its four
pastors. Yorkville: Yorkville Enquirer, 1879. 84 p.   MONT
                                                        SCL, YOCL
Latta Baptist Church, Latta.   An historical sketch of the Latta
Baptist Church of Latta, SC, in Dillon County, SC, 1891-1958.
NP: NPub, 1958? 45 p.   FURM
Laurel Baptist Church, Greenville County.   [History]...1879-1979
NP: NPub, 1979. 30 p.   FURM
Lavisky, Saul.   Golden anniversary, House of Peace Synagogue,
Beth Shalom Congregation, 1908-1959. Cola: Beth Shalom
Synagogue, 1958. 82 p.   SCL
Laurence, Mrs. C. Fred.   A history of the A.R.P. Church, Rock
Hill, SC...1895-1945. NP: NPub, 1945. 35 p.   MONT
Laurence, Jessie H.   A.R.P. Church, Rock Hill, SC...1896-1948.
NP: NPub, 1948. 34 p.   YOCL, MONT
Lawrence, W. H.   The centenary souvenir. Containing a history

of Centenary Church, Charleston, & an account of the life &
labors of Rev. R. V. Lawrence... Chstn, 1885. 383 p.   SCL
                                                         GRCL
Leathers, W. W. Shiloh Baptist Church [Oconee County]. NP:
typescript, 1916. 2 p.   FURM
Leawood Baptist Church [Greenville County]. 20th anniversary.
NP: NPub, 1967. 20 p.   FURM
Lebanon Presbyterian Church, Winnsboro [SpC]   FACM, FACL, MONT
Lebby, Anna R. James Island Presbyterian Church. James Island,
SC, 1956. 21 p.   SCL, SCHS
Ledford, J. Broadus. History of Southside Baptist Church, or-
ganized 1913. Anderson: the church, 1972. 9 p.   PIPD
Lee County Bicentennial Committee. Historical data - Lee County
churches [SpC]   LECL
Lee, Robert G. Payday everyday [First Baptist Church, Edge-
field]. Nashville TN: Broadman Press, 1974. 146 p.   EDTO
Leith, John H. Greenville Presbyterian Church: the story of a
people, 1765-1973. Greenwood County: the church, 1973. 156
p.   COMMON
Leith, John H. Supplement. Greenville Presbyterian Church: the
story of a people, 1765-1973. NP: typescript, 197? 14 p.MONT
Leland, Aaron W. A sermon, delivered on the 29th Dec., 1814, at
the dedication of the new [First] Scotch Presbyterian Church
in Charleston, SC. Chstn: Hoff, 1815. 25 p.   SCHS
Lemira Presbyterian Church, Sumter. Anniversary & homecoming,
November 4, 1973... NP: NPub, 1973. 20 p.   SCL
Lexington Baptist Church, Lexington County. History of old Lex-
ington Baptist Church. NP: NPub, nd. 11 p.   FURM
Lexington Methodist Church, Lexington. Lexington Methodist
Church & its century of progress: 1850-1950. NP: NPub, 1950.
15 p.   SCL
Libbey, Robert E. Brief history of the [St. Paul's] Episcopal
Church in Conway, SC. Conway: privately printed, 1970.
28 p.   EPDI, HOCL
Lide, Robert. Historical sketch of the First Baptist Church of
Georgetown, SC. NP: typescript, nd. 6 p.   FURM
Lilly, Edward G. & Clifford L. Legerton. Historic churches of
Charleston. Chstn: Legerton & Co., 1966. 171 p.   COMMON
Lilly, Edward G. Beyond the burning bush: First (Scots) Presby-
terian Church, Charleston, SC. Historical viewpoints with
brief sketches of the history, buildings & lives of the min-
isters. Chstn: Garnier, 1971. 73 p.   COMMON
Lisbon Presbyterian Church, Laurens County. ...Centennial Cel-
ebration, 1871-1972. Mountville: the church, 1972. 23 p.LRCL
Loftis, D. F. Historical sketch of Milford [Baptist] Church
[Greer]. NP: typescript, nd. 33 p.   FURM
Loftis, D. N. Motlow Creek Baptist Church [Greenville County].
4 p.   FURM
Logan, John R. Sketches, historical & biographical, of the
Broad River and Kings Mountain Baptist Associations of SC &
NC, from 1880-1882. Shelby NC: Babington, Roberts & Co.,

156

1887. 605 p.   SCL, SPCL
Long, Roswell C. The story of our church [Presbyterian Church
in the United States]. NP: NPub, 1932.   SPCL
Longtown Baptist Church [SpC]   FACM
Loris United Methodist Church, Horry County. A record of the
history & organization of Loris United Methodist Church, Loris
SC. NP: mimeo, 1976. 14 p.   HOCL
Lovell, Edward. History of Rocky River Baptist Church [Ander-
son County]. Anderson: the church, 1963. 8 p.   FURM
Lower Fairforest Baptist Church [Union County], 1762-1962.
NP: the church, 1962. 28 p.   FURM
Lowndes Hill Baptist Church, Greenville. 1871, a century of
progress; being the history of the Lowndes Hill Baptist
Church,... Greenville: NPub, 1974? 72 p.   SCL, GRCL
Lucas Avenue Baptist Church, Laurens. [History.] NP: NPub,
1964. 8 p.   FURM
Luppo, Mrs. J. C. & Mrs. R. S. Rogers. Piney Grove Baptist
Church, 1810-1960 [Dillon County]. NP: NPub, 1960. 26 p.FURM
Lutheran Church in the U. S. Synod of South Carolina. History
of the Evangelical Lutheran Synod of SC, 1824-1924... Cola:
the Synod, 1924? 318 p.   SCL, CHCO
Lutheran Church in America. South Carolina Synod. History of
the Synod Committee. A history of the Lutheran Church in SC.
Cola: S. C. Synod of the Lutheran Church in America, 1971.
966 p.   COMMON
Lutheran Church of German Protestants, Charleston. Rules & regulations...adopted on the 4th day of March, 1818. Revised...
1846 &...1869... Chstn: Courier Job Press, 1869. 19 p. SCL
Lyles, Thomas. First Baptist Church [Spartanburg]. Centennial
edition. NP: Williams Printing Co., 1939. 25 p.   SCL, FURM
Macaulay, Mrs. H. H. The Seneca Presbyterian Church, 1875-1968
... NP: NPub, 1968. 76 p.   PIPD, MONT
MacDonald, Donald F. A history of Carolina Presbyterian Church,
old Marion District, Dillon County, SC. 1849-1960. NP: NPub,
1960. 6 p.   SCHS
Macedonia Lutheran Church. A history of Macedonia Lutheran
Church, Lexington County, SC. 1847-1947. Lexington: the
church, 1947. 10 p.
MacStephens, Mary & Marie W. Glenn. A history of Kentyre Pres-
byterian Church, 1871-1971.   DICL
McArn, A. Douglas. Through the years: Bethesda [Presbyterian]
Church. Camden: the church, 1963. 93 p.   KECA
McCants, Charles S. Sion Presbyterian Church, Winnsboro, SC...
Founded 1809...Historical sketch, 1787-1959. Winnsboro: News
& Herald, nd. 32 p.   SCL, MONT
McCarrier, Herbert G. History of the missionary jurisdiction of
the south of the Reformed Episcopal Church, 1874-1970. 1970?
(Reprinted from the Historical Magazine of the P.E. Church)SCL
McClendon, Carlee T. Methodism in Edgefield County. Edgefield:
Hive Press, 1977. 18 p.   EDTO
McConnell, Thomas M. Hand-book of history of the Presbyterian

Church of Greenville, SC... Greenville: the church, 1898.
60 p.   SCL, MONT
McCrady, Edward. A historic church...a sketch of St. Philip's
Church, Charleston, SC...1665-1897. Chstn: W,E&C, 1901.
65 p.   COMMON
McCraw, Cornelia M. History of Mt. Zion Presbyterian Church,
Sandy Springs, SC, 1832-1976. 1976. 11 p.   ANCL
McCullough, Dorothy. A short history of Cedar Springs Baptist
Church of the Cedar Swamp community in Williamsburg County,
SC, 1859-1959. NP: NPub, nd. 11 p.   FURM
McCullough, H. A. The history of St. Paul's Evangelical Luth-
eran Church, Columbia, SC... NP: NPub, 1955. 12 p.   SCL
McCullough, John B. St. Paul's Lutheran Church, Aiken, SC,
1907-1977; a history. NP: NPub, 1977.   AICL
McFadden, George W. History of Midway Presbyterian Church,
Clarendon County, SC. NP: NPub, 1934. 8 p.   MONT
McGee, Joseph H. A brief sketch of the Second Presbyterian
Church of Charleston, SC. Chstn, 1949. 3 p.   SCL
McGee, Mike L. A history of Providence Baptist Church, Gaffney,
SC, 1803-1963. NP: NPub, 1963? 43 p.   FURM
McGill, F. T. & Maude S. Buford. Short history of the First
Presbyterian Church of Greer, SC, 1841-1941. NP: NPub, 1941.
49 p.   SCL, MONT
McIntosh, Samuel E. Salem Black River Presbyterian Church [May-
esville, Williamsburg County]. Bicentennial. 1759-1959.
Kingstree?: NPub, 1959. 7 p.   WMCL
McKoy, Henry B. History of the First Presbyterian Church in
Greenville, SC. Greenville: Keys Printing Co., 1962. 373 p.
                                               SCL, GRCL, MONT
McLean, Phillip J. History of the First Baptist Church at Aiken
SC. Aiken: Standard & Review, 1937. 34 p.   SCL
McLeod, Cliff H. History of the First Presbyterian Church, Sum-
ter, SC. Organized May 29, 1823. Sumter: Sumter Printing,
1973. 24 p.   SCL
McLin, J. L. Historical sketch of Pleasant Grove Presbyterian
Church [Chester County]. Chester: Chester Reporter Job Print,
1888. 3 p.   CSCL, MONT
McMaster, Fitz Hugh. History of First Presbyterian Church & its
churchyard, Columbia, SC. Cola: State Co., 1925. 26 p. MONT
                                                        SCL, SCHS
McMillan, Mrs. Keith. Centennial, 1880-1980. Mullins First
Baptist Church. Mullins: the church, 1980. 100 p. FURM, MACL
                                                        SCL, SCHS
McNeill, D. H. John Calvin Presbyterian Church. History of the
church presented upon the occasion of the tenth anniversary.
Florence: NPub, 1974. 14 p.   MONT
McTyeire, Holland N. History of Methodism, from its rise to
1884. Nashville TN: Southern Methodist Publ. House, 1884.
688 p.   SPCL
Magee. An account of the Unitarian scheme. Chstn: Protestant
Episcopal Society for the Advancement of Christianity in S.C.,
nd. 28 p.   SCHS

Mahaffey, James E. Some factors of Methodism... NP: NPub, nd.
16 p.   SCL
Mallard, Annie H. Religious work of SC Baptists among the
slaves from 1781 to 1830. Thesis (M.A.), U.S.C., 1946. 89 p.
                                                             SCL
Maloney, James. The first one hundred years. A history of Ab-
ingdon Creek Baptist Church, Gaffney, SC. NP: NPub, 1975?
67 p.   FURM
Manly, Basil. Mercy & judgement. A discourse containing some
fragments of the history of the Baptist Church in Charleston,
SC...1832. NP: Knowles, Vose & Co., 1837. 80 p.   SCL
Manning Baptist Church, Manning. [History.] NP: typescript,
1936. 1 p.   FURM
Manning, Edna A. History of Barnwell Presbyterian Church [Barn-
well]. NP: typescript, 1966. 24 p.   MONT
Marion Baptist Church, Marion. [History.] NP: typescript,
1936. 6 p.   FURM
Marion Baptist Church, Marion. An historical review commemo-
rating the one hundredth anniversary of Marion Baptist Church,
Marion, SC. NP: NPub, 1958? 48 p.   FURM
Marion, J. P. History of the Presbyterian Church, of Sumter,
SC. NP: NPub, nd. 8 p.   SCL
Marion Methodist Church, Marion. A history...one hundred and
seventy years, 1786-1956... NP: NPub, 1956. 49 p. SCHS, FLCL
Marlboro County Library. Special Collections - Churches:
Bennetsville Baptist Church; Bennetsville Baptist Tabernacle;
Blenheim Presbyterian Church; Boykin Church; Brownsville Bap-
tist Church; Bruton's Fork Baptist Church; Calvary Baptist
Church; Cash Baptist Church; Cheraw Hill Church, Welsh Neck;
Church of God; Dunbar Presbyterian Church; Ebenezer Church;
First Presbyterian Church; First United Methodist Church;
Freewill Baptist Church; Macedonia Missionary Baptist Church;
McColl Main Street Baptist Church; Mormon Church - L.D.S.;
Nazarene Church; Oak Grove Methodist Church; Pentecostal Holi-
ness Church; St. David's Episcopal Church, Cheraw; St. Dennis
Catholic Church; St. Luke Fire Baptist Holiness Church; St.
Matthews Baptist Church; St. Michael's United Methodist Church
St. Paul's Episcopal Church; Salem Baptist Church; Sawmill
Baptist Church; Shiloh Methodist Church; Thomas Memorial Bap-
tist Church.   [END]
Marsh, Robert T. The history of the Rock Hill Baptists... Rock
Hill: Author, 1909. 84 p.   SCL, COKL, FURM
Marshall, Anna W. 1861-1961. One hundredth anniversary of the
founding of the First Baptist Church, Belton, SC. Greenville:
Keys Printing Co., 1961. 47 p.   FURM, PIPD
Martin, Arthur M. From Indians to industry; historical paper
prepared for Piedmont Presbytery. 1961. 6 p.   SCL
Martin, S. Maner. Memorial exercises, Black Swamp, SC. April
29, 1942. Historical sketch of Black Swamp Church [Black-
ville]. NP: typescript, 1942. 5 p.   WOMA
Matheson, D. S. History of First Presbyterian Church, Cheraw,

SC. NP: NPub, 1943. 55 p.   FLMC, MONT, SCL
May, John A. Of thine inheritance: the history of Saint John's
    Methodist Church. Aiken: NPub, 1957. 41 p.   USAI, AICL, SCL
Mayes, George G. Sion Presbyterian Church, Winnsboro, SC.
    Historical sketch, 1799-1926. NP: NPub, 1926? 24 p.SCL, MONT
Mayo Baptist Church, Mayo. ...Fiftieth anniversary, 1971. NP:
    the church, 1971. 34 p.   FURM
Meadowcroft, Ralph S. The windows of Grace [Episcopal] Church.
    Chstn: NPub, 1973. 20 p.   SCL
Mechanicsville Baptist Church, Mt. Pleasant SC. Covenant of the
    Mechanicsville Baptist Church. NP: NPub, nd. 7 p.   SCL
Meixner, J. Edward. History of the Church of Christ in greater
    Greenville, SC. Greenville: NPub, 1978. 61 p.   GRCL
Memorial Baptist Church, St. George. The annual harvest day &
    home-coming...Nov. 22, 1953.   DOCL
Memorial Baptist Church, St. George. Historical sketch...Sept.
    11, 1966. 75th anniversary edition. NP: NPub, 1966? 18 p.
                                                         DOCL
Memorial Baptist Church, St. George. 75th anniversary service
    with special dedication services for the Memorial Baptist
    Church educational building...Sept. 11, 1966. St. George:
    the church, 1966. 16 p.   FURM, DOCL
Memorial volume of the semi-centennial of the Theological Semi-
    nary at Columbia, SC. Cola: Presbyterian Printing House, 1884
    440 p.   WOFF
Merchant, Marie. A brief history of Sardis Baptist Church [Sa-
    luda County]. Saluda: the church, 1954. 46 p.   FURM
Methodist Episcopal Church. South Carolina. Charleston Dist-
    rict. Exposition of the causes & character of the difficul-
    ties in the church in Charleston: in the year 1833; up to
    November 28, of that year. NP: NPub, nd. 48 p.   SCL
Methodist Episcopal Church. South Carolina. Charleston Dist-
    rict. Exposition of the late schism in the Methodist Episco-
    pal Church in Charleston, in which the conduct of the schis-
    matics, and the course of the church towards them, are fully
    set forth, and their complaints against the ministry answered
    ... Chstn: J. S. Burges, 1834. 63 p.   SCL, SCHS
Methodist Episcopal Church. South Carolina. Conferences. Pro-
    gram [of] sesqui-centennial celebration, South Carolina Meth-
    odism....1935. Cola: State Co., 1935. 15 p.   SCL
Metts, Ethel C. A church was planted: a history of Little Beth-
    el Baptist Church, Route 1, Mullins, SC, 1874-1974. Cola:
    RLB, 1974. 107 p.   FLMC
Milam, Jane C. & Mrs. L. G. McCraw. Shared memories, centered
    around Mt. Zion Presbyterian Church, Sandy Springs, SC. NP:
    mimeo, 1976. 14 p.   ANCL, PIPD
Miller, Frances C. Republican Baptist Church [Edgefield County]
    NP: typescript, 1957. 10 p.   FURM
Mills, W. H. Address...delivered on home-coming day at Mc-
    Dowell's Presbyterian Church, Greelyville, SC, May 24, 1936...
    NP: NPub, nd. 3 p.   MONT

Mills, W. H. Midway [Presbyterian] Church, Anderson County, SC. Centennial. July 1833-July 9, 1933 [covers 1833-1866]. NP: typescript, 19??. 15 p.   MONT
Mims, Florence A. The history of the Woman's Missionary Union, Edgefield Association. 1873-1914. Edgefield: Advertizer Press, 1914. 184 p.   DACL, EDTO
Mims, Nancy C. Horn's Creek Baptist Church, 1776-1970. Edge-field County: NPub, 1976. 150 p.   EDTO
Mizell, James H. The history of Hopewell Baptist Church, 1861-1968 [Seneca, SC]. NP: typescript, 1969. 25 p.   FURM
Moise, Harold. The Jewish cemetery at Sumter, SC. NP: NPub, 1942. 23 p.   SCL, SMCL
Monaghan Presbyterian Church history [Monaghan, SC], 1909-1959. NP: NPub, 1959. 3 p.   MONT
Montgomery, Mabel. A history of the Marion Methodist Church... 1786-1956... Marion: the church, 1956. 49 p. SCL, MACL, GWPL
Mood, Francis A. Methodism in Charleston: a narrative. Nash-ville TN: E. Stevenson & J. E. Evans, 1856. 207 p. WOMA, SCHS
                                                                              SCL
Moore, Alvin & Tommy Rogers. History of Northside Memorial Baptist Church [Sumter County]. NP: typescript, 1958. 3 p.
                                                                             FURM
Moore, G. B. A sketch of Brushy Creek Baptist Church from 1794 to 1901...Taylors, SC.   FURM
Moore, Thomas J. Reminiscences of Nazareth Church cemetery & family burial grounds [Spartanburg County]. Spartanburg: Band & White, 1909. 27 p.   SPCL, DOCL, SCL
Moorman, Robert. History & traditions of Trinity [Episcopal] Church, Columbia SC. NP: NPub, 1925? 15 p.   SCL
Morningside Baptist Church, Spartanburg. Decades of service. Spartanburg: Morningside Baptist Church, 1960. 6 p.   FURM
Morris, James K. The windows of St. John's Episcopal Church, Shandon. Cola: the church, 1972. 24 p.   SCL
Morris Street Baptist Church, Aiken. [History.] Aiken: type-script, 1976. 5 p.   SCHS
Moseley, Algie M. The Buncombe Street Methodist [Church] story. Greenville: Keys Printing Co., 1965. 296 p.   COMMON
Moss, Bobby G. A voice in the wilderness. A history of Buffalo Baptist Church. Gaffney: Gaffney Printing Co., 1972. 90 p.
                                                                        SCL, FURM
Moss, Katherine. A history of Cherokee Avenue Baptist Church, Gaffney, SC...1895-1970. NP: NPub, 1970. 98 p.   FURM
Moss, Marie T. Mount Paran Baptist Church, 1853-1977: a history Shelby NC: Shelby Printing Co., 1977. 48 p.   FURM
Mount Calvary Baptist Church, Elko. History of Mt. Calvary Bap-tist Church. One hundredth anniversary. NP: typescript, 1956 11 p.   FURM
Mount Calvary Lutheran Church, Johnston. Centennial...1830-1930 June 29, 1930. NP: NPub, nd. 29 p.   SCL
Mount Elon Baptist Church, Darlington County. Through the years: Mt. Elon Baptist Church. NP: typescript, 1961. 6 p.   FURM

Mount Herman Lutheran Church. Highlights...1910-1970. West
Columbia: the church, 1970. 10 p.   LXMU
Mount Horeb Lutheran Church, Chapin. History...1966. Chapin:
the church, 1966. 24 p.   LXMU
Mount Lebanon United Methodist Church. History... NP: NPub,
1974.   GNCL
Mount Moriah Baptist Church, Greenwood. 150th anniversary &
homecoming [& a brief history of the church]. NP: NPub, 1960?
12 p.   FURM
Mount Olive Baptist Church, Horry County. History... NP: type-
script, 1970. 3 p.   FURM
Mount Olivet Presbyterian Church, Chester County [SpC]   CSCL
Mount Olivet Presbyterian Church [SpC]   FACM
Mount Paran Baptist Church, Cherokee County. [History]...1853-
1977... Shelby NC: the church, 1977. 48 p.   CRCL
Mount Pisgah Baptist Church, Kershaw County. History...1837-
1931. NP: typescript, 1931. 3 p.   FURM
Mount Pleasant Baptist Church. Historical sketch... NP: type-
script, 1949.   SCL
Mount Tabor Lutheran Church, New Brookland. Celebrating the
fiftieth anniversary of the founding...1886-1936. June 19-21,
1936. Cola: State Co., 1936. 32 p.   SCL
Mount Tabor Lutheran Church Committee. Mt. Tabor Evangelical
Lutheran Church, 1886-1970. NP: typescript, 1970. 4 p. LXMU
Mount Zion A. M. E. Church, Lancaster. The one hundredth anni-
versary of Mount Zion A.M.E. Church, Lancaster, SC. NP: NPub,
1967. 56 p.   SCL
Mount Zion Baptist Church, Edgefield County. ...1829-1979:
150th anniversary church calendar, Nov. 4, 1979. Edgefield
County: NPub, 1979. 6 p.   EDTO
Mount Zion Presbyterian Church, St. Charles. Sesqui-centennial,
1809-1959. St. Charles: NPub, 1959. 8 p.   SCL, MONT
Mueller, William A. The history of the efforts to provide
chimes & tower-clock for St. Matthew's German Evangelical
Lutheran Church in Charleston, SC... NP: Rev. Wm. A. C.
Mueller and the Church Council, nd. 72 p.   SCL
Munnerlyn, Annie. Baptist churches of Pee Dee section & early
ministers [SpC]   MRCL
Murphy, Louise. History of the Joanna Baptist Church. NP:
NPub, 1949. 11 p.   LRCL
Murphy, Martin C. Short history of St. Peter's [Catholic]
parish from 1824 to 1958 [Columbia]. NP: NPub, 1958? 40 p.
                                                     SCL, CDIO
Murray, Chalmers S. Through historic ways of an ancient city.
A brief historical sketch of four Charleston churches & other
places of interest along the gateway walk. Chstn: Southern
Printing Co., 196? 24 p.   SCHS
Myers, David. A brief sketch of Pisgah United Methodist Church,
Florence, SC, 1806-1978. Florence: Pattillo Printing Co.
1978. 43 p.   DAHC, FLCL
Napier, J. M. Mechanicsville Baptist Church, Darlington County,

SC. NP: typescript, 1947. 7 p.   FURM, DAHC
Nash, Sara M. Lebanon United Methodist Church [Greenville Coun-
   ty]. Greenville: typescript, 1974. 5 p.   GRCL
Neely, Lucile B. Short history of First Presbyterian Church,
   Hartsville, SC...1867-1967. Clinton: Jacobs Press, 1967.
   32 p.   COMMON
Neely's Creek A.R.P. Church. From out of the past, 1790-1955.
   Lesslie: the church, 1955. 33 p.   YOCL
New Bethel A.M.E. Church, Plantersville. Souvenir program...
   Georgetown: Georgetown Times, 1968. 44 p.   SCL
New Harmony Presbyterian Church. One hundredth anniversary...
   Fountain Inn, SC. Tuesday, August 15, 1944. NP: NPub, 1944?
   12 p.   SCL
New Holland Baptist Church, Aiken County. [History.] NP: NPub,
   1966. 10 p.   FURM
New Hope Baptist Church, Lancaster County. Celebration of one
   hundredth anniversary... Kershaw: Kershaw Era, 1932. 18 p.
                                                             FURM
New Hope Church of Our Lord Jesus Christ of the Apostolic Faith,
   Sumter. [History.] NP: typescript, nd. unp.   SMCL
New Pleasant Baptist Church, Spartanburg County. From a mustard
   seed. New Pleasant Baptist Church, constituted in 1878. NP:
   NPub, nd. 88 p.   FURM
Nicholes, Cassie. Hickory Road Baptist Church [Donaldson]. NP:
   Santee Baptist Association, 1977. 1 p.   FURM
1959 directory [with historical sketch]. Good Hope Presbyterian
   Church, Iva, SC... NP: NPub, 1959. 30 p.   MONT
90th anniversary. Calvary Episcopal Church [Charleston]...1847-
   1937. Chstn: W,E&C, 1937. 12 p.   EPDI
North Augusta Baptist Church. Directory...1923. NP: NPub, 1923
   50 p.   FURM
North Charleston Baptist Church. Anniversary booklet...1936.
   NP: NPub, 1936. 28 p.   SCHS
Northgate Baptist Church, Greenville. ...Service of dedication.
   NP: NPub, 1960. 9 p.   FURM
Oak Grove Methodist Church. NP: typescript, 1965. 9 p.
O'Bannon, Joyce S. Healing Springs Baptist Church, 1772-1972.
   Blackville: NPub, 1972. 32 p.   SCL, FURM
O'Brien, Joseph L. A chronicle history of St. Patrick's parish.
   Chstn: NPub, 1937. 68 p.   SCL, CDIO, CHCO
O'Brien, Joseph L. A chronicle history...supplement number one.
   1937-1943. NP: NPub, 1943. 21 p.   CDIO
O'Connell, Jeremiah J. Catholicity in the Carolinas & GA:
   Leaves of its history, 1820-1875. 1879, rp Spartanburg: RPC,
   1972. 647 p.   COMMON
Old Brick Church [SpC]   FACM
Old Stone Church [SpC]   FACM
100 years of christian life & service. St. Matthew's Lutheran
   Church. 1840...1940. NP: NPub, 1940. 30 p.   SCL
100th anniversary. Abbeville Presbyterian Church. 1868-1968.
   Abbeville: NPub, 1968. 23 p.   MONT

One hundredth anniversary of the Carolina Presbyterian Church,
    Little Rock, SC, Oct. 30, 1949. NP: NPub, 1949. 8 p.   MONT
175th anniversary & diamond jubilee of the Baptist Church of
    Beaufort... Beaufort: the church, 1979. 12 p.   SCL
The 175th year history of Dry Creek Baptist Church, Ward, SC,
    1804-1979. Ward: the church, 1979. 11 p.   EDTO
O'Neal, Annie C. Brownsville Baptist Church. Organized 1757...
    Blenheim, SC. Blenheim: the church, 1980. 4 p.   SCHS
O'Neal, Carole L. Look unto the rock; a history of the First
    Baptist Church, Camden... NP: NPub, 1960. 21 p.   FURM
Oolenoy Baptist Church, Pickens County. Directory... Green-
    ville: Hudson Church Directory Co., 1968. 10 p.   FURM
Orangeburg Lutheran Church, Orangeburg, SC; a historical sketch;
    published in observance of the 100th anniversary. NP: NPub,
    1955. 40 p.   ORCL
Orangeburg Methodist Episcopal Church, South. Directory...1899.
    Orangeburg: Berry, 1899. 68 p.   SCHS
Outlaw, Cecil F. After a century, "to whom?"... Ellenton
    Christian Church. Augusta GA: Walton Printing Co., 1939.
    107 p.   SCL
An outline of the history of the Presbyterian Church, Sumter,
    SC...1823-1923. NP: NPub, 1923. 8 p.   SCL, MONT
Owen, Fred C. St. Paul United Methodist Church, Ninety-Six, SC.
    NP: Drinkard Printing Co., 1974.   GNCL
Owens, Loulie L. A history of the first twenty years of Ashley
    River Baptist Church [Charleston County]. NP: typescript,
    1963. 8 p.   FURM
Owens, Loulie L. A history of Ridge Spring Baptist Church.
    Greenville: Hiott Press, 1944. 20 p.   FURM
Owens, Loulie L. Memorial windows of Ridge Spring Baptist
    Church [Saluda County]. NP: NPub, 1944. 17 p.   FURM
Owens, Loulie L. Saints of clay. The shaping of SC Baptists.
    Cola: RLB, 1971. 146 p.   COMMON
Owens, Loulie L. Taproot of the SC back country: Fairforest
    Baptist Church. Greenville: A Press, 1980. 135 p. FURM, UNCL
Owens, Nancy. Seventy years a sentinel for God; a history of
    the First Baptist Church, Dillon, SC. NP: NPub, 1961. 66 p.
                                                        COMMON
Owens, Mrs. Ollin J. Fork Shoals Baptist Church [Fork Shoals].
    NP: typescript, 1960. 9 p.   FURM
Oxendine, Jacob. History, Long Branch Baptist Church, Sumter
    County, SC. NP: typescript, 1970. 2 p.   SMCL
Palmer, B. M. An address at the one hundredth anniversary of
    the organization of the Nazareth Church & congregation in
    Spartanburg, SC... Richmond VA: Shepperson & Co., 1872. 39
    p.   SCL, MONT
Palmer Presbyterian Church, Greenville. Manual... Greenville:
    Brewer Printing Co., nd. 10 p.   MONT
Park Street Baptist Church, Columbia. History... Cola: the
    church, 1960. 10 p.   FURM
Park Street Baptist Church, Columbia. 50th anniversary; 1910-

1960. Cola: NPub, 1960? 19 p.   FURM
Pascoe, C. F. Two hundred years of the S. P. G.; an historical
   account of the Society for the Propagation of the Gospel in
   Foreign Parts, 1701-1900. London, 1901.   SCHS
Patten, Mrs. C.R. A history of the First Baptist Church, Tim-
   monsville, SC. Timmonsville: Rutledge Printing Co., 1972.
   42 p.   FLMC
Patterson, William H. The pre-revival of the [Episcopal] Church
   in SC: 1785-1820. Chstn: Dalcho Historical Society, 1953.
   15 p.   SCL, SCHS, EPDI
Payne, Daniel A. History of the African Methodist Episcopal
   Church. 1891, rp NY: Arno Press, 1969. 502 p.   SCL
Paysour, Mary & Virginia Hawkins. The first fifty years of
   Park Baptist Church [York County]. NP: typescript, 1957.
   12 p.   FURM
Pendleton Methodist Church, Pendleton. A history...1834-1964.
   NP: NPub, 1964. 48 p.   PIPD, ANCL
Pennington, Edgar L. The earnest looking forward. Historical
   address in commemoration of the establishment of the parish of
   St. Michael, in Charles Town, SC, June 14, A.D. 1751... Mo-
   bile AL: Acme Printing Co., 1951. 24 p.   SCL, SCHS, SPCL
Pettigrew, George R. Annals of Ebenezer [Baptist Church, Flor-
   ence] 1778-1950; a record of achievement. Florence: NPub,
   1951. 150 p.   COMMON
Petty, Mrs. George B. & Samuel B. Hoyt, Jr. Historical sketch
   of Bethesda Presbyterian Church, McConnels, SC, organized
   1769. NP: NPub, 1960. 24 p.   MONT, SCL
Phillips, Lorena & others. History of State Line Baptist Church
   [Cherokee]. Cherokee: the church, 1957. 125 p.   FURM
Phillips, Raymond L. History of Trinity Episcopal Church, Abbe-
   ville, SC...organized 1842... NP: NPub, 195? 14 p. SCL, EPDI
Pickens, Monroe. Historical sketch: Buncombe Street Methodist
   Church, South, Greenville, SC. Greenville: Peace Printing
   Co., 1923. 16 p.   SCL
Pine Grove Baptist Church, Great Falls. Pine Grove's story...
   NP: NPub, 1973.   FACL
Pine Grove Evangelical Lutheran Church, Lone Star. One hundred-
   th anniversary...1847-1947. NP: NPub, 1947? 12 p. SCL
Pleasant Hill Baptist Church, Barnwell County. Yearbook.
   Pleasant Hill Baptist Church & Pleasant Hill W.M.U. NP: NPub,
   1961. 27 p.   FURM
Pleasant Hill Baptist Church, Bethune. A brief history... NP:
   NPub, 1971. 18 p.   FURM
Points of interest. The Old Stone Church [Presbyterian]. 1797.
   Pendleton & Clemson College. NP: NPub, nd. 6 p.   MONT
Porcher, Jennie R. The silver of St. Philip's [Episcopal]
   Church, Charles Town - Charleston, 1670-1970. Chstn: NPub,
   1970. 27 p.   SCL, CHCO
Porter, Anthony T. Anniversary address...delivered before the
   Protestant Episcopal Society for the Advancement of Christian-
   ity in SC, at Grace [Episcopal] Church, May 30, 1881, being a

resumé of the proceedings of that society from 1810 to 1880;
&, the 71st annual report of the trustees. Chstn: W,E&C,
1881. 74 p.   SCL, SPCL
Prater's Creek Baptist Church, Pickens County. History...1875-
1975. NP: NPub, 1975. 15 p.   FURM
Presbyterian Church in the U.S. Historical addresses & commemorative ode delivered in the Synod of S.C., in Purity [Presby-
terian] Church, Chester, Oct. 24, 1885. Richmond VA: Whittet
& Shepperson, 1886. 86 p.   SCL, SCHS
Presbyterian Church in the U.S.A. Bethel Presbytery. Manual of
the Presbytery of Bethel...1886. Richmond VA: Whittet & Shep-
person, 1886. 68 p.   SCL
Presbyterian Church in the U.S.A. Bethel Presbytery. Woman's
Foreign Missionary Union. History of the beginnings of the
Woman's Foreign Missionary Union of Bethel Presbytery. Organ-
ized in Yorkville, SC, Sept. 14, 1899. Chester: Lantern Job
Office, nd. 10 p.   SCL
Preston, Flora Y. A goodly heritage; a history of the Anderson/
Young Memorial Associate Reformed Presbyterian Church of An-
derson, SC...1904-1979. Anderson: Young Memorial A.R.P.
Church, 1979. 283 p.   ANCL
A protest against the admission of any other than the white race
in the councils of the Protestant Episcopal Church of the Diocese of SC. Chstn: Lucas & Richardson, nd. 26 p.   SCL
Protestant Episcopal Church Building Society of SC. Constitution & by-laws...to which are appended the act of incorporation and list of members. Chstn: W,E&C, 1858. 19 p. SCL, SCHS
Protestant Episcopal Society for the Advancement of Christianity
in SC. Acts of incorporation, constitution & standing resolu-
tions... Chstn: Lucas & Richardson, 1900. 19 p.   SCL
Providence M. E. Church, South, Orangeburg District. Facts &
figures... Orangeburg: C.C. Berry & Co., 1921? 21 p.SCL, SCHS
Pugh, John V. & Rebecca B. Pugh. The first one hundred fifty
years, 1828-1978. A history of St. Luke's Lutheran Church,...
Prosperity, SC... NP: NPub, 1978. 44 p.   SCL, NWRL, LTSS
Pulley, Mrs. Laura M. Centennial celebration, July 30, 1972,
Lisbon Presbyterian Church, organized May 20, 1871 [with in-
scriptions of the churchyard & the Dr. John Nichols family
graveyard]. NP: NPub, nd. 23 p.   MONT
Quattlebaum, Paul. Kingston Presbyterian Church of Conway, SC.
NP: typescript, 1957. 8 p.   MONT
Quattlebaum, Paul. The Kingston Presbyterian Church, Pee Dee
Presbytery, Conway, SC, 1858-1958. Conway: the church, 1958.
126 p.   COMMON
Quattlebaum, Paul. Presbyterian Church on the Waccamaw [River].
NP: typescript, 1953.   SCL, HOCL
Raisin, Jacob S. Centennial booklet commemorating the intro-
duction of Reform Judaism in America at Kahal Kadosh Beth
Elohim [Synagogue] of Charleston, SC, organized 1750. Chstn:
NPub, 1925. 68 p.   SCL, SCHS
Ramsay, David. History of the Independent or Congregational

Church in Charleston, SC, from its origin till the year 1814,
with an appendix containing the speech of the Rev. William
Tennent in the Commons House of Assembly...Jan. 11, 1777...
Philadelphia PA: author, 1815. 71 p.   SCL, GRCL
Randolph, W. S. Post centennial celebration, First Baptist
Church [Sumter County], 1868-1969. NP: NPub, 1969? unp. SMCL
Ratterree, Alma C. The history of First Baptist Church [Rock
Hill]. Rock Hill: the church, 1978. 47 p.   FURM
Rawlinson, Mrs. J. M. Historical sketch of Mt. Zion Baptist
Church, 1834-1974 [Chester County]. NP: typescript, 1974.
2 p.   FURM
Readling, James M. History of Hopewell Presbyterian Church,
Claussen, SC. 1770-1970. Cola: RLB, 1970. 103 p.   COMMON
Reames, J. Mitchell. The history of McLeod's Chapel Methodist
Church, Rembert, SC. NP: NPub, 1954. 11 p.   SCL, MACL
Reedy Creek Baptist Church, Marion County. History... NP:
typescript, nd. 3 p.   FURM
Reenstjerna, Otto. History of St. Stephen's Lutheran Church,
Lexington, SC, 1959. NP: typescript, 1959? 78 p.   LXMU
Register, C. S. History of Wesley Chapel Church. NP: type-
script, nd.   DAHC
Reid, R. H. A sermon by the Rev. R. H. Reid on the founding of
the Presbyterian Church in Spartanburg. NP: typescript.
19 p.   SPCL
Remount Baptist Church, North Charleston. A history... Chstn:
the church, 1974. 4 p.   FURM
A review of the history of the First Baptist Church in the
south. Charleston, SC. Chstn: J.J. Furlong & Son.   CHCO
Rice, Janie C. A history of the Chester Baptist Association,
1878-1973. Chester: Chester Baptist Assn., 1975. 149 p. FURM
Rice, Janie C. History of the First Baptist Church, Rock Hill.
NP: NPub, 1960. 29 p.   COMMON
Rice, Janie C. A history of York Baptist Association, 1868-1964
NP: York Baptist Assn., 1966. 136 p.   GWPL, YOCL
Richardson, Carol. Elliott Baptist Church [Lee County]. Lee
County: Elliott Baptist Church, 1976. 14 p.   FURM
Richardson, Laurence & Robert Richardson. History of Standing
Spring [Baptist] Church [Greenville County]. NP: typescript,
1935. 2 p.   FURM
Richardson, Mrs. M. B. & Mrs. D. Keys. The history of Lebanon
Baptist Church [Anderson]. NP: mimeo, 1979. 13 p.   FURM
Richey, Norine B. A history of Earle's Grove Baptist Church...
1911-1978. NP: NPub, 1978. 136 p.   FURM
Richland Presbyterian Church, Eastover, SC [historical sketch].
Cola: RLB, 1926. 7 p.   MONT
Riddle, Hazel. A history of Flat Rock Baptist Church [Anderson
County]. NP: typescript, 1971. 9 p.   FURM
Ridge Spring Baptist Church, Saluda County. Centennial anniver-
sary, 1856-1956. Cola: Sloan Printing Co., 1956. 9 p. FURM
Ridgell, Mrs. E. C. A historical sketch of the First Baptist
Church of Batesburg in Lexington County, SC, 1873-1973. NP:

NPub, 1973. 26 p.   SCL
Ridlehoover, Wayne. Dear old Rehobeth. A history of Rehobeth
  [Baptist] Church, [Edgefield]... NP: typescript, nd. 22 p.
                                                                    FURM

Riley, John A. The church of God which is at New Harmony.
  Clinton: Thornwell Orphanage Press, 1894. 16 p.   SCL
Riley, Mrs. Willie & Sarah Higgins. The history of Walnut Grove
  Baptist Church [Greenwood County]. Greenwood: the church,
  1976. 99 p.   FURM
Rivers, E. L. & Daniel W. Ellis. A history of St. James' Epis-
  copal Church, James Island. James Island?: NPub, 1930. 4 p.
                                                                    SCHS

Roberts Presbyterian Church, Anderson County. Historical sketch
  ...1789-1964. Anderson: Palmetto Publishing Co., 1964. 13 p.
                                                             PIPD, MONT
Robertson, Lucy H. The history of Red Hill Baptist Church
  [Edgefield County]...1835-1973. Edgefield: Advertiser Press,
  1973. 48 p.   EDTO
Robinson, Carlton M. History of Poinsett Baptist Church [Green-
  ville County]. NP: typescript, 1961. 3 p.   FURM
Rock Creek Baptist [Church, Fairfield County]. Fairfield: the
  church, 1950. 1 p.   FURM
Rock Presbyterian Church, Greenwood. Memorial of the one hun-
  dred and thirty-fourth anniversary: 1770-1904. Greenwood:
  News & Views Pub. Co., 1904. 41 p.   SCHS
Rocky Creek Baptist Church, Edgefield. Excerpts from minutes
  read at Rocky Creek centennial. Edgefield: Advertiser, 1931.
  1 p.   FURM
Rocky River Baptist Creek of Iva, SC, 1803-1963. NP: NPub,
  1963. 30 p.   PIPD
Rodgers, Hattie H. Lane Baptist Church [Williamsburg County].
  NP: mimeo, 1936. 1 p.   FURM
Rodgers, James A. Society Hill - a heritage. NP: typescript,
  1963. 6 p.   FURM
Rogers, James A. Ebenezer [Baptist Church, Florence]: the story
  of a church. Cola: RLB, 1978. 223 p.   COMMON
Rogers, John B. History of McColl First Baptist Church, 1772-
  1972... McColl: the church, 1972. 148 p.   FURM
Rogers, John B. History of the McColl First Baptist Church.
  NP: typescript, 1976. 7 p.   FURM
Rollins, J. L. History of Lake Swamp Baptist Church. 1883. DAHC
Rowell, Mrs. L. A. History of New Pisgah Baptist Church, 1884-
  1966. Spartanburg: the church, 1966. 47 p.   SPCL
Rudisill, Horace F. Bethel Methodist Church [history].
  NP: typescript, 1972.   DAHC
Rudisill, Horace F. Early history of Swift Creek Baptist Church
  NP: typescript, 1965.   DAHC
Rudisill, Horace F. History of Antioch Baptist Church. NP:
  typescript, 1964.   DAHC
Rudisill, Horace F. History of Black Creek Baptist Church. NP:
  typescript, nd.   DAHC

Rudisill, Horace F. History of Elim Methodist Church. NP:
typescript, 1967.   DAHC
Rudisill, Horace F. History of Liberty Chapel. NP: typescript,
1970.   DAHC
Rudisill, Horace F. History of Mount Elon Baptist Church. NP:
typescript, 1981.   DAHC
Rudisill, Horace F. History of Pisgah Methodist Church. NP:
typescript, 1964.   DAHC
Rudisill, Horace F. Sketch of Fair Hope Presbyterian Church.
NP: typescript, 1968.   DAHC
Rudisill, Horace F. Sketch of Mt. Carmel Baptist Church. NP:
typescript, 1968.   DAHC
Rutledge Avenue Baptist Church [Charleston]. Chstn: the church,
1967. 5 p.   FURM
St. Andrew's Lutheran Church, Charleston. Centennial: 1853-
1953. Chstn, 1953. 16 p.   SCHS
St. Andrew's Lutheran Church, Charleston. History. Chstn, 1978
32 p.   SCHS
St. Barnabas Lutheran Church, Charleston. Our fifty years.
Chstn: NPub, 1962. 4 p.   SCHS
St. Barnabas mission in St. Paul's parish, Summerville, SC. NP:
NPub, 1896. 16 p.   SCL
St. Cyprian's [Catholic] Church & School. Silver jubilee...
founded 1951...Georgetown, SC. NP: NPub, 1976. unp.   CDIO
St. David's [Episcopal] Church, Cheraw, SC, 1770-1947. Cheraw:
NPub, nd. 50 p.   SCHS, SCL, GRCL
St. David's Evangelical Lutheran Church, Lexington, SC, 1845-
1970. NP: the church, 1970. 16 p.   LXMU
St. Helena's Episcopal Church, Beaufort, SC: two hundredth anni-
versary, 1712-1912. Beaufort: the church, 1912. 16 p.   SCL
St. Helena's Episcopal Church, Beaufort. History... founded
1712. NP: NPub, nd. 7 p.   SCL, HOCL
St. Helena's Episcopal Church, Beaufort. Short historical
sketch of the parish from the first English settlement to the
present time. 1712-1912. NP: NPub, 1912. 13 p.   SCL, EPDI
St. James Episcopal Church, Greenville. ...Directory. Green-
ville: NPub, 1972. unp.   GRCL
St. James [Episcopal] Parish, Goose Creek. History. NP: NPub,
197?.   SCHS
St. Johannes Evangelical Lutheran Church, Charleston. Kirchen-
ordnung der deutschen evangelisch-lutherischen St. Johannes
Gemeinde, Gotteshaus: N.W. Ecke von Hasel und Anson Strasse...
Chstn: F. Melchers & Son, 1879. 16 p.   SCL
St. Johannes Evangelical Lutheran Church, Charleston. Jubilee
anniversary. Chstn: NPub, 1928. 14 p.   SCHS
St. Johannes Evangelical Lutheran Church...1878-1978. Chstn:
NPub, 1978. 24 p.   SCHS
St. John's Church, Florence. Directory. NP: NPub, 1914. SCL
St. John's Episcopal Church [SpC]   FACM
St. John's Evangelical Lutheran Church, Charleston. Anniversary
of the ordination of George J. Gongaware, observed...nineteen

hundred and forty-six. Chstn: NPub, 1946. 13 p.   SCL
St. John's Evangelical Lutheran Church, Charleston. Brief
  sketch. Chstn, 1958. 5 p.   SCHS
St. John's Evangelical Lutheran Church, Charleston. Services
  commemorating the centennial of the consecration of the present edifice... Chstn: NPub, 1918. 47 p.   SCL, CHCO
St. John's Evangelical Lutheran Church, Charleston. Services
  commemorating the 225th anniversary of its founding, 1742-
  1967. Chstn: Nelson's Southern Printing, 1967. 23 p.SCHS,ORCL
St. John's Evangelical Lutheran Church, Charleston. Yearbook...
  Chstn: Lucas & Richardson, 1887.   SCL
St. John's Evangelical Lutheran Church, Pomaria. Bicentennial
  booklet... Pomaria: the church, 1954. 23 p.   SCL
St. John's Evangelical Lutheran Church, Walhalla. Centennial
  celebration...1853-1953. Walhalla: NPub, nd. 22 p.   SCL
St. John's Lutheran Church, Clinton. The service of dedication
  ... NP: NPub, 1968? 8 p.   LTSS
St. John's Lutheran Church, Lexington. [History.] Lexington:
  the church, 1963. 16 p.   LXMU
St. John's Lutheran Church, Spartanburg. 50th anniversary,
  1902-1952... Spartanburg: Band & White, nd. 4 p.   SCL
St. John's Methodist Church, Rock Hill [SpC]   YOWC
St. John's Methodist Episcopal Church, Anderson [SpC]   PIPD
St. Joseph's Catholic Church...Anderson, SC. NP: NPub, nd.
  12 p.   CDIO
St. Luke's Episcopal Church, Charleston. Directory...1918. SCL
St. Luke's Episcopal Church, Charleston. Parish letter, Oct.
  1910 [includes history]. 8 p.   SCHS
St. Luke's Episcopal Church, Newberry. Program of the centen-
  nial celebration to commemorate the consecration.. NP: NPub,
  1955. 20 p.   SCHS, SCL
St. Martin's-in-the-Fields Episcopal Church, Columbia. The
  parish church of St. Martin's... Forest Acres, Columbia, SC.
  .. NP: NPub, 1962.   SCL
St. Mary's annual for Greenville missions. Upper South Carolina. 1922. NP: NPub, 1921. 216 p.   CDIO
St. Mary's annual...Greenville, Spartanburg, Anderson & mis-
  sions upper SC...1917. NP: NPub, 1916. 154 p.   SCL, CDIO
St. Mary's Catholic Church, Charleston. The Roman Catholic
  church of St. Mary's, Charleston, SC. Chstn: N. G. Duffy, nd.
  44 p.   SCL
St. Mary's Catholic Church, Charleston. Rules & regulations...
  1895. Chstn: Perry, 1895. 16 p.   SCHS
St. Mary's Help of Christians Church, Aiken. History...and the
  Aiken missions. Diamond jubilee, 1867-1942. NP: NPub, 1942?
                                                            AICL
St. Matthew's Episcopal Church, Darlington. History... NP:
  typescript, nd.   DAHC
St. Matthew's Lutheran Church, Charleston. 125 years of service
  ... Chstn: Nelson's Southern Printing Co., 1967. 50 p. SCHS
St. Michael United Methodist Church, Bennetsville. [History.]
                                                            MRCL

St. Michael's Episcopal Church, Charleston. Activities at the
  beginning of the third century of service...1761-1961. Chstn:
  Nelson's, 1961. 19 p.   SCL
St. Michael's Evangelical Lutheran Church ["Blue Church"].
  1814-1944 [history]. NP: NPub, 1944. 12 p.   LTSS
St. Paul's Episcopal Church, Radcliffeboro [Charleston]. Con-
  stitutional form of government & by-laws... Chstn: NPub,
  1870.   SCL
St. Paul's Episcopal Church, Radcliffeboro [Charleston]. Histo-
  ry... Chstn: Lucas & Richardson, 1878. 44 p. SCHS, SCL, FLCL
St. Paul's Episcopal Church, Pendleton. [History.] Pendleton :
  NPub, 1963. 6 p.   SCL, SCHS
St. Paul's Episcopal Church, Pendleton. ...established in 1819.
  Building erected in 1822. NP: NPub, 1969. 6 p.   SCL
St. Paul's Episcopal Church, Summerville. Yearbook...1893.
  Summerville: the church, 1893. 20 p.   SPCL
St. Paul's Evangelical Lutheran Church. 1886-1971...Columbia,
  SC. NP: NPub, 1971. 57 p.   SCL, LTSS
St. Paul's Evangelical Lutheran Church, Columbia. Fiftieth
  anniversary. 1886-1936... Cola: NPub, 1936. 25 p.   SCL
St. Paul's Evangelical Lutheran Church, Columbia. 1886-1962.
  Cola: NPub, 1962. 20 p.   SCL
St. Peter's Catholic Church, Columbia. Manual & directory...
  1901. Cola: RLB, 1901. 20 p.   SCL
St. Peter's Parish, Columbia. Short history...from 1824 to
  1958. Cola: NPub, 1958. 40 p.   SCL
St. Philip's Episcopal Church, Charleston. Special service set
  forth by the bishop for May 12, 1875, in commemoration of the
  planting of the Church of England within the province of
  Carolina. Chstn: W,E&C, 1875. 8 p.   SCL
St. Philip's Episcopal Church, Charleston. ...Special services
  held at St. Philip's church, Charleston, SC, on the 12th &
  13th of May, 1875, in commemoration of the planting of the
  Church of England in the province of Carolina. With the sermon preached by the Rt. Rev. W. B. W. Howe, bishop of the
  diocese, and the historical address delivered by J. H. Prin-
  gle Smith... Chstn: W,E&C, 1876. 172 p.   SCL, SCHS
St. Stephen's Episcopal Church [SpC]   FACM
St. Timothy Lutheran Church, Whitmire, SC. 25[th anniversary].
  1939-1964. NP: mimeo, 1964. 8 p.   LTSS
St. Timothy's Church, Columbia. 1892-1967. St. Timothy's
  Church...anniversary celebration... NP: NPub, 1967. 19 p.SCL
Saleeby, Mary. Historical sketch. Magnolia Heights Baptist
  Church [Florence]. NP: typescript, nd. 1 p.   FURM
Sampey, John R. Southern Baptist Theological Seminary: the
  first thirty years, 1859-1889. Baltimore MD: Wharton, Barron
  & Co., 1890. 217 p.   COKL
Sandridge Baptist Church, Dorchester County. A brief history...
  NP: typescript, 1967. 1 p.   FURM
Sands, Anna E. St. Paul's Mission, Horse Creek Valley. Gran-
  iteville: NPub, 1914. 19 p.   SCHS

Sans Souci Baptist Church, Greenville. [History.] NP: type-
script, nd. 2 p.   FURM
Saye, James H. Cedar Shoal [Presbyterian] Church & congregation
... NP: NPub. Reprint of 1878 ed. 18 p.   MONT, SCL
Scalf, Margaret B. A history of the First Associate Reformed
Presbyterian Church, Rock Hill, SC... In commemoration of
the 75th anniversary, 1895-1970. Rock Hill: NPub, 1970.
50 p.   LNCL, YOCL, SCL
Schirmer, Jacob F. Historical sketches of the Evangelical Luth-
eran Synod of SC, from its formation in 1824; also, a brief
history of the church in the state of SC, with other important
statistics... Chstn: A.J. Burke, 1875. 50 p.   SCL
Scott, Herschel K. Sardis Baptist Church, 1835-1964. Lexing-
ton: typescript, 1970. 32 p.   LXMU
Screven Baptist Church [Georgetown. History]. NP: typescript,
1957. 2 p.   FURM
Seaborn, Margaret M. Walhalla Presbyterian Church. 1868-1968..
. Westminster: Westminster News Press, 1968. 104 p.SCL, SCHS
Seabrook, E. M. History of the Protestant Episcopal Church of
Edisto Island. Chstn: Walker & James, 1853. 63 p. EPDI, SCL
Sease, Rosalyn S. A brief history of St. John's Lutheran Church
Pomaria, SC. Founded in 1754... NP: St. John's Lutheran
Church Historical Committee, 1970. 15 p.   LTSS, LXMU
Second Baptist Church, Clifton. Diamond jubilee... NP: NPub,
1976. 16 p.   FURM
Second Baptist Church, Rock Hill. [History.] NP: typescript,
nd. 5 p.   FURM
Second Presbyterian Church, Charleston. 1809-1909. Exercises
connected with the 100th anniversary... Chstn: Daggett, 1910.
105 p.   SCL, SCHS
Second Presbyterian Church, Charleston. Historical notes of
woman's societies & yearbook... Chstn: M.S. Heisser, 1924.
6 p.   SCL, SCHS
Second Presbyterian Church, Charleston. History. Chstn, 1837?
81 p.   SCL, SCHS
Second Presbyterian Church, Charleston. Manual for the communi-
cants...[includes membership roll]. Chstn: B. Jenkins, 1847.
34 p.   SCL, MONT, SCHS
Second Presbyterian Church, Charleston. Manual...prepared under
the direction of the Rev. Thomas Smyth... Chstn: Jenkins &
Hussey, 1838. v.p.   SCL
Second Presbyterian Church, Greenville [SpC]   MONT
Second Presbyterian Church, Greenville. History & manual...
Abbeville: Hugh Wilson, 1896. 12 p.   MONT
Second Presbyterian Church, Greenville. Manual...(various
years, 1912-19--).   SCL, MONT
Second Presbyterian Church, Greenville. Our 75th year, 1892-
1967. Greenville: NPub, 1967. 32 p.   GRCL
Second Presbyterian Church, West Columbia [SpC]   MONT
Sellers, Hazel C. Old SC churches. Cola: Crowson Printing Co.,
1941. 127 p.   COMMON

The Seneca Presbyterian Church, 1875-1968, Seneca, SC. NP: NPub
1968? 76 p.   MONT, NWRL
The sesquicentennial history of Associate Reformed Presbyterian
Church; mainly covering the period 1903-1951... Clinton:
Jacobs Bros., 1951.   SCL, FACL
The sesqui-centennial of Methodism in SC, 1785-1935. Addresses
& historical sketch. Cola: State Co., 1936. 180 p. SCL, WOFF
Seven Oaks Presbyterian Church [SpC]   MONT
75th anniversary services with special dedication services for
the Memorial Baptist Church educational building. St. George:
the church, 1966.   DOCL
1731-1931 - bicentennial, First (Scotch) Presbyterian Church.
NP: NPub, 1931. 20 p.   SCL, CHCO, MONT
1770-1904. Memorial of the one hundred and thirty-fourth anniversary of the Rock Presbyterian Church [Greenwood]. Greenwood: News & Views Publ. Co., 1904. 41 p.   MONT
Shaffer, Edward T. History of Bethel Presbyterian Church from
the founding in 1728 down to the present time - 1928. Walterboro: Press & Standard, 1928? 32 p.   COMMON
Shand, Peter J. Address at the laying of the corner stone of
the new Episcopal church, Columbia, SC, November 26th, 1845.
Cola: I. C. Morgan, 1845. 9 p.   SCL
Shandon Presbyterian Church, Columbia [SpC]   MONT
Shandon Presbyterian Church, Columbia. ...50th anniversary &
homecoming. 1916- May 8, 1966. NP: NPub, 1966. 8 p.   SCL
Sharon Methodist Church, 1852-1969. Lexington: typescript,
1970. 10 p.   LXMU
Shedd, Mary M. A history of Monticello Methodist Church, Monti-
cello, SC. NP: NPub, 1960. 12 p.   SCL
Shelor, John W. The Richland [Presbyterian] Church: early Pres-
byterianism in upper SC. Walhalla: Keowee Courier Press, 1915
24 p.   SCL, MONT
Shiloh Methodist Church. Lexington: typescript, 1969. 17 p.
                                                           LXMU
Shipp, Albert M. History of Methodism in SC. 1884, rp Spartanburg: RPC, 1972. 652 p.   COMMON
Short history of the [Episcopal] Diocese of SC. Chstn: Dalcho
Historical Society, 1953. 189 p.   EPDI
Shull, A. Harper. Origin & history of Mt. Hebron United Method-
ist Church, West Columbia, SC. West Columbia: typescript,
1976. 7 p.   LXMU
Siloam Baptist Church, Easley. A history...1791-1978. NP:
typescript, 1978. 28 p.   FURM
Silver Spring Baptist Church centennial history, 1874-1974.
Pendleton: NPub, 1974. 20 p.   PIPD
Simmons, Agatha A. Brief history of St. Mary's Roman Catholic
Church [Charleston]. Chstn: J.J. Furlong, 1961. 40 p. COMMON
Simmons, Mrs. H.F. Pine Level Baptist Church [Jasper County].
NP: typescript, 1972. 9 p.   FURM
Simms, W. E. & Hattie Simms. A brief history of the Washington
Baptist Church [Pelzer]. Pelzer: the church, 1956. 22 p.FURM

173

Simpson, Henry. Early history of the First Presbyterian Church
of Laurens, SC. 1932. LRCL
Simpson, Zera C. Fifty years of progress noted in the history
of Concord [Baptist] Church, Anderson, SC, 1907-1957. Anderson: author, 1957. 12 p. PIPD
Simrill, Belle. History of Bethel Methodist Church, Chester,
SC. Chester: the church, nd. unp. LNCL
Singleton, George A. The romance of African Methodism; a study
of the African Methodist Episcopal Church. NY: Exposition
Press, 1952. 251 p. SCL
Singmaster, Elsie. The story of Lutheran missions. Cola: Survey Publishing Co., 1917. 221 p. SCL
Sion Presbyterian Church [SpC] SCL, FACM
1695-1895. Services at the laying of the corner stone of the
new Presbyterian church of Summerville...with a sketch of the
origin & history of the organization. Chstn: W,E&C, 1895.MONT
1696-1911. Services at the celebration of the two hundred &
fiftieth anniversary of the Dorchester Independent [or Congre-
gational] Church by its legal successor, the Summerville Presbyterian Church. Summerville: NPub, 1911. 30 p. SCHS, MONT
A sketch of the Covenanters of Rocky Creek, Chester County, SC.
Chester, nd. 22 p. YOCL
Sketches of Bethesda Presbyterian Church and Bethesda community,
York County, SC. Yorkville: NPub, nd. 28 p. YOCL
Sloan, H. Thompson. A historical sketch of Cedar Spring & Long
Cane [A.R.P. Churches?], Abbeville District, SC. Due West:
Telescope Press, 1860. 36 p. SCL, MONT
Sloan, James P. History of Providence A.R.P. Church, September
10, 1836-July 10, 1977. Clinton: Printers Assoc., 1977. 68
p. SCL, LRCL
Smart, Robert L. Historical sketch of the old St. George
Baptist Church [Dorchester County]. St. George: the church,
1964. 9 p. DOCL, FURM
Smith, Mrs. C. M. History of Bush River Baptist Church, 1771-
1933. Kinards: NPub, 1934. 65 p. NWRL, SCL
Smith, George L. History of Saint Mary Help of Christians
Church & the Aiken missions...1867-1942. NP: NPub, 1942.
103 p. CDIO
Smith, Mendel L. Historical address at the centennial celebra-
tion of Camden Baptist Church, Camden, SC, Nov. 20, 1910.
Camden: Camden Chronicle, nd. 36 p. SCL, FURM
Smyth, Thomas. ...the late Charleston Union Presbytery: the
occasion of its division fairly stated; and the action of the
Presbytery fully justified... Chstn: Observer Office Press,
1840. 80 p. SCL
Smyth, Thomas. Manual...of the Second Presbyterian Church,
Charleston...[incl.] a list of all the former, and present
pastors, elders & officers...with a list of all its members in
1832...& also...since 1832. Chstn: Jenkins & Hussey, 1838.
236 p. SCL, MONT
Society for the Propagation of the Gospel in Foreign Parts.

Letters between the missionaries to the parish of Goose Creek
in the province of SC and the S. P. G. in London, England,
1702-1737. Typescript, 3 vol.   SCHS
Society for the Propagation of the Gospel in Foreign Parts.
Letters to the S. P. G. from the clergy of SC, 1716-1765.
Typescript.   SCHS
Society for the Relief of Elderly & Disabled Ministers of the
Independent or Congregational Church. Rules...1860. Chstn:
W,E&C, 1860. 33 p.   SCL
Society for the Relief of Elderly & Disabled Ministers of the
Independent or Congregational Church. A statement of some
evidence, facts, and arguments, in relation to the claims of
Wappetaw upon the Society for Relief, etc., in the state of
SC., together with the petition of the members and support-
ers of the said church to the legislature, in relation to the
charter of said society. NP: NPub, nd. 29 p.   SCL
Society for the Relief of the Widows & Orphans of the Protestant Episcopal Church in the State of SC. Rules...to which is
prefixed an historical account of the society. Chstn: W,E&C,
1910. 24 p.   SCL, SCHS
South Carolina Baptist Historical Society. SC: state of south-
ern Baptist beginnings. NP: author, 1958. unp. YOCL,FURM,SCL
South Main Street Baptist Church, Greenwood. History... Green-
wood: the church, 1957. 6 p.   FURM
Southern Bleachery Baptist [Church, Taylors]. NP: typescript,
1928. 3 p.   FURM
Sparks, Claude E. History of Padgett's Creek Baptist Church,
Union, SC. Union: Counts Printing Co., nd. 172 p.   COMMON
Speaks, Emma D. Memory sketches of long ago [Hopewell Baptist
Church, Hampton County]. NP: mimeo, 1935. 1 p.   FURM
Sparks, Fannie L. Yesterday & today. A look at one hundred
years. 1873-1973. Grace United Methodist Church, Union, SC.
Union: the church, 1973. 60 p.   SCL
Spears, Vera S. The Fairforest story: history of the (Lower)
Fairforest Baptist Church & community. Charlotte NC: Crabtree
Press, 1974. 172 p.   COMMON
Spence, Thomas H. Address delivered at the sesquicentennial
celebration of Concord Presbytery, Bethpage [Presbyterian]
Church, October 16, 1945... Morgantown NC: Concord Presby-
tery, 1945. 15 p.   SCL
Spence, Thomas H. The Historical Foundation [of the Presbyter-
ian & Reformed Churches] and its treasures. Montreat NC:
Historical Foundation Publications, 1960. 171 p.   COMMON
Spiesman, Henry L. The Anderson, SC, [Catholic] missions. NP:
NPub, nd. 15 p.   CDIO
Springfield Baptist Church, Greenville. History... Greenville:
author, 1955? 10 p.   SCL
Springfield Baptist Church, Greenville. Ninety-fifth anniver-
sary...souvenir bulletin - July, 1962. unp.   GRCL
Springfield Baptist Church, Greenville. ...1867-1967; a centu-
ry of service for Christ. Greenville: NPub, 1967. unp. GRCL

Sprunt, Alexander. A brief history of the Rock Hill Presbyterian Church...to April 1895... Abbeville: Hugh Wilson, 1895. 21 p.   YOCL

Stacey, Emily C. 175 years of Methodism in Georgetown, SC, 1785-1960. Georgetown: Duncan Memorial Methodist Church, 1960 12 p.   SCHS

Stackhouse, Robert E. Methodism on the Pee Dee. An address... at Darlington, SC, December 13, 1904... NP: NPub, 1904. 23 p.   DAHC, FLMC, WOMA

Stacy, James. History of the Midway Congregational Church, Liberty County, GA [formed from Independent or Congregational Church of St. George's Parish, SC]. Newman GA: Murray, 1899? 283 p.   SCL, SCHS

Stacy, James. History of the Midway Congregational Church... revised ed. Newman GA: Murray, 1903. 396 p.   SCL, SCHS

Stanley, Victor B., Jr. Marion churches & churchmen, 1735-1935. Chstn: Southern Printing Co., 1938. 109 p.   COMMON

Starnes, George E. History of St. John's United Methodist Church, Fort Mill, SC. NP: privately printed, 1972. 19 p.
                                                        SCL, YOCL

State Street Baptist Church, Cayce. A history...1941-1970. NP: typescript, 1970? 5 p.   LXMU

Steadman, Joseph E. A historical sketch of the Emory Methodist Church in Saluda County, SC. Edgefield: Edgefield Advertiser, 1965. 107 p.   COMMON

Steedman, Marguerite C. A short history of the French Protestant Huguenot Church, Charleston, SC. Chstn: Nelson's Southern Printing, 1970. 10 p.   COMMON

Stephens, Mary M. & Marie W. Glenn. A history of Kentyre Presbyterian Church, 1871-1971. NP: NPub, 1971. 18 p. DICL, MONT

Stevenson, Charles A. Historical sketch of Mt. Olivet Presbyterian Church...[near] Winnsboro... NP: NPub, 1947. 36 p.
                                                  SCL, MONT, GRCL

Stevenson, Evelyn R. The first ninety years: First Presbyterian Church, Bennettsville, SC. With a list of present & former members. NP: NPub, 1945. 26 p.   MONT

Stevenson, Mrs. Pearl M. Keeping the faith. A history of Upper Long Cane Presbyterian Church, Abbeville, SC. 1763-1976. Greenwood: Drinkard Printing Co., 1976. 56 p.   MONT

Stevenson, R. M. Philadelphia Church history. NP: typescript, 1976.   DAHC

Stevenson, R. M. Studies in [A.R.P.] church history... Due West: A.R.P. Company, 1916. 54 p.   SCL, MONT

Stewart, C. L. Historical sketch of the Presbyterian Church, of Pelzer, SC. NP: NPub, 1897. 9 p.   MONT

Still, Charles. First Baptist Church, St. Andrews Parish [Charleston County]. NP: typescript, 1974. 2 p.   FURM

Stinson, Daniel. Sketch of the Covenanters of Rocky Creek, SC. NP: typescript, nd. 27 p.   GWPL

Stoddard, Mrs. D. L. Padgett Corner Baptist Church. Enoree Church; West Springs Baptist Church. NP: typescript, nd.

26 p.   SCL, FURM
Stokes, John L. The march of democracy in the Methodist Episco-
     pal Church, South. Cola: State Co., 1912. 14 p.
Stoll, Elnita. First Baptist Church, Kingstree, SC, 1858-1958.
     NP: NPub, 1958. 35 p.   FURM
Stoney, Samuel G. Building a church on the Santee, 1804-1807.
     Chstn: Charleston Museum, 1945. 17 p.   SCL, SCHS
Story of exercises of first homecoming day. Unity Presbyterian
     Church, Fort Mill, SC...1924. NP: NPub, 192? 7 p.   MONT
Story of the memorial shrine of St. Andrew the Apostle Catholic
     Church at Barnwell, SC. NP: NPub, 1944. 58 p.   CDIO
Story of the SC branch of the Woman's Auxiliary, 1885-1935
     [Episcopal Diocese of SC]. Sumter: Sumter Printing Co., 1935.
     21 p.   EPDI
Stout, John. Historical sketch of the Welsh Neck Baptist Church
     Society Hill, SC... Greenville: Hoyt & Keys, 1889. 90 p.COKL
Strain, J. L. Historical sketch. Salem [Presbyterian] Church.
     The origin of "Old" and "New Salem". Gaffney: Ledger Print,
     nd. 8 p.   SCL, MONT
Strong, Elizabeth E. History of the Chester A.R.P. Church, July
     1869-July 1969. Clover: Clover Printing Co., nd. 61 p.   SCL
Stubbs, Thomas A. Early history of Sumter Churches. Sumter:
     Osteen-Davis Printing Co., 1951. 32 p.   COMMON
Sullivan, Claude T. Westminster Presbyterian Church, 1947-1972.
     Greenville: NPub, 1972. 12 p.   GRCL
Summerton Presbyterian Church, Summerton. Centennial. Summer-
     ton: NPub, 1975. 26 p.   SCL
Summerville Presbyterian Church, Summerville. Services at the
     celebration of the two hundred and fiftieth anniversary.
     Summerville: NPub, 1911. 30 p.   SCL, SCHS, MONT
Summerville Presbyterian Church. Services at the laying of the
     corner stone of the new Presbyterian church of Summerville,
     SC, May 7, 1895, and of the dedication of the new church Dec.
     15, 1895... Chstn: W,E&C, 1896? 24 p.   SCL, SCHS
Sumter Cemetery Association, Sumter. Bicentennial memorial
     publication. Sumter, 1976. 110 p.   SCL, SMCL, SCHS
Sumter Presbyterian Church. Exercises in connection with the
     dedication of the Sumter Presbyterian Church... Sumter: Her-
     ald Print, 1907. 8 p.   SCL
Sumter Presbyterian Church. An outline of the history of the
     Sumter Presbyterian Church, Sumter, SC. NP: NPub, 1923.
     3 p.   SCL
Sumter, John R. The Church of the Holy Cross [Episcopal],
     Stateburg, SC. Sumter, 1930.   SCL, SCHS
Sunset Boulevard Baptist Church. NP: typescript, 1970. 1 p.
                                                      LXMU
Surner, Meta A. The Lowndesville Baptist Church [Abbeville
     County]. NP: typescript, 1958. 1 p.   FURM
Swansea Baptist Church. From brush to brick. Swansea: L.
     Saylor, 1973. 49 p.   FURM, SCL
Sweeney, Robert. St. Joseph's Catholic Church, Chester, SC.

NP: NPub, nd. 6 p.   CDIO
Sweet, Malcolm S. Unto everlasting life: the history of the
    Hartsville Presbyterian Church, 1867-1952. Hartsville: the
    church, 1954. 241 p.   COMMON
Synod of South Carolina. Historical addresses and commemorative
    ode, delivered in the [Presbyterian] Synod of SC, in Purity
    [Presbyterian] Church, Chester, October 24, 1885, at the cen-
    tennial celebration of the Presbytery of South Carolina...
    Richmond VA: Whittet & Shepperson, 1886. 86 p.   SCL
Tabernacle Baptist Church, Union. The progress of Tabernacle
    Baptist Church. Union: the church, 1966. 28 p.   FURM
Taylor, Charles G. & Carolyn S. Taylor. Boiling Springs [Meth-
    odist] Church [history]. NP: typescript, 1964. 6 p.   WOMA
Taylor, H. A. Locust Hill Baptist Church [Greenville County].
    NP: mimeo, nd. 4 p.   FURM
Temple Baptist Church [Simpsonville] and how she grew. NP:
    typescript, 1957. 11 p.   FURM
Templeton, Mrs. William & Mrs. Meek Dickson. Directory of Beer-
    sheba Presbyterian Church cemetery, Route 1, York, SC. NP:
    NPub, 1969. 38 p.   LNCL, YOCL, MONT
Theus, Nita G. Presbyterian faith & churches in Beaufort, SC.
    NP: typescript, 1938. 74 p.   MONT
Thomas, Albert S. Church of the Cross, St. Luke's parish, Bluf-
    fton, SC. NP: NPub, 1954? 17 p.   SCL
Thomas, Albert S. The Diocese of SC. Past, present & future.
    A vision. Chstn: NPub, 1944. 11 p.   SCL, SCHS
Thomas, Albert S. The Episcopal Church on Edisto Island.
    Chstn: Dalcho Historical Society, 1953. 15 p. SCL, SCHS, EPDI
Thomas, Albert S. A historical account of the Protestant Epis-
    copal church in SC, 1820-1957, being a continuation of Dal-
    cho's account, 1670-1820. Cola: RLB, 1957. 879 p.   COMMON
Thomas, Albert S. Historical sermon [delivered in the] Church
    of the Cross, St. Luke's parish, Bluffton, SC. Bluffton?,
    1954. 17 p.   SCL, SCHS
Thomas, Albert S. A history of St. Peter's [Episcopal] Church,
    Charleston... Chstn: Dalcho Historical Society, 1955. 26
    p.   SCL, SCHS, EPDI
Thomas, Albert S. A short history of the [Episcopal] Diocese
    of SC. Chstn: NPub, 1953. 189 p.   SCL
Thomas, Albert S. A sketch of the history of the [Episcopal]
    Church in SC. 1935.   SCL
Thomas, Albert S. Trinity [Episcopal] Church, Society Hill.
    NP: typescript, nd.   DAHC
Thomas, Charles E. A brief history of St. Philip's Episcopal
    Church, Greenville, SC, 1914-1973. NP: NPub, 1973. 15 p.
                                               SCL, GRCL, SCHS
Thomas, Charles E. Historical sketch of Cedar Creek Mission,
    founded 1839; St. Stephen's Episcopal Church, consecrated
    August 4, 1854, Ridgeway, SC. NP: NPub, nd. 8 p.   SCL
Thomas, Charles E. Historical sketch of St. Stephen's Episco-
    pal Church, Ridgeway, SC. Indianapolis: 1934. 10 p. SCL, SCHS

Thomas, Charles E. Know your church [Christ Episcopal Church, Greenville]. Greenville: Christ Episcopal Church, 1968. 30 p.   SCL, GRCL

Thomas, Curtis. Foundation-stone of the second, or Wentworth Street Baptist Church [Charleston]. Chstn: B.B. Hussey, 1842. 16 p.   FURM

Thomas, Herman L. History of Sweetwater Baptist Church [Edge-field County]. NP: typescript, 1970. 42 p.   FURM

Thomas, John P. The life & labors of the Rev. Samuel Thomas; an epic of the infant [Episcopal] Church in SC, 1702-1706. Chstn W,E&C, 1904. 21 p.   SCL, SCHS

Thomas Memorial Baptist Church. Historical sketch...1820-1955. Bennettsville: NPub, 1955. 4 p.   SCL, FURM

Thomas, W. J. A history of Sandy Run Baptist Church [Hampton]. Hampton: the church, 1964. 4 p.   FURM

Tobin, R. M. Mount Arnon Baptist [Church, Allendale County]. NP: typescript, 1937. 3 p.   FURM

Townsend, Leah. Early [Baptist] Church discipline. NP: type-script, 1951. 11 p.   FURM

Townsend, Leah. South Carolina Baptists, 1670-1805. 1935, rp Baltimore MD: GPC, 1974. 391 p.   COMMON

Townsend, Leon. The history of the Mispah Baptist Church, 1834-1934. NP: typescript.   DAHC

A tract. History & doctrine of the A.R.P. Church... Due West: A.R.P. Print, 1885. 20 p.   MONT

Trapier, Paul. Incidents in my life: the autobiography of the Rev. Paul Trapier, with some of his letters. Chstn: Dalcho Historical Society, 1954. 66 p.   SCHS, SCL, EPDI

Traywick, Joseph B. The place of the local preacher in Method-ism. Cola: State Co., 1909. 14 p.   SCL

Trinity Episcopal Church, Abbeville. To the glory of God & in loving memory... NP: NPub, nd. 6 p.   SCL

Trinity Episcopal Church, Columbia. Service held in Trinity Church...in celebration of the rector's fiftieth anniversary. Rev. Peter J. Shand, D.D., 1834-1884. Cola: Charles A. Calvo, 1884. 60 p.   SCL, EPDI

Trinity Episcopal Church, Columbia. Observance of one hundred years of the building of Trinity Church. Cola: RLB, 1946. 32 p.   SCL

Trinity Episcopal Church, Columbia. One hundred twenty-fifth anniversary. Cola: State Co., 1937. 132 p.   COMMON

Trinity Episcopal Church, Columbia. 150 golden years. Cola: the church, 1962. 7 p.   SCL

Trinity Ev. Lutheran Church, Greenville. History... Fiftieth anniversary... Greenville: NPub, 1959. 34 p.   LTSS

Trinity Methodist Church, Anderson. We build a church to the glory of God. Anderson: the church, 195? 8 p.   SCL

Trinity Methodist Episcopal Church, South, Charleston. Direct-ory...1914 [also 1924].   SCHS

Trinity United Methodist Church, West Columbia, SC, 1960 to 1970 NP: typescript, 1970? 2 p.   LXMU

Tripp, Mrs. Henry. History of Bethel Baptist Church [Green-
    ville]. NP: typescript, 1950. 11 p.   FURM
Truluck, B. K. History of Earden Baptist Church, 1840-1940.DAHC
Truluck, Dr. The history of Sardis Baptist Church [Florence].
    Florence: the church, nd. 47 p.   FURM
Tucker, J. Powell. The great achievement of a loyal & noble
    people... The First Baptist Church, Rock Hill, SC. NP: NPub,
    nd. 8 p.   FURM
Tucker, Marie C. History of Big Creek Baptist Church [Anderson]
    1788-1971. NP: typescript, 1971. 11 p.   FURM
Tupper, Harold A. Two centuries of the First Baptist Church of
    SC, 1683-1883. Baltimore MD: R.H. Woodward & Co., 1889.
    351 p.   COMMON
25th anniversary history. Westminster Presbyterian Church
    [Florence]...organized December 14, 1947. NP: NPub, 1972?
    22 p.   MONT
Union between Zion [Presbyterian] Church, Glebe Street, & Cen-
    tral Presbyterian Church, Charleston, SC... Chstn: NPub, 1882
    9 p.   SCL
Union Memorial Presbyterian Church, Fairfield County [SpC] MONT
Union (Quaker) Baptist Church. Historical sketch.   LRCL
Unitarian Church, Charleston. The old & the new: or, discour-
    ses & proceedings at the dedication of the re-modeled Unitar-
    ian Church in Charleston, SC, on Sunday, April 4, 1852...
    Chstn: Samuel G. Courtenay, 1854. 148 p.   COMMON
Unitarian Church, Charleston. Woman's Alliance. The first
    bazaar of the Unitarian Church of Charleston, SC, 1836.
    Chstn: Archives Committee of the Woman's Alliance, 1960. 5 p.
                                                             SCL
Unity Baptist Church, Spartanburg. [History.] Spartanburg:
    Spartan Baptist Association, nd. 18 p.   FURM
Van Wyck Presbyterian Church, Lancaster. History...1884-1961.
    NP: mimeo, 1961. 3 p.   MONT
Vaughn, Thomas E. A brief history of the churches in the Lex-
    ington Baptist Association. Cola: McDonald Letter Shop,
    1978. 109 p.   FURM
Vedder, Charles S. A historical sketch of the [French Protest-
    ant] Huguenot Church...Charleston, SC, founded A.D. 1681-82.
    With a view of the present building... Chstn: News & Courier,
    1886. 19 p.   SCL, SCHS
Vedder, Charles S. The Huguenot Church of Charleston, SC. An
    apostolic & true church. Two discourses... Chstn: W,E&C,
    1880. 32 p.   SCL, CHCO
Voigt, Gilbert P. A history of Ebenezer Lutheran Church, Co-
    lumbia, SC. NP: NPub, 1930. 152 p.   SCL, SCHS, CHCO
Von Nessen, H. W. Augusta Street [Presbyterian] Church...[Co-
    limbia]...a brief history of the congregation. NP: NPub, nd.
    18 p.   MONT
The Walhalla Presbyterian Church, 1868-1915... Walhalla: Cour-
    ier Print, 1915. 8 p.   MONT
Walhalla Presbyterian Church, 1868-1968. Westminster: Westmin-

180

ster News Press, 1968. 104 p.   SCL, GRCL, SMCL, FLCL
Walkins, Louise. Brief history of Mt. Ebal Baptist Church [Ai-
ken County]. NP: typescript, nd, 2 p.   FURM
Wallace, David D. The historical background of religion in SC:
address delivered...Nov. 28, 1916. Florence: Upper South
Carolina Conference Historical Society, 1916? 34 p. SCL, SCHS
      COKL
Wallace, James A. History of Williamsburg [Presbyterian] Church
... Salisbury NC: Bell & James, 1856. 122 p.   COMMON
Walls, William J. The African Methodist Episcopal Zion Church:
reality in the black church. Charlotte NC: A.M.E. Zion Publ.
House, 1974? 669 p.   SCL
Walnut Grove Baptist Church. History...1826-1926.   GSGN
Walsh, Thomas T. The church of the middle way. Rock Hill: Lon-
don Printery, nd. 55 p.   SCL
Walter, Margaret C. Old Union Church [Orangeburg County]. Or-
angeburg: NPub, 1971. 9 p.   ORCL
Want, Leroy M. History of the Darlington Hebrew Congregation.
NP: typescript, nd.   DAHC
Ware, Charles C. SC Disciples of Christ: a history. Chstn:
Christian Churches of SC, 1967. 216 p.   SCL, GRCL, CLCC
Waring, Joseph I. St. James' Church [Episcopal], Goose Creek,
SC. A sketch of the parish from 1706 to 1896. Chstn: Lucas
& Richardson, 1897. 58 p.; also 1909, 70 p.   COMMON
Warlick, Hal C. From promise to fulfillment; the history of
Trinity Baptist Church [Seneca]. Seneca: the church, 1970.
27 p.   SCL, FURM
Warr, Mrs. O. L. Church history & church directory - Seventy-
fifth anniversary, 1891-1966 [Lamar Baptist Church]. NP: Par-
ter's Service Press, 1966. 34 p.   DAHC, FURM
Washington Avenue Baptist Church [Greenville]. NP: typescript,
1928. 1 p.   FURM
Washington Street Methodist Church, Columbia. Day of dedica-
tion: educational & administration building, May 6, 1945.
Cola: NPub, 1945. 24 p.   SCHS
Washington Street Methodist Episcopal Church. Sketch of...
Cola: NPub, nd. 6 p.   SCL
Washington Street Methodist Episcopal Church, South. History &
directory... Cola: NPub, 1925. unp.   SCL
Washington Street Presbyterian Church, Greenville. Manual...
Greenville: Shannon & Co., 1892. 20 p.   FURM
Wateree Presbyterian Church [SpC]   FACM
Watson, Carlos. A history of Kellytown Baptist Church, 1923-
1964. NP, 1964.   DAHC
Watson, Ellen B. A history of the Bethel Baptist Association.
Spartanburg: B. F. Long Printing Co., 1967. 38 p. SCL, SPCL
Watson, Emory O. A review of Methodist education in SC. NP:
NPub, nd. 21 p.   SCL
Watson, Emory O. Sesqui-centennial of Methodism in SC, 1785-
1935. Cola: State Co., 1936. 180 p.   MRCL
Watson, J. F. Brief history of Lamar Church. NP: typescript,

1920.   DAHC
Watson, J. Fred. History of Lamar Baptist Church. NP: type-
   script, 1934.   DAHC
Watson, J. N. A history of the First Baptist Church of Travel-
   er's Rest, SC. NP: NPub, 1963? 37 p.   FURM
Waxhaw Presbyterian Church, Lancaster County [SpC]   MONT
Way, Mrs. George K. A history of the Winnsboro First Methodist
   Church...1808-1958. NP: NPub, 1958. 24 p.   SCL
Way, William. The history of Grace [Episcopal] Church, Charles-
   ton, SC: the first hundred years. Chstn, 1948. 208 p. COMMON
Way, William. Seventy-fifth anniversary of the consecration of
   Grace [Episcopal] Church, Charleston, SC... History of the
   parish... Chstn: the congregation, 1923. 112 p.   COMMON
Weaver, Lansing, Lake Swamp Baptist Church [Darlington County],
   1819-1969; a bit of church history. NP: typescript, 1969.
   8 p.   FURM, DAHC
Webb, R. A. History of the Presbyterian Church of Bethel...
   [Bethel, SC]. Gastonia NC: Gazette Print, 1887. 56 p. COMMON
Weber, Samuel A. The auld lang syne of the South Carolina Con-
   ference [Methodist Church]. An address delivered before the
   Historical Society of the SC Conference...December 12, 1905.
   NP: NPub, nd. 13 p.   SCL
Weber, Samuel A. The [SC Methodist] Conference of 1859... An
   address delivered before the Historical Society of the SC Con-
   ference...December 8, 1903... NP: NPub, nd. 15 p.   SCL
Welsh Neck Baptist Association. Declaration of principles...
   with an appendix. Chstn: Walker & James, 1850. 68 p.   SCL
Welsh Neck Baptist Church, Society Hill. Historical sketch...
   together with addresses delivered at the one hundred and fiftieth anniversary, April 21, 1888. Greenville: Hoyt & Keys,
   1889. 90 p.   DAHC, SCL, GRCL
Welsh Neck Baptist Church, Society Hill. Historical sketch...
   two hundred and twenty-fifth anniversary, March 3, 1963. Cola:
   State Co., 1963. 60 p.   FLMC, FURM, DAHC
Wentworth Street Baptist Church, Charleston. Rules or by-laws..
       Chstn: Walker, Evans & Co., 1859. 16 p.   FURM
Wesberry, James P. Baptists in SC before the war between the
   states. Cola: RLB, 1966. 91 p.   COKL, ANCL
Wesley bi-centennial celebration. Charleston, SC, June 24-28,
   1903. Chstn: W,E&C, 1903. 15 p.   SCHS
West, H. Norman. History of the First Baptist Church of Moncks
   Corner. Moncks Corner: the church, 1970. 28 p.   FURM
West, Nannie L. & Vivian Boiter. Poplar Springs Baptist Church
   [Spartanburg County], the first one hundred years, 1874-1974.
   NP: NPub, 1974. 64 p.   FURM
West, W. Edgar. Berkeley County Baptists. NP: NPub, 1953.
   64 p.   SCL
Whatley, James F. The history of First Baptist Church, Mauldin,
   SC. NP: NPub, 1957. 16 p.   FURM
White, H. B. History of Red Bank Baptist Church [Saluda County]
   NP: typescript, 1934. 17 p.   FURM

182

White, William B., Jr. History of the First Presbyterian Church
of Rock Hill, SC, 1869-1969. Richmond VA: Whittet & Shepper-
son, 1969. 134 p.   COMMON
Whitmire, Mrs. J. C. History of First Baptist Church, Walhalla.
NP: typescript, 1954. 1 p.   FURM
Wigington, Jo Ann R. Historical sketch of Mount Pisgah Baptist
Church, 1791-1971 [Anderson County]. NP: typescript, 1971.
61 p.   FURM
Wilkes, E. Alston. The circuit riders' sketch book. Cola: RLB,
1907. 230 p.   COMMON
Willcox, Clarke A. Belin Memorial Methodist Church, Murrell's
Inlet, SC. Our benefactor, 1788-1859; commemorating 110 years
since his death on May 19th, 1859. Murrell's Inlet: the
church, 1974? 16 p.   CLCC
Williams, George W. St. Michael's [Episcopal Church], Charles-
ton, 1751-1951. Cola: USC Press, 1951. 375 p.   COMMON
Willis, George T. History of Mayer Memorial Evangelical Luth-
eran Church, 1899-1959... NP: NPub, 1959. 14 p.   SCL
Willow Swamp Baptist [Church, Orangeburg County]. NP: mimeo,
1936. 2 p.   FURM
Willson, John O. Methodism & education, especially in SC. Cola
State Co., 1914. 28 p.   SCL
Willson, John O. Sketch of the Methodist Church in Charleston,
SC, 1785-1887. Chstn: Lucas & Richardson, 1888. 32 p.   SCHS
                                                         SCL, GRCL
Winn, David J. An historical sketch of Methodism & roll of
Methodist preachers stationed on the Santee Circuit and Sumter
Station from the year 1786 to 1918... Sumter: Knight Bros.,
1918. 60 p.   SCL
Wise, Mrs. Mattie. History of New Bethel A.M.E. Church, 1865 -
1970. NP: typescript, 2 p.   LXMU
Wittenburg Lutheran Church, Leesville. The first hundred years,
1870-1970...   LXCL
Wolfe, W. M. & others. History of Providence Baptist Church
[Orangeburg County], 1868-1944. NP: typescript, 1944? 7 p.
                                                             FURM
Wood, Robert C. Parish in the heart of the city: Christ Church,
Greenville, SC. Greenville: Keys Printing Co., 1977. 136 p.
                                                   GRCL, SCL, SCHS
Woods, W. D. A sketch of Methodism in Darlington, SC. 1904.
                                                             DAHC
Woodson, Hortense. History of the Edgefield Baptist Associa-
tion, 1807-1957. Edgefield: Advertiser Press, nd. 346 p.
                                                           COMMON
Woodson, Hortense. Horn's Creek Baptist Church [Edgefield Coun-
ty]. Historic landmark. NP: typescript, nd. 9 p.   FURM
Woodson, Hortense. Publish glad tidings... A pageant depicting
the history of the Edgefield Baptist Church from its organization in 1823... Edgefield: Advertiser Print, 1945. 20 p.
                                                         SCL, EDTO
Woodson, Hortense. Red Oak Baptist Church [Edgefield County].

NP: typescript, nd. 14 p.   FURM
Woodward, J. Herbert. The Negro bishop movement in the Episco-
   pal Diocese of SC. McPhersonville: NPub, 1916. 45 p.SCL,SCHS
Work Projects Administration. Sermon by the Rev. R. H. Reid on
   the founding of the Presbyterian Church in Spartanburg [also:
   St. John's Theological Seminary, Spartanburg Female Academy].
   Spartanburg: typescript, nd. 19 p.   SPCL
Yarbrough, Mattie J. In part, a sketch given at Salem Baptist
   Church [Edgefield County] homecoming. NP: typescript, nd.
   1 p.   FURM
Yeadon, Richard. History of the Circular [Independent or Con-
   gregational] Church [Charleston]; its origin, building, re-
   building and recent ornamental renovation...as published in
   the Charleston Courier, July 16, 1853. With additions.
   Chstn: Nixon, 1853. 24 p.   SCL, SCHS
Young, Emory F. History of Kellytown Baptist Church.   DAHC
Young, Thomas J. The duty of combining religious instruction
   with every system of education. A sermon. Chstn: Miller,
   1841. 22 p.   SCHS
Zimmerman, Laura. History in brief of First Presbyterian Church
   Laurens, SC. NP: NPub, 1979. 2 p.   MONT
Zion-Olivet Presbyterian Church, Charleston. Tenth anniversary
   celebration. Chstn: John J. Furlong, 1974. 16 p.   SCL

PUBLISHED STATE & COLONIAL RECORDS

The following are commonly available published editions of colonial and state records. They have been compiled by the South
Carolina Department of Archives and History, its predecessors,
and by other institutions and individuals.

For checklists of other state records, see J. H. Easterby,
Guide to the study & reading of South Carolina history...with
supplement, 1975 (Spartanburg: the Reprint Co., 1975) 344 p.

For a guide to the holdings of manuscript state and colonial
records, see Marion C. Chandler & Earl W. Wade, The South Carolina Archives: a temporary summary guide. 2nd ed. (Columbia:
South Carolina Department of Archives & History, 1976) 161 p.

Since many of the publication titles are repetitive, the following format is used:

From	-To	Editor	Place	Publ.	Year	#pp

British Public Records Office.

Records in the British Public Record Office relating to SC:

From	To	Editor	Place	Publ.	Year	#pp
1663-	1684	Salley	Cola	HCSC	1928	325
1685-	1690	Salley	Cola	HCSC	1929	307
1691-	1697	Salley	Cola	HCSC	1931	252
1698-	1700	Salley	Cola	HCSC	1946	205
1701-	1710	Salley	Cola	HCSC	1947	344
1710-	1782	see SC Archives Microcopies.				

Commons House of Assembly

Journals of the Commons House of Assembly:

From	To	Editor	Place	Publ.	Year	#pp
20 Sep 1692-	15 Oct 1692	Salley	Cola	HCSC	1907	31
1693-	[4 sessions]	Salley	Cola	HCSC	1907	41
20 Nov 1695-	28 Nov 1695	Salley	Cola	HCSC	1943	18
30 Jan 1696-	17 Mar 1696	Salley	Cola	HCSC	1908	53
24 Nov 1696-	5 Dec 1696	Salley	Cola	HCSC	1912	20
1697-	[2 sessions]	Salley	Cola	HCSC	1913	24
1698-	[2 sessions]	Salley	Cola	HCSC	1914	40
30 Oct 1700-	16 Nov 1700	Salley	Cola	HCSC	1924	30
4 Feb 1701-	1 Mar 1701	Salley	Cola	HCSC	1925	25
13 Aug 1701-	28 Aug 1701	Salley	Cola	HCSC	1926	35
1702-		Salley	Cola	HCSC	1932	115
1703-		Salley	Cola	HCSC	1934	140
6 Mar 1705/6	9 Apr 1706	Salley	Cola	HCSC	1937	64
20 Nov 1706-	8 Feb 1706/7	Salley	Cola	HCSC	1939	53

From	-To	Editor	Place	Publ.	Year	#pp
5 Jun 1707-	19 Jul 1707	Salley	Cola	HCSC	1940	109
22 Oct 1707-	12 Feb 1707/8	Salley	Cola	HCSC	1941	74
2 Jun 1724-	16 Jun 1724	Salley	Cola	HCSC	1944	61
23 Feb 1724/5	1 Jun 1725	Salley	Cola	GenAs	1945	161
1 Nov 1725-	30 Apr 1726	Salley	Cola	GenAs	1945	116
15 Nov 1726-	11 Mar 1726/7	Salley	Cola	GenAs	1946	189
8 Nov 1734-	7 Jun 1735	Salley	Cola	HCSC	1947	255
10 Nov 1736-	7 Jun 1739	Easterby	Cola	SCAD	1951	764
12 Sep 1739-	26 Mar 1741	Easterby	Cola	SCAD	1952	613
18 May 1741-	10 Jul 1742	Easterby	Cola	SCAD	1953	620
14 Sep 1742-	27 Jan 1744	Easterby	Cola	SCAD	1954	607
20 Feb 1744-	25 May 1745	Easterby	Cola	SCAD	1955	626
10 Sep 1745-	17 Jun 1746	Easterby	Cola	SCAD	1956	291
10 Sep 1746-	13 Jun 1747	Easterby	Cola	SCAD	1958	444
19 Jan 1748-	29 Jun 1748	Easterby	Cola	SCAD	1961	457
28 Mar 1749-	19 Mar 1750	Easterby	Cola	SCAD	1962	549
23 Apr 1750-	31 Aug 1751	Olsberg	Cola	USC	1974	607
14 Nov 1751-	7 Oct 1752	Lipscomb	Cola	USC	1977	471
8 Jan 1765-	9 Aug 1765	Salley	Cola	HCSC	1949	210

Court of Chancery.

Gregorie, Anne K.   Records of the Court of Chancery of SC, 1671-
    1779. Washington DC: American Historical Assn., 1950.   676 p.

General Assembly.

Journals of the General Assembly of SC:
26 Mar 1776-	11 Apr 1776	Salley	Cola	HCSC	1906	89
17 Sep 1776-	20 Oct 1776	Salley	Cola	HCSC	1909	174

General Assembly & House of Representatives.

Journal of the General Assembly & House of Representatives:
1776-	1780	Hemphill	Cola	USC	1970 371

Grand Council.

Journal of the Grand Council of SC:
25 Aug 1671-	24 Jun 1680	Salley	Cola	HCSC	1907 91
11 Apr 1692-	26 Sep 1692	Salley	Cola	HCSC	1907 67

His Majesty's Council.

Journal of His Majesty's Council for SC:
29 May 1721-	10 Jun 1721	Salley	Atlanta	HCSC	1930 32

House of Representatives.

Journals of the House of Representatives:
8 Jan 1782-	26 Feb 1782	Salley	Cola	HCSC	1916	143
1783-	1784	Thompson	Cola	USC	1977	762
1785-	1786	Emerson	Cola	USC	1979	710

Indian Affairs.

Documents relating to Indian affairs:
21 May 1750-	7 Aug 1754	McDowell	Cola	SCAD	1958	592
1754-	1765	McDowell	Cola	SCAD	1970	657

Journal of the Commissioners of the Indian trade:
20 Sep 1710-	12 Apr 1715	Salley	Cola	HCSC	1926	91
20 Sep 1710-	29 Aug 1718	McDowell	Cola	SCAD	1955	368

Journal of Col. John Herbert, Commissioner of Indian affairs for the province of SC:
17 Oct 1727-	19 Mar 1727/8	Salley	Cola	HCSC	1936	34

Land.

Warrants for land in SC:
1672-	1679	Salley	Cola	HCSC	1910	222
1680-	1692	Salley	Cola	HCSC	1911	226
1692-	1711	Salley	Cola	HCSC	1915	264
1672-	1711	Olsberg	Cola	USC	1973	724

Jackson, Ronald V. Index to SC land grants, 1784-1800. Bountiful UT: Accelerated Indexing Systems, 1977. 163 p.

Lords Proprietors.

Commissions & instructions from the Lords Proprietors of Carolina to public officials of SC:
1685-	1715	Salley	Cola	HCSC	1916	292

Carolina Lords Proprietors' account of disbursements & receipts, 1663-1666. Winnabow NC: Charles Towne Preservation Trust, 1963. 28 p.   SCL

Military Service.

Salley, Alexander S. South Carolina provincial troops named in papers of the first Council of Safety of the Revolutionary Party in SC, June-November, 1775. Baltimore MD: GPC, 1977. 234 p.
Salley, Alexander S. South Carolina troops in Confederate service, vol. I. Cola: RLB, 1913. 783 p.
Salley, Alexander S. South Carolina troops in Confederate ser-

vice, vol. II. Cola: RLB, 1914. 743 p.
Salley, Alexander S. South Carolina troops in Confederate ser-
    vice, vol. III. Cola: HCSC, 1930.
Salley, Alexander S. Records of the regiments of the South Car-
    olina line in the Revolutionary War. Baltimore MD: GPC, 1977.
    86 p.

Navy.

Journals of the Commissioners of the Navy of SC:
  9 Oct 1776-   1 Mar 1779   Salley   Cola   HCSC 1912 269
 22 Jul 1779- 23 Mar 1780   Salley   Cola   HCSC 1913 91

Capt. Tollemache's journal of the proceedings of H.M.S. Scorpion
 21 Jun 1775- 18 Sep 1775   Salley   Cola   HCSC 1919 25

Privy Council.

Journals of the Privy Council:
      1783-   1789   Edwards   Cola   USC   1971 274

Provincial Congress.

Extracts from the journals of the Provincial Congresses of SC:
      1775-   1776   Hemphill   Cola   SCAD 1960 299

Extracts from the journals of the Provincial Congress of SC,
    held at Charles-Town, Feb. 1, 1776 [to April 11, 1776].
    Chstn: Peter Timothy, 1776.
Extracts of letters, etc., published by order of Congress.
    Chstn: Peter Timothy, 1776. 1 p.

Secretary of the Province & Register of the Province.

Records of the Secretary of the Province & Register of the Pro-
    vince of SC:
      1671-   1675   Salley   Cola   HCSC 1944 77

Senate.

Journal of the Senate of SC:
  8 Jan 1782- 26 Feb 1782   Salley   Cola   HCSC 1941 160

Surveyor General.

Account of plats for lands granted before the late war with
    Great Britain, which are now in the Surveyor General's office,
    but were never recorded. Cola: Young & Faust, 1796. Typed
    copy, 96 p.

Treasurer.

Accounts audited of Revolutionary War claims against SC:

Abbott-Allen	v. 1	Salley	Cola	HCSC	1935	192
Allison-Arnet	v. 2	Salley	Cola	HCSC	1938	181
Austin-Barnet	v. 3	Salley	Cola	HCSC	1943	177

[for complete series, see SC Archives Microcopies.

Stub entries to indents, issued in payment of claims against SC,
   growing out of the Revolution:

Book B		Salley	Cola	HCSC	1934	264
"	C-F	Wates	Cola	SCAD	1957	278
"	G-H	Wates	Cola	SCAD	1955	123
"	I	Salley	Cola	HCSC	1939	120
"	[J not used]					
"	K	Wates	Cola	SCAD	1956	60
"	L-N	Salley	Cola	HCSC	1910	376
"	O-Q	Salley	Cola	HCSC	1915	333
"	R-T	Salley	Cola	HCSC	1917	319
"	U-W	Salley	Cola	HCSC	1918	317
"	X, part 1	Salley	Cola	HCSC	1925	257
"	X, part 2	Salley	Cola	HCSC	1925	224
"	Y-Z	Salley	Cola	HCSC	1927	344
"	AA being prepared					
"	FEC "					
"	CT "					
Book RP	"					

South Carolina Department of Archives & History. South Carolina
   treasury; general index to ledgers, 1784-1791. Cola: USC
   Press, 1973. 55 p.

Misc. Records.

Lanning, J. T. The St. Augustine expedition of 1740: a report
   to the SC General Assembly. Cola: SCAD, 1954. 182 p.

South Carolina Archives Microcopies.

#1. Records in the British Public Records Office relating to
   SC, 1663-1782, with general index. 12 rolls.
#2. United States Census. Original agriculture, industry, soc-
   ial statistics, and mortality schedules for SC, 1850-1880.
   With a printed introduction. 22 rolls.
#3. Records of the Public Treasurers of SC, 1725-1776. With
   a printed introduction & tables. 2 rolls.
#4. Records of the SC Treasury, 1775-1780. With a printed in-
   troduction. 6 rolls.
#5. SC Treasury Ledgers & Journals, 1783-1791. With a printed
   introduction & index. 4 rolls.
#6. Duties on Trade at Charleston, 1784-1789. With a printed

introduction & tables. 1 roll.

#7. SC Treasury Ledgers & Journals, 1791-1865. With a printed introduction. 12 rolls.

#8. Accounts audited of claims growing out of the Revolution in SC. Printed guide in preparation. 165 rolls.

#9. SC Will transcripts (C.W.A.), 1782-1868. [Covers all of SC after 1782 except Charleston District] With a printed introduction. 31 rolls. Indexed in Mrs. John D. Rogers, Index to the county wills of SC (Washington DC: Martha Lou Houston, 1946), rp Baltimore MD: GPC, 1964 & 1975.

INDIANS

Atkin, Edmond. Indians of the southern colonial frontier. The
Edmund Atkin report & plan of 1775. Cola: USC Press, 1954.
108 p.   SCL, SPCL, SCHS
Bierer, Bert W. Discovering SC: a story about indians, their
ancient remains and trails. NP: author, 1969. 78 p.   COMMON
Bierer, Bert W. Indian arrowheads & spearheads in the Carolinas
a field guide. NP: Carolina Indian Lore Pub., 1974. 83 p.
                                                       SCL, SPCL
Bierer, Bert W. Indians & artifacts in the southeast. Cola:
State Co., 1980. 502 p.   SCL, SCHS
Bierer, Bert W. SC indian lore. Cola: State Co., 1972. 164 p.
                                                         COMMON
Bradford, William R. Report of representative William R. Brad-
ford for committee appointed to concurrent resolution H. 281
of the status of Catawba indians. Cola: General Assembly, nd.
                                                       SCL, YOCL
Bradford, William R. The Catawba indians of SC. Cola: General
Assembly, 1957. 31 p.   COMMON
Brown, John P. Old frontiers: the story of the Cherokee indians
from earliest times to the date of their removal to the west,
1838. NP: Southern Publishers, 1938.   KECA
Calmes, Alan R. The culture and acculturation of the Cusaba
indians, 1520-1720. Thesis (M.A.), U.S.C., 1964. 97 p.   SCL
Calmes, Alan R. Indian cultural traditions & European conquest
of the GA-SC coastal plain, 3000 B.C. - 1733 A.D.: a combined
archaeological & historical investigation. Thesis (Ph.D.),
U.S.C., 1968. 191 p.   SCL
Fundaburk, Emma L. Southeastern indians; life portraits, a cat-
alogue of pictures, 1564-1860. Luverne AL: author, 1958.
136 p.   GTML, SPCL
Green, Edwin L. Indians of SC. Cola: State Co., 1920. 81 p.
                                                         COMMON
Gregorie, Anne K. Notes on the Seewee indians & indian remains
of Christ Church parish, Charleston county. Chstn: Charleston
Museum, 1925. 23 p.   SCL, SCHS, SPCL
Hollingsworth, Dixon. Indians on the Savannah River. NP:
Partridge Pond Press, 1976. 83 p.   SCL, EDCL, GTML
Hudson, Charles M. The Catawba nation. Atlanta GA: University
of Georgia Press, 1970. 142 p.   SCL, SPCL, YOCL, KECL
Hudson, Charles M. The southeastern indians. Knoxville TN:
University of Tennessee Press, 1976. 573 p.   COKL
Jones, Charles C. Antiquities of the southern indians, partic-
ularly of the Georgia tribes. 1873, rp Spartanburg: RPC,
1972. 532 p.   COMMON

Lesesne, Joab M. The Catawba indians from earliest times to the
American revolution. Thesis (M.A.), U.S.C., 1932. 95 p. SCL
Malone, Henry T. Cherokees of the old south; a people in trans-
ition. Athens GA: University of Georgia Press, 1956. 238 p.
SCL, KECL, SPCL, COKL
Milling, Chapman J. Red Carolinians. Cola: USC Press, 1969.
438 p.   COMMON
Mooney, James. Catawba. Washington DC: Smithsonian, 1907.
213 p.   YOCL
Mooney, James. The Siouan tribes of the east. Washington DC:
GPO, 1894.   SCL, YOCL
Moore, Clarence B. Certain aboriginal mounds of the coast of
SC. Philadelphia PA: Academy of Natural Sciences, 1897.
2 vol.   SCL, BUCL
Parker, Thomas V. The Cherokee indians, with special reference
to their relations with the U.S. government. NY: Grafton
Press, 1907. 116 p.   SCL, SPCL
Sass, Herbert R. Hear me, my chiefs. NY: William Morrow & Co.,
1940. 256 p.   SCL, YOCL
Scaife, Hazel L. Catawba indians of SC: history & conditions...
Washington DC: GPO, 1930. 17 p.   YOCL
Speck, Frank G. Catawba hunting, trapping, & fishing. Phila-
delphia PA: University Museum, 1946.   ·   SCL, YOCL
Speck, Frank G. Catawba medicines & curative practices. Phila-
delphia PA: University of Pennsylvania Press, 1937.   YOCL
Speck, Frank G. Catawba texts. NY: Columbia University Press,
1934.   SCL, YOCL
Speck, Frank G. Siouan tribes of the Carolinas, as known from
Catawba, Tutelo, and documentary sources...   YOCL
Starkey, Marion L. The Cherokee nation. NY: Knopf, 1946.
355 p.   SCHS
Starr, Emmet. History of the Cherokee indians and their legends
and folk lore. Oklahoma City OK: Warden Co., 1921. 680 p.
CRCL
Swanton, John R. The indians of the southeastern U.S. Washing-
ton DC: Smithsonian, 1946. 2 vol.   SCL, SCHS
U.S. Congress. Senate. Subcommittee of the Committee on Indian
Affairs. Survey of the condition of the Catawba indians in
the U.S. Rock Hill, 1930.   YOCL
U.S. Bureau of Indian Affairs. Factual information on the Ca-
tawba indians & their lands...1958.   YOCL
U.S. Office of Indian Affairs. Constitution & by-laws of the
Catawba indian tribe of SC. Washington DC: GPO, 1946.   YOCL
U.S. Department of the Interior. Bureau of Indian Affairs.
Catawba indian tribe of SC; notice of final membership roll.
(in: Federal Register, v. 26, no. 37, Feb. 25, 1961.)   YOCL
Waddell, Gene. Indians of the SC lowcountry, 1562-1751. Cola:
Southern Studies Program, U.S.C., 1980. 484 p.   COMMON
Wade, Forest C. Cry of the eagle; history & legends of the
Cherokee Indians... Cumming GA: author, 1969. 151 p.   COKL
Wilkins, Thurman. Cherokee tragedy: the story of the Ridge fam-

ily and the decimation of a people. NY: Macmillan Co., 1970.
398 p.   KECA
Williams, Walter L. Southeastern indians since the removal era.
Athens GA: University of Georgia Press, 1979. 253 p.   SCHS

Abbott, Martin. The Freedmen's Bureau in SC, 1865-1872. Chapel
   Hill NC: UNC Press, 1967. 162 p.   COMMON
Afro-Americana, 1553-1906: author catalog of the Library of
   Philadelphia & the Historical Society of Pennsylvania. Bos-
   ton: G. K. Hall, 1973. 714 p.   PUBL
Bleser, Carol K. The promised land; the history of the South
   Carolina Land Commission, 1869-1890. Cola: USC Press, 1969.
   189 p.   COMMON
Brown, William. An oral history of Edisto Island: the life and
   times of Bubberson Brown. Goshen IN: Pinchpenny Press, 1977.
   110 p.   SCL
Bryant, Lawrence C. Negro lawmakers in the SC legislature, 1868
   to 1902. Orangeburg: S. C. State College, 1968. 142 p. GTML
Bryant, Lawrence C. Negro legislators in SC. Orangeburg: S. C.
   State College, 1967. 107 p.   SCL, GTML
Bryant, Lawrence C. Negro senators & representatives in the SC
   legislature, 1868-1902. Orangeburg: S. C. State College,
   1968. 196 p.   GTML
Campbell, Stephen C. An outline of some history of the Negro
   Baptists of SC. NP: NPub, 1953.   SCL
Charleston. Treasurer. Tax book of free persons of color.
   1864. 1 Ms. vol.   CHCA
Charleston County School District. The ethnic history of SC.
   Chstn: author, 1975. 296 p.   SCL, EDTO, SCHS
Crum, Mason. Gullah: Negro life in the Carolina sea islands.
   Durham NC: Duke University Press, 1940. 351 p. SCL,CTCL, BUCL
Gonzales, Ambrose E. The black border; gullah stories of the
   Carolina coast... Cola: State Co., 1922. 348 p.   SCL, SPCL
Gordon, Asa H. Sketches of Negro life & history in SC. 1929,
   rp Cola: USC Press, 1971.   COMMON
Hemmingway, Theodore. Beneath the yoke of bondage: a history of
   black folks in SC, 1900-1940. Thesis (Ph.D.), U.S.C., 1976.
   438 p.   SCL
Johnson, Guy B. Folk culture on St. Helena Island, SC...
   Chapel Hill NC: UNC Press, 1930. 183 p.   COMMON
Joyner, Charles W. Slave folklore on the Waccamaw Neck: ante-
   bellum Black culture in the SC lowcountry. Thesis (Ph.D.),
   University of Pennsylvania, 1977. 332 p.   SCL, UMBOD, GTML
Methodist Episcopal Church. Darlington Circuit. Names of the
   members of the colored class in the M.E. church in the Dar-
   lington Station, for the year 1843. 1 Ms. vol.   WOMA
Morgan, P. D. Afro-American cultural change; the case of colon-
   ial SC slaves. Typescript, 1979.   SCHS
Morse, Annie R. Keese barn: black history in Pendleton, SC.
   Pendleton: Black History & Culture Foundation of the Pendleton Area, Inc., 1979. unp.   PIPD
Newby, Indus A. Black Carolinians: a history of Blacks in SC
   from 1895-1968. Cola: USC Press, 1973. 388 p.   COMMON

Oubre, Claude F. Forty acres & a mule; the Freedmen's Bureau &
  black land ownership. Baton Rouge LA: Louisiana State University Press, 1978. 212 p.   SCHS
Rutledge, Archibald H. God's children. The Negroes of Hampton
  plantation. Indianapolis IN: Bobbs-Merrill, 1947. 159 p.
                                                             COMMON
Slave narratives; a folk history of slavery in the U.S., from
  interviews with former slaves. SC narratives. St. Clair
  Shores MI: Scholarly Press, 1976. 2 vol.   BUCL
South Carolina's blacks & native Americans, 1776-1976. 1976.
  254 p.   SCL, GTML, CTCL
Starobin, Robert S. Denmark Vesey: the slave conspiracy of
  1822. Englewood Cliffs NJ: Prentice-Hall, 1970.   SCL, CLCC
Tindall, George B. SC Negroes, 1877-1900. Cola: USC Press,
  1952. 336 p.   COMMON
Wilson, Miriam B. Slave days [Old Slave Mart museum lecture].
  Chstn: Old Slave Mart Foundation.   SCL, SCHS
Wirkramanayake, Marina. A world in shadow: the free black in
  antebellum SC. Cola: USC Press, 1973. 213 p.   COMMON
Wood, Peter H. Black majority; Negroes in colonial South Caro-
  lina from 1670 through the Stono Rebellion. NY: Knopf, 1974.
  346 p.   COMMON
Woofter, Thomas J. Black yeomanry; life on St. Helena Island.
  NY: H. Holt & Co., 1930. 291 p.   COMMON
Zimmerman, Samuel C. Negroes in Greenville, 1970. Greenville:
  Tricentennial Association, 1970. 47 p.   SCL, CLCC
Zamba. The life & adventures of Zamba, an African Negro king, &
  his experience of slavery in SC. Written by himself...
  London: Smith & Elder, 1847. 258 p.   SCL, SCHS

Alford, Robbie L. Two rice planters of Waccamaw. Georgetown:
  Rice Museum, 1976. 4 p.   SCHS
Andrews, Matthew P. The women of the south in war times. Nor-
  man ??: Remington, 1920 & 1923. 466 p.   COMMON
Bailey, James D. Some heroes of the American Revolution. 1924,
  rp Easley: SHP, 1976. 295 p.   COMMON
Bailey, James D. Some heroes of the American Revolution...
  index. Typescript, nd.   SPCL, UNCL
Biographies of York County physicians. Rock Hill: York County
  Medical Auxiliary, 1963. Typescripts. v.p.   YOCL
Boddie, Idella. South Carolina women: they dared to lead. Lex-
  ington: Sandlapper Store, 1978. 154 p.   COMMON
Bodie, Mrs. J. H. The Sabbath of years. History of the Woman's
  Missionary Society of Columbia District, upper SC conference,
  Methodist Episcopal church, south. NP: NPub, 1927? 32 p.SCHS
Boozer, Mary E. Bethel's pastors: biographical sketches of the
  pastors of Bethel Lutheran church, White Rock, SC. White
  Rock: the church, 1978. 67 p.   SCL
Brabham, A. McKay & others. United Methodist ministers in SC,
  1975; biographical sketches... Cola: RLB, nd. 270 p.   SPCL
Bradford, William R. Twenty-one governers of SC: Tillman to
  Byrnes. Cola: NPub, 1954. 88 p.   SCL, GTML, SCHS
Brooks, U. R. South Carolina bench & bar. Cola: State Co.,
  1908, 1926. 381 p.   COMMON
Burton, E. Milby. SC silversmiths, 1690-1860. Chstn: Charles-
  ton Museum, 1968. 311 p.   COMMON
The Carolinian. [Biographical sketches of SC artists & writers.
  May 1939].   SCL, SCHS
Catalogue of the Winthrop Normal College, 1892-93...including
  sketches of "Historic women of SC." Cola: Charles A. Calvo,
  1893.   SCL
Charles, Lois P. Sketches of SC missionaries & deaconesses in
  home & foreign fields, 1892-1933. NP: NPub, 1933. SCL, GRCL
The Citadel. After fifty years: the Citadel class of 1923 looks
  back. Chstn?, 1973? 85 p.   SCHS
Collier, Mrs. Bryan Wells. Biographies of representative women
  of the south, 1861-. NP: NPub, 192?. 5 vol.   SCL, SCHS
Conner, Mrs. James & others. SC women in the Confederacy.
  Cola: State Co., 1909. 2 vol.   SCL, EDTO
Cyclopedia of eminent & representative men of the Carolinas of
  the nineteenth century. Madison WI: Brant & Fuller; rp
  Spartanburg: RPC, 1971. 2 vol.   COMMON
Daniel, Sadie I. Women builders. Washington DC: Associated
  Publishers, 1931. 187 p.   SCL, SCHS
Devereux, Anthony Q. The rice princes: a rice epoch revisited.
  Cola: State Co., 1973. 125 p.   COMMON
Dill, Jacob S. Lest we forget: Baptist preachers of yesterday
  that I knew. Nashville TN: Broadman Press, 1938. 127 p. GRCL
DuBose, Louise J. South Carolina lives. NP: Historical Record

Association, 1963. 680 p.   SCL, MRCL, EDCL
Duncan, Watson B. Twentieth century sketches of the SC Confer-
ence, M. E. church, south. Cola: State Co., 1914. 486 p.
                                                             COMMON
Edgefield Advertiser. Ten governors of SC from Edgefield Coun-
ty. Edgefield: author, 1967. 16 p.   SCHS
Edgefield County Historical Society. Edgefield County judges.
Edgefield: Advertiser Press, 1942. unp.   EDTO
Faunt, Joan R. History of the class of 1910, U. S. C. Cola:
Vogue Press, 1961. 161 p.   SCL, GTML
Faunt, Joan R. History of the class of 1907, the Citadel.
Cola: State Co., 1965. 108 p.   SCL, SCHS, GTML
Forrest, Mary. Women of the south distinguished in literature.
NY: Richardson, 1866. 511 p.   SCL, SCHS
Garlington, J. C. Men of the time: sketches of living notables.
A biographical encyclopedia of contemporaneous SC leaders.
1902, rp Spartanburg: RPC, 1972. 467 p.   COMMON
Gist, Margaret A. Presbyterian women of SC. Greenville: Wom-
en's Auxiliary of the Synod of S.C., 1929. 785 p.   COMMON
Gramling, Andrew C. Men, in public life, from Orangeburg Coun-
ty, who attended Wofford College... Typescript, 1954. 32 p.
                                                              ORCL
Grier, Ralph E. SC & her builders... Cola: Carolina Biograph-
ical Association, Inc., 1930. 358 p.   SCL, SCHS, MRCL
Harris, Ray B. Eleven gentlemen of Charleston: founders of the
Supreme Council...accepted Scottish rite of Freemasonry.
Washington DC: The Supreme Council, 1959. 70 p.   COMMON
Hart, Bessie L. Pastors of Mulberry, 1826-1964. Macon GA:
Southern Press, 1964. 231 p.   SCL
Hemphill, James C. Men of mark in SC. Washington DC: Men of
Mark Publishing Co., 1907-1909. 4 vol.   COMMON
Hennig, Helen. Great South Carolinians. Chapel Hill NC: UNC
Press, 1940 & 1949. 2 vol.   COMMON
Irwin, W. J. [First Baptist Church, Chester.] Our church's
pastors, 1885-1958. NP: mimeo, 1958. 12 p.   FURM
Jackson, H. W. The southern women of the second American revo-
lution [SpC]   CSCL
Jaynes, R. T. Honoring the memory of two Revolutionary heroes:
Joseph Reid & John Gresham. Keowee Courier, 1935. 14 p. SCHS
Johnson, Leonard E. Men of achievement in the Carolinas; their
contributions to the rapid development of the two states.
Charlotte NC: Men of Achievement Publishing Co., 1952. 341 p.
                                                            COMMON
Kaminer, Gulielma M. A dictionary of SC biography during the
period of the royal government, 1719-1775. Thesis (M.A.),
U. S. C., 1926. 89 p.   SCL
Linder, Suzanne C. Medicine in Marlboro County, 1736-1980.
Bennettsville: Marlboro County Historical Society & Marlboro
County Medical Society, 1980. 206 p.   SCL, MRCL, SCHS
McKissick, J. Rion. Men & women of Carolina. Addresses & papers.
Cola: USC Press, 1948   SCL, UNCL

McLaurin, G. G.   Dillon County bar, 1888-1974.   NP: Herald
   Publishing Co., 1976.   24 p.   DICL
Meriwether, James B.   South Carolina women writers.   Proceedings
   of the second Reynolds conference, 1975.   Spartanburg: RPC for
   Southern Studies Program, U.S.C., 1975.   COMMON
Mills, William H.   Twelve great SC farmers.   Clemson: SC Agri-
   cultural Experiment Station, 1960.   44 p.   CLEM, CTCL, GWPL
Montgomery, Mabel.   Worth-while South Carolinians.   Cola: State
   Co., 1934.   48 p.   COMMON
New England Society of Charleston.   Mortuary, 1874.   Dunkin,
   Howland, Beach.   Chstn: W,E&C, 1874.   22 p.   SCL, SCHS
News & Courier, Charleston.   Our women in the war: the lives
   they lived; the deaths they died...   Chstn: News & Courier,
   1885.   482 p.   COMMON
Newberry County Medical Society.   Woman's Auxiliary.   Biograph-
   ies of deceased physicians of Newberry County...   NWRL
O'Neall, John B.   Biographical sketches of the bench & bar of
   SC.   1859, rp Spartanburg: RPC, 1975.   2 vol.   COMMON
Ravenel, Beatrice S.   Architects of Charleston.   Chstn: Carolina
   Art Assn., 1945.   329 p.   COMMON
Reynolds, Emily B. & Joan R. Faunt.   Biographical directory of
   the senate of the state of SC, 1776-1964.   Cola: SCDAH, 1964.
   358 p.   COMMON
Reynolds, Emily B. & Joan R. Faunt.   The county offices & offi-
   cers of Barnwell County, SC, 1775-1975.   A record.   Spartan-
   burg: RPC for Southern Studies Program, U. S. C., 1979.
   123 p.   COMMON
Reynolds, Emily B.   The senate of the state of SC, 1776-1962.
   Cola: 1962.   186 p.   SCHS
Rudisill, Horace F.   Doctors of Darlington County, SC, 1750-
   1912.   Darlington: Darlington County Historical Society, 1962.
   86 p.   COMMON
Sabine, Lorenzo.   Biographical sketches of loyalists of the
   American revolution.   Boston: Little & Brown, 1847 & 1864.
   2 vol.   SCL, EDTO, SCHS
Salley, Alexander S.   Delegates to the Continental Congress from
   SC, 1774-1789...   Cola: State Co., 1927.   36 p.   COMMON
South Carolina.   General Assembly.   House of Representatives.
   Research Committee.   Biographical directory of the SC House
   of Representatives.   Cola: USC Press, 1974.   2 vol.   COMMON
Temple, Wade.   Medical Doctors of Dillon County.   Dillon: NPub,
   1970.   DICL
Tolbert, Marguerite.   South Carolina's distinguished women of
   Laurens County.   Cola: RLB, 1972.   273 p.   COMMON
Union County men of medicine.   Monroe NC: Union County Medical
   Assn., 1968.   SCL, DICL
United Daughters of the Confederacy.   SC Division.   SC women in
   the confederacy.   Cola: State Co., 1903-1907.   2 vol.   COMMON
United Methodist ministers in SC.   Biographical sketches...
   Cola: RLB, 1975.   SCL
Utsey, Walker S.   Who's who in SC, 1934-1935.   Cola: Current

History Assn., 1935. 578 p.   COMMON
Walker, Jon L. Biographical dictionary of the confederacy.
  Westport CT: Greenwood Press, 1977. 601 p.   KECA
Wardlaw, Frank H. Men & women of SC. Selected addresses &
  papers by J. Rion McKissick. Cola: USC Press, 1948.GTML, SCL
Watson, E. O. Builders; sketches, Methodist preachers in SC,
  with historical data. Cola: Southern Christian Advocate, 1932
  268 p.   COMMON
Wauchope, George A. The writers of SC. With a critical intro-
  duction, biographical sketches... Cola: State Co., 1910.
  420 p.   SCL, MACL, MRCL, SCHS
Way, George K. Methodist ministers in SC, 1952: biographical
  sketches... Cola: S. C. Methodist Advocate Print, 1952?
  279 p.   SCL, USAI, SPCL
White, Henry A. Southern Presbyterian leaders. NY: Neale Publ.
  Co., 1911. 476 p.   SCL, FLCL
Who's who in America; a biographical dictionary...[var. eds.]
                                                               COMMON
Who's who in SC. Cola: McCaw, 1921. 226 p.   COMMON
Who's who in the south & southwest. A biographical dictionary
  ... [var. eds.]   COMMON
Williams, George W. Early ministers at St. Michael's [Episcopal
  church], Charleston. Chstn: Dalcho Historical Society, 1961.
  78 p.   COMMON
W.P.A. Federal Writer's Project. Palmetto pioneers: six stor-
  ies of early South Carolinians. 1938, rp Spartanburg: RPC,
  1972. 81 p.   COMMON
Young, Marjorie W. SC women patriots of the American revolution
  Anderson: Anderson Historical Society, 1978. unp. FACM, ANCL

Babbel, June A. Lest we forget: a guide to genealogical research in the nation's capital. Baltimore MD: GBC, 1976.
135 p.   SCL
Blockson, Charles L. & Ron Fry. Black genealogy. Englewood
Cliffs NJ: Prentice-Hall, 1977. 232 p.   COMMON
Cache [UT] Branch Genealogical Library. Handbook for genealo-
gical correspondence. Rev. ed. N: author, 1974. 274 p.
[distributor: GBC]   DIST
Colket, Meredith B. & Frank Bridgers. A guide to genealogical
records in the National Archives. Washington DC: GPO, 1964.
145 p.   COMMON
Côte, Richard N. The genealogists' guide to Charleston County,
SC. 1978, rp Easley: SHP, 1981. 44 p.   COMMON
Doane, Gilbert H. Searching for your ancestors: the how & why
of genealogy. 3rd ed. Minneapolis MN: University of Minne-
sota Press, 1960. 198 p.   COMMON
Everton, George B. The handy book for genealogists. 6th ed.
Logan UT: Everton publishers, 1971. 298 p.   COMMON
Everton, George B. The how book for genealogists. 7th ed.
Logan UT: Everton Publishers, 1976.   PUBL
Frazier, Evelyn M. Hunting for your ancestors in SC...a guide
for amateur genealogists. Walterboro: Florentine Press,
1974. 42 p.   COMMON
Genealogical Institute. Newspapers - were your ancestors front
page news? Salt Lake City UT: Gencor, Inc., 1974.   PUBL
Genealogical Institute. Tracing the immigrant ancestor. Salt
Lake City UT: Gencor, Inc., nd. 73 p.   PUBL
Greenwood, Val D. The researcher's guide to American genealogy.
Baltimore MD: GPC, 1973. 535 p.   SCL, CLEM
Groene, Bertram H. Tracing your Civil War ancestor. Winston-
Salem NC: Blair, 1973. 124 p.   SCL, GNCL, KECA
Holcomb, Brent. Brief guide to SC genealogical research &
records. Greenville: A Press, 1979. 29 p.   COMMON
Jacobus, Donald L. Genealogy as pastime & profession. 2nd ed.
Baltimore: GPC, 1968. 120 p.   COMMON
Jones, Vincent L. & others. Family history...[genealogical re-
search: a jurisdictional approach] Salt Lake City UT: Gencor,
Inc., 1972. 326 p.   SCL
Kirkham, E. Kay. The ABC's of American genealogical research.
Salt Lake City UT: Deseret Book Co., 1955. 123 p.   SCL
Kirkham, E. Kay. The handwriting of American records... Logan
UT: Everton Publishers, 1973. 106 p.   SCL
Kirkham, E. Kay. Record searching in the larger cities of the
U.S. Logan UT: Everton Publishers, Inc., 1974. 137 p.   PUBL
Kirkham, E. Kay. Research in American genealogy. A practical
approach... Salt Lake City UT: Deseret News Press, 1956.
447 p.   SCL
Meyer, Mary K. Directory of genealogical societies in the U.S.

& Canada, with an appended list of independent genealogical
    periodicals. Pasadena MD: author, 1976. 73 p.   SCL
Miller, Olga K. Migration, emigration & immigration. Logan UT:
    Everton Publishers, Inc., 1974. 278 p.   PUBL
Milner, Anita C. Newspaper genealogy columns: a preliminary
    checklist. Escondido CA: author, 1975. 94 p.   SCL
National Genealogical Society. Special aids to genealogical
    research on southern families. Washington DC: author, 1962.
    125 p.   SCL
Neagles, James & Lila Neagles. A guide to locating your immi-
    grant ancestor. Baltimore MD: GPC, 1975. 153 p.   PUBL
Rottenberg, Dan. Finding our fathers: a guidebook to Jewish
    genealogy. NY: Random House, 1977. 401 p.   CLEM
Rubincam, Milton. Genealogical research: methods & sources.
    Baltimore MD: GBC, 1977. 454 p.   SCL, CLEM
South Caroliniana Library, U. S. C. Are you hunting your ances-
    tors? A brief guide to genealogical material in the South
    Caroliniana Library. Cola: USC, var. ed.   COMMON
Stevenson, Noel C. Genealogical evidence: a guide to the stan-
    dard of proof relating to pedigrees, ancestry, heirship, &
    family history. Laguna Hills CA: Aegean Park Press, 1979.
    233 p.   PUBL
U. S. National Archives. Genealogical sources outside the Nat-
    ional Archives. Washington DC: National Archives, 1972.
    8 p.   SCL
Williams, Ethel W. Know your ancestors. Rutland VT: C.E. Tut-
    tle Co., 1960. 313 p.   CLEM

Abbeville County Family History. Clinton: Intercollegiate Press
    1980. 199 p.   SCL, NWRL
Abbey, Matilda O. The family of Lt. Thomas Tracy. Milwaukee
    WI: Harkness, 1889.   CHLS
Abbey Memorial. NP: Abbey Print Shop, 1916.   CHLS
Abbott Family [SpC]   PIPD
Abbott-Smith, G. & J. Bancroft. Charles Bancroft...his ances-
    tors and his descendants, 1640-1943. NP, NPub, 1943.   CHLS
Abee, Blanche H. Colonists of Carolina in the lineage of Hon.
    W.D. Humphrey. Richmond VA: William Byrd Press, 1938. 259 p.
                                                             CRCL
Account of the meeting of the descendants of Col. Thomas White
    of Maryland...June 7, 1877. Philadelphia PA: NPub, 1879. 211
    p.   SCHS
Acker, George H. Descendants of Peter Acker and his wife Jane
    Sutherland, settlers of 1787 in the Pendleton district of SC.
    NP: typescript, 1966. 75 p.   SCHS
Across the years. The name and family of Gamble. NP, NPub,
    1948. 38 p.   LNCL
Adair Family [SpC]   PIPD, YOWC
Adair, James B. Adair history & genealogy [incl. Dillard, Pitts
    Biggs, Little, Anderson, Copeland, Finney, Glenor, Nabors &
    King families] 1924, rp Easley: SHP, 1978. 408 p.   COMMON
Adams, Frank L. Notes for genealogist on the Adams family of
    northeast Georgia, 1820-1880. Tampa FL: author, 1964.   SCL
Adams, William F. James Hayward, b. April 4, 1750; killed in
    the Battle of Lexington, April 19, 1775; with genealogical
    notes relating to the Haywards of Springfield, Massachusetts.
    Springfield MS: author, 1911. 58 p.   SCHS
Adams, William F. James Hosmer, Cambridge, 1635. Settled in
    Concord, Mass., soon after. Springfield MS: author, 1911.
    63 p.   SCHS
Adams, William F. Wealtha Staples, with records relating to
    some of the Berkley-Taunton, Massachusetts, families. Spring-
    field MS: author, 1911. 70 p.   SCHS
Adcock, Robert M. Adcock kinfolks, families & ancestors [incl.
    Whitney, Shanks, Sellers, Cowart, Leveritt, Lowe, McClane,
    Hubbard, Killebrew, Isbell, Kennedy, Feaster, McCall & Arline
    families]. St. Petersburg FL: author, 1980. 566 p.   SCHS
Adger Family [SpC]   FACM
Adger family in the Pendleton district, SC. Clemson: typescript
    1960. 16 p.   SCL, CLEM
Adickes, Clarke W. Genealogy of the Adickes family. Rock Hill:
    Record Print, 1959. 84 p.   YOCL, SCL
Aiken, Augustus. A short sketch of ancestors & descendants of
    David & Nancy Aiken. NP: typescript, 1906. unp.   SCL
Albergotti, William G. Albergotti Creek, the chronicles of a
    colonial family of the SC sea islands. Cola: RLB, 1979. PRIV
Albert, Ethel E. The history of five southern families. Balti-

more MD: Gateway Press, 1970. 234 p.   SCHS
Aldrich, James. A short sketch of the lives of James Thomas Aldrich and his wife Mrs. Isabel Coroneus Aldrich. Aiken: NPub, 1903. 40 p.   SCL, SCHS
Aldridge, Eugene T. Some southern Talberts. Provo UT: J. Grant Stevenson, 1975. 220 p.   SCL, GWPL
Alexander, Charles C. Alexander kin. NP, NPub, 1979. 173 p.   SCHS
Alexander Family [SpC]   PIPD
Alexander, Henry A. Notes on the Alexander family of SC & GA, and connections. NP, NPub, 1954. 142 p.   COMMON
Alexander, Virginia W. Whitten and allied families. NP: Genealogical Publishing Co., 1966. 304 p.   SCL, LRCL
Alexander, Virginia W. The Wood-Woods family magazine. Columbia TN: 1973- .   SCHS
Alford, Lewis E. Alford family genealogy, 1774-1979. NP: typescript, 1979. 36 p.   HOCL
Alleger, Daniel E. The early Breckenridges of the deep south. Gainesville FL: Renaissance Printing Co., 1977. 105 p.   SCL
Allen, Clarence B. The Joel Allen house. NP: C.J. Allen, 1978. 76 p.   MACL
Allen, Clarence B. William Benjamin and Theodosia Allen family. Dillon: Herald Publishing Co., 1973. 23 p.   SCL, FLMC
Allen, Edna. Robert Harper, son of W.M. Harper, Sr. (a supplement to "William Harper, Irish immigrant to Lancaster county, SC.   SCL, LNCL
Allen, Penelope J. Genealogy of a branch of the Johnson family & connections, revised & continued. Chattanooga TN: Helen Betts Miller, 1967. 447 p.   SCL, NWRL
Allen, Penelope J. Leaves from the family tree...records of the Pettigrew family. Seneca? NPub, 1962. 10 p.   CLEM
Allison, J.B. The family of Dr. Robert Turner Allison & Martha Burnett Clinton... York: mimeo, 1941. 185 p. YOCL, SCHS, SCL
Allison, William F. The family: Colonel William Barry Allison & Mary Susan Currence, their ancestors & all of their descendants. York: NPub, 1968. 204 p.   SCL
Allston, Elizabeth D. The Allstons & Alstons of Waccamaw. Chstn: W,E&C, 1936. 99 p.   SCHS, SCL
Alston Family [SpC]   FACM
Alston-Williams-Boddie-Hilliard Society. Society & family book, vol. I: 1958-1961. Winston-Salem NC: Bradford Printing Service, 1961.   SCHS, CHLS, SCL
Ambrose, Lorene B. Jamie Seay and his descendants & other allied lines [incl. Wingo family]. Spartanburg: author, 1977. 187 p.   SPCL
Ames, Faber K. The Ames family of Bruton, Somerset, England... Los Angeles CA: NPub, 1969. 285 p.   CHLS, SCL
Ames, Joseph S. Six generations of the Cantey family of SC. Chstn: W,E&C, 1910. 56 p.   SCL, SCHS
Ames, Joseph S. The Williams family of Society Hill; with "Life on the old plantations", by N. William Kirkpatrick. Cola:

203

State Co. for the Pee Dee Historical Assn., 1910. 20 p.
                                        SCL, CLEM, SPCL, SCHS
Anderson, Edward L. A history of the Anderson family, 1706-1955
    through the descendants of James Mason Anderson & his wife
    Mary "Polly" Miller. Cola: RLB, 1955. 250 p.   COMMON
Anderson, Ethel M. Draper families in America, beginning with
    Thomas Draper, born about 1725, buried in Monck's Corner SC.
    1964. 514 p.   DEALER
Anderson Family [SpC]   GSGN, YOWC
Anderson Family Reunion. Twenty-fifth anniversary. Descendants
    of James Mason "Tyger Jim" Anderson & Polly Miller Anderson...
    NP: NPub, 1964. v.p.   SCL
Anderson, Frank P. Anderson family tree...1858-1955. NP: type-
    script, 1955. 43 p.   SCL
Anderson, Katie W. Standing in the doorway of a day long ago
    [incl. Anderson, Berry, Dew, Hampton, Weatherford, Booth &
    Wise families]. NP: Utah Printing Co., 1963. 145 p. COMMON
Anderson memorial association. William Anderson & Rebecca Denny
    & their descendants, 1706-1914 [incl. Old Antioch Church Ceme-
    tery & Nazareth Church Cemeteries, Spartanburg Co.]. Cola:
    RLB, 1914. 287 p.   SPCL
Anderson, Sarah T. Lewises, Meriwethers, and their kin...
    Richmond VA: Dietz Press, 1938. 652 p.   CLEM
Anderson, William P. Anderson family records. Cincinnati OH:
    NPub, 1936. 174 p.   SCHS
Andrea, Leonardo. Abstracts of divisions of estates of Stubbs &
    allied families of Marlboro Co., SC. NP: NPub, 1964. 323 p.
                                        SCL, MRCL, SCHS
Andrea, Leonardo. The forty-sixth annual Wyatt reunion combined
    with allied & associated families, June 15, 1952. Greenville
    Presbyterian Church, Donalds, SC. NP: NPub, 1952. 48 p.
                                                          COMMON
Andrea, Leonardo. Guyton family. NP: typescript, nd. 83 p.
                                                            SCHS
Andrea, Leonardo. The Leonardo Andrea Genealogical Collection.
    A collection of approximately 1,029 folders of compiled gene-
    alogical information and records on approximately 825 surnames
    including material from local and church records, family rec-
    ords and Bibles. The collection is on microfilm (57 rolls,
    35 mm.) at the South Caroliniana Library (SCL), University of
    South Carolina, Columbia. Special copying provisions apply.
    Contact the Manuscripts Curator, South Caroliniana Library.
    Families and institutions listed in the index to the collec-
    tion are:
Abbott, Adams, Addington, Adkins-Atkins, Adolph, Agnew, Aiken-
Akin-Akins-Eakin-Eakins, Albert-Albird, Albertson-Aluertson, Al-
bright, Alexander-Crow-Oates, Allen, Allston, Amaker, Anderson,
James Anderson, Andrews, Pinson Archibald, Ardis, Armstrong, Ar-
nold #1, Arnold #2, Ash-Ashe, Ashley, Ashmore, Family of James
Atkinson of Sumter County, The Name and Family of Atkinson, At-
kinson #3, Atterbury. (continued next page)

Andrea Genealogical Collection, continued:

Babb, Baber-Babers, Bachman, Bailey, Baker, Baldwin, Ball, Ballard-Bullard-Grimes-Sandlin in SC, Ballentine, Barfield, Barfield & Barefield, Barnes, Barnett, Barrington and Barronton, Barry-Berry, Baskin, Batson, Baugh, Baughman, Beacham, Beal, Beam, Bean, Beasley, Beaty, Beckham, Belcher, Bell, The Bell Family in SC, Bell Ancestors of Horry County (Virginia ancestors of Samuel Bell of Horry County, SC), Belton-Bolton, Benbow, Benson, Betterton-Betterson, Bettis #1, Bettis #2-Bettis-Bettison-Betterton, Bettison, Bickham, Bigby, Birdsong-Byrdsong, Black, Blackburn, Blackwell, Blain #1, Blain #2, Blake-Wier, Blassinghame, Boatner, Bobo, Boddie and Eidson, Bonneau, Boswell, Bowen, Bowman, Boyce, Boyd, Boyd in Augusta County VA, Braden, Bradford Bradley, Brake, Brandon, Brashier, Brazleton, Breazeale, Brent, Brewster-Buster, Brice, Bridges, Brightman, Brinson, Brisbane, Broadwater, Brock, Brockington, Brockman, Brown, Brownlee, Brunson, Bryan, Buckalew (2), Buford-Burford, Bullard, Bulloch-Hardin-Ivey, Bullock, Burch, Burnett, Burns, Burris, Burt, Burton, Busby.

Caldwell #1, Caldwell #2, Caldwell #3, Caldwell #4, Caldwell #5-Richey-Dunn-Caldwell-Agnew, Caldwell-Harshaw-McElwee, Calhoun #1, Calhoun #2-Calhoun of Abbeville County SC, Calhoun #3, Calhoun #4, Calhoun #5, Calhoun #6, Calhoun #7, Long Cane Calhoun & Allied Data, Calhoun-the ancestry of the Barnwell County SC set of Calhouns, Calhoun odds & ends, Calhoun-Barnwell Court of Equity data, Calhoun-William Calhoun of Abbeville County SC, Calhoun in PA, Calhoun-Alan T. Calhoun, Calhoun-Ladson, Calhoun-Sharp, Calhoun-Williamson, Camp-Kemp, Cantey, Carlton, Carlton-Crutchfield-Stapleton, Carmichael, Carroll, Carson, Carter, Carteret-Cartwright, Cartledge, Case, Casey, Cashin, Caskey, Cason, Casper-Cosper, Cato & Carter in SC, Causey, Chambers, Chancellor Chapman, Cherry, Chesnut-Chestnut, Chew, China-Chaney-Cheney, Chisholm, Clark, Clatworthy, Clayton, Cleckler-Kleckley-Clackler Kleckler, Clements-Clemmons, Clinkscales, Cloud, Coachman, Coate Cobb, Cobb & Kolb in SC archives, Cockrell, Coffee-Kennedy, Cohoon notes, Colding, Cole, Coleman in Marion County SC, Collins, Collins & allied data from Camden District SC, Wyatt Collins, Colson, Commander, Conant, Conyers, Cook, Cooper, Cooper by Yates, Conner, Cork, Couch, Coulter, Counts, Coursey-Causey #1, Coursey-Causey #2, Cowsert, Cox, Crapton, Craig, Creighton-Crayton, Crenshaw, Cribb, Crosby, Culp, Cunningham, Cureton.

Dalrymple, Darby #1, Darby #2, Darraugh-Dorroh, Darwin, D.A.R. Davis-Griffin-Williams and Reminiscences, Dawkins, Day, DeBarelben, DeBruhl, DeLashmet, DeLoach, Dandy, Denson, Devlin, Dial-Dyal, Dickerson-Dickson, Dingle, Dinkins, Dixon, Dobbins, Dobson, Dodson, Donehue, Donnelly, Douthit, Downes-Downs, Drakeford Draper, Draughn, DuBard, Dubber, Duggan, Dundas, Dunlap, Dunn, DuPre and DuPree Family, Du Rant, Duren, Durham.

Earle, Easterling, Edmundson, Edwards, Eikner, Elkin-Elkins, Elliott, Ellis #1, Ellis #2, Ennis-Innis, Entriken, Eppes, Etheridge, Eubanks, Evans-Evins, Everitt-Averitt.

Andrea Genealogical Collection continued:
Faris, Farwell, Faust, Few, Findley-Finley, Finney #1, Finney
#2, Fleming, Fletcher, Flewelling-The Flewelling Family of Laur-
ens (Flewellen-Fincher-Smith), Flowers, Floyd, Ford, Fore, Foreman, Fort, Foster, Fowler, Franklin #1, Franklin #2, Franklin
#3, Frazier, Frink, Furniss.
    Gaillard, Gaines, Gambrell, Gammill, Garrett, Garrison, Gary,
Gasper-Gosper, Gaston, Gause, Gay, Gayden, Geiger, Gentry, Geor-
ge, Gibson, Gibson-Sparks-Evans, Gilbert, Gilchrist, Gilder-
Guilder, Gilkey, Gill, Gillispie, Gilreath Family Data, Gilreath
and Gilreath, Given-Givens, Gladney, Glasgow, Glasier and Glazier, Glass, Glaze, Glenn #1, Glenn #2, Glenn and Glen in S.C.,
Glover, Godhold, Godfrey, Golightly, Goodlett, Goodwin, Gordon,
Gore by Prince, Gore and Goree, Gore of Horry, Gowens-Going,
Goza, Graddick-Creaddick-Gredig-Reddick, Graham, Gramling, Grant
Graves, Gray and Grey, Gray in Abbeville and Richland counties
in S.C., Green-Greene, Greenwood, Greer-Grier, Grice and Grist,
Grigsby-Paxton and Foster, Grimke, Guyton.
    Hadden-Haddon, Haddon, Hairston, Haley, Hall #1, Hall #2, Hall
in S.C. Archives, Hallum, Hamilton, Hampton, Hanks, Hanna and
Hannah, Hannah-James Hannah Data, Hardwick, Hardy, Hardy and
Hardee, Harper, Harris #1, Harris #2, Harrison, Harshaw, Hart-
ness, Hartness for D.A.R., Hartness-The Gurley Ancestry of
George Bowman Hartness, Hartley, Hartsfield, Haselwood, Hatcher,
Hawthorn, Hay-Hayes-Hays, Haynes, Haynie, Hazel-Hazle, Head,
Hearn and Hyrne, Helveston-Helfestein, Hemingway, Hemphill, Hen-
derson, Hendricks, Henry, Hesselius, Hester, Higgs, Hill #1,
Hill #2,-Stubbs-Hubbard-Chiles and Allied Lines, Hill #3, Hill-
iard, Hitch and Hitchcock, Holcombe, Hollingsworth, Hollis, Hol-
esonback-Holsombake-etc., Holston, Holtzclaw, Hood, Hopkins,
Horton, Houlditch-Hardwick, Houston, Howard, Howell, Howle, Hub-
bard, Hucks, Huddleston, Hudson, Huggins, Hughes, Humphrey, Humphries, Hunt #1, Hunt #2, Hunt "Miscellaney" #3, Hutto, Holman,
Holmes #1, Holmes #2, Holmes #3.
    Ingram, Irvin-Irwin, Isbell, Isbell Family, Ivey.
    Jackson, Jaggers, James-The James Family, Jamison, Jelks, Jen-
kins, Jennings, Jeter, Johns, Johnsey, Johnson-Johnston (2),
Jones #1, Jones #2-Adam Crain Jones Family, Jones #3 (Samuel
Jones), Jordan, Jordan in Horry County S.C., Joyner.
    Kaigler, Kay, Keels-Keel-Keels-Kell, Kelly, Kelso, Kemp, Ken-
drick, Kennedy, Kennerley, Kidd, Kilby, Kimbrough, Kinard, Kin-
caid-McMorries-Watt-Glazier-Rabb, Kinchen, Kinsler, Klough-Klug-
Klugh, Knight, Knox, Koch, Koger, Kolb.
    Lackey, Laird, Lambert, Landers, Lane, Lanford-Langford- Lea-
therwood, Lang, Langley, Langston, Larrimore-Larrimon, Latimer,
Law-Laws, Lawson, Lay, League, Leatherwood, LeBon, LeBon-LaBoon,
Ledbetter, Lee-Lea, Leeper, Leeper-Looper, Lennox, Lenoir, Leonard, LeRoy, Lester, Lewis #1, Lewis #2-Lewis and Hemingway in
S.C., Lightfoot, Lightwood, Limehouse, Lindley, Lindsay and
Lindsey, Lively, Livingston Family of Horry County, S.C., Lock-
hart, Loptis-The Loptis Family, Logan #1, Logan #2, Long, Long-

Andrea Genealogical Collection continued:
Thompson, Longshore, Lott, Love, Loveless, Lucas, Lykes, Lyles.
  McAlpin, McCain and McKain Data from S.C., McCaleb, McCall,
McCalla, McCants, McCarter, McCarty-McCarthy, McCarty-McCartney,
McCaskill, McClain, McClain-McLain-McLean, McClaren-McLaren in
S.C., McClendon #1, McClendon #2-Data and Letters from Samuel E.
McClendon, McClendon #3-Georgia Data, McClendon #4- Alabama,
Louisiana, and Mississippi Data; McClendon #5-North Carolina
and South Carolina Data, McClendon #6-Miscellaney and Unclass-
ified Data on McClendon, McClimon Notes and Confederate Letters
from McClimon, McClinton, McClinton in S.C.; McClure of Chester
County, S.C.; McClurken, McCord, McCreary, McCullough, McDaniel,
McDavid-McDade, McDonald Data From South Carolina Archives, Mc-
Donald-McDaniel, McDuffin-Vereen-Livingston for D.A.R., McElwee
#1, McElwee #2, McFaddin, McGrew, McKee, McKeown, McKinley, Mc-
Kinney, McKnight, McLaughlin, McLellan, McLemore, McLeurath, Mc-
Murray, McNeil, McWhorter, Machen, Mackey, Mackie, Madden, Madison of Virginia, Magee-McGehee, Major, Malone, Magum, Manly-Man-
ley, Mann, Mansfield, Mapp, Martin, Massey #1, Massey #2, Masters, John Moore, Mathis, Mattison, Mauldin, May-Mays, Mayfield
in S.C. Archives, Meadows, Meek, Mellett, Melton, Merck, Meredith, Messer, Michael-Michel, Michel Bible Entries, Mickle,
Miles, Milford, Miller #1, Miller #2, Miller #3, Miller #4 (Mil-
ler II), Miller #5 (Miller III), Miller #6 (Miller IV - 96 District, S.C.), Miller #7 (Miller Notes & Letters), Miller #8 (Mil-
ler Sheets), Miller #9 (Miller in Georgia), Miller #10 (Miller-
Muller from Switzerland), Milner, Milwee, Mishoe-Michaw, Mitchell #1, Mitchell #2, Mitchell #3, Mitchell Data by Mrs. Ernest
Mehringer, Mixom, Moak, Mobley (How the Mobleys Came To South
Carolina in a Cavalcade and Changed Spelling on Their Name...
The Affair at Mobley's Meeting House), Montgomery, Moody, Moon,
Moore of Newberry County, Moore from New Hampshire to S.C. in
1815, Moreland, Morgan, Morris, Morrison, Morrow & Morrah, Mos-
ley, Mouchet, Murff #1, Murff #2, Murff #3, Murphy, Murray, Mur-
ray-Koger-Cook.
  Nail, Nation, Naugher, Neal-Neale-Neel-Neil, Neely, Nelson-
Neilson, Nesmith, Nettles, Nettles-Cloud-Scofield #1 & 2, New-
man, Newton, Nicholls-Nickels, Norfleet, Norris, Norton, Nuck-
olls.
  O'Brient, O'Dell, Odom, Oestman, Oliver-Olliver, O'Neal, Ot-
terson, Overby, Owens.
  Palin, Palmer, John Palmer (Revolutionary Soldier #1), John
Palmer (Revolutionary Soldier #2), Park-Parks, Parker, Parrott,
Partain, Patterson, Patterson-Pattison, Patton, Paul, Pearce,
Peden, Pelham, Penn, Pennington, Perry, Perryman, Peterkin, Pet-
ers, Pettigrew, Pettway, Pickens, Pierson, Mrs. T.C. (Boyd-Mc-
Craven-Bonner), Pinson, Pitts #1-Data on Pitts-Belton-Findley-
Houlditch, Pitts #2, Pitts #3, Pitts #4-Pitts in S.C., Plumer &
Plummer in S.C., Plunkett, Poinsett, Pollard & Pollock in S.C.,
Ponder, Pool-Pettypool, Poore, Posey, Potts, Powell, Prater-Pra-
ther-Praytor, Pray-Pratt-Prater-Prator-Praytor-Prather-Praither,

Andrea Genealogical Collection continued:
Prescott, Preslar-Presley, Pruitt, Puckett, Pulley, Purdy, Pursley, Purvis, Putman, Putman Data by Mrs. Ernest Mehringer, Pyles
   Rabb, Rainey, Ramage (Mrs. J.T. Ramage), Rambo, Christian Raysor Family in S.C., Rasor-Notes on Rasor and Other Surnames Found in Pauline Young's Book, "Abstract of Abbeville", Ratcliff -Radcliffe, Read-Reed-Reid, Rees-Reese-Rea, Reily-Riley, Renfro, Reynolds, Rhodes #1, #2, & #3, Rhodus, Richardson, Richey in Abbeville County S.C., Rickman-Richman, Riddle-Riddel, Ridgell, Ridgeway #1, Ridgeway #2-Ridgeway & Ridgway in Sumter County S.C., Rippy, Riser-Preacher-Wise, Rish-Rich, Ritchie (Benjamin Linn-John Ritchie-John Gilkey), Rives, Robert-Roberts, Roberts-Griffith-Cartwright-Simpson (Ancestral Study of Four Families with Relationships), Robertson-Robinson-Robison, Robyns-Robins, Rochelle, Roddenberry-Rottenberry, Roddy, Roden, Rodgers-Roger-Rogers, Rogers-Giles (Giles Rogers Family), Roseborough, Ross, Rossville, Ruff, Rush, Russell, Rutherford #1, Rutherford #2, Rutherford #3, Rutherford #4-Rutherford in Edgefield S.C., Rutherford #5, Rutherford #6, Rutherford (Letters) #7, Rutherford (Notes) #8, Rutledge.
   Sadler, Sample, Sanders-Saunders, Sandiper, Sandlin-Sandland, Satterwhite #1, #2, #3, Savage, Sawyer #1, #2, Sawyer-Gaston and Sawyer Data, Scaipe, Scogin, Scott, Seaborn #1, #2, Seago-Sego, Seale-Sale, Sealey, Seawright #1, #2 & #3-The Seawright Family, Setzler-Seitzler, Severance, Sharp #1, #2, Shedd, Sheed, Sheffield, Shepherd-Sheppard, Sheppard in North Carolina, Sheriff, Sherrerd for the D.A.R., Sherrerd-Moore and Allied Families, Sherrill, Shields, Shirley-Shurley, Shivers, Short, Simons #1, #2, Simpson, Sims-Massey-Duncan-Sims, Skeen-Skene-Skine, Slay, Smart #1, #2, Smith #1-Smith in Union County S.C.-Ephriam Smith, Smith #2-Reuben Smith, Smith #3, #4-Smith in Pendleton District S.C., Smith #5-William Smith of Pennsylvania, Smith #6-U.S. Census for 1790 in the State of S.C., Smith #7-The Families of Reuben Smith and John D. Smith, Smith #8, #9-Smith, Wyatt and Swain for the D.A.R., Smith #10, #11-Silas Smith, Snead, Snow, Spears and Speers, Stack, Stock, Stall-Stoll, Stark, Starnes, Steinwinder-Stivender, Stephens-Stevens, Stevenson-Stephenson, Still and Cockroft, Stingley, Stinson, Stokes, Stribling-Talliferro-Kincheloe, Strickland, Stringer, Strother, Stubbs #1-Allied Families, #2-Stubbs in North Carolina and Virginia, #3-Stubbs in S. C., Sturgis, Sullivan, Summerville, Sutton, Swain, Swan-Swann, Swearingen, Swent-Swet-Sweet-Swete, Sylvester,
   Tallent, Talman, Tanner, Tarrant-Greenville S.C. R.M.C. Office Tate, Taylor, Terry, Theus, Thomas #1, #2, #3-Thomas of Union, Chester and Fairfield, #4-Thomas Family of Horry County S.C., #5-Thomas of Maryland to Carolina, Thompson, Thomson, Thorn, Thornhill, Thornton, Tidmore, Tidwell, Tidwell, Tidwell-Kennedy-Craig for D.A.R., Tindall, Tisdale, Tison, Titshaw, Tobler,Toney #1, #2, Torbert, Touchstone, Towles in S.C., Townsend, Trammell, Traylor, Trussell in S.C., Tubb, Tucker, Turbeville, Turk, Turner in S.C., Turnipseed, Turnipseed-S.C. Supreme Court Decis-

Andrea Genealogical Collection continued:

ion vs. Turnipseed et al.

Valentine, Various Surnames-Data from S.C. Columbia Archives, Vaughan-Vaughn-Vaun,Venters-Fenters, Vereen, Vereen and Livingston for the D.A.R., Vernon, Vice-Vise, Vince-Vance, Vineyard and Stephens Families, Vogt-Voigt.

Waggoner-Wagner, Walker, Wall, Waller #1, #2-McGehee-Waller, Walton-The Walton Family, Wardlaw, Warley and Worley in S.C., Waties, Watson #1, #2, Watt and Watts, Weathersbee, Weathersbee-The Weathersbee Family, Webb #1, #2, #3-Webb Records in Abbeville Co., #4, Wedgeworth, Welch with Variants, Wells #1-Wells from S.C. Archives, #2, Wesner in S.C. in the Columbia Archives, West, Wheeler, Whitaker, White-Norris, Whitley, Whitmire, Whittington, Wideman, Wigington, Wiley, Williams, Williamson, Williamson for D.A.R., Wilson, Wilson-Willson, Wyatt #14-Wyatt in S. C., #15-Wyatt in Spartanburg County, S.C., #16-Wyatt in Tennessee, Kentucky, Ohio, #17-Wyatt in Texas, #18-Wyatt in Virginia, #19-Wyatt in Virginia, #20-Data from Virginia Cavaliers, #21-Wyatt in States of: Alabama, Arkansas, Georgia, Kentucky, Mississippi, Missouri, Texas, Tennessee, #22-Wyatt and Allied Family Lineages, #23-Wyatt Lineage, #24-Wyatt Lineage, #25-The Wives of the Wyatts, Wimpey, Windham, Wing, Wingate, Winn #1, #2, Withers Witherspoon Family, Wofford, Wolfe, Wood-Woods, Woodberry, Woodruff, Woodson, Woodward, Workman, Worthy, Wren, Wyatt #1-A Short History of the Wyatt Family, #2-Wyatt History, #3-"At the Sign of the Crest", Wyatt Coat-of-Arms, #4-Wyatt in England, #5-Wyatt Bibles and Wills, #6-A Study in Wyatt Data in Georgia and Points West, #7-Wyatt in Henry and Newton Counties, Georgia, #8-Wyatt in Kentucky, #9-Wyatt in Maryland, Pennsylvania, New York, #10-Wyatt in Missouri, #11-Wyatt in North Carolina, #12-Wyatt in North Carolina, #13-The Wyatt Family, #26-Dr. Ed Wyatt, #27-The Ancestry of Elijah Wyatt, #28-Eugene Wyatt (Alabama), #29-Florence Wyatt Sparger, #30-Mrs. John W. Wyatt-Wyatt in Virginia, #31-James Foster Wyatt, #32-Redmond G. Wyatt, #33-Major William Wyatt of St. Stephen's, #34-Out-of-State Letters Containing Wyatt Data, #35-Wyatt News Letters, #36-Wyatt Notes from Leonardo Andrea's Personal Notebook, Wyrick-Wirick-Wyrich-Irick-Irig-Irigg.

Yarborough, Yeldell, Yonce, York, Young.

Zinn.

"A" Folder: Abercrombie, Aberly, Acruman, Addee-Ade-Adys-Adie-Addie-Adee, Addison, Addy-Dreher-Greer-Lorick, Ainslie, Alexander, Alford, Alldridge, Allgood, Allison, Alverson, Anthony, Appleby, Arendell, Arlidge, Ashpord, Atkin, Avery, Aull, Ayers.

"B" Folder: Backstrom, Baddely, Badgley, Barber, Barmore, Barnes, Bartlett, Barton, Bass, Batchelor, Baum, Beatson, Beck, Bedwell, Beeco, Bellune, Bender, Bennett, Bernard, Beverly,Bibb, Bigham, Bird, Bishop, Blalock-Blaylock, Blanchard, Boatner, Bogglas, Boggs, Bolick, Booker, Booth, Bowers, Bowyer, Brackin,

Andrea Genealogical Collection, continued:
Breeden, Brenan, Bridwell, Briggs, Bright, Bristow, Britton,
Brock, Bronson-Brownson, Buchanan, Buffington, Burgess, Burnell,
Bush, Butler, Byers, Bynum, Byrd.
   "C" Folder: Cain, Cairnes, Cannon, Canon, Carey, Cargill,Car-
ney, Carpenter, Carr, Carrel, Carruth, Carwile, Cauthen, Caven,
Champion, Chandler, Chapeau, Charles, Chastain, Cheatham, Cheek,
Chevillette, Chiles, Christian, Class, Cleland, Cleveland, Clip-
ton, Cloinger, Colclough, Collier, Coln-Conn, Colvin, Cone,Cook,
Copeland, Corker, Cornwell, Cortney, Cottingham, Cowan, Cozby,
Craighead, Crawford, Creech, Crocham, Crocker, Crockett, Cros-
land, Crowley, Crutchfield, Cumbe, Cumbo, Cutts.
   "D" Folder: Daniel, Daniell, Dargan, David, Davidson, Davis,
Davison, Dawson, Dedman, de Graffenried, Dennis, Dent, DeWitt,
Dickey, Docton, Dodds, Dominick, Donnon, Dorsey, Douglass, Down-
ing, Dozier, Drake, Drayton, Dreher, Drennan, Dudding, Duncan,
Dunovant.
   "E" Folder: Eakin, Earp, Eaton, Eddins, Eidson, Elam, Eller-
bee, Endsley, Ervin, Erwin, Esnard, Ewing.
   "F" Folder: Fairey, Faison, Farr, Farrar, Faucett, Feagin,
Ferguson, Filbay, Fincher, Fisher, Fox, Frederick, Freeman, Fri-
erson, Fuller, Fullingim, Fullwood.
   "G" Folder: Gaddy, Galbraith, Gallman, Galloway, Gamble, Gas-
soway, Geiglemann, Gillham, Gillis, Goforth, Goings-Gowins,Good,
Goodson, Gousdy, Gough, Goutcher, Gowen, Griffen, Griffin, Gri-
mes, Grimmer, Gruber, Gurley.
   "H" Folder: Haden, Hadley, Haile, Hainey, Halbert, Hamer,Ham-
iter, Hand, Harling, Harp, Harralson, Harrington, Harris, Hart,
Harwood, Hathorn, Hawkins, Hayden, Hayman, Heard, Heckendorn,
Henegan, Herndon, Haustiss, Hewitt, Hines, Hix, Hodges, Hoff,
Hogan, Hogge, Holland, Hollingshead, Hollinshed, Holloway, Hoop-
er, Hope, Horan, Horn, Hornsby, Hough, How, Howerton, Hoy, Hud-
gens, Huey, Huff, Huffman, Hughey, Hunter, Hutchinson, Hux, Hy-
man.
   "I" Folder: Isham and Randolph.
   "J" Folder: Joyce, Just.
   "K" Folder: Kenting, Kilgore, King, Kirkland, Knighton, Kuy-
kendall.
   "L" Folder: Lacey, Laney, Larkin, Lawhorn, Leathen, Leppard,
Lesesne, Lide, Light, Lincoln, Linn, Little, Loftis, Lorick,
Lowe, Lowrey, Lowther, Luther.
   "Mc" Folder: McAuslan, McBride, McBryde, McCaslan, McClellan,
McClelland, McCoy, McCullock, McCurdy, McCutchen, McDowell,Mack
Elduff, McGirt, McIlroy, McJunkin, McKelvy, MacKenzie, McKoy,
MacLand, McLeod, McLilley, McMillen, MacNair, McNarin, McNeeley,
MacTeer.
   "M" Folder: Mallard, Manning, Markham-Greer, Marsh, Marshall,
Mason, Mathias, Meadows, Means, Megee, Mellon, Mendenhall, Mic-
haux, Middleton, Millen, Mills, Minter, Mock, Moffatt, Moffatana
Bulletin, Moores, Moorhead, Mophet, Mordaugh, Mottrom, Murrell,
Myers.

Andrea Genealogical Collection, continued:
"N" Folder: Nairne, Nisbet, Nix, Noble, Norman, Northcutt, Norvell, Norwood, Nowell.
"O" Folder: Oakham, O'Bannon, O'Mahone.
"P" Folder: Padgett, Pagett-Padgett, Parish, Paschall, Pate, Patrick, Payne, Peatson, Pennell, Perkins, Person-Persons, Perritt, Phillips, Pickett, Pistole, Polk, Pooke, Porter, Preslar, Price, Prince, Pritchard, Pugh, Purnell, Purse.
"Q" Folder: Quarles.
"R" Folder: Rabon, Ragan, Raines, Randolph, Rasbuary, Ray, Renddick, Reeder, Register, Rhinehart-Rhinehardt, Richmond, Rosamond, Royal, Rust.
"S" Folder: Salmon, Salyars, Sarvis, Satcher, Saylor, Schumpert, Screven, Scurry, Seigler, Selden, Shaw, Shealy, Shearer, Shell, Sherer, Sherrod, Shine, Shipman, Sieling, Singleton, Sitler, Skelton, Skidmore, Skipwith, Small, Smarr, Smithwick, Smythe, Snipes, Spainhour, Sparks, Spell-Smith, Spence, Spight, Spivey, Splat, Stafford, Stallings, Standley, Stedman, Steel, Stewart, Stone, Stoutenmyer, Stovall-Tatum, Strain, Strange, Street, Stroud-Strowd-Strode, Stuart, Suggs.
"T" Folder: Tart, Taton-Tatum, Tatum, Terrell, Thomasson, Tilghman-Tillman, Toliver-Couch or Crouch, Treadwell, Tutt, Tweedwell, Tyler.
"U" Folder: Underwood, Utsey.
"V" Folder: Vandiver, Vaneavery-Van Eavery, Vining, Voss.
"W" Folder: Wadlington, Wallace, Walters, Ward, Warnock, Warren, Washington, Waters, Watkins, Way, Weatherly, Webster, Weir, Welborn-Waddell-Waddle-Huff-etc., Westmoreland, Wicker, Wiggins, Wilkes, Willingham, Willis, Windley, Wooley, Worrty, Wright.
"X-Y-Z" Folder: Yutzy-Utsey, Zeigler, Zubly.
List of folders...Containing Genealogical Data:
Abernathy, Mrs. Rustin; Acruman, Mrs. L.C.; Anderson, Paul V.; Artoe, Ethelina Edwards (Mrs. John); Ault, Mrs. Helene B.
Bayley, Mrs. Florence; Berry, C.B.; Bidez, Mrs. Thelma C.; Biggerstaff, Inez B. (Mrs. M.B.); Blaisdell, Gertrude G.; Boss, Mrs. Lula Reed; Bradley, Katherina J. (Mrs. James W.); Brice, Mrs. Charles P.; Bridwell, Ronald E.; Brock, Pope F.
Carnes, Mrs. Carl J.; Catrevas, Mrs. A.N.; Coddington, John I; Collins, Carl; Conner, Mr. & Mrs. Dudley; Conway, Louise Markham (Mrs. Lester H.); Crawford, Paul; Crowder, Mrs. J.W.; Croxton, Alma D. (Mrs. E.C.); Cupit, John T.; Cusimano, Grace Camulette (Mrs. Frank).
Davis, Miss Nora & Miss May-Milwee Hemphill-Legare Davis; Darden, Evelyn Baldwin (Mrs. Edward C.); Dotson, Flora B. (Mrs. Carl C.); Doughtie, Mrs. Charles E.; Draughan, Paul V.; Duggan, Mrs. Sam; Dunagin, Mae (Mrs. G.H.L.); Dundas, Francis de Sales; Duren, The Rev. W.L.; Durham, Com. O.H.
Early, Charles; Elliott, Lester, Elms, Alice Stroud; Ennis, Mrs. O.W.; Esker, Mrs. Jerome; Ervin, Mrs. Sarah S.; Evans, Eytive Long.
Fava, Mrs. F.J.; Floyd, Mary; Folk, Mrs. O.H. & Dr. Walter

Andrea Genealogical Collection, continued:
Wyatt; Fullingim, Glee.
   Gambrell, Raymond D.; Geupel, Mrs. Ruby T.; Giberson, Sallie
G.; Grass, Patty (Mrs. Frank); Guckes, Mrs. Sybil.
   Hall, Ruth C. (Mrs. Linwood B.); Hansen, Angie Boyd; Harkins,
Bobbye (Mrs. John P.); Harper, Milton J.; Harrell, Thelma (Mrs.
John W.); Hatfield, Teddie Carruth (Mrs. Charles H.); Havens,
Maryann (Mrs. Walter); Hawkins, Mrs. Ansel; Haynie, Mrs. Orsen;
Hearn, Estelle; Heverly, Earl L.; Hill, J. Ed; Hoagland, Henry
V.; Hollingsworth, Clyde D. (Mr. & Mrs.); Hollingsworth, Leon;
Holsonback, Mrs. J.C.; Houts, Alice (Mrs. Haile); Huchingson,
Mrs. John W.; Huckaby, Mrs. Sybil S.; Hussey, Eula; Huxford,
Folks.
   Johnston, E.F.; Jones, Mrs. Tillman.
   Kent, Fred H.; Kerrigan, Mrs. Adele C.; Keown, Mrs. Sue Matti-
son & Mrs. Joe Brown; Kinard, Hubert H.; Kincaid, B.J.,Sr.;
King, George H.S.; Knight, M.A.; Kretschmar, Mrs. W.P.
   LaBoon, Brant; Ladson, Jack E.; Lester, Memory A.; Long,Grace;
Lukhard, Catherine; Loyless, E.B.; Lyle, Jane B. & Georgia.
   McBee, May Wilson (Mrs. John Harbour); McClanahan, Marshall
L.; McCroskey, Mrs. Betty M.; McDavid, Mrs. E.R.,Sr.
   Martin, Davis S.; Martin, Mrs. V.G.; Mattison, Eileen (Mrs.R.
C.); Mattison, J.E. & Mrs. T.A. Gannaway; Mehringer, Mrs. Ern-
est; Meriwether, R.L. (South Caroliniana Society); Millar,Fran-
ces (Mrs. Ernie); Miller, Alice Davis (Mrs. Clement Harvey);
Mitchell, Boyce S.; Mitchell, M.; Mize, Mrs. Leila R.; Moore,
(Miss) Elizabeth.
   Neel, Oliver; Nicholson, Mrs. Robert W.
   O'Donnell, Mrs. Pearl Foster.
   Palmer, Etta S.; Palmer, Sue Gardiner (Mrs. J.B.); Palmerton,
Helen (Letters on Smith and Strange);Parker, Marie Hammond; Par-
son, Mary D.; Pasley, Robert B., Jr.; Peet, Helen Hanna (Mrs. T.
B.); Peteet, Mrs. Gayden Bennett; Picras, Sadie R. (Mrs. George
N.); Pierce, John H.; Pierson, Lucile Floyd (Mrs. L.C.); Price,
Lucie Gill; Primm, Mamie Perryman.
   Quattlebaum, Paul & Wm. Wade Hinshaw; Querries (Historical
Commission).
   Raines, Mrs. Gussie G.; Ramsay, Mrs. A.K.; Reed, Eddie K.;
Reed, Mollie (Mrs. Harrison M. Sr.); Reeves, Jonathan Floyd and
Emma; Richard, Edridge Fortier (Mrs. Earl A.); Ritchie, E.B.;
Robbins, Mary Lee Donaghey (Mrs. John C. Jr.); Roberts, Owen;
Robertson, Amanda Blaluck (Mrs. Benjamin Otis); Robinson, Shir-
ley Montgomery (Mrs. A.M.); Rogers, Frank M.; Rogers, Lois; Rog-
ers, Mary Caroline.
   Sallee, Mrs. Adelia Stewart; Sample, Mrs. A.D.; Sandipord,
Edward Raymond; Sarrazin, Jean; Scott, Marie G. (Mrs. B.K.);
Searcy, Margaret; Sharp, Rev. E.M.; Sheperd, Mrs. Coleman D;
Sitton, Eugene N.; Skelton, Caroline (Mrs. Steve); Sledge, Wil-
lie (Mrs. A.G.); Slimp, Altie (Mrs. Horace B.); Smith, Mr. &
Mrs. Charles Owen; Smith, H.E.; Smith, W. David; Spearman, Min-
nie Webb (Mrs. A.W.); Spencer, William M. Jr.; Stanley, Bess

Andrea Genealogical Collection, continued:
(Mrs. Eugene A.); Stokes, Laura H. (Mrs. R.M.); Strieby, Irene
M.; Stubbs, Thomas M..

Tanner, Myrtle and Sarah Green; Taylor, Robert; Thomas, Cornelius; Thompson, Eileen Lanier (Mrs. Cleveland); Tillman, Mamie
N.; Turner, George P. Jr..

Updike, Mrs. L.C.; Vereen, Jackson H..

Walker, Eloise Wingo (Mrs. L.W.); Walton, L. (Mrs. E.M.);
Wands, Beatrice (Mrs. Burton); Watkins, Mildred S.; Watson, Har-
ry L.; Webb, Elizabeth; Wepel, Willie May; Wells, Guy H.; Wheel-
er, Ellen; Williams, Dorothy W. (Mrs. Roger); Williams, Lillie
Burress (Mrs. S.D.); Williamson, Reba Calhoun; Willingham, Rob-
ert S.; Willis, Waid Scott Sr.; Wilson, Anna Saylor (Mrs. T.C.);
Wilson, Lola; Wimmer, Corrine Turley (Mrs. J. Ivan); Winter,
Mrs. Mary Carter; Wofford, Mrs. Charles; Wyatt, Tula Townsend
(Mrs. W.A.).

Yarborough, Charles D.; Yates, Gladys Collins and Adlai Robin
Yates; Young, Pauline.

List of Folders With Genealogical and/or Historical Data:
B: Bible Records #1, Bible Records #2 and other genealogical
data, Bible Records-S.C. Bible Records v. 1, 2, & 3; Blanding-
McFaddin Families.

C: Campbell-Bits of Information about the Argyll Campbell
Clan; Census, Arkansas; Census, North Carolina; Census, S.C.;
Census, Tennessee; Census, Texas; Charleston; Churches-Clear
Springs Baptist Church; Churches-Church of the Immaculate Con-
ception, Edgefield; Churches-Jackson Grove Methodist Church,
Greenville County; Churches-Misc.; Counties in S.C.; Counties-
Abbeville & Edgefield Counties; Counties-Greenville County;
Counties-Horry County; Counties-Laurens, Newberry & Abbeville
Counties; Counties-Spartanburg County; Court Records; Court of
Equity Records-Barnwell District-First Book; Court of Equity
Records-Barnwell District-Second Book.

D.A.R.-Texas; DuBose-William Porcher DuBose Reminiscences.

Early Catholics in South Carolina; The Ecclesiastes of Pro-
crustes, The.

The Free Negro in Ante-Bellum S.C., chapters I-IX, bibliography.

Genealogical and Historical Research in Georgia; Genealogists
and the Columbia Genealogical Society; Genealogy Exchange; Geor-
gia-Lands; Graveyards-Alabama, Georgia, Mississippi, North Carolina; Graveyards in Arkansas; Graveyards-Little River Cemetery,
Horry County; Graveyards-Miscellaneous S.C.; Graveyards-Old
Greenville Church Cemetery; Guerry-Rembert-Michau-DuPont-Crom-
well Families.

Heard [Family], James Henagen [Family], Highlights of History
of Covington and St. Timothy Parish, Louisiana; History of Old
Dorchester; History of the Pendleton District.

Immigrants; Index to Irish Wills; Ioor [Family]; Justices of
the Peace; Kinchelor [Family]; Land Grants; Lands on the Ridge,
S.C. (Land Plat Abstracts); Loyalists in S.C..

Andrea Genealogical Collection, continued:
  Maps; Marriage List, Deeds, Etc.; Marriage Lists-North Caroli-
na; Marriage Lists-South Carolina; Marriage Records-Ann Pamela
Cunningham Chapter, D.A.R.; Marriage Records-S.C. Volume III;
Marriages-S.C..
  Ninety-Six District Surrogate Records in S.C. with Index for
These Records; Norris & Kindred Families; North Carolina Notes.
  Palatine Settlers in North Carolina; Plantations-Belle Isle
Plantation by A.S. Salley, Jr.; Plantation Negro of Today, by
Francis Marion Hutson; Postoffices of Yesteryear (S.C.), by Olin
J. Salley.
  Revolution-General Francis Marion's Men-A List of Twenty-Five
Hundred; Revolution-Pay Lists; Revolution-Pension Lists by Coun-
ties; Revolutionary Pensions-Group Listings & Some Individual
Listings; Revolutionary Pensions-Individual Abstracts; Revolu-
tionary Soldier-Memoirs of Tarlton Brown.
  Smiths-Fullers-Cooks-McDavids-Shumates-McCulloughs; Soldiers-
Colonial Soldiers of S.C.; South Carolina Cemetery Epitaphs;
S.C. Constitutional Convention of 1868; South Carolina Society;
Spencer [Family]; St. Matthew's Parish S.C.-Minutes of the Vest-
ry; St. Stephen's Lutheran Church Cemetery Inscriptions to 1920,
Lexington, S.C.; Sullivan #1 & 2 [Families].
  Tax Payers (Commutation Tax) in Georgetown County for 1905;
Tax Roll of Hopkins County, Kentucky, for the Year 1807, pre-
pared by William Davis; Towns in S.C.-Pineville; Treutlen, John
Adam; Voters.
        * * *END OF LEONARDO ANDREA COLLECTION * * *
Andrea, Leonardo. Sitton-Aull-Bouneau genealogy. NP: NPub, nd.
                                                             SCHS
Andrea, Leonardo. The Vereens of Horry, an address delivered by
  Leonardo Andrea...[at] Vereen Family Cemetery, Little River SC
  ... NP: Vereen Family Association, nd. 20 p. SCL, HOCL, SCHS
Archdale, Henry B. Memoirs of the Archdales. Enniskillen ??,
  Trimble, 1925.   CHLS
Arledge Family [SpC]   FACM
Armstrong, Margaret N. Five generations: life & letters of an
  American family, 1750-1900 [Armstrong family]. NY: Harper,
  1930. 425 p.   COMMON
Armstrong, Zella. Notable southern families [incl. Armstrong,
  Banning, Blount, Brownlow, Calhoun, Deaderick, Gaines, Howard,
  Key, Luttrell, Lyle, McAdoo, McGhee, McMillan, Phinizy, Polk,
  Sevier, Shields, Stone, Turnley, VanDyke, Bean, Boone, Borden,
  Bryan, Carter, Davis, Donaldson, Hardwick, Haywood, Holliday,
  Hollingsworth, Houston, Johnston, Kelton, Magill, Rhea, Mont-
  gomery, Shelby, Vance, Wear, Williams, Armstrong, Trooper,
  Cockrill, Duke, Elston, Lea, Park, Parkes, Tunnell, Sevier,
  Crockett, & Doak families]. 6 vol., 1918-, rp Baltimore: GPC,
  1974. 3 vols.   COMMON
Arndt, John S. The story of the Arndts...antecedents & descend-
  ants of Bernhard Arndt... Philadelphia PA: Christopher Sower
  Co., 1922. 427 p.   CLEM

Arnold Family Association of the South. (Quarterly, 1970-.)
GSGN, LRCL
Arnold, Leonard W. Arnold-Luckey family ties...of the Drusilla
Arnold ancestors from...949...to 1931. NY: privately printed,
1931. 168 p.   SCHS
Arnold, Mildred L. Gladneys in America. Atlanta GA: Footprint
Co., 1966. 160 p.   FACL, SCL
Arrington, Charles. The Arringtons of Kirksey [SC]; sketch of
the Caleb Arrington family. NP: mimeo, 1958. 24 p.   GWPL
Arthur, Glenn D. Annals of the Fowler family, with branches in
VA, NC, SC, TN, KY, AL, MS, CA, TX. Austin TX: author, 1901.
327 p.   SCL
Ashford, Charlie R. Some of the ancestors and descendants of
James & George Ashford, Jr., of Fairfield County SC. Stark-
ville MS: author, 1956. 123 p.   COMMON
Ashley, Mabel I & Mary K. Ashley. Family history: descendants
of Millicent Anne Ashley & James Ashley Rosenblatt. NP: auth-
or, 1943. 153 p.   SCHS
Atkinson, Margaret L. The annual report of the Lindsay Associa-
tion of America...   SCHS
Attwater, Charles H. Atwater history & genealogy, 1956. Santa
Monica CA: Publisher's Hall, 1956. 316 p.   SCL
Atwood Family [SpC]   GSGN
Austin, Elizabeth R. & Helen R. Roberts. The Nathan Reids of VA
in the march of freedom. Tuscaloosa AL: authors, 1976. 176
p.   SCL, PIPD
Austin, James W. The Austin and allied families. 2nd ed. At-
lanta GA: Knight, 1972. 314 p.   SCHS
Autry, Mahan B. The family & descendants of Captain John Autry.
Corsicana TX: Morton's, Inc., 1964. 209 P.   SCL
Avant, David A. Florida pioneers and their AL, GA, NC, SC, MD &
VA ancestors [incl. Davis, Gamble, Tatum, Townsend, Wood fami-
lies], vol. I, revised. Spartanburg: RPC, 1979. 463 p. SCL
Avant, Fenton G. The Davis-Wood families of Gadsden County, FL,
& their forbears [incl. Gamble, Culber, Warfield, Pierpont,
Gauthier, LeGette & Dixon families]. Easley: SHP, 1978. 500
p.   SCHS
Avery, Samuel P. The Avery, Fairchild, and Park families of CT,
MS & RI... Hartford CT: privately printed, 1919. 151 p. SCHS
Babb, Robert E. 2161 of the Babb descendants of Phillip Babb,
Kittery, Maine. 1652... Chstn: author, 1976. v.p.   SCL
Baer, Mabel V. The Vandeveers of NC, KY & IN. Richmond VA:
Whittet & Shepperson, 1960. 180 p.   SCL, SCHS
The Bagnal clan, descendants of John Belton Bagnal & Harriet Ma-
tilda Pack. Married June 8, 1848. NP:NPub, nd. Unp.   SMCL
Bagwell, William F. Her first hundred years; the life & times
of Dora Martin Dodson [Dodson & Martin families]. NP: type-
script, nd. 44 p.   GWPL
Bailes, Samuel E. Bailes family history. NP:NPub, 1963. 23 p.
SCL
Bailey, J.D. History of Grindal Shoals & some early adjacent
215

families. Gaffney: Ledger Print, 1927. 85 p.   COMMON
Bailey, John C. & William B. White. The sesquicentennial of
   Hopewell Presbyterian Church, York County, SC, 1808-1958, con-
   taining histories of connected families [incl. Wherry, Davies,
   Dunlop & McFadden families]. Rock Hill: White Printing Co.,
   1958. 59 p.   MONT, SCL
Baines Family [SpC]   CRCL
Baker Family [SpC]   PIPD
Balch, Thomas W. The Brooke family of Whitchurch, Hampshire,
   England; together with an account of Acting-Governor Robert
   Brooke of MD, & Colonel William Beall of MD... Philadelphia
   PA: Lane & Scott, 1898. 64 p.   SCHS
Ball, Nan S. Ball family of Stoke-in-Teignhead, Devon, England.
   Chstn: NPub, 1944. 30 p.   SCHS
Ball, Nicholas. Edward Ball & some of his descendants. Newport
   RI: Mercury Print, 1891. 15 p.   SCHS
Ball, Roy H. Conquering the frontiers. A biography & history
   of one branch of the Ball family. Oklahoma City OK: Semcocol-
   or Press, 1956. 93 p.   SCL
Ballentine, 1822-1928. A brief sketch of the family of John
   William Ballentine & wife Mary Magdelene Derrick Ballentine &
   collateral family lines. Johnston: G.G. Waters, 1928. 37 p.
                                                                  SCL
Balliet, Stephen C. The Balliet, Balliett, Balliette, Balyeat,
   Bolyard and allied families. Baton Rouge LA: Moran's Sons,
   1968. 993 p.   SCL
Banister, Eme O. Daniel, Paul & Jeremiah Williams, their ances-
   tors & descendants. NP: author, 1968.   SCL, PICL
Banister, Eme O. The family of Rogers of the Piedmont section
   of SC, & allied families. Anderson: author, 1967 & 1969.
   400 p.   COMMON
Banister, Eme O. Hunt hunting. Several Hunt family lineages.
   Anderson: author, 1966. 400 p.   COMMON
Banister, Eme O. The Wood family of Laurens Co., SC. Anderson:
   author, 1966. 50 p.   NWRL
Banister, Eme O. The Rogers Line. NP: typescript, nd. unp.
                                                                 LRCL
Banister, Eme O. Williams records with allied families: Arm-
   strong-Brown-Eggleston-Chilton-Clark-Latham-Pemberton-Taylor-
   Warnard-Winslow. Anderson: author, 1966. 400 p.   EDTO
Bankhead, Eleanor G. Colonel Samuel Watson & his descendants.
   Silver Spring MD? author, 1966. 129 p.   CLEM, YOCL
Banta, R.E. Benjamin Fuller & some of his descendants, 1765-
   1958. Crawfordsville IN: Howell-Goodwin Co., 1958. 143 p.SCL
Barbee, James E. A brief history of the early Barbee families
   of Smith County TX. NP: typescript, nd. 45 p.   SCHS
Barekman, June B. The Barrackman-Barkman-Barekman family of
   Knox County IN. Chicago: NPub, 1961. unp.   SCL
Barekman, June B. Our Coker kin. Chicago: Genealogical Refer-
   ence Builders, 1967. 2 vol.   COKL, SCL

216

Barekman, June B. Some Dobbin(s)-Skiles lines. NP: mimeo, nd.
unp.   SCHS
Barksdale, James A. The descendants of Basil (Bazwell) Barksdale, c. 1790-1978. NP:NPub, 1979? 149 p.   LRCL, SCL
Barksdale, John A. Barksdale family history & genealogy, with
collateral lines... Richmond VA: William Byrd Press, 1940.
634 p.   LRCL, SCHS, SCL
Barnes, Clair E. Barnes; the westward migration of one line of
the Thomas Barnes' of Hartford & Farmington CT. Long Beach
CA: mimeo, 1966. 13 p.   SCHS
Barnes, Clair. Family records of Barnes, Brown, Lair & Wilson.
With references to Crays, Fee, Sherrill, Stark & Thornton.
NP: typescript, nd. 71 p.   SCHS
Barnes Family [SpC]   FACM
Barnhill, Edward S. The Beatys of Kingston. Chstn: J.J. Fur-
long, 1958. 143 p.   COMMON
Barnwell, Joseph W. Barnwell of SC. NP:NPub, 1946. 43 p. SCHS
                                                            CLEM
Barnwell, Joseph W. Dr. Henry Woodward, the first English set-
tler in SC, & some of his descendants... NP:NPub, 1907?
13 p.   SCL, SCHS
Barnwell, Stephen B. The story of an American family...[incl.
Barnwell, Cuthbert, DeVeaux, Elliott, Fuller, Heyward, Rhett,
Sams & Stuart families]. Marquette MI: NPub, 1969. 435 p.
                                                          COMMON
Barrett, M.C. A.J. Barrett & Evan Watkins, Jr., pioneers of
Craighead County AR: their families... NP: author, 1970.
431 p.   SPCL
Barringer, Brandon. The Wethered book. Petersborough NH: auth-
or, 1967. 201 p.   SCHS
Barringer, Laurence S. Family facts for the future... Cola:
RLB, 1958. 104 p.   SCL
Barron, James A. Barron family history - 1927. NP:NPub, 1927.
unp.   YOCL
Barry, Ruby M. The McKinseys.   NWRL
Bartlett, Marguerite B. Haley Talbot Blocker: his background &
life. St. Petersburg FL: Calaher's Letter Shop, 1970. 27 p.
                                                            EDTO
Bartlett, Marguerite B. Some of the Blockers: family of Michael
Blocker, the emigrant. St. Petersburg FL: Widers Printing Co.
1967. 45 p.   EDTO
Barton, Baynard & Fannie May Dooley Barton. Whaleys, 1660-1956.
Stonega VA: NPub, 1956. 143 p.   SCHS
Barton, Jason E. The Barton family of Tigersville SC. Pasadena
MD? NPub, 196? 577 p.   SPCL, SCL
Baskerville, Patrick H. Additional Baskerville genealogy; a sup-
plement... Richmond VA: Wm. Ellis Jones' Sons, 1917. 179 p.
                                                            SCHS
Baskerville, Patrick H. Genealogy of the Baskerville family...
from 1266 A.D. Richmond VA: Ellis Jones' Sons, 1912. 214 p.
                                                            SCHS

Baskerville, Patrick H. The Hamiltons of Burnside NC & their
ancestors & descendants. Richmond VA: Wm. Ellis Jones' Sons,
1916. 158 p.   SCHS
Bateman, Thomas H. DuPont & allied families; a genealogical
study. NY: American Historical Co., 1965. 497 p.   SCHS
Bauer, William R. The Sineath family & affiliated lineages [in-
cl. Alston, Bauer, Boineau, Davis, Farley, Metheringham, Mick-
ler, Rhame, Ulmer, Villepontoux, Warnock & Westbury families].
Cola: RLB, 1970 & 1971. 379 p.   COMMON
Beadles, Zada W. The Wades; the history of a family. Zachary &
Mary Hatton Wade. Their descendants & related lines in MD, VA
TN, SC, NC, etc. NP:NPub, 1963. 247 p.   DEALER
Beall, F.M.B. The Beall & Bell families. Washington DC: NPub,
1929. 296 p.   SCHS
Beattie, Archibald J. The Beattie clan. Bishopville: author,
1967.   LNCL
Beaty, James D. The Beaty family... NP: author, 1970. 52 p.
                                                         FACM
Beckham, William K. The Kinslers of SC... Cola: author, 1964.
90 p.   GWPL, LXMU, SCLB
Beckman, Ludwig A. Alexander Thompson of Fairfield District SC.
NP: author, 1950. 56 p.   SCL, FACM
Beckman, Ludwig A. A branch of the Beckman family. NP:NPub,
nd. 8 p.   SCL
Beckman, Ludwig A. Genealogy: John Stewart Rosberry [of] Ire-
land. Descendants through his son James... NP: author, 1979.
104 p.   CSCL, FACM
Belk-Smith, Gladys E. Brown & related families' records, TN,
SC, MD. NP: mimeo, 1975. 40 p.   SCHS
Bell, Maria B. The Bells & allied families... Cola: NPub, 1953
78 p.   SCHS, SCL
Bell, Raymond M. Andrew Baskin, Esq. Kershaw & Lancaster Counties, SC, and other Baskin notes. Washington PA: NPub, 1965.
12 p.   SCL
Bell, Raymond M. The Baskin-Baskins family. SC & PA. Washing-
ton PA: NPub, revised 1963. 85 p.   SCL, LNCL
Bell, Raymond M. The Clemson family of PA. Washington PA:
Washington & Jefferson College, 1971. 4 p.   CLEM
Bellinger, Lyle F. Genealogy of the Mohawk valley Bellingers &
allied families. NY: Herkimer County Historical Society,
1976. 124 p.   SCHS
Belser, William G. The Belser family of SC... NP:NPub, 1941.
67 p.   COMMON
Benedict, Clare. The Benedicts abroad. London: Ellis, nd.
651 p.   SCHS
Benedict, Clare. Constance Fenimore Woolson. Five generations
(1785-1923) being scattered chapters from the history of the
Cooper, Pomeroy, Woolson & Benedict families... London: Ellis
nd. 421 p.   SCHS
Benedict, Clare. Five generations. London: Ellis, 1929-30.
3 vol.   CHLS

Benedict, Clare. Voices out of the past. London: Ellis, nd.
332 p.   SCHS
Bennett, Grover G. The Asbill family history... Pulaski TN:
NPub, nd. 288 p.   SCL
Benta, R.E. Benjamin Fuller and some of his descendants. 1958.
                                                                 CHLS
Bentham family genealogy. NP: typescript, nd. unp.   SCHS
Benton, Josiah H. Samuel Slade Benton, his ancestors and de-
scendants. Boston MS: privately printed, 1901. 354 p.   SCHS
Berry, Connelly B. The Vaught family of Horry County. NP:
typescript, nd. unp.   HOCL
Berry, Connelly B. Gause family data...collected by Connelly B.
Berry. NP: typescript, 1972. 23 p.   HOCL
Berry, Connelly B. Withers family. NP: typescript, nd. unp.
                                                                 SCHS
Berry, Lloyd E. Hudson Berry & his descendants...a compilation
of the Berry, Gaines, and Harrison Families... Pelzer: Berry-
Gaines-Harrison Reunion, 1956. 106 p.   COMMON
Bethea, Mary B. Ancestral Key to the Pee Dee. Cola: RLB, 1978
                                                           SCL, CHLS
Bethea, Philip Y. Genealogy of the Bethea family of the south.
Cola: State Co., 1926. 29 p.   MACL, HOCL, SCL
Beusse, Jesse H. Sketches of the Beusse & Evans families and
items of interest to family & friends... NP: McGregor Co.,
1923. 118 p.   SCL
Bicentennial Book; North, Neeses, Woodford [&] Livingston fami-
lies. 1976. 75 p.   ORCL
Bigger, David A. Bigger family. NP: typescript, nd. unp. YOCL
Bigger, David A. Brief sketches of pioneer families of York &
adjoining counties. Rock Hill: typescript, 1930. unp.   YOCL
Bigger, David A. Sketch of the Neel-Johnson family of the new
acquisition. Rock Hill: London Printery, nd. 30 p.
                                                       YOCL, SCHS, SCL
Billings, John S. Descendants of James Henry Hammond of SC.
NY: J.S. Billings, 1934. 14 p.   GTML, SCL
Birnie, Joseph E. The Earles & the Birnies. Richmond VA: Whit-
tet & Shepperson, 1974. 235 p.   COMMON
Birnie, Joseph E. The Earles of Westmoreland. Atlanta GA:
typescript, 1972. 54 p.   SCHS
Bird Family [SpC]   CRCL
Black, James M. Families & descendants in America of Golsan,
Golson, Gholson, Gholston, also Golston, etc. Salt Lake City
UT: NPub, 1959. 815 p.   ORCL, SCHS, SCL
Black, Mary S. The Bush family as descended from Richard and
Elizabeth Beby Bush of Virginia... Augusta GA: NPub, 1968.
60 p.   SCL
Blackwell Family [SpC]   GSGN
Blake, Thomas S. The statistical record of John Blake's Green-
wood tree. Jacksonville FL: Greenwood Press, 1958. 112 p.
                                                           GWPL, SCL
Blake, Mrs. Tyther S. The Shaw brothers: Rev. Murdock Wesley

Shaw, Sr., & Roderick (Lodd) Shaw of Chesterfield County SC, & their descendants. NP: Colonial Printing Co., 1976.　　　CTCL
Blakemore, Mary S. A narrative genealogy of the Stewarts of Sequatchie Valley TN & allied families. Richmond VA: Dietz Press, 1960.　　　SCHS
Blanding, Abram L. Blanding-McFadden, 1553-1906. Fountain Inn: A.L. Blanding, 1927. 2 vol.　　　SCL, CLEM, SMCL, SCHS
Blanding, Abram L. The McFaddin dedication, Sardinia SC, 1936. Clinton: Jacobs Brothers, 1937. 91 p.　　　SCL, SCHS
Blanding, Abram L. The McFaddin/McFadden line of Williamsburg County. NP: typescript, nd. 58 p.　　　SCL, WMTR
Blanding, Abram L. McFaddin, 1730-1930. Clinton: Jacobs Brothers, 1931. 3 vol.　　　SCL, SCHS
Blanding, Abram L. Blanding-DeSaussure, 1440-1863. Fountain Inn: author, 1924. 38 p.　　　SCL, CLEM
Blanding, Abram L. Blanding Family [Blanding, DeSaussure, & McFaddin families]. Fountain Inn: author, 1924-. 6 vol. SCL
Blanton, William N. Reminiscences of a Texas frontier heritage as portrayed in the lives of Ransom Gwyn Blanton & Benjamin Franklin Blanton. Taylor TX: Merchants Press, 1969. 100 p.　　　SCL
Bloore, Helen L. A genealogical record of the Hancock, Cofer, Jones & Massie families of VA & KY. NP: privately printed, 1960. 52 p.　　　SCHS
Blum, Willetta B. The Baylis family of VA. Washington DC: NPub 1958. 669 p.　　　SCHS
Boddie, John B. Historical southern families. Baltimore: GPC, 1967-. 21 vols.　　　COMMON
Boddie, Mrs. John B. A genealogical history of the Rubel, White, Rockefeller, McNair & allied families. Baltimore MD: Gateway Press, 1977. 263 p.　　　GWPL
Boggan, Carrie L. The Pennington family: volume I. NP:NPub, nd. 196 p.　　　SCL, CRCL, SPCL, SCHS
Boggs Family [SpC]　　　PIPD
Boland, Lawson P. History of the John Boland family. Greenville MS: Porter Print, 1965. 89 p.　　　COMMON
Boling, Katharine. A piece of the fox's hide [incl. Bigham family]. Cola: Sandlapper Press, 1972. 361 p.　　　COMMON
Bolls, Kate M. The Daniel Townsends of the SC islands... Verona VA: McClure Printing Co., 1975. 109 p.　　　SCHS
Bolls, Kate M. The Townsends of Edisto Island. NP:NPub, 1977. 45 p.　　　SCHS
Bolt, Ernest C., Sr. Descendants of Abraham Bolt, Sr. Charlotte NC: author, 1978. 41 p.　　　LRCL
Bond, Henry. Genealogies of the families & descendants of the early settlers of Watertown MA, including Waltham & Weston. Boston: Little, Brown & Co., 1855. 1094 p.　　　SCHS
Bonham, Milledge L. Life & times of Milledge Luke Bonham [incl. Butler, Brooks, Griffin & Lipscomb families]. NP: typescript, nd. 1164 p.　　　EDTO
Bonnette, Mrs. Belvin. William Norton Bonnett family. Neeses:

NPub, 1976. 45 p.   ORCL
Bookhart, Emmie M. Records of the Burden & Barnes families.
NP: typescript, 1939. unp.   ORCL
Bookhart, Emmie M. The coming of the Bookhart family to Amer-
ica. Cola: The Letter Shop, nd. 21 p.   ORCL, SCL
The Boone Bulletin; a magazine of history & genealogy. v-.
1928-.   SCHS
Boone Family [SpC]   PIPD
Boone, Merritt A. Descendants of Henry Harrison Boon, including
partial histories on Curtner & Burgess families. NP:NPub,
1971. 96 p.   CLEM
Boozer, Alice B. Auntie Boozer's letters, 1860-1886;... NP:
mimeo, nd. 146 p.   GWPL
Boozer, Mary E. The Boozer family of SC...of Lexington & New-
berry counties... Cola: RLB, 1970. 360 p.   COMMON
Boozer, Mary E. The Boozer family of SC [supplement]. White
Rock: author, 1973. 20 p.   SCL, CLEM
Boozer, Simon Elbert. History of the Boozer family in America
from 1738 to 1955. NP:NPub, 1955? 44 p.   SCL
Bornemann, Vivian D. Genealogy. The families of Spinks, Worthy
& Davis. NP: mimeo, nd. 92 p.   SCL, SCHS
Boroughs Family genealogy [SpC]   PIPD
Boswell, F. Irene. Profiles & silhouettes of our ancestors.
NP: NPub, nd. 65 p.   FACM
Boughton, Willis A. Arnold, Redway & Earle families. Ann Arbor
MI: Edward Bros., 1948.   CHLS
Boughton, Willis A. Bouton, Boughton & Franham families. NP:
privately printed, 1949. 214 p.   SCHS
Boulware Family [SpC]   FACM, YOWC
Boulware, James R. The Boulware family genealogy, 1608. 1924-
1948. NP: mimeo, 1948. 56 p.   FACM, SCL
Boulware, James R. The Boulware family genealogy...with correc-
ted & added material...to 1979. NP: typescript, 1979. 56 p.
                                                   SCL, GWPL
Bowen, Catherine. Family portrait [Drinker family]. Boston:
Little, Brown & Co., 1970. 301 p.   CLEM, SCHS
Bowen Family [SpC]   PIPD
Bowen, Harold K. Book of Adam [King family]. Osceola MO: NPub,
1943. 14 p.   SCHS
Bowen, John M. The Bowen family (with McGowan & Brooks lineage)
of George's Creek, Pickens County SC. Decatur GA: Bowen Press
1962. 115 p.   CLEM, SCL
Bowen, John M. Louie Cassels & Hallie Jones; Cassels, Jones,
Endres, Mallard & Law lineage. Decatur GA: Bowen Press, 1964.
163 p.   CLEM, SCL
Bowers, Ralph L. The ancestors & descendants of Levi & Eliza-
beth Ann Young Bowers. Greenville: author, 1970. 30 p. NWRL
Bowie, Walter W. The Bowies & their kindred...[incl. Brooke &
Waring families]. Cottonport LA: Polyanthos, 1971. 523 p.
                                                          SCL
Boyd, Frederick T. History of the Boyd clan & related families.

Ft. Lauderdale FL: Regal Press, 1962. 106 p.   GWPL
Boyd, George H. Our Boyd family [incl. Boyd, DeGraffenreid,
    Tidwell, Milam, Patton families]. Danielsville GA: Heritage
    Papers, 1971. 82 p.   SCL
Boyd, John W. A family history: Wright-Lewis-Moore & connected
    families... Atlanta GA: Higgins-McArthur Co., 1968. 731 p.
                                                              COMMON
Boyd, Montague L. The Boyd family [incl. Boyd, Broyles, John-
    son, Lafitte, Fowke, Hewlett, Bush & Dunbar families]. Atlan-
    ta GA: Commercial Printing Service, 1964. 3 vol.   SCL
Boyd, Montague L. The Broyles, Lafitte & Boyd relatives & an-
    cestors of Montague Lafitte Boyd, Jr., M.D. Atlanta GA: auth-
    or, 1959. 130 p.   ANCL, SCHS, SCL
Boykin, Edward M. History of the Boykin family... Camden: Col-
    in Macrae, 1876. 27 p.   SCL
Brabham, Angus M. Mizpah, a family book [incl. Brabham, Kearse,
    Kirkland, McMillan & Moye families]. Cola: RLB, 1978. 302 p.
                                               CLEM, BACL, SCL
Brabham, Matthew M. A family sketch and else; or, Buford's
    Bridge and its people. Cola: State Co., 1923. 144 p. COMMON
Brainerd, Lawrence. Gary genealogy. The descendants of Arthur
    Gary of Roxbury MA, with an account of the posterity of Steph-
    en of Charleston MA, and also of a SC family of this name...
    Boston: T.R. Marvin & Son, 1918. 235 p.   SCHS, SCL
Bramlett, K.R. Bramlett line. Charlotte NC: typescript, 1978.
    31 p.   LRCL
Brasington, Juanita K. History of the Brasington family in the
    United States... NP: Brasington Family, 1958. 105 p.   CTCL
Bratton Family [SpC]   FACM
Brecht, Samuel K. The genealogical record of the Schwenkfelder
    families...who fled from Silesia to Saxony and thence to PA in
    the years 1731 to 1737. Pennsburg PA: Board of publication of
    the Schwenkfelder church, 1923. 1752 p.   SCHS
Brewer, Edward D. The house of Brewer. Tulsa OK: NPub, 1947.
    151 p.   MACL, SCHS
Brice, Agnes. History of the Brice family. Fort Worth TX:
    American Reference Publishing Co., 1972. 102 p.   SCL
Brice, Laurie S. The Brice family who settled in Fairfield
    County SC, about 1785. NP:NPub, 1956. 46 p.   FACM, SCL
A brief history of the Fee family from 1750 to the present time.
    Chester: Lantern Printing Co., 1901.   YOCL
A brief sketch of the family of John William Ballentine & wife
    Mary Magdalene Derrick Ballentine & collateral lines. John-
    ston: G.C. Waters, 1928. 37 p.   SCL
Broadwater, Mary J. David Rush & his descendants & stories of
    the community [incl. Rush, Adolph & Etheridge families].
    Greenwood: NPub, 1952. 238 p.   SCL, CLEM, GWPL, EDTO
Broadway, Bette I. The Broadway [& Bradway] family of SC. NP:
    NPub, 1974. 18 p.   SCL
Brockmann, Charles R. Adams, Caruthers, Clancy, Neely and Town-
    send descendants composing the Adams, Legerton, Wakefield,

222

Brockmann & other twentieth century families of the Carolinas. Charlotte NC: NPub, 1950. 118 p.   CLEM, CHLS, SCL

Brockman, Mary B.   Clarks of Edisto Island SC, and Clark family in America. NP:NPub, nd. 38 p.   SCL

Brockman, William E.   The Brockman scrapbook; Bell, Bledsoe, Brockman, Burrus, Dickson, James, Pedan, Putman, Sims, Tatum, Woolfolk & related families. Minneapolis MN: NPub, 1952. 442 p.   SCL, LRCL

Brockman, William E.   Early American history; Hume & allied families. Minneapolis MN: NPub, 1926. 2 vol.   SCL

Brooke, Francis H. A family narrative. NY: Arno Press, 1971. 43 p.   GTML

Brooks, Anna B.   Alexander Black of Northern Ireland & York County SC. NP: author, nd. 37 p.   SPCL

Broughton, M. Leon. Broughton memoirs, 3rd ed. Dallas TX: author, 1972. 403 p.   PRIV

Broun, Robert J.   History of the Broun family and related families [incl. Broun, Thomas, Deas, Singleton, Winthrop-Marston, Dudley, Harleston, LeJau, Olney, Reynolds & Petty families]. Tequesta FL: NPub, 1971. 288 p.   CHLS, SCL

Broun, Thomas L.   The Ball, Conway, Gaskins, MacAdam & other kindred of William & Janetta Broun, of Northern Neck VA. NP:NPub, nd. 4 p.   SCHS

Brown, Mrs. C.C.   The ancestry of Cyril Conrad Brown concerning Brown, Ferguson & Shirley families, Rock Hill SC area. NP: typescript, nd. unp.   YOCL

Brown Family [SpC]   PIPD

Brown, Gerry H.   John D. Brown, 1848-1918 & Irene Sanford, 1850-1919. Genealogical record of their descendants... NP: typescript, nd. 35 p.   HOCL

Brown, Richard L.   A Brown family of Spartanburg & Greenville counties, SC. Maplewood NJ: author, 1963.   SPCL

Brown, Richard L.   Cobb-Thompson & kindred families of Greenwood County SC. Maplewood NJ: typescript, 1964. 49 p.   GWPL

Brunson, Charlotte B.   Kershaw County cousins. Cola: RLB, 1978. 476 p.   MACL, KECA

Brunson, Marion B.   A backward look. A history of the Brunson reunion. NP:NPub, 1969. 72 p.   SCHS, SCL

Brunson, W.A.   History of old Ebenezer Church, with genealogy of the Dargan, Woods & other families. Weldon NC: Harrell Printing House, 1909. 16 p.   SCL

Bryan, Thomas R.   Name & family of Bryan or Brian. Edgefield: Shaffer Printing Co., 1970. 232 p.   SCL, EDTO

Bryant, Lawrence C.   The Bryant reporter; a compilation of old editions. Orangeburg: author, 1967. v.p.   SMCL, SCL

Bryant, Lawrence C.   The Bryant reporter and miscellaneous papers. Compilations of old editions, June 1967-June 1970. Vol. II. Orangeburg: author, 1970. v.p.   SCL

Bryant, Lawrence C.   A historical & genealogical record of Fanny Sills & related families of Nash County NC. Orangeburg: author, 1968. 84 p.   SCL, ORCC, SMCL

223

Bryant, Lawrence C. A historical & genealogical record of Law-
rence Bryant & Pattie Sessoms' five other sons of Nash County
NC. Orangeburg: author, 1968. 144 p.   SMCL, SCL
Bryant, Lawrence C. Pictures of Sessoms & Bryants. Orangeburg:
author, 1978. 51 p.   SCL
Buchanan Family [SpC]   FACM
Buckalew Family [SpC]   CRCL
Buffington, Ralph M. The Buffington Family in America. Houston
TX: Mary B. Webb, 1965. 433 p.   SCL
Buie, Robert B. The Scotch family Buie. NP: author, 1950.
82 p.   SCL
Bull, Charles M. Society of the Bull family of Ashley Hall.
Chstn: typescript, 1974. unp.   SCHS
Bull, Henry DeSaussure. The family of Stephen Bull of Kinghurst
Hall, County Warwick, England and Ashley Hall, SC, 1600-1960.
Georgetown: Winyah Press, 1961. 161 p.   COMMON
Bull, James H. John Bull of Perkiomen...PA & his descendants,
1674-1930. San Francisco CA: Shannon-Conmy Printing Co.,
1930. 436 p.   SCHS
Bull, Joseph C. Miscellaneous notes, pedigrees, etc., relating
to persons of the surname Bull. NP:NPub, nd. v.p.   SCHS
Bulloch, Joseph G. The Cuthberts, barons of Castle Hill, &
their descendants in SC & GA. NP:NPub, 1908. 100 p.SCHS, SCL
Bulloch, Joseph G. Genealogical & historical records of the
Baillies of Inverness, Scotland, and some of their descendants
in the U.S.... Washington DC: Potomac Printing Co., 1923.
84 p.   SCHS
Bulloch, Joseph G. A history & genealogy of the families of
Bayard, Houston of Georgia, and the descent of the Bolton fam-
ily from the families of Assheton, Byron & Hulton. Washington
DC: Dony, 1919. 76 p.   SCHS
Bulloch, Joseph G. A history & genealogy of the Bulloch & al-
lied families. Savannah GA: Braid & Hutton, 1892. SCL, SCHS
Bulloch, Joseph G. A history & genealogy of the family of Bail-
lie of Dunain, Dochfour & Lamington, with a short sketch of
the family of McIntosh, Bulloch, and other families...
Green Bay WI: Gazette Print., 1898. 111 p.   SCHS
Bulloch, Joseph G. A history & genealogy of the families of
Bulloch, Stobo, DeVeaux, Irvine, Douglass, Baillie, Lewis,
Adams, Glen, Jones, Davis, Hunter, with a genealogy of branch-
es of the Habersham, King, Stiles, Footman, Newell, Turner,
Stewart, Dunwoody, Elliott, with mention of the families of
Bryan, Bourke, Williams, Wylly, Woodbridge, and many other
families. NP: Braid & Hutton, 1892. 171 p.   SCL, SCHS
Bulloch, Joseph G. History & genealogy of the Stewart, Elliott
& Dunwoody families. Savannah GA: Robinson, 1895. SCL, SCHS
Bulloch, Joseph G. A history & genealogy of the families of
Bellinger & DeVeaux and other families. Savannah GA: Morning
News Print., 1895. 107 p.   SCL, UMBOD, SCHS
Bulloch, Joseph G. A history & genealogy of the families of
Bulloch & Stobo and of Irvine of Cults. Washington DC: Byron

224

& Adams, 1911. 95 p.   SCHS
Bulloch, Joseph G. A history of the Glen family of SC & GA [in-
  cl. Bayard & Polter families]. Washington DC: NPub, 1923.
  132 p.   SCHS, SCL
Bulloch, Joseph G. A history of the Habersham family. Cola:
  RLB, 1901. 245 p.   SCL, UMBOD
Bullock, Kenneth C. A genealogy of James Bullock & Mary Hill,
  Latter-Day Saint pioneers. Provo UT: NPub, 1964. 361 p. SCHS
Bullock, Kenneth C. A genealogy of McGee Harris, Latter Day
  Saint pioneer. Provo UT: NPub, 1962. 409 p.   SCHS
Burckhalter Family [SpC]   GSGN
Burgess, Barry H. Burgess genealogy. Kings County, Nova Scotia
  branch of the descendants of Thomas & Dorothy Burgess who came
  from England in 1630 and settled in Sandwich MA. NY: Chas. E.
  Fitchett, 1941. 77 p.   SCHS
Burgess, Marjorie C. A genealogy of the Cutler family of Lex-
  ington MA, 1634-1964. NP: privately printed, 1965. 104 p.
                                                                SCHS
Burgess, Sallie R. The Mayes family of VA & SC. Greenville:
  typescript, 1930.   SCHS, PRIV
Burns Family [SpC]   PIPD
Burns, James C., Sr. Burns [& Putnam] Family in old Ninety-Six
  District, SC. Greenwood: NPub, 1954. 35 p.   COMMON
Burress, David E. History of the Burriss [& Burress] family.
  Pendleton: NPub, 1940. 4 p.   CLEM
Burroughs, Eli. A limited genealogy of the Burroughs family of
  the Martin County NC branch. NP:NPub, nd. 39 p.   SCL
Burt, Evelyn R. Our family [Adicks-Marjenhoff]. NP: typescript
  nd. unp.   SCHS
Burt Family [SpC]   PIPD
Burton, William L. Remember, my children. The story of Solomon
  Burton & some of his descendants. Iowa City IA: author, 1973.
  211 p.   SCHS
Byars Family [SpC]   CRCL
Byerly, Wesley G. The Byerlys of Carolina. Hickory NC: Economy
  Printing Co., 1960. 69 p.   SCL
Cabell, James B. The Majors and their marriages. With collat-
  eral accounts of the allied families of Aston, Ballard,
  Christian, Dancy, Hartwell, Hubard, Macon, Marble, Mason, Pat-
  teson, Piersey, Seawell, Stephens, Waddill & others. Richmond
  VA: W.C. Hill Printing Co., 1915. 188 p.   SCHS
Caldwell, John H. The Thurstons of the old palmetto state...
  NY: J. Russell, 1861. 406 p.   SCHS, SCL
Calhoun, Edwin C. Archibald Calhoun & descendants [incl. Cal-
  houn, Patterson, Phillips & Baugh families]. San Antonio TX:
  NPub, 1974. 148 p.   SCL
Calhoun, Robert S. The Calhoun family: origin and activities.
  Fort Myers Beach FL: author, 1977. 43 p.   SCL, CLEM
Callahan, Anna D. A history of the Callahan [&Callaham] fami-
  lies. Charlotte NC: Delmar Publishers, 1976. 493 p. COMMON
Calvert, Bessie L. Climbing the family tree. Plant City FL:

NPub, 1966-67. 2 vol.   SCL
Camp, Max W. Our ancestors & kinsmen. The Shelbys, Polks, Mc-
Lartys, Perkersons, Tarpleys & Camps. Detroit MI: Harlo, 1976.
  126 p.   SCL, SCHS
Campbell, Julia A. Descendants of Joel Adams & Grace Weston of
  "the Fork", Richland County, SC. Charlottesville VA: NPub,
  1959. 38 p.   SCL, SCHS
Campbell, Julia Courtenay. The Courtenay Family; some branches
  in America. NP:NPub, 1964? 54 p.   SCL
Campbell, Leslie L. The Houston Family in VA. Lexington VA:
  NPub, 1956. 77 p.   CLEM
The Campbells came: a chronicle.   SCHS
Campbell, Simeon. Compilation [Campbell family]. Marion: NPub,
  1937. 291 p.   SCHS
Campbell, Thomas. The Campbell family chart & distaff line.
  Charlottesville VA: author, 1955.   NWRL
Campbell, Thomas. Descendants of Capt. Angus Campbell of Laur-
  ens SC. Charlottesville VA: NPub, 1955. v.p.   SCL
Canady, Phyllis B. Britton; basic facts of the first generation
  of the Brittons of Britton's Neck. NP: typescript, 1966.
  17 p.   WMTR
Candler Family [SpC]   PIPD
Cannon, Lyndon J. Happy heritage: genealogies of seven southern
  families [Lee, Benton, Singletary, Timmons, Myers, Harrell &
  Cannon families]. Cola: State Co., 1943. 203 p.   SCL
                                                            FLCL, DACL
Capers Family [SpC]   PIPD
Carlisle, Cecil A. Carlisle family history. NP:NPub, 1961.
  131 p.   SCL, MRCL
Carlisle Family [SpC]   FACM
Carlson, Avis D. Small world...long gone: a family record of an
  era [Dungan family]. Chicago: Chicago Review Press, 1977.
  154 p.   CLEM
Carmichael, Roderick L. The Scottish highlander Carmichaels of
  the Carolinas. Washington DC: author, 1935. 143 p.   COMMON
Carnahan, Alfred E. The Pyeatts & the Carnahans of Old Cane
  Hill. Fayetteville AR: Washington County Historical Society,
  1954. 51 p.   CLEM
Carnes, Dorothy S. Descendants of Andrew DuBose, Jr., and Eliz-
  abeth Mims DuBose. NP:NPub, nd.   DACL
Carroll, F. Julian. The Carroll family of SC. NP:NPub, 1952?
  32 p.   SCHS
The Carroll family. NP: typescript, nd. 14 p.   FACM
Carroll, J. Gregg. Abbeville County family history. Clinton:
  Intercollegiate Press, 1979. 199 p.   SCL
Carvill, H. C. Royal servants; an Episcopal heritage [Bruce
  family]. Little Rock AR: typescript, 1968. 20 p.   SCHS
Carvin, Ernest A. Genealogy of the Carvin-Istvan families. NP:
  typescript, 1972. 15 p.   SCL, SCHS
Casper, Mary K. Family history: Ashley, Bridgman, Hewitt, Shel-
  don, Symonds & Warner. NP: Typescript, 1943. 153 p.   SCHS

                                226

Cathcart Family [SpC]   YOWC
Chaffin, Encel A. & others. Abner Chaffin of Jackson County TN
  & sons. An account of their migrations to MO, IL, & MT...
  Provo UT: authors, 1966.   SCHS
Chamberlain, N.A. A record of one of the lines of descendants
  of Edmund Chamberlain (d. 1696), English emigrant. Chstn:
  NPub, 1912. 12 p.   SCHS
Chamberlain, George W. The Spragues of Malden. Boston MA:
  NPub, 1923. 317 p.   SCHS
Chandler, Charles H. The descendants of Roger Chandler of Con-
  cord MA. 1658. Provo UT: privately printed, 1949. 152 p.
                                                                  SCHS
Chandler, William H. Letters to Benjamin Britton of Williams-
  burg County SC. 44 p.   WMTR
Chaplin, Ellen P. The Chaplins & allied families [incl. Holman
  family]. Neeses: NPub, 1965. 119 p.   COMMON
Chapman, F.W. The Buckingham family; or, the descendants of
  Thomas Buckingham, one of the first settlers of Milford CT.
  Hartford CT: Case, Lockwood & Brainard, 1872. Part I.   SCHS
Chapman Family [SpC]   PIPD
Chapman, John V. Samuel Whatley Chapman & his wife, Missouri
  Ann Morris (Chapman) & allied families. Tallahassee FL:
  NPub, 1949. 52 p.   SCHS
Chappell, Buford S. The Chappell family in early SC. Cola: RLB
  1972. 98 p.   COMMON
Chappell, Buford S. The Winns of Fairfield County: Colonel John
  Winn, William Winn, General Richard Winn. Cola: RLB, 1975.
  122 p.   COMMON
Chappell, Philip E. A genealogical history of the Chappell,
  Dickie, & other kindred families of VA, 1635-1900. Kansas
  City MO: Hudson-Kimberly Publ. Co., 1900. 382 p.   SCL
Chart showing descendants of Johannes & Sarah Kolb [inc. Wilson
  family]. NP:NPub, 1932, revised 1960.   DACL
Chase, George B. Lowndes of SC... Boston: A. Williams & Co.,
  1876. 81 p.   COMMON
Chase, Guy B. Descendants of Samuel Chase of New Brunswick.
  St. Paul MN: NPub, 1976. 85 p.   SCHS
Cherry & Fee family: entries copied from Nancy Monica Cherry Mc-
  Gee's bible, 1873. NP: typescript, nd. unp.   YOCL
Cherry, Lina V. Ancestry of my three children [Cherry, Vande-
  grift, Denison, Williamson & Marbury families]. Little Rock
  AR: Npub, 1945. 743 p.   CLEM
Cherry, Lina V. McDonnell & allied families. 1959. 108 p.SCHS
Cherry, Marjorie L. The roots of the Cherry tree. NP: type-
  script, 1955. unp.   YOCL, SCHS
Child, Elias. Genealogy of the Child, Childs, & Childe families
  ...from 1630 to 1881[incl. May, Morse, Smith, Walker & West
  families]. Utica NY: Curtiss & Childs, 1881. 842 p.   SCL
Childs, Arney R. Planters & businessmen: the Guignard family of
  SC, 1795-1930. Cola: USC Press, 1957. 155 p.   COMMON
Chisholm, William G. Chisholm Genealogy. NY: Knickerbocker

Press, 1914. 95 p.   SCL, CLEM, SCHS
Christie, Susan C. The Cantrill-Cantrell genealogy. NY: Graf-
ton Press, 1908. 271 p.   SCL
Chute, George. Chute family in America in the 20th century.
Plymouth MI: NPub, 1967. v.p.   SCL
Clardy Family [SpC]   PIPD
Clark, Chovine R. Lineage of Chovine Richardson Clark, Manning,
SC [incl. Clark, Benbow, Humphrey, Long, Kimmel, Phillips,
Perdriau, Dupont, & Richardson families]. Sumter: Wilder &
Ward, 1969. 60 p.   COMMON
Clark, Eva L. Jacob Clark of Abbeville SC & some of his de-
scendants...& letters of Rev. Jacob Clark... NY: Downes
Printing Co., 1926. 121 p.   SCL, CHLS
Clark, John W. Some descendants of William Clark of Sabin Coun-
ty TX. Fort Worth TX: American Reference Publishers, 1971.
45 p.   SCL
Clark, Meribah E. The James & Eliza Ritchey family, 1700-1976.
Astoria IL: Stevens, 1976. 131 p.   SCL, SCHS
Clarke Family [SpC]   FACM
Clarke, George K. Genealogy of the descendants of Nathaniel
Clarke of Newbury MA. Boston: Marvin, 1883. 121 p.   SCHS
Clarke, Jane. Porcher family & other related lines. NP: Type-
script, nd. unp.   SCHS
Clarkson, Francis O. Thomas Boston Clarkson of SC: his forbears
& his descendants through his son William; including brief
genealogies of Simons, Heriot & Marion families of SC. NP:
NPub, 1973. 108 p.   SCL
Clary Family [SpC]   CRCL
Clawson Family [SpC]   YOWC
Clayton, Claud F. Family notes...by Claud Franklin Clayton.
Knoxville TN: Fine Printing Co., 1959. 1076 p.   SCL
Clem, Inus M. The Clem family: 1765-1976. Dallas TX: Ray Hope
Clem, 1976. 281 p.   SCL
Clement, Louise M. The McCown family of the PeeDee section of
SC. Cola: RLB, 1966. 246 p.   MACL
Clowney Family [SpC]   FACM
Cloyd, A.D. Genealogy of the Cloyd, Basye & Tapp families in
America. Omaha NB: NPub, 1912.   CHLS, SCHS
Clyburn, Margaret P. Anderson family directory, 1830-1958;
descendants of John & Rebecca Cobb Anderson [of Greenwood
County SC]. NP: mimeo, nd. 17 p.   GWPL
Cobb Family [SpC]   PIPD
Cockrell, Augustus W. Kanawha: descendants of Thomas "Kanawha"
Spratt. Jacksonville FL: NPub, 1908.   SCL, YOCL
Coffee, Isabelle Maxwell. The Grant-Ivie families... Baldwin
GA: NPub, 1961. 71 p.   SCL
Cogburn, Lewellyn E. The John Cogburn family. Cola: Npub, 1962
229 p.   EDTO
Coit, John E. Lineage of the descendants of John Calkins Coit
of Cheraw SC, 1799-1865. NP:NPub, 1945. 52 p.   SCL
Coker, Robert E. Caleb Coker, Jr., of Society Hill SC. NP:

NPub, 1965.   63 p.   COKL, SCL
Coker, W.C.   A visit to the grave of Thomas Walter.   (Reprinted
   from the Journal of the Elisha Mitchell Scientific Society,
   April, 1910).   12 p.   SCL, SCHS
Colby, Lydia.   The genealogy and history of the families of
   Francis Dodds & Margaret Craig Dodds of Spartanburg SC.   Gen-
   eseo IL: NPub, 1929.   177 p.   SPCL, SCL
Colcock, C.J.   The family of Hay; history of the progenitors &
   some descendants (in SC) of Col. Ann Hawkes Hay.   With later
   lines added by Mrs. T. D. Bateman.   NY: NPub, 1908, rp 1959
   [by ?].   SCL, SCHS, CHLS
Coleman, James P.   The Robert Coleman family from VA to TX, 1652
   to 1965 [incl. Coleman, Feaster, Mobley, Colvin, Stevenson &
   Yongue families].   Kingsport TN: Kingsport Press, 1965.   451
   p.   COMMON
Coleman, James W.   Robert Coleman family.   Reno NV: mimeo, 1970?
   37 p.   LRCL
Cole, Joada J.   Journal of the John family.   NP:NPub, 1959.
   158 p.   SCL, MRCL
Cole, Robert F.   The Captain A.B. Cole genealogy.   Miami FL:
   Sunshine Press, 1964.   v.p.   SCL
Coles, William B.   The Coles family of VA...   NY: privately
   printed, 1931.   SCHS
Collier, J.D.   History of a branch of the Collier family from
   the year 1781 to the present.   NP: author, 1911.   102 p.   EDTO
Collins, Archibald O.   "Ole Man Mose and his chillun": the story
   of Moses Collins of SC, GA, AL & MS, & his descendants.   Hou-
   ston TX: NPub, 1974.   485 p.   SCL
Collins Family [SpC]   GSGN
Collins, Herbert R.   History & genealogy of the Collins family
   of Caroline County VA & related families.   Richmond VA: Dietz
   Press, 1954.   222 p.   CLEM
Colvin, Ethelle & Baker Colvin.   Colvin & allied families.   El
   Dorado AR: Hurley Printing Co., 1965.   540 p.   CSCL, SCL
Combs, Bedford M.   Antecedents.   NP: typescript, 1976. unp.   YOCL
Comer Family [SpC]   GSGN
Committee for the Shealy Family History.   The Shealy family.
   Cola: RLB, 1976.   206 p.   LXMU
Conant, Frederick O.   A history & genealogy of the Conant family
   in England & America...also Connet, Connett & Connit families.
   Portland ME: privately printed, 1887.   639 p.   SCHS
Conley, Katherine L.   The genealogy of Major Francis Logan.
   Rutherfordton NC: NPub, 1970.   LNCL
Conyers Family [SpC]   GSGN
Coone, Lucille B.   Colonial Higdons & some of their descendants.
   NP:NPub, 1976.   167 p.   SCL
Cooper, James H.   A record of the descendants of Hugh McMillan
   & Jane Harvey from Scotland through Ireland to America.   Fair-
   born OH: Miami Valley Publ. Co., nd.   95 p.   LNCL
Copeland, Mary H.   Copeland family.   NP: typescript, 1965.
   11 p.   LRCL

Copeland, Mary H. Hughes [family]. Ware Shoals: author, 1965.
16 p.   LRCL
Corcoran, E. Emmons. The John Cunningham McDow, Sr., family of
Lancaster County SC. Asheville NC: Npub, nd. 46 p.   LNCL
Courtenay Family [Genealogy]. NP: typescript, nd. unp.   SCHS
The Courtenay family monument in Magnolia Cemetery, Charleston
SC, erected 1891. NP:NPub, nd. 4 p.   SCL
Courtenay, William A. The Courtenay family: some branches in
America. Charlottesville VA: J.C. Campbell, 1964. 54 p. CLEM
                                                          CHLS, SCHS
Cousar, James E. Physician turned planter: the evolution of a
southern family [Muldrow family]. Summerville: Presbyterian
Home of SC, 1976. 171 p.   COMMON
Cousar, James E., Jr. Down the Waxhaw road: the life story of
the Rev. John Cousar. Florence: NPub, 1953.   SCL, LNCL
Covington, William S. The Covingtons. Omaha NB: Citizen Print-
ing Co., 1941. 201 p.   SCL, MRCL
Cowan Family [SpC]   PIPD
Cowan, Zachary S. A history of the Cowan family, with list of
descendants of Dr. James Jones Cowan & Sarah Ann Cook Cowan.
NP:NPub, 1957. 71 p.   SCL
Cox Family [SpC]   GSGN
Coyle Family [SpC]. CRCL
Craig Family [SpC]   PIPD
Craig, Marion S. John Craig and some descendants, 1773-1976...
Little Rock AR: author, 1977. 102 p.   SCL
Craighead, James. The Craighead family...descendants of Rev.
Thomas & Margaret Craighead, 1658-1876. Philadelphia PA: NPub
1876. 173 p.   LNCL, SCL
Cravens, John P. Records of the ancestry of John Park Cravens.
Booneville AR: NPub, 1957. 17 p.   SCL
Crawford, Lee F. Forney forever. Birmingham AL: Commercial
Printing Co., 1967. 246 p.   CHLS, SCL
Creekmore, Robert. The Danielson family history [Edgefield &
Newberry Counties]. NP: typescript, 1979. 18 p.   SCHS
Creswell, John O. Creswell history & genealogy...1744-1967.
Maryland TN: Brazo Press, 1967. 256 P.   SCL
Crider, Gussie W. Four generations of the family of Strangeman
Hutchins & his wife, Elizabeth Cox... Kokomo IN: NPub, 1935.
20 p.   SCHS
Cronic, Josie W. Mattie Ball & William Jefferson Wells: their
forbears & descendants... NP:NPub, 1978. 23 p.   GWPL
Crooks Family [SpC]   PIPD
Crosleigh, Charles. Descent & alliance of Crosslegh, or Crossle
or Crossley, of Scaitcliffe, and Coddington of Old Bridge, and
Evans of Eyton Hall [incl. Colquhoun & Calhoun families].
London: De La More Press, 1904. 441 p.   SCL
Cross, Jesse C. The Jackson family; a history of Ephraim Jack-
son...and his descendants, 1684-1960. NP:NPub, 1961. 398 p.
                                                          SCHS
Crouch family of VA & Saluda County SC. NP:NPub, nd. 55 p. EDTO

230

Crouse, Maurice A. The Manigault family of SC, 1685-1783. M.A. thesis, Northwestern University, Evanston IL, 1964. 454 p.
                                                              UMBOD, CLEM, SCHS
Culbertson, Ambrose B. John Culbertson, Ransom Thacker, John Cummings & related families. Fort Worth TX: NPub, nd. v.p.
                                                              SCL
Culler, Emily. The family of Jacob Culler of the Orangeburg District, SC, 1735-1970. Orangeburg: NPub, 1970. 99 p. ORCL
Culler, Emily. Family records: Jacob H. Inabnit & Mary A. Houser, 1735-1953. Orangeburg: typescript, 1956. 60 p.   ORCL
Culler, Emily. Genealogy of the Lartigue, Grace, Stewart, Bull & Bellinger families. NP:NPub, 1956.   ORCL
Culler, Emily. The Inabnit family of Orangeburg, SC. Orangeburg: NPub, 1970. 245 p.   ORCL
Culler, Emily. The Inabnit family of Orangeburg...supplement. Orangeburg: Npub, 1973. unp.   ORCL
Culler, Emily. The Simmons family of Orangeburg & Charleston, SC. Orangeburg: NPub, 1970. 17 p.   ORCL
Culler, Hugh C. A history of the Culler family. Cola: RLB, 19?? 202 p.   SCL
Culler, Hugh C. A history of the Culler family. NP: typescript nd. 77 p.   SCL, ORCL
Cunningham, Caroline. Benjamin Jones & his descendants. NP: NPub, nd. 135 p.   SCL, LNCL
Cunyus, Walter H. Cunyus family [incl. Conyers family]. NP: NPub, 1970. 61 p.   SCL
Cupit, John T. A history of the Cupit family. DeRidder LA: Reliance Press, 1954. 204 p.   SCL
Cureton, Thomas K. The Curetons of Lancaster County SC. NP: mimeo, 1949. 16 p.   LNCL, GWPL
Curry, Annie H. Hughey genealogy. NP: mimeo, 1965. 8 p. GWPL
Dacus Family History [SpC]   YOWC
Danforth, Edward C. Fifteen generations of Danforths in England & America. NP: mimeo, 1970. 25 p.   SCL, SCHS
Dannelly Family [SpC]   GSGN
Dantzler, Daniel D. A genealogical record of the Dantzler family, from 1739 to the present time. Orangeburg: RLB, 1899. 52 p.   ORCL, SCL
Dantzler, David H. The David & Elizabeth Shuler Dantzler family [incl. Felder family]. Orangeburg: Quality Printing, Inc., 1970. 71 p.   COMMON
Darby, Rufus C. Genealogy of the Darby family. George Darby, 1726-1788, of Montgomery County MD. Atlanta GA: NPub, 1914. 159 p.   SCL, SCHS
Darby, Rufus C. Genealogy of the Darby family. Joseph Darby of Anne Arundel County MD. Atlanta GA: NPub, 1953. 107 p. SCL
Darden, Newton J. Darden family history with notes on the ancestry of allied families: Washington, Lanier, Burch, Strozier, Dodson, Pyles, McNair, & Barnett. Washington DC: NPub, 1953, revised 1957. 190 p.   PIPD
Darley, Lon J. Your Darley ancestors. Baltimore MD: Gateway

Press, 1979. 194 p.   SCL
Data on Norris & kindred families. (Bulletin of the Edgefield
County Historical Society, 1956). 40 p.   SCL, LNCL
Davenport, Charles W. Information on Davenport family [SpC]
29 p.   NWRL
Davidson, Chalmers G. Gaston of Chester. NY: author, 1956.
146 p.   COMMON
Davidson, Chalmers G. Major John Davidson of "Rural Hill",
Mecklenburg County NC planter. Charlotte NC: Lassiter Press,
1943. 93 p.   LNCL
Davis, Dudley C. & Martha D. Abernathy. Sketches of the John
Davis-Anne Byrd descendants. Phoenix AZ: Herald Press, 1969.
161 p.   LRCL
Davis Family [SpC]   FACM
Davis, Harry A. Davis Family History. NP: mimeo, 1927. unp.
                                                          MACL, MRCL
Davis, Harry A. Some Huguenot families of SC & GA. Peter La-
fitte, Andre Verdier, Samuel Montague, Henri Francois Bourquin
Jean Baptiste Bourquin, Peter Papot, Benjamin Godin...revised
& corrected... NP: mimeo, 1926. 100 p.   SMCL, SCL
Davis, Henry R. The Gordon family & allied families of William-
sburg County SC. NP: typescript, 1963. 12 p.   WMTR
Davis, Josephine. Origin & history of the black Sherards in SC.
NP: author, 1977. 9 p.   ANCL
Davis, Thomas F. A genealogical record of the Davis, Swann &
Cabell families of NC & VA. NP:NPub, 1934. 40 p.   SCHS
Dawsey, Cyrus B. The Dawsey family. NP: mimeo, nd. 29 p. HOCL
Deal, Fern W. Descendants of William Deal III and thirteen al-
lied & collateral family lineages of Sherrill, Pepper, Woods,
Kirkpatrick, Caldwell, Rutherford, Bayless, Champion, Barlett,
Ellis, Lindsay, Lack, & Tipton. Knoxville TN: Mannis Print-
ing Co., 1975. unp.   LNCL
Deas, Alston. Wigfall of Christ Church and St. Thomas & St.
Denis' parish, SC. 1978. 19 p.   SCHS
Deas, Anne S. Recollections of the Ball family of SC and the
Comingtee plantation. 1909, rp Chstn: SCHS, 1978. 189 p.
                                                             COMMON
DeForest, Louis E. Babcock & allied families. New Haven CT:
DeForest Publ. Co., 1928. 137 p.   SCHS
DeGraffenried, Thomas P. History of the DeGraffenried family
from 1191 A.D. to 1925. NY: Vail-Ballou Press, 1925. 282 p.
                                               LNCL, GWPL, SCHS
DeHuff, Elizabeth W. The Ashley family as compiled in 1962 by
Elizabeth Willis DeHuff. NP: mimeo, nd. 62 p.   SCL
DeHuff, Elizabeth W. The Boyd family. Augusta GA: mimeo, 1963.
55 p.   SCL
DeHuff, Elizabeth W. Brown family of VA & SC... NP: mimeo, 196?
24 p.   SCL
DeHuff, Elizabeth W. The Bush family as descended from John &
Mary Bryan Bush of NC... Augusta GA: NPub, 1967. 169 p. SCL
DeHuff, Elizabeth Willis. The family of James Dunbar.... NP:

232

mimeo, nd. 165 p. SCL

DeLancey, Edward F. The original family records: Cruger. NP:
NPub, 189? 12 p. SCHS

DeLorme, Harold M., Jr. Perry data. Compiled on Perrys in old
Camden District, SC. Grenada MS: NPub, 1952-53. SCL, LNCL

DeSaussure, James P. Some family lines of James Peronneau De-
Saussure and of his wife Annie Isabella Laurens. NP: Richard
Laurens DeSaussure, Sr., 1958. 40 p. SCL, SCHS

Descendants of James Boyd Magill, 1799-1880, emigrant from Ireland to Chester County, SC, in 1823...including allied families. Clinton: Jacobs Bros., 1963. 195 p. SCL, LNCL

Descendants of John Wesley Wiley...& Elizabeth Ray Washburn Wiley... Cola: RLB, 1966. 78 p. LNCL

Devereux, Margaret G. The Green girls. A memoir of our youth,
1898-1918... [Green family]. Saluda NC: typescript, 1970.
5 p. SCL

Devereux, Margaret G. The land & the people, an American heritage [incl. Green, Jones, Woods, Farnifold, Boylston, Moli-
neux, Taylor, DuBose families]. NY: Vantage Press, 1974.
395 p. EDTO, SCL

DeView, Donna H. Benjamin Cave, 1760-1842. Knoxville TN: typescript, 1960. v.p. SCL

Deviney, Esther G. A Gambrell album. Austin TX: AusTex Dupli-
cators, Inc., 1974. 282 p. ANCL

Diary of Mrs. Jennie I. Coleman [incl. Coleman, Feaster, Mobley,
Yongue & Stevenson families]. NP:NPub, nd. 138 p. FACM

Diary of Rosanna Law, Jan. 1 - Nov. 5, 1853 [incl. Glenn, Law,
Gillam & Blake families]. Greenwood: Greenwood County Historical Society, 1963. 64 p. SCL, DACL, MACL

Dicken, Emma. Our Burnley ancestors & allied families. NY:
Hobson Book Press, 1946. 261 p. PRIV

Dickey, Grover C. John & Alexander Dickey: immigrants, 1772.
Oklahoma City OK: author, 1976. 128 p. SCL, SCHS

Dickson Family [SpC] PIPD

Dinkins Family [SpC] YOWC

Dinkins, James. Genealogical...the Dinkins & Springs families
in connection with the Kendrick, Fox, Ball, Alexander, Riddick
Smith, Hart & others. New Orleans LA: Picayune Job Print,
1908. 24 p. SCL

The Dixon family. NP: American Genealogical Research Institute,
nd. 110 p. FACM

Dixon, William W. The Mobleys & their connections. NP: NPub,
1915. 146 p. SCL, UMBOD, FACM

Doliante, J. Sharon. Genealogical Serendipity, Vol. I: families
of Greene, Scoggin, White, Dyer, Griggs, Hurt, Mackey, Phillips & others. Alexandria VA: author, 1965. 346 p. LRCL

Dominick, Henry W. Henry Dominick, the Ist, & his family. Newberry County, SC. NP: NPub, 1921. 39 p. SCL

Donnald, Elizabeth. Donnald [Donald family]. Williamston: NPub
1975. 16 p. SCL

Donnald, Elizabeth. Genealogy of Major John Donnald, 1780-1855,

& Mary Houston, 1785-1846, of Donald's SC. NP: NPub, 1975.
17 p.   ANCL, GWPL
Donnelly, Shirley. The Thurmonds. A study...of Philip Thurmond
of Amherst County VA, & his descendants. NP: author, 1939.
47 p.   SCL
Dorman, John F. The Farish family of VA... Richmond VA: author
1967. 168 p.   SCHS
Dorman, John F. The Robertson family of Culpepper County VA.
Richmond VA: author, 1964.   SCHS
Dorsey, Jean M. Christopher Gist of MD & some of his descend-
ants. Chicago IL: John S. Swift Co., 1958. 296 p. SCL, SCHS
Doster, Elizabeth A. The Doster genealogy. Richmond VA: NPub,
1945. 286 p.   SCL, LNCL, SCHS
Doughtie, Beatrice M. The Mackeys & allied families. Decatur
GA: author, 1957. 1002 p.   SCL, LNCL, SCHS
Doughtie, Beatrice M. The Mackeys...errata sheet #2, including
supplemental data... NP: NPub, 1973. 173 p.   LNCL
Doughtie, Beatrice M. McDonald, Kimball, Wade & Lead [families]
Court, bible, church, cemetery [&] family records. NP: NPub,
1971. 682 p.   SCL, LNCL
Douglass, Hiram K. My southern families. Gillingham, Dorset,
England: World Nobility & Peerage, 1967. 405 p.   SCHS
                                                          SCL, CHLS
Dowling, R.A. A Dowling family of the south. NP: author, 1959.
133 p.   BACL, SCL
Dreyer, Gladys G. Our Gracen (Grayson) family of SC, 1775-1952.
NP: NPub, nd. 127 p.   SPCL, SCL
DuBin, Alexander. Five hundred first families of America [incl.
West family]. NY: Historical Publication Society, 1975.
400 p.   SCL, SCHS
DuBordieu, William J. Baby on her back: a history of the Hugu-
enot family DuBordieu... Lake Forest IL: author, 1967.
358 p.   SCL
DuBose, John W. The Witherspoons of Society Hill. Hartsville:
Bulletin of the Pee Dee Historical Assn., 1910. 21 p.SCL,FLMC
Dufford, Julius P. Dufford Family history. NP: NPub, 1979?
32 p.   SCL
Duke, Columbus W. & Gladys M. Williams. Sentimental journey to
the Duke, Shackelford, Crockett & more than four hundred al-
lied families. Lubbock TX: Keels, 1974. 143 p.   SCL
Dulles & related families records. NP: typescript, nd. 40 p.
                                                                 SCHS
DuMont, John S. DuMont de Soumagne & allied families... [incl.
duMont de Soumagne, duMont von Monten, duMont von Köln, Batt-
hyány von Gussing, Jones, Taliaferro, Merriwether, Waller,
Smith, Fettyplace, Van Vechter, Bunker, Stagg, De Peyster,
Washburn, Sweetser, Humphrey, Whitney, Daniels, Atkinson &
Ball families. Greenfield MA: NPub, 1960.   SCHS
Dunbar, Carl. ...They came...from across the sea & over the
hills: the forbears of four Dunbars... NP: NPub, 1976?
1 p.   SCL

Dunbar Family [SpC]   PIPD
Duncan Family [SpC]   CRCL
Dundas, Francis D. The Dundas genealogy. 2nd ed. Staunton VA:
    McClure, 1954. 186 p.   SCL
Dunlap Family [SpC]   GSGN, FACM
Dunlap Genealogical Collection: Dade, Dunlap, Haile, Massey,
    Miller, Decatur & White families [SpC]   YOCL
Dunn, Doris A. Allen & allied families. Greenville: A Press,
    1978. 117 p.   AJHR, MACL, SCL
Dunn, Monroe H. The genealogy of the Dunn, Crawford, Madden &
    Sanders families... Franklin Springs GA: Advocate Press, 1979
    26 p.   ANCL
Dupre Family [SpC]   PIPD
Dwight, Benjamin W. The history of the descendants of John
    Dwight, of Dedham MA... NY: author, 1874. 2 vol.   SCHS
Dyar, William H. The Dyar (Dyer) families. Jonesville NC:
    NPub, 1961. 120 p.   CLEM
Dyar, William H. Some Siebern (Seaborn) records. Greensboro
    NC: NPub, 1963. 71 p.   CLEM
Eaddy, Elaine Y. Genealogy of the Austin Stone & Jacob Bartell
    families of Marion County. NP: typescript, 1979. unp.   WMTR
Eaddy, Elaine Y. Johnsons & Johnsonville [Florence County] 1979
    [SpC]   WMTR
Eaddy, Elaine Y. Port-Humphries families of Marion County [SpC]
                                                                 WMTR
Eaddy, Elaine Y. The promised land: the James Eaddy family in
    SC. Cola: State Co., 1976. 359 p.   COMMON
Ealer, Frederick S. People; a history of the Ealer family. NP:
    author, 1968. 239 p.   SMCL
Earle, Charles L. Crouch family. Cola: NPub, 1973. 55 p. SCL
Earle Family [SpC]   PIPD
Earle, Isaac N. History & genealogy of the Earles of SeCaucus
    ... Marquette MI: Guelff Print. Co., 1925. 828 p. CLEM, SCL
Earle, Julius R. Earle. Short biographical sketches & family
    history. Hollands: NPub, 1899. 8 p.   SCL
Earle, Samuel B. Genealogy of the Earle family in SC. NP:
    author, nd. 145 p.   ANCL
Earley, Jesse K. Twelve generations of Farleys. Evanston IL:
    author, 1943. 79 p.   SCHS
An early manuscript copy of the Witherspoon family chronicles &
    later notes on related families. Kingstree: Kingstree Litho-
    graphic Co., nd. 39 p.   SCL, SCHS
Earnest family. Notes & U.S. census records, SC & nearby
    states. NP: typescript, nd. 5 p.   SCHS
Earp, Charles A. The Levi Chalk genealogy. Baltimore MD: mim-
    eo, 1965. 59 p.   SCHS
Eastman, Lucius R. Genealogy of the Eastman family for the
    first four generations. NP: Clapp, 1867. 10 p.   SCL
Edgefield County Historical Society. Bonham, Griffin, Lipscomb
    & Smith families. Edgefield: Edgefield Advertiser Print, 1941
    27 p.   SCL, GWPL

Edgefield County Historical Society. Data on Norris & kindred
    families. Edgefield: Edgefield Advertiser Press, 1956. 40 p.
                                                        SCL, SCHS
Edgefield County Historical Society. ...Genealogy of Nicholson &
    allied families: dedication of a monument to Wright Nicholson
    in the old Nicholson cemetery. Edgefield: Edgefield Adverti-
    ser Press, 1944. 68 p.   EDTO, SCL, SCHS
Edgefield County Historical Society. The Hammond family of
    Edgefield District... Edgefield: Edgefield Advertiser Press,
    1954. 16 p.   SCL, EDTO
Edgefield County Historical Society. The Martins of Martintown.
    Edgefield: Edgefield Advertiser Press, 1953. 16 p. SCL, EDTO
Edgefield County Historical Society. The Mims families of Edge-
    field. Edgefield: Edgefield Advertiser Press, 1951. 36 p.
                                                        SCL, EDTO
Edmonds Family [SpC]   PIPD
Edmunds, Elsie C. John Chapman of Spotsylvania County, VA;
    Thomas Powe of Cheraw, SC; & related families... Jackson MS:
    author, 1971. 421 p.   SCL, SCHS
Edwards Family [SpC]   CRCL
Edwards, John C. Sketch of the Garrison family, York County.
    Rock Hill: typescript, nd. unp.   YOCL
Elder, Clarice P. The Townsend family's unique history. NP:
    typescript, 1969. unp.   SCHS
Eldridge, Leila M. Bogle family records... Atlanta GA: NPub,
    1937. 50 p.   SCL
Elliott, Edwin E. Daniel Elliott, patriot, & a record of his
    descendants, 1769 to 1930... Portland OR: NPub, 1930. 260 p.
                                                             SCL
Elliott Family [SpC]   PIPD
Elliott, Rita J. The Herndon & Connor families... Chattanooga
    TN: author, 1961. 151 p.   GWPL, NWRL, LRCL
Elliott, Rita J. The John Jones family genealogy: including
    Benson, Chandler, Dunbar, Lester, Miles & Sibley. NP: author,
    1975. 91 p.   SCL, GWPL, NWRL
Ellis, Edmund D. Dr. Edmund Eugene Ellis & some of his descend-
    ants. NP: author, 1966. 235 p.   COMMON
Ellis, Edmund D. Nathaniel Lebby, patriot, & some of his de-
    scendants. NP: mimeo, 1967. 554 p.   COMMON
Ellis, Emily C. The flight of the clan; a diary of 1865. Being
    an account of how the Ellis family of SC, together with their
    kinsmen, the DeLoaches, Hays & Framptons fled before Sherman's
    raiders. Atlanta GA: NPub, 1954. 14 p.   SCL, SCHS
Ellis, Frampton E. Some historic families of SC [DeLoach, Fripp
    Grimball, & Ladson families]... 2nd ed. Atlanta GA: type-
    script, 1962. 92 p.   SCL, CLEM, SCHS
Ellis, McClintock T. Record of the family of Joseph Ellis.
    Fayetteville TN: NPub, 1939. 23 p.   CLEM
Elrod, Agnes H. The family of John C. Calhoun... NP: NPub,
    1963. 9 p.   CLEM
Elston, James S. George Walker & his descendants. West Hart-

ford CT: mimeo, 1952. 32 p.   SCHS
Emison, James W. The Emison families; with partial genealogies
   and notes on the following collateral families: Baird, Clarke,
   Holmes, Posey, Allen, Dunning, Rabb, Sinclair, Scott, Campbell
   McClellan, Patterson, Cullop, Mantle, Brevoort, Simpson, Mc-
   Cord, Hogue & Reily. Vincennes IN: NPub, 1947. 243 p.   SCHS
                                                            SCL
Engel, Beth B. The Middleton family...records from Wales, Eng-
   land, Barbados, and the southern United States. Jessup GA:
   Jessup Sentinel, 1972. 330 p.   SCL, FLCL, LNCL, CLEM
Enloe, E. E. Enloe Family. Sebastopol CA: NPub, 1948. 48 p.
                                                            SCL
Enloe, Thomas A. Enloe family. Washington DC: NPub, 1947.
   58 p.   SCHS
Ensworth, Sarah I. The Bradleys & allied families of SC. NP:
   Ensworth Printing Co., 1969. 428 p.   SMCL, KECA, LECL
Ephraim Family [SpC]   PIPD
Epton, Theodore. A history of the Epting & Epton families of SC
   New Tripoli PA: NPub, 1979. 300 p.   LXMU
Erath, Clara E. Descendants of John & Robert Ellison, Fairfield
   County, SC. Houston TX: NPub, 1972. 131 p.   SCL
Ervin, Sam J. The Conyers family of Clarendon County SC. NP:
   typescript, nd. unp.   SCHS
Ervin, Sam J. The Richbourg family of SC. NP: typescript, nd.
   27 p.   SCHS
Ervin, Sam J., Jr. The Ervins of Williamsburg, SC. NP: NPub,
   nd, 88 p.   SCHS
Ervin, Sara S. Genealogical survey of Anderson County Sullivan
   family. NP: Thomas A. Bolt, 1978. 15 p.   ANCL
Erwin, Lucy L. The ancestry of William Clopton of York County
   VA. Rutland VT: Tuttle Publ. Co., 1939. 333 p.   SCL, SCHS
Estes, Charles. Estes genealogies, 1097-1893. Salem MA: Eben
   Putnam, 1894. 397 p.   SCL
Estes Family [SpC]   GSGN
Etheridge, Hamlin W. Our Etheridge family circles. From 1753
   to 1953. Johnston: The Ridge Citizen, nd. 72 p.   SCL, NWRL
Eustis, Warner. The Eustis families in the United States from
   1657 to 1968. Newton MA: privately printed, 1968. unp. SCHS
Eustis, Warner & Mrs. Anthony Schilpp. Eustis families in the
   United States, volume III. NP: NPub, 1972. 12 p.   SCHS
Evans, Eytive L. A documentary history of the Long (Lang) fami-
   ly; Switzerland to SC, 1578-1956...of Newberry, Edgefield, &
   Saluda counties. Decatur GA: Bowen Press, 1956. 316 p.COMMON
Evans, James D. History of Nathaniel Evans of Cat Fish Creek,
   & his descendants... Williamsburg VA? NPub, 1905. 99 p.COMMON
Evans, Regina. Carville Tudoe Chalk & his descendants, 1784-
   1970. NP: author, 1970. 100 p.   SCL, CSCL, SCHS
Evard, Helen E. Descendants of Bartholomew Jacoby. Greenfield
   IN: Mitchell-Fleming Printing Co., 1955. 291 p.   SCHS
Ewing, Linda C. My forbears. History & genealogy of the Cun-
   ningham, Knox, Gibson, Borders & Ewing families. Auburn GA:

John T. Hancock, 1946. 112 p.   SCL
Ezell, Helen H. The Ezells of Buck Creek in Spartanburg County,
    SC. NP: author, 1970. 52 p.   GWPL, SPCL
Ezell, Mildred S. An aid to southern Corry research... NP:
    NPub, 1967. 2 vol.   SCL
Fagg, Jenny M. A family history of Thomas Martin, Sr., a NC
    American revolutionary soldier. Fort Worth TX: Arrow/Curtis
    Printing Co., 1976. 385 p.   SCL, CRCL
Fail, Welton B. The Fail-Faile-Fails family trail... Baltimore
    MD: Gateway Press, 1979. 485 p.   LNCL
Fair, Marielou R. Roach, Roberts, Ridgeway & allied families.
    NP: NPub, 1951. 258 p.   SCL
Fair, Mildred C. Llhuyd, Loyd, Lloyd, Lide: from Wales to PA,
    through VA to SC, with extensive records for Evan James Lide.
    Orangeburg: author, 1971. 94 p.   MACL, ORCL, GWPL
The family of Dr. Robert Turner Allison & Martha Burnett Clinton
    Their immediate ancestors & all of their descendants [incl.
    Meeks, Mason, Starr, McKinney & McCorkle families]. York:
    NPub, 1941.   SCL, LNCL
The family history of Saluda County, 1895-1980... Clinton:
    Intercollegiate Press, 1980. 408 p.   SCL, NWRL
The family of Isham & Mary Hayes Watson. NP: NPub, 1942. unp.
                                                               DICL
The family of Matthew Current who married Jane Wilson Call.
    Paris, KY: NPub, 1955. 15 p. Martha B. Hall, author. SCL, SCHS
Family reminiscences of the Pinckney, Brewton, Elliott, Oding-
    sells, Ramsay & Laurens families... Chstn: W,E&C, 1859.
    95 p.   SCL
Fanning, Lawrence. The Fannin(g) family & their kin [incl. Win-
    ningham, Phillips & Corbett families]. NP: NPub, 1968.
    350 p.   SCL
Fant, Alfred E. Fant genealogy. NP: author, 1975.   SCL, ANCL
Fant Family [SpC]   PIPD   SCL
Faris, Thomas M. Coltharp; descendants of John J. Coltharp &
    Melinda Cranford Coltharp... NP: mimeo, 1971.   YOCL
Faris, Thomas M. Faris line: Faries, Faries, Ferris, Farris,
    1698-1966; paternal genealogy of Thomas Murray Faris. Atmore
    AL: NPub, 1966.   YOCL
Farrell, Louis. McCallums: their antecedents, descendants &
    collateral relatives. NP: author, 1946.   SCL, SPCL, SCHS
Farrow, Audrey D. A genealogical history of the Farrow, Waters
    & related families... NP: Itawamba County Times, 1973. 104
    p.   SPCL
Faucette, Shirley & Joseph E. Steadman, Sr. Ancestors of the
    Fox family of Richland & Lexington counties, SC. NP: NPub,
    1972. 247 p.   SCL, DEALER
Feaster Family [SpC]   FACM
The Felder family of SC. NP: NPub, nd. 12 p.   SCL
Felder, Rice A. Descendants of James Addison Felder & Flavilla
    Shuler of Orangeburg County, SC. Cola: NPub, 1980. SCL, SCHS
Felkel, Nancy B. Felkel genealogical records. Midway ??:

mimeo, 1954. 70 p.   ORCL
Ferguson, Amelia C. Histories of the families of James & Martha
    Crawford & of John & Isabella Whitesides... NP: author, 1939.
                                                                YOCL
Ferrell, Hubbard O. Our Ferrell Genealogy. NP: mimeo, 1965.
    150 p.   SCL
Ferrin, Frank M. Captain Johnathan Farren of Amesbury MA, &
    some of his descendants. NP: author, 1941. 222 p.   SCHS
Ferris, Mary W. Dawes-Gates ancestral lines...the ancestry of
    Rufus R. Dawes. NP: author, 1943. 2 vol.   SCHS
Fetzer, John E. The men from Wengen & America's agony: the
    Wenger-Winger-Wanger history, including Christian Wenger,
    1718. Kalamazoo MI: John E. Fetzer Foundation, 1971. 446 p.
                                                                SCHS
Field, Nora D. Genealogy & history: Bowen-Field-Nimmons & kin-
    dred families. Greenville: Keys Printing Co., 1960. 351 p.
                                                          CLEM, SCHS
A Finley Genealogy: a compilation. NP: NPub, 1905. 18 p. EAST
Finnell, Woolsey. Reverend Daniel Brown of Culpepper County, VA
    & allied families: Webster, Finnell, McCain, & Pemberton.
    Tuscaloosa AL: NPub, nd. 72 p.   SCL, SCHS
Firestone, Eva M. Mead-Clark genealogy. Upton WY: privately
    printed, 1946. 88 p.   SCHS
Fishburne, Charles C. History of the Fishburne family. NP:
    typescript, 1979. unp.   SCHS
Fisher, Primrose W. One dozen pre-Revolutionary War families of
    eastern NC, & some of their descendants [incl. Fisher, Paquin-
    et, Pelletier, Dudley, Hunter, Dennis, Weeks, Watson, Jarratt,
    Morton, Mann & Bell families]. New Bern NC: New Bern Histori-
    cal Society Foundation, 1958. 629 p.   CLEM
Flagg, Ernest. Genealogical notes on the founding of New Eng-
    land... Hartford CT: Case, Lockwood & Brainard, 1926. 440 p.
                                                                SCHS
Flagg, Norman G. Family records of the descendants of Gershom
    Flagg (b. 1730) of Lancaster MA, with other genealogical
    records of the Flagg family descended from Thomas Flagg of
    Watertown MA... NP: privately printed, 1907.   SCHS
Fleming, Louise C. Caesar to Creswell & other families [incl.
    Fleming, Gibbes & Hunter families]. Laurens: typescript,
    1957. v.p.   CLEM
Fleming, Louise C. Genealogical data on the Butler, Brooks,
    Barratt & Fleming families of SC & allied lines. Greenwood:
    mimeo, nd. 57 p.   GWPL
The Flenniken family. NP: NPub, nd.   SCL, FACL
Fletchall, Gale F. The Fletchalls, early settlers on American
    frontiers. NP: NPub, 1971? 123 p.   SCHS
Fletcher, Azile M. Fletcher family history. NP: NPub, 1979.
    18 p.   SCL
Fletcher, Azile M. The Milling family of SC, 1771-1976. NP:
    mimeo, 1976. 174 p.   SCL, GWPL, FACM
Fletcher, William J. The Gee family; descendants of Charles Gee

                              239

(d. 1709) & Hannah Gee (d. 1728) of VA. Rutland VT: Tuttle
  Publishing Co., 1937. 158 p.   SCL
Floyd, Viola C. Caston & related families: descendants of Glass
  Caston of Lancaster County, SC. Lancaster: author, 1972.
  204 p.   COMMON
Floyd, Viola C. Descendants of William Harper, Irish immigrant
  to Lancaster County, SC. Lancaster: Lancaster Center Press,
  1965. 583 p.   LNCL, SCL, SCHS
Floyd, Viola C. Floyd-Ervin family of Lancaster County, SC.
  Summerville: NPub, 1963. 126 p.   SCL, LNCL
Floyd, Viola C. The record of Alexander Ingram of Augusta Coun-
  ty VA & Lancaster County SC... Lancaster: author, 1934-1957.
                                                              LNCL
Fludd, Eliza C. Biographical sketches of the Huguenot Solomon
  Legare & of his family... Chstn: E. Perry & Co., 1886. 142
  p.   SCL, CHCO, SCHS
Fogle, Leila H. Fogle's family history; Vogel, Fogel & Fogle...
  & Fogle, Fogal & Fogeler settlers of Orangeburg District...
  NP: Fogle Historical Society, 1966. 280 p.   DOCL, SCL, ORCL
Folger, Walter W. Family records. Barton, Breazeale, Folger,
  Ashworth, Hill, & Hurt. NP: NPub, 1966. v.p.   SCL, ANCL
Folger, Walter W. Family records, Bible records, letters...:
  Barton, Breazeale, Field, Folger, Hill, Hurt, Pegram, Anthony,
  & Gibbs. NP: NPub, 1976. 72 p.   SCL
Folmar, Laurie W. Colonial ancestors of the Fulmers of SC & the
  Folmars of AL... Pelham NY: NPub, 1972. 94 p.   SCL
Folmar, Laurie W. Colonial ancestors...addendum. Revised 1973.
  Pelham NY: NPub, 1973. 8 p.   SCL
Folmar, Laurie W. Colonial ancestors...addendum. Revised 1976.
  Pelham NY: NPub, 1976. 18 p.   SCL
Folsom Family [SpC]   GSGN
Fontaine Family...the Huguenot Matthew Fontaine Maury [SpC] SCHS
Foreman, James A. The Foreman genealogy. NP: mimeo, 1958.
  45 p.   SCL
Forrester, Wallace R. House of Forrester... Leesburg GA: For-
  rester Genealogical Association, 1966. 266 p.   SCL
Fort, Kate H. Memoirs of the Fort & Fannin families. Chatta-
  nooga TN: MacGowan & Cooke, 1903. 232 p.   SCHS
Foster, Catherine A. Aycock genealogies... York: mimeo, 1968.
  190 p.   SCL, YOCL
Foster, Talmage D. History of the Fosters of Spartanburg County
  SC & Amelia Court House, VA... NP: NPub, 1972. 96 p.SCL, SPCL
Foulke, Roy A. Crozier family. Bronxville NY: NPub, 1976.
  97 p.   SCHS
Fowler, Christine C. History of the Fowlers. 1950.   CHLS
Fowler Family [SpC]   CRCL
Fowler, Grover P. The house of Fowler. Hickory NC: Hickory
  Printing Co., 1940. 754 p.   COMMON
Fox, Frank B. Two Huguenot families: DeBlois-Lucas. Cambridge
  MA: Cambridge University Press, 1949. 120 p.   SCHS
Frazier, Irvin. The family of John Lewis, pioneer [incl. Maver-

ick & Conrad families]. San Marino CA: NPub, 1960. 108 p.
                                                          CLEM
French, Janie P. The Crockett family & connecting lines...
  1928, rp Spartanburg: RPC, 1974. 611 p.   SCL, AHJR
Friend, Carter W. The descendants of Captain Thomas Friend,
  1700-1760, Chesterfield County VA. NP: privately printed,
  1961   SCHS
Frierson, John L. The Friersons of Stateburg. NP: NPub, 1972.
  21 p.   EPDI
Frierson, Robert E. Rev. David Ethan Frierson, his ancestors &
  his descendants. NP: NPub, 1977. 42 p.   SCL
Fripp Family [SpC]   GSGN
Fugler, Madge Q. The family of Peter Quin. NP: NPub, nd. CRCL
Fuller, Theodore A. Early southern Fullers. Sylva NC: NPub,
  1967. 207 p.   SCL, LRCL
Fullerton, Gordon W. The Fullertons of North America... Hono-
  lulu HI: author, 1975. 491 p.   ANCL, SCL, LNCL
Fullwood Family [SpC]   SMCL
Fulmer, Verley L. The Lever family. NP: typescript, 1945.
  5 p.   LXMU
Fulmer, Verley L. Shealy family, 1752-1941: a genealogical &
  biographical record. NP: NPub, 1941. Bruner Press,1941 SCL
Funderburk, Guy B. Funderburk history & heritage. Salem WV:
  Salem Press, 1967. 544 p.   SCL, LNCL
Funderburk, Guy B. Laney lineage & legacy. Monroe NC: Cory
  Press, 1974. 302 p.   LNCL, KECL, CTCL
Furman, James D. The Furman legend. NP: author, 1978. 85 p.
                                    SCL, KECA, SMCL, ANCL
Gaffney Family [SpC]   CRCL
Gaillard Family [SpC]   FACM
Gaines, Lewis P. History of the Gaines family...featuring a
  compilation of the Henry Gaines family & allied lines. Rome
  GA: Brazleton-Wallis Printing Co., 1973. 369 p.   GWPL
Gaines, Thomas R. ...Francis Gaines of Albermarle County VA &
  Elbert County GA. Anderson: NPub, nd. 104 p.   SCL, ANCL
[Gamble Family] Across the years. The name & family of Gamble.
                                                          LNCL
Gambrell, Sarah E. Genealogical line of Mrs. Sarah Elizabeth S.
  Gambrell through Sitton-Aull-Smith-Simons. NP: typescript,
  nd. unp.   SCHS
Gantt Family [SpC]   PIPD
Garber: Virginia A. The Armistead family. 1635-1910... Rich-
  mond VA: Whittet & Shepperson, 1910. 319 p.   SCL
Gardner, Benjamin H. Genealogy of the Gardner family. Aiken:
  NPub, 1953. 25 p.   SCL
Gardner, William L. Gardner & allied families. Baltimore MD:
  Gateway Press, 1979. 294 p.   LNCL
Garner, Sam. Southern Garners. Rome GA: NPub, 1979.   UNCL
Garrett Family [SpC]   GSGN
Garrett, Hester E. Pucketts & their kin of VA, KY, & other
  southern states; including notes on Garrett, Weldon, Mayes,

Gentry, Allen, Vance, Horning, Fleming, Shelton, Wyatt, Sparrow, Womeck, Campbell, Milby & other southern families. NP:
author, 1960. 285 p.   GWPL
The Garrett line. NP: mimeo, nd. 4 p.   GWPL
Garrison, Harry C. Ancestors & descendants of Charles Cleveland
Garrison & Mary Virreaner Rasor. Westport CT: mimeo, 1955.
54 p.   SCL, ANCL
Garrou, Hilda W. The Whitener family, 1717-1971. NP: NPub, nd.
unp.   LNCL
Gaston, Thelma. A sketch of the Gaston family, Murfreesboro TN.
Sumter: mimeo, nd. 2 p.   SCL
Gaudelock Family [SpC]   CRCL
Gault, Charles B. Ashe genealogy: some descendants of John
Baptista Ashe of Carolina. Chapel Hill NC: typescript, 1968,
revised 1978. 44 p.   SCL
Gault, Charles B. Portrait album of the family of Mr. & Mrs.
Francis Beers Gault of Lake Waccamaw and Wilmington NC...
Chapel Hill NC: NPub, 1968. 30 p.   SCL
Gault, Pressly B. & Elizabeth P. Leighty. The William Gault
family history. Sparta IL: NPub, nd.   LNCL
Gee, Christine S. The ancestry & descendants of Amzi Williford
Gaston II (1841-1911) of Spartanburg County, SC. Charlottes-
ville VA: Jarman's, 1944. 48 p.   SCL
Gee, Christine S. Genealogical notes on the South family, from
the states of NJ, PA, MD, VA, SC, KY & TX. NP: privately
printed, 1963. 163 p.   SCL, SCHS, GWPL, LRCL
Gee, Christine S. John Daniel, Sr., 1724-1819, of Essex County
VA & Laurens County, SC... Cola: McDonald Letter Shop, 1970?
227 p.   GWPL, SCL, CLEM, LRCL
Gee, Christine S. The roots of the branches of the Puckett fam-
ily tree. Cola: State Co., 1958. 136 p.   COMMON
Gee, Christine S. Some of the descendants of Daniel Martin
(1745-1829) of Laurens County, SC, and...the Hudgens, McNeese,
Rogers, & Saxon families. Greenwood: Keys Printing Co., 1963.
97 p.   COMMON
Gee, Christine S. Some of the descendants of John Martin (ap-
prox. 1785-1867) & his wife, Mary Osborne Martin, of Laurens
County, SC. NP: privately printed, 1963. 85 p.   SCL, GWPL
Gee, Mary G. The ancestry & descendants of Amzi Williford Gas-
ton II (1841-1911) of Spartanburg County, SC. Charlottesville NA: Jarman's, 1944. 48 p.   SCL, SCHS
Gee, Wilson. The Gee family of Union County, SC. Charlottes-
ville NA: Jarman's, 1935. 29 p.   COMMON
Gee, Wilson. The Gist family of SC & its MD antecedents. Char-
lottesville VA: Jarman's, 1934. 101 p.   COMMON
Geiger Family [SpC]   FACM
Geiger, Percey L. The Geigers of SC. NP: privately printed,
1946? 191 p.   SCL, ORCL, GTML
Genealogical notes on Burrows, Hibbs, Gatchell, Sheppard, Graves
Dickens & Marshall families. NP: mimeo, nd. unp.   SCHS
Genealogical reference record of the descendants of Dielman Kolb

together with the descendants of other ancestors bearing the
name of Kolb, Kulp & Culp. Based in part on the history of
the Kolb-Kulp-Culp family by Daniel Kolb Cassel, 1895. NP:
NPub, 1936.   MRCL
Genealogy of the ancestors & descendants of John Thomas McColl
& other McColls. 1966.   MRCL
Genealogy of the Bissehl family, southern branch. NP: NPub, nd.
16 p.   SCL, EAST
Genealogy of the Moore family of Londonderry NH & Peterborough
NH; 1648-1924. Cola: RLB, 1976. 285 p.   COML
Genealogy of the VA family of Lomax...with references to the
Lunsford, Wormeley, Micou, Roy, Corbin, Eltonhead, Tayloe,
Plater, Addison, Tasker, Burford, Wilkinson, Griffin, Gwynn,
Lindsay, Payne, Pressley, Thornton, Savage, Wellford, Randolph
Isham, Yates & other prominent families of VA & MD. Chicago:
Rand, 1913. 79 p.   SCHS
Genealogy of the Wherry family. NP: typescript, nd. unp. YOCL
Gentry, David. The Pickens-Jenkins family of Tugaloo: family
records. Hickory NC: author, 1978. 51 p.   PIPD, CLEM
Gibbes, Robert W. & Caroline Elizabeth Guignard. Descendants of
Susan Gibbes Robinson. Cola: RLB, 1970. 63 p.   SCL, SCHS
Gibert, Anne C. The Gibert Family: part II, biographical. Cola:
mimeo, 1962. 186 p.   SCL, SCHS
Gibson Family [SpC]   FACM
Gibson, J. Preston. The Gibson family. Georgetown: Field
Publishing Co., 1905. 18 p.   SCL
Gibert, Anne C. Pierre Gilbert, Esq., the devoted Huguenot;
a history of the French settlement of New Bordeaux, SC. NP:
NPub, 1976. 131 p.   COMMON
Gilkey, George L. The Gilkeys... Merrill WI: mimeo, 1950?
467 p.   SCHS, SCL
Gilley Family [SpC]   CRCL
Gilman, Arthur. The Gilman family traced in the line of the
Hon. John Gilman, of Exeter, NH... Albany NY: Joel Munsell,
1869. 324 p.   SCL
Gilmore, Leroy H. Two great-grands: a factual story of two re-
markable people [Connor family]. Chstn: W,E&C, 1955. 127 p.
                                                           SCL, SCHS
Gladney Family [SpC]   FACM
Gladney, Samuel M. The Gladney family tree [incl. Polk & Lacey
families]. NP: NPub, nd. 30 p.   SCL
Glenn, Laurence M. Keys family sketches: four generations in
direct line from Peter Keys (1761-1835) through J.C. Keys
(1882-1936)... Greenville: Keys Printing Co., 1965. 101 p.
                                          SCL, CLEM, GNLN, ANCL
Gleston, Grace N. Genealogical record of Joe (Isaac) Gleaton,
our immigrant ancestor of London, England, & Orangeburg, SC,
with allied families [incl. Carmichael family]. NP: NPub,
1941. v.p.   SCL
Glover, Beulah. The high house Glovers.   COML
Glover, Charles M. Genealogy of Glover clans. Santa Barbara

CA: NPub, 1939. 90 p.   SCHS
Glover family. Land records. [SpC]   SCHS
Glover, William L. History of the Glover family, 1600-1800.
   Chstn: typescript, 1940. 123 p.   SCHS
Glover, William Lloyd. History of the Glover family...beginning
   in the year 1635... NP: typescript, nd. unp.   ORCL
Gnann, Pearl R. Georgia Salzburgers & allied families. NP:
   Georgia Salzburger Society, 1956. 537 p.   SCL, SCHS, ORCL
Gnann, Pearl R. Georgia Salzburgers & allied families. Revised
   ed. Easley: Georgia Genealogical Reprints, 1976. SCL, SCHS
Godfrey, Lucile N. Some historical facts about the Burroughs
   family, the business, & Horry County... NP: typescript, 1960.
   37 p.   HOCL
Golsan, Page E. The Golsan genealogy. NP: typescript, nd.
   unp.   SCHS
Gooch, Frank A. ...The Line of John Gooch from the records of
   the late Samuel Henfield Gooch... New Haven CT: privately
   printed, 1926. 160 p.   LNCL
Goode, G. Brown. Virginia cousins. A study of the ancestry &
   posterity of John Goode of Whitby, VA...from 1148 to 1887.
   Richmond VA: Randolph & English, 1887. 525 p.   SCHS
Goodlett, Mildred W. Links in the Goodlett chain. 1965, rp
   Easley: SHP, 1978. 274 p.   COMMON
Goodlett, Mildred W. Our heritage: a history of Smyrna church
   & of the Boozers of Smyrna. Greenville: Keys Printing Co.,
   1963. 272 p.   COMMON
Goodlett, Mildred W. Waterloo: a history of the Anderson family
   of old Laurens District, SC. Greenville: Hiott Press, 1961.
   239 p.   COMMON
Goodman, Hattie S. The Knox family; a genealogical & biograph-
   ical sketch of the descendants of John Knox of Rowan County,
   NC... Richmond VA: Whittet & Shepperson, 1905. 206 p.   CLEM
Goodnight, S.H. The Goodknight (Gutknecht) family in America.
   Madison WI: 1936. 29 p.   SCHS
Goodwin, Elizabeth I. Descendants of James Goodwin, born 1795
   in St. Bartholomew's parish, SC. NP: NPub, 1968.   SCL, COML
Gordon Family [SpC]   GSGN   SCL
Gossett Family [SpC]   PIPD
Graham, Charles P. The Grahams: a history of that family which
   settled in the Williamsburgh District of SC. NP: NPub, 1976.
   44 p.   WMCL
Graham, Emma H. Major John Moore's records... Memphis TN:
   author, 1965. 74 p.   LRCL
Graham Family history. NP: typescript, nd.   SCHS
Graham Family [SpC]   CRCL
Graham, Virginia W. Ancestral lineage; Mildred Olive Bates Mc-
   Cann, Adair County IA; & Prince George County, VA... Hopewell
   VA: NPub, 1964. 45 p.   SCL, CLEM
Green, Fletcher M. The Lides go south...and west; a record of
   a planter migration in 1835. Cola: USC Press, 1952. 51 p.
                                                                COMMON

                               244

Green, W. Hughson. The Green family of SC. NP: author, 1958.
LECL
Green, Mrs. Robert L. Kirkland source book of records. Green-
wood: NPub, 1978. 3 vol.   SCL, SCHS
Greer Family [SpC]   PIPD
Greer, Jack T. Leaves from a family album. Waco TX: Texian
Press,1975. 112 p.   SCL
Gregg, Eugene S. A crane's foot or pedigree of branches of the
Gregg, Stuart, Robertson, Dobbs & allied families. Hilton
Head Island: author, 1975. 681 p.   COMMON
Gregory, Lewis J. Willis Gregory family history, 1785-1968.
NP: NPub, 1968. 318 p.   SCL, LNCL
Griffin, Clarence. Descendants of Chisolm Griffin. Spindale NC
author, 1931. unp.   SCHS
Gross, Evelyn R. The Winstocks [incl. Rosenberg family] of SC.
Greenwood: NPub, 1961-2.   SCL, GWPL
Groves, Carnice J. Jennings-McMillan-Faulling-Whaley-Bluer &
other families of SC. NP: Daytona Beach Community College,
1971. 336 p.   ORCL
Groves, Joseph A. The Alstons & Allstons of North & South Caro-
lina [incl. LaBruce, Pawley & Ward families]. 1902, rp Easley
SHP, 1976. 534 p.   COMMON
Guerard, George C. A history & genealogy of the Guerard family
of SC from 1679-1896. Savannah GA?: NPub, 1896? 15 p. SCHS
Guess, Dorothy M. Genealogy of the Moore family of Londonderry
NH & Peterborough NH; 1648-1924. Cola: RLB, 1976. 285 p.COML
Guffey, Alvin J. The Robert Sylvanus Floyd ancestors & descend-
ants: Floyd, Hammond, Neal, Bailey, Mobley & Gay. Mechanics-
ville MD: author, 1977. 140 p.   SCL, LNCL
Guild, Mrs. Mary Stiles. The Stiles family in America. Geneal-
ogies of the MA family, descendants of Robert Stiles of Rowley
MA, 1659-1891. And the Dover NH family, descendants of Wil-
liam Stiles of Dover NH, 1702-1891. Albany NY, privately
printed, 1892. 683 p.   SCHS
Guittard, Lynn Bussey. The Bussey family genealogy. Fort Worth
TX: Miran Publishers, 1979. 423 p.   PRIV
Guttery, Florence K. Burton & Pratt [families]. Jasper AL:
NPub, 1960. 70 p.   SCL
Gwathney, Louise T. Moore & Worley family history. Fayette-
ville TN: mimeo, 1977. 74 p.   LRCL
The Habergham family. References to, and remarks upon, the
historical records by Matthew Henry Habershon (b. 1821). NP:
NPub, nd. 16 p.   SCL, SCHS
Hagood, Johnson. Meet your grandfather: a sketch-book of the
Hagood-Tobin family. Chstn: author, 1946. 165 p.   COMMON
Haight, Theron W. Three Wisconsin Cushings. A sketch of the
lives of Howard B., Alonzo H., and William B. Cushing, child-
ren of a pioneer family of Waukesha county [WI]. Wisconsin:
Historical Commission, 1910. 109 p.   SCHS
Haines, Clara M. Visit our family tree [incl. Denham, Burns,
Haines, Glaze, Osborn, Jaynes, Simmons, Pitts, Belton, Maret,

Fant, Harris, Cox, Grubbs, Suttles, Mayes, McClung, Reese,
Harris, Bruce families]. El Reno OK: author, 1976. 869 p.
ANCL, PIPD
Hale, Nathaniel C. Roots in VA; an account of Captain Thomas
Hale, VA frontiersman...[and] the families of Hale, Saunders,
Lucke, Claiborne, Lacy, Tobin... Philadelphia PA: privately
printed, 1948. 227 p. SCL, SCHS
Hall. David M. Six centuries of the Moores of Fawley, Berkshire
England... Richmond VA: printed for the committee by O.E.
Flanhart Printing Co., 1904. 96 p. SCHS
Hall Family [SpC] FACM
Hall, Lou M. Genealogy & family history: McDonald-Smith family.
NP: typescript, 1957. 63 p. MACL
Hall, Martha B & others. Family of Matthew Current who married
Jane Wilson Call. Paris KY: NPub, 1955. 15 p. SCL, CLEM
Hallman, Elmer B. Early Carolina Heilmans (Hallmans-Holmans),
1736-1800. Cola: NPub, 1972. 112 p. SCL, ORCL, SCHS
Hallman, Isaac D. Mills-Smith; a SC family. A genealogical
record of Hallman & related families in America who are de-
scendants of those who settled in SC between 1730 & 1750.
Centerville UT: author, 1974. PRIV
Hamilton Family [SpC] GSGN
Hammond, Joan M. & others. The Marbert heritage. Summerville:
Printing Associates, 1980. 98 p. EDTL
Hamrick Family [SpC] CRCL
Hanahan, Hardin D. A place in history: The Davant family.
Cola: RLB, 1972. COMMON
Hanks, Bryan. Nancy Hanks, of undistinguished families...
Kansas IL: author, 1960. 367 p. ANCL
Hanna, Frank A. The Hanna family of Enoree river. Durham NC:
author, 1969. 113 p. SCL, SPCL
Hanna, James A. The house of Dunlap. Ann Arbor MI: Edward
Bros., 1957. 412 p. SCL, FLMC
Hansen notes on the Wylie & Robertson families of Chester &
Fairfield Counties. Rock Hill: typescript, 1958. 18 p. YOCL
Hardy Family [SpC] CRCL
Hardy, Stella P. Colonial families of the southern states of
America. NY: T.A. Wright, 1911; rp Baltimore MD: GPC, 1974.
643 p. COMMON
Hardy, Stella P. Colonial families of the southern states of
America: a history & genealogy of colonial families who set-
tled in the colonies prior to the Revolution. 2nd ed. Balti-
more MD: Southern Book Co., 1958. 643 p. SCL,MACL, EDTO, DICL
Harley, Lloyd D. Lloyd D. Harley, Sr.: his history & genealogy.
Titusville FL: author, 1979. 186 p. SCL, SCHS, ORCL, COML
Harllee, William C. Kinfolks, a genealogical & biographical
record. New Orleans LA: Searcy & Pfaff, 1934. 4 vol. COMMON
Harmon, Lillian E. The plantation Marshes: a colony of Edge-
field County Marshes and the account of their lineage. Edgefield: Edgefield Advertiser, 1964. 153 p. SCL, CLEM
Harper, Annie L. The Mellett family. Sumter: author, 1959.

15 p.   SMCL
Harrington, Sarah R. The families of Jacob Franklin Rodgers &
  David Henry Hanna of Williamsburg County, SC. 1977. 43 p.
                                                         WMTR
Harris Family [SpC]   CRCL
Harris, Fielder B. The James Harris-Mary Cherry family... NP:
  author, 1935. 166 p.   YOCL
Harris, James. C. The personal & family history of Charles
  Hooks & Margaret Monk Harris... Rome? GA: author, 1911.
  116 p.   FLMC
Harrison Family [SpC]   FACM
Harrison Family records [SpC]   GSGN
Harrison, Hastings. Dial & related families. NP: typescript,
  1955. 31 p.   LRCL
Harrison, Margaret H. A Charleston album [Hayne family]. Ridge
  NH: Richard R. Smith Publishing Co., 1953. 122 p.   COMMON
Harrison, Thomas P. The Harrisons of Andersonville SC...
  Austin TX: author, 1973. 148 p.   COMMON
Harrison, Thomas P. The Harrisons of Andersonville SC: a sup-
  plement. Austin TX: author, 1975. 47 p.   ANCL, PIPD, GWPL
Hart, Charles G. James Hart: a genealogical & historical record
  of his descendants... Jacksonville FL: Marion Hart, 1976.
  435 p.   SCL, EDTO
Hart, Joseph E., Jr. An account of the descendants of James
  Moore & Rachel (Black) Moore. NP: typescript, 1964.   YOCL
Hart, Joseph E., Jr. Adams family, York County, SC. NP: type-
  script, 1972.   YOCL
Hart, Joseph E., Jr. Barron family: Archibald Barron & some of
  his descendants. NP: typescript, 1973.   YOCL
Hart, Joseph E., Jr. Barron family, York County, SC. NP: type-
  script, 1972.   YOCL
Hart, Joseph E., Jr. Black family. NP: typescript, 1966. YOCL
Hart, Joseph E., Jr. Brandon family. NP: typescript, 1973.YOCL
Hart, Joseph E., Jr. Burris family. NP: typescript, 1972. YOCL
Hart, Joseph E., Jr. Byers family. NP: typescript, 1966. YOCL
Hart, Joseph E., Jr. Caldwell family of York County, SC. NP:
  typescript, 1978.   YOCL
Hart, Joseph E. Carothers family. NP: typescript, 1966. YOCL
Hart, Joseph E., Jr. The Crawford family of Bethany. NP: type-
  script, 1969.   YOCL
Hart, Joseph E., Jr. Currence family. NP: typescript, 1973.
                                                         YOCL
Hart, Joseph E., Jr. Erwin family, York County, SC. York:
  typescript, 1965.   YOCL
Hart, Joseph E., Jr. The Garrison family in York County, SC.
  York: typescript, 1963.   YOCL
Hart, Joseph E., Jr. The Hanna family of York County, SC: a
  trial genealogy. York: typescript, 1973.   YOCL
Hart, Joseph E., Jr. Jackson family. York: typescript, 1971.
                                                         YOCL
Hart, Joseph E., Jr. Jones family: Daniel Jones & his descend-

ants. York: typescript, 1974.   YOCL
Hart, Joseph E., Jr. Joseph Palmer & allied families: Cahusac,
   Love, Moore, Sadler, etc. York: typescript, 1970.   YOCL
Hart, Joseph E., Jr. Lindsay family, York County, SC. York:
   typescript, 1968.   YOCL
Hart, Joseph E., Jr. The Marion family of SC. York: typescript
   1967.   YOCL
Hart, Joseph E., Jr. McCarter family. York: typescript, 1973.
                                                          YOCL
Hart, Joseph E., Jr. McElwee family, York County, SC. York:
   typescript, 1965.   YOCL
Hart, Joseph E., Jr. The McGill family of York County, SC.
   York: typescript, 1967.   YOCL
Hart, Joseph E., Jr. Neely family: records from Chester County,
   York County, etc. York: typescript, 1963.   YOCL
Hart, Joseph E., Jr. Sadler family, York County, SC. York:
   typescript, 1964.   YOCL
Hart, Joseph E., Jr. Sherer family. York: typescript, 1973.
                                                          YOCL
Hart, Joseph E., Jr. Some descendants of Alexander Moore, York
   County, SC. York: typescript, 1969.   YOCL
Hart, Joseph E., Jr. Some of the descendants of John & Mary
   (Beall) Moore. York: typescript, 1956. 13 p.   YOCL
Hart, Joseph E., Jr. Some of the Loves of York County, SC.
   York: typescript, 1965.   YOCL
Hart, Joseph E., Jr. The Starr family. York: typescript, 1969.
                                                          YOCL
Hart, Joseph E., Jr. Sturgis family of York County, SC. York:
   typescript, nd.   YOCL
Hart, Joseph E., Jr. The Sutton family in York County. York:
   typescript, 1968.   YOCL
Hart, Joseph E., Jr. York County genealogy. York: typescript,
   1964.   YOCL
Hartness, George B. By ship, wagon & foot to York County, SC
   [incl. Hartness, Ash, Burris, Bowen, Whitley, Mitchell, Car-
   son, Thomas, Neil, Irvin, Chesnut, Curley, Sutton, McClain,
   Waggoner, Eakins & Johnsey families]. Cola: author, 1966.
   116 p.   MRCL, FLCL, SCL
Hartwell, John F. The Hartwells of America. Saginaw MI: author
   1956. 212 p.   SCL, SCHS
Harvay family records [SpC]   SCHS
Hasell, Annie B. Baynard: an ancient family bearing arms...
   Cola: RLB, 1972. 252 p.   COMMON
Hasty, Liswa E. Ellerbe: descendants of.... NP: NPub, 1979.SCL
Hatch, Alden. The Byrds of VA. NY: Holt, Rinehart & Winston,
   1969. 535 p.   CLEM, CHLS
Hawkins, Essie M. A history of the Daniel & Julia Ann Moore
   family. Newberry? author, 1963. 30 p.   NWRL
Hawthorne Family [SpC]   PIPD
Hayes, Maude M. John Clarence Calhoun family: an appendix to
   the sketch of Miller & Calhoun-Miller families by Florence

McWhorter Miller, 1927. Hartwell GA: NPub, 1961. 56 p. CLEM
                                            SCL, ANCL, PIPD
Haynsworth, Hugh C. Ancestry & descendants of Sarah Morse
   Haynsworth: A SC supplement to the histories of the Morse
   (Moss), Tomlinson, Welles, Curtis, and Shelton families of
   CT. Sumter: Osteen Publishing Co., 1939. 52 p.SCL,COKL, SMCL
Haynsworth, Hugh C. Haynsworth-Furman & allied families, in-
   cluding ancestry & descendants of Sarah Morse Haynsworth.
   Sumter: Osteen Publishing Co., 1942. 333 p.   COMMON
Hays, Louise F. The Rumph & Frederick families. Atlanta GA:
   author, 1942. 242 p.   SCL, ORCL
Hays, Mary S. & Carolyn E. Sowell. A history of the John Alex-
   ander & Laura Hilton Sowell family. Houston TX: authors,
   1973. 106 p.   SCL, KECA
Hearst Family [SpC]   GSGN
Heller, J. R. The Willson family of Pendleton Discrict, SC.
   Anderson Co: typescript, 1979. 8 p.   PIPD
Henagen, John C. The James Henagen family. Dillon: mimeo,
   1960. 10 p.   SCL, DIDU
Hendrix, Carolyn S. Fee family history. NP: typescript, nd.
   unp.   LNCL
Hendrix, Mrs. P.B. Genealogical sketches of the Shealy family.
   NP: NPub, 1941. 201 p.   LTSS
Henley, S. W. The Cash family of SC: a truthful account of the
   many crimes committed by the Carolina cavalier outlaws.
   Wadesboro: Intelligencer print, 1884. 64 p. SCL, YOCL, SCHS
Henning, Helen K. History of the Blount, Miller, Scarborough,
   Murrell, DuBose, Barnwell, Stuckey, Asbill families. Cola:
   typescript, 1937. 46 p.   SCL
Henson Family [SpC]   PIPD
Hepburn, Henry F. The Clayton family. Wilmington DL: Histori-
   cal Society of Delaware, 1904. 41 p.   SCHS
Herman, Louise B. The descendants of Michael McGee...and Ann
   Melvina Sims...including tombstone inscriptions [etc.] Bur-
   bank CA: author, 1968. 108 p.   ANCL
Heyward, Barnwell R. The descendants of Thomas, 1st Landgrave
   Smith. NP: typescript, nd. 3 vol.   SCHS
Heyward, Barnwell R. Genealogical chart. Barnwell of SC.
   Albany NY: NPub, 1898. 1 p.   CHLS, SCL, SCHS
Heyward, Barnwell R. Genealogical chart. Heyward of SC.
   Albany NY: NPub, 1896.   SCHS
Heyward, Barnwell Rhett. Morrison, Campbell, Percy, Hamilton,
   Fuller & Bard families. NP: NPub, nd. unp.   SCHS
Heyward family genealogy. NP: typescript, nd. 4 vol.   SCHS
Heyward, James B. The genealogy of the Pendarvis-Bedon families
   of SC. Atlanta GA: Foote & Davies, 1905. 221 p. SCL, SCHS
Heyward, James B. Heyward [family]. Charleston?: Mrs.May Hey-
   ward Weems, 1968. 174 p.   SCL, SCHS
Hewell, Eleanor M. The Pedens of America: an outline history of
   the ancestry & descendants of John Peden & Margaret McDill
   Peden: Scotland, Ireland, America. Greenville: Hiott Press,

1961. 654 p.   CLEM, SPCL
Hibben Family. Tenth reunion, 1945-54, of the descendants of
   Andrew Hibben...1954. NP: mimeo, 1954? 12 p.   SCHS
Hickes Family [SpC]   CRCL
Hicklin Family [SpC]. FACM
Hickman Family [SpC]   PIPD
Hiers, James L. The Hiers genealogy (Hyer, Kier, Hire, Hires,
   Hiers) and allied families: Platts, Rentz, Fender, Varn, Car-
   ter, Parker, Croft, Kinard & others). Cola: RLB, 1974.
   606 p.   COMMON
Hill Family [SpC]   FACM
Hill, George A. Hill & Hill-Moberly connections of Fairfield
   County, SC. Ponca City OK: author, 1961. 326 p. UNCL, FACM
                                                               SCL, LNCL
Hill, Joseph E. Colonel Patrick McGriff of Chester County, SC
   & Montgomery County, GA; his children & grandchildren & some
   others named McGriff. Leesburg FL: author, 1973. 66 p. SPCL
                                                                     SCL
Hillers, Kathleen C. Kissin' kin... Rutherford NJ: mimeo,
   1967. 174 p.   SCL, CLEM, PIPD
Hillhouse, Albert M. Pierre Gibert, French Huguenot; his back-
   ground & descendants. Danville KY: author, 1977. 398 p.
                                                               COMMON
Hillhouse, Helen T. The Hillhouse family, SC branch. NP:
   author, 1959. 75 p.   SCL,ANCL, SCHS
The Hills of Wilkes County, GA, & allied families. Daniels-
   ville GA: Heritage Papers, 1972. 345 p.   SMCL
Historical & biographical sketch of the Verner-Varner family.
   NP: mimeo, 196?. 5 p.   CLEM
History of the Jackson family in America.   LNCL
History of the Norris, Prince, Burt & Walker family. NP: NPub,
   1976? 40 p.   ANCL
History of William King, Jr. NP: News & Press, 1960. DHML, DACL
Hoch, J. Hampton. Hoch-High Family in the United States & Can-
   ada... NP: Hoch-High Family Reunion, 1962.   SCHS
Hodges, Alica A. Ancestry & descendants of John Woodson Amis of
   Granville County, NC, and Scott County, MS. Pendleton: author
   1978. 31 p.   SCL, CLEM
Hodges, Carolyn W. The Widener family & friends. Reseda CA:
   mimeo, 1978. 77 p.   FACM
Hodgson, Sara L. Our family history: Venables, Hugenots, Shep-
   person, Liddell, Hudson, Baugh, Bennett. NP: NPub, 1968.
   v.p.   PIPD
Hoffman, Laban M. Our kin, being a history of the Hoffman,
   Rhyne, Costner, Rudisill, Best, Hovis, Hoyle, Wills, Shetley,
   Jenkins, Holland, Hambright, Gaston, Withers, Cansler, Clem-
   mer & Lineberger families. 1915, rp Baltimore MD: Gateway
   Press, 1976. 585 p.   SCL, LNCL
Hoke, Rachel H. The Stowe family: descendants of William & Mary
   Stowe, from VA to NC, 1718-1976. Myrtle Beach?: author, 1977.
   227 p.   SCL

Holcomb, Brent H. The Bedenbaugh-Betenbaugh family of SC.
   Easley: SHP, 1978. 67 p.   SCHS, SCL, LXMU
Holcomb, Brent H. Young family. NP: author, 1971. 75 p. LRCL
Holden, Pauline K. Information about the Bearden family of Oco-
   nee County, SC... Clemson: typescript, 1957. 9 p.   CLEM
Holladay, Elizabeth D. Dinwiddie family records, with especial
   attention to the line of William Walthall Dinwiddie, 1804-
   1882. Charlottesville VA: King Lindsay Printing Corp., 1957.
   191 p.   CLEM
Holland Family [SpC]   PIPD
Hollingsworth, Julia A. Descendants of Valentine Hollingsworth.
   Atlanta GA: Peachtree Printing Co., 1976. 211 p.   SCHS
Hollingsworth, Leon S. A history of the origin & development of
   our family in America, & a genealogy of the descendants of
   John Hunter, II. Decatur GA: NPub, 1962. 176 p.   SCL, LRCL
Hollingsworth, William B. & J. Adger Stewart. Descendants of
   Valentine Hollingsworth, Sr. Louisville KY: John P. Morton
   Co. 208 p.   SCL, UNCL
Hollingsworth, William B. Hollingsworth genealogical memoranda
   in the United States, from 1682 to 1884. Baltimore: NPub,
   1884. 144 p.   SCHS
Hollis Family [SpC]   FACM
Hood, Belle M. Genealogy of Dr. Allen Spivey & Mary Essie Col-
   lins. Myrtle Beach: author, 1980. 23 p.   HOCL
Hook, James W. Captain James Hook of Greene County, PA. Ann
   Arbor MI: privately printed, 1952. 164 p.   SCL, SCHS
Hooker, Flora J. John Hick Hamer: his antecedents, descendants
   & collateral families, 1765-1842. Spartanburg: Williams
   Printing Co., 1949. 350 p.   SCHS, DICL
Hooker, Flora J. & Louis Farrell. The Robersonian McCallums &
   collateral families. Spartanburg: Williams Printing Co.,
   1946. 234 p.   PRIV
Hope, Willie C. The truth about the McDonalds - historical.
   Charlotte NC: Herb Eaton, 1977. 164 p. SCL, ANCL, PIPD, CLEM
Hopkins, Laura J. Lower Richland planters: Hopkins, Adams,
   Weston, & related families of SC. Cola: RLB, 1976. 288 p.
                                                           COMMON
Hoppin, Charles A. The Washington ancestry, and records of the
   McClain, Johnson, & forty other colonial families... Green-
   field OH: privately printed, 1932. 3 vol.   SCHS
Hord, Arnold H. The Hord family of VA...a supplement. NP:
   privately printed, 1915. 119 p.   SCHS
Horlacher, Levi J. & Vaneta T. Horlacher. Family of Hans Mi-
   chael & Maria Veronica Horlacher. Lexington KY: authors,
   1968. 326 p.   SCL, CLEM
Horne Family [SpC]   CRCL
Houser, John. A genealogical sketch of the descendants of
   Andrew & Anna Christina (Palmer) Cook, 1769-1970. Printed in
   Canada: NPub, 197? 581 p.   SCHS
Houston-Donnald lines [SpC]   GSGN
Houston, Florence A. Maxwell history & genealogy, including the

allied families of Alexander, Allen, Bachiler, Batterton, Beveridge, Blaine, Brewster, Brown, Callender, Campbell, Carey, Clark, Cowan, Fox, Dinwiddie, Dunn, Eylar, Garretson, Gentry, Guthrie, Houston, Howard, Howe, Hughes, Hussey, Irvine, Johnson, Kimes, McCullough, Moore, Pemberton, Rosenmüller, Smith, Stapp, Teter, Tilford, Uzzell, Vawter, Ver Planck, Walker, Wiley, Wilson...also baptismal record of the Rev. John Craig, D.D., of Augusta County, VA, 1740-1749... Indianapolis IN: C.E. Pauley & Co., 1916. 642 p.   CLEM

Howard, Cecil Hampden. Genealogy of the Cutts family. Albany NY: Joel Munsell's sons, 1892. 658 p.   SCHS

Howard, John W. Record of Hogg & Howard families of St. Luke's Parish, Beaufort District, SC. NP: typescript, 1943. 15 p.
                                                                    SCHS

Howard, Nell H. & Bessie W. Quinn. Moragnes in America, & related families: Williams, Quarles, Read, Whorton, Forney, Abernathy, Young, Hughes, Hodges, Hillsman, Mynatt, Burns & Dobbins. Birmingham AL: Banner Press, 1971. 522 p. SCL, GWPL

Howard, Thomas D. Charles Howard family domestic history. Cambridge MS: author, 1956. 278 p.   SCL, BUCL

Howell, George R. Biographical sketch of Joel Munsell...to which is appended a genealogy of the Munsell family. Boston: New England Historic & Genealogical Society, 1880. 16 p. SCHS

Howell, William E. The Wayne family of South Carolina. NP: NPub, nd. 170 p.   MACL

Hubert, Sarah D. Genealogy of part of the Cody & Womack families of America. Atlanta GA: Franklin, 1902. 23 p.   ANCL

Hucks, Joseph H. As I knew them: Hucks & Hendrick [families]. NP: author, 197? 82 p.   HOCL, MRCL

Hudgens, Eugene S. The Simpson genealogy of two distinct families of Simpsons who married & emigrated from County Antrim, Ireland, & settled in Laurens County, SC, between 1770 and 1790. 2nd ed. NP: author, 1958. 49 p.   LRCL

Hudson, Joshua H. Genealogy of the Hudson family of Amherst County VA, and of Chester & York, SC, & autobiography of Joshua Hilary Hudson. NP: NPub, 1898? 19 p.   SCL, SCHS

Hudson, Thomas C., Jr. Charlton ancestry. Hopeville GA: author, 1978. 66 p.   KECA

Huey Family Records [SpC]   LNCL

Huey, Olga C. Huey family records. Cola: mimeo, 1970. 30 p.
                                                            SCL, YOCL

Huey, Olga C. Index of the family of Edward & Ann Snead Crosland, 1740-1957. Bennettsville: Marlboro Herald-Advocate, 1967. 37 p.   SCL

Huey, V. H. Huey family history. Birmingham AL? Birmingham Publishing Co., 1963-68. 2 vols.   LNCL

Huggin Family [SpC]   CRCL

Huidekoper, Frederic L. The American ancestry of Frederic Louis Huidekoper & Reginald Shippen Huidekoper of Washington DC... Geneva, Switzerland: A. Kundig, 1931. 62 p.
                                                            SCL, SCHS

Humbert, John B. History of the Giroud-Humbert families, 1630-
   1956. NP: author, 1957. 33 p.   LRCL
Humphreys, Peggy F. The Frink family in America...compiled from
   the records of Henry Farnsworth Frink & Wilbur Gustavus Frink.
   Ann Arbor MI: Edwards Bros., 1971. 41 p.   SCL
Humphries, John D. Descendants of Charles Humphries of VA,
   Nathaniel Pope of VA, Reuben Brock I of Ireland & Aaron Parker
   of VA. Atlanta GA: NPub, 1938. 63 p.   SCHS
Humphries, John D. Descendants of John Thurman of VA, William
   Graves of VA, & James Jones of SC. Atlanta GA: author, 1938.
   81 p.   SCHS
Hunt Family [SpC]   PIPD
Hunter, Billie G. Great old soldiers' sons [incl. Benjamin Goss
   family]. NP: NPub, 1977?   SCL
Hunter Family [SpC]   PIPD
Hunter, Gaillard. Copy of genealogical chart of the descend-
   ants of Pierre Gaillard & his wife Clermond LeClair...
   Pendleton: author, 1958. 1 p.   CLEM
Hutchins, James A. Descendants of William B. & Martha Scruggs
   Guill. NP: mimeo.   DIDU
Hutchinson, F. M. Hutchinson family of Laurens County, SC...
   1947. 263 p.   DEALER
Hutto, Edgar. Isaac (Otto) Hutto: from the German Rhine to the
   Edisto in Carolina. St. George: author, 1962. SCL, DOCL ORCL
Hutto, Edgar. Whence came Hans (In Aebnit) Inabnit & your
   Swiss kin. St. George: author, 1962. unp. SCL, DOCL, SCHS
The Hyatt family in Chester County, SC. NP: typescript, nd.
   20 p.   YOCL
Hydrick, Onan A. The descendants of Jacob Haysmith Hydrick
   (1819-1903) and his two wives, Margaret Jemima Hildebrand
   (1819-1877) and Mary Cornelia Pou (1862-1917), & the descend-
   ants of each... Cola: RLB, 1978. 134 p.   ORCL, CLEM
Isbell Family [SpC]   PIPD
Ivy, Emma P. As I find it...Butler...a partially documented
   history of some of the Butlers, early 1700's to 1968, includ-
   ing a few allied or related families. Atlanta GA: Peachtree
   Letter Service, 1968. 194 p.   SCL, EDTO, SMCL
Ivy, Emma P. Ten thousand Plunketts: a partially documented
   record of the families of Charles Plunkett of Newberry County
   SC; and his brother Peter Plunkett of old Barnwell District,
   SC... Atlanta GA: Peachtree Printing Co., 1970.   SCL, EDTO
Jackson, Ruth D. History of a Dunlap family: including addit-
   ions & corrections to "History of a Dunlap Family", by Evelyn
   Dunlap Potts. Greenville: author, 1966. 32 p. Also Rock
   Hill: typescript, 1977. 5 p.   YOCL
Jacob, Nancy V. Bradford Roots & Branches. NP: PBS Graphic
   Arts & Printing, 1975. 149 p.   SCL, LNCL, KECA
Jacobs, Thornwell. My people. Clinton: author, nd. SCL, LRCL
James, Kenneth M. James family of Wales, Ireland, and the Kings
   Tree, Williamsburg District, SC. NP: mimeo, 1968. 15 p. GWPL
Jaynes, Willard G. Jaynes family. NP: typescript, 1974. SPCL

Jeffcoat, Vera D. Seed of Jacob: a history & genealogy of the
  Jacob Jeffcoat family. Cola: Wentworth Printing Co., 1975.
  269 p.   SCL, LXMU, ORCL
Jeffers, William H. The Butler-Brooks line...of the John
  Morgan Timmons family. Florence: mimeo, 1967. 5 p.   GWPL
Jeffrey, Christine C. The Cannon clan. Lexington VA: Rock-
  bridge Printong Co., 1952. 28 p.   COKL
Johnson, Catherine B. Boyd family history: Archibald Boyd of
  PA & SC, 1758-1802, & related families: Young, Fair, Jones,
  Crow, Dickson, Goss. Roanoke AL: Yarborough Commercial Print-
  ing, 1979. 105 p.   SCL, NWRL
Johnson, Charles O. The genealogy of several allied families:
  Frazer, Owen, Bessellieu, Carter, Shaw, Wright, Landfair,
  Briggs, Neill, Tidwell, Johnson & others. New Orleans LA:
  Pelican Publishing Co., 1961. 543 p.   SCL, UNCL
Johnson, Evalyn P. The family of Wilkins. Marion: Marion
  Star, 1937. 88 p.   MACL
Johnson, Falba L. Ancestors & descendants of Chancellor William
  L. Dalrymple Johnson & his wife Sarah Elizabeth McCall. Cola:
  RLB, 1979. 328 p.   SCL, SMCL, MACL
Johnson Family of Laurens County, 1735-1970 [SpC]   LRCL
Johnson, Robert B. Genealogy of the McWillie & Cunningham fami-
  lies. Cola: RLB, 1938. 219 p.   COMMON
Johnston, Coy K. William Johnston of Isle of Wight County, VA,
  & his descendants, 1648-1964. West Hartford CT: author, 1965.
  376 p.   SCL, SCHS
Johnston, Edith Duncan. The Campbells came: a chronicle. NP:
  typescript, nd. 2 vol.   SCHS
Johnston, Henry P. Little acorns from the mighty oak [incl.
  Poellnitz, Rembert, Carter, & Rogers families]. Birmingham
  AL: Featon Press, 1962. 357 p.   COMMON
Johnston, Henry P. Pioneers in their own rights [incl. White,
  Cunningham, Morgan, Phillips, Simms, Doroh families]. Birm-
  ingham AL: Vulcan, 1964. 638 p.   SCL, SCHS, GTML
Johnstone, James D. Johnstones: the Annandale peerage case.
  NP: NPub, 1978.   SCHS
Johnstone, William C. The Johnston(e)s of coastal Carolina.
  Princeton KY: Lakewood Printers, 1971. 66 p. SCL, SCHS, FLMC
Jolly Family [SpC]   CRCL
Jones, Allen & Jane Clarke. Porcher family & other related
  lines. NP: NPub, nd.   SCHS
Jones, Cadwaller. A genealogical history of the Jones family.
  Cola: RLB, 1900. 78 p.   SCL, CHLS, YOCL
Jones Family [SpC]   FACM
Jones, Genevieve B. Children, meet your ancestors [incl. Ander-
  son, Smith, Exum, Motte, Summers, Broome families]. West
  Point GA: Broome, 1976. 274 p.   SCL
Jones, Hazel P. Descendants of James Boyd Magill, emigrant from
  Ireland to Chester Cove, SC, in 1823. Clinton: Jacobs Bros.,
  1963. 195 p.   SCL, SCHS, YOCL, KECL
Jones, Hazel P. The history of the Samuel Jones family, Kershaw

County, SC, 1756-1960... Kershaw: author, 1961.   SCL, YOCL
                                                         SCHS
Jones, Hazel P. Book two of the Samuel Jones family, Kershaw
  County, SC, 1756-1979... Clinton: Jacobs Bros., 1979. 396 p.
                                                 SCL, KECA, LNCL
Jones, Hazel P. Nathaniel Parker & his descendants... NP:
  Vogue Press, 1966. 128 p.   SCL, KECL
Jones, Mary E. History of Jeremiah Jones of Orangeburg District
  SC & his antecedants & descendants. Cola: RLB, 1967. 283 p.
                                             SCL, ORCL, DOCL
Jordan Family [SpC]   FACM
Jordan, Hattie. Family record of descendants of Frederic Red-
  wine & Barbara Stoner. Canon GA: NPub, 1938. 36 p.   LRCL
Joseph Edwards Rhoades Family Association. Genealogy. Darling-
  ton: author, 1955. 99 p.   DHML
Kauffman, Charles F. A genealogy & history of the Kauffman-
  Coffman families of North America, 1584 to 1937; including...
  allied families in Lancaster & York Counties of PA... Becker,
  Baer, Correll, Erisman, Fahs, Kuntz, Kneisley, Hershey, Hie-
  stand, Myers, Musselman, Neff, Martin, Ruby, Snavely, Shenk,
  Shirk, Sprenkle, Witmer & others. York PA: author, 1940.
  775 p.   SCL, CLEM, LXMU
[Kay Family] The family of Richard Butler Kay & Florence E.
  Wright, 1876-1976. [Belton, SC: V.Kay, 1976]   SCL, ANCL
Keen, Gregory B. The descendants of Jöran Kyn of New Sweden.
  Philadelphia PA: Swedish Colonial Society, 1913. 318 p. SCHS
Keese Family [SpC]   PIPD
Keith, Clayton. History of the Jackson family in America. NP:
  NPub, nd. 52 p.   LNCL
Kellam, Ida B. Brooks & kindred families. Wilmington NC:
  NPub, 1950. 384 p.   SCL, CLEM
Keller-Comer Family [SpC]   GSGN
Kelly, Margaret M. The Ricaud family, 1640-1976. Baltimore MD:
  Gateway Press, 1976. 115 p.   COMMON
Kelsey, Mavis P. & others. Benjamin Parrott, c. 1795-1839, &
  Lewis Stover, 1781-1850/60, of Overton County, TN, & their
  descendants. Houston TX: author, 1979. 133 p.   SCL, PIPD
Kelsey, Mavis P. & Mary W. Kelsey. The family of John Massie,
  1743-c. 1830, revolutionary patriot of Louisa County, VA...
  Houston TX: author, 1949. 241 p.   PIPD
Kenan, Robert G. History of the Gignilliat family of Switzer-
  land & SC. Easley: SHP, 1977. 285 p.   COMMON
Kennedy, Gayle M. My Kennedy ancestors of Fairfield County, SC.
  Spartanburg: author, 1969. 77 p.   SCL, SPCL, FACM
Kennedy, John T. The Funchess family: a brief record of the
  Funchess family of Orangeburg County, SC. Cola: NPub, 1962.
  48 p.   SCL, ORCL
Kennedy, John T. The Kennedy family: a brief record of the Ken-
  nedy family of Lenoir & Wayne Counties, NC. Cola: author,
  1963. 97 p.   SCL, ORCL
Kershaw, Peter G. A Kershaw family, 1670-1970. Port Charlotte

FL: author, 1974. 128 p.   SCL, NABL, KECA
Ketchen, Jane G. Ancestry & descendants of Sarah Ida Jackson
  Kitchens of Chester County, SC. Cola: privately printed,
  1967. 65 p.   SCL, YOCL, GWPL
Keys Family [SpC]   PIPD
Kiebling, Hermann. Patrick aus Trarbach an der Mosel. NP:
  Bergisch-Markischer Genealogisher, 1971. 74 p.   SCL, SCHS
Kilgore, Daniel E. The ancestors & descendants of William Rap-
  pleye Cole. Clarkwood TX: NPub, 1956. 31 p.   SCL
Kincaid Family [SpC]   FACM
King descendants. History of William King, Jr. Darlington:
  News & Press, 1960. 148 p.   SCL, DACL, DHML
King, Elbert A., Sr. The descendants of Jean Jacques LeRoy
  (John Jacob King) and Cannon & Pennington connections. NP:
  typescript, nd. 149 p.   NWRL
King, W. A. "Grandfather" Robert King, 1750(56)-1826 [King
  family]. Anderson: J. Mack King, 1937. 7 p.   SCL, CLEM
King, Willis A & Mrs. Henry K. Lowe. History of Robert King
  family of Anderson County, SC., 1772-1900. Clemson: authors,
  1978. 44 p.   PIPD
King, Willis A. Josiah King, Jr., family of Anderson County,
  SC. Clemson: author, 1979. 41 p.   PIPD, ANCL
Kip, Bishop. Historical notes of the family of Kip of Kipsburg
  & Kip's Bay, NY. Albany NY: Munsell, 1871. 49 p.   SCHS
Kip, Frederic E. History of the Kip family in America... Mont-
  clair NJ: privately printed, 1928. 440 p.   SCHS
Kirkland Family [SpC]   FACM
Kirkland, J. T. Richard Kirkland & his descendants. Jackson-
  ville FL: author, nd. 134 p.   EDTO
Kirksey, Sadie C. Graig family history. Pickens: author,
  1973? 258 p.   COMMON
[Kitchell Family] Lineal ancestors of Susan (Kitchell) Mulford,
  mother of Mrs. Susan (Mulford) Cory... NP: privately printed,
  1937. 2 vol.   SCHS
Knight, Edwin R. The Knight family of Cheraw, SC. Cheraw:
  Ted Morris, 1976. 35 p.   SCL SCHS, FLMC
Knox, John B. The Ballenger family of Oconee County, SC.
  Seneca: G. W. Ballenger, 1956. 32 p.   CLEM
Kohner, Bessie. Jay family index...from the workbook of Cassius
  Milton Jay, 1886-1953. NP: Jay Family Assoc., 1963. 111 p.
                                                         SCL SCHS
Kyles, Carolyne S. The Shooter family of Marion County, SC,
  1760-1973. Charlotte NC: author, 1974. 60 p.   SCHS, MACL
Laboon, Margaret E. Laboon (1720-1958), Foster (1770-1958);
  family history-genealogy. Athens GA: NPub, 1958.   SCL, SCHS
Lachicotte, Henry A. Genealogy of the Rossignol-Lachicotte
  family... NP: Julian W. Frier, 1950. 104 p.   SCHS
Ladd Family [SpC]   FACM
Lamb, Bessie P. Genealogical history of the Poole, Langston, &
  Mason families ...of upper SC. Enoree: author, 1931. 251 p.
                                                   SCL, SPCL, LRCL

Lamont, Corliss. The Thomas Lamonts in America. NP: A.S.
Barnes & Co., 1962. 255 p. SCL, SCHS, GNCL, FACM
Landers, Erma P. Poston family of SC. Atlanta GA: mimeo, 1965.
100 p. SCL, SCHS
Landers, John P. Poingdestre-Poindexter: a Norman family
through the ages, 1250-1977. Houston,TX: R.D. Poindexter,
1975. 199 p. SCL, CLEM
Lane, Mrs. Julian C. Key & allied families. Statesboro GA:
author, 1931. 495 p. SCL, SMCL
Lanford, Helen W. "Miss Minnie" [Westmoreland family]. Green-
ville: author, 1970. 144 p. SCL, SPCL, GRCL
Langley, Emimae P. The DuPre Trail... NP: NPub, 1965-66.
2 vol. SCL, SCHS
Lanphere, Edward E. Bates: descendants of Bates ancestors who
lived in VA. Chapel Hill NC: typescript, 1973. 104 p. SCHS
Lapham, Samuel. The Lapham family of Medford, MA, & Charleston
SC. SCHS
Latta, F. F. The Lord's vineyard, including the life of E. C.
Latta, 1831-1909. Shafter CA: mimeo, 1940. 91 p. LNCL
Lauderdale Family [SpC] FACM
Law, John A. Adger-Law ancestral notebook. Spartanburg: NPub,
1936. 159 p. COMMON
Law, Rosanna S. Diary of Rosanna Law, January 1 - November 5,
1853, Greenwood SC. Greenwood: Greenwood County Historical
Society, 1963. 64 p. SCL, GWPL, NWRL
Lawrence Family [SpC] PIPD
Lawton, Edward P. A saga of the south [Lawton family]. Ft.
Myers Beach FL: Island Press, 1966. SCL, SCHS, GTML, CHLS
Leach, Josiah G. Chronicles of the Yerkes family; with notes on
the Leech & Rutter families. Philadelphia: Lippincott, 1904.
261 p. SCHS
Leach, Josiah G. Genealogical & biographical memorials of the
Reading, Howell, Yerkes, Watts, Latham & Elkins families.
Philadelphia: Lippincott, 1898. 285 p. SCHS
Leach, Josiah G. Memoranda relating to the ancestry & family of
Hon. Levi Parsons Morton, Vice-President of the United States,
1889-1893. Cambridge MA: Riverside Press, 1894. 191 p. SCHS
Leach, M. Atherton. Some account of the Draytons of SC & Phila-
delphia. Lancaster ??: Wickersham Press, 1921. 26 p. SCHS
Lee Family [SpC] FACM, CRCL
Lee, Henry. History of the Campbell family. Chstn: Garnier &
Co., 1968. 156 p. SCL
Lee, Janice G. Keisler descendants of Lexington County, SC.
West Columbia: author, 1980. 127 p. SCL, LXMU, LXCL, SCHS
Lee, John G. Family reunion: an incomplete account of the Maxim
& Lee family history. NP: privately printed, 1971. 421 p.
SCHS
Lee, Lucy Chaplin. An American sojourn in China. Family memo-
ries. Annandale VA: Turnpike Press, 1968. 59 p. SCHS
Lefvendahl, Georgie I. The Inabnit family of SC [incl. Inabnet,
Inabinet, Inabinett families]. NP: author, 1970. 147 p.

[Lefvendahl, Georgie I., continued]   SCL, FLCL, ORCL, MACL
Lefvendahl, Georgie A. Lefvendahl, Smoak, & related family records. Orangeburg: author, 1966. 74 p.   SCL, ORCL, DOCL
Lefvendahl, Georgie A. Oliver-Sistrunk families: Orangeburg
  area, SC. Orangeburg: author, 1964. 73 p.   SCL, SCHS, ORCL
[LeGette Family] History: Legette-Wood family. NP: typescript.
                                                             SCHS
Leland, Sherman. The Leland magazine: or, a genealogical record
  of Henry Leland & his descendants...from 1653 to 1850. Boston MA: Wier & White, 1850. 278 p.   CLEM
L'Engle, Susan. Notes of my family & recollections of my early
  life... NY: Knickerbocker Press, 1888. 67 p.   SCL
Lenoir, Kate. The Whitakers & related family lines [inc. Ches-
  nut, Clarke, McRae, Goodwyn, English, Lenoir, & Dinkins fami-
  lies]. NP: author, 1965. 22 p.   KECA
Lentz, Azalee M. Records & history of descendants of James Mc-
  Knight Morrow. NP: NPub, nd. 25 p.   LNCL
Lesley, Agnes B. Bolding family: Jonathan Lee Bolding, 1806-
  1879, a pioneer citizen of the Pea Ridge section of Pickens
  County, SC... Pickens: Sentinel Press, nd. 80 p.   ANCL
                                                    SCL, PICL
Lesslie (Lessly) Family since 1750 [SpC]   YOCL
Lewis Family [SpCl]   PIPD
Lewis Family, [of] Lewis Turnout, Chester County, SC. Chester,
  1976. 13 p.   YOCL
Lewis, Fred H. Descendants of Olin & Viola Turner Lewis. NP:
  typescript, 1976. 6 p.   SCL, HOCL
Lewis, Mary S. Stoddard-Sudduth papers [incl. Gay, Power, Dial,
  Owen, Armstrong & Robertson families]. NP: NPub, 1961?
  281 p.   CRCL
Lewis, William T. Genealogy of the Lewis Family. NP: Courier-
  Journal Printing Co., 1893.   SCL, DIDU
Lidwin, Virginia P. Hicks, Pegues & related families from rec-
  ords in SC, NC, GA & MS. NP: mimeo, c.1960. 152 p. SCL, SCHS
Ligon, William D., Jr. The Ligon family & connections. Hart-
  ford CT: Bond Press, 1947. 2 vols.   SCL, CSCL
Ligon, William D., Jr. Proceedings, in two sections. NY: The
  Ligon Family & Kinsmen, 1937-39. 2 vol.   SCHS
A Limb from John Martin Hook, I (1755-1820). Lexington: NPub,
  1970. 5 p.   LXMU
Linder, Billy Royce. John Lewis Linder of SC, GA, & MS, 1765-
  1843. Vienna VA: typescript, 1975. 13 p.   SCL, SCHS
Lindsay, Elizabeth & Sue D. McLeod. The Duffies & related fami-
  lies. Chester: mimeo, 1968. 54 p.   SCL, CSCL
Lindsay, E. J. History of the Lindsay family. Milwaukee WI:
  NPub, 1925. 292 p.   SCHS
Lipscomb, James W. Lipscomb genealogy: Joel Lipscomb's descend-
  ants. Gaffney: DeCamp Publishing Co., 1959.   SCL, CRCL, SPCL
Littlejohn, James C. Ten generations of Littlejohns. Clemson:
  mimeo, 1951. unp.   CLEM
Livingston, Hazel M. West, Harvey, Smith & allied families.

Sylvania GA: author, 1959. 198 p. ORCL
Livingston, Lucius W. Historical & genealogical record of John
Livingston the first of Orangeburg County, SC. Orangeburg:
Walter D. Berry, 1940. 91 p. SCHS, MRCL, ORCL
Lloyd, Emma R. Clasping hands with generations past [Rouse,
Zimmerman, Tanner, Henderson, Porter & McClure families].
Cincinatti OH: privately printed, 1932. 228 p. SCHS
Locker, Ora B. McGregor genealogy. Paducah KY: author, 1962.
130 p. SCL, SPCL
Lockey, Iris M. Ancestors of our Maples & Adams families [incl.
Baguley, Budd, Catlett, Davis, Deone, Dye, Fowles, Gordon,
Graves, Hopkins, Knight, Mackmetion, Maris, Musgrove, Newman,
Proctor, Reynolds, Rudd, Simcock, Spearman, Tate, Worthington,
Wright families]. NP: typescript, 1974. 42 p. NWRL
Lodge, William J. A record of the descendants of Robert &
Elizabeth Lodge, English Quakers, 1682-1903. Geneva ??:
W.F. Humphrey Press, 1942. 150 p. SCHS
Logan, George W. A record of the Logan family of Charleston,
SC. 2nd ed., with biographical additions. Cincinnati, OH:
NPub, 1923. 70 p. SCL, SCHS
Loggins, Vernon. The Hawthornes/Hathornes... NY: Columbia
University Press, 1951. 365 p. CLEM
Logsdon, Mattie L. My Mothershead family. Ada OK: NPub, 1975.
184 p. LNCL
London, Hoyt H. A genealogical history of one branch of the
London family in America. Ancestors & descendants of Charles
Marion Henry London. Columbia MO: University of Missouri
Press, 1957. 52 p. SCHS
Long, Eugene W. A genealogical record of the John Jacob Long
family beginning with his landing in America about 1750.
Cola: author, 1970. 211 p. LXMU, NWRL
Long, Marilyn L. The Jordan book. Richmond KY: typescript,
1970. 54 p. HOCL
Love, Albert G. Our ancestors: the Love family of Trezevant
Carrol County, TN. Washington DC: author, 1953. 129 p. LNCL
Loveless, Richard W. Two hundred American ancestors: the pro-
genitors of Richard William Loveless. Oshkosh WI: Oshkosh
Press, 1968. 48 p. SCHS
Lucas, Silas E. The Dodson-Dotson family of VA, TN, OH, KY,
SC, NC, GA, AL, & the west. Easley: SHP, 1980. 500 p. SCHS
Lucas, Silas E. Supplement to the history of the Dodson-Dotson
family of southwest VA...with misc. deeds concerning the for-
bears of Sara Pyles Dodson, and a short history of the...Mad-
dux family of VA, MD, GA & AL. Swainsboro GA: Forest Blade
Publishing Co., 1966. 113 p; also Easley: SHP, 1965. 125 p.
GWPL, SCHS
Lucas, Silas E. Genealogy of the Dodson/Dotson, Lucas, Pyles,
Rochester & allied families. 1959, rp Easley: SHP, 1980.
959 p. SCL, SCHS, LRCL
Lucas, Silas E. Powell family of Norfolk and Elizabeth City
Counties, VA... NP: author, 1961. 305 p. SCL, LRCL

Lucas, Silas E. History of the Powell families of VA & the
south, an encyclopedia. 1969, rp Easley: SHP, 1977. 604 p.
SCL, SCHS
Luce, Robert F. Notes on the Earnest family...SC & nearby
states. NP: NPub, 1963.   SCHS
Lupo, Flora M. The Fords of the Pee Dee. Dillon: author, 1950?
7 p.   SCHS, FLMC, DIDU
Lyle, Jennie B. A brief history of the Fee family... Chester:
Lantern Printing Co., 1901. 55 p.   CSCL
Lyle, Jennie B. William & Barbara Moffatt. Little Rock AR:
typescript, 1959. 127 p.   CSCL
Lynch, Alma & Elizabeth Ellison. Echoes; Oolenoy-Pumpkintown,
1745-1980. Easley: Pace Printing Co., 1980. 206 p. SCL, PICL
MacDowell, Dorothy K. Descendants of William Capers & Richard
Capers & related families. Cola: RLB, 1973. 134 p. SCL, SCHS
MacDowell, Dorothy K. Descendants of William Capers & Richard
Capers...supplement I. Aiken: author, 1979. 91 p. SCL, SCHS
MacDowell, Dorothy K. DuBose genealogy. Descendants of Isaac
DuBose & wife Susanne Couillandeau, who settled on the Santee
river...about 1689. Cola: RLB, 1972. 533 p.   COMMON
MacDowell, Dorothy K. DuBose genealogy. Supplement I. Aiken:
author, 1975. 197 p.   SCL, SCHS, PIPD
MacDowell, Dorothy K. DuBose genealogy. Supplement II. Aiken:
author, 1980. 262 p.   SCL, SCHS
MacDowell, Dorothy K. Gaillard genealogy: descendants of
Joachim Gaillard & Esther Paparel Gaillard, 1625-1974. Cola:
RLB, 1974. 373 p.   COMMON
MacDowell, Dorothy K. Gaillard genealogy. Supplement I. Aiken
author, 1980. 100 p.   SCL, SCHS
MacElyea, Annabella B. The MacQueens of Queensdale. Charlotte
NC: Observer Printing House, 1916. 261 p.   DIDU
MacGregor, Amelia G. History of the clan Gregor. Edinburgh,
Scotland: Brown, 1898-1901. 2 vol.   SCHS
MacIvor, Hazel A. Edward family of SC... NP: NPub, nd. 73 p.
SPCL
MacIvor, Hazel A. Some ancestors & descendants of Benjamin Ar-
nold, of King William County, VA, & Greenville County, SC.
Lake Orion MI: Arnold Family Assn. of the South, 1974. 165 p.
COMMON
MacLaren, Margaret. The MacLarens: a history of Clan Labhran.
Stirling, Scotland: McKay, 1960. 147 p.   MRCL
MacMillan, Somerled. The clan MacMillan magazine of North Amer-
ica...   SCHS
MacMillan, Somerled. The emigration of Lochaber MacMilans to
Canada in 1802. Paisley, Renfrewshire, Scotland: NPub, 1958.
13 p.   SCHS
MacMillan, Somerled. Families of Knapdale...being a compendium
of information on the MacMillans... Ipswich MA: NPub, 1960.
68 p.   SCHS
McAllister, Annabelle. Brasfield-Brassfield genealogies. Cran-
ford NJ: author, 1959. 720 p.   SCL

McAlister, Frank D. Notes on the family of Alexander McAlister
of Pendleton, SC. Conway AR: Educators Consulting Service,
1979. 46 p. PIPD
McAllister, D. S. Genealogical record of the descendants of
Col. Alexander McAllister of Cumberland County, NC, & of Mary
& Isabella McAllister. Richmond VA: Whitter & Shepperson,
1900. 244 p. SCHS
McAllister, James G. Family records, compiled for the descend-
ants of Abraham Addams McAllister & his wife Julie Ellen
(Stratton) McAllister, of Covington VA... Easton PA: Press of
the Chemical Publishing Co., 1912. 88 p. CLEM
McBee Family [SpC] CRCL
McBride, Sarah C. History & genealogy of the Livingston family,
1068-1900. Jenkinsville: typescript, 1947. 27 p. FACM
McCaa, John. Dr. John McCaa of Camden, SC, 1793-1859; his de-
scendants [incl. Whitaker family]. Anniston AL: author, 1975.
267 p. SCL, CHLS, SCHS, FLMC
McCain, William D. Eight generations of the family of Henry Fox
(1768-1852) & his wife Sarah Harrell (1772-1848), of SC, TN,
AL & MS. 2 vol. 1975. DEALER
McCalla Family [SpC] YOWC
[McCann family] Ancestors & descendants of John J. Jones, who
married Mary Ellen Swartswelder (a McCann). Paris, KY: NPub,
1956. 19 p. SCHS
[McCann family] Ancestral lineage, Mildred Olive Bates McCann.
Hopewell, VA: Doutt's Printing, 1964. 32 p. SCL, SCHS
[McCann family] Family of Eliza R. McCann who married Lytle
Griffing. Hopewell, VA: Doutt's Printing SCL, CLEM, SCHS
[McCann family] Family of Wesley D. McCann, Bourbon County, KY.
NP: NPub, 1962. 12 p. SCL, CLEM, SCHS
[McCann family] Some descendants of John Keand of Whithorn,
Scotland, many of whom lived & died in Paris, Bourbon County,
KY, and were known as McCanns. Typescript, 1955. SCL, CLEM, SCHS
McCants, Elliott C. Family papers. I: Concerning myself; II:
McCants family history; III: My mother's family (Poole); IV:
Data on the Gilliam family; V: Descent of the Moore children;
VI: The Lipscomb family. Chapel Hill NC: typescript, 1954.
19 p. GWPL
McCarty, Louise M. Footprints: the story of the Greggs of SC.
Winter Park FL: Orange Press, 1951. 282 p. SCL, FLCL, FLMC
McCary, Ben C. McCary & several allied families [incl. Pace,
Wilson, White, King & Parrish families]. Richmond VA: Tide-
water Press, 1972. 142 p. EDTO
McCaslan, Ann A. Walker-McCaslan families. Greenwood: mimeo,
1959? 55 p. GWPL
McColl, Helen S. & Lila S. McColl. Genealogy of the ancestors &
descendants of John Thomas McColl & other McColls. NP: type-
script, 1966. 101 p. MRCL
McConnell, Richard B. Ancestral peregrinations [Bohun family].
Houston TX: C.S. Fleetwood, 1979. 55 p. SCL, CLEM
McConnell, Richard B. A genealogical chart of some of the de-

scendants of Colonel George Logan of Charles Towne, SC, & of
his wife, Frances Logan. NP: NPub, nd. unp.   SCHS
McConnell, Richard B. Glover cousins: a chart index of some of
the descendants of Colonel Joseph Glover (1719-1783) & Anne
Wilson Doughty (1730-1807). 1965. 88 p.   SCHS, ORCL, SCL
McConnell, Richard. Logan cousins [incl. Chalmers, Gantt, Per-
ry & Kennedy families]. NP: typescript, nd.   SCHS
McConnell, Richard. McConnell cousins. A chart index of some
of the descendants of Alexander Elbrige McConnell...& his wife
Margaret Neilson. NP: typescript, nd.   SCHS
McCormick, Colin D. Our clan of McCormicks, with supplement.
Laurin NC: McCormick Clan, 1972. 163 p. SCL, DICL, DIDU, MRCL
McCormick, Sarah G. Forbears & descendants of Reuben Henry
Tison & Rebekah Mary Jane McKensie... NP: privately printed,
1967. 75 p.   SCHS
McCrady, Louis D. & Mary DeB. Barnwell. Mrs. Edward McCrady, II
& her DeBerniere family papers. Charleston: typescript, 1960.
134 p.   SCHS
McCrary Family [SpC]   PIPD
McCreight Family [SpC]   FACM
McCullough, Rose C. Yesterday when it is past [incl. Chambers &
Goode families]. Richmond VA: William Byrd Press, 1957.
403 p.   CLEM
McCutchen, Elizabeth C. The genealogy of Hugh McCutchen & Isa-
bella Cooper of Williamsburg County. NP: typescript, nd.
6 p.   WMTR
McDaniel, Ruth B. Ancestors of Ruth Barr McDaniel & Raymond
Allen McDaniel [incl. Allen, Bollinger, Parker, Cayce, Barr,
Barre, Quattlebaum, Dowling, Zorn, Rice, McDaniel, Minnick,
Mitchell, Scurry & Abney families]. Taylors: Faith Printing
Co., 1977. 712 p.   SCL, BACL, LXCL, CLEM
McDonald, Clarinda P. Our pioneer heritage [McDonald family].
Dallas TX: author, 1961. 202 p.   CLEM
McDonald, E. W. The Muses. NP: typescript, nd. 26 p.   FACM
McDowell, John H. History of the McDowells & connections [incl.
Erwin & Irwin families]. Memphis TN: C.B. Johnston & Co.,
1918. 680 p.   CLEM
McElveen, Margaret. The ancestry & children of John Frierson of
Shiloh, SC, "proprietor" of the plantation described in the
book Life on the Old Plantation in Ante-bellum Days, by the
Rev. I. E. Lowery. Cola: State Co., 1911. 6 p.   SMCL
McGill, John. The Beverly family of VA: descendants of Major
Robert Beverly (1641-1687) & allied families. Cola: RLB,
1956. 111 p.   SCL
[McGowan family] Proceedings of the reunion of the McGowan fam-
ily. 1915.   SCL, LRCL
McHugh, Matthew L. Celena (Lena) Jane Russell Smith: her ancestors, descendants & collateral kinsmen [incl. Russell, Hamilton, Sitton, Norton, Walker, Kennedy & Leman families]. Cola:
author, 1974. 511 p.   SCL, ANCL, PIPD
McHugh, Matthew L. Some Goodmans & McHughs. Cola: author, 1968

262

240 p.   COMMON
McIntosh, Allie A. Genealogies: Anderson-Fullwood & related
   families. NP: author, 1970? 101 p.   LECL
McIntosh, Allie A. Genealogies: McCutchen- Anderson & related
   families. NP: NPub, 1974. 215 p.   SCHS
McIntyre, Katie L. Heritage of a squire. Dillon: typescript,
   1968. 69 p.   MRCL
McKenzie, Israel J. History of the DuBose family. 1000 A.D.-
   1955 A.D. Camden: NPub, 1957? 12 p.   SCL
McKeown Family [SpC]   FACM
McKinney Family [SpC] . . . . .CRCL
McKown Family [SpC]   YOWC
McKown, Iris L. Littlejohn genealogy: Oliver Littlejohn's de-
   scendants. Gaffney: Ledger Print, 1953.   SCL, CLEM, CRCL
McKoy, Henry B. The Carpenter-Wier family of upper SC & other
   ancestors... Greenville: Keys Printing Co., 1959. 305 p.
                                                           COMMON
McLaughlin Family [SpC]   YOWC
McLaurin, G. G. G.G. McLaurin & some of his kin... Dillon:
   author, 1970. 175 p.   FLMC, MRCL
McLees, John. The diary of Rev. John McLees, beginning in the
   year 1838; the early history of Greenwood, SC; & McLees/Mac-
   Lees family data. Gastonia NC: mimeo, 1971. 167 p.   GWPL
McLellan, Timothy R. Meet the Macs. NP: mimeo.   DIDU
McLeod, Claude A. Our McLeod ancestry. NP: author, 1942.
   60 p.   MACL
McLeod, William A. Fullinwider & McFarlend: pioneer Texas
   Presbyterians. Cuero TX: NPub, 1931.   SCL
McMaster, Fitz H. The Flenniken family... NP: NPub, nd.
   16 p.   SCL
McMaster, Fitz H. The history of the MacMaster-McMaster family.
   Cola: State Co., 1926. 142 p.   SCL, FACL, SPCL, CHLS
McMaster, Louise M. Ancestry of the Buchanan family of Fair-
   field County, SC. NP: NPub, 1945. 34 p.   SCL, SCHS, FACL
McMaster, Louise M. Roderick McIver & his family. NP: type-
   script, 1952. 45 p.   SCL, SCHS
McMillan Family [SpC]   CRCL
McMillan, Willis E. Genealogy: Willis Malcolm McMillan. NP:
   NPub, 1967. 83 p.   SCL, HOCL
McNees, Lucien L. Descendants of Alexander Power of Laurens
   County, SC. Lexington MS: mimeo, 1967. 195 p.   LRCL
McPherson, Hannah E. The Holcombes; nation builders... Wash-
   ington DC: author, 1947. 1346 p.   LRCL, CLEM, UNCL
McPherson, Jessie C. A history of the Coleman-Sloan-Johnston
   families. Cola: mimeo, 1970. 214 p.   SCL, GWPL
McPherson, Lewin D. The brotherhood of man, in some families of
   Reid, Gaston & Simonton. Washington DC: NPub, nd. 52 p. SCHS
McPherson, Lewin D. Calhoun, Hamilton, Baskin & related fami-
   lies. NP: NPub, 1957. 447 p.   COMMON
McPherson, Lewin D. Kincheloe, McPherson & related families...
   Washington DC: author, 1951. 505 p.   CLEM

                            263

McPike, Eugene F. Halley & Pyke families. Reprinted from Notes
& Queries, July 16, 1910. 6 p.   SCHS
McQueen, James. The McQueens of Queensdale. Maxton NC: Obser-
ver Printing Co., 1913. 261 p.   DICL
McSwain, Eleanor P. My folk, the first three hundred years,
1670-1970 [incl. Covington, Dockery, Walls, Thomas, Ellerbee,
Leake & Everett families]. NP: NPub, 1972. 226 p.   PRIV
McSwain, Eleanor D. Some descendants of David McSwain of Isle
of Skye. Mason GA: National Printing Co., 1974.   SCL, LRCL
Mace, Brice M. Brice Martin Mace & Ella Cook: their ancestors &
descendants. NP: mimeo, nd. 54 p.   SCHS
Madden, Merna T. The descendants of Edward Moroni Thurman.
Provo UT: Stevenson, 1964. 222 p.   SCHS
Manigault, Gabriel E. Historical sketch of the Manigault fami-
ly. NP: typescript, 1896. 41 p.   SCHS
Manning, Mrs. Wayland. The descendants of John Potter, 1765-
1906. Dedham MA: NPub, 1906. 28 p.   SCHS
Manning, W. H. Jr. & Edna Anderson. Our Kin. Augusta GA:
Walton Printing Co., 1958. 1678 p.   SCL, MRCL, DICL
Marbut, Laura P. David M. Chaney, 1809-1859. Allied families
& descendants [incl. Nettles family]. Danielsville GA: Heri-
tage Papers, 1971. 134 p.   SCL, EDTO
Maret, Marett, Bowen, Mason & Keese Families [SpC]   PIPD
Marks, Jeanette. The family of the Barrett. NY: McMillan, 1938
                                                           CHLS
Marsh, Lucius B. The genealogy of John Marsh of Salem MA & his
descendants, 1633-1888. Amherst MA: Williams, 1888. 283 p.
Marshall, Ermine N. Gordons of the deep south. Austin TX:
Steck Co., 1961. 302 p.   NWRL
Martin Family [SpC]   SPCL, PIPD
Martin, Samuel L. Genealogical record of Benjamin Martin, Sr.,
& memoirs of his son, Samuel Manner Martin [incl. Manner,
Bostick & Lawton families]. Clemson: NPub, 1957? 15 p. CLEM
Martin, Samuel D. Genealogical record of the Martin family from
1680-1886. Chstn: W,E&C, 1886. 20 p.   SCHS, EDTO
Martin, Mrs. Sophia. Mack genealogy, the descendants of John
Mack of Lyme, CT... Rutland VT: Tuttle Co., 1903. 2 vol.SCHS
Massengill, Samuel E. The Massengills, Massengales, & variants,
1472-1931. Bristol TN: King Printing Co., 1931. 908 p. SCHS
Massey family history. Rock Hill: Typescript, nd. unp.   YOCL
The Massey family of the Waxhaws, Lancaster County, SC [incl.
Cook, Lanier & Rives families]. Rock Hill: typescript, nd.
unp.   YOCL
Massie, Martha A. DeLoache-Axson family. NP: NPub, 1966?
54 p.   SCL
Massie, Martha A. DeLoache-Axson-Smoak-Golson. NP: NPub, 1962.
62 p.   ORCL
Mathias Family [SpC]   PIPD
Mathis, Robert B. The Mathew Burt family of VA & the deep south
NP: NPub, 1976. 242 p.   SCL, CLEM
Mathis, Robert B. The Thomas Charles Mathis family...Thomas

Charles Mathis...& Susanna Quarles Mathis. Edgefield: Adver-
tiser Press, 1968. 151 p.   COMMON
Matteson, David M. The Washington family...in England... & in
America. NP: NPub, nd.   SCHS
Matthews, William K. Luke Matthews of Brunswick County, VA,
1739-1788; & his descendants. Kobe, Japan: H. Kodama, nd.
150 p.   SCHS
Maxwell Family [SpC]   PIPD
Maxwell, Mary B. The genealogy of the Benson-Latimer-Reed-
Durham & associated families. NP: author, 1931. 59 p.   PIPD
Mayer, Harriet H. The Mayer family, 1604-1911. NP: NPub, 1911?
12 p.   SCHS
Mayes, Sarah S. Mayes family history. NP: typescript, 1917.
                                                             PRIV
Mayfield, George R. The living dream; a story of upper SC pio-
neers [Meherin family]. Cola: RLB, 1971. 239 p.   COMMON
[Mayham family] Family reunion & directory. With names, addresses & family lines of present members of the family.
1937.   SCHS
Mayo, Lawrence S. The Winthrop family in America. Boston MA:
Massachusetts Historical Society, 1948. 507 p.   SCHS
Mays, S. E. Jr. Genealogical notes on the family of Mays &
reminiscences of the war between the states...and some references to the Earle family. Plant City FL: Plant City Enter-
prise, 1927. 324 p.   DACL
Mays, Samuel E. Genealogy of the Mays family & related families
to 1929 inclusive. Plant City FL: author, 1929. 288 p. CLEM
                                                        SCL, GWPL
Mears, Neal F. A history of the Heverly family, including the
spellings Hever, Haverle, Heverly, Everle, Everley, Everleigh,
Eveleigh, Evelegh, Evely, Everly, & Eveleth. Chicago: Bates
Printing Co, 1945. 340 p.   SCL, SCHS
Media Research Bureau. The name & family of Tyler. Washington
DC: typescript, nd.   SCHS
Mehringer, Corinne P. Ancestors & descendants of Edward Gar-
rett (1733-1794), Laurens County, SC. Chicago IL: NPub,
1955-. 2 vol.   SCHS, CLEM
Mehringer, Corinne P. Descendants of William Boyd, Laurens
County, SC. Chicago IL: NPub, 1954. unp.   SCHS, CLEM
Mehringer, Corinne P. Genealogies presented by Mrs. Corinne
Putnam Mehringer [Mehringer family]. NP: typescript, 1954.
unp.   LRCL
Mehringer, Corinne P. House of Putnam [incl. Putnam & Burns
families]. Chicago IL: NPub, 1950. unp. SCL,SCHS, CLEM, GWPL
Mehringer, Corinne P. Louther Hitch (1750-1838): MD & SC.
Chicago IL: NPub, 1949. unp.   SCHS, CLEM, LRCL
Mehringer, Corinne P. Mitchell kith & kin. Chicago: mimeo,
1957. 37 p.   SCHS, GWPL, LRCL
Mell, Patrick H. The genealogy of the Mell family in the south-
ern states... Albany NY: J. Munsell's Sons, 1897. SCL, CHCO
Mellichamp Family [SpC]   FACM

Memorials of that branch of the Crawford family which comprises
the descendants of John Crawford of VA, 1660-1883. NY: NPub,
1883. 180 p. SCHS
Mendenhall, Samuel B. Genealogy of the Mendenhall family of
York County, SC. Rock Hill: typescript, nd. 12 p. YOCL
Mendenhall, Samuel B & William B. White, Jr. Plaxco-Robinson:
being an account of two of the ancient Presbyterian families
of upper SC (particularly situated in York & Chester coun-
ties). Richmond VA: authors, 1958. SCL, CSCL, YOCL, CHLS
Mendes, Lucia N. Descendants of George Alexander Norwood & Mary
Louisa (Wilkins) Norwood, 1859-1959. NP: NPub, 1959.SCL, FLCL
Mentzel, Laura W. Davis families of the Savannah river valley:
containing a record of the descendants of Van & Harmon Davis
from 1725-1978, covering the counties of Newberry, Anderson,
Pickens & Oconee of SC; & Habersham, Franklin, Hart, Stephens,
Polk, Paulding & Gwinnett counties of GA. Salt Lake City UT:
Bobby Press, 1978. SCL
Meredith, Doyle C. The families by the name of Meredith.
Phoenix AZ: mimeo, 1969. 104 p. FACM, LRCL
Meredith, Doyle C. The family by the name of Meredith. NP:
typescript, nd. 147 p. SCHS
Meredith, Gertrude E. The descendants of Hugh Armory. London,
England: Chiswick Press, 1901. 373 p. SCHS, CHLS
Merrill, Eleanor B. A Virginia heritage [Brown family]. Rich-
mond VA: Whittet & Shepperson, 1968. 186 p. SCHS
Mesick, John. A partial genealogy of John Godbold of SC. NP:
NPub, 1966? 100 p. MACL
Meyer, Leona. Francis Adams & Mary Elizabeth Hambrick. Hart-
ford KY: Sam McDowell, 1978. 135 p. SCL
Middleton, Margaret Simons. David & Martha Laurens Ramsay.
NY: Carlton Press, 1971. 117 p. SCL, SCHS
Mikell, Townsend. The Mikell genealogy of SC. Chstn: W,E&C,
1910. 24 p. SCHS
Milford, Charles P. Sands of time: genealogy & traditions of
the South family, Milford-Millford family, & other related
families... Baltimore MD: Gateway Press, 1976. SCL, ANCL
Miller, Allie E. Everhart-Miller & related families. West
Point MS: author, 1931. 191 p. SPCL
Miller, Annie E. Our family circle...[incl. Thomas Smith,
Pierre Robert, Bostwick, Joseph Lawton, Paul Grimball, Nathan-
iel Irwin, Daniels, William Stafford, & John Maner families]
Macon GA: J.W. Burke Co., 1931. 552 p. COMMON
Miller, Elbert H. T. Genealogies of Miller & Tillotson [incl.
Fraser, Christie, Smith & Wheeler families]. Scottsville NY:
NPub, 1951. 39 p.
Miller Family [SpC] YOWC
Miller, Florence M. Sketch of the Miller...& Calhoun-Miller...
families with their genealogy... Atlanta GA: Ruralist Press,
1927. 196 p. SCL, PIPD, CLEM, ANCL
Miller, Florence M. Sketch of the Miller...& Calhoun-Miller...
families...with appendix: John Clarence Calhoun Miller family,

266

by Maude Miller Hayes, 1961.   SCHS
Miller, Helen H. Yours of yesterday: The Millars of Ayrshire,
  [Scotland]. NP: NPub, nd. 83 p.   SCL, SCHS
Miller, Janis H. History of Ellis-Buckner & allied families...
  Washington DC: author, 1973. 103 p.   SCL
Miller, Joseph L. Ancestry & descendants of Lt. John Henderson
  of Greenbriar County, VA, 1650-1900. Richmond VA: Whittet &
  Shepperson, 1902. 37 p.   SCHS
Miller, Joseph L. The descendants of Capt. Thomas Carter of
  Barford, Lancaster County, VA, 1652-1912... Thomas WV:
  Miller, 1912? 4 p.   SCHS
Miller, Kenneth D. Barnard-Miller & allied families. NP: Des
  Plaines Publishing Co., 1952. 278 p.   SCHS
Milligan, Lou F. Some Loris families. NP: typescript, 1970.
  unp.   HOCL
Mills, Laurens T. A SC family: Mills-Smith & related lines.
  NP: Hawes & Norton, 1960. 158 p.   COMMON
Mills, Sarah E. Reminiscences [incl. Smith family]. NP: type-
  script, 1935. 16 p.   SCL, CLEM
Mims, Florence A. Miller records. Edgefield: typescript, 1954.
  91 p.   YOCL
Mitchell, Boyce S. Banister, DeJarnette, Kay, Latimer, Mitchell
  Pearman, Pruitt, Tucker & allied families of VA & SC; also
  Shirley family. Honea Path: mimeo, 1971. 11 p.   GWPL
Mitchell, Boyce S. Mitchell-Pearman families... Honea Path:
  author, 1967. v.p.   COMMON
Mitchell, Clarence B. Mitchell record. NP: privately printed,
  1926. 183 p.   SCHS
Mitchell, Ethel B. Judge Henry Pendleton of SC, 1750-1788.
  Clemson: author, 1968. 20 p.   PIPD
Mitchell, Virginia B. Gholson & allied families... Dallas TX:
  NPub, 1950. 97 p.   SCL
Mize, Leila R. & Jessie J. Mize. Threads of our ancestors:
  Telford, Ritchie, & Mize. Athens GA: University of Georgia
  Printing Dept., 1956. 273 p.   SCL, GWPL, NWRL
Moise, Harold. The Moise family of SC...descendants of Abraham
  & Sarah Moise who settled in Charleston, SC, in the year
  1791 A.D. Cola: RLB, 1961. 304 p. SCL,SCHS, SMCL, CHLS, SCLB
Monroe, Mary W. Alexander Simpson of County Antrim, Ireland.
  NP: mimeo, 1962. 28 p.   LRCL
Moody, Mary C. The Moodys & related families...[incl. Rushing,
  & Wayland families]. Arlington TX: author, 1979. 184 p.
                                              SCL, MACL, FLMC
Moore Family [SpC]   YOWC
Moore, George W. & others. Genealogy of the Moore family of
  Londonderry NH & Peterborough NH, 1648-1924. Cola: RLB, 1976.
  285 p.   SCL, EDTO
Moore, John W. Some family lines of James Peronneau DeSaussure
  & of his wife, Annie Isabella Laurens. Washington DC: NPub,
  1958. 40 p.   CHLS, SCL, SCHS, GWPL
Moore, John W. Some lines of the Andrew Chapel-Cokesbury Moore

family & of some related families [incl. Moore, Cobb, Waldrop, Vance, Ligon, Hodges & Wardlaw families]. Mt. Pleasant: typescript, 1964. 56 p.   SCHS, GWPL

Moore, Robart A. The ancestors of Richard Allan Moore & Calvin Cooper Moore. Brooklyn NY: privately printed, 1964.   SCHS

Moore, W. Allan. Mores, the first of our clan; notes on the Morrison clan. Chstn: Nelson, 1952. 4 p.   SCHS

Moore, W. Allan. Mohr-Moor-Moore and its family lore. NP: typescript, 1962. 24 p.   SCL, SCHS

Moorhouse, Robert W. Notes on the Wharton family: section one: descendants of George Wharton (1720?-1770). Bryn Mawr PA: typescript, 1960. 193 p.   GWPL

Moorhouse, Robert W. Notes on the Wharton family: section two: descendants of Col. Samuel Wharton (1740-1824). Bryn Mawr PA: typescript, 1958. 92 p.   GWPL

Morehead Family [SpC]   CRCL

Morris, Mike. History of the McConnell family, Williamsburg County, SC. The family of George McConnell (b. 1779) & his wife, Eliza Hewitt. NP: typescript, nd. 5 p.   WMTR

Morse, Sara H. The McCallums: our Scottish clan... Cola: RLB, 1978. 155 p.   SCL, FLMC, MRCL

Moseley Family [SpC]   PIPD

Moses, Herbert A. Pertaining to the Moses family. NP: author, 1963. 36 p.   SMCL

Moursund, Mary F. Stribling & related families. Austin TX: Von Boeckmann-Jones Co., 1967.

Münch, F. ...Das fünfzigjährige Hochzeits-Jubiläum des Gold-Jubelpaars I. C. Claussen und seiner Gattin Dorothea, geb. Fincken... Im Auftrage des Fest-Kommittees und nach dessen Berichten zuzammengestellt und beschrieben von Professor F. Münch. [trans: The fiftieth wedding anniversary of I.C. Claussen & his wife Dorothea Fincken...]. Chstn: NPub, 1898. 173 p.   SCL

Murff, Paul B. The genealogy of Randolph S. Murff, 1784-1955... Floydada TX: author, 1955. 372 p.   SCL, GWPL, LRCL

Murff, Vaughan W. Some descendants of Henry West. Floydada FL: typescript, 1961. 76 p.   CTCL

Murphy, Anne J. History & genealogy of the Boykin family... NP: mimeo, 1964. 148 p.   SCL

Murphy, Marion E. Early Leslies in York County, SC: their migration to TN, MO & AR... 3rd ed. San Diego CA: author, 1976 230 p.   SCL, YOCL

Nash Family [SpC]   PIPD

Nash, Sara M. Ancestors & descendants-- Edward & Lucinda Bell Nash; John & Ailsey Gray; John & Mary Fowler; George W. & Nancy King; Hugh & Elizabeth (Bridges) Bailey; the MaHaffeys; Solomon & Margaret Hopkins; the Curetons, & many others. Cola: RLB, 1972. 197 p.   SCL, SPCL, GWPL, LRCL

Nash, Shepard K. Nash family... Sumter: NPub, 1954. 18 p.YOCL

Nations, Loye E. The Alexanders of Pickens County, SC...[incl. Nations family]. Cola: mimeo, 1970. 19 p.   SCL

Nations, Loye E. Descendants of Mattison Nations & Cynthia Gar-
   rett. Cola: author, 1969. 173 p.   SCL, PICL
Neal, Carl B. The McQueen family of Johnson County, TN...
   Olympia WA: typescript, 1958. 147 p.   CLEM
Neal Family [SpC]   CRCL
Neal, John W. Neighbors [family]. Dallas TX: privatelt printed
   1976. 320 p.   LRCL
Neely Family [SpC]   YOWC
Neely, Juanita H. Neely family history, 1730-1959. NP: author,
   1959. 55 p.   SCL, GWPL, LNCL, YOCL
Nelson Family [SpC]   FACM
New Orleans Genealogical Research Society. Blanc cousins: a
   chart of some of the descendants of Louis Antoine Blanc (1758-
   1825) & Louise Gauvain (1760-1848). 2nd ed. New Orleans:
   author, 1959. 95 p.   SCHS
Newton, Clair A. History of the Newton families of colonial
   America... Naperville IL: NPub, 1927-1949. 2 vol.   SCHS
Newton, Clair A. Ralph Hemmenway of Roxbury MA, 1634, & his
   descendants: volume 2 of the Dietz family in America. Naper-
   ville IL: NPub, 1943. 274 p.   SCHS
Newton Family [SpC]   PIPD
Newton, Josephus H. Book of record & brief family history of
   John Wesley & Mary Alice Boggs Cochran. Pickens: author,
   1913 & 1915. 62 p.   PIPD
Nicholes, Cassie. The Brunsons of SC. Cola: RLB, 1973. 89 p.
                                           FLMC, SMCL, EDTO
Nichols, Clara S. ...History of the Smiths. Mt. Pleasant:
   Charles Towne Printing Co., 1976? 192 p.   MACL, CLEM
Nichols Family [SpC]   GSGN
Nimmons Family [SpC]   PIPD
Nisbet, Newton A. Nisbet narrations as collected by Newton Al-
   exander Nesbet. Charlotte NC: Crayton Printing Co., 1961.
   439 p.   SCL, LNCL
Norton, Sarah M. Generations back: Norton & related lines...
   Walhalla: author, 1977. 336 p.   COMMON
Norwood, Margaret D. Capt. John Norwood & Mary Warren Norwood;
   a family history. Goldsboro NC: Hilburn Printing Co., 1979.
   217 p.   SCL, DHML, SCHS
Norwood, William H. "General" John Norwood & related lines...
   Dallas TX: Trumpet Press, 1964. 424 p.   SCL, GWPL
[Oak family] Family register, Nathaniel Oak of Marlborough MA,
   & three generations of his descendants... Los Angeles CA:
   NPub, 1906. 84 p.   SCHS
O'Doherty, Mary K. Pioneers on the great Pee Dee: genealogical
   notes on Finklea & related families: Cain, Coleman, DeWitt,
   Exum, Finklea, Gibbs, Hyman, Keefe & Kirton. Myrtle Beach:
   Typescript, 1974. 47 p.   SCHS, SCL, HOCL
Olcott, Mary L. The Olcotts & their kindred from Anglo-Saxon
   times...and after. NY: National American Publ., 1956. 315 p.
                                                              SCHS
Oliver, Mrs. A.C. Arnold Harvey & descendants, 1754-1963.

Chstn: W,E&C, 1964. 208 p.   SCHS, BRCL
O'Neall, John B. Family reminiscences of the Pinckney, Brewton,
  Elliott, Odingsells, Ramsay & Laurens families. To which is
  added: notices of the Hon. Charles Pinckney, Benjamin Elliott,
  Sn., & Benjamin Elliott, Jr...also a sketch of the life of the
  Hon. Henry Laurens Pinckney. Chstn: Walker & Evans, 1859.
  95 p.   SCHS
Orr Family [SpC]   PIPD, CRCL
Orvin, Maxwell C. The Avinger & related families... Chstn:
  Nelson's Southern Printing, 1961. 144 p.SCHS, BKCL, SCL, CHLS
Osborn Family [SpC]   PIPD
Owen, Thomas M. Bryant Lester of Lunenburg County, VA, & his
  descendants. Baltimore MD: Friedenwald, 1897. 13 p.   SCHS
Owen, Thomas M. William Strother of VA & his descendants. Har-
  risburg PA: Harrisburg Publishing Co., 1898. 51 p.   SCHS
Owings, Addison D. Owings & allied families...descendants of
  Richard Owings I, of MD, 1685-1975. New Orleans LA: Polyan-
  thos, 1976. 434 p. Baltimore: Gateway Press, 1980 SCL, LRCL
Padgett, Dora A. The Howard Family of Ocracoke Island, NC.
  Washington DC: mimeo, 1955? 41 p.   SCHS
Padgette, Hattie L. History of Jacob Lindler, 1802, & his de-
  scendants. Cola: McDonald-Ashley Printing & Mailing Co.,
  1977. 223 p.   SCL, LXCL, LXMU, LTSS
Page, Leila B. History of George Washington Bowman & Fiser fam-
  ilies of Mooreville, Falls County, TX... Galveston TX: Paul
  C. Wilson, Jr., 1962. 25 p.   SCL
Page, Leila B. History of George Washington Bowman...supplement
  Galveston TX: typescript, 1962. 2 p.   SCL
Park, Lawrence. Major Thomas Savage of Boston & his descend-
  ants. Boston MA: Clapp, 1914. 78 p.   SCHS
Parker, Dorothy F. Franklin James Farrington, Jr., his ances-
  tors & descendants. Upper Montclair NJ: NPub, 1972. 93 p.SCL
Parker, Ellen. Record of the Parker family of the parish of St.
  James, Goose Creek, and of Charleston, SC. Chstn: NPub, 1930.
                                                           SCHS
Parker Family [SpC]   PIPD
Parker, Laurence H. The Barry family records, vol. I: Captain
  Charles Barry & his descendants. Boston MA: privately printed
  1951. 148 p.   SCHS
Parks, Frank S. Genealogy of Arthur Parke of PA & some of his
  descendants. Washington DC: NPub, 1922. 19 p.   SCHS
Partlow, Thomas E. The Partlow family & connections, part II.
  NP: typescript, 1974. 193 p.   SCL, SCHS, GWPL
Partridge, Croom. John Nathaniel Partridge...his descendants
  who followed him in the Methodist ministry. Atlanta GA:
  NPub, 1944. 5 p.   SCL, SCHS
Passmore, John A. Ancestors & descendants of Andrew Moore,
  1612-1897. Philadelphia PA: NPub, 1897. 2 vol.   SCHS
Pate, Julia C. Pate-Adams-Newton & allied families, principally
  in Richmond, Scotland & Robeson Counties, NC; & in Marlboro
  County, SC. Red Springs NC: NPub, 1958.   SCL, DICL, MRCL

Patterson Family [SpC]   GSGN
[Patterson family]   The Patterson & Pattison family association:
   1963, 1964, 1965. NP: mimeo, 1963-65. 3 vol.   SCL, SCHS
Patterson, Isabel C.   Builders of freedom & their descendants:
   a genealogy of related families...[incl. Adamson, Aldrich,
   Ayer, Bellinger, Black, Brown, Conoley, Crider, English, Fish-
   burne, Frizzell, Lyles, McNair, McTyeire, Mills, Poellnitz,
   Pritchard, Reynolds, Trotti & Wyman families]. Augusta GA:
   Walton Printing Co., 1953. 37 p.   COMMON
Payzant, Marion M.   A scrapbook with notes on the Payzant & al-
   lied Jess & Juhan families in North America. NP: typescript,
   1955. 3 vol.   SCHS
Pearson, Eugene L.   Pearson family history. NP: mimeo, 1962.
   57 p.   SCL, LRCL
Pearson Family [SpC]   FACM
Pearson, George M.   Benjamin & Esther (Furnas) Pearson: their
   ancestors & descendants. Los Angeles CA: Times- Mirror Print-
   ing House, 1941. 538 p.   NWRL
Peay Family [SpC]   FACM
Pedigree of the Capers family [SpC]   YOWC
Peebles, Anne B.   Peebles [family], ante-1600 to 1962. NP:
   J. Hughlett Peebles, 1962. 191 p.   SCL, SCHS
Pegues, A. D.   Families descended from Samuel Butler Pegues
   (1778-1835) & his wife Juliet (King) Pegues. NP: typescript,
   nd. 58 p.   SCL, SCHS, CHLS
Pepper Family [SpC]   PIPD
Perdue, Robert H.   Descendants of Dr. William Perdue, who set-
   tled in Chester County, PA, in 1737-38, and his wife, Susannah
   (Pim) Perdue. Part II: ancestors of Lucinda Maria (Smith)
   Perdue; giving the Smith, Potter & Hamilton lines of John Pur-
   due, founder of Purdue University. Cleveland OH: privately
   printed, 1934. 168 p.   SCHS
Perrine, William D.   Genealogy & records of the Perrines, 1665-
   1936.   SCHS
Perry, John B., Jr.   The Perry family of Lancaster & Kershaw
   (Old Camden district) SC, & Yalabousha & Grenada Counties, MS.
   Grenada MS: mimeo, nd. 49 p.   SCL, LNCL
Perry, Max.   The descendants of Perry-Peterson families. Mid-
   land TX: author, 1977. 93 p.   SCL, PICL
Perry, Max.   The descendants of the Simpson-Roach families of SC
   including...Berry, Bratton, Pickens, Moffett, Drennan, Boyd,
   Wylie, Macklin, Sadler, Farmer, Sanders, Nelson & Springs.
   Midland TX: author, 1973. 252 p.   COMMON
Peterson, John.   My family [Peterson family]. NP: NPub, 1976.
   62 p.   SCL, SCHS
Pettigrew Family [SpC]   GSGN
Peyton, Sue P.   Thomas Puckett of Travis County, TX: his ances-
   tors & descendants. Houston TX: author, 1955. 21 p.   GWPL
Phelps, James A.   The Wallace family in America. NY: Clemens,
   1914. 27 p.   SCL, SCHS
Phillips, Charles W.   Joseph Phillips family of [SC &] Calhoun

County, AL. NP: typescript, nd. 9 p.   SCHS
Phillips Family [SpC]   FACM
Phoenix, S. Whitney. The Whitney family of CT...descendants...
   of Henry Whitney... NY: privately printed, 1878. 3 vol. SCHS
Pickens Family [SpC]   PIPD
Pickens, Monroe. Cousin Monroe's history of the Pickens family.
   Easley: Kate Pickens Day, 1951. 279 p.   COMMON
Pierce, Elizabeth. Family records: (Turquand family of Chatel-
   leraut)... London: Chatfield, 1829. 128 p.   SCHS
Pilcher, Margaret C. Historical sketches of the Campbell, Pil-
   cher & kindred families. Nashville TN: Marshall & Bruce Co.,
   1911. 444 p.   UNCL, MACL
A pioneer descendant...by a descendant of Winifred Arnold Camp.
   Greenville?: typescript, nd. 4 p.   GWPL
Pitchford Family [SpC]   GSGN
Pitts, Esther H. Copeland family in Laurens County, SC. Clin-
   ton: typescript, 1963. 55 p.   LRCL
Pitts Family [SpC]   FACM
Plotts, Lois D. Breazeale kin, 1643-1880. NP: NPub, 1965.
   175 p.   SCL, ANCL
Plowden, J. S. History of descendants of Edward Plowden, I, in
   America. Greenville?: NPub, 197?. 82 p.   SCL, SCHS
Poe Family [SpC]   PIPD
Pompey, Sherman L. The Coker report. Chicago: NPub, 1964.
   134 p.   SCL, COKL
Pope, Jennings B. The Bryants of Spartanburg, 1780.   SCL
Pope, Jennings B. Pabst/Bobst/Pobst/Pope family in the south.
   Austin TX: NPub, 1978. 79 p.   SCL, SCHS
Pope, Jennings B. Some Jennings ancestors, their descendants, &
   allied families. Austin TX: author, 1977.   SCL, SCHS, EDTO
Postell, Phillip S. The Postells; chronicle of a southern fam-
   ily. Thesis, 1972. 236 p.   SCL, SCHS
Potter Family [SpC]   CRCL
Poyas, E. A. Our forefathers. Chstn: W,E&C, 1860.   SCL, SCHS
Prather, Emily. The Verdery's of GA, 1794-1942 A.D., a genealo-
   gical history of the descendants of Jean Jacques deVerdery...
   Atlanta GA: Williams Printing Co., 1942. 236 p.   SCL, PRIV
Pratt, T. Dennis. Joseph Hersey Pratt: a family memoir. Mt.
   Pleasant: author, 1979. 110 p.   PRIV
Prescott, Caroline W. Our family roots: genealogy records for
   the Woodbury family. NP: author, 1979. 155 p.   MACL
Preston, Thomas L. A sketch of Mrs. Elizabeth Russell: wife of
   General William Campbell; sister of Patrick Henry... Nash-
   ville TN: Methodist Episcopal Church, South, 1888.   SCL, PRIV
Price, Zelma W. The Colquitt Volume III.   SCL, SCHS
Price, Zelma W. The Gamble Volume IV   SCL, SCHS
Price, Zelma W. The Rish Volume II   SCL, SCHS
Price, Zelma W. The Robertson Volume VII   SCL, SCHS
Price, Zelma W. The Weatherbee-Norman Volume V   SCL, SCHS
Price, Zelma W. The Wells Volume I   SCL, SCHS
Price, Zelma W. The Wofford Volume VIII, pts. 1 & 2   SCL, SCHS

Prichard, MayBeth. McConnell-Roberts-Rudasill & allied families
  Atlanta GA: NPub, 1972. 50 p.   LNCL
Prince, Beiman O. Descendants of Lawrence & Christina Corley.
  Cola: author, 1970. 100 p.   LXMU
Prince, Beiman O. The Hardees of Horry. Cola: typescript,
  1961. 36 p.   SCL, HOCL
Prince, Beiman O. The Harmon family of Lexington & Newberry
  Counties. Cola: NPub, 1974. 200 p.   LXMU
Prince, Beiman O. Julius Cross Campbell & his kin. NP: mimeo,
  nd. 28 p.   SCL
Prince, Beiman O. Let's meet the Gores. The descendants of
  Joshua Gore... Cola: mimeo, 1962. 134 p.   SCL, HOCL
Prince, Beiman O. Nicholas Prince & his descendants. Cola:
  mimeo, 1961. unp. 83 p.   SCL, HOCL
Prince, Beiman O. The southern Frinks. Cola: mimeo, 1964.
  71 p.   SCL
Pringle, Alex. The records of the Pringles of Hoppingrills of
  the Scottish border. NP: Oliver & Boyd, 1933. 349 p.   SCHS
[Pringle family] Genealogy. As shown in letters between SC &
  Edinburgh, Scotland, 1846-196?. NP: typescript, nd.   SCHS
Prioleau Family [SpC]   PIPD
Proceedings of a special service held by the First Baptist
  Church of Hartsville, SC, honoring Mr. J. J. Lawton. Harts-
  ville: First Baptist Church, 1938. 39 p.   SCHS
Proceedings of the reunion of the McGowan family held at Liberty
  Springs [Presbyterian] Church. NP: NPub, 1915. 51 p.   WOFF
                                                          SCL, LRCL
Pulley, Laura M. John Madden family of Frederick County, VA,
  to Laurens County, SC, with collateral lines of Dial, Martin &
  Fleming. Laurens: mimeo, 1978. 17 p.   LRCL
Pumphrey, Pearl W. The story of Louis Lestargette. Gibsland LA
  NPub, nd.   PRIV
The Purvis family. NP: NPub, 1976. n.p. [121 p.]   SCL, SCHS
Putnam, Eben. Lt. Joshua Jones, a New England pioneer, & some
  of his descendants...& a sketch of Joseph Hewes, the signer.
  NY: privately printed, 1913. 656 p.   SCHS
Putnam family data: SC & VA. NP: mimeo, nd. 19 p.   SPCL
Quattlebaum, Manning M. Quattlebaum family history. Savannah
  GA: NPub, 1950. 280 p.   COMMON
Quattlebaum, Paul. Horry county families. NP: typescript,
  1960-64. 4 vol.   HOCL
Rabb Family [SpC]   FACM
Rabb, Horace. Biographical sketches of the Kincaid, McMorries,
  Watt, Glazier & Rabb families... NP: NPub, 1933. 39 p.   FACL
                                                    SCL, LNCL, FACM
Radcliffe, Elizabeth W. Capt. Edward Richardson: a memorial;
  with genealogical records of some of his ancestors & descend-
  ants. NP: privately printed, 1923. 81 p.   SCHS
Randall Family [SpC]   PIPD
Randolph, Wassell. George Archer I of the Umberslade Archers of
  Henrico County, VA, & his descendants. NP: typescript, nd.

63 p.

Randolph, Wassell. Henry Randolph I (1623-1673) of Henrico
County, VA, & his descendants. Preceded by a short review of
the Randolph family in early England... Memphis TN: NPub,
1952. 105 p.

Randolph, Wassell. Pedigree of the descendants of Henry Randolph I (1623-1673) of Henrico County, VA. This pedigree is
complementary to..."Henry Randolph & his descendants". Memphis TN: NPub, 1957. 277 p.

Randolph, Wassell. The Rev. George Robertson (1693-1739)...
& immediate descendants. Bristol Parish, VA: NPub, 194?.
45 p.

Randolph, Wassell. The Wassell family & its several branches.
Also a pedigree of one branch of the Spotts family... Memphis TN: typescript, 1962. 63 p.

Randolph, Wassell. William Randolph I of Turkey Island (Henrico County) VA, & his immediate descendants. Memphis TN:
Seebode Mimeo Service, 1949. 115 p.

Range, Ella M. The life of Rev. Philip Mulkey, his ancestors &
descendants, 1650-1950. Tryon, NC: NPub, nd. 15 p.

Raskob, John J. Raskob-Green record book. Claymont DL: Arch-
mere, 1921. 143 p.

Ravenel Family [SpC]

Ravenel, Henry E. Ravenel records. History & genealogy of the
Huguenot family of Ravenel of SC; with some account of the
Parish of St. John's, Berkeley, which was their principal location. Atlanta GA: Franklin Printing Co., 1898; rp 1964 &
1971.

Ravenel, William J. Ravenel records...supplements A, B, C, & D

Raymond, William O. Winslow papers, 1776-1826. St. John, New
Brunswick, Canada: New Brunswick Historical Society, 1901.
732 p.

Raypholtz, Mrs. H.F. Some of the descendants of Rene Julien &
his wife Mary Bullock. Salinas CA: author, nd. 136 p.

Read, Thomas C. The descendants of Thomas Lee of Charleston,
SC, 1710-1869: a genealogical-biographical compilation. NP:
author, 1964. 465 p.

Read, Thomas C. The Tower & Converse families. NP: NPub, 1962.
12 p.

Reade, Compton. The Smith family: being a popular account of
most branches of the name... London: Stock, 1904. 280 p.

Reason contents me: the Graham family. NP: mimeo, nd. 44 p.

Reaves, Caroline M. Grateful memories of James Robert Reaves
(184?-1940) & Sarah McMillan Reaves (1851-1941). Hartsville:
author, 1962. 132 p.

Redfearn, Daniel H. History of the Redfearn family. Miami FL:
author, 1954. 327 p.

Reed, Forrest F. A Reed family in America. With special refer-

ence to the family & descendants of William Reed (1818-1895)
whose ancestral home was in Itawamba County, MS. Nashville
TN: Tennessee Book Co., 1962. 83 p.   SCL, LNCL
Reeder, William M. A brief history of the Reeder family, with
emphasis on the AL line. Chattanooga TN: typescript, 1956.
251 p.   SCL, LRCL
Reese, Lee F. John Fleming: Carolina to California, some de-
scendants & in-laws, 1734-1972. San Diego CA: Goodway Copy
Center, 1972. v.p.   SCL
Reeves, Roy. Ancestral sketches. Lynchburg VA: Bell, 1951.SCHS
Reid family of Union & York Counties, SC. NP: typescript, 1965.
unp.   YOCL
Reid, John S. [Reid] family history. NP: typescript, 1921?
35 p.   MRCL
Reid, Mary R. & Elaine Y. Eaddy Brown. Two Brown lines of Wil-
liamsburg County, SC. Williamsburg: typescript, 1975. unp.
                                                           WMTR
Reid, Nell P. Darby record. NP: typescript, 1970. 78 p.   SCL
Rembert, Sallie H. & L.A. McCall. Remberts, by way of SC.
Chstn: NPub, 1979. 781 p.   SCL, SCHS
Re-union of the descendants of John & Ellen Smith, Duncans, SC,
Sept. 30th, 1891. Proceedings. Spartanburg: Warren DuPre,
1891. 20 p.   CLEM
Revill, Janie. Abstract of Moore records of SC, 1694-1865.
Cola: State Co., 1931. 46 p.   SCHS, SCL
Reyes, Jenness R. Jane Harris of Rocky River: she linked the
Carolinas [incl. Reese family]. NP: mimeo, 1964.   SCL, GWPL
Reynolds, Harriet D. Early Dickson history... Houston TX:
typescript, 1972. 80 p.   SCL
Rhame, Lee R. The lineage of Henry Wilton Rhame, April 14,
1851-April 30, 1911. NP: author, 1979. 31 p. SCL, SCHS, ORCL
Ricaud, Lulu C. The family of Edward & Ann Snead Crosland,
1740-1957. Cola: author, 1957. 546 p.   COMMON
Ricaud, Lulu C. Index of the family of Edward & Ann Snead
Crosland...revised ed. Bennetsville: Marlboro Herald-Advocate
nd. 40 p.   COMMON
Rice Family [SpC]   PIPD
Richardson, Elizabeth B. A genealogical record with reminis-
cences of the Richardson & Buford families. NP: J.W. Burke
Co., 1906. 150 p.   SCL, SCHS
Richey Family [SpC]   GSGN
Richmond, VA, Times-Dispatch. The Pickett family. 2 p.   SCHS
Riddlehoover, Wayne. The Winn family of Edgefield, SC. Green-
wood: privately printed, 1969. 18 p.   EDTO
Rion Family [SpC]   FACM
Roach, Henry A. William Roach, 1801-1879, & descendants. Glen
Rose TX: author, 1974. 47 p.   SCL, PIPD, ANCL
Robertson Family [SpC]   FACM
Robertson, Julian H. The Cox family: eight generations, 1736-
1979; the Bradford family: eleven generations, 1656-1979;
with brief biographies of all the descendants of Henry Clay

Cox, 1843-1898, & Julia D. Bradford, 1845-1913... Salisbury
NC: Salisbury Printing Co., 1979. 57 p.   CLEM
Robertson, Julian H. The story of Frederick Williams Robertson
& Charlotte (Reynolds) Hackett Robertson. With genealogical
references on the Robertson family. Salisbury NC: NPub, 1969.
17 p.   SCL, SCHS
Robinson Family [SpC]   FACM
Robinson, Robyna E. These are ours: about the ancestors & de-
scendants of Rebecca Moore Pennington. Cleburne TX: author,
1974. 231 p.   LRCL
Robinson, Susan G. Descendants of Robert Wilson Gibbes, M.D.,
& Carolina Elizabeth Guignard. Cola: RLB, 1970. 63 p.   GWPL
                                                                  SCL
Roddey, Wade B. The Fee Bible, copies of the entries in... LNCL
Rodman, Ida M. The McDow family in America. Lancaster: author,
1953. 109 p.   LNCL
Roddey Family [SpC]   LNCL, YOWC
Rogers Family [SpC]   PIPD
Rogers, Frank M. Rogers family of the Pee Dee, SC, & allied
families. Florence: author, 1958. 128 p.   COMMON
Rogers, Virgil M. Family history: Rogers-McCravy-Lanham, with
allied & descendant families. Strasburg VA: Shenandoah Pub-
lishing House, 1975. 184 p.   COMMON
Rohrbaugh, Lewis B. Rohrbach genealogy. Philadelphia PA:
Dando-Schaff, 1970-. 2 vol.   SCL, SCHS
Ronsheim, Edward J. The Stephen-Daniel line of the Noland fam-
ily. Anderson IN: mimeo, 1954. 76 p.   SCL, SCHS
Rose, Ben L. Alexander Rose of Person County, NC, & his de-
scendants. Richmond VA: Carter Composition Corp., 1979.
268 p.   SCL, SCHS
Rose, Christine. Ancestors & descendants of Anson Parmilee
Stone, descended from John Stone of Guilford, CT. San Jose
CA: NPub, 1963. 75 p.   SCHS
Ross Family [SpC]   CRCL
Ross, John G. Descendants of Caleb Garrison, Jr., & his wife,
Sarah Fleming. 1797-1966. Angleton TX: Times Printers, 1967.
305 p.   SCL
Rowe, William J. The Branton clan. NP: NPub, nd. 36 p.   HOCL
                                                                  SCHS
Rowell, P. E. Review of Grahams, Barnwell County, SC. Cola:
Berg, 1891? 25 p.   SCL, SCHS
Rowlett, William M. Genealogy...Rowletts, Blockers, Swifts, &
Mayos... NP: author, 1957. 145 p.   SCHS
Roy, Nancy R. The Jasper family from England to America. NP:
typescript, 1971? 67 p.   SCHS
Roystone, Agnes A. The descendants of Benjamin Porter Fraser &
Angelica Farquharson Fraser. Arlington VA: author, 1974.
35 p.   SCL
Roystone, Agnes A. The descendants of Benjamin Porter Fraser &
Angelica Farquharson Fraser. Warrenton VA: Sudduth, 1974.
70 p.   SCHS

Rucker, Elizabeth H. The genealogy of Peiter Heyle & his descendants. Shelby NC: Zolliecoffer-Jenks-Thompson, 1938.
1539 p.   MACL
Ruf, Alpha H. Ruf, Haight, Eddy, Sumner, Hatch & allied families... NY: American Historical Society, 1932. 175 p.SCL, SCHS
Ruff Family [SpC]   FACM
Ruff, Sara C. The Crosby family. 1969. 33 p.   FACM
Ruggles, Alice M. The story of the McGuffeys. NY: American
Book Co., 1950. 133 p.   CLEM
Rush, John D. Rush family history, Kershaw County branch in SC.
Spartanburg: author, 1970. 9 p.   SCL, SCHS, SPCL, CLEM
Russell, George E. Creswell-Criswell genealogical records.
Bowie MD: mimeo, 1966. 116 p.   GWPL
Rust, Ellsworth M. Rust of VA. Genealogy & biographical
sketches of the descendants of William Rust, 1654-1940. Washington DC: author, 1940. 463 p.   SCHS
Rutherford, William K. Genealogical history of our ancestors.
Revised ed. 2 vol. [Lexington, MO]: Rutherford, 1977.   SCHS
Ryerson, Albert W. The Ryerson genealogy...of Ryerson, Ryerse,
Ryerss; also Adriance and Martense families; all descendants
of Martin & Adriaen Reyersz (Reyerszen), of Amsterdam, Holland. Chicago: author, 1916. 433 p.   SCHS
Saddler Family [SpC]   PIPD
Saffold, Ruth. Cornelius [family] of Beaufort. Cola: RLB,
1969. 180 p.   KECL, SPCL
Salley, Alexander S. The Calhoun family of SC. Cola: NPub,
1906? 42 p.   SCHS, SCL, CLCM, LNCL
Salley, Alexander S. Genealogy of the Rumph family of SC.
Birmingham AL: Leslie Printing Co., 1903. 10 p.   COMMON
Salley, Alexander S. The Felder family of SC. NP: NPub, 1900.
18 p.   SCL
Salley, Alexander S. Ralph Bailey of Edisto Island & some of
his descendants. Chstn: NPub, 1902. 18 p.   SCL
Salley, Olin J. A history of the Salley family, 1690-1965.
Cola: Salley Family Historical Committee, 1977. 349 p. COMMON
Saluda Standard Sentinel. History Book Committee. The family
history of Saluda county, 1895-1980. Clinton: Intercollegiate
Press, 1980. 408 p.   SCL, UNCL, EDTO
Sanders family [SpC]   CRCL
Sarratt Family [SpC]   CRCL
Saunders, James E. Early settlers of AL...with notes & genealogies by...Elizabeth Saunders Blair Stubbs... New Orleans LA:
L. Graham & Son, 1899. 530 p.   SCL
Scalf, Henry P. The Stepp/Staff families of America: a source
book. Stanville KY: author, 1973. 421 p.   CLEM
Scarborough, Jewel D. Southern kith & kin; a record of my
children's ancestors. Abilene TX: Abilene Printing Co., 1957.
218 p.   SCL, SCHS
Schertz, Mary F. Descendants of John & Nancy Floyd. Provo UT:
J. Grant Stevenson, 1973. 578 p.   SCL, GWPL
Schroder, Ruth R. The story of a family: Amelia Jane Anderson &

Charles Pressley Roberts & their descendants. New Orleans:
NPub, 1972. 139 p.   GWPL
Schweizer, Charles B. James & Rhoda Sellers Faulk. Edwards-
ville IL: typescript, 1979. 40 p.   HOCL
Scogland, Thesta K. Garlington family. Baltimore MD: Gateway
Press, 1976. 873 p.   LRCL
Sease, Elberta. Aunt Kate: 100 years dear. The life & times of
an early Dutch Fork family [incl. Feagle, Monts, Sease, Kohn,
Wheeler, Houseal families]. NP: Dutch Fork Printing Co.,
1979. 60 p.   NWRL
Seaver, Jesse M. The Campbell genealogy... Philadelphia PA:
American Historical & Genealogical Society, 1929. 71 p. MACL
Seaver, Jesse M. The Cook genealogy. Philadelphia PA: American
Historical & Genealogical Society, nd. 32 p.   SCL
Seaver, Jesse M. ...Evans family records... Philadelphia PA:
American Historical & Genealogical Society, nd. 51 p.   SCL
Seaver, Jesse M. Gordon family records... Philadelphia PA:
American Historical & Genealogical Society, 1929. 52 p. MACL
Seaver, Jesse M. The Martin genealogy. Philadelphia PA: Ameri-
can Historical & Genealogical Society, nd. 58 p.   EDTO
Seaver, Jesse M. Moore family records... Philadelphia PA:
American Historical & Genealogical Society, 1929. 93 p. MACL
Seaver, Jesse M. ...Murray family records... Philadelphia PA:
American Historical & Genealogical Society, 1930. 63 p. CLEM
Seawright Family [SpC]   PIPD, GSGN
Selleneit, Minnie L. Daniel Cobia, 1714. Descendants in Amer-
ica. NP: author, 1979. 618 p.   SCHS
Sellers, Edwin J. An account of the Jaudon family. Philadel-
phia PA: Lippincott, 1890. 24 p.   SCHS
Sellers, Edwin J. DeCarpenter allied ancestry... Philadelphia
PA: NPub, 1928. 236 p.   SCHS
Sellers, Edwin J. Early history of the Draper family of Sussex
County, DL. Philadelphia PA: NPub, 1929. 25 p.   SCHS
Sellers, Edwin J. English ancestry of the Wayne family of PA.
Philadelphia PA: privately printed, 1927. 51 p.   SCHS
Sellers, Edwin J. Fenwick allied ancestry; ancestry of Thomas
Fenwick of Sussex County, DL... Philadelphia: Allen, Lane &
Scott, 1916. 191 p.   SCHS
Sellers, Edwin J. Jaudon family of PA. Philadelphia PA: NPub,
1924. 52 p.   SCHS
Sellers, Edwin J. Sellers family of PA. Philadelphia PA: NPub,
1925. 58 p.   SCHS
Sellers, Edwin J. Supplement to genealogies. Philadelphia PA:
author, 1922. 73 p.   SCHS
Sellers, Edwin J. Van Hecke allied ancestry; descendants of
Josin VanHecke, wife of Roeland deCarpentier, pensionary of
Ypres, grandparents of Maria De Carpentier, wife of Jean Paul
Jaquet... Philadelphia PA: author, 1933. 153 p.   SCHS
Sessions, Frederick. Notes of the history of the Sessions fami-
ly in England. Atlanta GA: typescript, 1976. 41 p.   HOCL
Shackelford, Robert B. The Shackelford family; its English &

American origins ... Charlottesville VA: author, 1940.   84 p.
                                                           SCHS
Shannon, William G.   Shannon family & connections.   Cola: author
   1973.   225 p.   SCL, CSCL, YOCL
Shannon, William & Sara B. Shannon.   The Smarr family.   1971.
   38 p.   SCL, FACM
Shannon, William & Sara B. Shannon.   The Smarr family [of VA &
   SC].   Cola: authors, 1971.   123 p.   SCL, SCHS
Sharp, E. M.   Cunninghams & allied families.   NP: typescript,
   1959.   16 p.   LRCL
Sharp, Eron M.   The descendants of William Calhoun of Coronaca
   & Siloam [Baptist] Churches in Old Abbeville County, SC [Now
   Greenwood County].   Starksville MS: typescript, 1953.   88 p.
                                                           GWPL
Sharp, Eron M.   A history of the Nathan Sims family of Coronaca
   community in Greenwood County, SC.   Memphis TN: typescript,
   1971.   96 p.   GWPL
Sharp, Eron M.   Pickens families of the south.   Memphis TN:
   typescript, 1963.   152 p.   SCL, SCHS
Shaw, Jessie O.   The Johnsons & their kin of Randolph.   Washing-
   ton DC: author, 1955.   214 p.   LNCL
Shealy family, 1752-1941: genealogical sketches of the Shealy
   family.   Cola: RLB, 1976.   205 p. [Lexington,SC 1941]SCL, LXCL
Shealy, Sara B.   The family of our maternal grandmother Sara B.
   Ruff.   Cola: mimeo, 1969.   31 p.   FACM
Shearer, James W.   The Shearer-Akers family combined with the
   Bryan line...   Somerville NJ: author, 1915.   171 p.   SCHS
Sheffield, Eileen B.   Tree of time.   Baytown TX: NPub, 1968?
   v.p.   SCL
Shelburne, Robert C.   Shelburne family.   Genealogical notes.
   NP: typescript, nd.   SCHS
Sheldon, Christine.   The Ezell family in America.   Descendants
   of George Ezell of old colonial Surry, VA.   1692-1961...
   NP: NPub, nd.   210 p.   SCL
Shepard, Jack.   The Adams chronicles; four generations of great-
   ness, 1750-1900.   Boston: Little, Brown, 1975.   CHLS
Sherman, Nellie C.   Taliaferro-Toliver family records.   Peoria
   IL: author, 1960.   39 p.   CLEM
Shields, John E.   A history of the Shields family...descent of
   William Shields (1728-1797).   Harrisburg PA: Triangle Press,
   1968.   116 p.   SCHS
Shields, John E.   Irish origins of the Shields family.   Gai-
   thersburg MD: Omega Print, 1975.   101 p.   SCHS
Shivers, Marcus O.   Shivers genealogy.   Salt Lake City UT:
   Deseret News Press, 1950.   347 p.   SCL, KECL, DACL
Shook, Mrs. Marion H.   Carolina roundup: Kay-Clinkscales-Pratt
   & related families.   NP: NPub, nd.   117 p.   SCL, ANCL
Shook, Patricia F.   The descendants of Nathaniel Thomasson.
   Indianapolis IN: mimeo, 1977.   103 p.   YOCL
Shuler, Christine W.   The history of the Shuler family: a gene-
   alogical survey.   Savannah GA: author, 1973.   SCL, DOCL, ORCL

Shull history, 1728-1900. Lexington: NPub, 1978. 4 p. LXMU
Shute, J. Ray. The Shute family of piedmont Carolina, 1778-
1978. Monroe NC: author, 1978. 66 p. SCL, LNCL
Sightler, Aubrey M. Genealogy of George (Seitler) Sightler &
scraps of family history... 1963. SCL, SMCL
Simmons, Agatha A. Charleston SC, a haven for the children of
Admiral de Grasse. Chstn: NPub, 1940. 16 p. SCHS
Simons, Robert B. Thomas Grange Simons, III; his forbears &
relations. Cola: RLB, 1954. 211 p. COMMON
Simpson, George L. The Cokers of Carolina: a social biography
of a family. Chapel Hill NC: UNC Press, 1956. 327 p. COMMON
Simpson, William R., Jr. Jones, Sitgreaves & Pride families:
taken from the Sitgreaves bible, Pride bible, and a genealogi-
cal history by Col. Cadwallader Jones. Rock Hill: 1972.
11 p. YOCL
Sims, Annie N. Francis Morgan, an early VA burgess... Savannah
GA: privately printed, 1920. 194 p. SCHS
Sims, Caldwell. Voices of the past. Union: Union County Hist-
orical Foundation, 1979. 230 p. SCL, UNCL
Singleton, Charles G. Capt. Richard Singleton & some descend-
ants. NP: privately printed, 1962. 99 p. SCL, SCHS
Singleton, Virginia E. Genealogy of the Singletons after their
emigration to America; also: old Kensington saved from the
torch; also: our women in the war. NP: author, 1914. 53 p.
SCL, SMCL
Singleton, Virginia E. The Singletons of SC. Cola: NPub, 1914.
53 p. SCL, SCHS
Skelton, Caroline N. Godfrey Ragsdale, from England to Henrico
County VA. Franklin Springs GA: Advocate Press, 1969. 48 p.
LRCL
Skelton, John W. John Skelton of GA: Charlottesville GA:
Bailey Printing, Inc., 1969. 975 p. SCL, GSGN, PICL
Sketch of the Gaston family. Murfreesboro TN: NPub., 1907.
Copied by Thelma Gaston, Sumter SC. 19 p. SCL
Skinner Family [SpC] CRCL
Slade, Leonard L., Sr. Samuel Slade of Cheraw District, SC, &
his descendants. Baltimore MD: Gateway Press, 1975. 193 p.
MRCL
Sloan Family [SpC] PIPD
Sloan, H. T. Autobiography of Rev. James Boyce, D.D. Abbeville
Hugh Wilson, 1892. 50 p. MONT
Smallwood, Marilu B. Birch, Burch family in Great Britain &
America...with an agenda of families allied to the Burch fami-
ly of England, VA, MD, GA, AL, MS, OR & other states. Macon
GA: Patten Publishers, 1957-59. 2 vol. SCHS, SCL
Smallwood, Marilu B. Burch, Harrell & allied families. Gaines-
ville FL: Storter Printing Co., 1968. 2 vol. SCHS, SCL
Smallwood, Marilu B. Related royal families [Burch family].
St. Augustine FL: privately printed, 1966. 451 p. SCL, SCHS
Smith, Arthur M. Some account of the Smiths of Exeter & their
descendants... Exeter [England]: W. Pollard & Co., 1896. SCHS

Smith, Carl B. Ancestors & related families...[incl. Breazeal,
Clark, Hudson, Jones, Major, Moore, Shirley, Smith & Terrell
families]. Tampa FL: Florida Grower Press, 1964. 77 p.   SCL
Smith, Edith G. Clan McCarrell: a genealogy... Richmond VA:
Lyceum Publications, 1977. 276 p.   CLEM
Smith, Emme E. ...Our family history... NP: typescript, nd.
18 p.   SCL
Smith, Emmet L. Bonham, 1631-1973; letters, quotations...
Yucaipa CA: author, 1973. 170 p.   SCL
Smith, Evelyn. F. One Futch family [incl. Allen, Kirkland &
Woods families]. Jacksonville FL: NPub, 1970? 70 p.   SCL
Smith Family [SpC]   CRCL, GSGN
[Smith family] Genealogy...descendants of 1st Landgrave Smith.
Typescripts.   SCHS
[Smith family] The descendants of Thomas, 1st Landgrave Smith
of SC. Typescript, 1897.   SCHS
Smith Gladys E. Waters family of VA & MD. NP: typescript, nd.
73 p.   SCHS
Smith, Harry C. The Darnall, Darnell family: including Darneal,
Darneille, Darnielle, Darnold, Dernall, Durnall, Durnell...
Los Angeles CA: American Offset Printers, 1954-55. 2 vol.CLEM
Smith, Hester Moore. William Pullen (1757-1845); an account of
his life in VA, GA, SC & AL. Baltimore MD: Logical Products,
1971. 39 p.   SCL
Smith, John J. The Penn family. Philadelphia PA: Pennsylvania
Historical Society, 1867?   SCHS
Smith, Rosten M. A historical & genealogical record of the Hen-
ry Smith & David Hallman families of Lexington County, SC.
NP: author, nd. 243 p.   SCL, SCHS, ANCL
Smith, Sadie M. Family record of Dr. John Bell Fennell & Eliza
Simpson Fennell... Chester: typescript, 1937. 113 p.   YOCL
Smith, Theodore W. Direct family lines of Theodore W. Smith &
Frances Gonzales Smith. San Jose CA: typescript, 1976. 73 p.
                                                           HOCL
Smoak, Uldean K. The Smoak history. NP: NPub, 1974. unp. ORCL
Soady, John W. Memoirs of a nonagenarian; some links with the
Charleston of colonial days through the Williams-Roper fami-
lies. Richmond VA: Dietz Press, 1940. 42 p.   SCHS
Sommerfeld, Mabel S. Andrew Edwards, revolutionary soldier: a
documentary. NP: mimeo, nd. 20 p.   LRCL
Soper, Mary W. The chronicle of a clan: 1045-1977 [Soper &
Shepherd families]. Sarasota FL: author, 1977. 218 p.   SCHS
South Carolina Historical Society. South Carolina General File:
Families. Family histories & genealogies compiled by various
persons, including genealogists Anne King Gregorie, Mabel
Webber & others. Files include the following families: Aber-
crombie, Adams, Adair, Aiken-Keirl, Aiken-Martin, Akin-Knight,
Albergotti, Alexander, Allan-Allen, Alford, Allison-Ellison,
Allston-Alston, Anderson, Andrea, Andress-Angel, Arden, Arm-
strong, Arnett, Arthur, Ash, Pope-Theus, Ashby, Ashe, Ashmead,
Atkinson, Avant, Axson, Axtell, Babb, Baber, Bachman-Baughman,

South Carolina Historical Society. South Carolina General File:
Families, continued:
Bacot-Huger, Badger, Bailey, Baker-Bullen, Baker-Nitingale,
Johnson, Millett, Ball-Veree, Teasdale, Heape, Barker, Bark-
ley-Montgomery, Baron, Barksdale, Barlow, Barnett, Barnette,
Barnwell, Barrett, Barry, Barton, Basden, Bass-Wilkes-Conyers,
Bateman, Battle, Batts-Flynn-Sapp, Baxter, Bay, Bayley-Bailes-
Bayle, Baynard-Vardell-Bailey, Bazar, Beale-Biel, Beardon,
Beattie, Beckham, Bee-Gadsden-Mellard-Beekman, Belin, Bell,
Bellinger, Benbow, Benbour, Bennett, Benson, Bentham, Beres-
ford, Cooke-Rhett, Berringer, Berry-Gause-Vaught-Bellamy-
Randall-Gore-Bryan-Vereen, Berry, Besselleau, Bessellieu,
Betts, Blackwood, Blair, Blake, Bland, Blewer, Blocker, Blount
Burton-Glover-Wilson, Boland, Blum, Boatwright-Goodwin,
Boatwright-Faust, Bochet, Bocket, Clarle-Coleman, Boisseau,
Bond, Bonham-Lipscomb-Waldo, Bonneau, Boone, Bordeaux, Bossard
Burns, Bossard-Cogdell, Bostwick, Bowen, Bower, Bower-Pope,
Bowles, Bowman-Booty-Morse, Box, Boyce, Boyd, Bradford, Brad-
ley, Brailsford, Branford, Brannen, Brixe, Brazeale-Curtis-
Walpole, Bremar, Brent-Turnipseed-Kaigler-Wells-Strange-
Whittington, Brewton, Brisbane-Deveaux-Seabrook, Brister,
Britton-Britaine, Broughton, Broughton-Gourdin, Brown-Broun,
Brown-Miller-Solano-Clastrier, Brunson, Bryan, Bryan-Bratton,
Brice-Bryce, Bissel, Buist, Bull, Bullock, Burdell, Burnet,
Burnkam-Elliot, Burnham, Burrows, Butler, Buyck, Cain, Calcote
Caldwell, Calhoun, Campbell, Canary, Cantey, Capers, Carothers
Carpenter, Carrière, Cassels-Corcoran, Caston, Cater, Chandler
Chaplin, Chaplin-Crovatt, Charles, Cherry, Chesney, Cheves,
Chicken, Chisholm, Clark, Clarkson, Cleveland-Conway, Clifford
Cobia, Cockfield, Coffin, ColClough, Collins, Parrott-Collins,
Conger, Conturier, Converse, Conyers-Couturier-Ray, Cooper,
Court, Courtney, Cox, Craig, Croskey, Cruger, Cuthbert-
Cuttino-Dammon, Cuthbert, Dalton, Daniel, Darby, Darrell-Tuck-
er, Davenport, Davis-Fabian-Foulke-Kinsey, DeHay, DeLoisseline
Desaussure, Devereux, Dickey-Dickson-Dixon, Plowden, McGill,
Dill, Dion, Dobbin, Dorchester, Doughty, O'Dougharty, Douglas,
Dozier, Drake-Witter, Drayton, DuBose-DuBoise, Dulles, Dunkin,
DuPont, Dupre, Durant-DuRant, Dwight-Singleton, East-Anderson,
Eaddings, Edings, Elliott, Ellis-Vanall-Ellford, Elmendorf-
Lamar, Elmes, Elmore-Eve-Kelly-Hanahan, Emms, Enloe-Enlow,
Ervin, Erwin, Evans, Eubank-Ewbank, Eustis, Eve, Fairchild,
Farnum, Fare, Fayssoux, Feemster, Fendid, Fenwick, Ferguson,
Field, Fitch, Fladger, Fleming, Folger, Ford-Leigh-Harvey-
Bonneau, Ford-Cater-Miles-Shaw-Wrench, Fort, Foster, Fourgeaud
Fowler, Frampton-Wilkins, Frazer, Fraser, Freeman, Freer,
Frink, Fripp, Frost, Fryer, Fuller, Gadsden, Gaillard, Gail-
liard-White-Alexander, Gaillard-Savage, Gallagher-Gay-Love-
Morrow-Wells, Galluchat-Ragin,·Garden, Garrett, Gatchell, Gee,
Gelzer-Hughes-Matthews, George, Gervais, Gibbes, Gibbs, Gibson
Gibbon, Gignilliat, Gilbert, Girardeau, Givhan-Winningham-
Garvin-Jackson-McNeese, Givhan, Glaze-Glover-North-Parker-Ioor

South Carolina Historical Society. South Carolina General File:
Families, continued:
Gleason, Glen-Glenn, Glover-Godfrey-Golden, Godfrey, Godfrey-
Woodward, Gooch, Gordon, Gough, Gough-Gwinnet-Lewis-Rhett-
Burnett, Grace, Grange, Graveley, Graves, Grayson, Green,
Greggs-Gregg, Gregorie, Grey-Greey-Gurney, Grimball, Guerard,
Guerin, Guerry, Guyton, Hackett, Hall, Hamilton, Hampton,
Hassell, Hanahan-Ogier-Barksdale-Macbeth-Grayson, Hard, Hardy,
Hart, Hartford, Hartley, Hartness, Harvey, Hayne, Haynes,
Hazlehurst-Hogg-Holliday-Matthews, Hazzard, Hearne-Hyrne,
Heatley, Hemmingway, Henagen, Hendricks, Herbert, Hernandez,
Heron-Howe, Herring, Hext, Heyward, Hibbs, Hicks, Hieronymous,
Hill, Hirons, Hogg, Holcomb, Hollingsworth, Holman, Holman-
Dalton, Holmes-Sandiford, Holmes, Hopkins, Horry, Horton-
Pope-Bower, Howard, Howe, Hoyt, Hull, Hume, Hunter, Hutchin-
son-Craig-Mathews, Hyrne, Hyrne-Massingberd, Ioor, Iredell,
Izard, Jackson, James, Moore-Singleton-Matthew, Jarrott, Jef-
fords, Jenkins, Johnson, Johnston, Johnstone, Jones, Juhan,
Klan, Keating, Kennedy-Kitchen, Kershaw, Kilpatrick, Kinloch-
Cleland, Knight, Knox-Pritchard, Koger-Cook-Murray, Kohler-
Durbec, LaBruce, Lacey, Lachicotte, Ladson, Lafitte, Lager-
quist, LaMotte, Lang, Langdon, Langley, Lanneau, Latta, Laur-
ens, Laval, Lawrence, Lawton, Lea, Lee, Legaré, Lempriere,
Lennon, LeSerurier, Lesesne, Lesesne-Blamyer-Frost, Lestar-
jette, Lewis, Lillington, Lindsay, Lindsey, Livingston, Lloyd,
Lockwood, Logan-Steele-Ewing, Logan, Lopez, Love, Lucas, Luke,
Lynch, Lynes-Lyons, McBeth-McBride, McCalla, McCants, McCor-
mick, McCaw, McClellan, McCrady, McGill-McIver-McIntosh,
McGirt, McGowan-Matthews, McLeod, McPherson, Macon-Martin-
Massey, Magwood-Marsh-Robinson, Maner- McKellar, Manigault,
Mannings, Marion-Wickham-Erwin, Marion, Marshall, Martin,
Mason, Massey, Mathews-Mathewes, Maverick, Maxwell, May-Miles,
Maybank-McFarlane-Wigfall, Mayer-Major, Mayes, Mayo, Mayrant,
Mazyck, Means, Merrill-Miller, Michel, Middleton, Mikell,
Miles, Miller, Milligan-Fraser-Flagg, Mills, Milner, Minnick,
Mobley, Moore-Barr, Miot, Mitchell, Mixon-Minson-Cox, Moffett,
Morf-Murf, Moise-Morawetz, Monk, Mood, Moore, Morrall, Mor-
ris, Morrison, Morse, Morton, Moseley, Moses, Motte, Murphee,
Murray, Musgrove-Myers, Nathan, Nelson, Neufville-Neyle-
Walter-Green, Neyle, Nicholson, Nisbet-Nisbett-Nesbit-Nesbitt,
Norwood, North, Norton-Johnson-Lewis, Oak, Oates, Ogier,
Oglivie, Osborn, O'Sullivan-Barrett, Owens, Page, Pagette,
Paine, Paisley, Parkenham, Palmer, Parker, Parminter, Pasque-
reau, Patrick-Parsons, Patterson, Paul, Pawley, Peacock, Pear-
son-Jefferson-Raiford, Pelot, Pemberton, Pendarvis, Pender-
grass, Pennington, Pepper, Perdrieau, Perkins, Peronneau,
Perret-Brunson-Varner, Perriman, Perritt, Perry, Peter, Petit,
Petigru, Pettigrew, Phillips, Pickett, Pickney, Platt, Polony,
Porcher, Porter, Postell, Potts, Powell, Poyas, Primrose-Mott,
Pringle, Prioleau, Pritchard-Fitzsimmons, Prior-Pryor, Pundt,
Purcell, Purdy, Purteets, Putman, Pyatt, Quask, Quattlebaum,

South Carolina Historical Society. South Carolina General File:
Families, continued:
Quincy, Raiford, Ragin, Railford-Pearson, Ramsey, Rose, Renfro
Randal, Ratcliff, Raven, Ravenel, Raysor-Rogers, Read-Reid,
Reily, Rembert, Rentz, Reynolds, Rhame, Rhett, Rice, Richard-
son, Richbourg, Riggins, Righton-Fullerton, Riley, Rippon,
Rivers, Roach, Robert, Roberts, Robinson-Thomas, Roper, Rose-
Guerard, Rose-Rowe, Royall, Rumph, Rush, Russell, Rutledge,
Sabin, Salley, Sams, Sanders, Sandiford, Satcher, Savage,
Schinkingh, Scott, Screven, Seabrook-Legare, Sealy-Pealot-
Harrison, Self-Sills-Sloan, Sere-Serre, Shackelford, Sessions,
Screven-Sibley, Severans, Shackelford-Bossard-Cogdell, White,
Sharples-Sleigh, Shedland, Shelburne, Shelton, Sheppard, Shu-
brick, Simmons, Simons, Sims, Singleton, Sinquefield, Sitton,
Skinner, Skirving, Slann, Sloan, Smart, Smith, Snell, Snipes,
Snowden, Somersall, Spencer, Spitzer, Splatt, Spry, Staats,
Stafford, Stanyarne, Staples, Stark, Starr, Starling, Steele,
Stevens, Stewart, Stiles, Stokes, Stone, Stoney, Stoudimire,
Strickland, Stroman, Stuart, Studebaker, Stukes, Sullivan,
Sumner, Surles, Swindershine-Miscally, Swinton, Tabb, Taber,
Tamplet, Taylors, Threadcraft, Theus, Thomas, Thompson-Stuart,
Thornton, Thurman, Tillinghast, Tims, Timms, Tobin, Toble,
Tomlinson, Toomers, Torquet, Townsend, Trail, Trapier, Trairs,
Trenholm, Trice, Trott, Troup, Tucker, Turquand, Tutt, Tyler,
Ulmer, Van Braam, Vanderhorst, Venning, Verdier-Vardier,
Vereen, Villepontoux, Wagner, Waight, Waites, Waight, Walker,
Wall, Walker, Walpole, Walter, Walters, Ward, Waring, Warley,
Waters, Way, Wayne, Weatherbee, Webb, Webster, Weissinger,
West, Weston, Weyman, Whaley, Wheeler, Whilden, Whippey,
White, Whitten, Whorton-Wharton, Wigg, Wigfall, Wightman,
Wilkes, Wilkins, Wilkinson, Williams, Willismson, Wilson,
Winborn, Winkler, Winn, Winningham, Winslow, Winslip, Winthrop
Withers, Witsell, Woodberry-Woodbury, Woodham, Wragg, Wright,
Wyatt, Wylly, Yates, Yeamans, Yongue, Younge-Young families.
[End of South Carolina General File: Families].

South Carolina Historical Society. Special Collections: Langdon
Cheves III Genealogical Collection. A collection of records
and compilations of Lowcountry family histories, including
the following families: Alston, Allston, Amory, Ashby, Baird,
Baker, Banbury, Barnwell, Bellinger, Beresford, Blake, Boone,
Boulerne, Bremar, Browning, Bull, Cantey, Cattell, Cheves,
Cleland, Cottin, Courtonne, Cuttino, Danniell, DeVeaux, DuBose
DuGué, Dulles, DuPuy, Elliot, Elliott, Ellis, Everleigh, Farr,
Fenwick, Fowell, Gaillard, Gibbes, Gignillat, Glen, Grimball,
Guiton, Haggard, Harleston, Harwood, Hayne, Heath, Heatley,
Hext, Howes, Huger, Hume, Izard, Jones, Kinloch,Lafons, Lang-
don, LeBoeuf, Legare, Lelas, Ligon, Lowndes, Lynch, Mayrant,
Manigault, Matthews, McCord, Megget, Merlat, Middleton, Miles,
Moore, Motte, Nelson, Nesbit, Page, Pages, Parker, Perry,
Pinckney, Prioleau, Raven, Ravenel, Reid, Rembert, Rivers,

South Carolina Historical Society. Langdon Cheves III Collect-
ion, continued:
Rose, Royer, Russell, Rutledge, Sabb, Sanders, Schenkinye,
Simmons, Singleton, Skotowne, Smith, Stanyarne, Summer, Tat-
nell, Taylor, Thomas, Thomson, Thorngood, Torquet, Turquand,
Vanderhorst, Vassell, Waring, Way, West, Williams, Woodward,
Wragg. [End of Langdon Cheves III Collection].

South Carolina Historical Society. Special Collections: Motte
Alston Read Collection. Genealogical papers and research on
approximately 100 colonial SC families, including: Adams,
Jenkins, Wilkinson, Mathews, Grimball, Aiken, Alston, Allston,
Ashe, Motte, LaBruce, Pawley, Warnock, Ash, Moore, Bailey,
Baker, Ball, Barker, Moore, Parker, Barksdale, Legare, Barnet,
Baynard, Bedon, Bee, Bellinger, Beresford, Ford, Cooke, Ber-
ringer, Blamyer, Boisseau, Bonneau, Boone, Bower, Branford,
Brewton, Broughton, Browne, Bruneau, Bryan, Burnham, Butler,
Cantey, Capers, Cattell, Chaplin, Ladson, Toomer, Clay,
Snipes, Brown, Garnier, Godfrey, Clifford, Coachman, Codner,
Cochran, Collins, Corner, Cooke, Trott, Cooke, Cooper, Wright,
Moore, Crichton, Blake, Dry, Weekley, Branford, Crosskeys,
Cuthbert, Daniel, Davis, Dean, Deas, DeBourdeaux, DeLiessel-
ine, Dennis, d'Harriette, Drayton, Duqué, Dubose, Durant,
DuPont, Odingsell, Robert, Tatnell, Rothmahler, Farr, Fenwick,
Ferguson, Fitch, Fitzsimons, Foissin, Foster, Norton, Cowen,
Ford, Edwaeds, Elliott, Elmes, Emms, Ellis, Freer, LeSerrur-
ier, Gignilliat, Mazyck, Fuller, Heape, Gibbes, Glaze, Ioor,
Jackson, Sanders, Glover, Godfrey, Gough, Graves, Griffith,
Grimball, Guerard, Hamilton, Bower, Pritchard, Harvey, Hext,
Hill, Holmes, Horry, Hutchinson, Hyrne, Hearn, LeGrand,
Lesesne, Lillington, Linkley, Little, Livingstone, Lynch, Wig-
fall, Miles, Marboeuf, Martin, Mathewes, Mazyck, McCall, Mc-
Gregor, McKewn, McPherson, Meggett, Mitchell, Monk, Moore,
Moseley, Motte, Moultrie, Norman, Nichols, Odingsell, Os-
borne, Oswald, Pamor, Palmer, Peyre, Parker, Parris, Patey,
Patterson, Pendarvis, Perriman, Perronneau, Perry, Peter,
Peters, Pight, Porcher, Porter, Postell, Poyas, Taylist,
Pritchard, Raven, Reynolds, Rippon, Rhett, Rivers, Rose, Rus-
sell, Rutledge, Sacheveral, Savage, Samways, Sanders, Saunders
Schenckingh, Screven, Scott, Seabrook, Simmons, Bee, Chardon,
Simons, Singleton, Slann, Smelie, Smith, Snipes, Clay, Stan-
yarne, Stock, Stocks, Stokes, Stone, Swann, Tatnell, Tauvron,
Toomer, Torquet, Townsend, Trapier, Trott, Tucker, Vanderhorst
Waight, Wallbank, Waring, Ward, Waties, Whitmarsh, Wigfall,
Wilkins, Wilkinson, Warnock, Warren, Weatherby. [End of Motte
Alston Read Collection].

Sowell, Carolyn E. & Mary S. Hays. History of the John Alexander & Laura Hilton Sowell family. NP:authors, 1973.SCL, KECA
Spencer, Margaret H. Miller-Cathcart-Roddey: notes on family
history. Rock Hill: typescript, 1956. 33 p.   YOCL

Spratt, Thomas D. Recollections of his family...July, 1875.
  Fort Mill: NPub, 1875. 110 p.   YOCL
Springs, Katherine. The squires of Springfield [Springs family]
  Charlotte NC: W. Lofton, 1965. 350 p.   COMMON
Sproule, Robert. Lineage of Robert Sproule, 1775-1966, with
  lineage of families allied by marriage. NP: typescript, nd.
  36 p.   SCHS
Stackhouse Family Association. The descendants of William
  Stackhouse, son of William & Mary (Bethea) Stackhouse, & his
  wife, Sarah Moody: the MS branch. Dillon: Herald Publishing
  Co., 1935. 34 p.   SCL, WOFF
Stackhouse Family Association. The Stackhouse family supple-
  ment. Dillon: mimeo, 1967.   SCL, DIDU
Stackhouse, William R. Stackhouse, an old English family, some-
  time of Yorkshire... Moorestown NJ: The Settle Press, 1906.
  107 p.   FLMC
Stackhouse, William R. The Stackhouse family: pt.1, history of
  Stackhouse from 1086 to 1935; pt. II, descendants of William
  & Mary (Bethea) Stackhouse from 1760 to 1930, by Walter F.
  Stackhouse. Dillon: Herald Publishing Co., 1935. 241 p.
                                                            COMMON
Stafford, George M. General Leroy Augustus Stafford, his for-
  bears & descendants... New Orleans LA: Pelican Publishing Co.
  1943. 474 p.   SCHS
Stafford, George M. The Wells family of LA & allied families.
  Baton Rouge LA: privately printed, 1942. 385 p.   SCHS
Stanley, Haywood A. Sands Stanley of the Pee Dee valley: a
  partial family history... Marion: author, 1978. 183 p.COMMON
Stanton Family [SpC]   PIPD
Starbird, Alfred A. Genealogy of the Starbird-Starbard family.
  Burlington VT: privately printed, nd. 179 p.   SCHS
Starnes, Herman. Antecedants & descendants of Richard Deese,
  1814-1872. Monroe NC: mimeo, nd. unp.   LNCL
Starnes, Herman. The Plyler genealogy, 1688-1965. Monroe NC:
  author, 1966. 189 p.   SCL, LNCL
Steadman, Joseph E. Ancestry of the Fox family of Richland &
  Lexington Counties, SC...and collection of data compiled by
  Shirley Faucette. Lexington: typescript, 1972. 166 p.   SCL
Steadman, Joseph E. History of the Fox family of Lexington,
  SC. NP: typescript, nd. 11 p.   SCL, LXMU
Steadman, Joseph E. & Johnson Bland Nobley. A history of the
  Minick family of the Dutch Fork of Lexington & Newberry
  Counties, SC. Cola: RLB, 1970. 249 p.   SCL, EDTO
Steadman, Joseph E. A history of the Spann family...with at-
  tached Hammond connections, compiled by Edward Spann Hammond
  from notes of James H. Hammond. NP: author, 1967. 90 p.
                                                            COMMON
Steadman, Joseph E., Sr. The Steedman/Steadman genealogy. Lex-
  ington: author, 1969. 4 p.   LXMU
The Steele family history. Lexington: typescript, 1970. 23 p.
                                                            LXMU

Steele, John M. The Steele family. Stephens City VA: mimeo,
1935. 30 p.   PRIV
Steele, Newton C. Archibald Steele & his descendants... Chattanooga TN: MacGowan & Cook Co., 1900. 222 p.   YOCL
Steen, Moses D. The Steen family in Europe & America... 2nd
ed. Cincinnati OH: Monfort & Co., 1917. 740 p.   SCL, SPCL
Stephens, Mary M. & Daisy M. Stephens. The genealogical record
of the descendants of Martha Christian Butler & Allen Thomas
Stephens, Jr. NP: mimeo, nd.   DIDU
Stephenson, Theodore F. The Friersons of Zion Church & their
descendants... Nashville TN: Parthenon Press, 1938. 235 p.
                                                            SCL
Stevens, Julia N. Genealogy: Jones, Dantzler, Felkel, Montgom-
ery, Bair, Bonnett, Baltzegar, McMichael. Boise ID: author,
1979. 26 p.   ORCL
Stevenson, Charlotte. The Stevenson reference book. Cola: RLB,
1973. 193 p.   COMMON
Stevenson Family [SpC]   GSGN
Stevenson, Mary L. William Lewis of Horry County, SC. Cola:
RLB, 1960. 181 p.   SCL, FLMC
Stevenson, Rev. Samuel & others. A history & genealogical rec-
ord of the Stevenson family from 1848-1926. NP: W.F. Steven-
son, nd. 238 p.   LNCL, CTCL, EDTO
Stewart, J. Adger. Descendants of Valentine Hollingsworth, Sr.
Atlanta GA: Peachtree Printing Co., 1976. 211 p.   SCL, EDTO
Stewart, J. Adger. Descendants of Valentine Hollingsworth, Sr.
Louisville KY: John P. Morton, 1925. 208 p.   SCL, SCHS
Stewart, J. Adger. Hollingsworth genealogy: from descendants of
Valentine Hollingsworth. Louisville KY: typescript, 1924.
4 p.   GWPL, CHLS
Stewart, John. The Stewarts: the Highland branches of a royal
name. Edinburgh, Scotland: W. & A. K. Johnston. 32 p.   GWPL
Stiles, Henry R. The Stiles family in America. Genealogies of
the CT family...and the southern (or Bermuda-Georgia) family,
1635-1894. Jersey City NJ: Doan & Pilson, 1895. 782 p. SCHS
Stockman, Mrs. Woodrow R. Notes on the Stockman name, sponsored
by Abner Pierce Stockman, Sr., Greenwood SC. Chapin: type-
script, 1978. 116 p.   COMMON
Stoddard, Mary S. Stoddard-Sudduth papers. Laurens: NPub,
1960? 281 p.   COMMON
Stokes, J. Lemacks. The book of Stokes, 1201-1915. Yorkville:
Enquirer Print, 1915? 28 p.   SCL, CLEM
Stoney, Samuel G. The Dulles family in SC...a keepsake publish-
ed on the occasion of a commencement address by the Hon. John
Foster Dulles... Cola: RLB, 1955. 29 p.   COMMON
Story family. Genealogy. NP: typescript, nd.   SCHS
Stoutmire, Ralph. Danial Stoutamire & Elizabeth C. Gardner
Stoutamire. Ancestry... Gainesville FL: NPub, 1951. 16 p.
                                                            SCHS
Stribling, Bruce H. Striblings of Walnut Hill & related fami-
lies: Alexander, Conger, Dendy, Dillard, Kincheloe, Knox,

Sloan, Taliaferro... Greenville: Keys Printing Co., 1979.
175 p.   CLEM, PIPD
Stringer, Mildred E. Blakeney, Stringer, Ware, Brunson, Heid-
elberg & McClammy [families]. NP: NPub, 1979. 35 p.   SCL
Strother Family [SpC]   FACM
Stroud, Agnes Blanding. The book of remembrance, 1841-1941;
historical facts of the Blanding family. Italy TX: W.E. Reid
& Co., 1941. 139 p.   SCL
Stubbs, Thomas M. Family album: an account of the Moods of
Charleston, SC, & connected families. Atlanta GA: Curtis
Printing Co., 1943. 246 p.   COMMON
Stubbs, William C. History of two VA families. NP: author,
nd.   CHLS
Suggs, Clarence E. Genealogical research of the Suggs family.
[Marietta, GA: 1975] 119 p.   SCL, YOCL
Sullivan, Hazel B. The Sullivan family: William Dunklin Sulli-
van line. NP: author, 1961. 43 p.   SCL, LRCL
Sullivan, William D. History of the Sullivan family, 1913.
Tumbling Shoals SC: NPub, 1960. 12 p.   SCL, GWPL, LRCL
Surles, Flora B. Surnamed Gregorie: eight generations in pro-
file, c. 1510-1852. Chstn: for the suthor, 1966. 22 p.COMMON
Sutherd, Calvin E. A compilation of Gaines family data with
emphasis on the lineage of William & Isabella (Pendleton)
Gaines. Ft. Lauderdale FL: author, 1969. 430 p.   GWPL
Sutherland, Henry C. Sutherland records. Crown Point IN: auth-
or, 1968. 245 p.   SCL, SCHS, PIPD
Symmes Family [SpC]   PIPD
Tally, Stephanie H. Genealogy of the Boggs family descendants
& related families... Corpus Christi TX: mimeo, 1965. v.p.
                                                          SCL
Tarble, Lee C. Nicholas Bean & some of his descendants. Mar-
shall IL: NPub, 1961. 36 p.   SCHS
Tate Family [SpC]   CRCL
Tatum, James R. Tatum [family]... Atlanta GA: author, 1959.
51 p.   SCL, CLEM
Taylor, Emily H. ...The Draytons of SC and Philadelphia. Phil-
adelphia PA: Genealogical Society of PA, 1921. 26 p.   COMMON
Taylor, George. A brief visit with the old folks [incl. Armour,
Harris, Boyd, Kappelmann, Toney, Taylor families]. NP: NPub,
1976. 224 p.   SCL
Teague Family Magazine [and indexes]   SCL, NWRL, LRCL
Tedcastle, Agnes B. The Beville family. Boston MA: privately
printed, 1917. 206 p.   SCHS, CHLS
Temple, Sarah E. Our Campbell ancestors, 1742-1937. Burbank CA
Deach, 1939. 225 p.   SCHS
Templeton, Leumas B. Templeton family history...Laurens County,
SC... NP: NPub, 1953. 155 p.   SCL, GWPL, LRCL
Tennent Family [SpC]   SCHS
Thomas, Albert S. The career & character of Col. John Peyre
Thomas, LL.D... [incl. Thomas family]. NP: typescript, nd.
60 p.   SCL, EDTO

Thomas, Albert S. Thomas family, SC. 1964. 43 p.   SCL, SCHS
Thomas Family [SpC]   PIPD
Thomas, Velma M. Historical genealogy of the Smith-Durham fami-
lies. NP: author, 1950. 95 p.   PIPD
Thompson Family Magazine.   SCHS
Thompson, Ruth M. The ancestors & descendants of Edward Traill
Horn, Harriet Chisolm, Henry Eyster Jacobs, & Laura Hewes
Downing. NP: privately printed, 1976.   SCHS
Three Rivers Historical Society. Family bible pages & other
genealogical data from Williamsburg, Florence & Georgetown
Counties, SC, for the following families: Brown, Graham, Gor-
don, Daniel, Newell, Lavender, Lifrage, McClary, Askins, Har-
dy, Durant, Baker, Bigham, Nesmith, Eaddy, Barr, Bartell, El-
more, Hewitt, Parrott, Britton, Scott, Keels, McKnight, Hem-
ingway, Skinner, Huggins, Floyd, McDaniel & Screven [SpC] WMTR
Tiernan, Charles B. The Tiernan & other families... Baltimore
MD: Wm. J. Gallery, 1901. 466 p.   SCHS
Tiernan, Charles B. The Tiernan family in MD... Baltimore:
Gallery & McCann, 1898. 222 p.   SCHS
Tiller family genealogy. 2 vol.   SCHS
Tiller family genealogy. Typescript, 1968.   SCHS
Tiller, Lorena Lavender. Lavender family [history]. 1967. SCHS
Tillman, James D. Tillman & Hamilton family records... Merid-
ian MS: author, 1959-63. 3 vol.   SCL, CLEM
Tillman, Stephen F. Reynolds family, 1530-1959. Chevy Chase
MD: author, 1959. 464 p.   GWPL
Tillman, Stephen F. Tilghman-Tillman family, 1225-1945. Ann
Arbor MI: Edwards Bros., 1946. 473 p.   SCL, FLMC
Tillman, Stephen F. The Tillman family. Richmond VA: William
Byrd Press, 1930. 134 p.   SCL, CLEM
Tims, Eugene C. Some descendants & antecedents of Nathan Tims
of Chester County, SC. Wolfe City TX: Henington Publishing
Co., 1967. 42 p.   SCL, CSCL
Tims, Eugene C. Some descendants of James Hanna of SC. Wolfe
City TX: Henington Publishing Co., 1969. 48 p.   CSCL
Tippin, Ernest E. A brief history of George Manton Tippin, Sr.,
of Ireland, York County, SC, and Washington County, IN, & his
descendants. Wichita KS: Preston Printing Co., 1952. 94 p.
                                                             SCL
Tippin, James J. Ancestry of Sanford Lathadeus Tippin family of
Henderson County, KY. Shreveport LA: M.L. Bath Co., 1940.
38 p.   SCL, SPCL
Todd, Joseph N. A short history of the Todds & Friersons, &
other related families: Warnock, McAlister, James, Kolb, Poun-
cey, & Crosland. Washington DC: NPub, 1951. 30 p.   ANCL
Tomlinson, Maude R. Reid family, 1776-1974. Shelbyville IL:
Austin, 1974. 112 p.   SCHS
Tompkins, Robert A. The Tomkins-Tompkins genealogy... Los An-
geles CA: author, 1942. 720 p.   SCHS
Toomey, Thomas N. The O'Toomeys of Croom & their descendants.
St. Louis MO: author, 1920. 17 p.   SCHS

Torrence, Clayton. Winston of VA & allied families. Richmond
VA: Whittet & Shepperson, 1927. 477 p.   SCHS
Torrence, Robert M. Torrence & allied families. Published un-
der the auspices of the Genealogical Society of PA, 1938.
559 p.   SCHS
Tracy, Sherman W. The Tracy genealogy...of Stephen Tracy of
Plymouth Colony, 1623... Rutland VT: Tuttle Publishing Co.,
1936. 242 p.   SCHS
Travis Family [SpC]   PIPD
Travis, Robert J. The Travis (Travers) families & its allies:
Darracott, Lewis, Livingston, Nicholson, McLaughlin, Pharr,
Smith, & Terrell... Savannah GA: author, 1954. 194 p.   SCHS
Treadway, Oswell G. Edward Treadway & his descendants. Chica-
go IL: privately printed, 1931, 1943. 14 p.   SCHS
Treadway, William E. Treadway & Burket families...through the
documented ancestry of Jonas Robert Treadway. NP: author,
1951. 148 p.   SCHS
Treat, John H. The Treat family: a genealogy of Trott, Traut &
Treat... Salem MA: Salem Press, 1893. 637 p.   SCHS
Trezevant, John T. The Trezevant family in the United States,
from the date of the arrival of Daniel Trezevant, Huguenot,
at Charles Town, SC, in 1685, to the present date. Cola:
State Co., 1914. 122 p.   SCL, CHLS, SCHS
Trezevant, John T. The Trezevant family in the United States...
facsimile reproduction of the 1914 edition, including some
additional family records. Chstn: Furlong, 1977.   SCL, SCHS
Tucker, Robert W. The descendants of the presidents. Charlotte
NC: Delmar Printing Co., 1975. 222 p.   CLEM
Twenty-fifth anniversary. Anderson family reunion. Descendants
of James Mason "Tyger Jim" Anderson & Polly Miller Anderson.
NP: NPub, 1964. v.p.   SCL
Updike, Ethel S. Armstrong, Branyon, Bryson & allied families
of the south [incl. Lindsay, Greer & Ellis families]. Salt
Lake City UT: Hobby Press, 1967. 419 p.   SCL, LRCL
Van Name, Elmer G. The Elwell family...southern NJ. Haddon-
field NJ: NPub, 1963. 40 p.   SCHS
Van Name, Elmer G. The Joseph Smith family of Gloucester &
Salem Counties, NJ. The James Dye family of Gloucester County
NJ. Haddonfield NJ: NPub, 1964. 32 p.   SCHS
Van Wyck Family [SpC]   PIPD
Vance genealogy. NP: NPub, nd. 6 p.   LRCL
Vogtle, Alvin W. The Stringer family & kin...pioneers of Law-
rence County, MS. Revised ed. Birmingham AL?: NPub, 1967.
20 p.   SCL, SCHS
Von Meister, Leila G. Some notes on the ancestors & descendants
of the Trapmans. NP: NPub, 1927? 24 p.   SCHS
Wade, Lottie F. Barry family of York County, SC. NP: typescript, 1972. unp.   YOCL
Wade, Ophelia R. The Box book, with McElroy & Floyd; the Box
families of SC, TN, AL, MS, TX... Bragg City MO: author,
1975? 241 p.   SCL

Waggoner Family [SpC]   FACM
Waggoner, John G. The Waggoner family; a list of the emigrant
Hans Waggoner & his descendants...1922, additions...1929. NP:
NPub, 1929. 58 p.   GWPL
Wait, Jane. History of the Wofford family. Spartanburg: Band &
White, 1928.   SPCL
Walker, Alice A. History of the Kincaid family & the invention
of the first cotton gin on his plantation. Winnsboro: NPub,
1965. 16 p.   FACM, CLEM
Walker, Anne K. Braxton Bragg Comer; his family tree from Vir-
ginia's colonial days [incl. Hammond, Drewry, Etheridge & Moss
families]. Richmond VA: Dietz Press, 1947. 364 p.   CLEM
Walker, Anne K. The storied Kendalls... Richmond VA: Dietz
Press, 1947. 163 p.   SCHS
Walker, Emmeline D. The Walkers of SC. Apalachicola FL: mimeo,
1931. 73 p.   SCHS
Walker, Joseph R. Walkers of SC & allied families [incl. Wood-
ward, Bull, Heyward, Guerard & Cuthbert families]. Petersburg
VA: privately printed, 1961. 73 p.   EDTO
Walker, Legare. The Walker family...of Edgefield County, SC.
Summerville: NPub, 1945. 60 p.   SCL, SCHS
Walker, Lucile G. The Friendly Swepson Geddings family of Pax-
ville SC... Macon GA: Rowland Printing Co., 1975. 140 p.
                                                            COMMON
Wall Family [SpC]   FACM
Wallace, George S. Wallace genealogical data pertaining to the
descendants of Peter Wallace & Elizabeth Woods, his wife.
Charlottesville VA: Michie, 1927.   SCHS
Wallace, Nettie S. Wallace-Feemster-Turner families of York
County, SC. NP: typescript, nd. unp.   YOCL
Waller Family [SpC]   GSGN
Wannamaker, John S. The Wannamaker, Salley, Mackay & Bellinger
families. Chstn: W,E&C, 1937. 485 p.   COMMON
Ward, Ebin J. Genealogy of the family of Josiah Ward, sixth
generation from William Ward. Ottawa IL: NPub, 1914.   SCHS
Wardlaw, Joseph G. Genealogy of the Wardlaw family... York:
author, 1929. 215 p.   GWPL, YOCL
Wardlaw, Joseph G. Genealogy of the Witherspoon family [incl.
Heathley, Donnom, Crawford, White, Dunlap, Jones families].
Yorkville: Enquirer Office, 1910. 229 p.   SCL, FLCL, YOCL
Waters, John J. The Otis family, in provincial & revolutionary
MA... Chapel Hill NC: UNC Press, 1968. 221 p.   VCOL, CLEM
Waters, Philemon B. A genealogical history of the Waters & kin-
dred families. Atlanta GA: Foote & Davies, 1902. 181 p. SPCL
                                                        SCL, SCHS
Watson, Harry L. Elihu Watson & Permelia Wright Niswanger Wat-
son & descendants... NP: Index-Journal, 1933. 57 p. SCL,GWPL
Watson, H. B. Risinger genealogy. NP: NPub, 1977. 17 p. LXMU
Watson, Louise M. Dr. & Mrs. Charles Richard Moseley & their
descendants [incl. Montague family]. NP: mimeo, 1962.
12 p.   GWPL

The Watts & their name [incl. Pollard, Taylor, Scurry, Watkins & Ball families]. NP: typescript, nd. 17 p.   GWPL
Weaver, Gustine C. The Boydstun family. Cincinnati OH: Powell & White, 1927. 145 p.   SCL, SCHS
Weaver, Gustine C. The Gustine compendium. Cincinnati OH: NPub 1929. 339 p.   SCHS
Weaver, Gustine C. The Howard lineage. The ancestry of Ida Ann Boydstun Welch through her mother Eoline Frances Howard Boyd-stun. Cincinnati OH: Powell & White, 1929. 230 p.   SCHS
Weaver, Gustine C. Welch & allied families. Cincinatti OH: Powell & White, 1932. 312 p.   SCL, SCHS
Webb Family [SpC]   PIPD
Webber, Mabel L. Descendants of John Jenkins of Charleston & of Colleton County, SC. Baltimore MD: Williams & Wilkins, 1920. 31 p.   SCHS
Weddington, Andrew S. The Cobbs of TN: descendants of John Cobb of Cobbs Court, County Kent, England, 1324-1968. Atlanta GA: Ruralist Press, 1968. 120 p.   CLEM, SCL
Weeks, Irma G. Kinsey coat of arms. NP: NPub, nd. 66 p. COML
Weise, O'Leva N. A. F. Carl Weise family. NP: author, 1979. 122 p.   FACM
Welles, Catharine J. Welles & allied families... NY: American Historical Society, 1929. 249 p.   SCHS
Wells, T. Tileston. Family notes. NY: NPub, 1927. 35 p. SCHS
Wells, T. Tileston. The Hugers of SC. NY: privately printed, 1931. 15 p.   SCL, CLEM, SCHS
Wells, T. Tileston. Les Huger de la Caroline du Sud; La Fayette a Olmutz. Paris France: Nourry, 1931. 42 p.   SCL, SCHS
West, Broadus B. Genealogy of Isaac West of Greenville County, SC. NP: NPub, nd. 53 p.   SCL, SPCL, ANCL, CHLS
Westen, Maryline C. Descendants of Thomas Cauthen, Sr., from VA to Warren County NC, to Lancaster District, SC.   LNCL
Westmoreland Family [SpC]   CRCL
Whaley, William E. The Baileys of Edisto Island, SC & some of their descendants ca. 1723 to 1970. Chstn: 1970. 84 p. SCHS
Wheeler, William A. Alden-Shedd families: Elwell, Grimes, Morse NP: privately printed, 1965.   SCHS
Whetsell, Elizabeth D. The Boyd [& Thompson] family. NP: type-script, nd. 20 p.   GWPL
Whetstone: a pamphlet. NP: NPub, 1971. 17 p.   SCL, ORCL
Whipple, Minnie N. Captain John Whipple, 1617-1685, & his de-scendants... Napierville IL: NPub, 1946. 286 p.   SCHS
Whisenhunt, Eph. Whisenhunt family genealogy. Lincolntown NC: NPub, 1975. 227 p.   SCL, ORCL, CRCL
White Family [SpC]   YOWC
White family. Account of the meeting of the descendants of Col. Thomas White of MD...June 7, 1877. Philadelphia PA: NPub, 1879. 210 p.   SCHS
White, Garner B. & others. The White family:...from the time of John White of County Antrim, Ireland, 1720, to...1968. 2nd ed Chester: NPub, nd. 115 p.   CSCL, LNCL

292

White, William B. The ancestral line of Iredell Jones, Rock
Hill, SC. Typescript, nd.   YOCL
White, William B. A brief genealogy of Alexander & Elizabeth
Campbell, of Neely's Creek, York County, SC. NP: typescript,
1973.   YOCL
White, William B. A brief sketch of the Hanna family of York
County... Typescript, 1968.   YOCL
White, William B. A brief sketch of the Strait family of Ches-
ter & York Counties, SC. Typescript, 1974.   YOCL
White, William B. Genealogical notes on the Davies family...
Rock Hill: typescript, 1957.   YOCL
White, William B. A genealogical outline of the descendants of
Col. William Hill, of York District, SC. Typescript, 1978.
unp.   YOCL
White, William B. A genealogical sketch of the descendants of
Matthew Hays (Hayes) of Fairfield County, SC. Rock Hill:
White Printing Co., 1965.   YOCL
White, William B. Genealogy of the Workman family of York Coun-
ty, SC. Typescript, 1973.   YOCL
White, William.   In re: Dundas family. Pedigree of Jane Dun-
das White. NP: privately printed, 1922. 16 p.   SCHS
White, William B. Notes on the Wylie family. Typescript.   YOCL
White, William B. The Sutton family of York County, SC. Type-
script, 1968.   YOCL
Whitfield, Emma M. Whitfield, Bryan, Smith, & related families
[incl. Hatch family]. Westminster MD: NPub, 1948?-1950. 2
vol.   CLEM
Whitley, Olga M. Colonel Joseph Howe, York County, SC... Com-
merce TX: author, 1960. 97 p.   SCL
Whitley, Olga M. The Howe line, PA, SC, KY. With connections:
Dunlap, McKenzie, Patrick & Biggers. Commerce TX: NPub, 1967.
316 p.   CLEM, YOCL, SCL
Widener Family [SpC]   FACM
Wier. The ten tribes of Wier in America; 1540-1940 [incl. Blake
family]. Atlanta GA: author, 1933, 1940. 38 p.   GWPL, CLEM
Wigg family in SC from 1700 to 1900. NP, 1959. 18 p.   SCHS
Wight, Charles H. Genealogy of the Claflin family, being a rec-
ord of Robert Mackclothlan, of Wenham, MA, & of his descend-
ants 1661-1898. NY: William Green, 1903. 473 p.   ORCC
Wigington, Elizabeth A. Allgood genealogy. Greenville: Poin-
sett Printing Co., 1963. 159 p.   COMMON
Wigington Family [SpC]   PIPD
Wilburn, Hiram Coleman. Welborn-Wilburn...the families in VA,
NC & SC. Waynesville NC: author, 1953. 104 p.   CLEM
Wilcox, Irene S. William Marion Wilcox, 1854-1940: his ances-
tors & descendants. NP: author, 1973. 44 p.   ANCL
Wilder, William M. Wilder & some connections (especially some
Ware families...3rd ed. Columbus GA: Columbus Office Supply
Co., 1969. 1312 p.   CLEM
Wiley, Robert G. Descendants of John Wesley Wiley...& Elizabeth
Ray Washburn Wiley. Cola: RLB, 1966.   YOCL

William Family [SpC]   PIPD
Williams, C. S. Descendants of Captain Joseph Miller of West
   Springfield, MA, 1698-1908. NY: privately printed, 1908.
   39 p.   SCHS
Williams, Charles C. Ancestors & posterity of Richard Williams
   & Frances Dighton, his wife, of Taunton, MA. Typescript,
   27 p.   SCHS
Williams, Frances L. A founding family: the Pinckneys of SC...
   NY: Harcourt, Brace Jovanovich, 1968, 1978. 533 p.   COMMON
Williams, Frank L. John Harrison of Ninety-Six District, SC,
   & Botetourt County, VA, 1771-1808. NP: mimeo, nd. 23 p. GWPL
Williams, I. Newton. The Rogers-Turfler family... Bradley Beach
   NY: Clarence W. Smith, 1946. 114 P.   SCHS
Williams, Joseph T. A genealogical sketch of the Williams fami-
   ly. Rock Hill: typescript, 1965.   YOCL
Williams, Wyman L. The Williams & Tyler families. Cola: author
   1980. 62 p.   SCHS
Williamson Family [SpC]   FACM
Williamson, Mary F. History of the Rogers family. Grant KY:
   mimeo, 1958. 51 p.   GWPL
Willie, Betty. League family of VA & SC. Amarillo TX: author,
   1976. 114 p.   LRCL
Williford, William B. Williford & allied families. Atlanta GA:
   Foote & Davies, 1962. 284 p.   SCL, SCHS, AHJR, COML
Willis, J. Ernest. House of Daniel Willis. Traveler's Rest SC:
   author, 1968. 49 p.   LRCL
Willison Family [SpC]   PIPD
Wilmeth, James L. Wilmot-Wilmoth-Wilmeth. Philadelphia PA:
   author, 1940. 373 p.   SCHS
Wilson Family [SpC]   GSGN
Wilson, Ida DeMay. The DeMay family & the Wilson family. Ag-
   win CA: Pacific Union College Press, 1974. 257 p.   SCL
Wilson, Robert. Genealogy of the Croft family. Aiken: Palmetto
   Press, 1904. 45 p.   SCL, USAI
Wilson, York L. A Carolina-Virginia genealogy of the Wilson-
   Chamberlayne-Stanyarne-Cave-Murray-Reade & Windebank families
   ... Aldershot, Hantshire, England: The Wellington Press,
   1962. 349 p.   SCL, SCHS
Wilson, York L. Wilson-Miller-Reade. A Carolina-Virginia gene-
   alogy. Aldershot, Hantshire, England: Gale & Polden, 1962.
   349 p.   COMMON
Winans, Inez. The Keasler book; descendants of Henry Kesler,
   planter of Newberry County, SC. Sacramento CA: author, 1977.
   151 p.   ANCL, NWRL
Wisda, Georgia G. Gosney family records, 1740-1940... NP:
   NPub, 1940? 325 p.   SCHS
Wishert, Mattie L. Descendants of David Johnathan Estes & Nan-
   nie Ruth Bobo Estes. NP: NPub, 1978. 37 p.   LRCL
Witherspoon, Robert. An early manuscript copy of the Wither-
   spoon family chronicle and later notes on related families...
   Cola: RLB, 1967, 1971. 39 p.   SCL, WMCL, FLCL, FLMC, MACL

Wolfe Family [SpC]   CRCL
Wolfe, Frank W. Genealogical record of James Russell Daniel
    Wolfe, Sr., of Orangeburg County, SC... NP: NPub, 1961. 55
    p.   ORCL
Wolfe, William C. A record of the Rowe family... NP: NPub, nd.
    11 p.   ORCL
Wolling Family [SpC]   FACM
Womack, Helen R. The book of Deason. Dallas TX: author, 1978.
    323 p.   SCL
Womack, Mildred C. Alston (Olsteen) Clark descendants of Lan-
    caster District, SC, 1771-1969... NP: NPub, 1969.   LNCL
Womack, Mildred C. Descendants of William Cauthorn, a Virginian
    from Warren County NC to Lancaster County, SC... NP: NPub,
    1968. unp.   LNCL
Womack, Mildred C. Meet your Hammond relatives. Descendants of
    Samuel Hammond & Mary Jenkins Hammond - Virginians of Camden
    District, SC. Atlanta GA: NPub, 1975. unp.   LNCL
Wood, Christine. Wood works...1100 descendants of William Wood
    ...in Spartanburg District, SC... NP: NPub, 1971.   SCL, SPCL
Wood, J. Wilbert. The Wood family of Laurens County, SC. NP:
    mimeo, nd. 50 p.   SCL, LRCL, ANCL, GWPL
Wood, Marie S. The Glen-Glenn family of Scotland, Ireland &
    America... Atlanta GA: Darby Printing Co., 1968. 205 p.
                                                            SCHS, SCL
Wood, Willie M. The family of George Marcus Dorn, one of 13
    children born to George Washington Dorn & Martha Timmerman
    Dorn of Edgefield County, S.C. NP: NPub, 1979. 15 p.   EDTO
Woodal Family [SpC]   PIPD
Woodburn, James A. Woodburn history... NP: Indiana University
    Press, 1935. 262 p.   CSCL
Woodruff, Caldwell. Heriots of Scotland & SC... NP: typescript
    1939. 341 p.   SCHS
Woodruff, Caldwell. Tucker Harris (1747-1821) of Charleston,
    SC... NP: typescript, 1938. 343 p.   SCHS
Woods, Gary D. Doyle & related families... Temple TX: NPub,
    1960. 184 p.   ANCL
Woodson, Hortense. Charles May & his descendants, who settled
    at May's Cross Roads in old Edgefield County, SC. Edgefield:
    May Family Assn., 1956. 287 p.   SCL, EDTO
Woodson, Hortense. Peter Outz, 1st, & his descendants. Edge-
    field: Advertiser Press, 1949. 345 p.   SCL, EDTO, NWRL, GWPL
Woolley, John B. John Bristow of Middlesex County, VA, & de-
    scendants...[incl. Davis family]. NY: Vantage Press, 1969.
    263 p.   SCL, SCHS
Worthy, Pauline M. A memoir of Ira B. Jones & Rebecca Wyse
    Jones.   SCL, LNCL
Wright, Anne M. A record of the descendants of Isaac Ross &
    Jean Brown, & the allied families of Alexander, Conger, Har-
    ris, Hill, King, Killingsworth, Mackey, Moores, Sims, Wade,
    etc. Atlanta GA: Conger Printing Co., 1977. 233 p. SCL, KECA
Wright Family [SpC]   CRCL

Wright family: ancestors & descendants [of] James Wilson Wright who married Cynthia Rebecca Jones. Paris KY: 1954. 21 p.SCHS

Wyatt, Lillian R. The Reeves, Mercer & Newkirk families: a compilation. Jacksonville ??: Cooper Press, 1956. 374 p.SCL,SCHS

Wylie Family [SpC]   FACM, YOWC

Wyrick Family [SpC]   FACM

Wyse, Frederick C. History of the Wise & Wyse families of SC... Richmond VA?: Wm. Brown & Son, 1944. 64 p.   SCL, CLEM, NWRL

Yates, Edward M. The Yates book: William Yates & his descendants. Old Orchard ME: author, 1906. 46 p.   SCHS

Yeadon, Richard. The Marion family and the widow of General Marion. Mimeo, nd.   SCHS

Yeamans Family [SpC]   YOWC

Young Family [SpC]   FACM

Young, Pauline. The Norris family of Abbeville, SC (old Ninety-Six District). Abbeville: author, 1948. 9 p.   CLEM

Youngblood, Georgia K. History of the Youngblood family of Carlowville AL. NP: NPub, 1953. 20 p.   SCHS

Zeigler, John A. The last of the Bighams... Florence: author, 1925. 230 p.   COMMON

Zink, Robert L. The Philip Zink family in America. Henderson NE: Service Press, 1975. 130 p.   SCHS

APPENDIX I

Articles and historical materials in the Yearbooks of the City of Charleston, 1880 - 1951 (courtesy City of Charleston Department of Archives & Records).

"An Account of the City of Charles-Town", from London Magazine, June, 1762, in CCYB 1882, pp. 341-342.

"Address delivered by Hon. Chas. H. Simonton on the unveiling of the Washington Light Infantry Monument, July 21st, 1891, in Washington Square", in CCYB 1891, pp. 143-153.

[Aiken, William] "In Memoriam", in CCYB 1887, pp. 283-287.

Aldredge, Robert Crumm. "A list of persons known to have been living in or near Charles Town in the year 1735", in CCYB 1939 pp. 184-210.

Aldredge, Robert Crumm. "Weather observers & observations at Charleston, S.C., 1670-1871", in CCYB 1940, pp. 190-257.

Andrews, Robert Armstrong. "Restoration and rededication of the Dock Street Theatre", in CCYB 1937, pp. 186-197.

Archer, Henry P. "A history of the public schools of Charleston", in CCYB 1908, pp. 21-40.

[Armstrong, Col. James] "In Memoriam", in CCYB 1930, p. 322.

"An artist's conception of Charleston in 1861, as seen from the Mount Pleasant shore". Reproduced from The South In The Building of the Nation, in CCYB 1936, p. 185.

"The Association of 1774, 'In favor of non-importation, non-consumption, and non-exportation', convened at Philadelphia. With the autographs of the forty-eight signers appended in fac-simile", in CCYB 1883, pp. 316-322.

[Ball, William Moultrie] "In Memoriam", in CCYB 1937, p. 185.

Barbot, Joseph C. "Municipal Art Gallery", in CCYB 1914, appendix pp. 443-465.

[Barbot, Joseph C.] "In Memoriam", in CCYB 1937, p. 182.

[Bird, John S.] "Mortuary", in CCYB 1887, pp. 290-292.

Bocock, Th. S., R.M.T. Hunter & Jefferson Davis. "Joint resolution of thanks to General Beauregard and the officers & men of his command, for the defence of Charleston, South Carolina", in CCYB 1895, p. 364.

Brackett, Gilbert R. "An historic sketch of the Second Presbyterian Church, of Charleston, S.C., from its beginning to the present time", in CCYB 1898, pp. 328-351.

Brale, Edward Othmel Gale. "A poem written in 1804, by Edward Othmel Gale Brale, describing a trip up the Cooper River", in CCYB 1903, appendix pp. 14-26.

Brewster, William Edward II. "A view of the public debt of the city of Charleston, South Carolina, 1914-1948", in CCYB 1948, pp. 179-196.

Browne, Rev. E.C.L. "A historical sketch of the Second Independent or Congregationalist, afterwards the Unitarian Church, established 1772", in CCYB 1882, pp. 406-426.

[Bruns, John Dickson] "Mortuary", in CCYB 1883, pp. 259-265.

[Bryan, George D.] "In Memoriam", in CCYB 1919, pp. 625-626.
[Bryan, Judge George S.] "A sketch of the life of Judge Geo. S. Bryan", in CCYB 1895, pp. 376-385.
[Bryan, J.P. Kennedy] "In Memoriam", in CCYB 1918, p. 521.
[Buist, Henry] "Mortuary", in CCYB 1887, p. 277.
[Buist, Samuel S.] "In Memoriam", in CCYB 1916, p. 528.
[Campbell, Celia] "Mortuary", in CCYB 1887, pp. 253-260.
[Campbell, James B.] "Mortuary", in CCYB 1883, pp. 278-280.
Cantwell, Edward P. "A history of the Charleston Police Force", in CCYB 1908, appendix pp. 3-19.
[Cappelmann, John D.] "In Memoriam", in CCYB 1930, p. 317.
"The centennial of the incorporation of the City of Charleston, August 13, 1-83", in CCYB 1883, pp. 325-380.
Chaffin, W.L., ed. "Extracts from the diary of Elder Wm. Pratt, relating to the founding of a Congregationalist Church at Dorchester, S.C., in 1695", in CCYB 1897, pp. 503-512.
Charleston Daily Courier, Aug. 29, 1868. "Charleston in olden times", in CCYB 1936, pp. 193-196.
"Charleston in war-time, 1861-1865", in CCYB 1908, appendix pp. 41-58.
Cheves, Langdon, ed. "A letter from Carolina in 1715, and journal of the march of the Carolinas into the Cherokee Mountains, in the Yemassee Indian War, 1715-16", in CCYB 1894, pp. 313-354.
[Chicco, Vincent] "In Memoriam", in CCYB 1928, p. 305.
Chichester, Rev. C.E. "Historical sketch of the Charleston Port Society", in CCYB 1884, pp. 313-334.
Chisolm, J. Bachman. "[Sketch of the] St. Andrew's Society, of Charleston, S.C., founded A.D. 1729", in CCYB 1894, pp. 274-294.
Clark, Eugene C. "A history of the first hundred years of the High School of Charleston, 1839-1939", in CCYB 1943, pp. 195-247.
[Cohen, Sidney Jacobi] "Tribute in respect. In Memoriam", in CCYB 1915, p. 448.
[Conlon, John H.] "In Memoriam", in CCYB 1921, pp. 635-636.
[Conlon, Thomas M.] "In Memoriam", in CCYB 1906, pp. 361-364.
"Confederate orders and communications to Col. J. B. Kershaw", in CCYB 1895, pp. 357-363.
[Conner, General James] "Mortuary", in CCYB 1883, pp. 265-276.
"Copy of signatures and seals of Bn. Smith, J. Rutledge, Henry Laurens, Peter Horlbeck, P. Manigault, M. Brewton, Thos. Lynch and Chas. Pinckney for the building of the Exchange and Custom House and the new Watch House", in CCYB 1898, p. 377.
"Correspondence - Lord Charles Montague with Gen. William Moultrie, Charles-Town, 1781", in CCYB 1884, pp. 309-312.
Cosgrove, James. "The Sanitary and Drainage Commission of Charleston County", in CCYB 1902, appendix pp. 89-104.
[Courtenay, William A.] "In Memoriam", in CCYB 1908, pp. 365-367.
[Cramer, Alderman A.F.C.] "In Memoriam" in CCYB 1908, p. 368.

Davis, Nora M. "Colonial hatchments in America", in CCYB 1946, pp. 182-193.

Davis, Nora M. "Public powder magazines at Charleston", in CCYB 1942, pp. 186-210.

[Davis, Gen. Zimmerman] "In Memoriam", in CCYB 1910, pp. 401-402

[Dawson, Francis Warrington] "In memory of Francis Warrington Dawson, born May 17th, 1840. Died March 12th, 1889. Editor, soldier, scholar, statesman", in CCYB 1889, p. ii.

[DeSaussure, Dr. H.W.] "Mortuary", in CCYB 1887, pp. 262-263.

[DeSaussure, General Wilmot G.] "Mortuary", in CCYB 1886, pp. 210-215.

DeSaussure, Wilmot G. "Charleston a century ago", in CCYB 1881, pp. 378-380.

DeSaussure, Wilmot G. "Names of the officers of the South Carolina regiments of the Continental Establishment", in CCYB 1893, pp. 205-237.

DeSaussure, Wilmot G. "The siege of Charleston, 1780", in CCYB 1884, pp. 282-308.

"Diary of Captain Bernard Elliott. Soldiers belonging to the Grenadier company of the Second Regiment...1775-1778", in CCYB 1889, pp. 151-262.

[Dibble, Rev. Virgil C.] "In Memoriam", in CCYB 1918, p. 517.

[Dingle, James H.] "In Memoriam", in CCYB 1938, p. 181.

"The earliest map of the Carolinas, made by order of the Lords Proprietors, 1672", in CCYB 1886, p. 248.

[Eason, James M.] "Mortuary", in CCYB 1882, pp. 295-297.

Endicott, Admiral M.J. and R. Goodwyn Rhett. "Notes of establishment of the Navy Yard at Charleston, So. Ca. Why the United States Government selected the port of Charleston", in CCYB 1901, appendix pp. 81-96.

"An exact prospect of Charlestown, the metropolis of the province of South Carolina", in CCYB 1882, p. 341.

"Extracts from a private manuscript written by Governor Paul Hamilton, Sr., during the period of the Revolutionary War, from 1776-1800", in CCYB 1898, pp. 300-328.

"Fac-simile of an old map of Carolina. Showing the settlements on the Cooper and Ashley [rivers] previous to 1700", in CCYB 1883, p. 376.

"A fac-simile of Sir Henry Clinton's 1780 map of the siege of Charles Town", in CCYB 1882, pp. 371-372.

[Fincken, E.H.] "In Memoriam", in CCYB 1908, pp. 371-373.

"Fort Sumter - corrected roll of commanders", in CCYB 1884, p. 403.

Fowler, William C., Ll.D. "The historical status of the Negro in Connecticut", in CCYB 1900, appendix pp. 3-64.

"Fragment of a journal kept by the Rev. William Tennent describing his journay, in 1775, to Upper South Carolina at the request of the Council of Safety, to induce the Tories to sign an association to support the cause of the colonists", in CCYB 1894, pp. 296-312.

[Frampton, L.A.] "Mortuary", in CCYB 1886, pp. 205-206.

299

"Franchise of the Charleston Northern Railway", in CCYB 1913, appendix pp. 461-476.

[Furchgott, Max] "In Memoriam", in CCYB 1921, pp. 636-639.

Gadsden, P.H. "Report to the Mayor of Charleston on immigration to the South", in CCYB 1907, appendix pp. 3-12.

[Geddings, Dr. J.F.M.] "Mortuary", in CCYB 1887, pp. 250-251.

"General William Moultrie's epitaph", in CCYB 1885, p. 341.

"The German Fusiliers in the war of American independence - founded 1775", in CCYB 1885, pp. 342-346.

Gilchrist, Major Robert C. "Confederate defence of Morris Island", in CCYB 1884, pp. 350-402.

Greene, Capt. B.D.; J.P. Allen; and T.M. Fischer. "Charleston Harbor improvements showing the sites of the north and south jetties, the progress made in their construction to June 30th, 1881, and the present depth of the bar", in CCYB 1881, front.

Gregorie, Anne King. "Notes on the 'Bedstead Tomb' at St. Michael's", in CCYB 1942, pp. 181-184.

Hale, Senator, ed. "Report of the hearings before the Committee on Naval Affairs relating to the proposed transfer of the Naval Station from Port Royal to Charleston, S.C.", in CCYB 1900, appendix pp. 83-205.

Halsey, Alfred O. "The passing of a great forest and the history of the mills which manufactured it into lumber", in CCYB 1937, pp. 198-218.

Hamilton, Gov. Paul, Sr. "Extracts from a private manuscript during the period of the Revolutionary War, from 1776-1800", in CCYB 1898, pp. 299-327.

[Hanckel, John] "Mortuary", in CCYB 1886, pp. 207-209.

Hart, Rev. Oliver. "The tornado of 1761", in CCYB 1885, pp. 389-392.

[Healy, John J.] "In Memoriam", in CCYB 1937, p. 183.

[Heffron, Robert C.] "In Memoriam", in CCYB 1927, p. 335.

Hemphill, J.C. "A short sketch of the South Carolina Interstate and West Indian Exposition", in CCYB 1902, appendix pp. 107-171.

Hemphill, J.C. "A story of the Coast Defense Squadron and the cruiser Charleston", in CCYB 1905, appendix pp. 29-56.

[Hennesy, Hugh B.] "In Memoriam", in CCYB 1946, p. 10.

[Hertz, John H.] "In Memoriam", in CCYB 1927, p. 336.

"The Hibernian Society celebrates its one hundredth anniversary" in CCYB 1901, appendix pp. 3-58.

"High School of Charleston", in CCYB 1910, appendix pp. 3-29.

"Hilton's voyage of discovery lately made on the coast of Florida, from lat. 31 to 33 deg. 45 min. north lat., together with proposals made by the commissioners of the Lords Proprietors to all such persons as shall become the first settlers on the rivers, harbors, and creeks there", in CCYB 1884, pp. 229-261.

[Hirsch, Isaac W.] "In Memoriam", in CCYB 1925, p. 358.

Historical Commission. "Some Charleston wharves", in CCYB 1936, pp. 183-192.

Historical Commission. "West Point rice mills", in CCYB 1937, pp. 211-218.

[Holmes, Frances Simmons] "In Memoriam", in CCYB 1882, pp. 335-338.

Holmes, George S. "The parish church of St. Michael in Charles Town, founded 1752", in CCYB 1886, pp. 281-327.

[Honour, John Henry, D.D.] "Mortuary", in CCYB 1885, pp. 231-235.

Hopke, J.G. August] "In Memoriam", in CCYB 1947, pp. 10-11.

Hopkins, Thomas F. "Historical sketch of St. Mary's Church", in CCYB 1897, pp. 427-502.

[Horlbeck, Dr. H.B.] "Official action of the City Council on the death of Dr. H.B. Horlbeck", in CCYB 1903, appendix pp. 7-8.

Horlbeck, Dr. H.B. "Address before the American Health Association, Nov. 1890, on maritime sanitation at ports of arrival", in CCYB 1890, pp. 135-159.

Horlbeck, Dr. H.B. "Report of the annual meeting of the American Public Health Association and recommendations for Charleston", in CCYB 1885, pp. 64-76.

Horn, Rev. E.T. "A historic sketch of St. John's Lutheran church, better known through two generations as 'Bachman's Church', covering a period of one hundred and fifty years", in CCYB 1884, pp. 262-279.

Horry, Elias. "An address respecting the Charleston and Hamburgh Railroad", delivered in Charleston at the Medical College, Oct. 2, 1883", in CCYB 1902, appendix pp. 5-38.

[Huger, Benjamin F.] "Mortuary", in CCYB 1887, pp. 263-264.

[Huger, William Harleston] "In Memoriam", in CCYB 1906, pp. 368-370.

[Hutchinson, Thomas Leger] "Mortuary", in CCYB 1883, pp. 276-278.

"The Ichnography of Charles Town, at High Water, 1739", in CCYB 1884, frontspiece.

[Ingraham, George Hall] "Mortuary", in CCYB 1887, pp. 292-295.

"Instructions for emigrants from Essex County, Massachusetts, to South Carolina, 1697", in CCYB 1899, appendix pp. 149-154.

"Interesting private letters written by Carolinians in the last century", in CCYB 1886, pp. 328-341.

[Irving, Agnes K.] "In Memoriam", in CCYB 1910, pp. 405-406.

[Israel, Morris] "In Memoriam", in CCYB 1911, p. 500.

[Jahnz, Julius H.] "In Memoriam", in CCYB 1928, p. 306.

The James S. Gibbes Memorial Art Gallery", in CCYB 1904, pp. 81-85.

Jesunofsky, L.N. "Notes on the cyclone of August 1893", in CCYB 1893, pp. 247-272.

Johnson, Rev. John. "Daily important events in Charleston and vicinity during the Civil War, 1860-'65", in CCYB 1888, appendix pp. i - xx.

[Johnson, Oscar Edward] "In Memoriam", in CCYB 1923, p. 264.

Kohn, August. "The Charleston of to-day", in CCYB 1909, appendix pp. 3-14.

Kohn, August. "Industrial Development", from the jubilee
    edition of the News and Courier, in CCYB 1909, pp. 38-66.
"The Ladies Benevolent Society", in CCYB 1896, pp. 418-423.
[Lapham, Samuel] "In Memoriam", in CCYB 1930, p. 318.
Lea, J.O. "Bonded Debt, Charleston, S.C.", in CCYB 1904, pp.
    15-41.
[Lebby, Robert, M.D.] "Mortuary", in CCYB 1887, pp. 251-253.
[Lee, A. Markley] "In Memoriam", in CCYB 1910, pp. 403-404.
[Lesesne, Chancellor Henry D.] "Mortuary", in CCYB 1886, p.
    224.
"Letters from General Francis Marion and General William Moul-
    trie, 1781-1788", in CCYB 1898, pp. 380-385.
"Letters from Major-General Nathaniel Greene to Brigadier Gen-
    eral Thomas Sumter, 1780-'83", in CCYB 1899, appendix pp.
    71-135.
"Letters from the Secretary of the Navy transmitting a report of
    the Board of Naval officers appointed for the purpose of exam-
    ining into the expediency of changing the location of the
    Naval Station now at Port Royal, S.C., to some point in the
    state of S.C. near the City of Charleston", in CCYB 1902,
    appendix pp. 41-88.
"Letters of the Hon. Rich[ar]'d Hutson", in CCYB 1895, pp. 313-
    325.
"Letters of General Francis Marion (1780)", in CCYB 1895, pp.
    326-332.
Levin, Nathaniel. "The congregation Beth Elohim of Charleston,
    S.C.", in CCYB 1884, pp. 280-281.
Levin, Nathaniel. "Historical sketch of the congregation Beth
    Elohim of Charleston, S.C., established 1750", in CCYB 1883,
    pp. 301-316.
[Lewis, John R.] "In Memoriam", in CCYB 1930, p. 320.
[Lockwood, Mayor Henry W.] "In Memoriam", in CCYB 1944, pp. 11-
    14.
[Lowndes, Charles T.] "Mortuary", in CCYB 1885, pp. 219-220.
[Lunz, Minnie Lofton] "A Resolution", in CCYB 1947, p. 170.
[Lynch, Rt. Rev. P. N., Bishop of Charleston] "Mortuary", in
    CCYB 1882, pp. 322-328.
[Macbeth, Charles] "Mortuary", in CCYB 1881, pp. 251-253.
[Manigault, General A.M.] "Mortuary", in CCYB 1886, pp. 225-226.
Manigault, G.E. "History of the Carolina Art Association", in
    CCYB 1894, pp. 243-273.
"Map of Charleston and vicinity - showing location of all forts,
    lines of defence &c, 1860-65", in CCYB 1885, p. 352.
"A map of Charleston showing Old Town and the early farms on
    the west bank of the Ashley [river], the present site of the
    city, up to Clements Ferry Road, with all the lines of forti-
    fications and historic points", in CCYB 1883, frontspiece.
"A map of Charlestown in 1704", in CCYB 1880, p. 243.
"A map of Charles Town in 1671, as originally settled on the
    west bank of the Ashley River, and also showing the present
    site", in CCYB 1880, p. 241.

"A map of Charles Town (without date)", in CCYB 1880, p. 257.
"A map of Charles Town with its entrenchments, and those made
during the siege by the English in 1780", in CCYB 1880, p.
264.
"Map of Charleston harbor", in CCYB 1890, p. 134.
"A map of Charleston - the harbor and vicinity - showing the location of the jetties now being constructed by the Congress of
the Unites States, upon plans of General G.A. Gilmore, U.S.
Engineer Corps, to which is appended valuable commercial
statistics", in CCYB 1880, frontispiece.
"Map of the improved part of Carolina, with the settlements
down to 1715", in CCYB 1886, p. 280.
"A map of the present city of Charleston", in CCYB 1880, p.
281.
"Map showing soundings at the jetties in Charleston harbor from
1884 to 1892", in CCYB 1893, p. 272.
[Marion, Francis] "A brief sketch of Gen. Francis Marion, with
his epitaph", in CCYB 1885, pp. 338-340.
[Marjenhoff, O. G.] "In Memoriam", in CCYB 1906, p. 365.
[Masters, R.M.] "In Memoriam", in CCYB 1918, p. 513.
[Mathews, Brice Howard] "In Memoriam", in CCYB 1937, p. 184.
Mazyck, William G. "The Charleston Museum, its genesis and de-
velpoment", in CCYB 1907, appendix pp. 13-51.
McCormack, Helen G. "A catalogue of maps of Charleston based on
the collection of engraved and photostatic copies owned by
Alfred O. Halsey", in CCYB 1944, pp. 179-203.
McCrady, Edward. "An historical address, delivered in Charles-
ton, S.C., by Gen. Edward McCrady, before the graduating
class of the Medical College of the state of South Carolina.
1885.", in CCYB 1895, pp. 386-424.
McCrady, Edward. "Historical sketch of St. Philip's Church", in
CCYB 1896, pp. 318-374.
McCrady, Louis DeB. "General Edward McCrady and some of the in-
cidents of his career", in CCYB 1904, pp. 43-85.
McKinley, Carl. "A descriptive narrative of the earthquake of
August 31, 1886", in CCYB 1886, pp. 343-441.
McKinley, Carl. "A descriptive narrative of the cyclone, August
1885", in CCYB 1885, pp. 371-388.
[McLaughlin, Bernard Anthony] "In Memoriam", in CCYB 1930, p.
319.
[McLeod, B.F.] "In Memoriam", in CCYB 1929, p. 353.
[Melchers, Alderman Theodore] "In Memoriam", in CCYB 1907, pp.
326-328.
Melchers, Franz. "Historical sketch of the German Artillery,
companies A and B", in CCYB 1898, pp. 352-356.
[Middleton, Henry A.] "Mortuary", in CCYB 1887, pp. 261-262.
Middleton, Margaret Simons. "A sketch of the Ladies Benevolent
Society, founded 1813", in CCYB 1941, pp. 216-256.
[Miles, Rev. Edward R.] "Mortuary", in CCYB 1885, pp. 220-222.
Missildine, Rev. A. M. "Historical sketch of the Independent
or Congregational (Circular) Church, from its origin to the

present time", in CCYB 1882, pp. 373-396.
[Mitchell, John S.] "Mortuary", in CCYB 1887, pp. 276-277.
[Mitchell, Julian] "In Memoriam", in CCYB 1907, p. 325.
[Moise, Benjamin F.] "Mortuary", in CCYB 1887, pp. 249-250.
[Morris, Richard J.] "In Memoriam", in CCYB 1925, p. 357.
[Mostin, J. Elmore] "In Memoriam", in CCYB 1921, p. 636.
"The Mount Sion Society, 1777", in CCYB 1887, pp. 325-345.
[Muckenfuss, Dr. B.A.] "In Memoriam", in CCYB 1919, p. 621.
[Murray, Andrew Buist] "In Memoriam", in CCYB 1929, pp. 349-352.
"Muster rolls of the Sixth Regiment, S.C. Continental Troops, to March 18th, 1779", in CCYB 1895, pp. 333-344.
Myers, T. Bailey. "Original letters, 1775-89 period", in CCYB 1882, pp. 343-371.
[Norhden, Julian F.] "In Memoriam", in CCYB 1918, p. 515.
[O'Conner, M. P.] "Mortuary", in CCYB 1881, pp. 244-250.
"Official action of City Council on death of Bernard O'Neill and Geo. W. Williams", in CCYB 1903, appendix pp. 12-13.
"Official action of City Council on death of Dr. H. B. Horlbeck" in CCYB 1903, appendix pp. 7-8.
"Official action of City Council on death of Dr. R. B. Rhett", in CCYB 1903, appendix pp. 3-6.
"Official action of City Council upon receiving the flag of steamers 'Chicora' and 'Palmetto' presented by General W.W.H. Davis, through Mayor pro tem C. W. Kollock at Philadelphia, June, 1901", in CCYB 1903, appendix pp. 9-11.
"Official correspondence between Brigadier General Thomas Sumter and Major-General Nathaniel Greene from A.D. 1780 to 1783", in CCYB 1899, appendix pp. 3-70.
"The old Postoffice (of Charleston)", in CCYB 1898, pp. 357-379.
[O'Neale, Robert Gourdin] "Tribute of true respect, in memoriam", in CCYB 1913, pp. 428-430.
"Original letter of petition on May 10, 1780, concerning the siege of Charleston", in CCYB 1897, pp. 394-399.
"Original letters from Gen. Francis Marion and Gen. William Moultrie, 1781-1788", in CCYB 1898, pp. 380-385.
Paltsits, Victor H. "Original papers relating to the siege of Charleston in 1780", in CCYB 1897, pp. 341-425.
[Pelzer, Dr. Anthony P.] "Mortuary", in CCYB 1886, pp. 216-218.
[Pelzer, Francis J.] "In Memoriam", in CCYB 1916, p. 527.
[Poinsett, Joel R.] "A biographical sketch of the Hon. Joel R. Poinsett, 1779-1851, of South Carolina", in CCYB 1887, pp. 380-424.
Porcher, F. A. "A brief history of the Ladies' Memorial Association of Charleston, S.C., 1866-1880", in CCYB 1944, pp. 204-215.
[Porter, William Dennison] "Mortuary", in CCYB 1883, pp. 249-258.
"Proceedings relative to the presentation and reception of the sword of the late Gen. G. T. Beauregard", in CCYB 1893, pp. 273-292.

"Proclamation by Sir Henry Clinton and Mariot Arbithnot, on June 1, 1780, to restore peace and good government to the colonies" in CCYB 1882, p. 369.

[Ravenel, Daniel] "In Memoriam", in CCYB 1947, p. 161.

[Ravenel, St. Julian, M.D.] "Mortuary", in CCYB 1882, pp. 328-335.

[Redding, Capt. James F.] "In Memoriam", in CCYB 1904, appendix p. 3.

"Report of John E. Lockwood, meteorologist in charge, United States Weather Bureau, on the tornadoes at Charleston, S.C., Sept. 29, 1938", in CCYB 1938, pp. 191-194.

"Report of Robert C. Aldredge, assistant, United States Weather Bureau, Charleston, S.C., on the five tornadoes of Thursday, Sept. 29, 1938", in CCYB 1938, pp. 195-201.

[Reynolds, Alderman Thomas H.] "In Memoriam", in CCYB 1919, pp. 623-624.

[Rhett, Dr. R.B.] "Official action of City Council on death of Dr. R. B. Rhett", in CCYB 1903, appendix pp. 3-6.

Rhett, R. Goodwyn. "The Charleston Navy Yard. Why the government selected the Port of Charleston", in CCYB 1901, pp. 87-96.

Rhett, R. Goodwyn. "The Charleston of tomorrow", in CCYB 1909, appendix pp. 15-38.

[Riddock, Edward J.] "In Memoriam", in CCYB 1918, p. 519.

[Riley, Andrew J.] "In Memoriam", in CCYB 1924, p. 334.

Ripley, General R.S. "The military defences of Charleston - 1860-1865", in CCYB 1-85, pp. 347-360.

[Ripley, General Roswell S.] "Mortuary", in CCYB 1887, pp. 265-276.

[Rittenburg, Sidney] "In Memoriam", in CCYB 1944, pp. 14-15.

[Rogers, Francis S.] "In Memoriam", in CCYB 1911, pp. 501-502.

"Roper Hospital", in CCYB 1905, appendix pp. 3-28.

Rutledge, Anna Wells. "Catalogue of paintings and sculpture in Council Chamber, City Hall, Charleston, S.C.", in CCYB 1941, pp. 195-214.

Rysn, Frank Winkler, Jr. "Travelers in South Carolina in the eighteenth century", in CCYB 1945, pp. 185-256.

Sandford, Robert. "Sandford's voyage on the coast of Carolina, 1666; succeeding Hilton's voyage, in 1663", in CCYB 1885, pp. 259-296.

[Schachte, Gen. Henry] "In Memoriam", in CCYB 1930, p. 323.

The Scientific Committee... "Artesian wells, 1823-1879, with analyses of artesian, cistern and well waters in and near the city of Charleston, S.C.", in CCYB 1881, pp. 257-315.

Shaftsbury Papers. "The voyage of the colonists, 1669-1670", in CCYB 1886, pp. 239-279.

[Shepard, Dr. Charles Upham] "Mortuary", in CCYB 1886, pp. 218-223.

Sheperd, Henry E. "Sketch of the College of Charleston", in CCYB 1883, pp. 238-246.

"A short story of the South Carolina Interstate and West Indian

Exposition", in CCYB 1902, pp. 107-171.

Shuck, Rev. L. H. "Historical sketch of the First Baptist
Church", in CCYB 1881, pp. 316-324.

[Simons, Dr. Manning] "In Memoriam", in CCYB 1911, p. 499.

[Simons, Dr. Thomas Grange] "In Memoriam", in CCYB 1927, p. 337.

[Simons, W. W.] "In Memoriam", in CCYB 1913, p. 427.

Simons, W. W. "Municipal officers of the city of Charleston,
1783-1882", in CCYB 1881, pp. 367-377.

Simons, W. W. "Special proceedings of the City Council - the
earthquake, 1886", in CCYB 1887, pp. 298-309.

Simons, W. W. "Roll of executive officers of South Carolina,
from March 1776...to the present time", in CCYB 1884, pp. 335-
337.

Simons, W. W. "Roll of representatives in United States Congress from South Carolina from 1789 to 1885", in CCYB 1884,
pp. 342-349.

Simons, W. W. "Roll of United States senators from South Carolina from 1789 to 1885", in CCYB 1884, pp. 338-341.

[Simonton, Judge Charles H.] "In Memoriam", in CCYB 1904, pp.
7-13.

Simonton, Charles H. "Address delivered by the Hon. Charles H.
Simonton on the unveiling of the Washington Light Infantry
monument, July 21st, 1891, in Washington Square", in CCYB
1891, pp. 143-153.

"Sketch of the history of Charleston, S.C.", in CCYB 1880, pp.
241-318.

"A sketch of the life of Gov. Andrew Gordon Magrath", in CCYB
1895, pp. 365-375.

"A sketch of the life of Judge George S. Bryan", in CCYB 1895,
pp. 376-385.

"Sketch of the South Carolina Military Academy", in CCYB 1892,
pp. 205-236.

Smith, H. A. M. "The administration of justice in South Carolina, 1670-1860", in CCYB 1885, pp. 314-330.

Smith, J. J. Pringle. "The government of the city of Charleston, 1682-1882", in CCYB 1881, pp. 325-377.

Smith, J. J. Pringle. "Sketch of the history of Charleston,
S.C.", in CCYB 1880, pp. 241-320.

[Smith, J. Lawrence] "Mortuary", in CCYB 1883, pp. 280-288.

Smythe, Augustine T., Jr. "Torpedo and submarine attacks on the
Federal blockading fleet off Charleston during the War of Secession", in CCYB 1907, appendix pp. 53-64.

[Smyth, Mayor James Adger] "In Memoriam", in CCYB 1920, pp.
635-637.

[Solomons, Dr. Joseph R.] "Mortuary", in CCYB 1887, pp. 289-290.

"Some brief remarks on the address of the Hon. Charles Francis
Adams, LL.D., pronounced on the occasion of the dedication of
a new library building for the use of the State Historical Society of Wisconsin", in CCYB 1900, appendix pp. 65-81.

[Sottile, Nicholas] "In Memoriam", in CCYB 1928, p. 307.

"The Stamp Act excitement in 1765", in CCYB 1885, pp. 331-337.

"The steam-frigate 'New Ironsides'", in CCYB 1888, appendix pp. 21-35.

[Strong, Alderman W. F.] "In Memoriam", in CCYB 1904, appendix p. 5.

[Sullivan, John P.] "In Memoriam", in CCYB 1938, p. 181.

[Taft, R. W.] "In Memoriam", in CCYB 1907, p. 325.

Tamsberg, A. J. "President Roosevelt's visit", in CCYB 1936, pp. 177-180.

Tamsberg, A. J. "The tornadoes of 1938", in CCYB 1938, pp. 182-190.

Tennent, Rev. William. "Fragment of a journal kept by the Rev. William Tennent, describing his journey, in 1775, to upper South Carolina, at the request of the Council of Safety, to induce the Tories to sign an association to support the cause of the colonists", in CCYB 1894, pp. 295-312.

[Thayer, James M.] "In Memoriam", in CCYB 1906, pp. 366-367.

[Thayer, Alderman William] "Mortuary", in CCYB 1885, pp. 224-231

[Thiele, John Henry] "Mortuary", in CCYB 1886, pp. 226-227.

Thompson, Rev. W. T. "Historical sketch of the First Presbyterian Church", in CCYB 1882, pp. 397-405.

[Tiedeman, Mrs. John C.] "In Memoriam", in CCYB 1930, p. 321.

"The Timrod Memorial Association", in CCYB 1901, appendix pp. 59-80.

"Transactions of the Sea Island Relief Committee for the sufferers by the cyclone of August 1893", in CCYB 1893, pp. 293-296.

[Turtletaub, Jacob] "In Memoriam", in CCYB 1927, p. 334.

[Ufferhardt, William] "Mortuary", in CCYB 1887, pp. 287-288.

Vedder, Rev. Charles S., D.D. "The Confederate Home and School, 1867-86", in CCYB 1885, pp. 361-370.

Vedder, Rev. Charles S.; Gen. Wilmot G. DeSaussure, and Daniel Ravenel. "A historic sketch of the Huguenot Church, 1681-1886", in CCYB 1885, pp. 297-313.

"A view from St. Michael's steeple, looking east, showing chooners in the Cooper [river], from Charleston, in 1883", in CCYB 1936, p. 193.

"A view from St. Michael's steeple, showing how little this section of the city has changed, in fifty years, from Charleston in 1883", in CCYB 1936, p. 193.

[Von Dohlen, J. Albert] "In Memoriam", in CCYB 1945, pp. 10-11.

Waring, Joseph Ioor. "The Marine Hospitals of Charleston", in CCYB 1939, pp. 172-182.

Waring, T. R. "Immigration from Europe through the Port of Charleston", in CCYB 1906, appendix pp. 2-26.

Whilden, William G. "Extracts from the diary of the Rev. Oliver Hart from 1740-1780", in CCYB 1896, pp. 375-401.

Whilden, William G. "Reminiscences of old Charleston", in CCYB 1896, pp. 401-417.

[Wightman, W. W.] "One of the bishops of the Methodist Episcopal Church, South", in CCYB 1882, pp. 317-321.

[Williams, George Walton] "In Memoriam", in CCYB 1923, p. 264.

[Williams, George Walton] "Official action of City Council on death of Bernard O'Neill and Geo. W. Williams", in CCYB 1903, appendix pp. 12-13.

Willson, Rev. John O. "Sketch of the Methodist Church in Charleston, S.C., 1785-1887", in CCYB 1887, pp. 347-379.

[Wilson, James M.] "Mortuary", in CCYB 1887, pp. 288-289.

Wilson, Robert. "Arts and artists in provincial South Carolina" in CCYB 1899, appendix pp. 138-147.

Wilson, Robert. "Chronicles of St. James Church, Goose Creek", in CCYB 1895, pp. 345-356.

[Wohltman, John] "In Memoriam", in CCYB 1923, p. 264.

[Wragg, William T.] "Mortuary", in CCYB 1885, pp. 222-224.

[Wynne, Edward W.] "In Memoriam", in CCYB 1909, pp. 374-375.

Youmans, LeRoy F. "A sketch of the life of Gov. Magrath", in CCYB 1895, pp. 365-375.

APPENDIX II

Articles and historical records in the South Carolina Historical and Genealogical Magazine, 1900-1940; continued as the South Carolina Historical Magazine, 1941-present.

Abbott, Martin & Elmer L. Puryear. "Beleagured Charleston: letters from the city, 1860-1864." 61:61-74, 164-175, 210-218.

Abbott, Martin. "County officers in SC in 1868." 60:30-40.

Abbott, Martin. "The Freedmen's Bureau and Negro schooling in SC." 57:65-81.

Abbott, Martin. "James L. Orr on congressional reconstruction." 54:141-142.

"Abstracts of records of the proceeding in the Court of Ordinary." 22:94-98, 124-139.

"Account of the loss of the Randolph as given in a letter from Rawlins Lowndes to Henry Laurens." 10:171-173.

"American prisoners in Mill Prison at Plymouth, in 1782. Captain John Green's letter." 10:116-124.

Ames, Joseph S. "Cantey family." 11:204-258.

Amundson, Richard J. "Trescot, Sanford, and sea island cotton." 68:31-36.

Anderson, H. George. "The European phase: John Ulrich Giessendanner's life." 67:129-137.

Andreano, Ralph Louis & Herbert D. Werner. "Charleston Loyalists: a statistical note." 60:164-168.

"Army correspondence of Col. John Laurens." 2:268-272; 3:16-23.

Armytage, W. H. G. "Letters on natural history of Carolina, 1700-1705." 55:59-70.

"Arrival of the Cardross settlers." 30:69-80.

"Augustus Taliaferro Broyles and the South Carolina College, 1856." 56:53-54.

"Autobiography of Daniel Stevens, 1746-1835." 58:1-18.

Baker, Frank. "John Wesley's last visit to Charleston." 78:265-271.

Bargar, B. D. "Charles Town loyalism in 1775: the secret reports of Alexander Innes." 63:125-136.

Barnhart, Eleanor L. "Thunderstorm of 1771." 74:37-38.

Barnhart, Mrs. William. "Inscriptions from the Independent or Congregational Church yard, Charleston, S.C." 69:253-261.

Barnwell, John. "Hamlet to Hotspur: letters of Robert Woodward Barnwell to Robert Barnwell Rhett." 77:236-256.

Barnwell, Joseph W. "Bernard Elliott's recruiting journal, 1775." 17:95-100.

Barnwell, Joseph W. "Correspondence of Charles Garth; Pitt statue." 28:79-93.

Barnwell, Joseph W. "Correspondence of Henry Laurens." 29:26-40, 97-114, 193-211, 280-294; 30:6-26, 90-104, 134-167, 197-214; 31:26-45, 107-123,209-227.

Barnwell, Joseph W. "Correspondence of Hon. Arthur Middleton,

signer of the Declaration of Independence." 26:183-213;
27:1-29, 51-80, 107-155.

Barnwell, Joseph W. "Diary of Timothy Ford." 13:132-147, 181-204.

Barnwell, Joseph W. "Dr. Henry Woodward, the first English settler in S. C., & some of his descendants." 8:29-41.

Barnwell, Joseph W. "European settlements on the east coast of North America." 25:88-93.

Barnwell, Joseph W. "The evacuation of Charleston by the British in 1782." 11:1-26.

Barnwell, Joseph W. "Fort King George." 27:189-203.

Barnwell, Joseph W. "Garth Correspondence." 28:226-235; 29:41-48, 115-132, 212-230, 295-305; 30:27-49, 104-116, 168-184, 215-235; 31:46-62, 124-153, 228-255, 283-291: 32:117-139, 262-280.

Barnwell, Joseph W. "Hon. Charles Garth, M.P., the last colonial agent of South Carolina in England, and some of his work." 26:67-92.

Barnwell, Joseph W. "Letter from Mrs. Charles Pinckney to Harriott Horry." 17:101-102.

Barnwell, Joseph W. and Mabel L Webber. "St. Helena's parish register." 23:8-25, 46-71, 102-151, 171-204.

Barnwell, Joseph W. "The second Tuscarora expedition." 10:33-48.

Barnwell, Robert Woodward, Jr. "George Harland Hartley's claim for losses as a Loyalist." 51:45-50.

"Barnwell of South Carolina." 2:47-88

Bartram, R. Conover. "The diary of John Hamilton Cornish, 1846-1860." 64:73-85, 145-157.

Baskett, Sam S. "Eliza Lucas Pinckney: portrait of an eighteenth century American." 72:207-219

"The Battle of Stono." 5:90-94.

Baumhofer, Hermine Munz. "Economic changes in St. Helena's Parish." 50:1-13

Baxley, Bennett. "Early artisans, the Gordons of Black Mingo." 81:122-188.

Baxter, Lucy W. "Through the Union lines into the Confederacy." 54:135-140.

Baylen, Joseph O. "A letter of James L. Orr, Minister of Russia, 1873." 61:225-231.

Beaty, Rives Lang. "Recollections of Harriet DuBose Kershaw Lang." 59:159-170, 195-205.

Beckham, Pauline M. "Sanders, Ford, Oswald, and Campbell records." 58:51-55.

Becker, Robert A. "Salus Populi Suprema Lex: Public peace and South Carolina debtor relief laws, 1783-1788." 80:65-87.

Beckwith, James P., Jr. "A short history of the A. E. O. C. by Thomas Pinckney Rutledge." 77:97-109.

Bedford, Henry F. "William Johnson and the Marshall Court." 62:165-171.

Bennett, Craig Miller. "Family records of Gov. Thomas Bennett."

51:51-54.

Bennett, John. "Charleston in 1774 as described by an English traveler." 47:179-180

Bennett, John. "List of noncommissioned officers and private men of the second South Carolina Continental Regiment of Foot." 16:25-33.

Bennett, John. "Marion-Gadsden correspondence." 41:48-60.

Bennett, Susan Smythe "The Cheves family of South Carolina." 35:79-95, 130-152.

Bennett, Susan Smythe. "The McCords of McCords' Ferry, South Carolina. 34:177-193.

Bennett, Susan S. "The return of the Mace." 58:243-245.

Bishop, Charles C. "The pro-slavery argument reconsidered: James Henley Thornwell, millennial abolitionist." 73:18-26.

Blackburn, George M. "A Michigan regiment in the Palmetto State." 68:154-164.

"Blake of South Carolina." 1:153-166; 39:103-109.

Blumberg, Arnold. "The strange career of Joseph Binda." 67:155-166.

Bond, Lula Sams and Laura Sams. "The Sams family of South Carolina." 64:39-52, 105-113, 169-177.

Brayton, Abbott A. "The south Atlantic blockading squadron: the diary of James W. Boynton." 76:112-117.

Breese, Donald H. "James L. Orr, Calhoun and the co-operationist tradition in South Carolina." 80:273-285.

Breibart, Soloman. "The synagogues of Kahal Kadosh Beth Elohim, Charleston." 80:215-235.

Bridenbaugh, Carl. "Charlestonians at Newport, 1767-1775." 41:43-47.

Brinsfield, John W. "Daniel DeFoe: writer, stateman, and advocate of religious liberty in South Carolina." 76:107-111.

Brittain, John Lafayette. "Two recently discovered letters of Charles Cotesworth Pinckney." 76:12-20

Brown, Douglas Summers. "Catawba Land Records, 1795-1829." 59:64-77, 171-176, 226-233.

Brown, Phillip M. "Early Indian trade in the development of South Carolina: politics, economics and social mobility furing the Proprietary Period, 1670-1719." 76:118-128.

Brown, Ralph H. "Governor Drayton's contribution to geography." 39:68-72.

Bryan, Richard Jenkins. "Epitaphs from family cemeteries on John's Island 50:163-166

Bryan, Richard J. "Epitaphs, the Gibbes family cemetery, John's Island." 50:68-70.

Bulger, William T. "Sir Henry Clinton's Journal of the seige of Charleston, 1780." 66:147-174.

Bull, Elias B. "Storm Towers of the Santee Delta." 81:95-101.

"The Bull Family of South Carolina." 1:76-90.

Bull, H. D. "Kinloch of South Carolina." 46:63-69, 159-165.

Bull, H. D. "The Waites family in South Carolina." 45:12-22.

Bull, Henry De Saussure. "Ashley Hall Plantation." 53:61-66.
Burgess, Mary Wyche. "Civil War letters of Abram Hayne Young." 78:56-70.
Burkette, Alice Gaillard. "Tombstone inscriptions at Walnut Grove Plantation Cemetery." 77:189-193.
"The Burning of Legareville." 51:117
Burton, E. Milby. "Ford, MacKewn, Carmichaell epitaphs." 52:132.
Bynum, Curtis. "Graves in Gillespie-Shipp family graveyard, Rose Hill Plantation, Marlboro County, near Kollock, S. C." 33:175-176.
Cain, Marvin R. "Return to Republicanism: a reappraisal of Hugh Swinton Legare and the Tyler presidency." 79:264-280.
Cann, Marvin L. "The end of a political myth: the South Carolina gubernatorial campaign of 1938." 72:139-149.
Cann, Marvin L. "Prelude to war: The first battle of Ninety Six, November 19-21, 1775." 76:197-214.
Cann, Marvin L. "War in the backcountry: The siege of Ninety-Six, May 22-June 19, 1781." 72:1-14.
Calmes, Alan. "The Lyttleton expedition of 1759: military failures and financial successes." 77:10-33.
Camp, Vaughn, Jr. "The War of Independence, North and South: the Diary of Samuel Catawba Lowry." 79:182-197.
Carroll, Kenneth L. "The Irish Quaker community at Camden." 77:69-83.
Carson, Louise and Mabel Runnette. "Orange Grove Plantation, Lady's Island, Beaufort County, S. C."
Cawley, Henry H. "Guillebeau Cemetery." 32:314-316.
Cawley, Henry H. "Inscriptions from cemetery, Old Presbyterian Church, Willington, S. C. " 28:246-255.
Cawley, Henry H. "Tombstone inscriptions from private cemeteries." 34:113-115.
Cawley, Henry H. "Tombstone inscriptions, Richardson Cemetery." 28:55-68.
Chadwick, Thomas W. "The diary of Samuel Edward Burges, 1860-1862." 48:63-75, 141-163, 206-218.
Chapman, Anne W. "Inadequacies of the 1848 Charleston Census." 81:24-34.
"A Cherokee War document." 1:151-153.
Chesnutt, David R. "South Carolina's penetration of Georgia in the 1760's: Henry Laurens as a case study." 73:194-208.
Chevalley, Sylvie. "The death of Alexandre Placide." 58:63-66.
Cheves, Langdon "William Smith's Marriage." 32:319-322.
Childs, Arney R. "William Hasell Gibbes' story of his life." 50:59-67.
Childs, St. Julien R. "The first South Carolinians." 71:101-108.
Childs, St. Julien R. "Honest and just at the court of Charles II." 64:27-38.
Childs, St. Julien R. "A letter in 1711 by Mary Stafford to her kinswoman in England." 81:1-7.

Childs, St. Julien R. "The naval career of Joseph West." 81: 109-116.

Childs, St. Julien R. "The Petit-Guerard Colony." 43:1-17, 88-97.

"Circular letter from Governor Guerard to Charles K. Chitty." 1:323-324.

Clark, E. Culpepper. "Sarah Morgan and Francis Dawson: Raising the woman question in reconstruction South Carolina." 81:8-23

Clendenen, Clarence C. "President Hayes' 'withdrawal' of the troops-an enduring myth." 70:240-250.

Clifton, James M. "The ante-bellum rice planter as revealed in the letterbook of Charles Manigault, 1846-1848." 74:119-127, 300-310.

Clower, George Wesley. "Letters from Mrs. James Steele of Anderson, 1856." 55:174-177.

Clower, George Wesley. "Notes on the Calhoun-Noble-Davis family." 53:51-53.

Coghlan, Francis. "Pierce Butler, 1744-1822, first senator from South Carolina." 78:104-119.

Cohen, Hennig. "Four letters from Peter Timothy, 1755, 1768, 1771." 55:160-165.

Cohen, Hennig. "John Esten Cooke to Paul Hamilton Hayne, 1873." 59:139-142.

Cohen, Hennig. "The journal of Robert Mills, 1828-1830." 52: 133-139, 218-224; 53: 31-36,91-100.

Cohen, Hennig. " 'Ossian' visits Charleston, 1765." 55:40-41.

Cohen, Hennig. "An unpublished diary by Robert Mills, 1803." 51:187-194.

Coker, Robert Ervin. "Springville: a summer village of old Darlington District." 53:190-211.

"The Collegiad" (poem) 63:83-85.

Coleman, Alan. "The Charleston bootlegging controversy, 1915-1918." 75:77-94.

"The Colleton family in South Carolina." 1:325-341.

"Colonel Robert Gray's observations on the war in Carolina." 11:139-160.

Cooper, William J., Jr. "Economics or race: an analysis of the gubernatorial election of 1890 in South Carolina." 73:209-219.

"Correspondence between Edmund Brailsford and his father." 8: 151-163.

"Correspondence between Hon. Henry Laurens and his son, John, 1777-1780." 6:3-11, 47-52, 103-110, 137-160.

Covington, James W. "Proposed Catawba Indian removal, 1848." 55:42-47.

Cox, Henry Miot. "Notes on the Boyce family of Laurens and Newberry." 61:82-85.

Cross, Jack L. "Letters of Thomas Pinckney, 1775-1780." 58: 19-33, 67-83, 145-162, 224-242.

313

Crouse, Maurice A. "Cautious rebellion:South Carolina's Opposition to the Stamp Act." 73:59-72.
Crouse, Maurice A. "Gabriel Manigault: Charleston merchant." 68:220-231.
Crouse, Maurice A. "The letterbook of Peter Manigault, 1763-1773." 70:79-96, 177-195.
Crouse, Maurice A. "Papers of Gabriel Manigault,1771-1784." 64:1-12.
Crowder, Louise Kelly. "Clinton and Hornsby family records." 59:50-53.
Curtis, Mary Julia, "Charles-Town's Church Street Theater." 70:149-154.
Curtis, Julia "A note on Henry Holt." 79:1-5.
Dabney, William M. "Drayton and Laurens in the Continental Congress." 60:74-82.
"David C. Ebaugh on the building of the David." 54:32-36.
Davis, Mary Katherine. "The featherbed aristocracy: Abbeville District in the 1790's, by Mary Katherine Davis." 80:137-155.
Davis, Richard Beale. "The Ball papers: a pattern of life in the low country, 1800-1825." 65:1-15.
Davis, Richard Beale. "An uncollected elergy by Paul Hamilton Hayne." 52:52-54.
Davis, Robert Scott, Jr. "The Loyalist trials at Ninety-Six." 80:172-192.
Deas, Alston. "A ball in Charleston." 75:49
Deas, Alston. "Eleanor Parke Lewis to Mrs. C. C. Pinckney." 63:12-17.
Deas, Alston "Letters from Dr. Rush of Philadelphia to Wm. Allston of S. C." 39:145-150.
Deas, Alston. "Washington Allston to Charles Sumner, 1841." 62:24-26.
Denney, William H. "South Carolina's conception of the Union in 1832." 78:171-183.
DeSaussure, Charlton, Jr. "Memoirs of General George Izard, 1825." 78:43-55.
DeSaussure, Henry A. "Death records (1829-1865)" 59:47-49, 114-116, 177-179.
"A description of Osceola" 65:85-86.
DeTreville, Marie and William L. Glover. "Registers of Sheldon Church, Prince William's Parish, 1826-1947." 56:151-156, 226-228; 57:51-54, 103-106, 179-181.
"Diary of John Berkley Grimball 1858-1865." 56:8-30, 92-114, 157-177, 205-225; 57:28-50, 88-102.
Dismukes, Camillus J. "Inventory of a planters estate." 73:37-38.
Dismukes, Camillus J. "The William Hervey Davis marriage register, 1837-1880." 77:41-48.
"Documents concerning Mrs. Samuel Thomas, 1707-1710." 5:95-99.
"Documents concerning Rev. Samuel Thomas, 1702-1707." 5:21-55.
Duffy, Charles. "A southern genteelist: letters by Paul Hamil-

ton Hayne to Julia C. R. Dorr." 52:65-73, 154-165, 207-217; 53:19-30

Duffy, John. "Yellow fever in colonial Charleston." 52:189-197.

Duncan, John E. "The correspondence of a Yankee prisoner in Charleston, 1865." 75:215-224.

Dunlop, J. G. "Capt. Dunlop's voyage to the southward." 30:127-133.

Dunlop, J. G. "Letter from Edmund White to Joseph Morton." 30:1-5.

Dunlop, J.G. "Letters from John Stewart to William Dunlop." 32:1-33, 81-114, 170-174.

Dunlop, J. G. "Spanish depredations, 1686." 30:81-89.

Dunlop, J. G. "William Dunlop's mission to St. Augustine in 1688." 34:1-30.

Dunn, Richard S. "The English Sugar Islands and the founding of South Carolina." 72:81-93.

Durden, Robert F. "The ambiguous antislavery crusade of James S. Pike." 56:187-195.

Durden, Robert F. "The establishment of Calvary Protestant Episcopal Church for Negroes in Charleston." 65:63-84.

Dwight, C. Harrison. "Count Rumford: his Majesty's Colonel in Carolina." 57:23-27.

Dewight, H. R. "Inscriptions from tombstones in graveyard at Hanover Plantation, St. John's Parish, Berkeley County, S.C." 41:74

Eaddy, Elaine Y. "Browntown: early industry on Lynches River." 80:236-241.

"The earthquake in Charleston, 1886, as reported in letters of the Smythe family." 49:69-75.

"Early letters from South Carolina upon natural history." 21:1-9

Easterby, J. H. "Captain Langdon Cheves, Jr. and the Confederate silk dress balloon." 45:1-11,99-110.

Easterby, J. H. "Charles Cotesworth Pinckney's plantation diary, April 6-December 15, 1818." 41:135-150.

Easterby, J. H. "The constitution of the Winyah and All Saints Argicultural Society." 44:52-54.

Easterby, J. H. "Internal improvements in South Carolina." 42:53-54.

Easterby, J. H. "Letters of James Warley Miles to David James McCord." 43:185-200.

Easterby, J. H. "Public poor relief in colonial Charleston." 42:83-86.

Easterby, J. H. "The St. Thomas Hunting Club, 1785-1801." 46:123-131, 209-213.

Easterby, J. H. "Shipbuilding on St. Helena's Island in 1816." 47:117-120.

Easterby, J.H. "The South Carolina education bill of 1770." 48:95-111.

Easterby, J. H. "South Carolina through New England's eyes."

315

45:127-136.

Edgar, Walter B. "Notable libraries of colonial South Carolina" 72:105-110.

Edgar, Walter B. "Robert Pringle and his world." 76:1-11.

Edgar, Walter B. "Some popular books in colonial South Carolina." 72:174-178.

Edwards, Katherine Bush. "Bush Hill Cemetery." 78:148-149.

Edwards, Katherine Bush. "Inscriptions from Mt. Bethel Baptist and Ebenezer Methodist Church Cemeteries, Anderson County." 79:138-166.

Eichert, Magdalen "John C. Calhoun's land policy of cession." 55:198-209.

Eisterhold, John A., M. D. "Charleston: lumber and trade in a declining southern port." 74:61-72.

Ellen, John C., Jr. "Political newspapers of the South Carolina up country, 1850-1859: a compendium." 63:86-92, 158-163.

Ellis, Mrs. M. Brantley. "Addition to the Brewton genealogy." 48:164-166.

"Elizabeth Heyward Jervey, 1883-1968" 70:64.

"The English ancestors of the Bull family of South Carolina." 36:36-41.

English, Elizabeth D. "Home furnishings of the 1830's as described in the letters of Martha Keziah Peay." 43:69-87.

English, Elizabeth D. "Marriage and Death notices from the Edgefield Hive." 41:25-27.

Enright, Brian J. "An account of Charles Town in 1725." 61:13-18.

Ervin, Sam Jr. "Entries in Colonel John Ervin's Bible." 79:219-252.

"Richard Xavier Evans, M. A. " 39:110-124.

Ewing, Gretchen Garst. "Duff Green, John C. Calhoun, and the election of 1828." 79:126-137.

"Extracts from Harriott Horry's receipt book." 60:28-29, 106, 169, 228.

"Excerpts from the wartime correspondence of Augustine T. Smythe." 62:27-32.

"The excommunication of Joseph Ash." 22:53-59.

"Exhumation of the body of John C. Calhoun, 1863." 57:57-58.

"An eye witness account of the occupation of Mt. Pleasant." 66:8-14.

Fagg, Daniel W. Jr. "St. Giles' Seigniory: the Earl of Shaftesbury's Carolina plantation." 71:117-123.

"Family Bible in possession of Miss Olivia Moore, Kollock, South Carolina." 33:177-179.

Farley, M. Foster. "The South Carolina Negro in the American Revolution 1775-1783." 79:75-86.

Fenhagen, Mary Pringle. "John Ashmead and some of his descendents in Pennsylvania and South Carolina." 47:133-142, 232-242.

Farley, M. Foster. "Three letters of William Henry Trescot to

Howell Cobb, 1861." 68:22-30.

Fenhagen, Mary Pringle. "Descendents of Judge Robert Pringle."
62:151-164, 221-236.

Fenhagen, Mary Pringle. "John Edwards and some of his descendents." 55:15-27, 103-115.

Fenhagen, Mary Pringle. "Letters and will of Robert Pringle,
(1702-1776)." 50:91-100, 144-155.

Fields, Joseph F. "Lynch autographs in South Carolina." 53:129-
132.

Florance, John E., Jr. "Morris Island: victory or blunder?"
55:143-152.

Floyd, Viola Caston. "The fall of Charleston." 66:1-7.

Flynn, Jean Martin. "South Carolina's compliance with the
Militia Act of 1792." 69:26-44.

Folger, Walter Weston. "Hill-Hurt family records." 65:45-47.

"Folio Bible of John Gaillard." 41:39-41.

Foote, William A. "The South Carolina Independents." 62:195-
199.

Foran, William A. "The Weimar letters of Mary Orr." 56:77-84.

Ford, C. Ford. "Letters of Ralph Izard." 2:194-204.

Fraser, Walter J., Jr. "Reflections of 'democracy' in revolutionary South Carolina?; the composition of military organizations and the attitudes and relationships of the officers
and men, 1775-1780." 78:202-212.

Frech, Laura P. "The republicanism of Henry Laurens." 76:69-
79.

Fripp, William Edward. "Minutes of the vestry, St. Bartholomew's Parish." 51:10-23, 78-96, 145-163, 229-242; 52:34-47.

"A funeral at the Horry house." 59:224-225.

Galbraith, J. E. H. "All Saints Waccamaw." 13:162-176.

Gallardo, Jose Miguel. "The Spaniards and the English settlement in Charles Town." 37:49-64, 91-99, 131-141.

Gatell, Frank Otto. "Postmaster Huger and the Incendiary Publications." 64:193-201.

Gatewood, Williard B. "Theodore Roosevelt and southern Repub-
licans: the case of South Carolina, 1901-1904." 70:251-266.

Geiger, Florence Gambrill. "St. Bartholomew's Parish, as seen
by its rectors, 1713-1761." 50:173-203.

Gelston, Arthur Lewis. "Radical versus straight-out in post-
reconstruction Beaufort County." 75:225-237.

"General Thaddeus Kosciuszko to Maj. Alexander Garden." 2:126-
127.

"Georgetown Library Society." 25:94-100.

"Gibson family records." 75:245-248.

Gildea, Michael M. "A letter from Samuel Maverick." 75:177-179

Glover, Miss Beulah. "Tombstone inscriptions, Colleton County."
40:36-39.

Glover, William L. "Bolan family records." 41:162-166.

Glover, William L. "Colonel Joseph Glover and his descendents."
40:1-10.

Glover, Wm. L. "Extracts from a Glover Bible." 40:105-107.

Glover, Wm. L. "The Heyward Family Burying Ground at Old House near Grahamville, S. C." 41:75-80.

Glover, William L. "Tombstones at Holy Trinity Episcopal Church Grahamville, S. C." 41:94-95.

Gormly, James L. "Secretary of State James F. Brynes, an initial British evaluation." 79:198-205.

Gould, Christopher. "Robert Wells, colonial Charleston printer." 79:23-49.

Graydon, Nell S. "Some letters from John Christopher Schulz, 1829-1883." 56:1-7.

Green, Mary Fulton. "A profile of Columbia in 1850." 70:104-121

Green, Ruth S. "The South Carolina Archives copy of the Fundamental Constitutions, dated July 21, 1669." 71:86-100.

Greene, Jack. "Slavery or independence: some reflections on the relationship among liberty, black bondage and equality in revolutionary South Carolina." 80:193-214.

Greene, Jack P. "The political authorship of Sir Egerton Leigh" 75:143-152.

Greene, Jack P. "South Carolina's colonial constitution: two proposals for reform." 62:73-81.

Greene, Jack P. "The South Carolina quartering dispute, 1757-1758." 60:193-204.

Gregorie, Anne King. "Cemetery inscriptions from Christ Church Parish." 21:132-135.

Gregorie, Anne King. "Diary of Captain Joseph Julius Wescoat, 1863-1865." 59:11-23, 84-95.

Gregorie, Anne King and Flora Belle Surles. "Inscriptions from family burying ground at Yeamans Hall." 38:99-103.

Gregorie, Anne King. "Inscriptions from Oldfield and Mayham plantations, St. Stephens Parish." 27:215-218.

Gregorie, Anne King. "John Witherspoon Ervin." 46:166-170.

Gregorie, Anne King. "Micajah Adolphus Clark's visit to South Carolina in 1857." 54:15-31.

Griffin, Inez H. "Marriage and death notices from the Charleston Gazette, 1828." 75:184-186.

Griffin, Inez. "Marriage and death notices from the City Gazette, 1827." 67:46-49.

Griffin, Inez H. "Marriage and death notices from the City Gazette of Charleston, 1825." 60:43-47, 107-110, 170-172, 229-232; 61:51-54, 114-116.

Griffin, Inez H. "Marriage and death notices from the City Gazette and Commercial Daily Advertiser, 1826." 61:176-179, 233-236; 62:55-57, 115-117, 183-184, 238-240; 63:52-54, 112-114, 182-184.

Griffin, Inez H. "Marriage and death notices from the City Gazette of Charleston, 1827." 64:114-116, 178-180, 227-229; 65:48-51, 114-117, 233-235; 66:125-129.

Griffin, Richard W. "Poor white laborers in southern cotton factories, 1789-1865." 61:26-40.

Grimke, Mrs. John Drayton. "Eighteenth century receipts." 34: 170-172.

Grimke, John Fauchereau. "Journal of the campaign to the southward." 12:60-69, 118-134, 190-206.

Grinde, Donald A., Jr. "Building the South Carolina railroad." 77:84-96.

Hahn, Stephen S. "Lexington's Theological Library, 1832-1859." 80:36-49.

Hall, Wm. B. "The marriage license of Claudius Pegues,1719-1790." 38:104-106.

Hanahan, Mrs. John. "Tombstones in Cypress Trees Plantation-Edisto." 40:108-109.

Halliburton, R., Jr. "Free black owners of slaves: a reappraisal of the Woodson Thesis." 76:129-142.

Harleston, John. "Battery Wagner on Morris Island, 1863." 57: 1-13.

Harrison, Lowell. "South Carolina's educational system in 1822." 51:1-9.

Hartwell, Richard B. "The Hot and Hot Fish Club of All Saints." 48:40-47.

Haywood, C. Robert. "Mercantilism and South Carolina agriculture, 1700-1763." 60:15-27.

Hemperley, Marion R. "Federal naturalization oaths; Charleston, South Carolina 1790-1860." 66:112-124, 183-192, 218-228.

Hemphill, Mrs. James C. "Epitaphs from Martin-Aiken Family Cemetery, Fairfield County." 54:215

"Henry Laurens on the Olympic Games." 61:146-147.

"Henry Ward Beecher and St. Michaels." 60:145-146.

Herd, Elmer Don, Jr. "Laurence M. Keitt's letters from the Provisional Congress of the Confederacy, 1861." 61:19-25.

Herd, Elmer Don, Jr. "Sue Sparks Keitt to a northern friend, March 4, 1861." 62:82-87.

Hesseltine, William B. and Larry Gara. "Sherman burns the libraries." 55:137-142.

Heyward, Barnwell Rhett. "Descendents of Col. William Rhett of South Carolina." 4:37-74, 110-188.

Heyward, James B. "The Heyward family of South Carolina." 59: 143-158, 206-223.

Heyward, Marie H. and Alice R. Huger Smith. "Inscriptions from the Baptist Church Yard, Beaufort, S. C." 35:118-121; 36: 25-27, 99-101; 37:71-76.

Heyward, Marie H. and Alice R. H. Smith. "Inscriptions from St. Helena Churchyard, Beaufort, South Carolina." 32:131-147, 205-237.

Heyward, Marie H. "Tombstone inscriptions from Holy Cross Church, Stateburg, S. C." 30:50-59.

Higgins, W. Robert. "Charles Town merchants and factors dealing in the external Negro trade." 65:205-218.

Higgins, W. Robert. "The South Carolina Revolutionary debt and its holders, 1776-1780." 72:15-29.

Hillman, E. Haviland, F.S.G. "The Brisbanes." 14:115-133, 175-197.

Hine, William C. "The 1867 Charleston streetcar sit-ins: a case of successful Black protest." 77:110-114.

"Historical relation of facts delivered by Ludovick Grant, Indian trader, to His Excellency, the governor of South Carolina." 10:54-68.

Hogue, L. Lynn. "Nicholas Trott: man of law and letters." 76:25-34.

Hollis, Daniel W. " 'Cotton Ed Smith'- Showman or statesman?" 71:235-256.

Hollis, Daniel W. "Samuel Chiles Mitchell, social reformer in Blease's South Carolina." 70:20-37.

Hough, Perry B. Bennett. "Hammond, Hughes, and Connors family record." 64:220-226.

Hollis, Daniel W. "Cole Bease: the years between the governorship and the Senate, 1915-1924." 80:1-17.

Hollis, Daniel Walker. "Robert W. Barnwell." 56:131-137.

Holman, Harriet R. "Charleston in the summer of 1841: the letters of Harriott Horry Rutledge." 46:1-14.

Holmes, Henry Schulz. "The Trenholm family." 16:151-163.

Holmes, Henry S. Robert Gibbes, Governor of South Carolina and some of his descendents." 12:78-105.

"Hon. Henry A. M. Smith." 29:67-69.

Hough, Perry B. Bennett. "Inscriptions from Beaver Creek Church Yard, Kershaw County." 60:205-207.

Hoyt, James A. "The Confederate Archives and Felix G. DeFontaine." 57:199-203.

Hoyt, William D., Jr. "To Coosawhatchie in December 1861." 53:6-12.

Hutson, Mrs. R.W. "Register kept by the Rev. Wm. Hutson, of Stoney Creek Independent Congregational Church and (Circular) Congregational Church in Charles Town, S. C. 1743-1760." 38:21-36.

Hutson, William Maine. "The Hutson family of South Carolina." 9:127-140.

Inglesby, Charlotte. "Tombstone inscriptions, May River Plantation." 74:31-36.

"Inscriptions from the Allston Burying Ground at Turkey Hill Plantation near Waccamaw." 10:181-183.

Inscriptions from the Church yard of the Independent or Congregational Church at Wappetaw, Christ Church Parish." 25:136-142.

"Inscriptions from the church yard of Old Prince Frederick Winyah, at Brown's Ferry, Black River." 18:91-95.

"Inscriptions from the Independent or Congregational (Circular) Church Yard, Charleston, S. C." 29:55-66, 133-150, 238-257, 306-328.

"Inscriptions on the gravestones at Sheldon Church." 18:180-183.

"Inscriptions on tombstones, private burying grounds on the Santee River, in Old St. Stephen's Parish, S. C." 26:113-121.

"Inscriptions from St. John's in the Wilderness, Flat Rock, N. C." 40:52-57.

"The inscriptions on the tombstones at the Old Parish Church of St. James's Santee, near Echaw Creek." 12:152-158.

"Items from a McPherson Bible." 40:110-111.

"Items relating to Charles Town, S. C., from the Boston News Letter." 40:73-78.

Ivers, Larry E. "Scouting the inland passage." 73:117-129.

"Izard-Laurens correspondence." 22:1-11, 39-52, 73-88.

"Izard of South Carolina." 2:205-240.

Jackman, Sydney W. "John C. Calhoun to David Bates Douglass." 60:83-85.

"James Sutherland to my lord." 68:79-84.

January, Alan F. "The South Carolina Association; an agency for race control in antebellum Charleston." 78:19-201.

Jarrott, Emory. "Tombstone inscriptions at Strobhar and DuPont Cemeteries, Purrysburg." 79:60-71.

Jellison, Richard M. and Phillip S. Swartz. "The scientific interests of Robert W. Gibbes." 66:77-79.

Jellison, Richard M. "Paper currency in colonial South Carolina: a reappraisal." 62:134-147.

Jenkins, Charles F. "An account of a new portrait of Thomas Lynch, Jr." 28:1-7.

Jervey, Elizabeth Heyward. "Death notices from the Gazette of the state of South Carolina, Charleston." 50:127-130, 204-208; 51:24-28, 97-102, 164-170.

Jervey, Elizabeth Heyward. "Marriage and death notices from the City Gazette of Charleston, S. C. " 38:43-48, 95-98, 137-141; 39:42-45, 91-95, 130-133, 168-172; 40:28-32, 65-69, 100-104, 151-155; 41:19-22, 69-73, 130-134, 157-161; 42:20-24, 76-80, 141-145, 199-202; 43:47-49, 98-102, 156-160, 213-218; 44:11-16, 81-86, 148-154, 220-227; 45:23-29, 71-79, 137-145; 46: 15-24, 70-77, 132-139, 190-197; 47:21-28, 76-82, 143-149, 205-213; 48:12-19, 76-83, 134-140, 198-205; 49:15-22, 76-87, 155-162, 208-215; 50:14-18, 71-76: 51:243-246; 52:48-51, 107-111, 180-182, 233-236; 53:47-50, 113-115, 172-175, 241-243; 54:54-56, 97-100, 159-163, 211-214; 55:48-51, 123-126, 170-173, 221-224; 56:50-52, 120-122, 178-180, 229-231; 57: 54-56, 107-108, 182-184, 223-225; 58:48-50, 114-116, 183-185, 266-270.

Jervey, Elizabeth H. "Marriage and death notices from the City Gazette and Daily Advertiser of Charleston, S.C." 38:66-71.

Jervey, Ellen Heyward. "Items from a South Carolina almanac." 32:73-80.

Jervey, Henrietta P. "The private register of the Rev. Paul Trapier." 58:94-113, 163-182, 246-265.

Jervey, Theo D. "Reverend Robert Cooper." 38:120-125.

Jervey, Theo. D. "The white indented servants of South Carolina." 12:163-171.
Jervey, Theodore. "Barlow Trecothick." 32: 157-169.
Jervey, Theodore D. "The Butlers of South Carolina." 4:296-311.
Jervey, Theodore. "Chief Justice Nicholas Trott's first wife." 42:187-188.
Jervey, Theodore D. "The Harlestons." 3:150-173.
Jervey, Theodore D. "The Hayne family." 5:168-188.
Jervey, Theodore D. "Yates Snowden." 34:175-176.
"John Rutledge to Benjamin Lincoln." 25:133-135.
Johnson, Elmer Douglass. "David Ramsey: historian or plagiarist?" 57:189-198.
Johnson, Elmer Douglas. "A Frenchman visits Charleston in 1777" 52:88-92.
Johnson, Louise R. and Julia Rosa. "Inscriptions from the churchyard of Prince George Winyah Georgetown, S. C." 31:184-208, 292-313.
Jones, Claude E. "Charles Woodmason as a poet." 59:189-194.
Jones, James P. "Charleston harbor, 1860-1861; a memoir from the Union garrison." 62:148-150.
Jones, Lewis Pinckney. "Ambrosio Jose Gonzales, a Cuban patriot in Carolina." 56:67-76.
Jones, Lewis P. "Two roads tried-and one detour." 79:206-218.
Jones, Newton B. "The Charleston Orphan House, 1860-1876." 62:203-214.
Jones, Newton B. "The Washington Light Infantry at the Bunker Hill Centennial." 65:195-204.
Jones, Newton B. "Writings of the Reverend William Tennent, 1740-1777." 61:129-145, 189-209.
Jordan, Laylon Wayne. "Police and Politics: Charleston in the Gilded Age, 1880-1900." 81:35-50.
"Josiah Smith's diary." 33:1-28, 79-116, 197-207, 281-289; 34:31-39, 67-84, 138-148, 194-210.
"Journal of Arthur Brailsford Wescoat, 1863, 1864." 55:71-102.
"Journal of Robert Pringle, 1746-1747." 26:21-30, 93-112.
Jumper, Charles F. "Hair Family Cemetery." 76:234
Kelsey, R. W. "Swiss settlers in South Carolina." 23:85-91.
Kennett, Lee. "Charleston in 1778: a French intelligence report." 66:109-111.
Kenney, William Howland, III. "Alexander Garden and George Whitefield: the significance of revivalism in South Carolina." 71:1-16.
Keys, Thomas Bland. "The Federal pillage of Anderson, South Carolina: Brown's Raid." 76:80-86.
King, Mrs. Louise C. "Journal of a visit to Greenville from Charleston in the summer of 1825 by Caroline Olivia Laurens." 72:164-173, 220-233.
Klebaner, Benjamin Joseph. "Public poor relief in Charleston, 1800-1860." 55:210-220

Klingberg, Frank L. "Commissary Johnston's Notitia Parochialis" 48:26-34.

Klingberg, Frank J. "Early attempts at Indian education in South Carolina: a documentary." 61:1-10.

Klingberg, Frank L. "The mystery of the lost Yemassee prince." 63:18-32.

Koch, Adrienne. "A family crisis: letters from John Faucheraud Grimke and Thomas Smith Grimke to Henry Grimke, 1818." 69: 171-192.

Koch, Adrienne. "Two Charlestonians in pursuit of truth: the Grimke brothers." 69:159-170

Kramer, Eugene F. "Senator Pierce Butler's notes on the debates on Jay's Treaty." 62:1-9.

Kyte, George W. "General Greene's plans for the capture of Charleston, 1781-1782." 62:96-106.

Kyte, George W. "Francis Marion as an intelligence officer." 77:215-226.

Lambert, Robert S. "A Loyalist odyssey: James and Mary Cary in exile, 1783-1804." 79:167-181.

Lander, Ernest M. Jr., "Antebellum milling in South Carolina." 52:125-132.

Lander, Ernest M. Jr., "The Calhoun-Preston feud, 1836-1842." 59:24-37.

Lander, Ernest M. "Columbia in the doldrums, 1836." 62:200-202

Lander, Ernest M. Jr. "Dr. Thomas Cooper's views in retirement" 54:173-184.

Lander, Ernest M. Jr. "General Waddy Thompson, a friend of Mexico during the Mexican War." 78:32-42.

Lander, Ernest M. Jr. "The South Carolinians at the Philadelphia Convention, 1787." 57:134-155.

Lander, Ernest M. Jr. "Two letters by William Mayrant on his cotton factory." 54:1-5

Lapham, Samuel, Jr. "Notes on Granville Bastion." 26:221-227.

Lawrence, Major Robert DeTreville. "Family Bibles of Lawrence Brothers of Charleston." 53:77-89.

Lawton, Thomas O., P. "Captain William Lawton: eighteenth century planter of Edisto." 60:86-93.

"A leaf from the South Carolina Commons House Journal." 57:109-110.

Leary, Lewis. "Phillip Freneau in Charleston." 42:89-98.

Lebby, Robert, M. D. "The first shot on Fort Sumter." 12:141-145.

Lee, Charles E. and Ruth S. Green "A guide to the Commons House Journals of the South Carolina General Assembly, 1692-1721." 68:85-96.

Lee, Charles E. and Ruth S. Green. "Guide to the Commons House Journals of the South Carolina General Assembly, 1721-1775." 68:165-183.

Lee, Charles E. and Ruth S. Green. "A guide to South Carolina Council Journals, 1671-1775." 68:1-13.

Lee, Charles E. and Ruth S. Green. "A guide to the Upper House

Journals of the South Carolina General Assembly, 1721-1775."
67:187-202.
Leiding, Hariette K. "Inscriptions from the church yard at
Wiltown Bluff." 27:104-106.
Leland, Harriott Cheves. " 'Robbing the owner or saving the
property from destruction?' : paintings in the the Middleton
Place House." 78:92-103.
Leland, Isabella Middleton. "Middleton correspondence, 1861-
1865." 63:33-41, 61-70, 164-174, 204-210; 64:95-104, 158-
168, 212-219; 65:33-44, 98-109
Lesesne, J. M. "Marriage and death notices from the Pendleton
Messenger of Pendleton, S. C." 47:29-31, 109-116, 163-170,
228-231; 48:35-39, 112-114.
Lesesne, J. M. "Marriage and death notices from the Greenville
Mountaineer of Greenville, S. C." 49:57-60, 119-122; 50:101-
105, 156-162, 216-220
"A letter from Bachman, London, 1838." 63:211-213.
"A letter from Bleak Hall, 1861." 62:193-194.
"A letter from Francis Marion to General Greene." 36:111-112.
"Letter from General Christopher Gadsden to Mr. Thomas Morris,
May 30th, 1790." 2:44-45
"A letter from John Laurens to his uncle James Laurens." 10:49-
53.
"Letter from Lord Charles Greville Montagu to Barnard Elliott."
33:259-261.
"Letter from Thomas Jefferson to Judge William Johnson." 1:1-12
"Letter from Wm. Charles Wells to Dr. James Currie." 26:41-44.
"A letter of 1783." 21:30.
"Letters concerning Peter Manigault." 21:39-49.
"Letters from Col. Lewis Morris to Miss Ann Elliott." 40:122-
136; 41:1-14.
"Letters from Commodore Alexander Gillon in 1778 and 1779." 10:
1-9. 75-82. 131-135.
"Letters from Henry Laurens to William Bell of Philadelphia."
24:2-16, 53-68; 25:23-35, 77-87.
"Letters from Hon. Henry Laurens to his son John, 1773-1776."
3:86-96, 139-149, 207-215; :26-35, 99-107, 215-220, 263-278.
"Letters from John C. Calhoun to Francis W. Pickens." 7:12-19.
"Letters from Judge William Johnson to Thomas Jefferson." 1:
206-212.
"Letters from the Marquis DeLafayette to Honorable Henry Laurens
1777-1780." 7:3-11, 53-68, 115-129; 8:1-18, 57-68, 123-131,
181-188; 9:3-11, 59-66, 109-114, 173-180.
"Letter from Joseph Lord." 21:50-51.
"Letters of John Rutledge." 17:131-146; 18:42-49, 59-69, 131-
142, 155-167.
"Letters of Rev. Samuel Thomas, 1702-1710." 4:221-230, 279-285.
"Letters of William Smith, Minister to Portugal." 25:57-76,
113-132, 159-172; 26:1-20.
"Letters to General Greene and others." 16:97-108, 139-150;
17:1-13, 53-57.

Lewis, Bessie M. "The Wiggs of South Carolina." 74:80-97.
"The lineage of Daniel Deupree (1768-1848)." 71:283
"List of the upper district of St. John's Parish." 23:92-93
Lloyd, Richard W. "Inscriptions from cemeteries in and near
  Camden." 25:47-55.
Lokke, Carl Ludwig. "Three letters of Charles Cotesworth Pinck-
  ney during the XYZ mission." 35:43-48.
Lord, C. W. "Young Louis Wigfall: South Carolina politician
  and duelist." 59:96-112.
"Lord Charles Greville Montagu's tombstone." 41:38.
"A loyalist Revolutionary claim." 39:82-83.
"A Lucas memorandum." 69:193.
McCormack, Helen G. "The Fireproof Building: new home of the
  South Carolina Historical Society." 44:205-211.
McCormack, Helen G. "A provisional guide to manuscripts in the
  South Carolina Historical Society." 45:111-115, 172-176; 46:
  49-53, 104-109, 171-175, 214-217; 47:53-57, 171-178; 48:48-
  52, 177-180.
McCowan, George C. Jr. "Chief Justice John Rutledge and the
  Jay Treaty." 62:10-23.
McCully, Robert S. "Letter from a reconstruction renegade."
  77:34-40.
McGrew, G. E. "Epitaphs from Duncan's Creek Presbyterian
  Church." 49:225-230.
McGriel, Paul. "William Fuller: Charleston's gentleman boxing
  master." 54:6-14.
McIver, Mrs. Edward H. "Tombstones in the Lartigue Family
  Graveyard in Blackville, S.C." 40:156.
McIver, Petrona Royall. "Josias and Martha DuPre and some of
  their descendents." 71:46-60
McIver, Petrona Royall. "Wappetaw Congregational Church."
  58:34-47, 84-93.
McIver, Petrona R. "Oliver Hart family record." 60:41-42.
McLaurin, Melton A. "Early labor union organizational efforts
  in South Carolina cotton mills, 1880-1905." 72:44-59.
McLeod, Minna. "Inscriptions from the family burying ground at
  Stiles Point, James Island." 38:74.
McMullen, Edna J. "Ramage and Sheppard family cemetery." 65:
  181-183.
McMurtrie, Douglas C. "A bibliography of South Carolina im-
  prints, 1731-1740." 34:117-137.
McMurtrie, Douglas C. "The correspondence of Peter Timothy,
  Printer of Charlestown, with Benjamin Franklin." 35:123-129.
McMurtrie, Douglas C. "Some nineteenth century South Carolina
  imprints, 1801-1820." 44:87-106, 155-172, 228-246.
Macaulay, Neill W., Jr. "South Carolina reconstruction histor-
  iography." 65:20-32.
Maclear, J. F. "Thomas Smyth, Frederick Douglass and the Bel-
  fast antislavery campaign." 80:286-297.
Marchione, William P., Jr. "Go South, young man! reconstruction
  letters of a Massachusetts Yankee." 80:18-35.

"Marriage notices from Negrin's Sociable Magazine and Quarterly
Intelligencer, January and April, 1804." 63:238-239.
Marszalek, John F., Jr. "The Charleston fire of 1861 as de-
scribed in the Emma E. Holmes diary." 76:60-67.
Martin, Julien Dwight. "The letters of Charles Caleb Cotton."
52:17-25, 132-144, 216-228.
Martin, Sidney Walter. "Ebenezer Kellogg's visit to Charleston,
1817." 49:1-14.
Maslowski, Pete. "National policy toward the use of black
troops in the Revolution." 73:1-17.
Mathews, Maurice. "A contempory view of Carolina in 1680."
55:153-159.
Mathis, Robert Neil. "Preston Smith Brooks: the man and his
image." 79:296-313.
Matteson, Robert S. "Francis LeJau in Ireland." 78:83-91.
May, Commander W.E., R.N. "Captain Charles Hardy on the Caro-
lina Station, 1742-1744."
May, Commander W. E., R.N. "His Majesty's ship on the Carolina
Station."
Mellon, Knox, Jr. Christian Priber and the Jesuit myth." 61:
75-.1.
Melvin, Patrick. "Captain Florence O'Sullivan and the origins
of Carolina." 76:235-249.
Meriwether, Robert L. "Preston S. Brooks on the caning of
Charles Sumner." 52:1-4.
Meroney, Geraldine M. "William Bull's first exile from South
Carolina, 1777-1781." 80:91-104.
Merrens, H. Roy. "A view of coastal South Carolina in 1778:
the journal of Ebenezer Hazard." 73:177-193.
"Middleton of South Carolina." 1:228-262.
Miller, Randall M. "A backcountry loyalist plan to retake
Georgia and the Carolinas, 1778." 75:207-214
Minchinton, Walter E. "Richard Champion, Nicholas Pocock, and
the Carolina trade." 65:87-97.
Minchinton, Walter E. "Richard Champion, Nicholas Pocock, and
the Carolina trade: a note." 70:97-103.
"The mission of Col. John Laurens to Europe in 1781." 1:13-41,
136-151, 213-222, 311-321; 2:27-43, 108-125.
"Miscellaneous papers of the General Committee, Secret Commitee
and Provincial Congress, 1775." 8:132-150, 189-194; 9:67-72,
115-117, 181-186.
Moffatt, Lucius Gaston and Joseph Medard Carriere. "A Frenchman visits Charleston, 1817." 49:131-154.
Mohl, Raymond A. "The grand fabric of republicanism: a Scots-
man describes South Carolina, 1810-1811." 71:170-188.
Moore, James W. "The Lowcountry in economic transition, Charleston since 1865." 80:156-171.
Moore, John Hammond. "The Abiel Abbott journals, a Yankee
preacher in Charleston society, 1818-1827." 68:51-73, 115-
139, 232-254.
Moore, John Hammond. "The Deas-Thomson papers in Austrailia."

71:189-196.

Moore, John Hammond. "Jared Sparks visits South Carolina." 72: 150-160.

Moore, John Hammond. "The last officer-April 1865." 67:1-14.

Moore, John Hammond. "Private Johnson fights the Mexicans, 1847-1848." 67:203-228.

Moore, Margaret DesChamps. "A northern professor winters in Columbia, 1852-1853." 60:183-192.

Moore, W. O., Jr. "The largest exporters of deerskins from Charles Town, 1735-1775." 74:144-150.

Morgan, Philip D. "Profile of a mid-eighteenth century South Carolina parish; the tax return of Saint James' Goose Creek" 81:51-92.

Morgan, Thurman T. "John Rivers and the voyage of the 'Three Brothers.' " 80:267-272

Morris, Richard B. "White bondage in antebellum South Carolina" 49:191-207.

Morse, H. Newcomb. "General Beauregard and the Colonel Rhett controversy." 78:184-190.

Moultrie, Rev. Gerard. "The Moultries." 5:229-260.

Mouzon, Harold A. "The Carolina Art Association: its first hundred years." 59:125-138.

Mouzon, Harold A. "The ship Prosper, , 1775-1776." 59:1-11.

Murdoch, Richard K. "Correspondence of French consuls in Charleston, South Carolina, 1793-1797." 74:1-17, 73-79.

Murdoch, Richard K. "A French account of the Siege of Charleston, 1780." 67:138-154.

Murdoch, Richard K. "A note on 'A French account of the Seige of Charleston, 1780.' " 69:57-58.

Mustard, Harry S. "On the building of Fort Johnson." 64:129-135.

Nadelhaft, Jerome. "Ending South Carolina's war: two 1782 agreements favoring the planters." 80:50-64.

Newton, Craig A. "Three patterns of local history: South Carolina historians, 1779-1830." 65:145-157.

Nielsen, J. V., Jr. "Post-Confederate finance in South Carolina." 56:85-91.

Norton, Barbara. "A sketch of St. Paul's Church, Pendleton." 63:42-51.

"Notes on some colonial governors of South Carolina and their families." 11:107-122.

O'Donnell, James H. "A loyalist view of the Drayton-Tennent-Hart mission to the upcountry." 67:15-28.

"Officers of the South Carolina Regiment in the Cherokee War, 1760-1761." 3:202-206

Ogg, David. "New College, Oxford, and South Carolina: a personal link." 59:61-63.

O'Hear, John. "Jones Bible notes, and Proayer Book, 1759." 41:32-33.

Ohline, Howard A. "Georgetown, South Caroina: racial anxieties and militant behavior, 1802." 73:130-140.

Olsberg, R. Nicholas. "Ship registers in the South Carolina Archives, 1734-1780." 74:189-299.

Olson, Gary D. "Dr. David Ramsay and Lt. Colonel Thomas Brown: patriot historian and loyalist critic." 77:257-267.

Olson, Gary D. "Loyalists and the American Revolution: Thomas Brown and the South Carolina backcountry, 1775-1776." 68:201-219; 69:44-56.

" 'On Liberty-Tree' : a revolutionary poem from South Carolina." 41:117-122.

"On Woman (poem)." 63:239

"An order book of the 1st Regiment, S. C. Line, Continental Establishment." 7:75-80, 130-142; 8:19-28, 69-87.

"Order book of John Faucheraud Grimke, August 1778 to May 1780" 13:42-55, 89-103, 148-153, 205-212; 14:44-57, 98-111, 160-170; 16:39-48, 80-85, 123-128, 178-183: 17:26-33, 82-86, 116-120, 167-174; 18:78-84, 149-153, 175-179; 19:101-104, 181-188.

"Original rules and members of the Charlestown Library Society." 23:163-170

Ott, Joseph K. "Rhode Islanders in Charleston: social notes." 75:180-183.

Otten, James T. "Disloyalty in the upper Districts of South Carolina during the Civil War." 75:95-110.

"Papers of the first Council of Safety of the Revolutionary Party in South Carolina, June-November, 1775." 1:41-76,119-135, 183-205, 279-310; 2:1-26, 97-107, 167-193, 259-267; 3:3-15, 69-85, 123-138, 193-201.

"Papers of the Second Council of Safety of the Revolutionary Party in South Carolina, November 1775-March 1776." 4:1-25, 83-98, 195-214.

Parker, F. L. "The Battle of Fort Sumter as seen from Morris Island." 62:65-71.

Parker, Mattie Erma E. "The first fundamental constitutions of South Carolina." 71:78-85.

"Paul Grimball's losses by the Spanish Invasion." 29:231-237.

Pearson, Fred Lamar, Jr. "Anglo-Spanish rivalry in the Chattahoochee Basin and West Florida, 1685-1704." 79:50-59.

Pease, Jane H. and William H. "The blood thirsty Tiger: Charleston and the psychology of fire." 79:281-295.

Peck, I. Heyward. "The Villepontoux family of South Carolina." 50:29-45.

Peeples, Robert E. H. "Family records from Bible of George Rhodes." 54:101-103.

Peeples, Robert E. H., Rev. "A Miles genealogy." 66:229-240; 67:29-45.

"Pendleton in the Eighteen Thirties." 47:69-75.

Pennington, Edgar Legare. "The confederate Episcopal Church in 1863." 52:5-16

Pennington, Edgar Legare. "The Reverend Thomas Morritt and the free school in Charles Town." 32:34-45.

328

Pennington, Edgar Legare. "The South Carolina Indian War of 1715, as seen by the clergymen." 32:251-269.
"Petition for roads from Black River, 1758." 26:122-123.
"Petitions of citizens of Orangeburg Township in behalf of Rev. John Giessendanner, 1749." 24:48-51.
"Phillip May Hamer (1891-1971) 72:238.
Pinckney, Elsie. "Letters of Eliza Lucas Pinckney, 1768-1782." 76:143-170.
Pinchney, Elise. "Register of St. John-in-the-Wilderness, Flat Rock." 63:105-111, 175-181, 232-237.
"A plantation in Goose Creek in 1781." 38:62-63.
"Poll lists Charleston Municipal Elections 1787." 56:45-49.
Porcher, Anne Allston. "Minutes of the Vestry of St. Stephen's Parish, South Carolina, 1754-1873." 45:65-70, 157-171; 46: 49-53, 93-102.
Postell, William Dosite. "Notes on the Postell family." 54: 48-53.
Prior, Mary Barbot. "Letters of Martha Logan to John Bartram, 1760-1763." 59:38-46.
Prior, Linda T. "Ralph Waldo Emerson and South Carolina." 79: 253-263.
Puryear, Elmer L. "The confederate diary of William John Grayson." 63:137-149, 214-226.
Pyburn, Nita Katherine. "The public school system of Charleston before 1860." 61:86-98.
Quattlebaum, W. Dan. "Epitaph of Thomas Taylor of Union County" 54:140.
Quattlebaum, Paul. "German Protestants in South Carolina." 47: 195-204.
Quattlebaum, Paul. "Quattlebaum: a Palatine family in South Carolina." 48:1-11, 84-94, 167-176, 219-226; 49:41-56, 104-118, 170-186, 231-245.
Quattelbaum, Paul. "The Presbyterian Church on the Waccamaw." 54:61-69.
Quattlebaum, Paul. "Some German Protestants in South Carolina in 1794." 51:75-77.
Radford, John. "The Charleston planters in 1860." 77:227-235.
Raiford, Norman Gasque. "South Carolina and the Second Bank of the United States: conflict in political principle or economic interest?" 72:30-43.
Ravenel, Beatrice St. J. "Notes on John and George Lucas." 46:185-189.
"The Rebel (Columbia), January 28, 1863." 64:13-15.
"Recollections of Samuel Gourdin Gaillard." 57:119-133.
"Record from the Bible of Daniel Horry." 39:129.
"Records from a White family Bible." 32:301-313.
"Records kept by Colonel Issaac Hayne." 10:145-170, 220-235; 11:27-38, 92-106, 160-170; 12:14-23.
"Records of marriages by the Reverend William States Lee from 1816-1871." 10:174-180.

"Records of the regiments of the South Carolina line, Continental Establishment." 5:15-20, 82-89, 144-160, 209-217; 6:13-19, 54-61, 111-113, 161-168; 7:20-26, 69-74.

Register, Jeannie Heyward. "Marriage and death notices from Charleston Courier for 1806." 29:258-263, 329-338; 30:60-68, 117-124, 185-191.

Register, Jeannie Heyward. "Marriage and death notices from the City Gazette." 25:101-112, 148-157, 179-192; 26:45-58, 128-135, 162-171, 228-236; 27:42-50, 95-103, 172-180, 219-230; 28:44-54, 132-137, 198-205, 236-245; 29:49-54, 151-163.

"Register of Independent Congregational (Circular) Church of Charleston, S. C. 1784-1815." 33:29-54, 154-174, 216-227, 306-316; 34:47-54, 96-102, 157-164.

"Register of marriage licenses granted, December, 1765 to August, 1766." 22:34-37.

"Register of St. Andrews Parish, Berkeley County, S.C. 1719-1774." 13:21-41, 104-113, 154-162, 213-223.

Reichart, Walter A. "An unpublished letter of Senator Ralph Izard to George Livius, Esq." 41:34-38.

"Revolutionary letters." 38:1-10, 75-80.

"A Revolutionary War rhyme." 46:103

Ricards, Sherman L. and George M. Blackburn. "A democratic history of slavery: Georgetown County, South Carolina, 1850." 76:215-224.

Richardson, Emma C. "Copy of family records from Bible John Maynard Davis." 39:102.

Richardson, Emma B. "Dr. Anthony Cordes and some of his descendants." 43:133-155, 219-242; 44:17-42, 115-123, 184-194.

Richardson, Emma B. "Letters of William Richardson, 1765-1784." 47:1-20.

Richey, Mattie Francis. "Certificate of character for Joseph Francis." 55:178

Riley, Edward M. "Historic Fort Moultrie in Charleston harbor." 51:63-74

Ringold, May Spencer. "William Gourdin Young and the Wigfall Mission-Fort Sumter, April 13, 1861." 73:27-36.

Robbins, Walter L. "John Tobler's description of South Carolina (1753)." 71:141-161, 257-265.

Robillard, Douglas J. "Henry Timrod, John R. Thompson, and the ladies of Richmond." 62:129-133.

Robinson, Emmett. "Dr. Irving's reminiscenses of the Charleston stage." 51:125-131, 195-215; 52:26-33, 93-106, 166-179, 225-232; 53:37-47.

Rogers, George C. Jr. "Aedanus Burke, Nathanael Green, Anthony Wayne and the Birtish merchants of S. C." 67:75-83.

Rogers, George C., Jr. "The Charleston Tea Party: the significance of December 3, 1773." 75:153-168.

Rogers, George C., Jr. "The first Earl of Shaftesbury." 68:74-78.

Rogers, George C., Jr. "Letters from Russia, 1802-1805." 60:

94-105, 154-163, 221-227.

Rogers, George C., Jr. "Letters of Charles O'Hara to the Duke of Grafton." 65:158-180.

Rogers, George C., Jr. "The letters of William Loughton Smith to Edward Rutledge (June 6, 1789 to April 28, 1794)" 69:1-25, 101-138, 225-242; 70:38-58.

Rogers, George C., Jr. "The papers of James Grant of Ballindalloch Castle, Scotland." 77:145-160

Rogers, George C., Jr. "South Carolina Federalists and the origins of the nullification movement." 71:17-32.

Rogers, George C., Jr. "Two Joseph Wragg letters." 65:16-19.

Rogers, Tommy W. "The great population exodus from South Carolina, 1850-1860." 68:14-21.

Rudisill, Horace. "Marriage licenses issued by the Court of Ordinary, Marion County, 1800-1829." 64:53-55.

"Rules of the St. Coecilia Society." 1:223-227.

Rundell, Walter, Jr. " 'If fortune should fail' : Civil War letters of Dr. Samuel D. Sanders." 65:129-144, 218-232.

Runnette, Mabel. "Epitaphs from Beaufort County." 51:171-174.

Runnette, Miss Mabel. "Grahamville Cemetery." 41:84-93.

Runnette, Mabel "Gravestones inscriptions from a private burial ground at Roseland Plantation, near Grahamville, Beaufort County, S.C." 38:72-73.

Runnette, Mabel. "Inscriptions from the grave stones at Stoney Creek Cemetery near Yemassee, Beaufort County, S. C." 37:100-110.

Runnette, Mabel. "Inscriptions from graveyards in Beaufort County." 38:16-20.

Runnette, Mabel. "Tombstone inscriptions from St. Helena Island." 35:34-39.

Rutledge, Anna Wells. "Four letters of the early nineteenth century." 43:50-56.

Rutledge, Anna Wells. "Letters from Thomas Pinckney to Harriott Pinckney." 41:99-116.

Ryan, Frank W., Jr. "The role of South Carolina in the First Continental Congress." 60:147-153.

Ryan, Harold W. "Diary of a journey by George Izard, 1815-1816" 53:67-76, 155-160, 223-229

"The St. George's Club." 8:88-94.

Salley, A. S., Jr. "Abstracts from the records of the Court of Ordinary of the Province of South Carolina, 1692-1700." 8:164-172, 195-210; 9:73-77, 118-121, 187-188; 10:10-19, 83-91, 136-144, 236-244; 11:50-56, 123-128.

Salley, A. S., Jr. "Abstracts from the records of the Court of Ordinary of the Province of South Carolina, 1700-1712." 12:70-77, 146-152, 207-214; 13:56-63, 84-88.

Salley, A. S., Jr. "Abstracts from the records of the Court of Ordinary of Greenville County, Ninety Six District, 1787-1789" 26:214-220; 27:91-94.

Salley, A.S. "A Broughton record." 35:77-78.

Salley, A. S., Jr. "The Calhoun family of South Carolina." 7: 81-98, 152-169.

Salley, A. S., Jr. "Capt. John Colcock and some of his descendents." 3:216-241.

Salley, A.S., Jr. "Captain William Capers and some of his descendents." 2:273-298.

Salley, A. S., Jr., "Col. Miles Brewton and some of his descendents." 2:128-152.

Salley, A. S., Jr. "Col. Moses Thomson and some of his descendents." 3:97-113.

Salley, A. S., Jr. "The Creek Indian tribes in 1725." 32:241-242.

Salley, A. S., Jr. "Daniel Trezevant, Hugenot, and some of his descendents." 3:24-56.

Salley, A. S., Jr. "Diary of William Dillwyn during a visit to Charleston in 1772." 36:1-6, 29-35, 73-78, 107-111.

Salley, A. S., Jr. "Dr. James Lynah, a surgeon of the Revolution." 40:87-90.

Salley, A. S., Jr. "Dunbar records." 41:30-31.

Salley, A. S., Jr. "DuPre records." 38:81-82.

Salley, A. S., Jr. "The family of the First Landgrave Thomas Smith." 28:169-175.

Salley, A. S., Jr. "The final Grand Council." 33:297-298.

Salley, A. S., Jr. "Fraser family memoranda." 5:56-58.

Salley, A. S., Jr. "Governor Joseph Morton and some of his descendents." 5:108-116.

Salley, A. S., Jr. "The grandfather of John C. Calhoun." 38:50

Salley, A. S., Jr. "Hext family records." 40:97-99.

Salley, Alexander S. "Horry's notes to Weems's Life of Marion." 60:119-122.

Salley, A. S. "The house at Medway." 33:245-246; 34:218-220.

Salley, A. S., Jr. "Hugh Hext and some of his descendents." 6:29-40.

Salley, A. S., Jr. "John Alston." 6:114-116.

Salley, A. S., Jr. "John Rutledge." 33:317

Salley, A. S. "Journal of General Peter Horry." 38:49-53, 81-86, 116-119; 39:46-49, 96-99, 125-128, 157-159; 40:11-14, 43-47, 91-96, 142-144; 41:15-18; 42:8-11, 72-75, 118-121, 191-193; 43:57-60, 125-128, 181-184, 251-255; 44:55-58, 124-129, 196-199, 255-257; 45:51-55, 116-119, 177-181; 46:54-59, 110-114, 176-179, 218-222; 47:58-60, 121-123, 181-183, 243-244; 48:53-54, 115-116.

Salley, A. S., Jr. "The Jervey family of South Carolina." 7: 31-46.

Salley, A. S., Jr. "Joseph Barnwell, a sketch." 31:324-329.

Salley, A. S., Jr. "Landgrave Daniel Axtell." 6:174-176.

Salley, A. S. "A letter by the Second Landgrave Smith." 32:61-63.

Salley, A. S., Jr. "Letter from Dr. Tucker Harris to his children." 27:30-35.

Salley, A. S. "Letters from the Schenckingh Smiths of S. C. to the Boylston Smiths of Massachusetts." 35:1-12.
Salley, A. S. "The Maybank family." 40:115-121.
Salley, A. S., Jr. "Members of the Commons House of Assembly, 1702-1711." 27:170-171.
Salley, A. S. "Note on the Bull family." 39:174-175.
Salley, A. S., Jr. "Notes on the Lucas and Mikell families of the Pee Dee country by William Lucas." 27:212-214.
Salley, A. S. "Order book of Colonel Peter Horry." 35:49-57, 112-117.
Salley, A. S. "A puzzle solved." 32:317-318.
Salley, A. S. "A quaint record." 32:296-300.
Salley, A. S. "Records from a Bible of the Wilson family of Williamsburg District." 34:173-174.
Salley, A. S. "Snipes family data." 34:85-87.
Salley, A. S. "Some early Simons records." 37:142-150.
Salley, A. S. "The Spanish settlement at Port Royal, 1565-1586" 26:31-40.
Salley, A. S., Jr. "Stock marks recorded in South Carolina, 1695-1721." 13:126-131, 224-228.
Salley, A. S. "Stukes records." 39:143.
Salley, A. S., Jr. "Tombstone inscriptions at Belle Isle Plantation." 26:158-161.
Salley, A. S., Jr. "William Smith and some of his descendants." 4:239-257.
"Samuel Gaillard Stoney, 1891-1968." 69:267-269.
"Sanders Bible." 32:243.
Scherr, Arthur. "The significance of Thomas Pinckney's candidacy in the election of 1796." 76:51-59.
"The Schirmer diary." 67:167-171, 229-233; 68:37-41, 97-100; 69:59-65, 139-144, 204-208, 262-266; 70:59-63, 122-125, 196-199; 72:115-118, 236-237; 73:97, 156-158, 220-221; 74:39-40, 103-104, 170-172, 311-315; 75:50-52, 121-122, 187-188, 249-251; 76:35-37, 87-88, 171-173, 250-252; 77:49-51, 127-129, 194-195; 78:71-73; 79:72-74, 166, 250-252; 80:88-90, 192, 256-266; 81:92-94.
"Extracts from the Schirmer diary, 1860." 61:163, 232; 62:54, 113-114, 182, 237.
Schmidt. Albert J. "Hyrne family letters " 63:150-157.
Scott, Kenneth. "Some counterfeiters of Provincial currency." 57:14-22.
Scott, Kenneth. "Some sufferers in the Charleston Fire of 1740" 64:203-211.
Senese, Donald J. "The free Negro and the South Carolina courts 1790-1860." 68:140-153.
Seybolt, Robert Francis, "South Carolina schoolmasters of 1744." 31:314-315; 38:64-65.
Shankman, Arnold. "A jury of her peers: the South Carolina woman and her campaign for jury service." 81:102-121.
Sharrer, G. Terry. "Indigo in Carolina, 1671-1796." 72:94-103.

Shearer, James J. "Augustin de Letamendi: a Spanish expatriate in Charleston, S. C., 1825-1829." 43:18-27.
Shingleton, Royce Gordon. "South from Appomatox: the diary of
Abner R. Cox." 75:238-244.
Sifton, Paul G. "La Caroline Méridionale: some French sources
of South Carolina Revolutionary history, with two unpublish-
ed letters of Baron de Kalb." 66:102-108.
Simmons, Slann L. C. "Diary of Abram W. Clement, 1865." 59:
78-83.
Simmons, Slann Legare Clement. "Records of the Willtown Pres-
byterian Church, 1747-1841." 61:148-162, 219-224; 62:33-50,
107-113, 172-181.
Simons, Albert. "The Fireproof Building: a project in preser-
vation." 62:51-53.
Simons, Harriett P. and Albert. "The William Burrows House of
Charleston." 70:155-176.
Simons, R. Bentham. "A Charleston Forty-niner." 57:156-178.
Simons, Robert Bentham. "Regimental book of Captain James Bent-
ham, 1778-1780." 53:13-18, 101-112, 161-171, 230-240; 54:
37-47, 88-96, 143-155.
Simons, S. Lewis. "Inscriptions from churchyard at St. George's
Dorchester, S. C. " 40:112-113.
"Six letters of Peter Manigault." 15:114-123.
Skeen, C. Edward. "Calhoun, Crawford and the politics of re-
trenchment." 73:141-155.
Skelton, Lynda Worley. "The Importing and Exporting Company of
South Carolina (1862-1876)" 75:24-32.
Skemer, Don C. "The papers of William A. McDowell: a New Jer-
sey Presbyterian in Charleston." 79:19-22.
Smith, Alice R. Huger. "Daniel Elliott Huger Smith."
Smith, D. E. Huger. "An account of the Tattnall and Fenwick
families in South Carolina." 14:1-19
Smith, D. E. Huger. "Broughton letters." 15:171-196.
Smith, D. E. Huger. "The Luxembourg claims." 10:92-115.
Smith, D. E. Huger "Wilton's Statue of Pitt." 15:18-38.
Smith, D. E. Huger. "Commodore Alexander Gillon and the frigate
South Carolina." 9:189-219.
Smith, D. E. Huger. "Nisbett of Dean and Dean Hall." 24:17-29.
Smith, Edward Leodore. "Landgrave Thomas Smith's visit to
Boston." 22:60-64.
Smith, Henry A. M. "Ashepoo Barony." 15:64-72.
Smith, Henry A. M. "Ashley Ferry Town." 14:203-206.
Smith, Henry A. M. "The Ashley River: its seats and settlement-
s." 20:1-51, 75-122.
Smith, Henry A. M. "Beaufort-the original plan its earliest
settlers." 9:141-160.
Smith, Henry A. M. "Boone's Barony." 13:71-83.
Smith, Henry A. M. Charleston and Charleston Neck: the orig-
inal grantees and the settlements along the Ashley and Cooper
Rivers." 19:1-76.
Smith, Henry A. M. "Charleston-the original plan and its earl-

iest settlers." 9:12-27.
Smith, Henry A. M. "Childsberry or Childsbury." 14:198-203.
Smith, Henry A. M. "Childsbury." 15:107-112.
Smith, Henry A. M. "The Cypress Barony." 12:1-13.
Smith, Henry A. M. "Entries in the old Bible of Robert Pringle." 22:25-33.
Smith, Henry A. M. "French James Town." 9:220-227.
Smith, Henry A. M. "Georgetown, the original plan and the earliest settlers." 9:85-101.
Smith, Henry A. M. "Goose Creek." 29:1-25, 71-96, 167-192, 265-279.
Smith, Henry A. M. "Hobcaw Barony." 14:61.
Smith, Henry A. M. "Hog Island and Shute's Folly." 19:87-95.
Smith, Henry A. M. "Inscriptions on the monuments in the church yard of the Parish Church of St. John's, Berkeley." 11:171-183.
Smith, Henry A. M. "Joseph West: Landgrave and Governor." 19:189-193.
Smith, Henry A. M. "Landgrave Ketelby's Barony." 15:149-165.
Smith, Henry A. M. "The Oketee or Devils Elbow Barony." 13:119-125.
Smith, Henry A. M. "Old Charles Town and its vicinity, Accabee and Wappoo, where indigo was first cultivated, with some adjoining places in old St. Andrews Parish." 16:1-15, 49-67.
Smith, Henry A. M. "The Orange Quarter and the first French settlers in South Carolina." 18:101-123.
Smith, Henry A. M. "Purrysburgh." 10:187-219.
Smith, Henry A. M. "Quenby Barony and the eastern branch of the Cooper River." 18:1-36.
Smith, Henry A. M. "Radnor, Edmundsbury, and Jacksonborough." 11:39-49.
Smith, Henry A. M. "Raphor Barony." 15:1-17.
Smith, Henry A. M. "St. Andrews Town." 14:206-208.
Smith, Henry A. M. "The Seewee Barony." 12:109-117.
Smith, Henry A. M. "Somerton." 14:134-146.
Smith, Henry A. M. "The town of Dorchester, in South Carolina-a sketch of its history." 6:62-95.
Smith, Henry A. M. "The upper Ashley; and the mutations of families." 20:151-198.
Smith, Henry A. M. "Wadboo Barony." 12:43-52.
Smith, Henry A. M. "Willtown or New London." 10:20-32.
Smith, Henry A. M. "Winyah Barony." 13:1-20.
Smith, Henry A. M. "Wragg of South Carolina." 19:121-123.
Smyth, William D. "Travelers in South Carolina in the early eighteenth century." 79:113-125.
"Some records kept by Rev. Paul Turguand of St. Matthews Parish" 33:180.
"South Carolinians at the Partridge Military Academy, 1826." 61:11-12.
"South Carolina Historical and Genealogical Magazine." 31:1-6

Spaulding,Phinizy. "South Carolina and Georgia: the early days." 69:83-96.

Staite, Paul. "Samuel F. B. Morse in Charleston, 1818-1821." 89:87-112.

Stanley, Victor B., Jr. "Grave stone inscriptions from family cemeteries in Marion County." 39:100-101.

Starr, Raymond. "Letters from John Lewis Gervais to Henry Laurens, 1777-1778." 66:15-37.

Staudenraus, P. J. "Letters from South Carolina." 58:209-217.

Staudenraus, P. J. "Occupied Beaufort, 1863: a war correspondents view." 64:136-144.

Steen, Ivan D. "Charleston in the 1850's: as described by British travelers." 71:36-45.

"Steven Mazyck to Peter Porcher." 38:11-15.

Stoesen, Alexander R. "The British occupation of Charleston, 1780-1782." 63:71-82.

Stokes, Durward T. "The Baptist and Methodist clergy in South Carolina and the American Revolution." 73:87-96.

Stokes, Durward T. "The Presbyterian clergy in South Carolina and the American Revolution." 71:270-282.

Stokes, Durward T. "Thomas Reese in South Carolina." 74:151-163.

Stoney, Samuel Gaillard. "The autobiography of William John Grayson." 48:125-133, 189-197; 49:23-40, 88-103, 163-169, 216-224; 50:19-28, 77-90, 131-143, 209-215; 51:29-44, 103-116.

Stoney, Samuel Gaillard "The Great Fire of 1778 seen through contemporary letters." 64:23-26.

Stoney Samuel Gaillard. "The De Tallenare grave inscription." 40:34-35.

Stoney, Samuel Gaillard. "The memoirs of Frederick Augustus Porcher." 44:65-80, 135-147, 212-219; 45:30-40, 80-98,146-156; 46:29-39, 78-92, 140-158, 198-208; 47:32-52, 83-108, 150-162, 214-227; 48:20-25.

Stoney, Samuel G. "A note on a eighteenth century cypher." 59:113.

Stoney, Samuel Gaillard. "The Poinsett-Campbell correspondence" 42:31-52, 122-136, 149-168; 43:27-35.

Stoney, Samuel Gaillard. "Prioleau inscriptions." 40:33-34.

Stoney, Samuel Gaillard. "Robert N. Gourdin to Robert Anderson." 60:10-14.

Stoney, Samuel Gaillard. "Silk culture in Stateburg." 52:112.

Stroup, Rodger E. "Before and after: three letters from E. B. Heyward." 74:98-102.

Stubbs, Thomas McAlpin. "The fourth estate of Sumter, South Carolina." 54: 185-200.

"Studies of Rebecca and Catherine Edwards for the year 1841." 55:127-128.

Stumpf, Stuart O. "Edward Randolph's attack on proprietary government in South Carolina." 79:6-18.

Stumpf, Stuart O. "Implications of King George's War for the Charleston mercantile community.." 77:161-188.
Sturgill, Claude C. and Charles L. Price. "McCabes impression of the bombardment of Charleston, 1863." 71:266-269.
Suber, Edward D. "The French theatre in Charleston in the eighteenth century." 42:1-7.
Takaki, Ronald. "The movement to reopen the African slave trade in South Carolina." 66:38-54.
"Taken from the historical records of the 30th Regiment in South Carolina, 1775." 40:43-47.
Tatnall, Walter G. "Inscriptions from the graveyard of Lewisfield Plantation, on Cooper River." 42:81-82.
Taylor, Antoinette Elizabeth. "South Carolina and the enfranchisement of women: the early years." 77:115-126.
Taylor, Antoinette Elizabeth. "South Carolina and the enfranchisement of women; the later years." 80:298-310.
Taylor. B. F. "Abstracts of wills of South Carolinians recorded in Savannah, Ga." 41:81-83.
Taylor, B. F. "Col. Thomas Taylor." 27:204-211.
Taylor, B. F. "General William Henderson." 28:108-111.
Taylor, B. F. "John Taylor and his Taylor descendents." 8:95-119.
"Thomas Bromley's tombstone." 35:40-41.
Thomas, Charles E. "The diary of Anna Hasell Thomas (July 1864-1865)." 74:128-143.
Thomas, John P. Jr. "The Barbadians in early South Carolina." 31:75-92.
Thompson, Lawrence S. "Books in foreign languages about South Carolina, 1900-1950." 54:70-74.
"Three letters from Ford and Ravenel papers." 26:146-150.
"Three letters of Rawlins Lowndes." 12:24-26.
Tindall, George B. "The Liberian exodus of 1878." 53:133-145.
Tischendorf, Alfred P. "A note on British enterprise in South Carolina, 1872-1886." 56:196-199.
Tison, John Laurens, Jr. "Recollections of John Safford Stoney, Confederate surgeon." 60:208-220.
Tobias, Thomas J. "Charles Town in 1764." 67:63-74.
Todd, John R. "Inscriptions from Brewton Plantation, near Yemassee." 32:238-240.
"Tombstone inscriptions from Buck Hall Plantation, St. James's Santee, formerly owned by Richard Shackelford." 40:113-114.
"Tombstone inscriptions from Northampton Plantation, Sampit." 39:173.
"Tombstone inscriptions from a private cemetery on the seashore near the causeway to Pawleys Island." 40:64.
Toms, Carolina Smith. "LaFayette-Huger letters, 1795-1820." 60:57-65.
Townsend, Leah. "The confederate gunboat, Pedee." 60:66-73.
Townsend, Leah. "Discipline in early Baptist churches." 54:129-134.

"The Tuscarora Expedition letters of Colonel John Barn-
well." 9:28-54.
"Two letters from Charles Cotesworth Pinckney to Ralph Izard."
21:150-152.
Ulmer, S. Sidney. "Some eighteenth century South Carolinians
and the duel." 60:1-9.
"A Union soldier at Fort Sumter, 1860-1861." 67:99-104.
"An unpublished letter of George Washington." 39:151-156.
"Upcountry tombstone inscriptions." 65:110-113.
Valentine, Ida Massie. "A memoir of the Thomson family." 62:
215-220.
Valley, Seabrook Wilkinson. "The parentage of Governor Morton."
74:164-169.
Vaughn, William P. "South Carolina University-1876 of Fisk
Parsons Brewer." 76:225-231.
Ver Steeg, Clarence L. "Stacy Hepburn and company:enterprisers
in the American Revolution." 55:1-6.
Villers, David H. "The Smythe Horses Affair and the Associa-
tion." 70:137-148
Vipperman, Carl J. "The brief and tragic career of Charles
Lowndes." 70:211-225.
Voight, Gilbert. "Cultural contributions of German settlers to
South Carolina." 53:183-189.
Voight, Gilbert P. "The 'Periclean Age' of Beaufort." 58:218-
223.
Voight, Glibert P. "Religious conditions among German-speaking
settlers in South Carolina 1732-1774." 56:59-66.
Voight, Gilbert P. "Swiss notes on South Carolina." 21:93-104.
Waddell, Gene. "Robert Mills' Fireproof Building." 80:105-135.
Wakelyn, Jon L. "The changing loyalties of James Henry Ham-
mond: a reconsideration." 75:1-13.
Wakelyn, Jon L. "Party issues and political strategy of the
Charleston Taylor Democrats of 1848." 73:72-86.
Walker, William E. "The South Carolina College Duel of 1833."
52:140-142.
Wallace, Sarah Agnes. "Confederate exiles in London, 1865-1870:
the Wigfalls." 52:74-87, 143-153, 198-206.
Wallace, Sarah Agnes. "Some letters of the Barnard Elliott Hab-
ersham family 1858-1868." 54:201-210; 55:28-39, 116-122,
166-169.
Walsh, Richard. "The Charleston mechanics: a brief study: 1760-
1776." 60:123-144.
Walsh, Richard. "Christopher Gadsden: radical or conservative
revolutionary? 63:195-203.
Walsh, Richard. "Letters of Morris and Brailsford to Thomas
Jefferson." 58:129-144.
Walsh, Walter Richard. "Edmund Egan: Charleston's rebel brewer"
56:200-204.
Waring Alice Noble. "Five letters from Francis W. Pickens to
Patrick Noble, 1835-1836." 54:75-82.

Waring, Joseph Ioor, M.D. "An account of the invasion of South Carolina by the French and Spainards in August 1706." 66: 98-101.

Waring, Joseph I. "The Carolina Herald" 72:161-163.

Waring, Joseph I., M.D. "Chief medical officers of the South Carolina Militia." 71:33-36.

Waring, Joseph I., M. D. "Correspondence between Alexander Garden, M. D., and the Royal Society of Arts." 64:16-22, 86-94.

Waring, Joseph Ioor. "The diary of William G. Hinson during the War of Secession." 75:14-23, 111-120.

Waring, J. I., M. D. "John McKenzie, a Carolina herb doctor of the early 19th century." 69:97-100.

Waring, Joseph I. "Letter of William Henry Timrod." 76:232-233.

Waring, Joseph Ioor, M. D. "Lieutenant John Wilson's 'Journal of the siege of Charleston.' " 66:175-182.

Waring, Joseph I. "A report from the Continental General Hospital in 1780." 42:147-148.

Waring, Joseph I. "Tombstone inscriptions." 27:36-41.

Waring, Joseph Ioor. "Waring family." 24:81-100.

Watson, Alan D. "Henry McCulloh: Royal Commissioner in South Carolina." 75:33-48.

Watson, Alan D. "A letter from Charles Williames to Lord Dartmouth, July, 1766." 77:1-9.

Watson, Alan D. "Placemen in South Carolina: the receiver Generals of the Quitrents." 74:18-30.

Watson, Charles S. "Jeffersonian republicanism in William Ioor's 'Independence,' the first play of South Carolina." 69:194-203.

Watson, Charles S. "Stephan Cullen Carpenter, first drama critic of the Charleston Courier." 69:243-252.

Weaver, John C. "Lawyers, lodges and kinfolk: the workings of a South Carolina political organization, 1920-1936." 78:272-317.

Webber, Mabel L. "Abstracts from marriage bonds of South Carolina." 19:95-100, 130-135, 162-169.

Webber, Mabel L. "Abstracts from an old account book of Georgetown District." 26:151-157.

Webber, Mabel L. "Abstracts from the records of the proceedings in the Court of Ordinary, 1764-1771." 23:34-38, 77-83, 158-161, 212-222; 24:101-115; 25:143-147; 26:124-127; 30:236-240; 31:63-66, 154-158; 32:291-295; 35:25-28; 36:102-104; 38:126-130; 40:137-141; 42:137-140, 194-198; 43:61-68, 118-124, 175-180, 243-250; 44:43-51, 107-114, 173-183, 247-254; 45:41-50.

Webber, Mabel L. "Baker records." 34:62-66.

Webber, Mabel L. "Berringer notes." 25:173-178.

Webber, Mabel L. "A bill of complaint in chancery, 1700." 21:139-143.

Webber, Mabel L. "The Bond family of Hobcaw Plantation, Christ Church Parish." 25:1-22

Webber, Mabel L. "Colonel Alexander Parris, and Parris Island."
26:137-145.
Webber, Mabel L. "Col. Senfs' account of the Santee Canal." 28
8-21, 112-131.
Webber, Mabel L. "Copy of some loose papers found among Manigault papers, in the handwriting of Dr. Gabriel Manigault,
October 25, 1888." 40:15-20.
Webber, Mabel L. "Death notices from the South Carolina Gazette
from September 29, 1766 to December19, 1774." 34:55-61, 88-
95, 149-156, 211-217.
Webber, Mabel L. "Death notices from the South Carolina and
American General Gazette, and it continuation the Royal Gaz-
ette, May 1766-June 1782." 16:34-38, 86-92, 129-133, 184-187;
17:46-50, 87-93, 121-128, 147-166.
Webber, Mabel L. "Descendents of John Jenkins of St. John's
Colleton." 20:223-251.
Webber, Mabel L. "Dr. John Rutledge and his descendents." 31:
7-25, 93-106.
Webber, Mabel L. "The early generations of the Seabrook Family"
17:14-25, 58-72.
Webber, Mabel L. "Extracts from the journal of Mrs. Ann Mani-
gault, 1754-1781." 20:57-63, 128-141, 204-212, 256-259; 21:
10-23, 59-72, 112-120.
Webber, Mabel L. "The first governor Moore and his children."
37:1-32.
Webber, Mabel L. "Gaillard notes." 39:72-80
Webber, Mabel L. "Grimball of Edisto Island." 23:1-7, 39-45,
94-101.
Webber, Mabel L. "Hyrne family." 22:101-118.
Webber, Mabel L. "An Indian land grant in 1734." 19:157-161.
Webber, Mabel L. "Inscriptions from the church yard at Strawberry Chapel." 21:161-170.
Webber, Mabel L. "Joseph West, Landgrave and Governor." 40:79-
80.
Webber, Mabel L. "Marriage and death notices from the Charles-
ton Morning Post and Daily Advertiser and the City Gazette."
20:52-56, 142-146, 213-219, 260-263; 21:24-29, 77-87, 121-131
153-160; 22:19-24, 65-72, 89-93, 119-123; 23:26-33, 72-76,
152-157, 205-211; 24:30-39, 69-80; 25:36-46.
Webber, Mabel L. "Marriage and death notices from the South
Carolina Weekly Gazette." 18:37-41, 85-90, 143-148, 184-189;
19:77-79, 105-113, 136-145, 170-180.
Webber, Mabel L. "The Mayrant family." 27:81-90.
Webber, Mabel L. "Moore of St. Thomas' Parish." 27:156-169.
Webber, Mabel L. "Notes relating to Georgetown, S.C." 32:193-
204.
Webber, Mabel L. "Parish register of St. James Santee." 15:
133-143, 197-203; 16:16-24, 68-79, 109-122, 164-177; 17:34-
45, 73-81, 103-115.
Webber, Mabel L. "Peter Manigaults letters." 31:171-183, 269-
282; 32:46-60, 115-130, 175-192, 270-280; 33:55-62, 148-153

247-250.
Webber, Mabel L. "Presentment of the Grand Jury, March 1733-34" 25:193-195.
Webber, Mabel L. "Records from the Blake and White Bibles." 36:14-19, 42-55, 89-93, 113-121; 37:38-44, 65-70.
Webber, Mabel L. "The records of the Quakers in Charles Town." 28:22-43, 94-107, 176-197.
Webber, Mabel L. "The register of Christ Church Parish." 18: 50-53, 70-77, 124-130, 168-174; 19:114-119, 124-129; 20:64-71, 123-127, 199-203, 252-255; 21:31-35, 52-58, 105-111, 144-149; 22:12-18
Webber, Mabel L. "Register of the Independent or Congregational (Circular) Church, 1732-1738." 12:27-37, 53-59, 134-140.
Webber, Mabel L. "Register of St. Andrews Parish, Berkeley Co., South Carolina, 1719-1774." See page 343 for citations.
Webber, Mabel L. "Sir Nathaniel Johnson and his son, Robert Johnson." 38:109-115.
Webber, Mabel L. "South Carolina almanacs to 1800." 15:73-81.
Webber, Mabel L. "South Carolina Loyalists." 14:36-43.
Webber, Mabel L. "The Thomas Elfe account book 1768-1775." 35: 13-24, 58-73, 96-106, 153-165; 36:7-13, 55-66, 79-88, 122-133; 37:24-32, 77-83, 111-122, 151-156; 38:37-42, 54-61, 87-94, 131-136; 39:36-41, 83-90, 134-142, 160-167; 40:21-27, 58-63, 81-86, 145-150; 41:23-29, 61-68, 123-129, 151-156; 42:12-19.
Webber, Mabel L. "The Thomas Pinckney family of South Carolina" 39:15-35.
Webber, Mabel L. "Williams Hart's journal." 24:40-47.
Weber Bernard C., and Brooks Thompson. "Letter from Mrs. Margaret Manigault to Mrs. Alice Izard, 1814." 54:156-158.
Weber, Ralph E. "Joel R. Poinsett's secret Mexican Dispatch Twenty." 75:67-76.
"Wedding menu, 1856" 64:202.
Wehmann, Howard H. "Noise, novelties and nullifiers: a U.S. Navy officer's impressions of the Nullification Controversy." 76:21-24.
Weidner, Paul R. "The journal of John Blake White." 42:55-71, 99-117, 169-186; 43:35-47, 103-117, 161-174.
Weir, Robert M. "Muster rolls of the South Carolina Granville and Colleton County Regiments of the Militia, 1756." 70:226-239.
Weir, Robert M. "Two letters by Christopher Gadsden, February 1766." 75:169-176.
Wells, Lawrence K. "Marriage and obituary notices from the Pioneer and Yorkville Weekly Advertiser, 1823-1824." 72:111-114.
Wells, Lawrence K. "Marriage and obituary notices from the Yorkville Compiler, 1840-1841." 72:179-183, 234-235.
Welsh, John R. "Washington Allston: Expatriate South Carolinian." 67:84-98.

White, Anne A. and Frances H. Leonard. "Records of the George-
town Methodist Church, 1811-1897." 61:41-50, 101-113.
West, Frances D. "John Bartram and slavery." 56:115-119.
White, Frank F., Jr. "The evacuation of Fort Moultrie, 1860."
53:1-5.
Wight, Williard E. "Some letters of William Dunlap Simpson,
1860-1863." 57:204-222.
Wight, Williard E. "Two Lutheran missionary journals, 1811,
1813." 55:6-14.
Williams, Frank B. "From Sumter to the wilderness: letters of
Sergeant James Butler Suddath, Co. E., 7th Regiment, S.C.V."
63:1-11, 93-104.
Williams, George W. "Early organists at St. Phillip's, Charles-
ton." 54:83-87.
Williams, George W. "Eighteenth century organists of St. Mich-
aels, Charleston." 53:146-154, 212-222.
Williams, George W. "Letters to the Bishop of London from the
Commissaries of South Carolina." 78:1-31, 120-147, 213-242,
286-317.
Williams, George W. "Two maps of Charleston in the Revolution."
76:49-50.
Williams, Horace G. "John Miller and his descendents." 72:104
Williams, Jack Kenny. "The Code of Honor in ante-bellum South
Carolina." 54:113-128.
Williams, Jack Kenny. "The criminal lawyer in ante-bellum
South Carolina." 56:138-150.
Williams, Samuel C. "General Richard Winn's notes, 1780." 43:
201-212; 44:1-10.
Williams, W. R. "British-American officers, 1720-1763." 33:183
-196, 290-296.
Winberry, John J. "Reputation of Carolina indigo." 80:242-255.
Withington, Lathrop. "South Carolina gleanings in England." 4:
231-238, 286-295, 100-107, 161-167, 218-228; 6:20-28, 116-
125, 169-173; 7:27-30, 143-152; 8:211-219; 9:78-94, 122-
126; 11:129-132; 15:91-96.
Wooster, Ralph. "Membership of the South Carolina Secession
Convention." 55:185-197.
Wright, David McCord. " 'Mr. Ash'- a footnote in constitution-
al history." 63:227-231.
Wright, David McCord. "Petitioners to the Crown against the
Proprietors, 1716-1777." 62:88-95.
Wright, David McCord. "Records and notes of the Scott family of
St. Helena Island." 66:55-59.
Wright, Nathalia. "Francis Kinloch: a South Carolina artist."
61:99-100.
Wynes, Charles E. "T. McCants Stewart: peripatetic black South
Carolinian." 80:311-317.
Young, Rogers W. "Castle Pinckney, silent sentinel of Charles-
ton Harbor." 1:14, 51-67.
Zahniser, Marvin R. "Edward Rutledge to his son, August 2,
1796." 64:65-72.

Zahniser, Marvin R. "The first Pinckney mission to France."
66:205-217.

Zornow, William Frank. "State aid for indigent families of
South Carolina soldiers, 1861-1865." 57:82-87.

Zornow, William Frank. "Tarriff policies in South Carolina,
1775-1789." 56:31-44.

* * *

Webber, Mabel L. "Register of St. Andrew's Parish, Berkeley
Co., South Carolina, 1719-1774 (from page 341)." 12:172-189;
13:21-41, 154-162, 213-223; 14:20-35, 81-97, 147-159,
209-218; 15:39-50, 97-106.

Articles and historical records in the South Carolina Historical Society <u>Collections</u>, volumes I-V (1857-1897).

Volume I

"Address pronounced at the inauguration of the South Carolina Historical Society, June 28th, 1855, by Prof. F. A. Porcher", pp. 1-17.
"A narrative of the capture of Henry Laurens, of his confinement in the Tower of London, &c., 1780, 1781, 1782,--", pp. 18-68.
"Appendix, containing documents, letters, &c., relating to Mr. Lauren's imprisonment in the Tower,--", pp. 69-83.
"A list and abstract of documents relating to South Carolina, now existing in the State Paper Office, London. Prepared for the South Carolina Historical Society by an authorized agent, in London", pp. 87-307.

Volume II

"Oration delivered on the third anniversary of the South-Carolina Historical Society, Thursday evening, May 27th, 1858. By James Louis Petigru, president of the society", pp. 9-21.
"Journal of the Council of Safety, for the Province of South Carolina, 1775", pp. 22-64.
"Illustrations", pp. 65-74.
"The French Protestants [Huguenots] of Abbeville District, South Carolina, 1761-1765", pp. 75-103.
"Oration delivered on the first anniversary of the South Carolina Historical Society, June 28, 1856. By J. Barrett Cohen", pp. 104-117.
"List and abstract of papers in the State Paper Office, London, relating to South-Carolina. Done under authority for the South Carolina Historical Society, 1857. Continued from volume I", pp. 118-330.
"Vocabulary of the Catawba language, with some remarks on its grammar, construction and pronunciation. By Oscar M. Lieber, State Geologist of S.C.", pp. 327-342.

Volume III

"Oration delivered before the South Carolina Historical Society, Thursday, May 19, 1859. By W. H. Trescott, Esq.", pp. 9-34.
"Journal of the second Council of Safety, appointed by the Provisional Congress, November, 1775", pp. 35-271.
"Lists and abstracts of papers in the State Paper Office, London, relating to South Carolina (1699-1743), done under authority for the South Carolina Historical Society, 1857. Papers of the Board of Trade", pp. 272-343.

Volume IV

Volume V

Articles in the Proceedings of the South Carolina Historical
Association, 1931-1978. Only articles pertaining to South
Carolina are listed.

Abbott, Martin. "The Freedmen's Bureau and its Carolina crit-
ics." 1962:15-23.
Ackerman, Robert K. "Colonial land policies and the slave pop-
ulation." 1965:28-35.
"Alvin Laroy Duckett." 1967:4.
Anderson, J. Perrin. Public education in Ante-Bellum South
Carolina." 1933:3-11.
Bailey, Hugh C. "The Up-country academies of Moses Waddell."
1959:36-44.
Barnwell, Robert W., Jr. "Addresses of Clinton & Arbuthnot."
1939:44.
Barnwell, Robert W., Jr. "The migration of Loyalists from
South Carolina." 1937:34-42.
Barnwell, Robert W., Jr. "Report on Loyalist exiles from South
Carolina, 1783." 1937:43-46.
Barnwell, Robert W., Sr. "Bentonville - the last battle of
Johnston & Sherman." 1943:42-54.
Bass, Robert D. "The last campaign of Major Patrick Ferguson."
1968:16-28.
Bass, Robert D. "The South Carolina Rangers: a forgotten
Loyalist regiment." 1977:64-71.
Bender, Jay. "Olin D. Johnston & the highway controversy."
1972:39-54.
Bennett, Susan S. Some early settlers of Calhoun County."
1938:16-24.
Bonham, Milledge L., Jr. "A convention that made history."
1940:3-9.
Bourne, Ruth. "The exchange of prisoners." 1944:3-20.
Brewster, Lawrence F. Planters from the Low-country & their
summer travels." 1943:35-41.
Brewster, Lawrence Fay. "Ante-Bellum planters & their means of
transportation." 1948:15-25.
Buchanan, G. A., Jr. "Xenophobia in the south." 1947:21-35.
Burnside, Ronald D. "Racism in the administration of Governor
Cole Blease." 1964:43-57.
Cann, Marvin. "Burnet Maybank & Charleston politics in the New
Deal era." 1970:39-48.
Carlisle, Jean Todd. "The State's editorial policy relative to
South Carolina, 1903-1913." 1951:29-40.
"Charles Edward Cauthen, 1897-1964." 1965:4.
Childs, St. Julien Ravenel. "Notes on the history of public
health in South Carolina, 1670-1800." 1932:13-22.
Cole, David. "A brief outline of the South Carolina colonial
militia system." 1954:14-23.

Copeland, J. Isaac. "The tutor in Ante-Bellum south." 1965: 36-47.

Daniel, Lucia. "The teaching of high school history - a point of view." 1949:25-35.

Davis, Nora Marshall. "Jefferson Davis's route from Richmond, Virginia, to Irvinville." 1941:11-20.

DeRosier, Arthur H. "John C. Calhoun & the removal of the Choctaw indians." 1957:33-45.

DesChamps, Margaret B. "Antislavery Presbyterians in the Carolina Piedmont." 1954:6-13.

Dickson, Maxcy Robinson. "Sources for South Carolina history in the nation's capital." 1942:50-54.

Douglas, W. Ernest. "Retreat from conservatism." 1958:3-11.

Easterby, J. H. "The Granger movement in South Carolina." 1931:21-32.

Easterby, J. H. "The study of South Carolina history." 1950: 49-70.

Edmunds, John B. Jr. "Francis W. Pickens and the war begins." 1970:21-29.

Ellen, John C. Jr. "Richard Yeadon, Confederate patriot." 1960:32-43.

Epting, Carl L. "Inland navigation in South Carolina and the Columbia Canal." 1936:18-28.

Fisher, Mrs. George. "John Barnwell and British western policy." 1956:23-33.

"Francis Butler Simkins, 1897-1966." 1966:4.

"Frank Watts Ashley." 67:4.

Gayle, Charles Joseph. "The nature and volume of exports from Charleston, 1724-1774." 1937:25-33.

Geer, William M. "Francis Lieber at the South Carolina College." 1943:3-22.

Gergel, Richard Mark. "Wade Hampton and the rise of one party racial orthodoxy in South Carolina." 1977:5-16.

Gilpatrick, D. H. "Nativism in American journalism, 1784-1814." 1948:3-14.

Gilpatrick, D. H. "Samuel Slater, the father of American manufactures." 1932:23-34.

Godbold, E. Stanley. "Christopher Gadsden: radical idealist." 1976:14-23.

Green, Fletcher Melvin. "Writing and research in southern history." 1942:3-17.

Gregorie, Anne King. "The first decade of the Charleston Library Society." 1935:3-10.

Hemphill, W. Edwin. "The Calhoun papers project: one editor's valedictory." 1977:28-36.

Henderson, William C. "The slave court system in Spartanburg County." 1976:24-38.

Hendrick, Carlanna. "John Gary Evans against the Columbia State." 1970:30-38.

Hollis, Daniel W. "Cole L. Blease and the senatorial campaign of 1924." 1978:53-68.

Hollis, Daniel W. "Costly delusion: inland navigation in the South Carolina Piedmont." 1968:29-43.

Hollis, Daniel W. "James H. Thornwell and the South Carolina College." 1953:17-36.

Howard, Laura Ellen. "William Prynne, a portrait." 1932:35-43.

Huff, Archie Vernon. "Langdon Cheves and the War of 1812: another look at 'national honor' in South Carolina." 1970: 8-20.

Hughes, Horatio. "The Elliott Society." 1938:25-31.

Jarrell, Hampton M. "William Gilmore Simms - almost a historian." 1947:3-8.

Jennings, Thelma. "South Carolina leadership in the southern unification movement, 1849-1850." 1978:31-41.

Jones, F. Dudley. "The Grimké sisters." 1933:12-21.

Jones, Newton B. "The role of the Commons House of Assembly in proprietary South Carolina." 1976:5-13.

Jones, Newton B. "Social consciousness in South Carolina during Reconstruction: imported or indigenous?" 1962:24-31.

Lander, E. M. Jr. "The South Carolina textile industry before 1845." 1951:19-28.

Lander, Ernest M., Jr. "The Palmetto Regiment goes to Mexico." 1973:83-93.

Leemhuis, Roger P. "William W. Boyce: a leader of the southern peace movement." 1978:21-30.

Lesesne, J. M. "The Nesbitt Manufacturing Company's debt to the Bank of the State of South Carolina." 1960:15-22.

Lesesne, J. Mauldin. "The nullification controversy in an Up-country district." 1939:13-24.

Levett, Ella Pettit. "Loyalism in Charleston, 1761-1784." 1936:3-17.

Link, Eugene P. "The Republican Society of Charleston." 1943: 23-34.

Logan, S. Frank. "Francis Warrington Dawson, 1840-1889; South Carolina editor." 1952:13-28.

McCowen, George S., Jr. "The Charles Town Board of Police, 1780-1782: a study in civil administration under military occupation." 1964:25-42.

McDowell, William L. "The indian books: important documents in the South Carolina Archives." 1955:15-21.

McKissick, J. Rion. "Some observations of travelers on South Carolina, 1800-1860." 1932:44-51.

Mills, W. H. "The thoroughbred in South Carolina." 1937:13-24.

Moore, Jamie W. "Ben Tillman and government for Hawaii." 1973:5-19.

Moore, John Hammond. "South Carolina's reaction to the photoplay, 'The Birth of a Nation'." 1963:30-40.

Moore, Robert J. "Governor Chamberlain and the end of Reconstruction." 1977:17-27.

Moore, Robert J. "Robert C. Winthrop: conservative opponent of Lincoln." 1961:8-24.

Moore, Winfred B., Jr. "'Soul of the south': James F. Byrnes and the racial issue in American politics, 1911-1941." 1978: 42-52.

Moss, Bobby G. "Wilbur Joseph Cash: iconoclast." 1967:43-54.

Mulkey, Floyd. "Rev. Philip Mulkey, pioneer Baptist preacher in upper South Carolina." 1945:3-13.

Neal, Diane. "Ben Tillman - no apologies for lynching." 1971: 5-15.

Needham, David C. "William Howard Taft and the Republican party in South Carolina." 1972:18-38.

Oliphant, Mary C. Sims. "The genesis of an Up-country town." 1933:50-62.

Patton, James Welch. "John Belton O'Neall." 1934:3-13.

Patton, James Welch. "The work of soldiers' aid societies in South Carolina during the Civil War." 1937:3-12.

Poole, Bernard L. "The presidential election of 1928 in South Carolina." 1953:5-16.

Prior, G. T. "Charleston pastime and culture in the Nullification decade, 1822-1832." 1940:36-44.

Rogers, George C., Jr. "The Laurens papers - half way." 1977: 37-48.

Rogers, George C., Jr. "South Carolina ratifies the federal constitution." 1961:41-62.

Roper, John Herbert. "A reconsideration: the University of South Carolina during Reconstruction." 1974:46-57.

Ryan, Frank W. "The opinions of editor William Gilmore Simms of the Southern Quarterly Review, 1849-1854." 1959:25-35.

Salley, A. S. "The Fundamental Constitutions of Carolina." 1934:25-31.

Sanders, Albert N. "Jim Crow comes to South Carolina." 1966: 27-39.

Sanders, Albert N. "Teaching American history with a South Carolina accent." 1956:34-42.

Scheer, George F. "Some events of the American Revolution as recorded by the Rev. James Jenkins." 1945:23-34.

Scott, Florence Johnson. "Letters and papers of Governor David Johnson and family, 1810-1855." 1939: appendix.

Shaffer, E. T. "The rejected Laurens." 1934:14-24.

Sherriff, Florence Janson. "The Salzburgers and Purrysburg." 1963:12-22.

Sherrill, George R. "Legislative domination in South Carolina." 1941:31-36.

Singleton, Kathleen. "The Grand Council of South Carolina." 1934:32-47.

Sisson, Charles N. "The report of the French minister." 1944:26-32.

Sirmans, M. Eugene. "Politicians and planters: the Bull family of colonial South Carolina." 1962:32-41.

Skipper, O. C. "J. D. B. DeBow, statistician of the old south." 1938:3-15.

Slaunwhite, Jerry. "Tillman's lieutenant: John Laurens Manning Irby." 1975:30-47.

Smith, Clarence McKittrick, Jr. "William Porcher Miles, pro-
gressive mayor of Charleston, 1855-1857." 1942:30-39.
Smith, Selden K. "'Cotton Ed' Smith's response to economic
adversity." 1971:16-23.
Steirer, William F. Slavery and the presence of free will."
1974:36-45.
Stroup, Rodger. "Tillman's lieutenant: John Lowndes McLaurin."
1975:48-57.
Taylor, Rosser H. "The mud-sill theory in South Carolina."
1939:35-43.
Tucker, Robert C. "James H. Hammond and the southern conven-
tion." 1960:4-14.
Tuttle, Jack E. "Tillman and the South Carolina Dispensary."
1961:63-74.
Vandiver, Frank E. "The South Carolina Ordnance Board, 1860-
1861." 1945:14-22.
Venable, Austin L. "William L. Yancey and the League of United
Southerners." 1946:3-12.
Voight, Gilbert P. "The Germans and the German-Swiss in South
Carolina, 1732-1765." 1935:17-25.
Wallace, D. D. "Some unexploited fields in South Carolina
history." 1935:26-35.
Walsh, Richard. "The South Carolina Academy, 1800-1811."
1955:5-14.
Ware, Lowry P. "Attorney General Isaac W. Hayne and the South
Carolina Executive Council of 1862." 1952:5-12.
Wates, Wylma. "The South Carolina public records as sources for
revisionist interpretation of the American Revolution."
1959:18-24.
Watson, Harry L. "Early newspapers of Abbeville District, 1812-
1834." 1940:18-35.
Williams, Jack K. "The southern movememt to reopen the African
slave trade, 1854-1860: a factor in secession." 1960:23-31.
Williams, Jack K. "William Edward Dodd: historian of the old
south." 1950:18-29.
Williamson, Gustavus G., Jr. "South Carolina cotton mills and
the Tillman movement." 1949:36-49.
Wiltse, Charles M. "Calhoun: an interpretation." 1948:26-38.
"Winston Chandler Babb." 1968:4.
Woody, Robert H. "Christopher Gadsden and the Stamp Act."
1939:3-12.
Wolfe, John Harold. "The South Carolina constitution of 1865 as
a democratic document." 1942:18-29.
Wright, E. Baskin. The problem of Negro education in the south."
1949:50-61.
Wright, Marion A. "A pre-requisite to progress." 1946:32-37.

APPENDIX V

Historical and genealogical articles in the <u>Transactions</u> of the
Huguenot Society of South Carolina, volumes 1-84 (1886-1979).
Notes and non-historical addresses have been omitted.

"Account book of Nicholas deLonguemare 1703-1711." 55:43-69.
"An account of the Porcher family in their old and new homes,
  with the story of two remarkable men, and one strange coinci-
  dence." 18:12-31.
Achurch, Col. Robert W. "Huguenots and Camisards." 69:5-15.
"Address by William Jay Schieffelin, president of the Huguenot
  Society of the American." 35:39-41.
"Address delivered by Harold A. Mouzon, esq. at the unveiling of
  the mural tablet to George Washington, in the Huguenot Church
  in Charleston, S.C." 38:82-87.
"Address delivered by M. Raymond Bosquet, Secretary of the
  French Embassy." 35:45-48.
"Address delivered by Major Alfred Huger, Huguenot anniversary
  celebration." 35:21-23.
"Address of Col. H. A. DuPont before the Huguenot Society of
  South Carolina at its annual meeting at Charleston, S.C.,
  April 13, 1917." 23:24-36.
"Address of Col. Richard L. Maury, of Richmond, Va." 9:8-39.
"Address of president T.W. Bacot at the twenty-eighth anniver-
  sary meeting of the Huguenot Society of South Carolina on the
  13th day of April, 1923." 28:15-26.
"Address prepared by St. J. Allison Lawton for the occasion of
  the unveiling of the granite cross marking the site of the old
  Huguenot Church of French Santee." 36:20-28.
"Alexander Mazcyk." 3:33-34.
"Alfred Ford Ravenel." 3:29.
"American pedigree [Quince-Heyward.]" 72:50.
"Ancestry of Captain Christopher Wilkinson." 80:111-112.
Anger, Charles L. "Charles Pelot Summerall: a sketch of the
  man." 61:5-16.
"Appeal on behalf of the library of the French Protestant Church
  of London." 70:40-42.
Ashford, Elizabeth Jeanette. "The Bellunes." 81:31-46.
"Bacot records." 77:93-126; 78:139-162
Bacot, T.W. "Abstract of the title of the Huguenot Society of
  South Carolina to the site of the old Huguenot Church and
  churchyard of 'Orange Quarter' (St. Denis)." 27:26-40.
Bacot, Thomas W. "Orange Quarter (St. Denis). 23:37-60
Bacot, Thomas W. "St. John's Berkeley" 24:27-35
Baumeister, Margaret Kilpatrick and Margaret Grant Plumb. "The
  Berrien family genealogy." 73:36-111; 74:47-76
Baumeister, Margaret Kilpatrick and Margaret Plumb. "In-
  troduction to the Berrien family genealogy." 72:53-76
Beck, Henry L. "Purrysburg, as it is today." 39:40-44

"Benjamin Huger Rutledge." 3:26-28
Bennett, Susan Smythe. "The Courtonnes of South Carolina."
  39:45-57.
Bennett, Susan Smythe. "Paul Turquand." 32:33-36.
Bennett, Susan Smythe. "The Turquands." 38:37-64.
Berry, Michael West. "Flournoy pedigree, and the Reverend
  Robert Flournoy line." 80:52-53.
"Bill of sale for a lot at French Jamestown, 1706." 61:30-24.
Black, Emma C. "The Isle of Oleron." 15:33-58.
Boardman, Hollis. "The French Huguenots." 80:65-69.
Bradley, Rev. S. Hugh. "How they kept the faith." 46:61-71.
Brandt, Rev. F. William. "Christain liberty." 49:44-48.
"A brief memorial to Francis Marion." 11:12-13.
"Bruneau." 79:161-163.
Burkette, Alice G. "Goose Creek cross repaired." 84:58
Burkette, Alice Gaillard. "Warning: water will cover these
  graves." 81:25-27.
Burns, Martha B. and Alice G. Burkette. "Peyre records." 79:
  164-176.
Burns, Martha B. "Point Farm." 80:124-132.
Burns, Martha Bailey. "Early Jaudon 'Pauls'." 68:49-52.
Burns, Martha Bailey. "Very affectionately, H. S. Legare"
  71:50-53.
Burns, Martha Bailey. "Vincent Guerin of St. Thomas and St.
  Denis." 69:37-45.
Butt, Mary McLure. "Belin genealogy." 67:61-64.
Carte, Carrie C. "James Jarrett, I." 80:57-64.
"Ceremonies held in the South Carolina Society Hall, Monday,
  April 12, 1920." 25:67
"Character of the Huguenots." 5:52-60.
Childs, St. Julien Ravenel. "French origins of Carolina." 50:
  24-44.
"The church at Charleston." 7:49-50.
"Church in St. Dennis Parish, Orange or French Quarter." 5:63-
  66.
"The church in St. John's Parish, Berkeley." 5:62-63.
Clark, Chovine R. "Count Casimar Pulaski." 82:114-116.
Clark, Chovine R. "David DuBose Gaillard." 83:62-63.
Clark, Chovine R. "John Richbourg and the American Revolution"
  82:50-53.
Clark, Chovine R. "An open letter to the town of Manning,
  South Carolina." 84:52-57.
Clark, Chovine R. "The Pony Express." 83:126-128.
Clearwater, Hon. A. T. "The Huguenots in America." 17:18-27.
Clearwater, Alphonso Trumpbour. "The Huguenot in America, and
  his successor." 25:81-94.
"Cleland Kinloch Huger." 3:19.
"Clement." 80:112-121.
Colcock, William Ferguson. "The Huguenots in northern Italy."
  83:52-58.
Cole, Brigadier General Eli K. "Charles Fort, South Carolina,

352

built by Ribualt in 1562." 29:15-25.

"Colonel Francis Pickens Miller." 56:5.

"Commemorative services in the Huguenot Church, Charleston,
S. C." 33:50-52.

Coombs, Miss Elizabeth. "Abstracts of Dewalt wills." 54:35-36.

Cordes, Alexander Watson. "The Cordes on that side...and the
Cordes' family tree." 79:86-101.

Coussons, John S. "The Huguenot spirit." 83:1-8.

Cuttino, G. P. "The descendents of William Cuttino." 83:79-123
84:116-139.

Cuttino, G.P. "Further notes on the history of the Cuttino
family." 65:23-32.

Cuttino, G. P. "The Huguenots in America: a reappraisal."
68:1-7.

Cuttino, G. P. "Notes on the history of the Cothonneau family."
45:42-51.

"Daniel Le Gendre." 11:32-34.

Davis, Curtis Carroll. "The several-sided James Matthewes Legare: poet." 57:5-12.

Davis, Curtis Carroll. "That elusive Mr. Legare: author and artist." 78:58-60.

De Coligny, Col. William Gaspard. "Admiral Gaspard de Coligny."
25:18-33.

De Coligny, Col. William Gaspard. "The ancestry of Admiral de
Coligny." 25:110-115.

"De La Roche." [genealogy] 80:36-45.

De Saussure, Henry A. "Huguenots on the Santee River." 14:14-
25.

De Saussure, Isabelle. "Ribault's Fort." 14:48-52.

"The dedication ceremonies at Purrysburgh, South Carolina." 46:
36-37.

"Deed of conveyance of old Huguenot Goose Creek Church site to
the Society." 20:28-30.

"Deed of conveyance to the Society of old 'Orange Quarter' (St.
Denis) Huguenot Church site." 27:21-25.

Demarest, Donald W. "New Jersey's oldest house as it appears
today." 81:28.

"Details pertaining to the Santee settlement" 5:70-76.

Dovell, Elizabeth Mazyck Simons. "A Simons tombstone comes
home." 78:53-54.

Du Bose, Lucile. "Fourth international reunion of Huguenots."
81:67-75.

Du Bose, Rev. Dr. William Haskell. "A Huguenot in the winning
of the west." 40:37-57.

Duffield, Rev. Howard. "The burning bush."

Duffield, Rev. Howard. "The Huguenot spirit." 25:73-80.

Druham, Francis Marion. "Dubose Heyward: English-French Huguenot." 58:5-12.

"Early generations of the Gaillard family." 44:36-44.

"Early generations of the Legare family in South Carolina." 46:
72-81.

"The Edict of Toleration, 1787." 20:32-38.
"Edmund Mazyck, M.D." 3:28.
"Edward Lightwood Parker." 3:20-21.
"Eighteenth century affidavit to prove the descent of the Gig-
nilliat family." 64:25-27.
"English pedigree." [Mellish] 72:51
Ervin, Senator Sam J., Jr. "Contributions of the Huguenots to
America." 78:1-7
Ervin, Sam J., Jr. "The Conyers family of Clarendon County,
South Carolina." 79:106-127.
Ervin, Sam J., Jr. "The Richbourg family of South Carolina."
77:61-79.
"Family record." [Legare' family.] 71:102-115.
Fercken, F. Harold "Chronological biography of General Daniel
Roberdeau." 43:37-44.
"The first Huguenot immigrants, 1670-1700." 5:7-18.
Fishburne, John I. "Protestantism in France in the nineteenth
and twentieth centuries." 47:26-33.
Fitch, Girdler B. "Agrippa D'Aubigne, Huguenot and poet." 55:
5-17.
Fitz Simons, Mabel Trott. "Burdell." 68:58-61.
Fitz Simons, Mabel Trott. "Perdriau [family]." 68:72-86.
Fitz Simons, Mabel Trott. "Some descendents of Henry Mouzon,
mapmaker and surveyor." 69:46-50.
Fitz Simons, Mabel Trott. "Tamplet (Tample) family." 61:40-44
Foelsch, Rev. Dr. Charles B. "The spirit of the Huguenots and
the faith of today." 37:34-42.
"Francis Marion Burdell." 3:21
"Frederick A. Porcher." 1:47-49.
"The French Hospital." 64:20-24.
"The French Huguenot Church of the parish of St. James, Goose
Creek." 16:42-47.
"The French Protestant church." 13:13-14.
"The French Protestants of Abbeville District, South Carolina,
1761-1765." 19:14-23.
"A Gaillard among the settlers at Abbeville." 5:79.
Gaillard, Edward McCrady. "A brief outline of my family back-
ground." 82:85-109.
"Gaillard list." 68:43-45.
Gaillard, Mr. Thomas. "List of French names of refugees arriv-
ing in Carolina." 4:21.
Gaillard, Thomas. "Copious extracts by the committee on public-
ation from the history of the Huguenots in South Carolina,
and their descendents." 5:7
Gaillard, W. Lucas. "Directions to Huguenots markers." 71:44-
49.
"Gaston Doumergue." 29:26-28.
"Gendron family." 4:20.
"General Richard Richardson." 81:47-52.
Gibbes, John E. "Huguenot traits." 53:27-37.
Gibert, Anne C. "The Admiral Gaspard de Coligny memorial pil-

354

grimage-England, Holland, Germany, Switzerland and France." 78: 42-50.

Gibert, Anne C. "The legacies of John De la Howe and John Lewis Gervais." 82:78-84.

Gourdin, Virginia. "Huguenot research abroad for amateur genealogists." 84:42-51.

Grove, Michael Motte. "Motte family." 72:42-49.

Guerry, Edward Brailsford. "The faith of the Huguenots." 82: 1-7.

Guerry, The Rev. Edward B. "In memoriam, The Right Reverend Albert Sidney Thomas, LL.D, DD." 73:23-25.

Guerry, The Rev. Edward B. "The pedigree tables of Guerry, Rembert, Michau, Du Pont and Cromwell." 76:74-75.

Guerry, Rt. Rev. William Alexander. "The search for General Moultrie's grave." 79:64-77.

Hadsel, Fred Latimer. "Huguenot immigration to England after the revocation of the Edict of Nantes." 46:45-58.

Hamer, Philip M. "Henry Laurens-neglected patriot." 70:1-15.

Hamilton, John A. "A Christian view of U.S. foreign policy." 60:5-13.

Hanahan, Hardin Davant. "Davant family history." 74:77-119; 75:101-165, 170-230.

Harper, J. Ernest, Jr. "Isaac Caillabeuf and some descendents." 71:54-56.

Harrison, James G. "Colonial Carolina's Huguenots." 75:1-13.

Harrison, James Geraty. "Sidney Lanier as a man of letters." 51:25-32.

Hasell, Annie B. "Some generations of the Louis Mouzon family." 70:45-55.

Hasell, Annie B. "Tombstone inscriptions from Oak Hill plantation burying ground." 68:62-64.

Hasell, N. Ingraham. "An incident of a sword." 79:102-103.

"Henry Lewis Chisholm." 3:17.

"Henry William De Saussure, M.D." 1:41-42.

"Henry William Ravenel." 1:42-43.

Hinton, Josephine Du Bose. "John Du Bose family." 79:138-160.

"Historical sketch of the Prioleau family in Europe and America." 6:5-16, 71:80-101.

Hodges, James B., Jr. "The Elias Bonneau family." 84:77-79.

Hoff, Henry Bainbridge. "The Gignilliat history." 79:78-85.

Hoff, Henry Bainbridge. "The Le Serrurier family." 82:75-77.

Hoff, Henry Bainbridge. "Monfort-Monfoort." 81:29-30.

"Hon. Hugh Swinton Legare." 4:9

Horlbeck, Elizabeth Miles. "John Gendron, a notable officer of the militia of provincial South Carolina." 62:48-51.

Horlbeck, Elizabeth Miles. "Notes from the Crottet manuscripts" 69:65-67.

"Hostility of the English settlers to the French." 5:19-42.

Huger, Dr. Wm. H. "Huger family record." 72:35-41.

Huger, Dr. Wm. H. "Paper describing the first generations of the Huger family in South Carolina." 4:11-19.

Huger, Major Alfred. "A triumph of spirit." 27:41-56.
"Huger pedigree." Enclosure to vol. 72.
"Huguenot belief in religious liberty is a part of the American heritage." 66:33-34.
"The Huguenot churches in South Carolina." 5:60-62.
"A Huguenot episode of the Revolution." [a play] 37:20-24.
"A Huguenot exhortation, 1677." 26:34-38.
"Huguenot immigration in South Carolina." 12:16-29.
"The Huguenots." 20:43-47.
"Huguenots in America." 19:27-60.
"The Huguenots of Abbeville, South Carolina." 5:76-77.
"Huguenots, the first textile manufacturers." 20:48-49.
"The Huguenots of South Carolina." 11:14-20.
"Huguenots on Laurel Hill, appendix I." 80:106-108.
"The Huguenots pilgrimage to French Santee." 36:29-30.
"Index to the Berrien family genealogy." 76:109-117.
"The influence of the Huguenots in the United States of America." 21:30-58.
"An interesting and valuable old record." [Record book of Probate Judge, 1685]. 21:60-62
"Interesting features of the unveiling of the monument by the Society." 27:57-69.
"The Isaac Du Dosc family of South Carolina." 77:46-69; 78:80-114.
"Jacob Ford Prioleau." 1:46-47.
"James Louis Petigru-notice of." 5:78-79.
"James Laird Jervey." 1:44.
"James Mazyck Wilson." 1:44-45.
"Jean Robert and some of his descendents." 77:70-92; 78:115-138.
"Jeanne D'Albert, a Huguenot queen." 38:19-33.
Jeffery, Rev. L. Stanley. "The value of memory to the cause of freedom." 51:41-46.
Jenkins, C. Bissell. "The first fifty years of the Huguenot Society of South Carolina." 40:31-36.
Jervey, W. St. Julien. "The causes which led to the emigration of the Huguenots from France." 1:55-76
Jones, Mrs. Tyre. "Copy of old paper on family of Elias Du Bose." 70:43-44.
"La Cevenole" [Huguenot song]. 25:66.
La Roche, Francis H., Sr. "La Roche tombstones, St. Paul's Episcopal Church, Meggett, South Carolina." 78:51-52.
Lart, Charles E. "The state of the French Protestants after 1685." 16:25-41.
"The last of the Huguenots." 15:31-33.
"The late David Du Bose Gaillard, Lieutneant Colonel, U.S. Army." 20:39-42.
"Laurel Hill plantation." 80:103-104.
Lawton, Alexander R. "The influence of religious persecution on Huguenot colonization." 22:19-36.

Layord, Ida H. "A short story of three brothers." 12:30-38.
"Le Conte." [family] 80:56.
Le Fevre, Ralph. "The Huguenots of New Paltz." 25:103-109.
"Le Noble family." 4:20.
LeRoy, Lansing Burrows, Sr. "Leroy ancestry-historical and gen-
    ealogical." 49:32-42.
Lee, E. Lawrence. "History and archeology." 65:5-14.
"Legare family." 4:20
"The Legare family of South Carolina." 4:7-9.
Leiding, Harriette DuBose Kershaw. "Purrysburg, a Swiss-French
    settlement of South Carolina on the Savannah River." 39:27-
    39.
Leland, Jack. "The Huguenots [poem]." 83: 59-61.
Lesesne, J. M. "The French Huguenots of New Bordeaux." 77:1-8.
"A letter from Captain Gignilliat, 1864." 80:70-72.
"Letter from the Honorable Alfred Huger, upon the death of Mr.
    Petigru, to his brother Dr. Benjamin Huger." 8:25-27.
"Letter of Voltaire." 4:10-11.
"Letters from Robertsville." 80:54-55.
"Lettres d'extraction et origin...David Giroud...par la commune
    du petit Bayard au Verrieres, 26 Fevrier 1732." 47:34-47.
Lilly, Rev. Edward Guerrant. "The revival of Protestantism in
    France in the eighteenth century." 43:26-36.
"List of South Carolina names in the parish registers of the
    French churches at Bristol, Stonehouse and Plymouth and that
    of the French church at Thorpe-Le-Soken, England." 19:24-27.
"Lists of the names of the Abbeville settlers, taken when they
    were at Plymouth, England." 5:77-78; 68:45-46.
"Louis Daniel De Saussure." 1:47.
Lumpkin, H. Henry. "The Huguenot as warrior." 80:1-11.
Lumpkin, Rev. William L. "The meaning and practice of religious
    freedom." 47:37-40.
"M. Le Pasteur Nathanael Weiss." 34:62-63.
MacDowell, Dorothy Kelly. "Miss Mary Huger Ravenel." 80:88-90.
"Major Hasell laid to rest, gallant Confederate sleeps at Mag-
    nolia Cemetery." 79:104-105.
Mahler, Jane Gaston. "Huguenots adventuring in the Orient: two
    Manigaults in China." 76:1-42.
Mahler, Jane Gaston "Our Huguenot heritage: homes, houses of
    worship and public buildings." 79:1-43.
"The Manigault family of South Carolina from 1685 to 1886." 4:
    48-84.
Manigault, Gabriel E., M.D. "Address." 3:37-69.
"The Marion family." 4:22-26.
"The Marion family." 22:37-49.
[General Francis] "Marion's last home." 80:35.
"Martha Gourdin DeSaussure." 3:20.
Mauzey, Armand Jean. "On to glory." 82:117-132.
"Mazyck family." 4:21.
Mazyck, Katharine B. "The European background of the Huguenots

settlements in South Carolina during the eighteenth century, Purrysburg (1734), New Bourdeaux (1764)." 42:27-30.

Mazyck, Katharine Barnwell. "Notes on the Mazyck family." 37: 43-62.

Mazyck, Katharine B. "Some notes on the descendents of Daniel Horry and Elizabeth Garnier who came to Carolina about 1692." 47:31-35.

McCrady, Edward. "The de Bernieres of Normandy." 74:1-10.

"Memorial tablets in the French Protestant (Huguenot) Church in Charleston, South Carolina." 75:51-93.

Merrill, John Lenord. "Address on the occasion of the unveiling of the cross marking the site of the old Huguenot church of St. John's Berkeley." 33:30-37.

Miller, Col. Francis Pickens. "America's role in the North Atlantic community." 56:6-12.

Milling, Chapman J. "The Arcadian and San Domingan French." 62:5-36.

"The minutes of the church in Charlestown." 7:56-74.

"Miss Mary Coffin Ravenel." 3:32-33.

"Miss Celia Campbell." 1:41.

"Miss Mary Butler Campbell." 3:16.

Missroon, Clelia Porcher. "A modern pilgrimage." 33:38-39.

Missroon, Clelia Porcher (Legare). "Three episodes: noted Huguenots women of the sixteenth century." 38:34-36.

"A monument to Jean Ribault, Dieppe, Normandy." 40:58-60.

Moore, Caroline T. "Early generations of the Rembert family of South Carolina." 68:65-71.

Moore, Caroline T. "Rembert and DuBose family Bible records." 69:68-70.

Moore, W. Allen, Jr. "The Bonneau family." 52:38-39.

Moore, W. Allen, Jr. "The Bonneau family, newly found data." 68:47-48.

"Moreau of Knightsbridge, London." 57:26.

"The Motte family: Shubrick line." 75:45-48.

"Mr. Bayard's address." 2:37-64.

"Mrs. Eliza C.K. Fludd." 1:52.

"Mrs. Hannah Ainsle Lawrence." 3:17-18.

"Mrs. Hariet Porcher Stoney." 3:30.

"Napoleon L. Coste." 1:40.

"Naturalization of Huguenot ancestors of members of the Huguenot Society of South Carolina." 50:51-54.

Nielsen, J.V. "The Oxford, Massachusetts, memorial celebration and William H. Potter's lost check." 84:59-61.

"Notes on the Besselleu family." 51:33-36.

"Notes on Dr. Joseph La Brosse De Marboeuf and some of his descendents-the Labruce family of South Carolina." 69:51-64.

"Notices of conspicuous members of the Gaillard family." 5:91-102.

Ogg, David. "France of the Revocation." 63:5-17.

"Old church's site marked." 20:30-32.

"On the death of Dr. Peter Porcher Bonneau: Bishop Seabury to

Reverend Gadsden." 81:76-77.
Osterhout, Major George H. "The sites of the French and Spanish forts in Port Royal Sound." 42:22-35.
"Our Huguenot ancestors: their homes in France." 75:94-98.
Owings, Nettie Smith. "Francis Marion's hunting lodge." 80:91-13.
Owings, Nettie Smith and Marvin Alpheus Owings. "Lesesne genealogy." 84:140-162.
"Pageant of the Richmond [play]." 35:9-16.
"Papers contributed by Miss Emma C. Black." 4:38-47.
"A pastor for the parish of St. Peter, Purysburg, South Carolina." 28:37-44.
Du Pasquier, J. Thierry. "France and the Huguenots today." 81:1-8.
"Peidgree of the Huger family of South Carolina." 4:84.
"Peidgree of the Marion family by Richard Yeadon." 4:22.
Peeples, Rev. Dr. Robert E. H. "The memoirs of Benjamin Spicer Stafford." 82:63-74; 83:64-74; 84:100-115.
Perry, De Wolf. "The Huguenots and the idea of toleration." 55:19-23.
"Peter Charles Gaillard." 1:50-52.
Peyre, Elizabeth "Peyre records." 80:133-153.
"Peyre family." 4:21.
"The Peyre family." 61:35-39.
"Pierre de St. Julien." 11:34-44.
"The planters of St. John's." 21:16-30.
Pope, Thomas H. "James Louis Petigru." 84:108.
Popell, Margaret Wiltse. "Phillipe Maton...first Wiltse in America." 84:65-68.
Poppell, Margaret Wiltse. "Round Robin...roadsign of history." 84:62-64.
Porcher, Catherine Cordes Porcher. "Porcher, a Huguenot family of ancient lineage." 81:90-186.
Porcher, Prof. Frederick A. "Upper beat of St. John's, Berkeley." 13:31-78.
"The Prioleau family in America." 6:17-35.
Prior, Granville Torrey. "Huguenot descendents in ante-bellum South Carolina." 52:25-37.
"Private journal kept by Mamie Huger Ravenel while in Darien, Georgia 1884-1885." 80:73-87.
Puryear, Elmer L. "Huguenots of the upper South." 66:5-11.
Ravenel, Catherine P. "Rene Ravenel." 15:30-31.
Ravenel, Daniel. "Historical sketch of the Huguenot congregations of South Carolina." 7:7-48.
Ravenel, Dr. Wm. C. "Copy of Francis G. Delieseline's narrative-the original having been forwarded to Hon. Thos. Butler King." 8:27-34.
"Ravenel family." 4:21.
"The Ravenel family in France and in America." 6:38-54.
"The real estate held by our church." 7:50-56.

"The remarkable application of N. H. R. Dawson." 80:46-50.
"Report of Simons and Lapham, architects for the Charlesfort monument." 31:38-41.
"Reverend Francis Lejau, first rector of St. James' Church, Goose Creek, South Carolina." 34:25-43.
"Robert E. Lee and Jefferson Davis to John B. Lafitte." 75:43-44.
"Robert Newman Gourdin." 3:30-32.
Roelker, Nancy Lyman. "A sympathetic view of the Huguenots in the Paris of Henri IV." 63:27-52.
Rogers, George C., Jr. "The conscience of a Huguenot." 67:1-11.
Rowland, Grattan Whitehead, Sr., "Berrien excerpts from the Whiteheads of Burke County, Georgia series." 84:74-76.
Ruff, Frances. "A sentimental journey." 84:69-73.
Sadler, Catherine Elizabeth "Additions to the Louis Mouzon family." 80:51.
"St. Julien family." 4:21.
Salley, A. S., Jr. "A certificate of naturalization." 21:59.
Salley, A. S., Jr. "Documents concerning Huguenots, 1686-1692." 27:70-76.
Salley, A. S., Jr. "The marriage bond of Daniel Horry and Elizabeth Garnier." 32:37-38.
Salley, A. S. "The settlement of New Bourdeaux." 42:38-54.
"Samuel David Stoney." 3:18-19.
"Sermon delivered in the French Protestant (Huguenot) Church, Charleston, Oct. 23, 1933, in commemoration of the 247th anniversary of the revocation of the edict of Nantes." 38:67-82.
"Settlement and church on the Santee." 5:66-70.
Short, Shelton H. III. "Hampden-Sydney College in Virginia and Patrick Henry's Huguenot heritage." 84:80-82.
"A short sketch on Peter Givert of New Bourdeaux." 66:39-42.
Simmons, Slann Legare Clement. "Clement's Ferry." 80:121-123.
Simmons, Slann Legare Clement. "Early Manigault records." 59:24-42.
Simmons, Slann Legare Clement. "Elizabeth Curtis, widow and the Mortons, Wilkinsons and Slanns." 81:53-66.
Simmons, Slann Legare Clement. "Porcher family records." 60:25-29.
Simmons, Slann Legare Clement. "Recorded burials in the Huguenot churchyard of Charleston." 57:31-64.
Simmons, Slann Legare Clement. "The two houses on Governor Morton's Togoodoo plantation." 83:75-78.
Simmons, Slann Legare Clement. "Wilkinson descendents of the Second Landgrave Morton." 80:109-110.
"Simons and allied families." 61:46.
Simons, Katherine Drayton Mayrant. "French Huguenots at the Cape in South Africa." 68:41-56.
"Sixteen Eighty-Five- and the penalty for intolerance." 71:1-17
Skipper, O. C. "J. D. B. De Bow." 44:23-35.
Snowden, Prof. Yates. "Letter concerning Rev. Mons. Pouderous."

17:28-29.

"Some Abbeville Huguenots." 5:80-90.

"Some descendents of the Reverend Francis Lejau." 34:44-47.

"Some heroes of the French reformation in the sixteenth century" 46:23-35.

"The South Carolina Society of Charleston." 5:90-91.

"South Carolina's part in the Huguenot-Walloon celebrations." 29:29-31.

South, Stanley. "The General, the Major, and the angel: the discovery of General William Moultrie's grave." 82:31-49.

"Speech of Dr. William De Beaufort, counselor of the Netherlands legation in Washington." 25:68-72.

Steedman, Marguerite Couturier. "The Huguenots' singing ride to victory." 82:54-56.

Steedman, Marguerite Couturier. "Theodore de Biza." 78:55-57.

Steedman, Marguerite Couturier. "A visit to Honilton." 83:40-45.

Stephenson, Nathaniel Wright. "The meaning of the World War." 24:14-26.

Stoney, Samuel Gaillard. "Jamestown on the Santee River." 61:27-29.

Stoney, Samuel Gaillard. "Nicholas de Longuemare, Huguenot goldsmith and silk dealer in colonial South Carolina." 55:38-42.

Stoney, Samuel Gaillard. "Some Huguenot achievements in South Carolina." 73:1-7.

Stoudt, Rev. John Baer. "The Huguenot Cross." 25:95-102.

Summerall, Gen. Charles Pelot. "Huguenot descendents in the Revolutionary War." 37:25-32.

Taylor, Eloise Lanier. "Little Britain. the story of an island" 79:135-137.

Taylor, Marie. "Canterbury Cathedral." 81:78-79.

Taylor, Marie. "A historic event is remembered [Keville family.]" 83:124-125.

Taylor, Rev. James H. "The spirit of the Huguenots and the maintenance of a great tradition." 35:54-75.

Terry, E. G. B. "The Huguenots of upper South Carolina." 32:20-32.

"Thad S. Burdell." 1:45-46.

Thomas, Rev. John N. "The Edict of Toleration, 1787." 43:46-52.

Thomas, Right Rev. Albert S. "The Huguenot dispersion." 35:91-98.

"Tombstones in Strobhar and du Pont cemeteries, Jasper County, South Carolina." 82:110-113.

"Trapier correspondence." 77:33-34.

Trapier, Rev. Paul. "Notices of ancestors and relatives, paternal and maternal." 58:29-54.

Travers, Rev. Marshall. "Faith of our fathers." 50:46-50.

Tyler, Dr. Lyon G. "The Huguenots of Virginia." 28:27-36.

"Unveiling the monument on the site of Charlesfort, Parris Island, South Carolina." 31:5-36.

Vedder, Charles S. "Huguenot character." 2:12-27.

Vurpillot, Rev. Florian. "Coligny: the patriot-the christian." 25:6-11.

Wallace, David Duncan. "Henry Laurens, Huguenot and American." 54:5-13.

Waring, Alice Noble. "Pickens genealogy: southern branch." 71: 57-79.

Waring, Joseph Ioor. "Medical Huguenots in South Carolina." 72:5-11.

Waters, William Arthur. "Notes on the Miot family in South Carolina." 51:37-39.

Werking, F. Woody. "The Huguenot settlements in Ireland." 47: 23-30.

Wickham, Julia Porcher. "Mathew Fontaine Maury: pathfinder of the seas." 36:35-59.

Wiles, A. G. D. "Sir Philip Sidney: the English Huguenot." 45:24-37.

Wilkerson, Constance. "Summit plantation, [poem]." 80:105.

Wilkinson, Constance Jenkins. "Huguenots on Laurel Hill." 79: 128-134; 80:94-109; 82:57-62; 84:83-99.

"Will of Benjamin Marion." 22:50-58.

"Will of Caesar Moze." 23:61-63.

"William C. Miller, Esq." 32:19.

"Wm. R. Caldwell." 1:40-41.

"William Ravenel." 1:49-50.

Williams, George W. "Charles Frederick Morreau (1735-1784): second rector of St. Michael's, Charleston." 57:27-30.

Williams, Rev. Merritt F. "Gallicanism and its effect on the French Reformation." 42:56-67.

Willis, Eola. "Antoine Gabeau." 13:84-88.

Willis, Eola. "Dr. J. L. E. W. Shecut." 14:44-48.

Wilson, Rev. Robert. "The Huguenot influence in colonial South Carolina." 4:26-38.

Wilson, Rev. Robert. "The Huguenots in Dublin." 10:15-53.

Wilson, Rev. Robert. "The pedigree tables of the Guerry, Rembert, Michau, Du Pont, Cromwell families." 76:76-108.

Wood, Rev. Raymond D. "The church's one foundation." 52:43-48.

Yeo, Cedric A. "The influence of the Huguenots in England." 49:25-32.

Butt, Mary McLure. "The Buford family in South Carolina." 68: 53-57.

Material pertaining to South Carolina in the Carolina Genealogist, courtesy of Mary Bondurant Warren, editor.

"Abbeville County: Long Cane": 16:1-2.
"Abbeville County: Long Cane A.R.P Church, 1797": 33:1-4.
"Abbeville County: maps of 1820 and 1966": 10:1-2.
"Abbeville County: newspaper article, Sample family": 21:1-4.
"Abbeville County: 1800 census, sojourners": 2:1-2.
"Acadians of 1755 in the SC Council journal": 4:1-6
"Aiken County cemeteries: Nail-Neal, Low, Bradford, Mims; Sum-
    merhill; Lamar; Hamburg; Hankinson; Dunbar, Galphin, Ardis;
    Gray; Church; Hammond; Clarke, Miller, Zubly": 5:1-8.
"Attainders & confiscations, 1783, Ninety-Six District": 2:1-4;
    3:5-6; 4:7-10.
"Beaufort County: Episcopal chapel cemetery at Hilton Head":
    7:1-2.
"Beaufort County: maps, Conveyance Book 1": 15:1-10.
"Berkeley County cemeteries: Bethlehem Baptist church, Grooms-
    ville Baptist church, Smyrna Methodist church": 16:1-2.
"Bible records: White & Prince families": 1:1-2.
"Bible records: Bryan & Crockett families": 2:3-6.
"Bible records: Brannon & Wilkinson families": 3:7-10.
"Bible records: McCants & Edwards families": 5:11-16.
"Bible records: Thompson family": 6:17-20.
"Bible records: Henry & Standefer families": 10:21-22.
"Bible records: North & Mitchel families": 15:23-26.
"Bible records: Mitchel & Lynes families": 16:27-28.
"Bible records: McCaskill & Murchison families": 24:29-32.
"Bible records: Murchison & Galphin families": 25:33-36.
"Bible records: James family": 26:37-38.
"Camden District Equity case files": 21:1-6.
"Camden District Equity proceedings, 1791-1817": 21:1-6; 33:7-10
    34:11-14; 35:15-18; 36:19-20; 37:21-24; 38:25-26; 39:27-28;
    40:29-32.
"Camden District Wills Book "A-1", 1781-1823: index": 17:1-4;
    18:5-8; 19:9-16; 20:17.
"Cherokee War: frontier forts payments, 1762-4": 21:1-4.
"Chester County cemeteries: Revolutionary soldiers buried in
    Catholic Presbyterian Churchyard": 8:1-4.
"Chester County cemeteries: old Anderson cemetery": 10:5-6.
"Chester County Court minutes, 1785-1788": 35:11-14; 36:15-18;
    37:19-22; 38:23-24; 39:25-30; 40:31-32.
"Chester County miscellaneous information: John Franklin estate"
    23:1-5.
"Clarendon county cemeteries: Calvary Baptist church": 10:1-4.
"Colleton County Conveyances Book I: re-recorded deeds": 19:1-2.
"Corps of Engineers cemeteries, Aiken County": 5:1-10; 6:11-20.
"Corps of Engineers cemeteries, Hartwell": 7:21-28.

"County formations in SC": 4:1-2.
"Darlington County: indexes to Will Book I (1791-93); Adminis-
tration Book "CC" (1792-3); Will Book 2 (1803-16); marriages
in Book 4 and Administration Book "E" (1807-13; Conveyances
Book "A" (1806-1808); also Conveyances Book "B": 1:1-4;
2:5-6; 3:7-10; 4:11-16.
"E & R Baptists: Cashaway Baptist Church, Darlington (1767-1805);
Mechanicsville Baptist Church, Mt. Pleasant (1803-4); Sandy
Run Baptist Church, in Bertie County, NC (1773-1804)": 10:1-10
"E & R Baptists: Friendship Baptist Church, Spartanburg County
(1802-35)": 13:19-20.
"E & R Baptists: Turkey Creek, Abbeville County (1785-93)":
14:21-22; 15:23-26.
"Edgefield County deeds index, Conveyance Book 1 (1786-1790)":
28:1-2.
"Edgefield County deeds index, Conveyance Book 2 (1787-1788)":
29:3-4.
"Edgefield County Equity Court record: Isaac Mathews": 22:1-3.
"Edgefield County probate index to 1900": 32:1-6; 33:7-12;
34:13-16; 35:17-20; 36:21-22; 37:23-28; 38:29-38; 39:39-48;
40:49-56.
"Edgefield County Record Book "A" (1800-1802)": 12:1-6; 14:7-12
15:13-16; 16:17-26; 17:27-28; 18:29-32; 19:33-38; 20:39-46;
21:47-56.
"Edgefield County Record Book "A", index": 22:57-60.
"Emigrants from England to colonial ports, 1774-5": 5:1-10;
6:11-20; 7:21-30; 8:31-38; 9:39-42; 10:43-44.
"Fairfield County Wills Book, 1787-1792": 14:1-10; 15:11-16;
16:17-26; 17:27.
"Florence County cemeteries: Salem Methodist": 6:1-6.
"Georgetown newspapers, 1791-1816": 16:1-6.
"Hampton County cemeteries: Bostick cemetery": 10:1-2.
"Jasper County cemeteries: Purrysburg": 11:1-3.
"Kershaw County: Camden Journal, 1842-1844": 11:1-8; 12:9-14;
13:15-16; 14:17-20; 15:21-22; 16:23-24; 17:25-26; 18:27-28;
19:29-30; 21:31-34; 22:35-38.
"Kershaw County cemeteries: Scotch cemetery": 1:1-4; 2:5-8;
3:9-10.
"Kershaw County tax list, 1784": 13:1-3.
"Kershaw County Will Book "A-1", "B-C" indexes": 3:1-2.
"Laurens County cemeteries: Upper Duncan Creek Baptist Church":
21:1-3.
"Lexington County equity cases, #1-7": 13:1-6; 14:7-8; 15:9-10.
"Lives & legends": 2:1-4; 10:5-6; 13:7-8.
"Loyalty oaths, Tar River, Granville County, Craven County
(1778); Regulators after Alamance (1771)": 5:1-6.
"Map of British ports of immigration, 1774-5": 5:7-8.
"Map of SC circuit court districts, 1769, and counties, 1785":
6:9-10.
"Marion County marriages, 1803-1859": 21:1-3.
"Marlboro County Court of Common Pleas, 1785-1807": 14:1-6;

15:7-10; 16:11-14; 17:15-16; 18:17-18; 20:19-20; 28:21-26; 29:27-28; 30:29-30.
"Marlboro County Court of Common Pleas, additions": 31:16-30; 32:31-32; 33:33-34; 34:35-36; 35:37-38; 37:39-40; 38:41-44.
"Marriages & deaths in SC newspapers, 1780-1782": 3:1-6; 4:7-12; 5:13-16; 7:17-18.
"McCormick County cemeteries: Willington Presbyterian cemetery": 11:1-2.
"McCormick County cemeteries": 22:3-6.
"Naturalizations in Charleston Federal District Court, 1790-1833": 1:1-8; 2:9-16; 3:17-22; 4:23-24; 6:25-26; 7:27-36; 8:37-40; 9:41-50; 10:51-52.
"Newberry County wills index, Book "A" (1787-1796); Book "B" (1796-1800); Book "C" (1800-1803); Book "D" (1803-1810)": 13:1-6.
"Newberry County wills index, Book "E" (1809-1814); Book "H-2" (1815-1818); Book "H" (1835-1839); Book "N" (1839-1840); Book 1839-1842 O.N.D.": 13:1-6; 14:7-8; 15:9-10; 17:11-12; 18:13-14.
"Ninety-Six District: Calhoun journal, Ordinary record of 1781": 30:1-10, 31:11-16; 32:17-22; 33:23-24; 34:25-30; 36:31-34; 37:35-38.
"Ninety-Six District: grand & petit jurors, 1777": 21:1-4.
"Ninety-Six District: miscellaneous information": 21:1-4; 22:5.
"Ninety-Six District: notes": 8:1-2.
"Ninety-Six District Plats Book "A", 1784-1785": 8:1-10; 9:11-20; 10:21-30; 11:31-32; 13:33-40; 15:41-42; 16:43-44; 18:45-50; 19:51-52; 20:53-58; 22:59-68; 23:69-77.
"Ninety-Six District: Saluda Plats Book "A", 1784-1794 and map": 11:1-8.
"Orangeburg Distr.: Rev. Bryan's marriages, 1784-1825": 7:1-3.
"Orangeburg Distr.: Equity Commissioner's Book, 1824": 12:1-12; 13:13-20; 14:21-22; 15:23-24; 16:25-28; 17:29-30; 18:31-32.
"Orangeburg Distr.: Giessendanner register, 1737-1760: 6:1-12; 7:13-22; 8:23-32; 9::33-38; 10:39-46; 11:47-50; 14:51-54; 15:55-56; 16:57-58; 17:59-60; 18:61-62; 19:63-66; 23:67-76.
"Orangeburg Distr.: mortgages & conveyances, 1818-1820": 24:1-17.
"Orangeburg: Willow Swamp Baptist Church, 1805-1882": 25:1-10.
"Orangeburg County: Youn family documents": 23:1-2.
"Original land grant: Thomas Rivers, 1771": 2:1-2.
"Passengers on the ship "Carolina": 2:1-2.
"Pendleton District Estates Record Book, 1793-1799": 11:1-4; 12:5-14; 14:15-29; 15:21-24; 16:25-28; 17:29-30; 18:31-32; 19:33-34; 20:35-36; 28:37-40; 29:41-44.
"Pendleton Messenger, 1807-1814": 30:1-10; 31:11-20; 32:21-30; 33:31-38; 34:39-42; 35:43-48; 36:49-52; 37:53-60; 38:61-70; 39:71-76; 40:77-82.
"Revolutionary private claims: Federal records to 1836": 2:1-6; 3:7-10; 4:11-14; 7:15-24; 8:25-28; 9:29-32; 10:33-38.

"Revolutionary War units: guide to NC & SC troops": 32:1-4.
"Revolutionary War officers": 2:9-16.
"Revolutionary War pensioners, 1820": 1:1-8; 3:17-20; 4:21-28;
11:29-30.
"Revolutionary War soldiers: Federal rolls, 1780, and SC bounty
lands to soldiers, 1784-1787": 25:31-40.
"SC aliens: War of 1812, records 1789-1815": 29:1-10; 30:11-12;
31:13-14; 32:15-16.
"SC Council Journal, 1751": 21:1-8; 22:9-12; 23:13-22; 24:23-
30; 25:31-32; 26:33-40; 27:41-50; 28:51-60; 29:61-70; 30:71-
76.
"SC Council Journal, 1752": 31:77-80; 32:81-82; 33:83-84; 34:
85-86; 35:87-88; 36:89-90; 37:91-92; 38:93-94; 39:97-98; 40:
99-102.
"SC customs records, 1787-89": 24:1-12.
"SC Equity abstracts, 1784-1800": 19:1-10; 20:11-20; 22:21-23.
"SC equity laws & district maps, 1791, 1799, 1808, 1819, 1824,
1836": 27:1-2; 28:3-10.
"SC Inventories Book "AA", 1762-1777": 26:1-8.
"SC mark registrations, 1694-1721": 24:1-6.
"SC natives in Cumberland County, IL 1850 census": 6:1-2.
"SC newspapers, 1770: South Carolina Gazette and Country Jour-
nal": 1:1-10.
"SC newspapers, 1770-71: South Carolina Gazette and Country
Journal": 2:11-20.
"SC newspapers 1776-78: American General Gazette": 3:1-10.
"SC newspapers, 1779-1781: American General Gazette and
Royal Gazette": 4:11-20.
"SC newspapers, 1781-82: Royal Gazette": 5:21-30.
"SC Ordinary: marriages - 1765": 3:1-2.
"SC private acts, 1777-90": 30:1-10; 31:11-20; 32:21-24.
"SC State Revolutionary Pensioners Acts of 1791-1806":
36:59-64.
"SC State Revolutionary pensioners, 1783-1833": 26:1-10; 27:
11-24; 28:25-34; 29:35-44; 30:45-48; 31:49-50; 32:51-52;
33:53-54; 34:55-56; 35:57-58.
"Spartanburg County 1790 census": 3:1-6.
"Spartanburg County Court Minutes, 1784-1787": 34:1-4; 35:5-8;
36:9-12; 37:13-14; 38:15-16; 39:17-22; 40:23-26.
"Spartanburg Distr. Deeds Book "C", 1754-1795": 3:1-4; 4:5-10;
5:11-20; 6:21-30; 7:31-38; 8:39-48; 9:49-58; 10:59-68; 12:69-
73.
"State maps: SC in 1799, and the Mitchell map of the southeast,
1755": 3:5-6.
"Sumter County cemeteries: Troublefield, Wedgefield, Ardis":
7:1-3.
"Union District Equity proceedings, 1801-1841": 27:1-8; 28:9-14;
29:15-16; 30:17-18; 31:19-20; 32:21-22; 33:23-28; 34:29-32;
35:33-38; 36:39-42; 37:43-46; 38:47-48; 39:49-56; 40:57-60.
"Union District Record Book 1+2, 1785-1800": 13:1-2; 14:3-4;
15:5-8; 16:9-12; 17:13-14; 18:15-16; 20:17-20; 21:21-24;

23:25-26.
"Unrecorded land grants prior to the Revolution, recorded 1817-
1818": 1:1-6; 2:7-10; 3:11-12; 4:13-14; 5:15-20; 6:21-24;
7:25-34; 8:35-42; 9:43-52.
"Winton County wills, 1787-1791": 11:1-10; 12:11-20; 13:21-30;
14:31-32; 15:33-34; 16:35-36; 17:37-40.
"York District Estates Record Book "A", 1787-1799": 34:1-4;
35:5-8; 36:9-12; 37:13-18; 38:19-24; 39:25-32; 40:33-36.

APPENDIX VII

Articles & historical source material in the South Carolina Magazine of Ancestral Research, courtesy of Brent H. Holcomb, editor.

"Abstracts of colonial inventory book I-I": VI:175-178, 307;
   VIII:102-104.
"Another source for marriage records": VIII:155.
"Applications for Confederate States pensions, Abbeville County"
   V:309.
"Applications for Confederate service pensions, Horry County":
   V:212-219.
"A Beaufort District equity suit": III:233-236.
"Bethesda Presbyterian churchyard tombstone inscriptions":
   II:17-23.
"Buffalo Baptist churchyard": VII:204-215.
"Capt. John Ryan of Edgefield": II:26.
"Cemeteries (Newberry County)": VII:11-17.
"Charles Humphries of VA, NC & SC": VII:188-190.
"Charles Slage, runaway": VII:216.
"Charleston deed book T-3": IV: 37-39, 195-201.
"Charleston District marriage licenses": V:148-151.
"Chesterfield District equity suit": V:223.
"Children received at the Charleston Orphan House": IV:67-71.
"Collins family Bible record": VIII:163.
"Colonial writs of partition": I:3-10, 71-78; 127-132, 195-202.
"Compensation for Revolutionary service": I:59-70, 156-160.
"Darlington County marriage licenses & bonds": V:199-203.
"Darlington County memorialized records": VII:72-80, 144-158.
"David Daniel & his family troubles": II:217-219.
"Death notices from the Hamburg Gazette": V:204.
"Dying confession of Willis Daniel": VI:73-76.
"An early Freshley document": VII: 121-122.
"An early Georgetown estate notice": VI:39.
"An early Orangeburg District deed": VII:203.
"Early records of Bethlehem Lutheran Church (Newberry County)":
   V:16-25.
"Early records of Rosemary Baptist Church (Barnwell District)":
   VII: 131-139, 217-220; VIII:83-86, 152-154, 208-211.
"Early records of St. Jacob's Lutheran Church": VI:195-205.
"Early records of St. Michael's Lutheran Church": IV:131-138,
   232-255.
"Early wills of Camden District": II:3-16, 93-101, 143-150,
   179-186; III:37-46, 147-154, 242-248; IV:46-52, 87-96;
   VI:77-78, 166-174.
"Edgefield District murders": V:78.
"1809 Marion District tax list": VIII:67-72.
"1829 census of Laurens District": IV:103-113, 139-151.
"1832 tax list for the town of Camden": VIII:27-28.

"1851 Orangeburg District tax list": VII:18-28, 109-114.
"An equity suit from the Middle District": VII:92-93.
"Estate partitions in the Washington District Court of Equity":
  III:9-18, 122-127, 183-188; IV:31-38, 79-85; VII:181-187.
"Extracts from the diary of Rev. John McLees": VIII:195-203.
"Fairfield County Will Book 1, 1787-1792": I:11-20, 89-96,
  139-147.
"Fragments of Equity records": III:206.
"Genealogy: Research resources of the Winthrop [College] Ar-
  chives": VIII: 164-168.
"German Reformed Church in Newberry County": VIII:151.
"Graves of Rev. William Leak and wife": VI:223.
"Houseal Bible record": VIII:207.
"Isaac Dubose Whitworth family Bible record": IV:86.
"James and Joseph Jamieson, patriot brothers": I:10.
"James Moore, impunctual juror": IV:45.
"A Kingston County petition": VIII:73-75.
"Lancaster County Deed Book A": I:21-28, 105-109, 161-165,
  202-206; II:44-49.
"Laurens County Estate Book A-1": VI:25-29, 224-226; VII:221-
  225; VIII:47-49, 140-145.
"Letters to John Hunter by F. H. McKelvey": II:39-41.
"Liberty Hill Evangelical Lutheran Church Cemetery, Laurens
  County": V:10-12.
"List of prisoners, Ninety-Six Jail, 1779": V:195-198.
"A lone grave": VI:163.
"Lost relatives": VI:127.
"Lost will of John Green": VIII:122.
"Marion family record": IV:178.
"Mark Derden family Bible record": II:92.
"Marriage & death notices from the Cheraw Gazette": VI:62-67,
  151-157, 211-213; VII:29-34.
"Marriage & death notices from the Columbia Telescope": VIII:
  29-33.
"Marriage & death notices from early Columbia newspapers": IV:
  72- ; V:248-253.
"Marriage & death notices from the Southern Christian Herald":
  V:152-156, 233-242.
"Marriage & death notices from the Southern Whig (Sumter, SC)":
  VI:23-24.
"Marriage & death notices from the Southron (Orangeburg, SC)":
  IV:202.
"Marriage & death notices from the Sumter Gazette": VIII:96.
"Marriage & death notices from the Wesleyan Journal": VI:30-33.
"Marriage & obituary notices from the Chester Standard": I:100-
  104, 123-126, 189-192; II:35-38, 75-78, 139-142, 203-206;
  III:33-36, 117-121.
"Marriage & obituary notices from the Cheraw Intelligencer and
  Southern Register": I:115-118, 179-184; II:27-30.
"Marriage & obituary notices from the Columbia Free Press &
  Hive": I:97-99.

"Marriage & obituary notices from the Columbia Telescope, and from the South Carolina State Journal": I:119-122, 185-188; II:31-34, 71-74.
"Marriage & obituary notices from the South Carolina Weekly Museum": VII:94-98.
"Marriage, death & estate notices from the Lancaster Ledger": VII:67-71, 165-169; VIII:37-41, 76-82, 146-150, 213-217.
"Marriage & obituary notices from the Darlington Flag": I:41-47
"Marriage & obituary notices from the Edgefield Advertiser": IV:203-207; V:31-36, 110-114.
"Marriage & obituary notices from the Greenville Mountaineer": II:129-134, 193-198; III:29-32, 111-116, 142-146, 215-219; IV:13-22, 73-78, 168-177, 223-231; V:46-51, 102-107, 177-183, 244-247; VI:51-57, 119-126, 179-188, 227-234; VII:49-58, 115-120, 170-172, 232-234; VIII:42-46, 97-101, 156-162, 212-213.
"Marriage & obituary notices from the Marion Star": II:66-70, 135-138, 199-202.
"Marriage & obituary notices from the Unionville Journal": I:37-41.
"Marriage & obituary notices from the Unionville Journal & Unionville Times": III:214.
"Marriages performed by Rev. Basil Manly": VIII:3-12.
"Marriages performed by Rev. James Erwin Rodgers": VI:131-143.
"Marriages performed by Rev. Samuel Smoke": VII:140-143.
"Memoir of Major Thomas Young": IV:181-190.
"Moore-Lindsay family Bible": III:131.
"Nates Bible record": V:101.
"Notes on the McWhorter family": IV:41-45.
"Officers of the South Carolina Line": II:42-43.
"Orangeburg District abstracts of deeds": III:131-141, 220-227.
"Orangeburg District equity suit": V:108-109.
"Orangeburg District intestates, 1819": VI:144-145.
"Payments for colonial services": IV:114-123, 155-167, 213-222; V:52-61, 115-124, 184-190.
"Pendleton County Court minutes": VI:8-22, 79-97, 147-150, 214-222; VII:35-48, 100-108, 173-180; VIII:53-59, 90-95.
"Pendleton County, S.C., Conveyance Book A, 1790-1792": III:66-104.
"Petition from Coosawhatchie Baptist Church": IV:212.
"Petition from Zion Lutheran Church": VIII:34-35.
"Records from burnt counties (Lexington & Orangeburg)": VIII:131-139, 204-205.
"Records of St. Luke's Lutheran Church": II:59-65, 157-163.
"Records of St. Matthew's Lutheran Church (Calhoun County)": V:131-136, 224-232; VI:40-50, 101-118, 158-162.
"Rehobeth cemetery": I:193-194.
"Revolutionary pension applications: William Venable & John Venable": II:79-84.
"Revolutionary soldiers aboard the frigate South Carolina": VI:164.

"Robert Lattimore & his descendants": I:29-36, 79-84, 151-155, 217-221.
"Royal grants, volume 41, 1734-1738": I:171-178; II:50-52, 85-91, 123-128; III:53-56, 169-172, 228-232; IV:53-60.
"Ruling elders of Fishing Creek [Presbyterian] Church, 1786": III:177.
"St. Matthews 1818 tax list": I:148-150, 214-215.
"St. Matthews voters, 1811": I:215-216.
"1779 jury list for Cheraws District": V:13-15.
"Shaw tombstones": II:122.
"Snowden & Nelson family Bible records": III:195-200.
"Some Abbeville County deeds": V:243.
"Some Beaufort accounts due, 1756": VII:87-91.
"Some Claremont & Sumter deeds": VI:146.
"Some early Lexington District documents": VIII:23-26.
"Some early settlers on Fishing Creek (York & Chester Counties)" VII:3-10, 73-86, 159-164, 226-231.
"Some Episcopalians in Claremont County, 1788": IV:124.
"Some equity cases appealed": V:205-211.
"Some lapsed colonial plats": V:67-77.
"Some miscellaneous records: VIII:22.
"Some old South Carolinians in 1808": VIII:87-89.
"Some Orangeburg records in Mississippi": VI:206-210.
"South Carolina equity records": VI:235-238.
"Spartanburg District Will Book B": V:79-88, 169-176.
"State pensions to Revolutionary survivors": IV:3-8.
"Stephenson & Byers family Bible records": IV:9-12.
"Stroud family Bible": V:157-158.
"Tax collectors of the Revolutionary period": V:26-30.
"Tax returns, 1783-1786": II:171-178; III:24-28, 178-182, 201-206; IV:208-211; V:89-93, 159-168, 220-222; VIII:50-52, 152-155.
"Three deceased witnesses": VII:143.
"Tombstone inscriptions from Sharon Associate Reformed Presbyterian Church, York County": III:3-8, 105-110, 161-168, 237-241.
"Trinity Methodist churchyard, York, SC": VIII:105-109.
"Turnipseed family Bible": VI:165.
"Two hidden marriage records": IV:30.
"Two York County cemeteries": VII:99.
"Union Methodist churchyard tombstone inscriptions": II:24-25.
"Waddle tombstones": II:65.
"War of 1812 service in SC for James Deer": IV:179-180.
"Wells obituaries": I:213.
"Western Circuit Equity Journal (Union, Spartanburg, York & Chester Counties)": VII:195-202; VIII:13-21, 110-121, 169-176, 218-223.
"William Henry of Henry's Knob": II:115-122, 207-213; IV:23-30
"William Rose family Bible record": I:211-213.
"Williamsburg County cemetery inscriptions": I:48-52, 84-88.
"Williamsburg County Will Book A": I:133-138, 207-210;

W. P. A. TYPESCRIPTS OF
TOMBSTONE INSCRIPTIONS AT THE
SOUTH CAROLINIANA LIBRARY

Abbeville County: Episcopal churchyard, Long Cane cemetery, Melrose cemetery.

Aiken County: Bethany cemetery, Darien Baptist cemetery, First Baptist churchyard, Glover cemetery, Hammond private graveyard, Hardy's Baptist churchyard, Kimball cemetery, Levels Baptist churchyard, Montmorenci Methodist cemetery, Millbrook Baptist churchyard, Montmorenci cemetery, North Augusta cemetery, Old Langley cemetery, St. John's Methodist cemetery, St. Thaddeus Episcopal churchyard, Sweetwater Baptist churchyard, Turner-Hatcher family cemetery, Wade private burying ground, Williams family cemetery.

Allendale County: Boyles & Brown family cemetery, Fairfax cemetery, Allen family cemetery, Swallow Savannah cemetery.

Anderson County: Barker's Creek Baptist churchyard, Bennett family cemetery, Bethany Baptist churchyard, Big Creek cemetery, Boggs burying grounds, Byrum family cemetery, Cedar Grove Baptist churchyard, Concord Baptist cemetery, Concord Baptist Churchyard, Dorchester Baptist churchyard, Ebenezer churchyard Eureka Baptist churchyard, First Presbyterian cemetery, Flat Rock cemetery, Hopewell Baptist churchyard, Long Branch cemetery, Midway Presbyterian churchyard, Mt. Bethel Baptist churchyard, Mt. Zion Presbyterian churchyard, Neal's Creek Baptist churchyard, Old Concord Presbyterian churchyard, Old Hopewell Baptist churchyard, Old Lewis burying ground, Pendleton Baptist churchyard, Pendleton Methodist churchyard, Presbyterian Church cemetery, Rice cemetery, St. Paul's Episcopal churchyard, Sandy Springs Methodist churchyard, Trinity Methodist churchyard, Union Grove Methodist churchyard, Watkins family burying ground, Welcome Baptist churchyard, Whitaker Smith burying ground, Whitefield Baptist churchyard, Williamston cemetery.

Barnwell County: Barnwell Baptist churchyards (2), Blackville Baptist churchyard, Blackville cemetery, Barnwell Catholic churchyard, Blackville Catholic churchyard, Barnwell Episcopal churchyard, Friendship churchyard, Blackville Methodist churchyard.

Beaufort County: First Tabernacle Baptist churchyard, St. Peters Catholic churchyard.

Berkeley County: Belle Isle cemetery, Pooshee Plantation cemetery. Smith family cemetery at Yeaman's Hall, Goose Creek: see Charleston County.

Calhoun County: Bochette cemetery, Cattle Creek Church cemetery, David Wannamaker cemetery, First Baptist churchyard (at St.

Matthews), Heatly/Richardson cemetery, Keller cemetery, Mizpah Baptist churchyard (at Fort Motte), St. Matthew's First
Baptist churchyard, St. Matthew's Episcopal churchyard, Tabernacle cemetery, West Bethel Methodist Episcopal churchyard.
Charleston County: Bethany cemetery, Bethel Methodist Episcopal
churchyard, Comstock tombstone on Broad St., Stadium cemetery,
Magnolia cemetery, Confederate monument at Magnolia cemetery,
Circular Congregational churchyard, French Protestant Huguenot
churchyard, First Baptist churchyard, Edisto Island Presbyterian churchyard, James Island Presbyterian churchyard, St. Andrew's Parish Episcopal churchyard, St. Andrew's Lutheran
churchyard, St. James Episcopal churchyard on James Island,
St. John's Episcopal churchyard, St. John's Lutheran churchyard, St. Lawrence Catholic cemetery, German Artillery Memorial Assn. cemetery, St. Mary's Catholic churchyard, St. Patrick's Catholic churchyard, St. Paul's Episcopal churchyard,
St. Peter's Episcopal churchyard, St. Philip's Episcopal
churchyard, St. Stephen's Episcopal Chapel on Anson St., First
(Scots) Presbyterian churchyard, Second Presbyterian churchyard, Styles Point burial ground on James Island, Trinity
Episcopal churchyard on Edisto Island, Trinity Episcopal
churchyard in Charleston, Unitarian churchyard, German cemetery, Smith family cemetery at Yeaman's Hall in Goose Creek.
Clarendon County: Brown family cemetery, Butler family burying
ground, Calvary Baptist churchyard, Conner burial ground, Elliott family cemetery, Evergreen cemetery in Summerton, Home
Branch Baptist churchyard, Lawson family cemetery, Manning
cemetery, Paxville cemetery, St. Paul's cemetery, Ragin family
cemetery, Summerton Baptist cemetery, Ridgill family burying
ground, Tisdal family burying ground, Trinity Methodist
churchyard.
Colleton County: Island Creek cemetery.
Darlington County: Antioch Baptist cemetery in Hartsville, Bethel Methodist churchyard, Bethlehem M.E. churchyard in Hartsville, Centre Point graveyard, Chapel Hill Baptist cemetery in
Hartsville, Damascus Methodist churchyard, First Baptist
churchyard in Hartsville, Grove Hill cemetery, Hebron Methodist cemetery, Jewish cemetery, Kellytown Baptist churchyard,
Magnolia cemetery in Hartsville, Methodist cemetery, Mt. Elon
Baptist cemetery in Lydia, New Providence Baptist churchyard
Pawley Swamp Baptist churchyard, Presbyterian cemetery, Presbyterian churchyard, Swift Creek Baptist churchyard in Hartsville, Wesley Chapel Methodist churchyard in Lydia.[New Providence Baptist churchyard & Pawley Swamp Baptist cemeteries
are in Horry County.]
Dillon County: Bass cemetery, Bethesda M.E. cemetery in Latta,
Buck Swamp cemetery in Bethea, Dothan cemetery, Harllee ceme-
tery, Hays burying ground in Latta, Little Rock Methodist cem-
etery, Magnolia cemetery, Sweat Swamp cemetery in Bethea, Union cemetery in Latta, William Rogers cemetery.
Edgefield County: Baker cemetery, Brick Church in Fairfield

374

County, Catholic Cemetery, Ebenezer cemetery, Harmony cemetery
Hatcher family cemetery, Little River Baptist cemetery in
Fairfield County, Mims-Tut cemetery, Posey cemetery, Willow-
brook cemetery.
Fairfield County: A.R.P. cemetery in Winnsboro, Antioch
    Methodist churchyard, Beaver Creek Baptist churchyard, Bethel
    Church cemetery, Brick River A.R.P. churchyard, Chappell fami-
    ly cemetery, Coleman family cemetery, Cook family cemetery,
    Cool Branch M.E. churchyard, Feaster family cemetery, Free
    family cemetery, Furman & Davis family cemetery, Horeb Presby-
    terian Church cemetery, Jeffares family cemetery, Little River
    Baptist cemetery, Lyles family cemetery, Kirkland family ceme-
    tery, Methodist churchyard, Monticello cemetery, Methodist
    cemetery, Episcopal cemetery, Pearson family cemetery, Presby-
    terian cemetery in Winnsboro, Shelton family cemetery, McMeek-
    in family cemetery, Shiloh M.E. cemetery in Jenkinsville,
    Winnsboro cemetery, Winnsboro Court House tablet, Winnsboro
    Confederate Memorial tablet, Woodward family cemetery. (For
    Brick Church cemetery & Little River Baptist cemetery, see
    Edgefield County list.) Alston family cemetery.
Georgetown County: Georgetown Hebrew cemetery, Georgetown Bap-
    tist cemetery, Prince Frederick's Episcopal Parish cemetery,
    Prince George Winyah Episcopal churchyard.
Greenville County: Springwood cemetery, Christ Episcopal Church
    cemetery.
Greenwood County: Rehobeth Church cemetery.
Horry County: Baker's Chapel Baptist churchyard, Beaty burying
    ground, Buck graveyard at Hebron Church in Bucksville, First
    Baptist churchyard in Conway, Fleming's Field cemetery at
    Savannah Bluff, Green Sea Baptist cemetery, Jack's Branch
    graveyard, Kingston Presbyterian churchyard in Conway, Lake-
    side cemetery in Conway, Conway M.E. churchyard, Mincey bury-
    ing ground, Old Camp burying ground, Pleasant View Baptist
    cemetery, Waccamaw Presbyterian churchyard, Singleton's grave-
    yard in Conway, Union Methodist churchyard in Conway, Pauley
    Swamp Baptist Church cemetery, Hebron Methodist Church cemete-
    ry. (New Providence Baptist churchyard: see Darlington Coun-
    ty.)
Kershaw County: Ancrum grave, Boykin burying ground, Chesnut
    cemetery, Hanging Rock Church cemetery, Kershaw grave, Quaker
    cemetery - old section.
Lancaster County: Old Presbyterian cemeteries I & II in Lancas-
    ter, West Side cemetery in Lancaster.
Laurens County: Laurens cemeteries I & II.
Marion County: Centenary M.E. churchyard, Davis family cemetery
    at Britton's Neck, First Methodist Church at Marion, Giles
    family cemetery, Godbold-Haseldon-Ellerbee cemetery, Legette
    family cemetery at China Grove Plantation, Munnerlyn graveyard
    Rose Hill cemetery at Marion, Tabernacle Methodist churchyard.
Marlboro County: Adams cemetery, Beauty Spot cemetery, Beaverdam
    cemetery, Bennett graveyard, Bethel churchyard, Breedin grave-

yard, David graveyard, Drake churchyard, Easterby cemetery,
Easterling graveyard, Fletcher's cemetery, Fletcher graveyard,
Hamer burial ground, Hebron cemetery, Hodges cemetery, Holy
Road cemetery, Lester cemetery, Liles graveyard, Manship grave
yard, Moore cemetery, Mossy Bay cemetery, Munford cemetery,
Murchison cemetery, Old Welsh Neck cemetery, Parker's cemetery
Parnassus cemetery, Robertson & Ellerbee cemetery, Rogers cem-
etery, Salem cemetery, Saw Hill churchyard, Smyrna cemetery,
Spears & Edens graveyard, Tatum cemetery, Webster graveyard.
Newberry County: Ashford cemetery at Strother's Bridge, Baxter
cemetery at Newberry, Boland burying ground, Nance graveyard
at Cannonville, Newberry Village graveyard, Reagin & Kinard
cemetery, Rosemont cemetery, King's Creek Presbyterian churchyard, St. Paul's Lutheran churchyard, Newberry Court House
memorial tablet.
Pickens County: Bethel Presbyterian cemetery, Choehee Baptist
cemetery at Tamassee, Day burying ground, Mountain Grove
Southern Baptist churchyard, Nicholson family graveyard, Old
Stone churchyard, Oolenoy churchyard, Pickens Mill cemetery,
Presbyterian churchyard, Secona Baptist churchyard, Sunrise
cemetery.
Richland County: Crescent Hill Baptist cemetery, Ebenezer Luth-
eran cemetery, Elmwood cemetery, First Baptist churchyard in
Columbia, First Presbyterian churchyard in Columbia, St.
Peter's Catholic churchyard, St. Peter's churchyard, Taylor
cemetery, Trinity Episcopal churchyard in Columbia, Trinity
Episcopal churchyard, Washington Street M.E. churchyard.
Spartanburg County: Oakwood cemetery, Magnolia cemetery in
Spartanburg.
Sumter County: Andrews Chapel M.E. churchyard, Bethel Baptist
churchyard, Bethel cemetery, C.P. Elliott grave at Bradford
Springs, Fulton cemetery, Hodge burial ground, Jewish cemetery
Providence Baptist churchyard, Reynolds burying ground, St.
Lawrence Catholic Church cemetery, St. Mark's Episcopal Church
at Sumter, Skinner cemetery, Weeks cemetery.
Union County: Episcopal cemetery at Union, Forest Lawn cemetery
at Union, Grace Methodist cemetery, Presbyterian cemetery,
Rosemont cemetery at Union.
Williamsburg County: Black Mingo Baptist churchyard, Baptist
cemetery, Baptist churchyard at Kingstree, Bethany Baptist
churchyard, Bethesda Methodist churchyard, Black Mingo Presby-
terian cemetery, Britton's burying ground, Cedar Lane cemete-
ry & Montgomery burying ground, Frierson burying ground, Gren-
och cemetery, Indiantown cemetery, McDonald burying ground,
McClary burying ground, Midway Presbyterian churchyard, Mt.
Hope cemetery at Greeleyville, Mt. Vernon Methodist cemetery,
New Market cemetery, Poplar Hill Freewill Baptist cemetery,
Richburg burying ground, Sutton Methodist churchyard, Union
Presbyterian churchyard, Williamsburg cemetery at Kingstree,
Witherspoon burying ground.
York County: Rose Hill cemetery, Adnah Church cemetery, McIlwain
& McAllum cemetery.

APPENDIX IX

Papers of the Beaufort County Historical Society in the Beaufort
County Library (BUCL), Beaufort.

1. Danner, Howard E. "The forts of Beaufort. Pre-revolutionary. Why they were there when they were there." 50 p.
2. Danner, Howard E. "The College of Beaufort - with a glimpse
   into its background." 23 p.
3. Danner, Ruby C. "Spanish explorations & settlements." 78 p.
4. Danner, Howard E. "Beaufort in the Civil War." 53 p.
5. Danner, Howard E. "Beaufort & the wars with England." 42 p.
6. Martin, Chlotilde Rowell. "An account of the towns of Radnor & Edmundsbury." 32 p.
7. Barnwell, Nathaniel Berners. "The battles of Beaufort."
   17 p.
8. Ramsay, Frank H. "Beaufort's battles."
9. Danner, Howard E. "Byways to '65." 55 p.
10. Dowling, George Geddes. "Wippy Swamp Guards." 13 p.
11. Rogers, E. Bert. "Reminiscences of Beaufort storms."
12. Bailey, Cmdr. Warren E. "Paul Hamilton & Henry DeSaussaure"
    5 p.
13. Elliott, William W. "Gillisonville." 9 p.
14. McDowell, Rebecca DesChamps. "John Barnwell & the Tusca-
    roras." 56 p.
15. Christensen, Frederick Holmes. "Coosawhatchie." 20 p.
16. Hall, Mary Fuller. "Joseph Rogers Walker, D.D., 1796-1879,
    rector of St. Helena's Episcopal Church, Beaufort, from
    1823-1878." 12 p.
17. "Autobiography of William John Grayson, 1788-1863." 127 p.
18. Ramsay, Frank H. "Beaufort County newspapers." 20 p.
19. Seay, Dr. W. M. "English explorations." 24 p.
20. Scheper, Margaret Raney. "The Golden Age in Beaufort." 25 p.
21. Paul, Ora Crofut. "Robertsville." 19 p.
22. Foster, Etta C. "Old families of Beaufort: the Stuarts &
    the Bulls." 17 p.
23. Foster, Etta C. "Old families of Beaufort: the Talbirds,
    the Barnwells & the Chaplins of St. Helena's Island." 40 p.
24. Theus, Nita Grimsley. "Stuart Town, 1684-1686." 21 p.
25. Theus, Nita Grimsley. "Religion in the 18th century." 19 p.
26. Hutson, Francis Marion. "Beaufort District landmarks &
    early historical sites." 12 p.
27. Voigt, Gilbert P. "Beaufort's galaxy of great men." 15 p.
28. Voigt, Gilbert P. "Beaufort's contribution to the Church."
    14 p.
29. McTeer, Lucille. "Purrysburg." 11 p.
30. Fripp, Nellie Hasell. "Bluffton & the Okatie." 20 p. plus
    pictures & clippings.
31. Fripp, Nellie Hasell. "Grahamville." 18 p. plus clippings
    & pictures.
32. Turnbull, Robert J. "Early French explorations & settle-

ments." 35 p.
33. Runnette, Mabel. "Early settlement of Beaufort Town, 1700-1725." 36 p.
34. Howard, John Webb. "Grahamville & its people." 50 p.
35. Busch, James W. "The Beaufort Baptist Church." loose-leaf.
36. Hardy, John W. "Prince William's Parish." 9 p.
37. Harris, Edna Macauley. "New frontiers of 1562." 14 p.
38. Ramsey, Frank H. "General Isaac Ingalls Stevens." 12 p.
39. "St. Helena's contribution to the ministry. Prepared from source material in the Beaufort Township library."
40. Theus, Nita Grimsley. "Catholicity in Beaufort." 28 p.
41. Runnette, Mabel. "Libraries of Beaufort, SC." 33 p.
42. Theus, Nita Grimsley. "The Presbyterian Church of Beaufort, SC." 79 p.
43. Colcock, Charles J. "The Battle of Honey Hill." 48 p.
44. Busch, James W. "Beaufort from secession to its capture & occupation by the Federals."
45. Harvey, W. Brantley. "'The Great Port Royal Experiment' following the War between the States." 16 p.
46. Andrews, Beatrice. "The Catholic church and the houses on New Street & vicinity." 21 p.
47. Hardy, Susan Martin. "Old houses on the bluff." 21 p.
48. Fickling, Evan Edwards. "Eight Beaufort homes." 65 p.
49. Barnum, Charles N. "Records of public transportation in Beaufort County."
50. Wall, Mr. & Mrs. W. O. "The storm of 1893."
51. Trask, John M., Jr. "Thoughts and recommendations on the preservation of Beaufort's cultural & historical resources."
52. Rosenblath, Katharine Mazyck. "Refugeeing from Beaufort."
53. Pinckney, Roger. "Occupation of the Beaufort area by northern forces during the war."
54. Weir, Robert M. "Beaufort & the British during the era of the American Revolution."

APPENDIX X

Material relating to South Carolina in the <u>Georgia Genealogical Magazine</u>, 1970 - 1980 (issues #35-78), courtesy of the Rev. Silas Emmett Lucas, Jr., editor.

Abbeville County
    Marriage records, 1837-1880: 65/66:284-288.
    Misc. equity records: 49/50:382-388.

Chester County
    Deed Book "A": 37:265-268, 38:363-368, 40:222-229.
    Deed Book "B": 46:400-405, 47:55-60, 68/69:179-188, 70:295-
       304, 75/76:125-136.
    Deed Book "B" & beginning of Deed Book "C": 77/78:273-282.
    Revolutionary War pensions: 74:303-304.
    Wills: 35:70-84, 36:183-188.

Edgefield County
    Deaths, 1829-1851: 39:77-84.
    Deaths & marriages: 40:211-221.

Greenville County
    Deed Book "A": 52/53:189-198, 54:296-305.
    Deed Book "B": 55/56:99-106, 58:300-308, 59:62-67, 60/61:
       193-196.
    Estate records: 65/66:289-299, 68/69:189-196.

Laurens County
    Bible & family records: 44:338-340, 42:457-466.
    Deed Book "A": 36:171-182, 37:277-284.
    Deed Book "B": 41:340-343, 48:181-183.
    Deed Book "B" & equity records: 49/50:377-381.
    Deed Book "C", 1789-1791: 55/56:107-114, 57:212-217, 62:
       309-313, 63/64:121-126.
    Guardians returns & misc. records: 35:85-96.
    Jury list: 47:61-64.
    Marriages: 58:299-300.
    Marriages & jury list: 46:406-409.
    Men in gray: 77/78:269-273.
    Miscellaneous records: 38:369-374, 60/61:197-204.
    Naturalizations: 43:57-64.
    Plat Book "A": 44:343-347.
    Revolutionary War pension applications: 67:55-56.

Laurens District
    Some equity records: 59:75-76.

Lexington County
    Miscellaneous equity records: 41:327-337.

Newberry County
  Miscellaneous equity records: 48:184-188.
  Will Book "A": 44/45:286-293, 46:410-413, 47:65-69.

Newberry District
  Equity records: 59:68-72.

Pendleton County
  Coroner's inquests: 57:231-236.
  Deed Book "B": 73:225-240.

Pickens County
  Estate records: 60/61:205-220, 62:314-317, 65/66:300-301.
  Miscellaneous records: 71/72:105-112.
  Real estate sales: 37:269-276, 38:375-378, 39:85-92.

Pickens District
  Naturalizations: 57:227-230.

Spartanburg County
  Nazareth Church cemetery: 74:305-312.

Union County
  Deed Book "A": 41:348-352, 43:65-72, 44/45:298-309, 47:70-73,
    48:189-196.
  Deed Book "B": 52/53:206-212, 55/56:115-122, 60/61:187-192,
    63/64:127-136, 65/66:302-307, 67:67-70, 68/69:197-202,
    71/72:113-122.
  Probate records, books 1 & 2: 49/50:389-395, 75/76:137-144.
  Wills: 52/53:213-214, 55/56:123-125.

Washington District
  Miscellaneous equity records: 59:73-74.

Winton (Barnwell) County
  1787 tax list: 49/50:396-401.

York County
  Deed Book "A", 1786-1788: 46:414-421, 51:67-72, 52/53:215-
    219.

APPENDIX XI

Churches for which a historical records survey was compiled during the course of the W. P. A. "Inventory of Church Archives",
1937-1939.

The original records and historical data survey sheets may be
found in the Manuscripts Division, South Caroliniana Library
(SCL), Columbia. In 1980, the collection of 12,000+ pages was
microfilmed by the South Carolina Historical Society, Charleston, through a grant from the South Carolina Committee for the
Humanities, an agent of the National Endowment for the Humanities. Microfiche copies of the survey for each county were made
available without charge to a library in each county. In addition, five sets of the complete "Inventory" for the entire state
were distributed to the following research libraries: The
South Carolina Historical Society, Charleston; The South Caroliniana Library, U. S. C., Columbia; The Winthrop College Archives, Rock Hill; Francis Marion College, Florence; Furman
University, Greenville; and The Historical Foundation of the
Presbyterian Church, Montreat, North Carolina.

Abbeville County: Abbeville A.R.P.; Abbeville Southern Baptist;
    Abbeville Congregational Holiness; Abbeville Pentecostal Holi-
    ness; Abbeville Presbyterian; Allen Chapel A.M.E.; Bell's
    Chapel M.E.; Bethel M.E.; Bethia Presbyterian; Bethlehem A.R.
    P.; Beulah Southern Baptist; Broadmouth S.B.C.; Brownah A.M.E.
    Calhoun Falls Methodist; Calhoun Falls Presbyterian; Campfield
    Negro Baptist; Cedar Springs A.R.P.; Abbeville Church of God;
    Church of God, Abbeville; Clear Spring A.M.E.; Cypress Chapel
    A.M.E.; Donalds S.B.C.; Donalds M.E.S.; Donalds Presbyterian;
    Due West A.R.P.; Due West S.B.C.; Ebenezer M.E.; Fairfield
    Negro Baptist; First S.B.C., Abbeville; Flatrock A.M.E.;
    Forksville Negro Baptist Church of Christ; Friendship Negro
    Baptist; Gilgal M.E.S., Grace Chapel A.M.E.; Grace M.E.S., Ja-
    cob Chapel A.M.E.; John's Creek Negro Baptist; Keowee S.B.C.;
    Lebanon Presbyterian; Little Mountain A.M.E.; Little Mountain
    Presbyterian; Little River S.B.C.; Little Rock Buffalo Negro
    Baptist; Long Cane A.M.E.; Lowndesville S.B.C.; Main Street
    M.E.S.; Midway S.B.C.; Moor's Chapel Fire Baptism Holiness
    Church of God of America (Negro); Mt. Calvary Negro Baptist;
    Mt. Canaan Negro Baptist; Mt. Clement Negro M.E.; Mt. Lebanon
    A.M.E.; Mt. Olive A.M.E.; Mt. Olive Negro Baptist; Mt. Pleas-
    ant Negro Baptist; Mt. Zion A.M.E.; Mt. Zion Presbyterian (Ne-
    gro); Mulberry A.M.E.; Pleasant Grove A.M.E.; Poplar Grove
    Negro Baptist; Providence Presbyterian; Rocky River Presbyter-
    ian; Rocky River S.B.C.; St. James A.M.E.; St. John's A.M.E.;
    St. John's A.M.E., St. Luke C.M.E.; St. Mary Negro Baptist;
    St. Peter A.M.E.; Salem Negro Baptist; Salem Negro Baptist;
    Shady Grove A.M.E.; Sharon M.E.S.; Shiloh Methodist; Smyrna
    M.E.; Southside S.B.C.; Springfield Negro Baptist; Springfield

381

Negro Baptist; Tabernacle A.M.E.; Trinity Episcopal; Union
Negro Baptist; Upper Long Cane Presbyterian; Walnut Grove Ne-
gro Baptist; Warrenton Presbyterian; Washington Street Pres-
byterian (Negro); Wilson Creek Negro Baptist #2; Zion Fire
Baptized Holiness Church of God of America (Negro).
Aiken County: St. John's M.E.S., Aiken; Aiken First Baptist
  (formerly Treadway S.B.C.); Aiken Presbyterian; Adeth Jeshurun
  Jewish Congregation, Aiken; St. Paul's Ev. Lutheran, Aiken;
  St. Thaddeus Episcopal, Aiken; Bell Grove Negro Baptist;
  Springfield Negro Baptist; Mt. Sinai Negro Baptist; Church of
  God, Holiness, Langley; Church of God, Holiness, Warrenville;
  Eureke S.B.C.; Shiloh S.B.C.; Vaucluse S.B.C.; Vaucluse M.E.S;
  Friendship Negro Baptist, Aiken; Cumberland A.M.E.; Union Ne-
  gro Baptist; Randol Branch Negro Baptist; Zion Hill Negro
  Baptist; Mt. Calvary Ev. Lutheran; Union Negro Baptist; Anti-
  och Negro Baptist, Vaucluse; Jerusalem Negro Baptist; Beaver
  Dam Negro Baptist; Mt. Pleasant S.B.C.; St. Luke A.M.E., Vau-
  cluse; Rocky Grove S.B.C.; Wagner S.B.C., Wagner; Mt. Ebal
  S.B.C.; Mt. Pleasant S.B.C..
Allendale County: St. Mary's Roman Catholic; Allendale First
  S.B.C.; Swallow Savannah M.E.S.; Smyrna S.B.C.; Happy Home
  Negro Baptist, Allendale; Allendale Presbyterian; Bethlehem
  S.B.C., Fairfax; Lower Three Runs S.B.C.; Mt. Arnold S.B.C.;
  Paul's Chapel Negro Baptist, Ulmers; Sycamore S.B.C., Syca-
  more; St. John's Holiness Church of God (Negro); St. John's
  Negro Baptist, Sycamore; Mt. Calvary Negro Baptist; Miller
  Swamp Negro Baptist; New Zion Negro Baptist, Seigling; Rock
  Hill Disciples of Christ (Negro), Sycamore; Virgin Mary Negro
  Baptist; Irvington Negro Baptist; St. Nicholas' United Evan-
  gelical Lutheran; Bethel S.B.C.; Harmony S.B.C.; Mt. Pleasant
  Primitive Baptist; Antioch Disciples of Christ; Galilee Negro
  Baptist, Appleton; Beulah Negro Baptist, Baldock; Bentley A.
  M.E., Appleton; New Hope Negro M.E.; Allen Chapel A.M.E.;
  Second Calvary Negro Baptist; Seigling C.M.E., Seigling;
  Great Salkehatchie S.B.C., Ulmers; Beautiful Gate Negro Bap-
  tist; St. Mark Negro Baptist; Holy Communion Episcopal, Allen-
  dale.
Anderson County: Sandy Springs M.E.S., Sandy Springs; Mt. Zion
  Presbyterian; Mt. Bethel S.B.C.; Diamond Hill A.R.P.; Concord
  A.R.P.; Hopewell Presbyterian, Pendleton; Midway Presbyterian;
  First Presbyterian, Anderson; Roberts Presbyterian; Church of
  God, Holiness, Anderson; Anderson A.R.P.; Bethel M.E.S., An-
  derson; Riverside S.B.C., Anderson; Gluck Mill M.E.S., Ander-
  son; Gluck Mill S.B.C., Anderson; Holy Trinity (Kreps Memor-
  ial) Lutheran, Anderson; Anderson Second S.B.C., Anderson;
  Concord S.B.C.; L.D.S. (Mormon), Anderson; Pentecostal Fire
  Baptist Holiness, Anderson; New Hope M.E.S.; Smith's Chapel
  M.E.S.; St. John's M.E.S., Anderson; New Prospect S.B.C.; Oak-
  wood S.B.C., Anderson; Verennes Presbyterian; St. Paul's
  Episcopal, Anderson; Trinity M.E.S.; Toxaway M.E.S.; Refuge
  S.B.C.; Pendleton S.B.C.; Lebanon S.B.C.; Salem S.B.C.; Mt.

Tabor S.B.C.; Sharon M.E.S.; Zion M.E.S.; Orrville M.E.S., Anderson; Orrville S.B.C., Anderson; King David Negro Baptist; New Prospect Negro Baptist; Six and Twenty S.B.C.; Pendleton S.B.C., Pendleton; Church of God, Holiness, LaFrance; LaFrance S.B.C., LaFrance; White Field S.B.C.; Eureka S.B.C.; Friendship S.B.C.; Pendleton M.E.S., Pendleton; Welfare Negro Baptist; Mountain Springs Negro Baptist, Anderson; Deep Creek M.E. (Negro); Bethesda M.E.S.; Mt. Airy S.B.C.; Neal's Creek S.B.C.; Shiloh M.E.S.; Wesley Chapel M.E.S.; Union Grove M.E. S., Anderson; Dorchester S.B.C.; Beulah M.E.S.; White Plains S.B.C., Anderson; Belton First S.B.C., Belton; Belton M.E.S., Belton; Shady Grove S.B.C.; Belton Presbyterian, Belton; Mt. Pisgah S.B.C.; Beaverdam S.B.C.; Corinth First S.B.C.; Friendship S.B.C.; Fairview Methodist Protestant; Cedar Grove S.B.C. New Hope Missionary Baptist (Negro); New Hopewell Missionary Baptist (Negro); B'Nai Israel Orthodox & Reform Jewish Congregation, Anderson; Church of God, Honea Path; Chignola S.B. C., Honea Path; Honea Path S.B.C., Honea Path; Trinity M.E.S., Honea Path; Chignola M.E.S., Honea Path; Big Creek S.B.C., Williamston; Church of God, Holiness, at Kelley's Crossing, Williamston; Williamston First S.B.C., Williamston; Williamston Presbyterian, Williamston; Williamston Second S.B.C., Williamston; Wesley Methodist (Wesleyan Methodist), Williamston; Piedmont Presbyterian, Piedmont; Wesleyan Methodist Church (Wesleyan Methodist), Piedmont; Williamston Mill Methodist, Williamston; Grace Methodist, Williamston; Tabernacle S.B.C., Pelzer; Wesleyan Methodist, Pelzer; Victoria Holiness, Williamston; Anderson First S.B.C., Pelzer; Pelzer Presbyterian, Pelzer; Anderson Methodist, Pelzer; Church of God, Holiness, Pelzer; Church of God, Holiness, West Pelzer; Brown-Salem M.E. Belton; Holiness, Belton; Bethlehem A.M.E., Belton; Springfield Negro Baptist, Belton; New Broadmouth Negro Baptist; St. James M.E. (Negro); Liberty Negro Baptist, Honea Path; Mt. Zion Negro Baptist, Belton; St. Paul C.M.E., Honea Path; Bethel M.E. (Negro), Williamston; New Prospect Negro Baptist, Williamston; Pleasant Hill Negro Baptist; Cedar Grove Baptist; Wesleyan Methodist, Iva; Grove A.R.P.; Barker's Creek S.B.C.; Honea Path Presbyterian, Honea Path; Starr S.B.C., Starr; Martin Grove Fire Baptized Holiness; Poplar Springs S.B.C.; Good Hope Presbyterian, Ira; Ira Pentecostal Holiness, Ira; Ira S.B.C., Ira; Good Hope S.B.C.; Good Will C.M.E., Starr; St. Paul A.M.E., Ira; Cross Roads C.M.E.; Mountain View C.M.E. Shiloh Negro Baptist; Bethlehem C.M.E.; Generostes A.R.P.; Triangle S.B.C.; Flat Rock S.B.C.; Flat Rock Presbyterian; Ira A.R.P., Ira; New Bethlehem Methodist; Double Springs S.B.C.; Pleasant Grove Negro Baptist; Jefferson Chapel A.M.E.; Providence Methodist; Bethel Methodist, Ira; Ruhamah Methodist; Mt. Sinai Methodist (Negro); New Harmony Methodist (Negro); Mt. Olive Negro Baptist; Springfield Methodist (Negro); Mt, Moriah Negro Baptist; Mountain Creek S.B.C.; Union S.B.C.; Liberty S.B.C.; Fellowship S.B.C.; Hebron Methodist; Fellowship Wes-

leyan Methodist; New Bethlehem Lutheran, Townville; Mt. Herman
Negro Baptist; Generostee Negro Baptist; Evergreen M.E. (Ne-
gro); McNeely Holiness; Oakdale Baptist; Wilson's Creek Negro
Baptist No. 1; Pleasant View Negro Baptist; New Mt. Pisgah Ne-
gro Baptist; Fairfield C.M.E.; Evergreen Negro Baptist; Salem
Negro Baptist; St. Peter A.M.E.; Mt. Sinai A.M.E.; Mt. Abel
Negro Baptist; New Light Negro Baptist; Holly Springs Negro
Baptist; Oak View Negro Baptist; Holly Creek Negro Baptist;
Shiloh S.B.C. (also known as Shockley's Ferry Baptist, Big
Generostee Baptist); Carswell S.B.C.; Barnett's Grove Fire
Baptized Holiness; Oak Grove S.B.C.; Guthrie Grove Church of
God of Abrahamic Faith; New Hope S.B.C.; King's Chapel A.M.E.,
Pendleton; Welcome S.B.C.; North Side S.B.C., Anderson; St.
Joseph Catholic, Anderson; Sunset Forest Negro Baptist; Sweet
Canaan Negro Baptist; Bethel Methodist (Negro), Pendleton; New
Mt. Grove Baptist; Wilson Calvary Negro Baptist, Anderson;
Rock Hill Negro Baptist; New Prospect Negro Baptist No. 2;
Fair View A.M.E.; Ebenezer Negro Baptist; Townville S.B.C.,
Townville; Bethany S.B.C.; Starr Methodist, Starr; Asbury
Methodist; Pine Grove Baptist; Long Branch S.B.C.; Thompson
Centennial Methodist (Negro), Anderson; Salem Presbyterian
(Negro), Anderson.
Bamberg County: St. James M.E.S., Erhardt; Erhardt S.B.C., Er-
hardt; Erhardt Memorial United Evangelical Lutheran, Erhardt;
First Christian (Disciples of Christ. Negro.), Erhardt; Bam-
berg Presbyterian, Bamberg; Bamberg Pentecostal Holiness, Bam-
berg; Savannah Creek Negro Baptist, Erhardt; Bamberg S.B.C.,
Bamberg; Trinity M.E.S., Bamberg; Mt. Carmel Methodist, Bam-
berg; Thankful Negro Baptist, Bamberg; Denmark Presbyterian,
Denmark; Bethel Park M.E.S, Denmark; Bethel M.E.S., Olar,
Ghents Branch S.B.C.; Denmark S.B.C., Denmark; Bethel A.M.E.,
Denmark; Central Negro Baptist, Denmark; Rome Negro Baptist,
Denmark; Franklin M.E. (Negro), Denmark; Govan S.B.C., Govan,
South Side M.E.S., Bamberg; Colston Branch S.B.C.; Mt. Herman
Negro Baptist; St. John's Negro Baptist, Bamberg; Ebenezer
C.M.E.; Springtown Negro Baptist; Mizpah M.E.S.; Salem M.E.S.;
Kearse's Chapel M.E.S..
Barnwell County: Barnwell Presbyterian, Barnwell; Barnwell M.E.
S., Barnwell; Church of the Holy Apostles Episcopal, Barnwell;
Barnwell S.B.C., Barnwell; St. Andrew's Roman Catholic, Barn-
well.
Beaufort County: Baptist Church of Beaufort (S.B.C.), Beaufort;
Beaufort First Presbyterian, Beaufort; Berean Presbyterian
(Negro), Beaufort; Beth Israel Jewish Congregation, Beaufort;
Carteret Street M.E.S., Beaufort; Central Negro Baptist, Beau-
fort; Church of the Living God Pillar & Ground Truth, Sancti-
fied, Beaufort; First African Negro Baptist, Beaufort; Grace
Chapel A.M.E., Beaufort; Lebeco M.E.S., Lebeco; C.M.E., Beau-
fort; St. Helena's Island Chapel of Ease (Episcopal); St. An-
drew's Roman Catholic, Pritchardville; St. Anthony's Roman
Catholic, Hardeeville; St. Helena's Episcopal, Beaufort; St.

384

Peter's Roman Catholic, Beaufort; Sheldon Church ("Burnt
Church") of Prince William's Parish, Sheldon Township.
Berkeley County: Apii Methodist Episcopal, South; Berea M.E.S.;
Bethel Negro M.E., Bethlehem Negro Methodist Protestant; Black
Creek M.E.S.; Bonneau Missionary Baptist; Chapel of Our Sav-
iour, Mt. Holly; Christian Church (Disciples of Christ), St.
Stephens; Church of Jesus Christ of Latter-Day Saints, Bethera
Cordesville Southern Baptist; Day Dawn Negro Missionary Bap-
tist, Pineville; Ebenezer M.E.S.; Ebenezer African Methodist
Episcopal; Emanuel A.M.E., Monck's Corner; Emanuel Reformed
Episcopal; Epiphany Protestant Episcopal, Eutawville; First-
born Church of the Living God- Holiness; Grace Reformed Epis-
copal; Green Hill A.M.E., Bonneau; Greenland Negro Missionary
Baptist; Good Shepherd Reformed Episcopal; Grove Hall A.M.E.;
Grove Hall Holiness (Negro); Holy Comforter Reformed Episco-
pal, Monck's Corner; Irving Chapel A.M.E., Monck's Corner;
Jamestown Missionary Baptist; Jehovah A.M.E.; Jehovah Negro
Baptist, St. Stephens; Jerusalem A.M.E.; Jerusalem Missionary
Baptist, Jamestown; Jerusalem Missionary Baptist; Lebanon M.
E.S.; Liberty Reformed Episcopal; Macedonia Christian; Messiah
Reformed Episcopal; Moncks Corner Christian (Disciples of
Christ; Moncks Corner M.E.S.; Moncks Corner Missionary Baptist
Moncks Corner Negro Missionary Baptist; Mt. Olivet Missionary
Baptist, Pinopolis; Mt. Pisgah A.M.E.; New Hope A.M.E.; Oak
Grove Negro M.E.; Oak Grove Pentecostal Holiness; Pineville
M.E.S.; Pompoin Hill Protestant Episcopal; Reconciliation Re-
formed Episcopal; Redeemer Negro Protestant Episcopal, Pine-
ville; Redeemer Reformed Episcopal, Pineville; Rehobeth M.E.
S., McBeth; Russellville Christian (Disciples of Christ);
St. James M.E.S.; St. John (Strawberry Chapel) Protestant
Episcopal; St. John's Berkeley Protestant Episcopal (Biggin
Church); St. Luke's A.M.E.; St. Luke Negro M.E., Moncks Cor-
ner; St. Mark A.M.E.; St. Mary's A.M.E.; St. Matthew A.M.E.;
St. Matthew's Negro Baptist; St. Michael's Reformed Episcopal,
St. Stephens; St. Paul Negro M.E., St. Stephens; St. Philip's
Reformed Episcopal; St. Stephens M.E.S., St. Stephens; St.
Stephens Negro Baptist; St. Stephens Protestant Episcopal, St.
Stephens; St. Stephens S.B.C.; St. Thomas & St. Denis Protest-
ant Episcopal, Cainhoy; Sand Ridge S.B.C.; Smith Chapel C.M.E.;
Smyrna M.E.S.; Solomon Temple M.E., Moncks Corner; Spring Hill
M.E.S.; Sumter Class Room- Negro M.E.; Taveau Negro M.E.;
Trinity Chapel Protestant Episcopal, Pinopolis; Trinity Pro-
testant Episcopal; Unity Negro Missionary Baptist; Wassamassaw
Missionary Baptist; Zion A.M.E.; Zion Negro M.E., St. Steph-
ens.
Calhoun County: St. Paul A.M.E., Creston; Mt. Zion M.E.S.; Mt.
Pisgah A.M.E.; Beulah M.E.S., Sandy Run; Fort Motte M.E.S.,
Fort Motte; St. Paul M.E.S., St. Matthews; St. Matthews Pro-
testant Episcopal; Sandy Run United Evangelical Lutheran;
Congaree Missionary Baptist; Mt. Zion A.M.E.; Pine River Uni-
ted Evangelical Lutheran, Lone Star; Cameron Missionary Bap-

tist, Cameron; Cameron M.E.S., Cameron; Church of the Resur-
rection Evangelical Lutheran, Cameron; St. John Negro Baptist;
Brown's Chapel Negro Baptist; New Bethany Negro Baptist; Mt.
Pleasant Negro Baptist; St. Mark's Negro Baptist; Cedar Grove
Negro Baptist, Lone Star; Union A.M.E.; Hayne's Chapel A.M.E.,
Lone Star; St. Peter's A.M.E., Cameron; Bethel A.M.E., St.
Matthews; St. Matthews Negro Baptist, St. Matthews; Friendship
Negro Baptist, St. Matthews; Mt. Carmel Negro Baptist; Mispah
Missionary Baptist; Providence Missionary Baptist; Shady Grove
M.E.S.; Andrews Chapel M.E.S.; Jericho M.E.S.; Canaan A.M.E.;
St. Peter A.M.E.; Shiloh Negro Baptist; Providence A.M.E.; Mt.
Zion Negro Baptist, Fort Motte; Gethsemane Missionary Baptist;
Ebenezer A.M.E.; St. Matthews First S.B.C., St. Matthews; E-
mancipation Negro Baptist, Riley; St. Matthews Presbyterian,
St. Matthews; St. Matthews Evangelical Lutheran, St. Matthews;
Epiphany Evangelical Lutheran, St. Matthews; Bethlehem Negro
M.E., St. Matthews; St. Luke's A.M.E.; Fort Motte Presbyter-
ian; Wesley Chapel M.E.S.; Heyward A.M.E.; Bethel M.E.S.; St.
Luke A.M.E.; Mt. Nebo Negro Presbyterian.
Charleston County: Calvary Protestant Episcopal (Negro); Ebene-
zer A.M.E., Charleston; Hebron Presbyterian (Negro), John's
Island; Promise Land Reformed Episcopal, John's Island; Plymouth Congregational (Negro), Charleston; Edisto Island Presbyterian, Edisto Island; Gethsemane Negro Baptist, Charleston;
King Street S.B.C.; Church of God-Holiness (Negro), Charleston; Jerusalem A.M.E., Wadmalaw Island; Calvary S.B.C., Meggett; First Christian, Charleston; Edisto Island Presbyterian
(Negro), Edisto Island; Union Negro Missionary Baptist, Charleston; Mt. Zion A.M.E., Charleston; Holy Communion Protestant Episcopal, Charleston; Zion Presbyterian (Negro), Charleston; Shiloh Negro Missionary Baptist, Edisto Island; Westminster Presbyterian, Charleston; Macedonia A.M.E., Charleston;
Centenary Negro M.E., Charleston; Morris Brown A.M.E., Char-
leston; Bethel M.E.S., Charleston; Wallingford Presbyterian,
Charleston; Olivet Presbyterian (Negro), Charleston; Israel
Reformed Episcopal, Charleston; Rutledge Street S.B.C., Charleston; Refuge Church of Our Lord Jesus Christ-Apostolic Faith
Charleston; Trinity M.E.S., Charleston; Mt. Hermon Reformed
Methodist Union Episcopal, Charleston; Francis Brown Methodist
Protestant (Negro), Charleston; Emanuel A.M.E., Charleston;
Jordan Negro Missionary Baptist; Lovely Hill Negro Missionary
Baptist; Jerusalem A.M.E., Maryville; Emanuel A.M.E., Mary-
ville; North Charleston M.E.S.; Payne Chapel A.M.E., James Is-
land; Cherokee M.E.S., Charleston; Graham Chapel A.M.E.; Wes-
ley Negro M.E., Charleston; Midland Park M.E.S., North Char-
leston; Asbury Memorial M.E.S., Charleston; Vanderhorst Memor-
ial C.M.E., Charleston; Rockville Presbyterian, Rockville;
James Island Presbyterian, James Island; Morris Street Negro
Baptist, Charleston; Calvary Negro Baptist, Charleston; Pilgrim Negro Baptist; Mt. Moriah Negro Baptist; John's Island
S.B.C., John's Island; Jerusalem Negro Baptist; Mt. Olivet Ne-

gro Baptist; North Charleston S.B.C., North Charleston; First
Negro Missionary Baptist, Maryville; James Island Negro Baptist, James Island; Charleston Heights S.B.C., Charleston; Oak
Grove Negro Baptist; Hampstead Square S.B.C., Charleston; Holy
Trinity Reformed Episcopal, Charleston; Christ Church Protestant Episcopal, Wilton-Adams Run; Church of the Good Shepherd
Protestant Episcopal, North Charleston; Calvary Pentecostal-
Assembly of God, Charleston; Fourth Negro Missionary Baptist,
Charleston; Wesley Negro M.E., John's Island; Bethel Negro
M.E., Charleston; Bethel A.M.E.; Citadel Square S.B.C., Charleston; Grace Protestant Episcopal, Charleston; Circular
Congregational, Charleston; French Protestant (Huguenot),
Charleston; First (Scotch) Presbyterian, Charleston; Beth Elohim Synagogue, Charleston; Rosemont S.B.C.; Grace Chapel
Protestant Episcopal, Rockville; Chapel of the Holy Cross Protestant Episocpal, Sullivan's Island; Church of Jesus Christ
of Latter-Day Saints (Mormon), Charleston; Brith Shalom Synagogue, Charleston; Green Street Negro Baptist, Charleston;
First Baptist, Charleston; Unitarian Church of Charleston;
First Church of Christ-Scientist, Charleston; Beth Israel
Synagogue, Charleston; St. John the Baptist Catholic, Charleston; Our Lady of Mercy Roman Catholic, Charleston; Second
Presbyterian, Charleston; Trinity Greek Orthodox, Charleston;
McClellanville M.E.S., McClellanville; Tibwin A.M.E., Tibwin;
Bethel A.M.E., McClellanville; Union A.M.E., Awendaw; New Wappetaw Presbyterian, McClellanville; Wrens M.E.S.; Ocean Grove
M.E.S., Awendaw; Johnson Chapel A.M.E.; Lovely Mountain Negro
Baptist; Jerusalem Negro Baptist, Charleston; Ashley Negro
Baptist, Edisto Island; Trinity C.M.E., Charleston; St. Andrew's Episcopal Mission, Charleston; St. Andrew's Lutheran,
Charleston; St. Andrew's Protestant Episcopal, St. Andrew's
Parish; St. Barnabas Evangelical Lutheran, Charleston; St.
Frances M.E.S., Meggett; St. James A.M.E.; St. James A.M.E.,
John's Island; St. James A.M.E.; St. James Bethel A.M.E., Wadmalaw Island; St. James Presbyterian, James Island; St. James
Protestant Episcopal, James Island; St. James Protestant Episcopal, McClellanville; St. Johannes German Lutheran, Charleston; St. John's Lutheran, Charleston; St. John's Protestant
Episcopal, Charleston; St. John's Protestant Episcopal, John's
Island; St. John's Reformed Episcopal, Charleston; St. Joseph's Roman Catholic, Charleston; St. Jude A.M.E.; St. Philip's Protestant Episcopal, Charleston; St. Luke's A.M.E., Wadmalaw Island; St. Luke's Reformed Episcopal, Charleston; St.
Luke's Protestant Episcopal, Charleston; St. Mary's Roman
Catholic, Charleston; St. Mark's A.M.E.; St. Mark's Protestant
Episcopal (Negro), Charleston; St. Matthew A.M.E., John's Island; St. Matthew's Evangelical Lutheran, Charleston; St.
Michael's Protestant Episcopal, Charleston; St. Patrick Roman
Catholic, Charleston; St. Paul A.M.E.; St. Paul Negro Baptist,
Charleston; St. Paul's Protestant Episcopal, Charleston; St.
Paul's Protestant Episcopal, Meggett; St. Peter's-by-the-Sea

Protestant Episcopal, North Charleston; St. Peter's Episcopal, Charleston; St. Peter's Protestant Episcopal, Charleston; St. Peter's Reformed Episcopal; St. Peter's Roman Catholic, Charleston; St. Stephen's A.M.E., John's Island; St. Stephen's Chapel Protestant Episcopal, Charleston; Sacred Heart of Jesus Roman Catholic, Charleston; Salem Negro Baptist, Charleston; Salem Negro Baptist, Wadmalaw Island; Salem Presbyterian (Negro), Wadmalaw Island; Seventh Day Adventist, Charleston; Shiloh A.M.E.; Spring Street M.E.S., Charleston; Star Gospel Mission, Charleston.
Cherokee County: Limestone Presbyterian, Gaffney; State Line S.B.C.; Broad River Baptist, Blacksburg; Love Springs S.B.C.; Church of the Incarnation Protestant Episcopal, Gaffney.
Chesterfield County: Elizabeth S.B.C., Mt. Croghan; Mt. Croghan S.B.C.; Timmonsville Negro Baptist; Zion A.M.E., Chesterfield; Mt. Level Negro Baptist; Chesterfield Presbyterian (Negro), Chesterfield; Grand View Presbyterian (Negro), Chesterfield; Ruby Presbyterian (Negro), Ruby; Pageland Presbyterian (Negro) Pageland; Gum Spring Negro Baptist; Sweet Home Negro Baptist; New Zion Negro Baptist, Chesterfield; Davidson Grove Negro Baptist; Thompson Creek S.B.C.; White Oak Presbyterian, Ruby; Pageland S.B.C., Pageland; Providence S.B.C.; Long Branch S.B.C.; Westfield S.B.C.; Bethlehem S.B.C.;Ruby S.B.C., Ruby; Rocky Creek S.B.C.; Antioch S.B.C.; Ebenezer M.E.S.; Salem Negro Baptist, Chesterfield; Wesley Chapel A.M.E.; Pleasant Hill S.B.C.; Mt. Olive M.E.S.; Lower Macedonia S.B.C.; Zoar Methodist; St. Paul Negro Baptist; Union Hill Negro Baptist; John Wesley Negro M.E., Pageland; Peniel M.E.S.; High Point S.B.C.; Rivers Chapel Negro Baptist; Drucilla Zion Methodist (Negro), Chesterfield; Clanton Plains S.B.C.; Liberty Hill S.B.C., Pageland; Wolf Pond S.B.C.; St. Mary Negro Baptist, Chesterfield; Flint Ridge Negro Baptist; McBee S.B.C., McBee; McBee M.E.S., McBee; McBee Presbyterian, McBee; St. Paul M.E.S., Chesterfield; Providence M.E.S., McBee; Union M.E.S., McBee; Angelus M.E.S., Angelus; Beauford S.B.C.; Hopewell Negro Baptist; McBee Chapel A.M.E. Zion, McBee; Sandy Run Negro Baptist; Galilee Negro Baptist, McBee; Clark's Chapel A.M.E. Zion; Mt. Elon Negro M.E.; Salem M.E. Zion, Pageland; Wilks Chapel M.E.S.; Prospect M.E.S.; Hebron M.E.S.; Middendorf S.B.C.; Zion Hill Negro Baptist; Bethel A.M.E.; Brown Springs S.B.C.; Cedar Creek S.B.C.; Shiloh M.E.S.; Patrick Presbyterian, Patrick; Morning Star Negro Baptist, Patrick; Jefferson S.B.C., Jefferson; Fort Creek M.E.S.: Mt. Olivet S.B.C.; Patrick S.B.C., Patrick; Tabernacle M.E.S., McBee; Zoar M.E.S.; Jefferson M.E.S., Jefferson; Hopewell Negro M.E., Jefferson; Mt. Canon Negro Baptist, Jefferson; Palmetto S.B.C.; Bethel S.B.C.; White Plains S.B.C.; New St. David Protestant Episcopal, Cheraw; Pentecostal Holiness, Cheraw; Mt. Taber M.E.S., Chesterfield; Mt. Zion C.M.E.; Wesley Negro M.E., Cheraw; Teal's Chapel Negro Baptist; Second Presbyterian (Negro), Cheraw; Chesterfield S.B.C., Chesterfield; Pine Grove S.B.C.;

David Grove S.B.C.; McDonald Presbyterian Mission (Negro);
Powe Presbyterian Mission (Negro); Westside S.B.C, Cheraw;
Cheraw First Presbyterian, Cheraw; Mt. Hebron A.M.E. Zion,
Cheraw; Triumph Holiness Church of God (Negro), Cheraw; Union
Pee Dee Negro Baptist, Cheraw; Cheraw S.B.C., Cheraw; Cheraw
First M.E.S., Cheraw; St. Peter's Roman Catholic, Cheraw;
Friendship M.E.S..
Clarendon County: First Negro Baptist, Sardinia; Gable A.M.E.
Mission; Melina Presbyterian (Negro); Old Nathan's Pres-
byterian (Negro); St. Matthews A.M.E.; Harmony Elizabeth
Presbyterian (Negro); Reevesville A.M.E.; New Hope A.M.E.;
Fellowship Negro Baptist; A.M.E. Chapel, Alcolu; Howard
A.M.E. Chapel; Good Hope (Negro), Brogdon; Fourth Cross
Roads (Ridgell Shed) Baptist (Negro); Hickory Grove -
African Free Will Baptist (Negro); Shiloh A.M.E., Forreston;
St. Peter's Baptist (Negro), Brodgon; Westminster Pres-
byterian (Negro); Rock Hill Baptist (Negro); King's Chapel -
Christian Faith (Negro); Williams Chapel - Christian Faith
(Negro); Trinity A.M.E., Manning; St. James A.M.E.; Lib-
erty Hill A.M.E.; New Hope-Union M.E. (Negro); St. Mark's-
A.F.W.; Ebenezer Baptist (Negro), Manning; Fire Baptized
Holiness (Negro), Manning; Taw Caw Baptist (Negro); Briggs
Chapel (Negro Baptist); Mt. Zero Baptist (Negro); Mt. Siani-
Fire Baptized Holiness (Negro), Bloomville; Mt. Hope-
Pentecostal Holiness (Negro); New Zion A.M.E., Forreston;
St. Mark's A.M.E., Summerton; Union Hill A.F.W. Baptist;
Antioch Baptist (Negro); St. James A.M.E.; Light Hill-
African Hard Shell Baptist; Mt. Zion A.M.E.; New Hope-
Reformed M.E. (Negro); Sardinia Presbyterian U.S. (Negro),
Sardinia; Trinity Methodist M.E.S. (Negro); Home Branch
S.B.C.; Clarendon S.B.C., Alcolu; Midway Presbyterian U.S.;
New Harmony Presbyterian U.S.; New Harmony Presbyterian U.S.;
Manning Presbyterian U.S., Manning; Brewington Presbyterian
U.S., Manning; All Saints Prot. Episcopal (Negro), Manning;
Summerton Presbyterian U.S., Summerton; Pinegrove M.E.S., Tur-
beville; Horse Branch Free Will Baptist (Negro); Rehobeth M.E.
S.; Turbeville S.B.C., Turbeville; Oak Grove M.E.S.; Live Oak
M.E.S.; Manning S.B.C., Manning; St. Paul Holiness Church of
God (Negro); Mt. Carmel Presbyterian (Negro), Manning; Jordan
Presbyterian (Negro), Jordan; Pisgah Pentecostal Holiness (Ne-
gro); Paxville S.B.C., Paxville; St. Mary's Roman Catholic
Chapel, Summerton; Tump Spring or First Negro Baptist; Union
M.E.S., Wilson's Hill; Summerton S.B.C., Summerton; Forreston
M.E.S., Forreston; Forreston S.B.C., Forreston; Friendship
Presbyterian (Negro); Manning M.E.S., Manning; Green Savannah
Free Will Baptist (Negro); Mulberry Negro Baptist; Union Cy-
press A.M.E.; Calvary S.B.C.; Spring Hill A.M.E.; Bethel Mis-
sion A.M.E.; Coley A.M.E. Chapel, Jordan; Green Hill Negro Bap-
tist, Alcolu; Jordan M.E.S., Jordan; Dudley (Moriah) S.B.C.,
Harvin; Oakland M.E.S., Harvin; Paxville M.E.S., Paxville;
Rock Hill Negro Baptist; Society Hill A.M.E.; Calvary Negro

Baptist; St. Paul's M.E.S.; Summerton M.E.S., Summerton; Mt.
Moriah Union M.E. (Negro); Goodwill African Free Will Baptist,
Bloomville; St. John's Negro Baptist, Jordan; New Life Negro
Baptist, Davis Station; New Branch Union M.E.; Antioch-R.Union
M.E., Rimini; Mt. Chapel Negro Baptist; New St. Philip's A.M.E;
St. Phillips A.M.E.; St. James A.M.E.; Jerusalem Negro Baptist;
Mt. Pleasant R.U.M.E. (Negro), Panola; Briggers A.M.E.; Andrews
Chapel M.E.S.; Mother Church-Free Will Baptist; Hopewell Bap-
tist S.B.C.; Bethlehem M.E.S.; New Zion Negro Baptist; Wilson's
Grove-African Free Will Baptist; Millwood Chapel-Sanctified
Holiness (Negro); DeLain A.M.E.; Macedonia Negro Baptist; San-
tee A.M.E.; A.M.E. Chapel, Paxville; New Rehobeth M.E.S.; Tri-
umph Sanctified-non-denom., Manning; Mt. Carmel African Free
Will Baptist, Manning; New Light Negro (Hardshell) Baptist,
Manning; Holly Hill Negro Baptist; New Jerusalem Free Will Bap-
tist; Lodobar A.M.E.; Laurel Hill A.M.E.; Mt. Nebo Negro Bap-
tist; St. Philip R.M.U.E. (Negro); St. Philip R.M.U.E. (Negro).
Colleton County: Black Creek S.B.C.; Smoaks S.B.C., Smoaks; St.
Anthony's Roman Catholic, Walterboro; Great Swamp S.B.C., Wal-
terboro; Ruffin S.B.C., Ruffin; Cottageville S.B.C., Cottage-
ville; Shiloh Primitive Baptist; Peniel Primitive Baptist
Church (No. 2); Bethel S.B.C.-Round O; Ashton M.E.S., Ashton;
Bethel Presbyterian, Walterboro; St. Jude's Protestant Epis-
copal, Walterboro; Hendersonville S.B.C., Hendersonville; Zion
S.B.C., Walterboro; Bethlehem S.B.C., Walterboro; Spring Hill
S.B.C.; Pine Grove S.B.C.; Carter's Ford S.B.C.; St. John's
A.M.E., Ruffin; Bedon's S.B.C.; Walterboro S.B.C., Walterboro;
Peniel S.B.C.; Williams S.B.C., Williams; Williams M.E.S., Wil-
liams; Doctor's Creek S.B.C.; Bethel M.E., Walterboro; St. Bar-
tholomew Protestant Episcopal; Mt. Carmel M.E.S.; Ruffin M.E.S.;
Pleasant Grove S.B.C.; Canaan S.B.C.; Mt. Tabor M.E.S.; Mt.
Zion Negro Baptist; Evergreen Negro Baptist, Williams; Marion
S.B.C., Williams; St. James Roman Catholic (Negro), Colleton;
Walterboro Jewish Congregation, Walterboro.
Darlington County: Hartsville First S.B.C., Hartsville; Wesley
M.E.S., Hartsville; Bethel M.E.S.; St. Bartholomew Prot. Epis.,
Hartsville; Wesley Chapel M.E.S.; Hartsville Presbyterian,
Hartsville; Church of Jesus Christ-Latter Day Saints, Darling-
ton; Trinity M.E.S., Darlington; Darlington Presbyterian,
Darlington; Darlington First S.B.C., Darlington; St. Matthew's
Protestant Episcopal, Darlington; Central S.B.C., Darlington;
Welsh Neck S.B.C., Society Hill;Christian Science Society, Dar-
lington; Black Creek S.B.C., Dovesville; Fourth Street S.B.C.,
Hartsville; Latter Day Saints or Mormon, Hartsville; East Side
S.B.C., Hartsville; Twitty Chapel M.E.S., Hartsville; Kelley-
town S.B.C., Kelleytown; Gum Branch S.B.C.; New Providence S.
B.C.; Antioch S.B.C.; Antioch Baptist Mission (Negro); Kay
Branch Negro Baptist, Hartsville; Lawson Grove Negro Baptist;
Mt. Pisgah Presbyterian (Negro), Hartsville; Jerusalem Negro
Baptist, Hartsville; Centenary A.M.E., Hartsville; Mt. Calvary
A.M.E., Hartsville; Centerville A.M.E., Hartsville; Church of

God-Undenom.; Congregational Holiness, Congregational; Mt.
Elon S.B.C.; Nathan's Temple - Fire Baptized Holiness Church
of God of America (Negro); Wesley A.M.E. Chapel; Bethlehem
Methodist; The Church of God- Church of God - Darlington;
Kelly Bell A.M.E.; Friendship Negro Baptist, Darlington; St.
James A.M.E., Darlington; Mt. Teman Negro Baptist; Darlington
Second S.B.C., Darlington; Macedonia Negro Baptist (Nat'l Bap.
Convention), Darlington; Josey A.M.E. Chapel; Mt. Calvary Ne-
gro Baptist; Kingsville A.M.E.; Pentecostal Holiness-Holiness,
Darlington; Chapel Hill S.B.C.; Bethel A.M.E., Darlington;
Green Hill Negro Baptist; Salem M.E.S.; Prospect M.E.S.; Free
Will S.B.C., Darlington; Lamar Presbyterian, Lamar; Pine Grove
M.E.S.; Philadelphia M.E.S.; Lake Swamp S.B.C.; Shiloh M.E.;
Mechanicsville S.B.C., Mechanicsville; Lamar S.B.C., Lamar;
Lamar M.E.S., Lamar; Epworth M.E.S., Darlington; Elim M.E.S.,
Savannah-African M.E.; St. Johns A.M.E.; Church of God-Church
of God-Darlington; Zion M.E.S.; Pleasant Grove Negro Baptist;
New Providence Negro Baptist; Mt. Olive Holiness-Apostolic
Faith Church of God and Christ, Hartsville; Mt. Olive S.B.C.,
Patrick; New Hopewell Negro Baptist; Bethney Negro Baptist,
Lamar; Mt. Zion Negro Baptist; Union M.E. Church; Church of
God- Pentecostal Holiness; Friendship Chapel-Pentecostal Holi-
ness; St. Pauls A.M.E.; Union Negro Baptist, Society Hill;
Trinity-Prot. Epis., Society Hill; Newman Swamp Meth. Epis.
Mt. Beulah C.M.E. (Negro); Bethany Negro Baptist, Lamar; New
Market M.E.S.; Cross Roads Free Will Baptist; Mont Clare Mis-
sion-non-denom., Mont Clare; Cherry Grove Negro Baptist; Be-
thesda Negro Baptist, Society Hill; Darlington Jewish Congre-
gation-Reform, Darlington; Round O Negro Baptist, Mont Clare;
John Wesley M.E.(Negro), Lamar; Society Hill Presbyterian,
Society Hill.
Dillon County: Main Street Lower M.E.S., Dillon; Bowling Green
A.M.E.; New Harley A.M.E.; Latta S.B.C., Latta; Dillon Main
M.E.S., Dillon; Pine Hill A.M.E.; Catfish S.B.C.; Dillon S.B.
C., Dillon; Little Rock S.B.C., Little Rock; Dillon Presby-
terian, Dillon; Sardis S.B.C.; Pyerian S.B.C.; St. Paul A.M.E.
Floydale; Lake View S.B.C., Lake View; Mt. Andrews M.E.S.;
Reedy Creek Presbyterian; Bear Swamp S.B.C.; Pentecostal Holi-
ness Mission, Lake View; Kentyne Presbyterian; Latta Presby-
terian, Latta; Indian New Hope-Holiness Meth; St. Barnabus-
Prot. Epis., Dillon; Latta M.E.S., Latta; Little Zion Negro
Baptist; Mt. Calvary S.B.C.; Pleasant Grove S.B.C.; Bermuda
S.B.C.; Mt. Zion S.B.C.; Hamer Presbyterian, Hamer; Dillon
Mill S.B.C., Dillon; Shady Grove Negro Baptist; Piney Grove
S.B.C.; Fork S.B.C., Fork; Pleasant Hill S.B.C.; Kemper S.B.C.
Kemper; Union A.M.E. Chapel; Ohav Shalom-Reform-Masonic Temple,
Dillon; Hopewell M.E.S., Fork; Andrews Chapel C.M.E. (Negro),
Latta; St. Stephens C.M.E. (Negro), Dillon; Weston A.M.E.
Chapel, Latta.
Dorchester County: Bethel A.M.E., St. George; St. George M.E.S.,
St. George; Memorial S.B.C., St. George; Summerville Presby-

terian, Summerville;. St. Matthews Negro Baptist, Reevesville;
Reevesville S.B.C., Reevesville; St. George's Prot. Epis., Dorchester; Dorchester Congregational (or Independent), Dorches-
ter; Jedburg Presbyterian, Jedburg; Mt. Tabor M.E.S., Ridgeville; Zion S.B.C.; Limestone S.B.C.; Ridgeville S.B.C., Ridgeville; Grover M.E.S., Grover; Trinity M.E.S., Givan; Appleby's
M.E.S.; Shepherd S.B.C.; Church of Christ-Christian-Harley-
ville; Harleyville M.E.S., Harleyville; Red Bank A.M.E. (Negro);
Bethel A.M.E., Ridgeville; Rock Hill Negro Baptist; Jerusalem
C.M.E., Harleyville; Church of Christ-Hol. (Negro); St. Luke
A.M.E.; Jerusalem Negro Baptist; Zion M.E.S.; Salem M.E.S.,
Dorchester; Jedburg S.B.C., Jedburg; Indian Field M.E.S., Ro-
sinville; Reevesville M.E.S., Reevesville; Duncan M.E.S. Chap-
el; Pine Grove No. 2 S.B.C., Givan; New Hope M.E., St. Pauls
Prot. Epis., Summerville; St. Matthews S.B.C.; Pregnall M.E.S.,
Pregnall; St. Barnabas Prot. Epis., Summerville; Beulah S.B.C.;
St. George S.B.C.; St. Lukes Evang. Lutheran, Summerville; St.
John The Beloved-Roman Cath., Summerville; Harvey Chapel Negro
Baptist; Jericho Negro Baptist; St. Peters M.E.; Greenville M.
E.; First Baptist (Negro), Summerville; Pregnall Baptist (Ne-
gro); Branch M.E.S.; Bethany M.E.S., Summerville; Summerville
S.B.C., Summerville; Stallsville M.E.S., Stallsville; Boone
Hill M.E.S.; Cypress M.E.S.; Church of the Epiphany-Prot.Epis.
(Negro), Summerville; Bethel Seventh Day Adventist (Negro),
Summerville; St. Stephens-Ref.Epis. (Negro), Summerville; Shady
Grove C.M.E.; A.M.E., Summerville.
Florence County: Hebron S.B.C., Friendfield; Olanta S.B.C., O-
lanta; Central M.E.S., Florence; Central M.E.S., Florence;
Cumberland A.M.E. Zion, Florence; Ebernezer Baptist, Ebernezer;
Church of Jesus Christ of Latter Day Saints-Mormon, Florence;
McGill Memorial Presbyterian; St. John's Prot. Epis., Florence;
Immanuel Baptist, Florence; Pentecostal Free Will Baptist Mis-
sion, Florence; Magnolia Heights S.B.C., Florence; Florence
First S.B.C., Florence; Trinity Nat'l Bap. Con. (Negro), Flor-
ence; Bethel Temple or Bethel Tabernacle-Assemblies of God-
Pent. Holiness, Florence; St. Lukes United Evang. Lutheran,
Florence; St. Anthony Roman Catholic, Florence; Salvation Army-
Undenom., Florence; Lake City Southern Presbyterian, Lake City;
Gate City Mission A.M.E., Florence; Mt. Zion A.M.E., Florence;
Florence First Presbyterian, Florence; Seventh Day Adventist
(Negro), Florence; Independent Pentecostal Holiness; Mt. Carmel
Fire Baptized Holiness, Florence; Ebenezer Second Baptist-Nat'l
Bap.Con.Inc., Florence; Kingsburg S.B.C., Kingsburg; Holiness
Tabernacle-Pent. Holiness, Lake City; Pentecostal Church of
First Born-Pent. Holiness, Lake City; Wesley M.E. Chapel (Ne-
gro), Lake City; Immanuel M.E.S., Lake City; Red Hill A.M.E.,
Lake City; Lake City S.B.C., Lake City; Church of First Born-
Church of God Holiness (Negro), Lake City; Gilead Free Will
Baptist; Cameron M.E.S.; Scranton M.E.S., Scranton; Scranton
Pentecostal Holiness Tabernacle, Scranton; Lake City Presby-
terian, Lake City; Mt. Clair Negro Baptist, Lake City; Ninevah

C.M.E.; Lake Point C.M.E.; Beulah A.M.E.; John's Tabernacle-
Apostolic Holiness, Lake City; Paran S.B.C.; Cook's Pent. Holi-
ness Chapel; New Zion S.B.C.; Mt. Moriah S.B.C., Scranton; New
Zion Negro Baptist; Shady Grove Free Will Baptist (Negro),
Scranton; Scranton S.B.C., Scranton; Hick's Pent. Holiness;
Tabernacle Free Will Baptist, Cowards; Matthews Pent. Holiness
Tabernacle; Savannah Grove African Free Will Baptist; St. Mark
A.M.E.; Believers Church-Pent. Holiness (Negro); Lee's Pente-
costal Holiness Tabernacle; Mt. Seale S.B.C.; St. Matthews Free
Will Baptist; St. Peter's Union American (Negro);First Born of
the Living God-Pent. Holiness (Negro); Bethlehem Negro Baptist;
High Hill Free Will Baptist; St. John Free Will Baptist; Stone
Pentecostal Holiness Chapel; Jerusalem Free Will Baptist (Ne-
gro); St. John M.E.S.; Prospect M.E.S.; Liberty S.B.C.; Little
Star Free Will Baptist; Brown's Chapel M.E.S.; Olanta Pent.
Holiness Mission (Negro); West Church-Pent. Holiness (Negro);
St. Paul A.M.E.; St. Paul Negro Baptist; St. Mark A.M.E.; Sand
Hill Free Will Baptist; True Light; Pamplico M.E.S., Pamplico;
New Prospect Free Will Baptist; Beulah Free Will Baptist; Bax-
en's Pentecostal Holiness Chapel; Pamplico Pent. Holiness (Ne-
gro), Pamplico; Jordan A.M.E. Chapel, Pamplico; St. John Ne-
gro Baptist; Olive Grove Negro Baptist; Union S.B.C.; Salem
M.E.S., Salem; Evergreen S.B.C., Evergreen; St. Luke C.M.E.,
Ephesus S.B.C.; Prosser's Pent. Holiness Chapel; Heyward A.M.E.
Chapel, Poston; St. Mark A.M.E.; St. Matthews Negro Baptist,
Pamplico; Mt. Zion S.B.C.; Mt. Zion Negro Baptist, Hyman; Aim-
well Negro Baptist; House of Prayer-undenom.; Little Bethel
Free Will Baptist; Lake City Church of God; Trinity A.M.E., Hy-
man; Bethany Pent. Holiness Church; Hebron S.B.C.; Bethsadia
Prot. Meth., Effingham; Bethlehem M.E.S.; Trinity M.E.S., Kings-
burg; Goodland A.M.E.; Elizabeth Negro Baptist; Piney Grove A.
M.E.; St. Peter's Holiness-Believers' Holiness Church, Florence;
Community Pent. Holiness Chapel; Olanta Presbyterian, Olanta;
Olanta M.E.S., Olanta; Mt. Olive Pent. Holiness Church of God
of America (Negro), Florence; Timmonsville Presbyterian, Tim-
monsville; Willow Creek Prot. Methodist; Bethel Original Free
Will Baptist; Lake City S.B.C.; Mispah S.B.C., Mars Bluff Com-
munity; Nazareth A.M.E., Johnsonville; St. Beulah Holiness-Be-
lievers Holiness; White Chapel-Free Will Baptist (Negro); Beu-
lah S.B.C., Hyman; Effingham Presbyterian, Effingham; New Hope
Free Will Baptist; Johnsonville S.B.C.; Mt. Moriah Free Will
Baptist; Old Johnsonville M.E.S.; Mt. Elim Free Will Baptist;
New Prospect M.E.S.; Pamplico First S.B.C., Pamplico; Mill
Branch A.M.E.; Bethel A.M.E.; Peniel S.B.C.; Mt. Zion M.E.(Ne-
gro), Timmonsville; Zion Temple-Pent. Holiness, Timmonsville;
Bethlehem Baptist (Negro), Timmonsville; Mt. Zion C.M.E.; Bow-
ers Chapel C.M.E.; Bethel S.B.C.; Scranton Free Will Baptist,
Scranton; Union Grove Negro Baptist; Welch A.M.E. Chapel, Tim-
monsville; Ebernezer No. 2 Negro Baptist; Timmonsville S.B.C.,
Timmonsville; Mt. Rouah Negro Baptist; Sardis S.B.C.; Jordan

Chapel-Free Will Baptist (Negro); Beth Israel Jewish Congregation-Reform, Florence; Tabernacle M.E.S.; Friendship M.E.S.;
Pisgah M.E.S.; Savannah Grove Negro Baptist; Liberty M.E.S.;
Bay Branch Free Will Baptist; Timmonsville M.E.S., Timmonsville;
Hopewell Presbyterian; Cartersville S.B.C.; Mt. Carmen Northern
Baptist Convention (Negro).
Greenville County: Pendleton Street S.B.C., Greenville; Holmes
Memorial-Pent. Holiness, Greenville; Earle Street S.B.C.,
Greenville; Triune M.E.S., Greenville; First Church of Christ-
Scientist Christian Science, Greenville; First Presbyterian,
Greenville; Associate Reform Presbyterian, Greenville; River-
side S.B.C., Greenville; Augusta Road S.B.C., Greenville; Rock
Creek Negro Baptist; Popular Spring Negro Baptist, Simpsonville;
St. James Memorial-Prot. Epis., Greenville; Buncombe Street M.
E.S., Greenville; Third Presbyterian, Greenville; Central S.B.
C., Greenville; Trinity Lutheran, Greenville; Greenville First
S.B.C., Greenville; Christ Church-Prot. Epis., Greenville; St.
Andrews-Prot. Epis., Greenville; Bethel M.E.S., Greenville;
Morgan Memorial S.B.C., Greenville; Fourth Presbyterian, Green-
ville; Poe Mill S.B.C., Greenville; Poe Mill M.E.S., Greenville;
Brandou M.E.S., Greenville; St. Paul M.E.S., Greenville; Monga-
han Baptist S.B.C., Greenville; Woodside M.E.S., Greenville;
Monaghan M.E.S., Greenville; St. Mary's Catholic, Greenville;
Choice Street M.E.S., Greenville; Mills Mill M.E.S., Green-
ville; Dunean M.E.S., Greenville; Judson M.E.S., Greenville;
St. George Greek Orthodox, Greenville; First Church of Christ
(Disciples of Christ)-Non-denom., Greenville; Dunean S.B.C.,
Greenville; Judson S.B.C., Greenville; Poinsette S.B.C., Green-
ville; West Greenville S.B.C., Greenville; Monaghan Presbyter-
ian, Greenville; Beth Israel Synagogue-Orthodox, Greenville;
Union Bleachery S.B.C., Greenville; St. John M.E.S., Greenville;
Washington Avenue S.B.C., Greenville; Welcome S.B.C., Green-
ville; Park Place S.B.C., Greenville; Woodside Baptist, Green-
ville; Temple of Israel-Orthodox, Greenville; Sans Souci S.B.C.
Greenville; Emmanuel S.B.C., Greenville; Franklin S.B.C.,
Greenville; Church of Good-General Assembly, Greenville; Cal-
vary S.B.C., Greenville; St. Marks M.E. Church, Greenville.
Greenwood County: Connie Maxwell Orphanage S.B.C., Greenwood,
Bradley A.R.P., Bradley; Pine Grove A.M.E.; Main Street M.E.S.,
Greenwood; Lowell Street M.E.S., Greenwood; South Greenwood
M.E.S., Greenwood; Galloway Memorial M.E.S., Greenwood; First
Christian Church-Disciples of Christ, Greenwood; Our Lady of
Lourdes-Roman Catholic, Greenwood; Rock Church Presbyterian;
Greenwood A.R.P., Greenwood; Greenwood First Presbyterian,
Greenwood; Lockhart Negro Baptist; Immanuel Evang. Lutheran
Church, Greenwood; Greenwood First S.B.C., Greenwood; West Side
S.B.C., Greenwood; Jordan Street S.B.C., Greenwood; South
Greenwood S.B.C., Greenwood; Greenwood South Main Street S.B.C.
Greenwood; Church of Resurrection-Prot. Epis., Greenwood; Beth-
lehem M.E.S., Coronaca; Asbury M.E.S., Verdery; Ninety-Six
Presbyterian, Ninety Six; Coronaca S.B.C., Coronaca; Siloam

S.B.C.; Bradley S.B.C., Bradley; Kinards M.E.S.; St. Pauls
M.E.S., Ninety Six; Cedar Springs A.R.P.; Mt. Zion A.M.E.;
Cross Road Negro Baptist; St. Paul A.M.E., Cokesbury; Mt. Si-
nai; Friendship Negro Baptist; White Oak Negro Baptist, Cokes-
bury; Bethlehem Negro Baptist, Ninety Six; Big Mt. Zion Negro
Baptist; Macedonia C.M.E.; Dunham Temple C.M.E., Greenwood;
Marshall Negro Baptist Chapel; Mt. Zion Negro Baptist; Trinity
M.E., Greenwood; Cedar Grove A.M.E., Bradley; Troy A.R.P.,
Troy; Duke Street S.B.C., Ninety Six; Horeb S.B.C.; Troy S.B.
C.; Greenville Presbyterian; Walnut Grove S.B.C.; Hodges Pres-
byterian, Hodges; St. James-Prot. Epis., Ninety Six; Church of
God, Ware Shoals; Friendship Pent. Holiness; Mt. Lebanon M.E.
S.; Epworth Tabernacle M.E.S., Epworth; Ware Shoals M.E.S.,
Ware Shoals; Troy M.E.S., Troy; Ninety Six First S.B.C., Nine-
ty Six; Hodges S.B.C., Hodges; Donalds Creek Negro Baptist;
Mulberry Negro Baptist; Friendship A.M.E., Troy; Second Negro
Baptist, Troy; New China Negro Baptist, Troy; Piney Grove A.M.
E.; Enoree Negro Baptist; Mt. Pisgah A.M.E., Greenwood; Taber-
nacle Negro Baptist, Greenwood; Hodges M.E.S., Hodges; Moun-
tain Creek S.B.C.; Fellowship S.B.C.; Mt. Moriah S.B.C.; Memo-
rial Presbyterian, Ware Shoals; Bethel M.E.S.; Pent. Holiness,
Ninety Six; Cambridge M.E.S., Ninety Six; Salem M.E.S., God-
sey; Tranquil M.E.S.; Rehoboth M.E.S.; Turkey Creek S.B.C.;
Bold Spring S.B.C.; Ware Shoals S.B.C., Ware Shoals; Trinity
M.E. (Negro), Ninety Six; Wesley Chapel M.E. (Negro); Allen
A.M.E. Chapel; Weston A.M.E. Chapel, Greenwood; Mt. Pleasant
A.M.E., Ninety Six; Young's Negro Baptist Chapel; Mt. Pisgah
Negro Baptist; Antioch Negro Baptist; Mt. Olive Negro Baptist;
Damascus Negro Baptist; Flint Hill Negro Baptist; Morris Negro
Baptist Chapel, Greenwood; Mt. Moriah Negro Baptist; Damascus
S.B.C.; Old Cokesbury M.E.S., Cokesbury.
Hampton County: Second Thankful Negro Baptist; New Castle Negro
Baptist; Steep Bottom S.B.C.; St. Marks A.M.E., Shirley; Cy-
press S.B.C.; St. John's M.E.S., Garnett; Sand Hill Baptist,
M.E.S.; Harmony Presbyterian, Crocketville; Sandy Drain Prim.
Baptist; Mt. Carmel M.E.S.; Mill Creek Primitive Baptist; San-
ders Branch Primitive Baptist; Deep Branch S.B.C.; St. Paul
Negro Baptist; Jackson Branch Negro Baptist; Shady Grove Ne-
gro Baptist; Cedar Grove Disciples of Christ; First African
Baptist; Jones Chapel C.M.E.; Pilgrim's Ford Negro Baptist,
Yemassee; Cherry Grove Disciples of Christ; Heavenly Rest-
Prot. Epis; Estill Presbyterian, Estill; Estill M.E.S., Estill;
Miley Community-undenom., Miley; Brunson Christian-Disciples
of Christ, Brunson; Spring Hill Negro Baptist; Mt. Zion Negro
Baptist; Second Negro Baptist, Brunson; St. Paul's Primitive
Baptist; Bethlehem Negro Baptist, Early Branch; Zion Fair Ne-
gro Baptist; Scotia S.B.C., Scotia; St. John's A.M.E., Brun-
son; Brunson M.E.S., Brunson; Martin Temple, C.M.E., Estill;
Varnville Christian-Disciples of Christ, Varnville; Faith Chap-
el-Prot.Epis., Estill; Hampton S.B.C., Hampton; Prospect United Evang. Lutheran, Early Branch; Varnville M.E.S., Varnville;

Luray Christian Church-Disciples of Christ, Luray; Black Creek
Primitive Baptist; Mt. Olive Negro Baptist; Varnville S.B.C.,
Varnville; Nixville S.B.C.; Brunson S.B.C., Brunson; Hopewell
S.B.C.; Prince William Primitive Baptist; Samaritan Negro Baptist, Varnville; Bethlehem Negro Baptist; Huspah Negro Baptist;
Hampton M.E.S., Hampton; Furman M.E.S., Furman; Mt. Zion A.M.
E.; Brunson C.M.E. Chapel, Brunson; St. Peter's A.M.E., Estill; Lawtonville S.B.C., Estill; Blount C.M.E. Chapel, Varnville; Stafford S.B.C.; Furman S.B.C., Furman; St. John's Negro Baptist; Sinai Negro Baptist; First Estill Negro Baptist,
Estill; Ridgeville S.B.C.; Antioch Christian Church-Disciples
of Christ; Harmonia Negro Baptist; Black Swamp M.E.S.; Wilkerson Negro Baptist; Jerusalem Negro Baptist, Early Branch; Stoney Creek Independent Presbyterian, McPhersonville; Hickory
Grove S.B.C.; Whippy Swamp Primitive Baptist; Sandy Run Baptist; St. Luke or Blake A.M.E., Blake Plantation; Eferson Negro Baptist; Lovewell Negro Baptist; Sweet Rose Negro Baptist;
Union Negro Baptist, Valentine; Thompson A.M.E. Chapel; Long
Branch Negro Baptist; Emanuel R.M.U.E.; Macedonia Negro Bap-
tist; St. Peter's A.M.E.; Wish Well Negro Baptist, Gifford;
Annie Laurie Negro Baptist; St. Luke Negro Baptist; Sand Hill
Negro Baptist; King's Branch Negro Baptist; Happy Home Negro
Baptist, Scotia; Mt. Pleasant A.M.E.; Hopewell C.M.E.; Good
Hope Negro Baptist; Mt. Zion Negro Baptist; Old Thankful Ne-
gro Baptist; Kenyon Negro Baptist; Ebernezer A.M.E.; New Hope
Negro Baptist; Gaines Hill Negro Baptist; Good Will Negro Bap-
tist; Second Point Savannah Negro Baptist; Silver Hill Negro
Baptist; Browning Disciples of Christ; Early Branch M.E.S.,
Early Branch; Beach Branch (Coosawhatchie) S.B.C.; Roberts-
ville Baptist; House of Prayer for All.
Horry County: Red Oak S.B.C.; Good Hope S.B.C.; Beaulah S.B.C.,
Daisy; Mt. Leon S.B.C., Hammond; Pleasant Hill S.B.C., Hammond,
Simpson Creek Prim. Baptist, Daisy; Buck Creek S.B.C., Longs;
Ebernezer M.E.S., Longs; Pleasant Plains S.B.C., Brookville;
Mt. Ararot S.B.C., Ocean Drive; Salem S.B.C., Cook Springs;
Cedar Creek M.E.S., Little River; Cool Springs M.E.S., Cool
Springs; First S.B.C., Myrtle Beach; Aynor M.E.S., Aynor;
Pleasant Meadow S.B.C., Green Sea; Collins S.B.C., Burgess;
White Oak Bay S.B.C., Conway; Berea S.B.C., Cool Springs; Ju-
niper Bay S.B.C.; Cane Branch S.B.C., Allsbrook; Sweet Water
Branch S.B.C., Savannah Bluff; Pee Dee Prim. Bapt.; Green Sea
S.B.C., Green Sea; Hickory Grove S.B.C.; Bayboro S.B.C., Bay-
boro; New Light S.B.C., Gurley; Pine Grove S.B.C., Conway;
Galivant's Ferry S.B.C., Galivants Ferry; New Yome No. 2 S.B.
C., Galivants Ferry; Cedar Grove S.B.C., Cedar Grove; Conway
First S.B.C., Conway; Pee Dee S.B.C., Pawley Swamp; Ridgefield
S.B.C., Conway; Grace S.B.C. Chapel, Bucksport; Antioch Church
of Christ S.B.C., Galivants Ferry; Maple S.B.C.; Pleasant Hill
Prim. Baptist, Myrtle Beach; Oakie Swamp S.B.C.; Mt. Ariel
Freewill Baptist, Homewood; Aynor S.B.C., Aynor; Red Hill M.E.
S., Galivants Ferry; Conway M.E.S., Conway; Antioch M.E.S.,

Willow Springs M.E.S.; Mineral Springs M.E.S.; Centenary M.E.
S., Savannah Bluff; El Bethel M.E.S.; Union M.E.S., Toddville;
Brown's Swamp; Minutes of Waccamaw Circuit 1836-1855; First
Presbyterian, Myrtle Beach; Waccamaw Presbyterian; Skippers
Chapel-Undenom., Juniper Bay; Pentecostal Holiness, Conway;
Bayboro Presbyterian, Bayboro; Loris Presbyterian, Loris;
Greenwood S.B.C., Conway; Union Valley S.B.C., Wampee; Bethle-
hem S.B.C., Shell; Carolina S.B.C., Green Sea; Tilley Swamp
S.B.C., Tilley Swamp; Sharon S.B.C., Hand; United S.B.C., Hand;
Socastee M.E.S., Socastee; Zoan S.B.C.O., Lake Swamp; Durants
M.E.S., Hickory Grove; Loris S.B.C., Loris; Loris M.E.S., Lo-
ris; Cherry Hill S.B.C., Daisy; Macedonia S.B.C.; Free Light-
Ind.Mis.Baptist, Daisy; New Home No. 1, S.B.C., Allsbrook;
Sweet Home S.B.C., Longs; Sandy Plains M.E.S., Galivants Ferry,
Rehobeth M.E.S., Galivants Ferry; Rehobeth S.B.C., Aynor; Mt.
Hermon S.B.C., Aynor; Jordanville M.E.S., Jordanville; High
Point S.B.C., Jordanville; Pisgah M.E.S., Aynor; Kingston Pres-
byterian, Conway; Mitchell Mis.Bap. (Negro), Green Sea; St.
Elizabeth Mis.Bap., Aynor; New Hope A.M.E., Bayboro; Chesterfield Mis. Bap. (Negro), Wampee; St. John Free Will Bap. (Ne-
gro), Aynor; St. Joseph No. 2 Mis.Baptist, Wampee; Pent. Holi-
ness (Negro), Bucksport; Free Vine Negro Baptist, Conway; St.
John's Pent. Holiness (Negro), Conway; Mt. Zion Holiness (Ne-
gro), Conway; Savannah Bluff Pentecostal Holiness (Negro), Sa-
vannah Bluff; Salem A.M.E. Zion, Bucksport; Bethel A.M.E., Con-
way; St. James A.M.E., Conway; Mt. Zion A.M.E., Wampee; Poplar
A.M.E., Wampee; Iona M.E.S.; Mt. Zion A.M.E.; St. John A.M.E.,
Chestnut Cross Roads; Ebenezer A.M.E., Toddville; St. James A.
M.E., Free Woods; Browns Chapel A.M.E. Zion, Bucksville; Cher-
ry Hill-Carey Lott Mis. Baptist, Conway; Mt. Pisgah Baptist,
Conway; Jerusalem Negro Mis. Baptist, Bucksport; Bethlehem
Mis.Baptist, Conway; Mt. Moriah Mis. Baptist, Bucksport; Salem
Mis.Baptist, "Free Woods";; St. Peter Mis.Baptist (Negro),
"Free Woods"; Mt. Olive Mis.Baptist (Negro), Bayboro; Doctor's
Chapel Free Will Baptist (Negro), Conway; St. Paul's Mis. Bap.
(Negro), Conway; Hemingway Chapel A.M.E., Conway; Sandy Grove
Mis. Baptist (Negro), Myrtle Beach; Mt. Olive A.M.E., Myrtle
Beach; St. Paul A.M.E., Little River; St. Peter's A.M.E., Cool
Springs; St. Matthew's Mis. Baptist (Negro), Cool Springs; Mc-
Neal Chapel-Mis.Bap. (Negro), Allsbrook; Little Lamb-Free Will
Baptist, "Caw Ford"; Hill's Chapel-Mis. Bap.(Negro), Cedar
Creek; Hickory Grove-Mis.Bap.(Negro), Cedar Creek; Oak Grove
S.B.C., Fair Bluff; Spring Branch S.B.C., Fair Bluff; Floyds
M.E.S., Floyds; Wannamaker S.B.C., Duford Cross Roads; Mt.
Olive S.B.C., Mt. Olive; Bakers Chapel S.B.C., Conway; New
Hope Independent Baptist, Conway; Wampee M.E.S., Wampee;
Browns Chapel-Baptist, Conway; Little River M.E.S., Little
River; Homewood M.E.S., Conway; Salem M.E.S., Conway; Cedar
Creek S.B.C., Nichols; Pleasant View S.B.C., Green Sea; He-
bron M.E.S.; Zion Ch. M.E.S., Galivants Ferry; Poplar M.E.S.,
Maple.

Jasper County: Church of Jesus Christ of Latter Day Saints-
Mormon, Ridgeland; Ridgeland S.B.C., Ridgeland; Lovely Hill
Negro Baptist, Ridgeland; Pine Level S.B.C.; Black Swamp S.B.
C., Robertville.
Kershaw County: Camden S.B.C., Camden; Our Lady of Perpetual
Help-Roman Catholic, Camden; Lyttleton Street M.E.S., Camden;
Trinity Methodist (Negro), Camden; Second Presbyterian (Negro)
Camden; Bethesda Presbyterian, Camden; Mt. Moriah Negro Bap-
tist, Camden; Grace Protestant Episcopal-Prot.Epis., Camden;
Kershaw M.E.S., Kershaw; Kershaw First S.B.C., Kershaw; Church
of God-Holiness, Camden; Union S.B.C.; Harmony S.B.C.; Good
Aim Negro Baptist; Shady Grove A.M.E.; Blaney S.B.C.; Spring
Vale S.B.C.; Ebernezer M.E.S.; Shiloh M.E. (Negro); Mt. Josh-
ua M.E.(Negro); Beulah M.E.S.; Concord S.B.C.; St. Matthews
M.E.(Negro); Hermitage S.B.C.; Antioch S.B.C.; Temple Bethel-
Hebrew Benevolent Society, Camden; Bethlehem Negro Baptist,
Lugoff; Gum Springs Negro Baptist; Pentecostal Holiness, Cam-
den; Chapel Church-Prot.Epis., Camden; Emanuel M.E. (Negro),
Camden; Belmont Negro Baptist, Westville; Unity Negro Baptist,
Kershaw; Bingham Chapel A.M.E., Westville; Sardis Negro Bap-
tist, Camden; Edward's Chapel A.M.E. Zion, Camden; Betheny
(Old Hickory Head) Baptist S.B.C., Westville; Rowan Presbyte-
rian, Lugoff; Kershaw Presbyterian, Kershaw; Liberty Hill Pres-
byterian; Swift Creek S.B.C., Boykin; Tabernacle Negro Bap-
tist; Second Presbyterian (Negro), Liberty Hill; First Baptist
(New Light) (Negro), Liberty Hill; Mt. Olivet S.B.C.; Mt.
Prospect M.E.; Clinton A.M.E. Zion, Kershaw; Macedonia Negro
Baptist; St. Stephen Negro Baptist; Mt. Zion Neg. Baptist;
Broom Hill (Green Hill) Negro Baptist; Mt. Pilgrim Negro Bap-
tist; Nazareth Negro Baptist; Mt. Zion Negro Baptist, Camden;
Wesley Chapel-M.E.; Bethune S.B.C., Bethune; Pine Tree Presbyterian, Cassatt; Hanging Rock M.E.S.; Wateree S.B.C., Water-
ee Mill Village; St. Paul M.E.; Red Hill Negro Baptist; Sandy
Level Negro Baptist, Bethune; Cassatt S.B.C.; Refuge S.B.C.,
Beaver Creek Presbyterian; Abney S.B.C.; Sweet Home Negro Bap-
tist; Kershaw Second S.B.C.; Kershaw First Negro Baptist, Ker-
shaw; Ephesus First Baptist (Negro); Smyrna M.E.; Zion Hill,
DeKalb; Rock Hill M.E.; Bethune M.E.S., Bethune; Bethune Pres-
byterian, Bethune; New Hope S.B.C.; Providence S.B.C.; Damas-
cus M.E.S., Westville; Macedonia M.E., Camden; Buffalo S.B.C.;
St. Paul M.E.S.; Free Will Baptist, Camden; Malvern Hill S.B.
C.; Malvern Hill-Prot.Epis.; Beaver Dam S.B.C.; Rock Hill M.
E.S.; Smyrna M.E.S.; DeKalb S.B.C., DeKalb; Mt. Zion Negro
Baptist; Mt. Pilgrim Negro Baptist; Flat Rock Negro Baptist;
Second Calvary Negro Baptist; Cedar Rock Negro Baptist; St.
John Negro Baptist; Mill Creek Negro Baptist, Bethune; Mt.
Joshua Negro Baptist; Hyco Negro Baptist; Pate Mission M.E.
(Negro); Weeping Mary Negro Baptist; Sanders Creek Negro Bap-
tist.
Lancaster County: Free Will African Methodist-A.M.E. Independ-
ent Church of God; St. Paul A.M.E., Lancaster; Zion Pilgrim

Baptist (Negro); Frazer's Temple-A.M.E.Zion; Zion Methodist
M.E.S.; Pentecostal Holiness Church, Lancaster; David's Stand
A.M.E.Zion; Hopewell M.E.S.; Union S.B.C.; Pleasant Grove-Na-
tional Baptist Convention; White Bluff S.B.C.; Lancaster Sec-
ond S.B.C., Lancaster; Tabernacle M.E.S.; White Springs S.B.C.
Charlesboro S.B.C.; Bethlehem S.B.C.; Pentecostal Holiness
Church of Kershaw; Christ Church-Prot.Epis., Lancaster; Fork
Hill S.B.C.; Oak Hill S.B.C.; Rich Hill S.B.C.; Flat Creek
S.B.C.; Flint Ridge S.B.C.; Pleasant Hill S.B.C., Pleasant
Hill; Gill's Creek-A.R.P.; Heath Springs Presbyterian, Heath
Springs; Douglas Presbyterian; Lancaster; Lancaster A.R.P.,
Lancaster; Lancaster Presbyterian, Lancaster; Pleasant Hill-
A.R.P.; Belair M.E.S.; Camp Creek (Lower) M.E.S.; Mt. Zion A.
M.E.Zion, Lancaster; St. Luke M.E.S.; Van Wyck M.E.S., Van
Wyck; Calvary S.B.C., Lancaster; Salem M.E.S., Heath Springs;
Grace M.E.S., Lancaster; Old Waxhaw Presbyterian; Lancaster
First S.B.C., Lancaster; New Hope S.B.C.; Center Grove S.B.C.;
Heath Springs S.B.C., Heath Springs; Pleasant Ridge Presbyter-
ian, Lancaster; Bethel S.B.C.; Antioch S.B.C.; High Point S.
B.C.; Tirzah (Lower) Presbyterian; Shiloh A.R.P.; Unity A.R.P.
Camp Creek S.B.C.; Six Mile Presbyterian; Midway S.B.C.; Van
Wyck Presbyterian, Van Wyck; Lancaster M.E.S., Lancaster;
First Washington-Union Bright Light Assn. (Negro), Lancaster;
Warrior's Chapel-A.M.E.Zion; Centennial A.M.E.Zion; Carup
Creek-A.M.E.Zion; Spring Hill A.M.E.Zion; Bethlehem A.M.E.;
Pleasant Hill A.M.E.Zion, Heath Springs; Salem A.M.E.Zion;
Spring Hill A.M.E.Zion; North Corner-A.M.E.Zion; Steel Hill
A.M.E.Zion; Mt. Moriah A.M.E.Zion; Bright Light Negro Baptist,
Pleasant Hill; Black Jack Negro Baptist, Kershaw; Spring Hill
S.B.C.; Osceola M.E.S.; Beaver Creek S.B.C.; Taxahaw S.B.C.,
Taxahaw; Pleasant Plain S.B.C.; Pentecostal Holiness, Lancas-
ter; The Church of God-The Ch. of God Holiness, Lancaster;
New Bethel or Second S.B.C., Lancaster; Ebernezer S.B.C., St.
John Negro Baptist; St. Paul Negro Baptist; El Bethel A.M.E.
Zion; Mt. Carmel A.M.E.Zion; Gold Hill A.M.E.Zion; Holiness
(or Sanctified)-Holiness; Cross Roads Negro Baptist; New Zion
Negro Baptist; Gethsemane Negro Baptist; New Hope A.M.E.Zion;
White Oak A.M.E.Zion.

Laurens County: Ora A.R.P., Ora; Providence A.R.P., Clinton;
Laurens A.R.P., Laurens; St. John's Evan. Lutheran, Clinton;
Pentecostal Holiness, Goldville; Reedy Grove-Pent; Pentecostal
Holiness; Church of God Holiness; Langston S.B.C.; Poplar
Springs S.B.C.; Durbin Creek S.B.C.; Warrior Creek S.B.C.; Ra-
bun S.B.C.; Highland Home S.B.C.; Friendship S.B.C.; New Har-
mony S.B.C.; Cedar Grove S.B.C.; Mount Olive S.B.C.; Gray
Court S.B.C., Gray Court; First S.B.C., Laurens; Laurens Sec-
ond S.B.C., Laurens; Lucas Ave. S.B.C., Watts Mill; First Bap-
tist S.B.C., Clinton; Lydia S.B.C., Clinton; Goldville S.B.C.,
Goldville; Hurricane Baptist Church of Christ; Mountville S.
B.C., Mountville; Cross Hill S.B.C., Cross Hill; Bethabara S.
B.C.; Princeton S.B.C., Princeton; Mt. Gallagher S.B.C.; Eno-

ree S.B.C., Enoree; Lanford S.B.C., Lanford; Holly Grove Baptist; Hopewell M.E.S.; King's Chapel-M.E.S.; Patterson's Chapel-M.E.S., Lanford; Princeton M.E.S., Princeton; Pentecostal Holiness; Trinity M.E.S.; Gray Court M.E.S., Gray Court; Owings M.E.S., Ownings; Mt. Bethel M.E.S.; Shiloh M.E.S.; Bramlett's M.E.S.; Cross Hill M.E.S., Cross Hill; Epworth M.E.S., Goldville; Bethlehem M.E.S.; Bailey Memorial M.E.S., Clinton; Lydia M.E.S., Lydia Mill; Leesville M.E.S.; St. James M.E.S., Watts Mill; Central M.E.S.; Little River Presbyterian; Duncan's Creek Presbyterian; Rocky Springs Presbyterian; Liberty Springs Presbyterian, Cross Hill; Friendship Presbyterian; Bethany Presbyterian; First Presbyterian, Clinton; New Harmony Presbyterian; Shady Grove Presbyterian; First Presbyterian, Laurens; Todd Memorial Presbyterian, Laurens; Lydia Presbyterian, Clinton; Goldville Presbyterian, Goldville; Lisbon Presbyterian; Mountville Presbyterian, Mountville; Dorroh Presbyterian, Gray Court; Presbyterian Church, Owings; Watts Mill Presbyterian, Watts Mill; Mt. Pleasant S.B.C.; New Prospect S.B.C., Madden; New Harmony M.E.S.; Laurel Hill Negro; St. Paul's Negro Baptist, Laurens; St. John's Negro Baptist; White Plain Negro Baptist, Mountville; Flat Ruff Negro Baptist; Zion Hill Negro Baptist; Hopewell Negro Baptist; Center Rabun Negro Baptist, Gray Court; Church of God-Evening Light (Negro), Laurens; Bethel A. M.E., Laurens; Mt. Pisgah Presbyterian (Negro), Laurens; Church of the Epiphany-Prot.Epis., Laurens; Sandy Springs M.E.S.; Thornwell Memorial Presbyterian, Clinton; First M.E.S., Laurens; Dials M.E.S., Laurens; Rock Bridge Presbyterian; Old Fields Presbyterian, Ora; Chestnut Ridge S.B.C.; Memorial Presbyterian Church, Ware Shoals; Broad Street Methodist, Clinton; Soul's Chapel M.E.S.; Calvary S.B.C., Clinton Mill; Waterloo S.B.C., Waterloo; Beaverdam S.B.C.; Rocky Springs (Negro); Cedar Grove (Negro); Good Hope Negro Baptist; Bethel A.M.E.; Smyrna A.M.E.; New Hope A.M.E., Mountville; Head Springs A.R.P.; Mount Zion Negro Baptist; New Grove Negro Baptist; Pitt's Presbyterian (Negro); Brown's Tabernacle-Church of God (Negro), Laurens; Duncan's Creek Negro Baptist; Union S.B.C.

Lee County: Bishopville Presbyterian, Bishopville; Lynchburg Presbyterian, Lynchburg; Bishopville S.B.C., Bishopville; Lynchburg S.B.C., Lynchburg; St. Philip's Prot.Epis.; Bethany M.E.S.; Mt. Zion Presbyterian; Bishopville (New Bethlehem) M.E.S., Bishopville; St. Matthew A.M.E., Lynchburg; Warren Chapel C.M.E.; Lynchburg M.E.S., Lynchburg; Bishopville Presbyterian (Negro), Bishopville; Savannah Advent Christian Church; Liberty Hill S. B.C.; Hebron M.E.S.; St. Phillip's A.M.E.; Ashland M.E.S.; Scope Avenue A.M.E.; Cedar Creek S.B.C.; Turkey Creek Presbyterian; Pate's Chapel-Negro Baptist; Little Brown Chapel-Reformed Mis. Baptist; Shaw's Mission A.M.E.; Bethany M.E.S.; St. Matthew M.E.S.; Smart Mission A.M.E.; High Hill-True Lights Church of Christ; Jerusalem Negro Baptist; Gum Springs Negro Baptist; New Hope Negro Baptist, Lucknow; Mt. Zion C.M.E., Bishopville, St. Matthew Negro Baptist; Little Zion Negro Baptist, New Jeru-

salem Negro Baptist; Salem M.E.S.; Negro-Interdenominational;
Lucknow M.E.S., Lucknow; Mt. Pleasant Primitive Baptist; Sandy
Grove C.M.E.; New Hope Presbyterian; Kelly Church of God Holi-
ness; Mt. Herman Negro Baptist, Bishopville; Wayside S.B.C.,
Concord Methodist Protestant; Liberty Negro Baptist; Ebernezer
C.M.E.; Mispah S.B.C.; Church of God-Holiness (Negro); Sanders
Bluff M.E. (Negro); Pleasant Hill-Meth.Protestant; Calvary-All
Saints Holiness; Savannah Negro Baptist, Elliott; Philadelphia
M.E. (Negro); St. Paul No. 2 M.E. (Negro); Mt. Olive-A.M.E.;
Elizabeth Negro Baptist; Marshall M.E.S.; Spring Hill A.M.E.;
Hepzibah Presbyterian; St. John M.E.S.; Bethlehem Negro Bap-
tist; Unionville ("Flemmon's Shade" 1869) A.M.E.; St. John A.M.
E.; Mt. Moriah M.E. (Negro); St. Luke M.E.S., Elliott; Elliott
S.B.C., Elliott; St. Andrew's Chapel-Holiness Church of God;
Mt. Sinai Presbyterian (Negro); Mt. Lisbon Presbyterian (Negro);
New Bethel Negro Baptist; New Zion A.M.E.; Mt. Beulah M.E. (Ne-
gro); Emanuel A.M.E.; St. Mark Negro Baptist; New Bethel A.M.E.;
Barnettville Negro Baptist; St. Paul No. 1-M.E.(Negro); New
Heaven; Green Bay Negro Baptist; King Emanuel Negro Baptist;
Rembert M.E.S.; Bethlehem Negro Presbyterian; Mt. Pleasant A.M.
E.; Pate's Grove-Holiness Church of God (Negro); St. John's
Catholic-Roman Catholic, Bishopville; Bishopville Hebrew Congre-
gation-Orthodox, Bishopville.
Lexington County: St. Stephen's Unit.Evang.Lutheran, Lexington;
Pisgah Unit.Evang.Lutheran; Mt. Hermon Unit.Evang.Lutheran; Mt.
Hebron M.E.S.; Red Bank M.E.S., Red Bank; Mt. Horeb M.E.S.;
Red Bank S.B.C., Red Bank; Lexington S.B.C., Lexington; Old
Lexington S.B.C.; Round Hill S.B.C.; Mt. Pleasant Negro Baptist;
Providence Evang.Luth.(Negro); Mt. Zion A.M.E.; Nazareth Evang.
Luth.; St. James United Evan.Luth., Red Bank; Mt. Olive Evang.
Luth., Irmo; Zion Unit.Lutheran; Lexington M.E.S., Lexington;
St. John's Unit.Evang.Luth.; Pilgrim Evang.Luth.; Bethany Unit.
Evang.Luth.; St. David's Evang.Luth; Cayce M.E.S., Cayce; First
S.B.C., West Columbia; Cayce S.B.C., Cayce; Mt. Tabor Unit.
Evang.Luth., W. Columbia; Holy Trinity Evang.Luth., W. Columbia;
Swansea S.B.C., Swansea; Oak Grove M.E.S.; Mt. Pleasant Negro
Baptist, Swansea; Zion Holiness (Negro), Gaston; Swansea M.E.S.,
Swansea; Calvary M.E.S.; Sardis S.B.C.; Good Shepherd Evang.
Luth., Swansea; Ebernezer M.E.S.; Kings Grove S.B.C.; Pelion
M.E.S., Pelion; Hall Hill Negro Baptist; Sandy Run S.B.C., Gas-
ton; Grace Evang.Luth., Gilbert; Brookland M.E.S., W. Columbia;
St. Peter's (Meetzes) Evan.Luth.; St. Matthews Evang.Luth.;
St. Paul's Evang.Luth.; Holy Trinity Evang.Luth., Pelion; Mt.
Horeb Evang.Luth., Chapin; Beulah M.E.S.; Shiloh M.E.S., Dixi-
ana; Gilbert M.E.S., Gilbert; St. John's Evang.Luth; Florence
S.B.C.; Cedar Grove Evang.Luth; Macedonia Negro Baptist, Irmo;
St. Paul's Negro Baptist, Lexington; Zion Hopewell Negro Bap-
tist; Bethel A.M.E., Lexington; St. Anne's Prot.Epis., Cayce;
Young Chapel A.M.E., Irmo; Emanuel A.M.E.; Pleasant Spring A.M.
E.; Irmo Presbyterian (Negro), Irmo; St. John C.M.E.; Calvary
A.M.E., Leesville; Friendship Negro Baptist, Leesville; Oak

Oak Grove S.B.C.; Steedman S.B.C., Steedman; Convent S.B.C.;
Pine Grove S.B.C.; Pond Branch M.E.S.; St. Jacobs Evang.Luth.;
Ebernezer M.E.S.; Leesville M.E.S., Leesville; St. John's M.E.
S., Batesburg; Boiling Springs M.E.S.; Shiloh M.E.S.; Bethel M.
E.S.; St. James Evang.Lutheran, Summit; St. John's Evang.Luth.;
(Poplar Spring) Enon-Evang.Luth.; Union Evang.Luth.; St. An-
drews Evang.Luth; Wittenburg Evang.Luth., Leesville; Emanuel
Evang.Luth., Long Branch Community; Leesville S.B.C., Leesville;
Faith Evang.Luth., Batesburg; Batesburg-Leesville Presbyterian,
Batesburg-Leesville; Harmony S.B.C.; Samaria S.B.C.; Batesburg
S.B.C., Batesburg; New Hope S.B.C.; Antioch S.B.C.; Sharon M.E.
S.; Olive Branch Negro Baptist, Batesburg; Mt. Zion Negro Bap-
tist, Batesburg; St. Matthew C.M.E., Leesville; Pisgah A.M.E.,
Dixiana; St. James C.M.E., Batesburg; St. Michaels (Blue Chur-
ch) Evang.Luth.; Salem M.E.S.; St. Peters Evang.Luth.; Bethle-
hem S.B.C.; Middleburg M.E.S., Batesburg; Middleburg S.B.C.,
Batesburg; Providence S.B.C.; St. Paul's Prot.Epis., Batesburg-
Leesville; Union Church M.E.S., Irmo; Pleasant Hill S.B.C.; W.
Columbia Presbyterian, W. Columbia; Batesburg Christian, Bates-
burg.
Marion County: Marion Presbyterian, Marion; Church of England,
Prot.Epis.; Beulah C.M.E., Mullins; Church of God-Holiness (Ne-
gro), Sellers; House of God-Pent.Holiness (Negro), Mullins; St.
John Free Will Baptist (Negro); Christ Church Negro Baptist;
Eulonia S.B.C.; St. John Free Will Baptist, Sellers; St. Paul
Negro Baptist, Mullins; Ebenezer A.M.E., Mullins; First M.E.S.,
Marion; Sellers M.E.S., Sellers; St. Matthews Negro Baptist;
Beulah Negro Baptist; St. Stephens Free Will Baptist; Buck
Swamp Freewill Baptist; Reedy Creek S.B.C.; New Life-Interde-
nom.; Friendship Negro Baptist, Nichols; Williams Chapel A.M.E.,
Nichols; Mt. Olive Negro Baptist, Mullins; St. John's Negro
Baptist; Nelson's Church-Holiness (Negro), Marion; Marion S.B.
C., Marion; First S.B.C., Nichols; St. John Negro Baptist, Ni-
chols; Page's Mill-Meth.Prot.; Church of God-Holiness; Zion
Hill-Apostolic Faith, Mullins; Church of England Chapel-Prot.
Epis., Sandy Bluff Section; Tabernacle-Interdenom., Mullins;
Mullins Presbyterian, Mullins; First S.B.C., Mullins; Centena-
ry M.E.S., Centenary; Church of the Advant-Prot.Epis., Marion;
Millers M.E.S.; Pleasant Hill M.E.S.; Spring Branch M.E.S.;
Olivet M.E.S., Rains; Tranquil M.E.S.; Friendship S.B.C.;
Spring Street Church M.E.S., Marion; Pee Dee S.B.C., Gresham;
Old Ark M.E.S.; Little Bethel S.B.C.; Wahee M.E.S.; Ariel S.B.
C.; Pine Grove S.B.C.; Emanuel S.B.C.; Oak Grove S.B.C.; Brit-
ton's Neck S.B.C.; Nebo S.B.C.; St. Paul Holiness Church-Ch. of
God (Negro), Marion; Bethlehem Negro Baptist, Marion; Carolina
Hol.-Ch.of God (Negro), Marion; Seventh Day Adventist (Negro),
Marion; St. James Reformed Methodist (Negro), Marion; Ellen
Chapel-Free Will Mission Holiness (Negro), Mullins; Mount Car-
mel Negro Baptist, Mullins; James Chapel-Fire Baptised Hol. of
God (Negro), Marion; Six Mt. Zion Negro Baptist, Mullins; Mt.
Pisgah Negro Baptist, Marion; St. John A.M.E., Marion; Bethel

Bethel A.M.E., Marion; Christ Church-Prot.Epis., Mullins;
Nichols S.B.C., Nichols; Gapway S.B.C.; Mill Creek Negro Bap-
tist, Mullins; Second Presbyterian (Negro), Marion; Old Field
Negro Baptist, Mullins; New Life Freewill Mission Holiness (Ne-
gro); Holy Church-Freewill Negro Baptist, Marion; Nazarene Ne-
gro Baptist, Mullins; West Marion Negro Baptist Chapel, Marion;
Center M.E.S., Mullins; Nichols M.E.S., Nichols; Terrells Bay
S.B.C., Centenery; St. Mary's A.M.E.; Bethlehem A.M.E.; Effing-
ham Negro Baptist; Jerusalem Negro Baptist, Rains; Centerville
Negro Baptist, Centenary; Pleasant Grove Negro Baptist; Red
Hill Negro Baptist; White Hill Negro Baptist; Libera-Carolina
Holiness (Negro); St. James A.M.E.; Bethel A.M.E.; Zion-Caro-
lina Holiness (Negro); Nebo M.E.S.; Shiloh M.E.S.; Church of
God, Marion; Macedonia M.E.S., Mullins; Union S.B.C.; Zion M.E.
S.; John Wesley A.M.E.; St. Paul Negro Baptist; Good Hope A.M.
E., Centenary; Soule's Chapel A.M.E.; Mt. Zion A.M.E., Zion;
Friendship A.M.E.; St. Paul-Fire Baptized Holiness (Negro),
Sellers; Weeping Willow Negro Baptist; Johnson Chapel-Fire Bap-
tized Hol.(Negro); Central M.E.S.; Soule's Chapel M.E.S., Gres-
ham.
Marlboro County: The Church of God-Holiness, Bennettsville; Pine
Grove M.E.S.; New Harley Negro Baptist; Evans A.M.E. Zion Chap-
el; Smyrna M.E.S.; Reedy Branch A.M.E.; Ashbury M.E.S.; Tatum
S.B.C., Tatum; Bethlehem M.E.S., Brownship Township; Shiloh M.
E.S., Bennettsville; St. Daniel's African Zion, Dunbar; Clio S.
B.C., Clio; Macedonia Negro Baptist, Bennettsville; Antioch M.
E.S.; Mt. Zion Tabernacle-Hol.(Negro), Bennettsville; Saren S.
B.C.; Second Negro Baptist, Bennettsville; Triumph-Hol.Ch.of
God (Negro); Salem S.B.C.; Mt. Olive Holiness Church (Negro),
Bennettsville; Beaver Dam Mis.Baptist, McColl; Hopewell M.E.S.,
Tatum; First Ch. of the Nazarene, Bennettsville; Freewill Bap-
tist; Ebenezer M.E.S.; Fair Plains A.M.E.; Level Green M.E.S.;
Boykin M.E.S.; Bruton's Form S.B.C.; St. Mathews Chapel-Free
Will Baptist (Negro); Tatum Presbyterian, Tatum; Hickory Grove
S.B.C.; St. Michael's Methodist (Negro), Bennettsville; Mt. Ta-
bor Negro Baptist; St. Peter's Chapel, A.M.E. Zion, Clio; Shi-
loh Baptist, Bennettsville; Tatum M.E.S., Tatum; Clio M.E.S.,
Clio; Hebron M.E.S.; McColl Presbyterian, McColl; Dunbar Pres-
byterian, Dunbar; Saw Mill Mis.Baptist; Parnassus M.E.S.; Mt.
Zion S.B.C.; New Zion A.M.E., Clio; St. Michael's Methodist
(Negro), Bennettsville; St. Paul's Prot.Epis., Bennettsville;
Mt. Hebron Pres. (Negro); Great Pee Dee Presbyterian; Clio
Presbyterian, Clio.
McCormick County: Pressley Memorial A.R.P., McCormick; McCormick
M.E.S., McCormick; McCormick S.B.C., McCormick; Asbury M.E.S.,
Meriwether; Bethlehem S.B.C., Clarks Hill; Plum Branch S.B.C.,
Plum Branch; Modoc S.B.C., Modoc; St. Paul M.E.S., Plum Branch;
Springfield A.M.E.; Bethany Negro Baptist, Meriwether; Hope-
well Negro Baptist; The McKissick Memo.-Undenom.-DeLaLowe
School; St. Stephens-Prot.Epis., Willington; Willington Bap-
tist-SBC-, Willington; Buffalo S.B.C.; Parksville SBC, Parks-

ville; Mt. Carmel Presbyterian, Mt. Carmel; Mt. Carmel A.R.P.,
Mt. Carmel; Laurel Grove Negro Baptist; Hosannah Negro Baptist,
Modoc; Holy Springs Negro Baptist; St.Mary A.M.E.; New Hope Ne-
gro Baptist; Harper's Chapel-Ch. of God, Mt. Carmel; Bethany
Negro Baptist, McCormick; Pine Grove A.M.E.; Bordeau M.E.S.,
Hopewell Presbyterian; Shiloh A.M.E.; Bethany S.B.C.; Republi-
can M.E.S.; Mt. Vernon M.E.S.; Long Cane A.R.P.; Spring Grove
Negro Baptist.

Newberry County: Sumner Memorial-Unit.Evang.Lutheran, Newberry,
Mayes Memorial-Lutheran, Newberry, Church of the Redeemer-Luth.,
Newberry; First S.B.C., Newberry; East Side S.B.C., Newberry;
West End S.B.C., Newberry; Oakland S.B.C., Newberry; Aveleigh
Presbyterian, Newberry; O'Neall Street M.E.S., Newberry; Epting
Memorial M.E.S., Newberry; Bethesda M.E.S., Newberry; Central
M.E.S., Newberry; Oakland M.E.S., Newberry A.R.P., Newberry;
St. Luke's Epis., Newberry; Bethlehem Lutheran, Pomaria; Can-
non's Creek A.R.P.; Central M.E.S., Newberry; Bush River Bap-
tist; Pleasant Grove A.M.E.; St. Matthew A.M.E.; Fairview Ne-
gro Baptist; Miller's Chapel A.M.E., Newberry; Calvary Presby-
terian, Newberry; St. Marks A.M.E.; Fellowship Negro Baptist;
Morris Chapel M.E.S., Pomaria; St. Johns Evang.Lutheran; Grace
Evang.Lutheran, Prosperity; Holy Trinity-Evang.Lutheran, Little
Mountain; Mt. Tabor Evang. Lutheran; Mt. Pleasant M.E.S.; Ebe-
nezer M.E.S.; Whitmire M.E.S., Whitmire; New Hope M.E.S.; Smyr-
na Presbyterian; Bethany Evang.Lutheran, Oakland Mill Village;
St. Matthews Evang.Luth; Mt. Hermon Evang.Luth., Peak; Unity
A.R.P.; Pomaria Evang.Luth., Pomaria; Prosperity S.B.C., Pros-
perity; Prosperity A.R.P., Prosperity; Bethlehem Negro Baptist,
Newberry; St. James A.M.E.; St. Paul A.M.E.; St. John Negro
Baptist; New Hope Negro Baptist; Metropolitan Negro Baptist;
Sims Chapel-Negro Baptist; Whitmire First S.B.C., Whitmire;
Zion M.E.S.; Whitmire Presbyterian, Whitmire; Bethel S.B.C.;
Saluda S.B.C., Chappels; Beth Eden-Evang.Lutheran; Bethel M.E.
S., Silverstreet; Enoree S.B.C., Keitts Cross Roads; Silver-
street Lutheran-Evang.Luth., Silverstreet; St. Philips Evang.
Lutheran; Kings Creek A.R.P.; St. Lukes Evang.Lutheran; Leba-
non M.E.S.; Wightman M.E.S., Prosperity; Wesleyan Meth.-Wel.
Meth., Whitmire; Welsh Zion Negro Baptist; St. Matthews Negro
Baptist, Newberry; Enoree Negro Baptist; St. Pauls Evang.Luth.;
Mt. Olivet Evang.Luth.; Backman Evang.Luth. Chapel; Mt.Pilgrim
Evang.Luth.; Colony Evang.Luth; St. James Evang.Luth., Jalapa;
Cannon's Creek Mission-A.R.P.; Trinity M.E.S.; New Chapel M.E.
S.; Ebenezer M.E.S.; Cross Roads S.B.C.; Mt. Zion S.B.C.; Mt.
Mariah A.M.E.; Vaughnville Cross Road Negro Baptist; Elisha A.
M.E.; Bush River Negro Baptist; Little River Negro Baptist;
Brown's A.M.E. Chapel, Helena; Shiloh A.M.E., Prosperity; Mt.
Olive A.M.E.; Capers M.E.S. Chapel; Lebanon M.E.S.; Bethel M.E.
S.; Scurry's Spring Hill Negro Baptist.

Oconee County: Shole Creek S.B.C., Clemson; Old Stone Presbyterian Church; Westminster Baptist, Westminster; Fair Play Presbyterian; Richland Presbyterian, Richland; Westminster Presby-

terian; Bethel Presbyterian, Walhalla; Fort Hill Presbyterian, Clemson College; Walhalla M.E.S., Walhalla; Choie A.M.E., Westminster; Wesleyan Methodist Ch.; Westminister M.E.S., Westminster; St. John's Luth.-United Evang.Luth., Walhalla; Seneca S. B.C., Seneca; (Old) Pickens Ch., Presbyterian; Seneca First Presbyterian, Seneca.

Orangeburg County: Orangeburg Presbyterian, Orangeburg; Bethany Christian; Gerezion M.E.S.; Target M.E.S.; Shiloh M.E.S.; Springfield Negro Baptist; Friendship A.M.E.; Bethel A.M.E., Holly Hill; Eutawville M.E.S., Eutawville; Elloree M.E.S., Elloree; Holly Hill M.E.S., Holly Hill; St. Paul A.M.E.; Shiloh A. M.E., Elloree; Live Oak A.M.E.; Bethlehem M.E.S.; Tabernacle Negro Baptist; Waring Chapel-Negro Baptist, Orangeburg; Lovely Hill Negro Baptist, Holly Hill; St. James Negro Baptist, Eutawville; Providence Negro Baptist; Holly Hill S.B.C., Holly Hill; Eutawville S.B.C., Eutawville; Corinth S.B.C.; Four Hole S.B.C.; Spring Hill Negro Baptist; Mt. Hebron Negro Baptist; Oak Grove Negro Baptist; Santee S.B.C., Elloree; St. Paul Negro Baptist, Elloree; Mt. Hebron Negro Baptist; Church of Jesus Christ-Apostolic Faith; Shiloh A.M.E., Eutawville; White House M.E.S.; Ebenezer A.M.E.; Providence M.E.S.; Ebenezer M.E.S.; Jericho A.M. E.; Silas A.M.E.Chapel; Wightman M.E.S., Bowman; Mt. Olivet A. M.E.; Pineville A.M.E.; Trinity Unit.Evan.Lutheran, Elloree; Liberty Hill Negro Baptist; Mt. Pisgah Neg. Baptist; Emancipation Negro Baptist; Bowman S.B.C., Bowman; Jerusalem M.E.S.; Macedonia A.M.E., Cope; William Chapel A.M.E., Orangeburg; Good Home A.M.E.; St. Paul Negro Baptist, Orangeburg; Trinity M.E. (Negro), Orangeburg; Bethlehem M.E.U.; Wesley Grove M.E.S.; Salvation Army-Undenom., Orangeburg; Church of God-Holiness- (Negro), Orangeburg; First S.B.C., Orangeburg; Orangeburg Lutheran-Evan., Orangeburg; Church of the Redeemer-Prot.Epis., Orangeburg; Union M.E.S., Cope; Holy Trinity Roman Catholic, Orangeburg; Sawyer Memorial S.B.C., Cope; Edisto S.B.C.; North M. E.S., North; St. John's M.E.S., Woodford; Shiloh M.E.S.; Ebernezer S.B.C., Cordova; Prospect M.E.S., Jamison; Wesley A.M.E., North; Shiloh Negro Baptist, Orangeburg; Bull Swamp Negro Baptist; Cedar Grove A.M.E.; Felderville A.M.E.; Red Hill Negro Baptist; Mt. Pisgah Negro Baptist, Orangeburg; Mt. Zion A.M.E.; St. Peters A.M.E.; Cedar Grove Negro Baptist; Liberty Hill Negro Baptist, Norway; Beauty Hill Negro Baptist; Hickory Hill Negro Baptist; Bethel A.M.E., Livingston; Turkey Branch Negro Baptist; St. Darcus Negro Baptist; Nazarath A.M.E.; St. Stephens A.M.E.; Church of God in Christ-Holiness (Negro); Mt. Olive A.M.E.; Double Branch S.B.C.; Pine Hill M.E.S., Pine Hill; Bethel S.B.C.; Calvary S.B.C.; Neeses S.B.C., Neeses; Norway S.B.C., Norway; St. John's M.E.S., Norway; Willow Swamp S.B.C.; Mt. Carmel S.B.C., Jamison; Canaan S.B.C.; North Baptist S.B.C., North; Pleasant Negro Baptist; Sardis M.E.S.; Prospect M.E.S.; Limestone M.E.S.; St. Paul M.E.S., Orangeburg; Neeses M.E.S., Neeses; Livingston M.E.S., Livingston; New Hope M.E.S., Rowesville; Branchville M.E.S., Branchville; St. George

S.B.C.; Bethany S.B.C.; Mt. Tabor S.B.C.; Salem S.B.C.;
Walnut Grove S.B.C.; Springfield S.B.C., Springfield; Two Mile
Swamp S.B.C.; Crosland Memorial S.B.C., Rowesville; Wilson
Chapel M.E., Branchville; Mt. Zion M.E., Branchville; St. Mi-
chael M.E.(Negro), Bowman; St. Stephens M.E.; Mayes Chapel M.
E. (Negro); Central M.E. (Negro), Rowesville; Hickory Grove
Negro Baptist, Rowesville; Mt. Calvary Negro Baptist; Jones
Negro Baptist Chapel; St. John A.M.E., Rowesville; St. Luke
Presbyterian, Orangeburg; Sean Swamp S.B.C.; Beaver Creek S.B.
C.; Pleasant Hill S.B.C.; Lebanon M.E.S.; Epiphany Chapel-Prot.
Epis., Eutawville; St. Stephen Negro Baptist; St. Luke Negro
Baptist; Bethel A.M.E., Branchville; Calvary A.M.E.; Samaria
Negro Baptist; Canaan Negro Baptist, Branchville; Butlers A.M.
E. Chapel, Wolfton; Nebo M.E. (Negro); St. Stephen M.E.(Negro);
Rocky Swamp M.E.S., Neeses; Springfield M.E.S., Springfield;
Orange Chapel-Evang.Lutheran, Springfield; Cattle Creek M.E.S.,
Branchville; Bull Swamp S.B.C.; Gethsemane (Penn Swamp) M.E.S.;
Trinity M.E.S.; Mack Branch Negro Baptist; Macedonia Negro Bap.,
Orangeburg; Fort Chapel M.E. (Negro), Orangeburg.
Pickens County: Bethlehem M.E.S., Pickens; Pickens First Presby-
terian, Pickens; Dacusville M.E.S., Dacusville Village; Mt.
Carmel S.B.C., Dacusville Village; Pickens First S.B.C., Pick-
ens; Carmel Presbyterian; Liberty Presbyterian, Liberty; Grace
Methodist M.E.S., Pickens; Mt. Bethel M.E.S.; Six Mile Baptist
S.B.C., Six Mile; Secona S.B.C.; Easley Presbyterian, Easley;
Keowee S.B.C.
Richland County: St. Andrews Unit.Evang.Luth; Oak Grove M.E.S.,
Taylor's Chapel A.M.E.; Bethel Negro Baptist, Blythewood; Rich-
land Presbyterian (or McKenzie); Brown's M.E.S. Chapel; Beulah
S.B.C.; Zion Negro Baptist; Wesley Mem.(or Waverly)M.E.S., Co-
lumbia; Shandon M.E.S., Columbia; Washington St. M.E.S., Colum-
bia; St. Paul's Evang.Luth., Columbia; Shandon Presbyterian,
Columbia; Mill Creek M.E.S., Lykesland; Ebenezer M.E.S.; St.
Timothy's Prot.Epis., Columbia; Trinity Prot.Epis., Columbia;
Cleaves Chapel C.M.E., Columbia; Congaree S.B.C.; Shandon S.B.
C., Columbia; Eason Memorial S.B.C., Eastover; Union Baptist
(Negro), Columbia; Macedonia Negro Baptist, Columbia; Gilbert's
Negro Baptist Chapel, Columbia; Jehovah Negro Baptist, Colum-
bia; Bethlehem Negro Baptist, Columbia; First Nazareth Negro
Baptist, Columbia; Second Calvary Negro Baptist, Columbia; Zi-
on Negro Baptist, Columbia; Antioch Negro Baptist, Columbia;
Tabernacle S.B.C., Columbia; Southside S.B.C., Columbia; Riv-
erside S.B.C., Columbia; Park St.S.B.C., Columbia; Columbia
First S.B.C., Columbia; Eau Claire S.B.C., Columbia; Colonial
Heights S.B.C., Columbia; Broadway S.B.C., Columbia; Whaley
Street M.E.S., Columbia; Green Street Methodist M.E.S., Colum-
bia; Zion Benevolent Negro Baptist; College Place M.E.S., Co-
lumbia; McLeods M.E.S. Chapel; Bethel A.M.E.; Crescent Hill S.
B.C., Columbia; Bishop's Memorial A.M.E. Zion Chapel, Colum-
bia; Sidnay Park A.M.E. Zion, Columbia; Jones Chapel-A.M.E.
Zion, Columbia; St. James-A.M.E. Zion, Columbia; Chappelle Sta-

tion-A.M.E. Zion, Columbia; Zion-Prot. Epis., Eastover; Trin-
ity Mission-Prot.Epis., Columbia; St. Matthews-Prot.Epis., Co-
lumbia; St. John's Prot. Epis., Columbia; Good Shepherd-Prot.
Epis., Columbia; St. John's Prot.Epis.;Saint Anna-Prot.Epis.,
Columbia; St. Luke's Reformed Prot.Epis., Columbia; St. Peters
Roman Catholic, Columbia; Mission of the Blessed Martin De Pol-
les-Roman Catholic, Columbia; St. Francis de Sales-Roman Cath.,
Columbia; Church of the Ascension-United Evan.Luth, Columbia;
Ebenezer United Evan.Luth., Columbia; Church of the Reforma-
tion-United Evan.Luth., Columbia; Church of the Incarnation-
United Evan.Luth., Columbia; St. Luke's Unit. Evan.Luth., Co-
lumbia; Church of Jesus Christ of Latter Day Saints-Mormon,
Columbia; Seventh Day Adventist, Columbia; House of Peace-Or-
thodox Hebrew, Columbia; Salvation Army-Undenom., Columbia;
Arsenal Hill Presbyterian, Columbia; A.R.P. Church, Columbia;
Central Church of Christ-Undenom., Columbia; Columbia First
Presbyterian, Columbia; Rose Hill Presbyterian, Columbia; Wood-
fin S.B.C., Columbia; Eau Claire Presbyterian, Eau Claire;
Main Street M.E.S., Columbia; Trinity M.E.S., Blythewood; St.
Mark's United Evan.Luth., Blythewood; Beulah M.E.S.; Mt. Zion
Negro Baptist; Pleasant Grove Negro Baptist; St. Philip A.M.E.;
Shiloh A.M.E.; St. Thomas-Prot.Epis.(Negro); Mt. Ararat or
Bush Arbor A.M.E.; Jerusalem Negro Baptist, Hopkins; Mt. Mori-
ah Negro Baptist; Mt. Nebo Negro Baptist, Wateree; Raleigh A.
M.E. Chapel; Red Hill Negro Baptist; St. John's Negro Baptist,
Hopkins; Bethel Evang. Lutheran, White Rock; Hopkins Presby-
terian, Hopkins; Lebanon M.E.S.; Church of God-Holiness, Co-
lumbia; Nazarene Tabernacle-Holiness, Columbia; Killian S.B.C.,
Killian; Mt. Olive S.B.C.; Mt. Elon; Good Hope S.B.C.; St.
Louis A.M.E., Wateree; Mt. Pilgrim Negro Baptist, Killian; Ch.
of God-Sanctified; Daughter of Zion Negro Baptist; Mt. Zion
Negro Baptist; St. Paul Negro Baptist; Mill Creek Negro Bap-
tist, Lykesland; Good Will Negro Baptist; Zion Pilgrim Negro
Baptist, Arthur; Dabney's Pond Negro Baptist; Piney Grove Ne-
gro Baptist, Wilson's Mill; Mt. Pilgrim Negro Baptist; Dau-
ghter of Matthew A.M.E.; Sandy Level S.B.C., Blythewood; Free
Will Baptist, Columbia; Oak Grove Original Free Will, Wilson's
Mill; Mt. Pleasant or Camp Ground M.E.S.; Jackson Creek S.B.C.,
Colonels Creek S.B.C.; Springdale Memorial S.B.C.; Spears
Creek S.B.C.; Rehoboth M.E.S., Dentsville; Antioch A.M.E.Zion;
Logs M.E.S.; Edgewood M.E.S., Edgewood; Zion Negro Baptist
Chapel; St. Peters Negro Baptist; Church of Jesus Christ Lat-
ter Day Saints-Mormon; Pisgah M.E.S.; Bethlehem Evang.Luth.,
Piney Grove A.M.E.; Free Hope A.M.E.; Bethlehem Negro Baptist,
College Place; St. Peters Negro Baptist; Stover A.M.E. Chapel,
Columbia; Epworth Orphanage M.E.S., Columbia; St. Paul A.M.E.,
St. James-Holiness; Zion Canaan Negro Baptist, State Park;
Pine Grove A.M.E.; Shady Grove M.E.S.; Zion M.E.S.; Tree of
Life Jewish, Columbia; St. John Negro Baptist, Columbia.
Saluda County:
Mt. Pleasant Luth.-Evang.Luth., Saluda; St. Paul's M.E.S., Sa-

luda; St. Paul's M.E.S., Saluda; Bethlehem M.E.S.; Red Bank
Baptist SBC, Saluda; Nazareth M.E.S.; Mt. Hebron-Evang.Luth.;
Bethel S.B.C.; Grace Prot.Epis., Ridge Spring; Rehoboth M.E.S.,
Spann M.E.S., Ward; Ridge Spring M.E.S., Ridge Spring; Ward S.
B.C., Ward; Providence M.E.S.; Clyde M.E.S.; Dry Creek S.B.C.;
Ridge Spring S.B.C., Ridge Spring; Sardis S.B.C.; First Calva-
ry Negro Baptist; Ridge Branch Negro Baptist; Cross Road A.M.E.;
Mine Creek Negro Baptist; Shiloh Negro Baptist; Pine Pleasant
S.B.C.; Hickory Grove Seventh Day Adventist; Speigner S.B.C.,
Chestnut Hill S.B.C.; Good Hope Evang.Lutheran; Trinity-Evang.
Luth.; Emory M.E.S. Chapel; Zoar M.E.S.; Shiloh M.E.S.; Butler
M.E.S.; Bethany M.E.S.; St. Williams Roman Catholic; Branch
Hill A.M.E.; Young Mt. Zion Negro Baptist; Pleasant Hill Ne-
gro Baptist; Mt. Moriah Neg.Baptist; Mt. Enon. Negro Baptist;
Mt. Alpha Negro Baptist, Ward; St. Paul Negro Baptist; Wesley
Zion-Holiness.
Spartanburg County: Whitney Community M.E.S. Church, Whitney Mill
Village; Whitney Community S.B.C. Church, Whitney Mill Village;
Arkwright S.B.C., Arkwright Mill Village; St. Paul A.M.E., Spar-
tanburg; Northside (formerly Gentry Memorial) Baptist, Spartan-
burg; Ligon Memorial S.B.C., Arcadia Mill Village; Whitney Free
Will Baptist, Whitney Mill Village; New Westminster Presbyte-
rian (Negro), Spartanburg; Mt. Moriah National Baptist (Negro),
Spartanburg; Landrum First S.B.C., Landrum; Majority National
Baptist (Negro), Spartanburg; Bethel-Fire Baptized Hol.Ch. of
God of the Americas (Negro), Spartanburg; Hayne S.B.C.; Bethle-
hem S.B.C.; Fairforest S.B.C.; Thompson St. Nat'l Baptist,
Spartanburg; Metropolitan A.M.E.Zion, Spartanburg; Silver Hill
M.E.(Negro), Spartanburg; Trinity A.M.E., Spartanburg; Smith M.
E.(Negro), Spartanburg; Epiphany Mission-Prot.Epis., Spartan-
burg; Mount Zion Unit. Pentecostal Holiness-Ch. of God(Negro),
Spartanburg; Holy Divine Tabernacle-Holiness, Spartanburg;
First Pentecostal Assembly-Holiness; St. Paul The Apostle-Ro-
man Catholic, Spartanburg; Beaumont M.E.S., Beaumont Mill; Wal-
ker Memorial C.M.E., Spartanburg; B'Nai Israel Temple-Orthodox
& Reformed Jewish, Spartanburg; Spartanburg First S.B.C., Spar-
tanburg; Calvary S.B.C., Spartanburg; Southside S.B.C., Spartan-
burg; Green Street S.B.C., Spartanburg; Switzer First S.B.C.,
Bethel M.E.S., Spartanburg; Everybody's Mission-Undenom., Spar-
tanburg; First Church of God, Spartanburg; El Bethel M.E.S.,
Spartanburg; Second Presbyterian, Spartanburg; Spartanburg
First Presbyterian, Spartanburg; Associate Reformed A.R.P.,
Spartanburg; Woman's Memorial-Evang.Luth., Spartanburg; Church
of The Advent-Prot.Epis., Spartanburg; Seventh Day Adventist,
Spartanburg; Citadel Salvation Army, Spartanburg; Summings St.
Baptist (Negro), Spartanburg; Beaumont S.B.C., Spartanburg; St.
Luke's Evang.Luth., Spartanburg; Church of Christ Scientist-
Christian Science, Spartanburg; St. Nicholas Greek Orthodox,
Spartanburg; Duncan Memorial M.E.S., Spartanburg; Glenn Springs
Presbyterian, Glenn Springs Village; Central M.E.S., Spartan-
burg; Wesleyan Methodist, Spartanburg; Billy Sunday Club, Inter-

denom-Y.M.C.A., Spartanburg; Drayton S.B.C., Spartanburg; Saxon Baptist S.B.C., Spartanburg; Saxon Church of God, Saxon Mill Village; Stephen Grove A.M.E. Zion; Nativity Lutheran United Evang.Luth.; Piedmont S.B.C.; Sloan's Grove; Campobello S.B.C., Campobello; Walnut Hill S.B.C.; Inman M.E.S., Inman; Inman Mill M.E.S., Inman; Inman First S.B.C. (formerly Mt. Calvary), Inman; Zion Hill (formerly Double Spring) Negro Baptist, Inman; Mount Pleasant S.B.C.; Chesnee First S.B.C., Chesnee; Cowpens Mills (formerly Central) S.B.C., Cowpens; Zion S.B.C.; Mt. Calvary Nat'l Negro Baptist; First S.B.C., Cowpens; Pleasant View M.E.(Negro); Salem M.E.S., Cowpens; Bethel M.E.S.; Trinity M.E. S., Spartanburg; Gospel Tent First Assembly of God, Spartanburg; Pentecostal Holiness Tabernacle-Pent.Hol.; Saxon Ave. Free Will Baptist, Spartanburg; Ben Avon S.B.C.; Boiling Springs S.B.C.; Zion Hill S.B.C.; Liberty M.E.S.; Davis Wesleyan Methodist Chapel; Drayton M.E.S., Spartanburg; Saxon M.E.S., Saxon Mill Village; Cole Free Will Baptist Chapel, Arcadia Mill Village; Roebuck S.B.C.; Inman Mill S.B.C., Inman Mill Village; New Prospect A.M.E. Zion; Golden Street Nat'l Baptist (Negro), Spartanburg; Macedonia Nat'l Baptist (Negro), Spartanburg; Nazareth Presbyterian; Hardy Negro Baptist Chapel; Sardis M.E., Forest C.M.E. Chapel, Spartanburg; Cherokee Springs S.B.C.; Mountain View S.B.C.; Cherokee M.E.S.; Foster's Grove Nat'l Baptist; Glendale Wesleyan Methodist, Glendale Mill Village; Lyman M.E.S., Lyman Mill Village; Arcadia M.E.S., Arcadia Mill Village; Clifton Presbyterian, Clifton No. 1 Mill Village; Chesnee Mill S.B.C., Chesnee Mill Village; Church of Jesus Christ of Latter Day Saints, Spartanburg; Holiness Tabernacle-Christ's Sanctified Holy Church, Spartanburg; Glendale Pentecostal Holiness; Graham's Wesleyan Methodist Chapel; Chesnee M.E.S., Chesnee; Oak Grove S.B.C.; Mount Olive (formerly Mountain View) S. B.C.; Lyman First S.B.C., Lyman; Glendale (formerly Bivingsville) S.B.C., Spartanburg; Brown's C.M.E. Chapel; Foster's National Baptist Chapel (Negro); Friendship Nat'l Baptist; St. Timothy's Prot.Epis. Mission, Spartanburg; All Souls Prot.Epis. Chapel, Spartan Mill Village; Arrowood S.B.C.; Trinity (formerly Hope) M.E.S.; Second S.B.C.; Olive Four Square Gospel-International Four Square; St. Andrews M.E.S., Clifton #2 Mill Village; Central M.E.S., Clifton No. 1 Mill Village; Fairforest Nat'l Baptist Boyd's Convention, Fairforest Village; Glendale M.E.S., Glendale; Clifton Wesleyan Methodist, Clifton #2 Mill Village; Converse (formerly Clifton #3 Baptist) S.B.C., Converse Mill Village; Roebuck Presbyterian, Roebuck Village; Canaan S.B.C.; Tucapau S.B.C., Tucapau; Assembly of God-First Assembly of God, Spartanburg; Faith Tabernacle (formerly Whosoever Gospel Mission)-Interdenom.; Allen's M.E. Chapel (Negro); Mt. Sinai Negro Baptist; Shiloh Nat'l Negro Baptist; Cedar Springs S.B.C.; New Pisgah S.B.C.; Philadelphia S.B.C.; Ben Avon M.E.S.; Chesnee Wesleyan Methodist, Chesnee; Converse M.E. S., Converse Mill Village; Tucapau Wesleyan Methodist, Tucapau Mill Village; Clifton No. 1 S.B.C., Clifton Mill Village No. 1;

Tucapau M.E.S., Tucapau Village; Valley Falls S.B.C., Valley
Falls Mill Village; Valley Falls Free Will Baptist, Valley
Falls Mill Village; Bethesda S.B.C.; Mount Zion S.B.C.; Well-
ford S.B.C., Wellford Village; New Trinity Nat'l Negro Baptist;
Bowers's Presbyterian Chapel (Negro); Florence M.E. Chapel (Ne-
gro); Wellford Presbyterian, Wellford; Whitestone M.E.S.,
Whitestone Village; Fairmont (formerly Crawfordville) M.E.S.,
Fairmont Mills Village; Pacolet(formerly Pleasant Grove) S.B.
C., Pacolet Village; Mt. Sinai Fire Baptized Holiness (Negro),
Mt. Calvary Nat'l Baptist (Negro); Travelers Rest Nat'l Bap-
tist (Negro); Bethel (formerly Arthur's Chapel) C.M.E.; Jones
Tabernacle A.M.E.Zion; Gethsemane Nat'l Baptist (Negro); Ab-
ner's Creek S.B.C.; Holly Springs S.B.C.; Duncan (formerly
Middle Tyger) S.B.C.; Jackson S.B.C., Jackson Mills Village;
Friendship S.B.C.; Shell-Anderson Memorial M.E.S., Jackson Mill
Village; Liberty Hill-Meth.Prot.; Pacolet Presbyterian, Paco-
let; Pacolet Mills Pentecostal Holiness, Pacolet Mills; Paco-
let Mills Baptist (formerly Trough Shoals) S.B.C., Pacolet
Mills; Montgomery Memorial (formerly Trough Shoals) M.E.S.,
Pacolet Mills; Brown's Chapel-S.B.C., Pacolet Mills; Harrison
Grove (formerly Harrion's Stand) Nat'l Baptist (Negro); May-
field Nat'l Baptist Chapel (Negro); Moore's Nat'l Baptist Cha-
pel (Negro); Calvary Prot.Epis., Glenn Springs Village; Inman
Presbyterian, Inman; Pacolet Methodist (formerly Zion) M.E.S.,
Church of God, Pacolet Mills; Montgomery Chapel-Nat'l Baptist
(Negro); Cleveland Chapel-Nat'l Baptist (Negro) ; Piney Grove
Nat'l Baptist (Negro); New Shady Grove Nat'l Baptist (Negro);
Lewis Chapel Nat'l Baptist (Negro); New Zion Nat'l Baptist;
Monk's Grove Nat'l Baptist; Kansas Nat'l Baptist Chapel(Negro);
New Salem Nat'l Baptist (Negro); Fairmont (formerly Bivings-
ville, later Crawfordsville) S.B.C.; Fairmont Mill Village;
Jones Chapel-Fire Baptized Holiness Church of God of the Amer-
icas, Spartanburg; Maxwell Nat'l Baptist Chapel, Spartanburg;
Asbury M.E. (Negro); Mt. Calvary Presbyterian; Shiloh M.E.S.;
Eirvin A.M.E.Zion Chapel, Inman; New Prospect S.B.C., New Pros-
pect Village; Soul Winning Tabernacle-Interdenom., Converse
Village; White Spring Pentecostal Holiness; The Church of God-
Congregational Holiness, Tucapau Village; United House of Pra-
yer-Interdenom. (Negro), Spartanburg; Hopewell Nat'l Baptist
(Negro); Landrum M.E.S., Landrum; Fairview No. 2 S.B.C.; Hol-
den Nat'l Baptist Chapel (Negro); Mountain View S.B.C.; Par-
ris Grove-Holiness; Gethsemane Nat'l Baptist (Negro); Cross
Anchor M.E.S., Cross Anchor; Yarborough Meth.Prot. Chapel; Mt.
Zion C.M.E., Cross Anchor; North Pacolet S.B.C.; Bethel S.B.C.;
Fairview #1 S.B.C.; Rock Hill S.B.C.; Engleside S.B.C.; Appa-
lache S.B.C., Appalache Mill; Cooley Springs S.B.C.; Reidville
Presbyterian, Reidville; Antioch S.B.C.; Carlisle Wesley Meth-
odist; Woodruff Presbyterian, Woodruff; Emma Gray Memorial
(formerly Woodruff, First) M.E.S., Woodruff; Grace M.E.S.,
Brandon Mill Village; Woodruff A.R.P., Woodruff; Woodruff
First (formerly Janey's Creek & Bethel) S.B.C., Woodruff; Mills

Mill S.B.C., Mills Mill Village; Unity (formerly Floyd's Meeting House) S.B.C.; Green Pond S.B.C.; Poplar Springs S.B.C.; Church of God-Pent.Hol., Brandon Mill
Sumter County: Church of the Holy Cross-Prot.Epis., Statesburg; Church of the Holy Comforter-Prot.Epis., Sumter; St. James Evan.Luth., Sumter; Trinity M.E.S., Sumter; Hebron Presbyterian, Oswego; Bethel (Black River) S.B.C.; Salem Black River Presbyterian; First S.B.C., Sumter; Sumter Presbyterian, Sumter; Concord Presbyterian; Christian Disciples of Christ, Sumter; Pinewood M.E.S., Pinewood; St. Anne's Roman Catholic, Sumter; Pinewood S.B.C., Pinewood, Graham S.B.C.; Fraser Memorial Presbyterian; St. Mark's Chapel-Prot.Epis., Pinewood; Pinewood Tabernacle-Interdenom; Zoar M.E.S.; St. James A.M.E., Pinewood; St. Matthew Negro Baptist; Pearson's A.M.E. Chapel; Mt. Olive A.M.E., Pinewood; St. John's Negro Baptist, Pinewood; Pinewood Presbyterian, Pinewood; Stone Hill A.M.E., Sumter; Shepherd A.M.E.; Shiloh First Baptist (Negro), Sumter; Apostolic Mission-Hol.Ch. of America (Negro), Mayesville; Berry Spring Sanctified Holiness Ch. of God (Negro); Evening Light Reformation-Hol. Ch. of America (Negro), Sumter; Apostolic Holiness-Hol.Ch. of America, Mayesville; Temple Sinai-Soc. Israelites, Sumter; Grace S.B.C., Sumter; Broad Street M.E.S., Sumter; Providence S.B.C.; Salem S.B.C., Sumter; Wedgefield S.B.C., Wedgefield; St. Mark's Upper Prot.Epis.; Wedgefield M.E.S., Wedgefield; Lewis M.E.S. Chapel; Bethesda Negro Baptist; Mt. Zion Negro Baptist, Sumter; New Bethel Negro Baptist; Queen's Chapel A.M.E.; Good Will Negro Epis; Congruity Presbyterian (Negro); St. Mark's A.M.E.; Bethel A.M.E., Sumter; Mulberry Negro; St. Paul A.M.E.; St. Mark's A.M.E., Mayesville; Clark's A.M.E., Oswego; Trinity Negro Baptist, Sumter; Pine Hill A.M.E.; Orange Hill Ref. M.E. (Negro); Orange Hill A.M.E.; St. James A.M.E.; Mt. Moriah Negro Baptist; Antioch A.M.E.; Ebenezer A.M.E., Mayesville; Salem A.F.W.B., Sumter; Brown Negro Baptist Chapel; Trinity Presbyterian (Negro), Mayesville; Bethel M.E.S.; Rembert M.E.S.; Mayesville S.B.C., Mayesville; Wedgefield Presbyterian; Galilee Negro Baptist, Mayesville; Beulah A.M.E.; Dalzell M.E.S., Dalzell; Providence M.E.S.; Union Negro Baptist; Long Branch S.B.C.; Horeb S.B.C.; Horeb S.B.C., Dalzell; Tirzah Presbyterian, Dalzell; Seventh Day Adventist, Sumter; Mt. Pisgah Negro Baptist; Mt. Pisgah A.M.E., Sumter; Union Sta.-A.M.E., Sumter; Ebenezer Presbyterian (Negro); Joshua Negro Baptist; Elizabeth M.E. (Negro), Borden; Grant Hill Negro Baptist; Hill Hills of Santee S.B.C.; Church of the Accension-Prot.Epis., Hagood; Good Hope M.E.; Second Presbyterian, Sumter; Rafting Creek Negro Baptist; Antioch A.M.E.; Mt. Bethel Negro Baptist; Rembert Negro Baptist Chapel, Rembert; Willow Grove A.M.E.; Apostolic St.Rest-Hol.Ch.of God (Negro), Mayesville; St. Mary's Prot.Epis.Chapel, Rimini; Pisgah S.B.C., Pisgah Cross Roads; Church of God by Faith, Sumter; Bethlehem Negro Baptist, Sumter; Bethesda M.E.S.; High Hills A.M.E.; High Hills Negro Baptist; Hopewell Negro Baptist; Mt. Carmel Negro Baptist; Weyman

A.M.E. Chapel, Stateburg.
Union County: West Side S.B.C., Union; Upper Fair Forest S.B.C.;
Hebron S.B.C.; Grace M.E. Ch., M.E.S.; Union Jonesville M.E.S.,
Jonesville; Augsburg Evan.Lutheran, Union; Fairforest Presbyte-
rian, Jonesville; Epis. Ch. of Nativity-Prot.Epis., Union;
First Presbyterian, Union; First S.B.C., Union; Seventh Day Ad-
ventist, Union; Monarch Presbyterian, Union; Bethel M.E.S.,
Mon-Aetna S.B.C., Union; Church of Christ-Christian, Union;
Padgett's Creek S.B.C., Union; Tabernacle S.B.C.; Church of
God, Union; Green St. M.E.S., Union; Sardis M.E.S.; Holy Trin-
ity-Roman Catholic, Union; Sulphar Springs S.B.C.; West Springs
S.B.C., West Springs; Phillipi S.B.C.; Mt. Lebanon S.B.C.; Put-
man S.B.C.; Lower Fairforest S.B.C.; Prospect S.B.C.; Beulah S.
B.C.; Mt. Joy S.B.C., Kelton; Salem S.B.C., Santuc; Carlisle
Baptist S.B.C., Carlisle; Jonesville S.B.C., Jonesville; Mt.
Vernon Presbyterian; Cane Creek Presbyterian, Santuc; Monarch
Presbyterian, Monarch Mill Village; Bethesda Negro Baptist;
James Negro Baptist Chapel, Carlisle; Maple Ridge Negro Bap-
tist; Foster Negro Baptist Chapel; Brown's Chapel S.B.C.; Mt.
Olive Negro Baptist; Thompson Negro Baptist Chapel; Galilee
Negro Baptist; Emanuel Negro Baptist Chapel; Jerusalem Negro
Baptist; Bethany Negro Baptist, Jonesville; Mt. Calvary Negro
Baptist; Beatey's A.M.E. Zion Chapel; Thomas A.M.E. Chapel;
Clinton A.M.E. Zion Chapel, Union; Bethel Negro Baptist; Jeter
A.M.E. Chapel; Spring Hill C.M.E.; Evergreen A.M.E.; Paradise
A.M.E.; Mt. Eden A.M.E., Carlisle; Williams A.M.E.Zion Chapel,
Carlisle; Lockhart M.E.S., Lockhart; Lockhart S.B.C., Lockhart;
Enoree Presbyterian, Sedalia; Gillams M.E.S. Chapel; Rogans-
ville M.E., Buffalo; Lower Fairforest Baptist, Union; Carlisle
M.E.S., Carlisle; New Hope M.E.S.; Bogansville M.E.S.; Union
Holiness, Union; Flat Rock M.E.S.; Quaker M.E.S., Sedalia;
Bethlehem M.E.S.; Buffalo S.B.C., Buffalo; Gilead S.B.C.; Buf-
falo M.E.S., Buffalo; Fairview S.B.C.; Foster's Chapel M.E.S.,
Kelton; Unity M.E., Union; Beulah S.B.C., Union; Flat Rock M.
E.; Buffalo Meth.Epis., Buffalo; Bethlehem M.E.; Salvation Ar-
my-Prot., Union; Lockhart M.E., Lockhart; New Hope M.E.S.
Williamsburg County: Greeleyville S.B.C., Greeleyville; McDow-
ell Presbyterian, Greeleyville; Williamsburg Presbyterian,
Kingstree; Friendship A.M.E.; Kingstree M.E.S., Kingstree; In-
diantown Presbyterian, Indiantown Community; St. Ann's Roman
Catholic, Kingstree; St. James A.M.E.; Marion Negro Baptist;
Jerusalem A.M.E., Sutton; Jehovia A.M.E., Salters; St. Philips
A.M.E., Salters; St. Mary A.M.E., Salters; Bethel A.M.E.; Naz-
areth A.M.E.; Great Pleasant A.M.E.; St. Peter's Negro Baptist;
Charity Negro Baptist; Cedar Grove Negro Baptist; Johnson
Swamp Pent.Holiness; St. John A.M.E., Trio; New Jerusalem C.M.
E., Blakeley; St. Matthew Negro Baptist, Salters; Macedonia
No. 1 Negro Baptist; Central Negro Baptist; Wesley C.M.E.;
Black Mingo Presbyterian; Union Negro Baptist; Black River Ne-
gro Baptist; St. Luke Negro Baptist; Laurel Swamp Negro Bap-
tist; Mt. Pilgrim Negro Baptist; Oak Grove Negro Baptist; Beth-

lehem Negro Baptist; St. Luke A.M.E.; Workman M.E.S., Workman;
Beulah M.E.S.; Earls M.E.S., Earls; Elim M.E.S.; Hemingway M.
E.S., Hemingway; Lane S.B.C., Lane; First Baptist S.B.C., Hem-
ingway; Lane Presbyterian, Lane; Bethel M.E. (Negro); St.
Mark A.M.E.; Brewington A.M.E. Chapel; Asbury M.E. (Negro); Mt.
Zion A.M.E.; St. John Negro Baptist; Good Hope Negro Baptist,
Greeleyville; Allan Freewill Baptist Chapel (Negro); Mt. Zion
A.M.E.; Millwood M.E.S.; Pergamas M.E.S.; Lane M.E.Ch.S.,
Lane; Trio M.E.Ch.S., Trio; Central Presbyterian; Mouzon Pres-
byterian; Union Presbyterian; Bethel Presbyterian; Greeley-
ville M.E.S., Greeleyville; Mt. Vernon M.E.S.; Spring Gully S.
B.C.; Oak Ridge Pent.Hol.,Andrews; Concord M.E.S.; St. Mary
C.M.E.; Siloan Negro Baptist, Kingstree; Beulah A.M.E.; Cades
S.B.C., Cades; Ebenezer S.B.C.; St. Stephen Negro Baptist;
Long Branch C.M.E.; Trinity Negro Baptist, Greeleyville; Wil-
son M.E. Chapel (Negro), Greeleyville; Sutton M.E.S.; Black
Mingo Church S.B.C., Rhems; Bloomingvale S.B.C.; Nesmith S.B.
C., Nesmith; Antioch Negro Baptist; St. Michel A.M.E.; Mt. Zi-
on M.E. (Negro), Kingstree; Harmony M.E.S.; Salters M.E.S.,
Salters; Bethel A.M.E., Kingstree; St. John Negro Baptist; St.
John M.E.S.; St. Luke A.M.E.; St. James Negro Baptist; Vox Me-
morial M.E.S.; St. Paul A.M.E.; Bethesda C.M.E.; Elizah A.M.E.;
St. Stephen Union Methodist; St. Paul C.M.E.; Wilson's C.M.E.
Chapel; Hebron M.E.S.; Sandy Grove African Freewill Baptist;
Good Will African Freewill Baptist; Hickory Grove A.M.E.; Mid-
way S.B.C.; Chavis A.M.E. Chapel; Bethesda M.E.S.; Cades M.E.
S., Cades; Lower St. Marks M.E.S.; St. Albans Prot.Epis., King-
stree; St. Asia Negro Baptist; Promised Land Negro Baptist;
Dickey Negro Methodist Chapel; New Bethel Negro Baptist; Mt.
Zion Negro Baptist; Antioch Negro Baptist, Lane; Rock Negro
Baptist; Bethel A.M.E.; Lanes A.M.E. Chapel; Midway Baptist A.
F.W.B.; Cedar Grove S.B.C.; Kingstree S.B.C., Kingstree; Free-
will Baptist, Greeleyville
York County: York First S.B.C., York; York A.R.P., York; Fil-
bert Presbyterian, Filbert: Bethlehem First Presbyterian (Ne-
gro); Olivet Presbyterian, McConnellville; Hopewell Presbyte-
rian, Leslie; Tirzah A.R.P.; St. Paul M.E.S.; Rock Grove A.M.
E.Zion; Flint Hill Negro Baptist; St. Matthew A.M.E.Zion; The
Ch. of Our Saviour-Prot.Epis., Rock Hill; Grace Evan.Luth.,
Rock Hill; Bethesda Presbyterian; St. John's Meth.Epis.South,
Rock Hill; Rock Hill First S.B.C., Rock Hill; Flint Hill S.B.
C.; Fort Mill First S.B.C., Fort Hill; Oakland Ave. Presbyte-
rian, Rock Hill; Highland Park M.E.S., Rock Hill; Hill's A.M.
E. Chapel; Adnah M.E.S.; Ezelle A.M.E.Zion; North Side S.B.C.,
Rock Hill; Smith's Presbyterian, Smith's Turnout; West Main
Street M.E.S., Rock Hill; Park Baptist S.B.C., Rock Hill; Ch.
of the Nazarene-Holiness, Rock Hill; St. John's M.E.S., Fort
Mill; Cedar Grove A.M.E.Zion, Smith's Turnout; Trinity M.E.S.,
York; Clover Presbyterian, Clover; Mt. Prospect Negro Baptist,
Rock Hill; Flat Rock Negro Baptist; Center Attraction A.M.E.
Zion, Clover; Liberty Hill Negro Baptist; Neely's Creek A.R.P.

Leslie; Tirzah Presbyterian, Tirzah; Clover A.R.P., Clover; Unity Presbyterian, Fort Mill; Ebenezer Presbyterian, Ebenezer; Smyrna A.R.P., Smyrna; Good Shepherd Prot.Epis., York; Clover First S.B.C., Clover; King's Mt. Chapel M.E.S.; White Street S.B.C., Rock Hill; Catawba S.B.C.

ADDENDA

In addition to the manuscript church records given in Section 6, the South Caroliniana Library, University of South Carolina (SCL) holds the following church records or copies of church records:

Aimwell Presbyterian Church, Ridgeway. Records of work of church women, c. 1905.
All Saint's Episcopal Church. Records 1819-1954.
Allendale Baptist Church. Records 1868-1902.
Allendale Episcopal Church. Records 1874-1900.
Antioch Baptist Church, Kershaw County. Marriage records 1852-1884.
Aveleigh Presbyterian Church, Newberry District. Records 1835-1853.
Barnwell Baptist Association. Records 1867.
Barnwell Baptist Church, Barnwell County. Records 1803-1912.
Beaulah Baptist Church, Laurens County. Records 1883-1904.
Beech Branch Baptist Church, Hampton County. Records 1814-1918.
Bennettsville Methodist Church, Bennettsville. Records 1846-1925.
Bennettsville Presbyterian Church. Records 1855-1898.
Bethabara Baptist Church, Laurens County. Records 1801-1881.
Bethel Baptist Church, Newberry County. Records 1841-1910.
Bethel Presbyterian Church, Williamsburg District. Minutes 1811-1828.
Bethesda Baptist Church, Kershaw County. Records 1823-1905.
Bethesda Presbyterian Church, Camden. Records 1806-1937.
Bethesda Presbyterian Church, York County. History 1769-1885.
Bethlehem Lutheran Church, Newberry County. Records 1816-1936.
Big Creek Baptist Church, Anderson County. Records 1801-1936.
Black Creek Baptist Church, Beaufort County. Records 1828-1922.
Bramlette Methodist Church, Laurens County. Records 1842-1878.
Browning Christian Church, Brunson. Records 1886-1927.
Bush River Baptist Church, Newberry County. Records 1792-1923.
Bushy Creek Baptist Church, Greenville County. Records 1794-1927.
Camden Baptist Church. Misc. records 1907-1933.
Camden Methodist Church. Records 1828-1894.
Canaan Baptist Church, Orangeburg County. Records 1923-1910.
Cannon Creek Presbyterian Church, Newberry County. Records 1875-1895.
Cashaway Baptist Church, Craven County. Records 1756-1778.
Central Methodist Church, Newberry. Records 1868-1901.
Chestnut Ridge Baptist Church, Laurens County. Records 1816-1939.
Christ Baptist Church, Horn's Creek. Records 1824-1854.
Christ Church Society (Episcopal), Florence County. Records

415

1907-1908.
Church of the Atonement, Episcopal, Blacksburg. Material re:
reconstruction plans, 1958.
Church of Christ Baptist Church, Abner Creek. Records 1834-70.
Church of Christ Baptist Church, Mountain Creek. Records 1833-
1854.
Church of Christ Baptist Church, Poplar Springs. Records 1878-
1911.
Church of the Holy Comforter, Episcopal, Sumter. Newspaper
clippings, 1934-35.
Church of the Redeemer, Episcopal, Orangeburg. Records 1734-
1885.
Church of the Redeemer, Lutheran, Newberry. Misc. records
1854-1899, 1953.
Columbia Baptist Church. Sunday School records, 1876-1878.
Concord Baptist Church, Greenville County. Records 1880-1903.
Coosawatchie Baptist Church. Records 1814-1864.
Cypress Methodist Church, Darlington. Sunday School records
1853-99.
Darlington Methodist Church. Records 1841-1867.
Darlington Presbyterian Church. Records 1827-1853.
Duncan Memorial Methodist Church, Georgetown. Marriage & bap-
tism records 1811-1846.
Ebenezer Baptist Church, Darlington County. Records 1823-1908.
Edmundsbury Episcopal Chapel. Records 1854-1856.
Elim Baptist Church, Effingham, Florence County. Records
1836-1927.
Enon Christian Church, Hampton. Records 1825-1911.
Epiphany Lutheran Church, St. Matthews. Records 1912-1963.
Euhaw Baptist Church, Beaufort County. 1831-1908.
Fair Forest Baptist Church, Union County. Records 1820-1899.
Fairview Presbyterian Church, Greenville. Centennial, 1768-
1886.
First Baptist Church, Charleston. Records 1847-1875.
First Baptist Church, Columbia. Records 1809-1840.
First Presbyterian Church, Columbia. Misc. records 1827-1952.
First Presbyterian Church, Greer. Minutes 1924-1939.
Fishing Creek Presbyterian Church, Chester County. Records
& minutes, 1799-1937.
Flint Hill Baptist Church, York County. Records 1792-1899.
Georgetown Presbyterian Church. Records 1897-1926.
Grace Episcopal Church, Camden. Records 1830-1938.
Grace Lutheran Church, Prosperity, Newberry County. Records
1859-1936.
Great Saltketcher Baptist Church, Barnwell County.
Greer Presbyterian Church. Records of Ladies Aid Society,
1901-1924.
Gum Branch Baptist Church, Lower Ford of Lynches Creek, Chester-
field County. Records 1796-1887.
Holy Cross Episcopal Church, Stateburg. Records 1770. 1936.
Hopewell Baptist Church, Chester County. Records 1871-1895.

416

Horn's Creek Baptist Church, Edgefield County. Records 1824-
1859.
Huntsville Baptist Church, Laurens County. Records 1838-1871.
Incarnation Lutheran Church, Columbia. Records 1921-1965.
Independent or Congregational (Circular) Church, Charleston.
Records 1695-1935.
James Island Presbyterian Church. Records 1833-1845.
John's Island and Wadmalaw Island Presbyterian Church. Records
1856-1911.
Kingston Presbyterian Church, Horry County. Minutes, 1903-1936.
Kingstree Baptist Church, Williamsburg County. Records 1858-
1894.
Little Pee Dee Baptist Church, Pauley's Creek, Horry County.
Records 1868-1887.
Lutheran Church. Conference minutes, 1939-1940.
Lutheran Church of German Protestants, Charleston. Records
1826-1937.
Lutheran Church. New Central Conference of the Evangelical
Lutheran Synod. Records 1930-1938.
Mechanicsville Baptist Church, Darlington County. Records
1803-1867.
Methodist Church, Black River & Kingstree Circuits. Records
1857-1869.
Methodist Church, Darlington Circuit, Florence County. Minutes
1831-1878.
Methodist Church, Lynch's Creek Circuit, Darlington County.
Records 1787-1897.
Methodist Church, Lynchburg. Records 1855-1938.
Methodist Church, Mars Bluff. Records of Missionary Society,
1890-1915.
Methodist Church, Newberry. Records 1820-1883.
Methodist Church, Newberry County. Records 1823-1886.
Methodist Church. Upper SC Conference. Minutes 1917-1940.
Methodist Church, Waccamaw Circuit, Horry County. Records
1836-1855.
Milford Baptist Church, Greenville County. Records 1832-1869.
Mineral Springs Baptist Church, Marlboro County. Records
1867-1905.
Mount Aron Baptist Church, Allendale County. Records 1839-1937.
Mount Moriah Baptist Church, Camden. Misc. records 1922-34.
Mt. Pleasant Baptist Church, Laurens County. Historical sketch,
1949.
Mount Tabor Presbyterian Church, Greer. Records 1841-1912.
Mountain Creek Baptist Church, Spartanburg County. Records
1833-1854.
Neal's Creek Baptist Church, Anderson County. Records 1832-
1901.
New Allendale Baptist Church, Allendale County. Records 1882-
1922.
New Hope Methodist Church, Chester County. Records 1832-1931.
New Providence Baptist Church, Hartsville. Records 1808-1922.

Ninety-Six Presbyterian Church. Records 1860-1936.
North Santee Episcopal Church. Minutes & records 1853-
1862.
Old Buffalo Presbyterian Church. Records 1833-1924.
Old Mispah Baptist Church, Mars Bluff, Florence County. Records
1830-1862.
Padget's Creek Baptist Church, Union County. Records 1784-1874.
Parnassus Methodist Church, Marlboro County. Records 1883-1915.
Perfect Baptist Church. Records 1859-1939.
Pleasant Grove Baptist Church. Records 1859-1939.
Pleasant Grove Presbyterian Church, Chester County. Records
1847-1929.
Poplar Springs Baptist Church, Union County. Records 1794-1937.
Presbyterian Church. Misc. records, c. 1935.
Presbyterian Church, Marlboro County. Records 1833-1924.
Primitive Baptist Church, Beaver Dam, Kershaw County. Records
1844-1882.
Primitive Baptist Church, Crooked Run, Edgefield District.
Records 1840-1843.
Prince George Winyah Episcopal Church, Georgetown County. Rec-
ords 1813-1916.
Prince Frederick Winyah Episcopal Church. Records (includes
Black River [Episcopal chapel]), 1729-1763.
Prince William's Baptist Church, Hampton County. Records 1812-
1937.
Protestant Episcopal Church, Charleston County. Records 1754-
1790.
Raburn Creek Baptist Church, Laurens County. Records 1828-1913.
St. Andrew's Evangelical Lutheran Church, Columbia. Records
1860-1938.
St. Bartholomew's Parish Episcopal Church, Colleton County.
Records 1840-1854.
St. David's Episcopal Church, Cheraw. Records 1768-1832.
St. James' Santee Episcopal Church. Records 1806-1886.
St. John's Episcopal Church, John's Island. Records 1834-1917.
St. John's Evangelical Lutheran Church, Charleston. Records
1778-1937.
St. John's Parish, Berkeley Episcopal Church. Records 1753-
1853.
St. Luke's Episcopal Church, Clarendon. Records 1840-1936.
St. Luke's Episcopal Church, Newberry. Records 1846-1923.
St. Luke's Lutheran Church, Stoney Battery, Newberry District.
Records 1932-1957.
St. Luke's Parish Episcopal Church, Charleston. Records 1866-
1905.
St. Mark's Lutheran Church, Fort Motte. Records 1895-1924.
St. Matthew's Lutheran Church, Orangeburg. Records 1767-1897.
St. Matthew's Episcopal Church, Calhoun County. Records 1767-
1838.
St. Michael's Episcopal Church, Charleston. Records 1759-1930.
St. Paul's Episcopal Church, Charleston. Records & church

history, 1810-1879.

St. Paul's Methodist Church. Records 1891-1914.

St. Peter's Episcopal Church. Records 1874-1930.

St. Philip's Episcopal Church, Bradford Springs. Records 1846-1855.

St. Philip's Episcopal Church, Charleston. Records 1732-1910.

St. Philip's Lutheran Church, Newberry County. Records 1881-1923.

St. Stephen's Episcopal Church, Craven County. Records 1754-1885.

St. Stephen's and St. John's Episcopal Church, Charleston. Records 1754-1935.

St. Thomas & St. Dennis Episcopal Church, Berkeley County. Records 1693-1794.

Salem Baptist Church, Marlboro County. Records 1797-1930.

Salem Presbyterian Church, Black River. Records 1759-1860.

Sandy Level Baptist Church, Fairfield County. Records 1817-1908.

Sandy River Methodist Church, Fairfield County. Records 1810-1874.

Sandy Run Baptist Church, Lexington District. Records 1881-1909.

Second Presbyterian Church, Charleston. Records 1809-1908.

Smyrna Baptist Church, Hampton County. Records 1870-1927.

Smyrna Presbyterian Church, Blenheim, Marlboro County. Records 1833-1924.

South Cypress Methodist Church, Charleston County. Records 1844-1888

Stoney Creek Independent Presbyterian Church, Prince William's Parish. Records 1722-1910.

Swallow Savannah Methodist Church. Records 1856-1889.

Swift Creek Baptist Church, Kershaw County. Records 1827-1868.

Tabernacle Methodist Church. Records 1861-1888.

Thomas Memorial Baptist Church, Marlboro County. Records 1832-1924.

Trinity Episcopal Church, Columbia. Records 1860-1925.

Trinity Methodist Church, Charleston. Records 1792-1888.

Tyger River Baptist Association, Greenville County. Records 1870.

Union Baptist Church, Spartanburg County. Records 1804-1843.

Union Presbyterian Church. Records 1864-1938.

Wambaw Church (St. James Episcopal Church, Santee). Records 1887-1935.

Warrior's Creek Baptist Church, Laurens County. Records 1843-1932.

Washington Street Methodist Church, Columbia. Misc. records 1831-86, 1923-1939.

Welsh Neck Baptist Church, Society Hill. Records 1737-1952.

Williamsburg Presbyterian Church, Kingstree. Records 1834-1931.

Zion Lutheran Church, Lexington County. Records 1861-1929.

INDEX

This index lists all proper, place and personal names shown as authors or subjects of publications in the bibliographies, the appendices and the addenda section of this book.

When using the index to locate family or personal names, check all possible variant spellings, as they have not been cross-referenced.

Regardless of the number of times a subject may appear on a page of the text, it has received only one index citation for that page.

Bennett, Addie O.: 51
Bennett, Craig Miller: 310
Bennett family: 209,250,282
Bennett graveyard: 375
Bennett, Grover G.: 219
Bennett, John: 311
Bennett School: 68
Bennett, Susan Smythe: 311, 346,352
Bennett, Gov. Thomas: 310
Bennettsville Baptist Church: 159
Bennettsville Baptist Tabernacle: 159
Bennettsville Methodist Church: 125,415
Bennettsville Presbyterian Church: 415
Bennettsville, SC: 8,67,108, 117,130,133,170,176, 403,415
Benson family: 205,236,265,282
Benta, R.E.: 219
Bentham family: 219,282
Bentham, Captain James: 334
Bentley A.M.E. Church: 382
Benton family: 219,226
Benton, Josiah H.: 219
Benton, Samuel Slade: 219
Bentonville, SC: 346
Berea Baptist Church: 125,396
Berea First Baptist Church: 146
Berea, M.E. Church, South: 385
Berean Presbyterian Church (Negro): 384
Beresford family: 282,284,285
Bekeley County: 22,41,51,54,68, 72,81,95,107,110,114,121,182, 315,330,341,363,373,385,419
Bermuda: 287
Bermuda Baptist Church: 391
Bernard family: 209
Bernheim, Gothardt D.: 125
Berretta, Randolph W.: xiv
Berrien family: 351,356,360
Berringer family: 282,285,339
Berry, Annie M.: 52
Berry, C.B.: 211
Berry, Connelly B.: 219
Berry family: 204,205,219,271, 282
Berry, Hudson: 219
Berry, James R.: 52
Berry, Lloyd E.: 219
Berry, Michael West: 352
Berry Spring Sanctified Holiness Church of God (Negro):411
Besselleau family: 282,358
Bessellieu family: 254,282
Best family: 250
"Best Friend" (railroad train): 84
Betenbaugh family: 251
Beth Elohim Synagogue: 126,138, 302,387
Beth Israel Jewish Congregation: 384
Beth Israel Jewish Congregation-Reform: 394
Beth Israel Synagogue: 387
Beth Israel Synagogue-Orthodox: 394
Beth Shalom Congregation: 155
Bethabara Baptist Church: 16, 125,399,415
Bethany: 247
Bethany Baptist Church: 398,406, 404
Bethany Baptist churchyard: 376
Bethany cemetery: 31,36,373,374
Bethany Christian Church: 405

Bethany Evangelical Lutheran Church: 404
Bethany M.E. Church, South: 392,400,408
Bethany Negro Baptist Church: 403,404,391,412
Bethany Pentecostal Holiness Church: 393
Bethany Presbyterian Church: 400
Bethany Southern Baptist Church: 384
Bethany United Evangelical Lutheran Church: 401
Bethea Family: 219
Bethea, Mary B.: 16,219
Bethea, Phillip Y.: 219
Bethea, SC: 374
Beth-Eden. Evangelical Lutheran Church: 404
Bethel A.M.E. Church: 384,386, 387,388,391,392,393,397,400, 401,402,403,405,406,411,412, 413
Bethel A.M.E. Church (Negro): 400,401
Bethel African Methodist Episcopal Church: 126
Bethel A.R.P. Church: 126
Bethel Baptist Church: 16,126, 180,388,390,393,399,404,405, 408.415
Bethel Baptist Church cemetery: 16
Bethel Baptist churchyard: 376
Bethel (Black River) Baptist Church: 411
Bethel C.M.E. Church: 410
Bethel cemetery: 42,376
Bethel Church cemetery: 16,375
Bethel churchyard: 375
Bethel Evangelical Lutheran Church: 134,407
Bethel Fire Baptized Holiness Church of God of the Americas (Negro): 408
Bethel Lutheran Church: 196
Bethel M.E. Church: 42,381,390
Bethel M.E. Church (Negro): 383,413
Bethel M.E. Church, South: 382, 384,386,390,394,395,402,404, 408,409,411,412
Bethel Methodist Church: 126, 168,174,383
Bethel Methodist Church (Negro) 384
Bethel Methodist churchyard: 374
Bethel Methodist Episcopal churchyard: 374
Bethel Mission (A.M.E.): 389
Bethel Negro Baptist Church: 401,406,412
Bethel Negro M.E. Church: 385, 387
Bethel Original Free Will Baptist Church: 393
Bethel Park M.E. Church, South: 384
Bethel Presbyterian cemetery: 376
Bethel Presbyterian Church: 16, 152,173,182,390,405,413,415
Bethel Presbyterian Church cemetery: 16,40
Bethel Southern Baptist Church: 410
Bethel Seventh Day Adventist Church (Negro): 392
Bethel, SC: 182
Bethel Southern Baptist Church: 382

Bethel Tabernacle Assembly of God-Pentecostal Holiness: 392
Bethel Temple: 392
Bethel United Methodist Church: 126
Bethera Cordesville Southern Baptist Church: 385
Bethesda Baptist Church: 16,124, 410,415
Bethesda C.M.E. Church: 413
Bethesda Community: 174
Bethesda M.E. Church, South: 404,411,383,413
Bethesda M.E. cemetery: 374
Bethesda Methodist churchyard: 376
Bethesda Negro Baptist Church: 391,411,412
Bethesda Presbyterian Church: 16,35,126,157,165,174,398,413, 415
Bethesda Presbyterian churchyard: 368
Bethia Presbyterian Church: 381
Bethlehem A.M.E. Church: 403, 383
Bethlehem A.M.E. Church (Negro): 399
Bethlehem A.R.P. Church: 381
Bethlehem Baptist cemetery: 39
Bethlehem Baptist Church: 126, 388,390,397,399,402,403,408
Bethlehem Baptist Church cemetery: 363
Bethlehem Baptist Church (Negro) 393
Bethlehem Baptist churchyard:28
Bethlehem C.M.E. Church: 383
Bethlehem First Presbyterian Church (Negro): 413
Bethlehem Lutheran Church: 126, 368,404,415
Bethlehem M.E. Church: 390,412
Bethlehem M.E. churchyard: 374
Bethlehem M.E. Church, South: 393,394,400,403,405,406,408, 412
Bethlehem M.E.U. Church: 405
Bethlehem Methodist Church: 391
Bethlehem Missionary Baptist Church: 397
Bethlehem Negro Baptist Church: 393,395,396,398,401,402,404, 406,407,411,412,413
Bethlehem Negro M.E. Church:386
Bethlehem Negro Methodist Protestant Church: 385
Bethlehem Negro Presbyterian Church: 401
Bethlehem Southern Baptist Church: 382
Bethney Negro Baptist Church: 391
Bethpage Presbyterian Church:175
Bethsadia Protestant Methodist Church: 393
Bethune Baptist Church: 393
Bethune M.E. Church, South: 398
Bethune Presbyterian Church: 398
Bethune, SC: 165,398
Betterson family: 205
Betterton family: 205
Bettis family: 205
Bettison family: 205
Betts, Albert D.: 126
Betts family: 282
Beulah A.M.E. Church: 393,411, 413
Beulah Baptist Church: 393
Beulah Baptist Church: 122,392, 393,396,406
Beulah C.M.E. Church: 402

Brewster Lawrence Fay: 346
Brewster, William Edward II:
297
Brewton family: 238,270,282,
285,316,332
Brewton, M.: 298
Brewton, Col. Moses: 332
Brewton, Miles: 72
Brewton plantation tombstone
inscriptions: 337
Brian family: 223
Brice, Agnes: 222
Brice, Mrs. Charles P.: 211
Brice family: 205,222,282
Brice, Laurie S.: 222
Brick Church cemetery: 374,375
Brick River A.R.P. churchyard:
375
Bridenbaugh, Carl: 311
Bridgers, Frank: 200
Bridges, Elizabeth: 268
Bridges family: 205
Bridges, Mrs. Louree: 128
Bridgman family: 226
Bridwell family: 210
Bridwell, Ronald E.: 53,211
Briggers A.M.E. Church: 390
Briggs Chapel (Negro Baptist):
389
Briggs family: 210,254
Brigham, Clarence S.: 1
Bright family: 210
Bright Light Negro Baptist
Church: 399
Brightman family: 205
Brinsfield, John W.: 311
Brinson family: 205
Brisbane family: 205,282,320
Brissie, Margia Lou: 128
Brister family: 282
Bristol, Roger P.: 1
Bristow, Mrs. C.D.: 53
Bristow family: 210,295
Bristow, John: 295
Bristow, Mollie: 128
Britaine family: 282
Brith Shalom Synagogue:
387
British Empire: 122
Brittain, John Lafayette: 311
Britton, Benjamin: 227
Britton family: 53,210,226,282,
289
Britton's burying ground: 376
Britton's Neck Baptist Church:
402
Britton's Neck, SC: 53,226,375
Brixe family: 282
Broad River Baptist Church: 388
Broad St., Charleston: 374
Broad Street M.E. Church,
South: 411
Broad Street Methodist Church:
400
Broaddus, Luther: 128
Broadmouth Southern Baptist
Church: 381
Broadwater family: 205
Broadwater, Mary J.: 222
Broadway, Bette I.: 222
Broadway Baptist Church: 406
Broadway family: 222
Broadway Presbyterian Church:16
Brock family: 205,210
Brock, Pope F.: 211
Brock, Reuben Ist: 253
Brockington family: 205
Brockington Funeral Home: 21
Brockman family: 205,223
Brockman, Mary B.: 223
Brockman, William E.: 223
Brockmann, Charles R.: 222
Brogdon, SC: 389

Broom Hill Negro Baptist
Church: 398
Bromwell, William J.: 13
Bronson family: 210
Bronson, Patricia: 10
Brooke family: 216,221
Brooke, Francis H.: 223
Brooke, Gov. Robert: 216
Brookgreen: 49
Brookgreen Garden: 53
Brookgreen, SC: 53
Brookland M.E. Church, South:
401
Brookland United Methodist
Church: 150
Brooks, Anna B.: 53,223
Brooks family: 220,221,239,254,
255
Brooks, J.L.: 128
Brookville, SC: 396
Brooks, Preston S.: 326
Brooks, Preston Smith: 326
Brooks, U.R.: 196
Brooks, Ulysses R.: 53
Broome family: 254
Bromley, Thomas: 337
Broughton: 334
Broughton family: 223,282,285,
331
Broughton, M. Leon: 223
Broun family: 282
Broun, Janetta: 223
Broun, Robert J.: 223
Broun, Thomas L.: 223
Broun, William: 194,223
Browder, Georgia G.: 128
Brown, Bubberson: 86,194
Brown, C.C.: 128
Brown, Carl H.: 53
Brown, Clinton C.: 53,128
Brown, Cyril Conrad: 223
Brown, Douglas S.: 53
Brown, Douglas Summers: 311
Brown, Elaine Y. Eaddy: 275
Brown family: 205,216,217,223,
232,252,266,271,275,282,285,
289,295
Brown family cemetery: 373,374
Brown, Frances H.: 53
Brown, Gerry H.: 223
Brown, Irene Sanford: 223
Brown, Jean: 295
Brown, John D.: 223
Brown, John P.: 191
Brown, Julie.: 1
Brown, Phillip M.: 311
Brown, Mrs. C.C.: 223
Brown, Mrs. Joe: 212
Brown Negro Baptist Chapel:411
Brown, Ralph H.: 311
Brown, Rev. Daniel: 239
Brown, Richard L.: 17,223
Brown, Richard M.: 53
Brown-Salem M.E. Church: 383
Brown Springs Baptist Church:
388
Brown Swamp United Methodist
Church: 128
Brown Swamp Methodist Church
cemetery: 28
Brown, Tarlton: 214
Brown, Lt. Colonel Thomas: 328
Brown, Varina D.: 53
Brownah A.M.E. Church: 381
Browne family: 285
Browne, Rev. E.C.L.: 297
Browne, Henry B.: 128
Browning Christian Church: 415
Browning Disciples of Christ
Church: 396
Browning family: 284
Brownlee family: 205
Brownlow family: 214

Brown's A.M.E. Chapel: 404
Brown's C.M.E. Chapel: 409
Brown's Chapel A.M.E. Zion:397
Brown's Chapel M.E. Church,
South: 393
Brown's Chapel - Baptist: 397
Brown's Chapel Negro Baptist
Church: 385
Brown's Ferry,SC: 320
Brown's M.E.S. Chapel: 406
Brown's Raid: 322
Brown's Southern Baptist Cha-
pel: 410,412
Brown's Swamp: 397
Brown's Tabernacle-Church of
God (Negro): 400
Brownship Township, SC: 403
Brownson family: 210
Brownsville Baptist Church: 147,
159,164
Browntown, SC: 315
Broyles, Augustus Taliaferro:
309
Broyles family: 222
Bruce family: 226,246
Bruce, Winnie J.: 128
Brumley, Blanche: 54
Bruneau family: 285,352
Bruns, John Dickson: 297
Brunson Baptist Church: 128,396
Brunson C.M.E. Chapel: 396
Brunson, Charlotte B.: 223
Brunson Christian-Disciples of
Christ Church: 395
Brunson M.E. Church, South: 395
Brunson, Eva H.: 54
Brunson family: 205,223,269,
282,283,288
Brunson, Marion B.: 223
Brunson, Mrs. C.N.: 128
Brunson, Nolan L.: 129
Brunson, SC: 128,395,396,415
Brunson, W.A.: 129,223
Brushy Fork Baptist Church: 129
Bruton's Fork Baptist Church:
159
Bruton's Fork Baptist Church:
403
Bryan, Evelyn M.: 17
Bryan family: 205,214,223,224,
279,282,285,293,363
Bryan, George D.: 298
Bryan, Judge George S.: 298,306
Bryan, Irene A.: 54
Bryan, J.P. Kennedy: 298
Bryan, Mary L.: 54
Bryan, Rev.: 365
Bryan, Richard J.: 311
Bryan, Richard Jenkins: 311
Bryan, Thomas R.: 129,223
Bryan, Wright: 54
Bryant family: 223,224,272
Bryant, Hal: 54
Bryant, Lawrence: 224
Bryant, Lawrence C.: 194,223,
224
Bryant, Pattie Sessoms: 224
Bryant Reporter: 223
Bryce, Mrs. Campbell: 54
Bryce family: 282
Bryce, James H.: 17
Brynes, Sec. of State James F.:
318
Bryson family: 290
Bryson, Iva C.: 54
Buchanan family: 210,224,263
Buchanan, G.A., Jr.: 346
Buchholz, Mrs. L.E.: 129
Buckalew family: 205,224
Buck Creek: 238
Buck Creek Baptist Church: 396
Buck graveyard: 375
Buck Hall plantation: 337

Buck Swamp Freewill Baptist
Church: 402
Buckingham family: 227
Buckingham, Thomas: 227
Buckner family: 267
Bucksport, SC: 396,397
Bucksville, SC: 25,375,397
Buck Swamp cemetery: 374
Budd family: 259
Buffalo Baptist Church: 161,
398,403,412
Buffalo Baptist churchyard:368
Buffalo M.E. Church: 412
Buffalo M.E. Church, South:412
Buffalo Presbyterian Church:
418
Buffalo, SC: 412
Buffington family: 210,224
Buffington, Ralph M.: 224
Buford family: 205,262,275
Buford, Maude S.: 158
Buford's Bridge: 222
Buie family: 224
Buie, Robert B.: 224
Buist, A.J.: 54
Buist family: 282
Buist, Henry: 298
Buist, Samuel S.: 298
Bulger, William T.: 311
Bull, Charles M.: 224
Bull, Elias: 54
Bull, Elias B.: 17,311
Bull, Emily L.: 54
Bull family: 224,231,282,284,
291,311,316,333,349,377
Bull, H.D.: 311
Bull, Henry D.: 54
Bull, Henry DeSaussure: 224,
312
Bull, James H.: 224
Bull, John: 224
Bull, Joseph C.: 224
Bull, Stephen: 224
Bull Swamp Baptist Church: 40,
145,406
Bull Swamp Negro Baptist
Church: 405
Bull, William: 326
Bullard family: 205
Bullen family: 282
Bulletin: 7
Bulletin for Genealogists: 7
Bullock Creek Cemetery Associ-
ation: 17
Bullock Creek Church: 17,37
Bullock family: 205,224,282
Bullock, James: 225
Bullock, Joseph G.: 224,225
Bullock, Kenneth C.: 225
Bullock, Mary: 274
Bullock, Mary Hill: 225
Bullock's Creek Presbyterian
Church: 17
Bull's Island: 107
Buncombe Street M.E. Church,
South: 394
Buncombe Street Methodist
Church: 161
Buncombe Street Methodist
Church, South: 165
Bunker cemetery: 28
Bunker family: 234
Bunker Hill, Massachusetts.
Centennial: 322
Bunting, Elizabeth B.: 54
Burch family: 205,231,280
Burckhalter family: 225
Burdell family: 282,354
Burdell, Francis Marion: 354
Burdell, Thad S.: 361
Burden family: 221
Burford family: 205,243
Burges, Samuel Edward: 312

Burgess, Barry H.: 225
Burgess, Dorothy: 225
Burgess family: 210,221,225
Burgess, James M.: 129
Burgess, Mrs. James: 129
Burgess, Marjorie C.: 225
Burgess, Mary Wyche: 312
Burgess, Robert H.: 54
Burgess, Sallie R.: 225
Burgess, SC: 396
Burgess, Thomas: 225
Burke, Aedanus: 330
Burket family: 290
Burkette, Alice G.: 352
Burkette, Alice Gaillard: 312,
352
Burkhead, J.D.: 129
Burkhead, Rev. J. DeWitt: 130
Burnell family: 210
Burnet family: 282
Burnett family: 205,283
Burney, Eugenia: 54
Burnham family: 282,285
Burnkam family: 282
Burnley family: 233
Burns, Annie W.: 17
Burns family: 205,225,245,252,
265,282
Burns, James C.: 129
Burns, James C., Sr.: 225
Burns, Martha B.: 352
Burns, Martha Bailey: 352
Burnside, Ronald D.: 346
Burnt Church (see also Sheldon
Church)
Burnt Church: 385
Burnt Meeting House cemetery:
44
Burress, David E.: 225
Burress family: 225
Burris family: 205,247,248
Burriss family: 225
Burrough family: 244
Burroughs, Eli: 225
Burroughs family: 225
Burrough's Graded School: 95
Burrows family: 242,282
Burrows, William (house): 334
Burrus family: 223
Burt, Evelyn R.: 225
Burt family: 205, 225,250
Burt, Mathew: 264
Burton, E. Milby: 54,196,312
Burton family: 205,225,245,282
Burton, Solomon: 225
Burton, William L.: 225
Busby family: 205
Busch, James W.: 378
Bush Arbor A.M.E. Church: 407
Bush, C.J.: 54
Bush, Elizabeth Beby: 219
Bush family: 210,219,222,232
Bush Hill cemetery: 316
Bush, John: 232
Bush, Mary Bryan: 232
Bush, Richard: 219
Bush River Baptist Church: 17,
129,174,404,415
Bush River Baptist Church
cemetery: 20
Bush River Baptist Church &
cemetery: 40
Bush River Negro Baptist
Church: 404
Bush River, SC: 148
Bushy Creek Baptist Church:
17,161,415
Bussey family: 245
Buster family: 205
Butler family: 210,220,239,
253,254,282,285,322
Butler family burying ground:
374

Butler, Harriet J.: 54
Butler M.E. Church, South: 408
Butler, Martha Christian: 287
Butler, Pierce: 313
Butler, Senator Pierce: 323
Butlers A.M.E. Chapel: 406
Butler's Brigade: 55
Butler's Cavalry: 53
Butt, Mary McLure: 352,362
Butt, Winnie J.: 129
Buyck family: 282
Buzhardt, Beaufort S.: 54
Byars family: 225
Bydaleck, Bernard: 54
Byerly family: 225
Byerly, Wesley G.: 225
Byers family: 210,247,371
Bynum, Curtis: 17,312
Bynum family: 210
Byrd, Anne: 232
Byrd, E.J.C.: 129
Byrd family: 210,248
Byrd, Lucille C.: 55
Byrdsong family: 205
Byrnes [Gov.]: 196
Byrnes, James F.: 348
Byron family: 224
Byrum family cemetery: 373

- C -

Cabell family: 232
Cabell, James B.: 225
Cache, Utah Branch Genealogical
Library: 200
Cades M.E. Church, South: 413
Cades, SC: 413
Cades Southern Baptist Church:
413
Caesar: 134
Caesar family: 239
Caesar's Head, SC: 55,108
Cahusac family: 248
Caillabeuf family: 355
Caillabeuf, Isaac: 355
Cain family: 210,269,282
Cain, Marvin R.: 312
Cainhoy, SC: 108,385
Cairnes family: 210
Calcote, Claude A.: 129
Calcote family: 282
Calcott, W.H.: 55
Caldwell family: 205,232,247,
282
Caldwell, James F.: 55
Caldwell, John H.: 225
Caldwell, May: 129
Caldwell, Wm. R.: 362
Calhoun: 334,365
Calhoun, Alan T.: 205
Calhoun, Archibald: 225
Calhoun, C.: 55
Calhoun, C.M.: 55
Calhoun community: 64
Calhoun County: 39,55,271,272,
346,370,373,385,418
Calhoun County Historical Com-
mission: 10
Calhoun, Edwin C.: 225
Calhoun Falls Methodist
Church: 381
Calhoun Falls Presbyterian
Church: 381
Calhoun family: 205,214,225,
230,248,263,266,277,279,282,
313,332
Calhoun, Grace W.: 55
Calhoun, John C.: 236,311,316,
321,324,332,347,350
Calhoun, John C. Shrine: 63
Calhoun, John Clarence: 248
Calhoun Land Company: 55
Calhoun monument: 64,78,84

Carter's Ford Baptist Church: 129,390
Cartersville Baptist Church: 394
Cartledge family: 205
Cartwright family: 205,208
Carup Creek A.M.E. Zion Church (Negro): 399
Caruthers family: 222
Carvill, H.C.: 226
Carvin, Ernest A.: 226
Carvin family: 226
Carwile, John B.: 56
Carwile family: 210
Cary, James: 323
Cary, Mary: 323
Case family: 205
Casey family: 205
Cash Baptist Church: 159
Cash, Ellerbe B.: 56
Cash family: 249
Cash-Shannon duel: 56,93
Cash, Wilbur Joseph: 349
Cashaway Baptist Church:364,415
Cashin family: 205
Caskey family: 205
Cason family: 205
Cason, Mollie T.: 130
Casper family: 205
Casper, Mary K.: 226
Cassatt Baptist Church: 398
Cassatt, SC: 34,398
Cassel, Daniel Kolb: 243
Cassels family: 221,282
Cassels, Hallie Jones: 221
Cassels, Louie: 221
Cassels, Louis: 56
Cassels, Louise: 56
Castle Hill: 224
Castle Pinckney: 342
Caston family: 240,282
Caston, Glass: 240
Cat Fish Creek: 237
Catawba: 192
Catawba and Wateree Company: 56
Catawba Indian Nation: 191
Catawba Indians: 21,191,192,311, 313,313,344
Catawba Male Academy:56
Catawba Region: 85
Catawba Regional Planning Council: 56
Catawba Southern Baptist Church: 414
Cater family: 282
Catfish Baptist Church: 391
Catfish Creek Baptist Church: 122
Cathcart family: 227,285
Cathedral of St. John the Baptist, Charleston: 130
Catholic cemetery: 42,375
Catholic Diocese of Charleston: 138
Catholic gravestones: 18
Catholic Presbyterian Church: 15,18,41,124,130
Catholic Presbyterian churchyard: 363
Catlett family: 259
Cato family: 205
Catoe, Bernice R.: 56
Catrevas, Mrs. A.N.: 211
Cattell family: 284,285
Cattle Creek Church cemetery: 373
Cattle Creek M.E. Church, South: 406
Caughman, Joseph Ansel: 56
Causey, Beth: 57
Causey, Beth G.: 57
Causey family: 205
Causey, Malcolm L.: 57

Cauthen, Charles E.: 57
Cauthen, Charles Edward: 346
Cauthen family: 210
Cauthen, Henry F.: 80
Cauthen, Thomas, Sr.: 292
Cauthorn family: 295
Cauthorn, William: 295
Cave, Benjamin: 233
Cave family: 294
Caven family: 210
Caw Ford, SC: 397
Cawley, Henry H.: 312
Cayce Baptist Church: 401
Cayce Church of the Nazarene: 130
Cayce family: 262
Cayce M.E. Church, South: 401
Cayce Methodist Church: 130
Cayce, SC: 57,130,176,401
Cedar Creek Baptist Church: 388,400
Cedar Creek Episcopal Mission: 178
Cedar Creek M.E. Church, South: 396,397
Cedar Creek, SC: 397
Cedar Grove A.M.E. Church: 395, 405
Cedar Grove A.M.E. Zion Church: 413
Cedar Grove Baptist Church: 383,396,399,413
Cedar Grove Baptist churchyard: 373
Cedar Grove Church (Negro): 400
Cedar Grove Disciples of Christ Church: 395
Cedar Grove Evangelical Lutheran Church: 401
Cedar Grove Negro Baptist Church: 386,398,405,412
Cedar Grove, SC: 56,396
Cedar Grove Southern Baptist Church: 383
Cedar Lane cemetery: 376
Cedar Shoal Presbyterian Church: 172
Cedar Shoals Baptist Church:155
Cedar Spring [A.R.P. Church?]: 174
Cedar Spring Baptist Church:149
Cedar Springs A.R.P. Church: 381,395
Cedar Springs A.R.P. Church cemetery: 31
Cedar Springs Baptist Church: 158
Cedar Springs Southern Baptist Church: 409
Cedar Swamp community: 158
Centenary A.M.E. Church: 390
Centenary Church: 156
Centenary M.E. Church, South: 397,402
Centenary M.E. churchyard: 375
Centenary Methodist Church cemetery: 28
Centenary Negro M.E. Church:386
Centenary, SC: 402,403
Centennial A.M.E. Zion Church: 399
Centennial A.R.P. Church: 130
Center Attraction A.M.E. Zion Church: 413
Center Church cemetery: 33
Center Grove Baptist Church:399
Center M.E. Church, South: 403
Center Methodist Church: 152
Center Rabun Negro Baptist Church: 400
Centerville A.M.E. Church: 390
Centerville Negro Baptist Church: 403

Central Association for the Relief of South Carolina Soldiers: 57
Central Baptist Church: 131,390, 394,409
Central Church of Christ: 407
Central M.E. Church (Negro):406
Central M.E. Church, South: 392 400,404,408,409
Central Methodist Church: 18, 131,415
Central Midlands Regional Planning Commission: 57
Central Negro Baptist Church: 384,412
Central Piedmont Regional Planning Commission: 57
Central Presbyterian Church: 127,131,134,180,413
Central, SC: 49,122
Central United Methodist Church: 131,146
Centre Point graveyard: 374
Chadwick, Nancy G.: 57,105
Chadwick, Thomas W.: 312
Chaffin, Abner: 227
Chaffin, Encel A.: 227
Chaffin family: 227
Chaffin, W.L.: 298
Chalk, Carville Tudoe: 237
Chalk family: 235
Chalk, Levi: 235
Chalmers family: 262
Chamberlain, Edmund: 227
Chamberlain family: 227
Chamberlain, George W.: 227
Chamberlain, Gov.: 348
Chamberlain, N.A.: 227
Chamberlayne family: 294
Chambers family: 205,262
Chambers, Gladys N.: 57
Champion family: 210,232
Champion, Richard: 326
Chancellor family: 205
Chandler, Charles H.: 227
Chandler family: 210,236,282
Chandler, Harry: 131
Chandler, Helen D.: 57
Chandler, Marion C.: 5,131,185
Chandler, Roger: 227
Chandler, William H.: 227
Chaney, David W.: 264
Chaney family: 205
Chapeau family: 210
Chapel, Andrew: 267
Chapel family: 267
Chapel Hill Baptist cemetery: 374
Chapel Hill Baptist Church: 391
Chapel of Ease, Pineville, SC:32
Chapel of Our Savior: 385
Chapel of the Holy Cross: 22
Chapel of the Holy Cross (Protestant Episcopal): 387
Chapin, George H.: 58
Chapin, SC: 149,162,401
Chapley, Samuel Whatley: 227
Chaplin, Ellen P.: 58,131,227
Chaplin family: 227,282,285,377
Chapman, Anne W.: 312
Chapman, F.W.: 227
Chapman family: 205,227,236
Chapman, John: 236
Chapman, John A.: 58,95
Chapman, John V.: 227
Chapman, Missouri Ann Morris: 227
Chappell, Buford S.: 227
Chappell family: 227
Chappell family cemetery: 375
Chappell, Phillip E.: 227
Chappelle Station A.M.E. Zion Church: 406,407

Chester Standard: 369
Chesterfield Baptist Church:388
Chesterfield County: 10,11,108,
112,220,388,416
Chesterfield County Tricenten-
nial Committee: 60
Chesterfield District: 368
Chesterfield Missionary Baptist
Church (Negro): 397
Chesterfield Presbyterian
Church(Negro): 388
Chesterfield, SC: 38,60,388
Chesterville Presbyterian
Church: 136
Chesterville, SC: 136
Chestnut family: 205
Chestnut Cross Roads, SC: 397
Chestnut Hill Baptist Church:
408
Chestnut Hill church cemetery:
40
Chestnut Ridge Baptist Church:
19,131,400,415
Chevalley, Sylvie: 312
Cheves family: 282,284,311
Cheves, Langdon: 298,312,345,
348
Cheves, Captain Langdon Jr.:315
Cheves, Langdon. Langdon Cheves
III Genealogical Collection:
284,285
Chevillette family: 210
Chew family: 205
Chicco, Vincent: 298
Chichester, C.E.: 60
Chichester, Rev. C.E.: 298
Chick Springs, SC: 71,108
Chick Springs Baptist Church:
132
Chicken family: 282
"Chicora" (steamer): 304
Chicora Wood plantation: 98
Chidsey, Donald B.: 60
Chignola M.E. Church, South:383
Chignola Southern Baptist
Church: 383
Child, Elias: 227
Child family: 227
Childe family: 227
Childs, Arney R.: 5,227,312
Childs family: 227
Childs, St. Julien R.: 60,312,
313
Childs, St. Julien Ravenel: 346,
352
Childsbury, SC: 335
Childsbury Town: 107
Chiles family: 206,210
Chiles, James M.: 60
Chilton family: 216
China: 257,357
China family: 205
China Grove plantation: 375
Chiquola United Methodist
Church Committee on History &
Records: 133
Chisholm family: 205,227,282,
289
Chisholm, Harriet: 289
Chisholm, Henry Lewis: 355
Chisholm, J. Bachman: 298
Chisholm, William G.: 227
Chitty, Charles K.: 313
Choctaw Indians: 347
Choehee Baptist cemetery: 376
Choie A.M.E. Church: 405
Choice Street M.E. Church,
South: 394
Chreitzberg, Abel M.: 132
Chrestomathic Society: 91
Christ Baptist Church: 415
Christ Church (Episcopal): 22,
132,134,147,179,387,394,399,
403

Christ Church Negro Baptist
Church: 402
Christ Church Parish: 22,33,
147,183,318,320,339
Christ Church Parish Agricul-
tural Society: 61
Christ Church Society (Episco-
pal): 415
Christ Episcopal Church ceme-
tery: 375
Christensen, Frederick Holmes:
377
Christian Church: 385
Christian Disciples of Christ
Church: 411
Christian family: 210,225
Christian Science Society of
Sumter: 132
Christie family: 266
Christie, Faye: 61
Christie, Susan C.: 228
Christopherson, Merrill G.: 61
Chronicles of St. Mark's
Parish: 129
Church cemetery: 363
Church, Henry F.: 61
Church of the Ascension Protes-
tant Episcopal: 411
Church of the Advent-Protestant
Episcopal: 402,408
Church of the Ascension: 22,138
Church of the Ascension-United
Evangelical Lutheran: 407
Church of the Atonement, Epis-
copal: 416
Church of Christ: 160
Church of Christ Baptist
Church: 416
Church of Christ-Christian:
392,412
Church of Christ-Holiness
(Negro): 392
Church of Christ-Scientist-
Christian Science: 408
Church of the Cross: 178
Church of England (see also
Anglican Church, Protestant
Episcopal Church)
Church of England: 122,139,171
Church of England Chapel-Prot-
estant Episcopal: 402
Church of England (Protestant
Episcopal): 402
Church of the Epiphany: 32
Church of the Epiphany [Epis-
copal]: 127,400
Church of the Ephany-Protestant
Episcopal (Negro): 392
Church of First Born-Church of
God Holiness (Negro): 392
Church of God: 381,383,390,391,
395,403,410,412
Church of God by Faith: 411
Church of God-Congregational
Holiness: 410
Church of God-Evening Light
(Negro): 400
Church of God-General Assembly:
394
Church of God, Holiness: 382,
383,398,399,402,403,407
Church of God-Holiness(Negro):
386,401,402,405
Church of God in Christ-Holi-
ness (Negro): 405
Church of God-Pentecostal Holi-
ness: 391,411
Church of God-Sanctified: 407
Church of the Good Shepherd
(Protestant Episcopal): 148,
387
Church of the Holy Apostles: 19
Church of the Holy Apostles,
Episcopal: 384

Church of the Holy Comforter:
132
Church of the Holy Comforter
[Episcopal]: 122,411,416
Church of the Holy Communion,
Episcopal: 151
Church of the Holy Cross, Epis-
copal: 112,145,177,411
Church of the Immaculate Con-
ception: 213
Church of the Incarnation
(Protestant Episcopal): 388
Church of the Incarnation-
United Evangelical Lutheran:
407
Church of Jesus Christ-Aposto-
lic Faith: 405
Church of Jesus Christ of
Latter-Day Saints (Mormon):
385,387,390,392,398,407,409
Church of the Living God Pillar
and Ground Truth, Sanctified:
384
Church of the Messiah: 22
Church of the Nazarene: 130
Church of the Nazarene-Holi-
ness: 413
Church of Our Savior, Episco-
pal: 139
Church of Our Savior (Protes-
tant Episcopal): 413
Church of the Redeemer: 19,22,
132
Church of the Redeemer, Epis-
copal: 45,136,405,416
Church of the Redeemer-Luther-
an: 404,416
Church of the Reformation-
United Evangelical Lutheran:
407
Church of the Resurrection: 154
Church of the Resurrection E-
vangelical Lutheran Church:386
Church of Resurrection (Protes-
tant Episcopal): 394
Church Street Theatre: 314
Churches of Christ: 39
Chute family: 228
Chute, George: 228
Circular Church (see also Inde-
pendent or Congregational
Church...)
Circular Church: 137
Circular Congregational Church:
320,387
Circular Congregational church-
yard: 374
"Circular" Independent or Con-
gregational Church: 146,184
The Citadel (see also SC Mili-
tary Academy): 52,85,197
The Citadel. Association of
Citadel Men: 15
The Citadel. Class of 1923:196
The Citadel. Memorial Military
Museum: 1
Citadel Salvation Army: 408
Citadel Square Southern Baptist
Church: 132,387
City Gazette (Charleston): 321,
330,340
City Gazette & Commercial Daily
Advertiser (Charleston): 318
City Gazette & Daily Advertiser
(Charleston): 321
Civil War (see also Confederate
States of America, SC Military
Units, SC Volunteer Army)
Civil War: 19,36,49,53,55,56,
62,64,66,73,75,76,82,83,90,94
107,108,117,118,120,136,139,
198,200,301,312,328,331,349,
377,378

Claflin family: 293
Claiborne family: 246
Clan Labhran: 260
Clan Mac Millan family of North America: 260
Clancy family: 222
Clanton Plains Baptist Church: 388
Clackler family: 205
Clardy family: 228
Claremont County: 371
Claremont, SC: 22,371
Claremont Theological Scholarship Society: 61
Clarendon Baptist Church: 389
Clarendon County: 61,84,95,107, 158,237,354,363,374,389
Clarendon County Historical Society: 61
Clarendon, SC: 418
Clark, Alston (Olsteen): 295
Clark, Chovine R.: 132,228,352
Clark, Chovine Richardson: 228
Clark, E. Culpepper: 313
Clark, Eugene C.: 298
Clark, Eva L.: 228
Clark family: 205,216,223,228, 239,252,281,282,295
Clark family burial: 43
Clark, G. Dewey: 61
Clark Hill Resevoir & Reservation: 61
Clark, Jacob: 228
Clark, Rev. Jacob: 228
Clark, John W.: 228
Clark, Marguerite: 19
Clark, Mary C.: 61
Clark, Meribah E.: 228
Clark, Micajah Adolphus: 318
Clark, Olsteen: 295
Clark, Thomas D.: 61
Clark, W.A.: 61
Clark, William: 228
Clarke cemetery: 363
Clarke, Erskine: 132
Clarke family: 228,237,258
Clarke, George K.: 228
Clarke, Jane: 228,254
Clarke, Nathaniel: 228
Clarke, Philip G.,Jr.: 132
Clark's A.M.E. Church: 411
Clark's Chapel (A.M.E. Zion): 388
Clarks Hill, SC: 403
Clarkson family: 228,282
Clarkson, Francis O.: 228
Clarkson, Thomas Boston: 228
Clarkson, William: 228
Clarle family: 282
Clary family: 228
Class family: 210
Clastrier family: 282
Clatworthy family: 205
Claussen, Dorothea Fincken: 268
Claussen, I.C.: 268
Claussen, SC: 167
Clawson family: 228
Clay family: 285
Clayton, Claud F.: 228
Clayton, Claude Franklin: 228
Clayton family: 205,228,249
Clayton, Frederick V.: 61
Clayton, Frederick Van: 114
Clayton, Glenn: 132
Clayton, W.F.: 61
Clear Spring A.M.E. Church: 381
Clear Spring Baptist Church:146
Clear Springs Baptist Church: 20,213
Clearwater, Hon. A.T.: 352
Clearwater, Alphonso Trumbour: 352
Cleaves Chapel C.M.E.: 406

Cleckler family: 205
Cleland family: 210,283,284
Clem family: 228
Clem, Inus M.: 228
Clemens, William M.: 19
Clement, Abram W.: 334
Clement family: 352
Clement, Louise M.: 228
Clements family: 205
Clement's Ferry: 360
Clements Ferry Road: 302
Clemmer family: 250
Clemmons family: 205
Clemson Agricultural College: 132
Clemson Baptist Church: 123
Clemson College: 88,134,150, 165,404
Clemson family: 218
Clemson, SC: 42,53,64,91,108, 144,404
Clemson University: 54,87
Clendenen, Clarence C.: 313
Cleveland family: 210,282
Cleveland National Baptist Church (Negro): 410
Clifford family: 282,285
Clifton cotton factory: 120
Clifton, James M.: 313
Clifton No.1 Mill Village, SC: 409
Clifton No.1 Southern Baptist Church: 409
Clifton No.2 Mill Village, SC: 409
Clifton No.3 Southern Baptist Church: 409
Clifton Presbyterian Church:409
Clifton Wesleyan Methodist Church: 409
Clifton, SC: 172
Clingstone: 7
Clinkscales family: 205,279
Clinscales, John G.: 61
Clinton: 108,114
Clinton A.M.E. Zion Chapel: 412
Clinton A.M.E. Zion Church (Negro): 398
Clinton Chamber of Commerce: 61
Clinton family: 314
Clinton, Sir Henry: 61,79,299 305,311,346
Clinton Lodge No.60, A.F.M.: 72
Clinton, Martha Burnett: 203, 238
Clinton Mill, SC: 400
Clinton Presbyterian Church:152
Clinton, SC: 38,87,122,152,170, 399,400
Clinton United Methodist Church: 132
Clio Baptist Church: 403
Clio M.E. Church, South: 403
Clio Presbyterian Church: 403
Clio, SC: 108,403
Clipton family: 210
Cloinger family: 210
Clopton, William: 237
Cloud family: 205,207
Cloud's Creek Baptist Church: 133
Clover A.R.P. Church: 414
Clover First Southern Baptist Church: 414
Clover Presbyterian Church: 19, 152,413
Clover, SC: 8,19,49,413,414
Clower, George Wesley: 313
Clowney family: 228
Clowse, Converse D.: 61
Cloyd, A.D.: 228
Cloyd family: 228
Clute, Robert F.: 19

Clyburn, Margaret P.: 228
Clyde, Mrs. E.: 133
Clyde M.E. Church, South: 408
C.M.E. Church: 381
Coachman family: 205,285
Coast Defense Squadron: 76
Coate family: 205
Cobb family: 205,223,228,268, 292
Cobb, Howell: 317
Cobb, John: 292
Cobe, M.L.: 133
Cobia, Daniel: 278
Cobia family: 278,282
Cochean Town cemetery: 28
Cochran family: 285
Cochran, Mary Alice Boggs: 269
Cockfield family: 282
Cockrell, Augustus W.: 228
Cockrill family: 205,214
Cockroft family: 208
Coddington family: 230
Coddington, John I.: 211
Code of Honor: 342
Codner family: 285
Cody family: 252
Cofer family: 220
Coffee family: 205
Coffee, Isabelle Maxwell: 228
Coffin family: 282
Coffman family: 255
Cofitachique: 50
Cogburn family: 228
Cogburn, John: 228
Cogburn, Lewellyn E.: 228
Cogdell family: 282,284
Coghlan, Francis: 313
Cohen, Hennig: 19,61,62,313
Cohen, J. Barrett: 62,344
Cohen, Sydney Jacobi: 298
Cohh, Alice: 133
Cohoon family: 205
Coit, John C.: 133
Coit, John Calkins: 228
Coit, John E.: 228
Coker, Caleb Jr.: 228
Coker College: 62,96
Coker, Edwin C.: 62
Coker family: 216,272,280
Coker, Hannah L.: 62
Coker, J.L.: 133
Coker, J.L.& Co.:118
Coker, James L.: 62
Coker, Leon W.: 133
Coker, Lois W.: 62
Coker, Robert E.: 62,228
Coker, Robert Ervin: 313
Coker, Thomas H.: 62
Coker, W.C.: 229
Cokesbury family: 267
Cokesbury M.E. Church, South:395
Cokesbury Presbyterian Church:19
Cokesbury, SC: 53,77,92,395
Colby, Lydia: 229
Colclough family: 210,282
Colcock, C.J.: 229
Colcock, Charles J.: 378
Colcock, Erroll H.: 62
Colcock family: 332
Colcock, Capt. John: 332
Colcock, William Ferguson: 352
Colcough, Emma: 133
Colding family: 205
Cole, Captain A.B.: 229
Cole, David: 346
Cole, David W.: 62
Cole, Brigadier General Eli K.: 352
Cole family: 205,229,256
Cole Free Will Baptist Chapel: 409
Cole, Joada J.: 229
Cole, Robert F.: 229

Converse College: 83,120
Converse family: 274,282
Converse M.E. Church, South:409
Converse Mill Village, SC: 409
Converse Southern Baptist
 Church: 409
Converse Village, SC: 410
Conway Baptist Church: 125
Conway Chamber of Commerce: 63
Conway family: 223,282
Conway family: 282
Conway First Baptist Church:396
Conway, Mrs. Lester H.: 211
Conway, Louise Markham: 211
Conway M.E. Church, South: 396
Conway M.E. churchyard: 375
Conway, SC: 28,30,63,78,95,108,
 128,141,156,166,375,396,397
Conwayboro Academy: 95
Conyers family: 205,229,231,
 354,237,282
Cook, Andrew: 251
Cook, Anna Christina Palmer:251
Cook, Ella: 264
Cook family: 205,207,210,214,
 264,278,283
Cook family cemetery: 375
Cook, George L.: 63
Cook, Harriet H.: 63
Cook, Harvey T.: 63
Cook Springs, SC: 396
Cook, T.: 133
Cooke family: 282,285
Cooke, Howard, & Co.: 19
Cooke, John Esten: 313
Cook's Pentecostal Holiness
 Chapel: 393
Cool Blow Village: 108
Cool Branch M.E. churchyard:375
Cool Springs M.E. Church, South:
 396
Cool Springs Methodist ceme-
 tery: 28
Cool Springs, SC: 396,397
Cooley, Rossa B.: 63
Cooley Springs Southern Baptist
 Church: 410
Coombs, Miss Elizabeth: 353
Coone, Lucille B.: 229
Cooper family: 205,218,282,285
Cooper, Isabella: 262
Cooper, James F.: 133
Cooper, James H.: 229
Cooper River: 80,118,297,299,
 307,334,335
Cooper, Rev. Robert: 321
Cooper, Dr. Thomas: 323
Cooper, William J.,Jr.: 313
Coosawhatchie Baptist Church:
 370,416
Coosawhatchie, SC: 320,377
Cope, SC: 405
Copeland, D. Graham: 63
Copeland family: 202,210,229,
 272
Copeland, J. Isaac: 347
Copeland, Mary H.: 229,230
Corbett family: 238
Corbin family: 243
Corcoran, E. Emmons: 230
Corcoran family: 282
Cordes, Alexander Watson: 353
Cordes, Dr. Anthony: 330
Cordes family: 330,353
Cordle, Charles G.: 63
Cordova, SC: 405
Corinth Baptist Church: 405
Corinth First Southern Baptist
 Church: 383
Corinth Presbyterian Church: 19
Cork family: 205
Corker family: 210
Corkran, David H.: 63

Corley, B.F.: 133
Corley, Christina: 273
Corley family: 273
Corley, Lawrence: 273
Cornelia, William E.: 63
Cornelius family: 277
Corner family: 285
Cornish, John Hamilton: 310
Cornwell family: 210
Coronaca Baptist Church: 279,
 394
Coronaca community, SC: 279
Coronaca Presbyterian Church:19
Coronaca, SC: 394
Correll family: 255
Corry family: 238
Cortney family: 210
Cosgrove, John I.: 63
Cosgroves, James: 298
Cosper family: 205
Coste, Napoleon L.: 358
Costner family: 250
Coté, Richard N.: xi,xiv,5,200
Cothonneau family: 353
Cothran, Grange S.: 133
Cothran, Lily G.: 133
Cottageville Baptist Church:390
Cottageville, SC: 390
Cottin family: 284
Cottingham family: 210
Cotton, Charles Caleb: 326
Cottrell, Joseph E.: 63
Couch family: 205,211
Couillandeau, Susanne: 260
Coulter family: 205
Council of Safety: see S.C.
 Council of Safety
Counts family: 205
Coursey family: 205
Court family: 282
Courtenay family: 226,230
Courtenay Family Monument: 230
Courtenay school: 100
Courtenay, William A.: 63,230,
 298
Courtney family: 282
Courtonne family: 284,352
Cousar, James E.: 135,230
Cousar, James E.,Jr.: 230
Cousar, Rev. John: 230
Coussons, John S.: 353
Couturier family: 282
Covenanters: 111,133
Covenanters of Rocky Creek:
 174,176
Covington: 133
Covington family: 230,264
Covington, James W.: 313
Covington, William S.: 230
Cowan family: 210,230,252
Cowan, Dr. James Jones: 230
Cowan, Sarah Ann Cook: 230
Cowan, Zachary S.: 230
Cowards, SC: 393
Cowart family: 202
Cowen family: 285
Cowpens Centennial Committee:
 64
Cowpens First Baptist Church:
 133
Cowpens-Guilford Courthouse
 Campaign: 65
Cowpens Mills Baptist Church:
 409
Cowpens, SC: 50,63,64,65,78,
 133,409
Cowsert family: 205
Cox, Abner R.: 334
Cox, Elizabeth: 230
Cox family: 205,230,246,275,
 282,283
Cox, Henry Clay: 275,276

Cox, Henry Miot: 313
Cox, James R.: 64
Cox, Julia D. Bradford: 276
Cox, Mrs. L.D.: 133
Cox, Leland H.: xiii
Coyle family: 230
Cozby family: 210
Craig, Eloise: 19
Craig family: 205,208,230,282,
 283
Craig, John: 230
Craig, Rev. John: 252
Craig, Marion S.: 230
Craighead family: 210,230
Craighead, James: 230
Craighead, Margaret: 230
Craighead, Rev. Thomas: 230
Cramer, Alderman A.F.C.: 298
Crane, Verner W.: 64
Crapton family: 205
Craven County: 22,67,77,107,
 364,415,419
Craven, Delle M.: 64
Craven, Mrs. H.H.: 134
Cravens family: 230
Cravens, John P.: 230
Cravens, John Park: 230
Crawford: 334
Crawford family: 210,235,239,
 247,266,291
Crawford, James: 239
Crawford, John: 266
Crawford, Lee F.: 230
Crawford, Martha: 239
Crawford, Paul: 211
Crawford, Samuel W.: 64
Crawfordsville Southern Baptist
 Church: 410
Crawfordville M.E. Church,
 South: 410
Crays family: 217
Crayton family: 205
Creaddick family: 206
Creech family: 210
Creek Indians: 332
Creekmore, Robert: 230
Creighton family: 205
Crenshaw family: 205
Crescent Hill Baptist cemetery:
 376
Crescent Hill Baptist Church:406
Creston, SC: 385
Creswell family: 230,239,277
Creswell, John O.: 230
Creswell, Michael D.: 134
Cribb family: 205
Crichton family: 285
Crider family: 271
Crider, Gussie W.: 230
Criswell family: 277
Crittenden, Stephen S.: 64,134
Crocham family:
Crocker family: 210
Crockett family: 210,214,234,
 241,363
Crockett, Nancy: 20
Crocketville, SC: 25,146,395
Croft Baptist Church: 134
Croft family: 250,294
Cromer, Willie S.: 134
Cromwell family: 213,355,362
Cronic, Josie W.: 230
Crooked Run Baptist Church: 134
Crooked Run Primitive Baptist
 Church: 418
Crooks family: 210
Cropper, Mariam D.: 64
Crory, Susan: 256
Crosby family: 205,277
Croskey family: 282
Crosland, Ann Snead: 252,275
Crosland, Edward: 252,275
Crosland family: 210,289

Crosland Memorial Baptist
  Church: 406
Crosleigh, Charles: 230
Cross, Jack L.: 313
Cross, SC: 134
Cross Anchor M.E. Church, South:
  410
Cross Anchor, SC: 410
Cross Hill Baptist Church: 399
Cross Hill M.E. Church, South:
  400
Cross Hill, SC: 31,40,153,399,
  400
Cross, J. Russell: 134
Cross, Jesse C.: 230
Cross Road A.M.E. Church: 408
Cross Road Negro Baptist
  Church: 395
Cross Roads Baptist Church:
  136,404
Cross Roads C.M.E. Church: 383
Cross Roads Free Will Baptist
  Church: 391
Cross Roads Negro Baptist
  Church: 399
Crosskeys family: 285
Crossle family: 230
Crosslegh family: 230
Crossley family: 230
Crottet family: 355
Crouch, C.W.: 64
Crouch family: 211,230,235
Crouch, Katy A.: 64,134
Crouse, Maurice A.: 231,314
Crovatt family: 282
Crow family: 204,254
Crowder, Mrs. J.W.: 211
Crowder, Louise K.: 20,134
Crowder, Louise Kelly: 314
Crowley family: 210
Croxton, Alma D.: 211
Croxton, Mrs. E.C.: 211
Crozier family: 240
Crozier, William A.: 20
Cruger family: 233,282
Crum, George Milton: 134
Crum, Mason: 194
Cruse, Guy C.: 134
Crutchfield family: 205,210
C.S.S. David (ship): 106
Culber family: 215
Culbertson, Ambrose B.:231
Culbertson, B.Y.: 134
Culbertson family: 231
Culbertson, John: 231
Culbertson, W.P.: 134
Culler, Emily: 231
Culler family: 231
Culler, Hugh C.: 231
Culler, Jacob: 231
Cullop family: 237
Culp family: 205,243
Cults: 224
Cumbe family: 210
Cumberland A.M.E. Church: 382
Cumberland A.M.E. Zion Church:
  392
Cumberland M.E. Church, South.
  Sunday School Society: 134
Cumbo family: 210
Cumming, William P.: 1
Cummings family: 231
Cunningham, Ann Pamela: 119
Cunningham, Mrs. C.D.: 134
Cunningham, Carolina: 231
Cunningham, Clarence: 64
Cunningham family: 205,237,254,
  279
Cunyus family: 231
Cunyus, Walter H.: 231
Cupit family: 231
Cupit, John T.: 211,231
Cureton family: 205,231,268

Cureton, Thomas K.: 231
Curley family: 248
Currence family: 247
Currence, Mary Susan: 203
Current family: 246
Current, Jane Wilson Call:238,
  246
Current, Matthew: 238,246
Currie, Dr. James: 324
Curry, Annie H.: 231
Curtis, Elizabeth: 360
Curtis family: 249,282
Curtis, Julia: 314
Curtis, Mary B.: 20
Curtis, Mary Julia: 314
Curtner family: 221
Cusaba Indians: 191
Cusabo: 67
Cushing, Alonzo H.: 245
Cushing, Howard B.: 245
Cushing, William B.: 245
Cushion Swamp cemetery: 28
Cusiman, Mrs. Frank: 211
Cusimano, Grace Camulette: 211
Cuthbert family: 217,224,282,
  285,291
Cutler family: 225
Cuttino family: 282,284,353
Cuttino, G.P.: 353
Cuttino, Marguerite A.: 134
Cuttino, William: 353
Cutts family: 210,252
Cypress Baptist Church: 395
Cypress Barony: 335
Cypress Campground: 108,134
Cypress cemetery: 16,127
Cypress Chapel A.M.E. Church:
  381
Cypress M.E. Church, South:392
Cypress Methodist Church: 134,
  416
Cypress Methodist Episcopal
  Church, South: 127
Cypress Tree plantation: 319

- D -

Dabbs, Edith M.: 64
Dabbs, James McBride: 3
Dabney, William M.: 64,314
Dabney's Pond Negro Baptist
  Church: 407
Dacus family: 231
Dacusville M.E. Church, South:
  406
Dacusville Village, SC: 406
Dade family: 235
Daisy, SC: 396,397
D'Albert, Jeanne: 356
Dalcho, Frederick: 64,134
Dalcho, Rev. Frederick:
Dalcho Historical Society: 134
Dallas, James M.: 134
Dalrymple family: 205
Dalton family: 282,283
Daly, Charles P.: 64
Dalzell M.E. Church, South:411
Dalzell, SC: 411
Damascus Baptist Church: 395
Damascus M.E. Church, South:398
Damascus Methodist churchyard:
  374
Damascus Negro Baptist Church:
  395
Dammon family: 282
Dana, William C.: 134
Dancy family: 225
Dandridge, Danske: 20
Dandy family: 205
Danforth, Edward C.: 231
Danforth family: 231
Daniel family: 210,276,282,285,
  289

Daniel, J.W.: 134
Daniel, John Sr.: 242
Daniel, Lucia: 347
Daniel, Robert N.: 65,135
Daniel, Sadie L.: 196
Daniell family: 210
Daniels family: 234,266
Daniels, Johnathan: 65
Danielson family: 230
Dannelly family: 231
Danner, Howard E.: 377
Danner, Ruby C.: 377
Daniel, David: 368
Daniel, Willis: 368
Danniell family: 284
Dantzler, Daniel D.: 231
Dantzler, David H.: 231
Dantzler, Elizabeth Shuler: 231
Dantzler family: 231,287
D.A.R. (see also National Soci-
  ety, Daughters of the American
  Revolution; also South Caroli-
  na Society, Daughters of the
  American Revolution.)
Darby family: 205,231,275,282
Darby, George: 231
Darby, Joseph: 231
Darby, Rufus C.: 231
Darden, Mrs. Edward C.: 211
Darden, Evelyn Baldwin: 211
Darden family: 231
Darden, Newton J.: 231
Dargan family: 210,223
Darien Baptist cemetery: 373
"Dark Corner" of Greenville
  County: 79
Darley family: 231
Darley, Lon J.: 231
Darlington Christian Science
  Society: 390
Darlington Circuit, M.E. Church:
  194
Darlington County: 20,21,32,65,
  69,93,96,101,108,116,133,154,
  155,161,162,182,198,364,368,
  374,375,390,416,417
Darlington County Agricultural
  Society: 93
Darlington County Historical
  Society: 7,65
Darlington Court House: 20
Darlington District: 62,313
Darlington First Baptist Church:
  390
Darlington Flag: 370
Darlington Guards: 58
Darlington Hebrew Congregation:
  181
Darlington Jewish Congregation-
  Reform: 391
Darlington Methodist Church:416
Darlington Presbyterian Church:
  20,139,416
Darlington riot of 1894: 78,112
Darlington Second Baptist
  Church: 391
Darlington, SC: 20,108,129,133,
  139,170,176,364,390,391,416
Darlington Station, M.E. Church:
  194
Darnall family: 281
Darneal family: 281
Darneille family: 281
Darnell family: 281
Darnielle family: 281
Darnold family: 281
Darracott family: 290
Darraugh family: 205
Darrell family: 282
Dartmouth, Lord: 339
Darwin family: 205
Datha Island: 103
D'Aubigne, Agrippa: 354

438

439

Ephraim family: 237
Epiphany Chapel (Protestant Episcopal): 406
Epiphany Evangelical Lutheran Church: 386
Epiphany Lutheran Church: 416
Epiphany Mission (Protestant Episcopal): 408
Epiphany Protestant Episcopal Church: 385
Episcopal cemetery: 375,376
Episcopal Church Home for Children: 22
Episcopal Church in SC: 165
Episcopal Church of the Advent: 40
Episcopal Church of Our Savior: 22
Episcopal Church of the Nativity: 412
Episcopal Churches of Columbia: 139
Episcopal churchyard: 373
Episcopal Diocese of SC: see Protestant Episcopal Church in the United States. Diocese of SC.
Episcopal Diocese of Upper SC: see Protestant Episcopal Church in the U.S. Diocese of Upper SC.
Eppes family: 205
Epting, Carl L.: 347
Epting family: 237
Epting Memorial M.E. Church, South: 404
Epton family: 237
Epton, Theodore: 237
Epworth M.E. Church, South: 391, 400
Epworth Orphanage M.E. Church, South: 407
Epworth, SC: 395
Epworth Tabernacle M.E. Church, South: 395
Erath, Clara E.: 237
Erhardt Memorial United Evangelical Lutheran Church: 384
Erhardt, SC: 384
Erhardt Southern Baptist Church: 384
Erisman family: 255
Erskine College: xiii,83,86,104
Ervin, Eliza C.: 69
Ervin family: 210,237,240,282
Ervin, Col. John: 316
Ervin, Julia: 139
Ervin, Sam J.: 237
Ervin, Sam, Jr.: 316
Ervin, Sam J., Jr.: 237
Ervin, Senator Sam J., Jr.: 354
Ervin, Sara S.: 237
Ervin, Sarah S.: 23
Ervin, Mrs. Sarah S.: 211
Erwin family: 210,247,262,282, 283
Erwin, Lane E.: 69
Erwin, Lucy L.: 237
Esker, Mrs. Jerome: 211
Esker, Katie-Prince W.: 23
Esnard family: 210
Estes, Charles: 237
Estes, David Jonathan: 294
Estes family: 237,294
Estes, Frank B.: 139
Estes, Nannie Ruth Bobo: 294
Estill M.E. Church, South: 395
Estill Presbyterian Church: 395
Estill, SC: 395,396
Etheridge family: 205,222,237, 291
Etheridge, Hamlin W.: 237
Etiwan Lodge: 69

Eubank family: 282
Eubanks family: 205
Euhaw Baptist Church: 23,137, 138, 139, 416
Eulalie: 54
Eulonia Baptist Church: 139, 402
Eureka Baptist Church: 139
Eureka Baptist churchyard: 373
Eureka Southern Baptist Church: 382,383
Eustis family: 237,282
Eustis, Warner: 237
Eutaw Springs: 116
Eutawville Baptist Church: 405
Eutawville M.E. Church, South: 405
Eutawville, SC: 73,107,385,405, 406
Evangelical Lutheran Charities Society: 69
Evans A.M.E. Zion Chapel: 403
Evans, Charles: 1,2
Evans, Clement A.: 70
Evans, E.G.: 139
Evans, Eytive L.: 237
Evans, Eytive Long: 211
Evans family: 205,206,219,230, 278,282
Evans, James
Evans, James D.: 70, 237
Evans, John Gary: 347
Evans, Nancy B.: xiii
Evans, Nathaniel: 237
Evans, Regina: 237
Evans, Richard Xavier: 316
Evard, Helen E.: 237
Eve family: 282
Evelegh family: 265
Eveleigh family: 265
Eveleth family: 265
Evely family: 265
Evening Light Reformation Holiness Church of America (Negro): 411
Everett family: 264
Evergreen A.M.E. Church: 412
Evergreen Baptist Church: 393
Evergreen cemetery: 29,39,374
Evergreen M.E. Church (Negro): 384
Evergreen Negro Baptist Church: 384,390
Evergreen, SC: 393
Everhart family: 266
Everitt family: 205
Everle family: 265
Everleigh family: 265,284
Everley family: 265
Everton, George B.: 200
Everybody's Mission - Undenominational (Church): 408
Evins family: 205
Eubank family: 282
Ewing family: 210,237,283
Ewing, Gretchen Garst: 316
Ewing, Linda C.: 237
Exchange & Custom House: 117
Exum family: 254,269
Eylar family: 252
Eyton Hall: 230
Ezell A.M.E. Zion Church: 413
Ezell family: 238,279
Ezell, George: 279
Ezell, Helen H.: 238
Ezell, Mildred S.: 238

- F -

Fabian family: 282
Fagg, Daniel W. Jr.: 316
Fagg, Jenny M.: 238
Fahs family: 255

Fahs family: 255
Fail family: 238
Fail, Welton B.: 238
Faile family: 238
Faile, J.A.: 139
Fails family: 238
Fair Bluff, SC: 397
Fair family: 254
Fair Forest Presbyterian Church cemetery: 41
Fair Hope Presbyterian Church: 23,169
Fair, Marilou R.: 238
Fair Plains A.M.E. Church: 403
Fair Play Presbyterian Church: 404
Fair View A.M.E. Church: 384
Fair View Industrial Home: 98
Fairchild family: 215,282
Fairey family: 210
Fairey, Robert T.: 70
Fairfax cemetery: 373
Fairfax, SC: 141, 382
Fairfield C.M.E. Church: 383
Fairfield Baptist Church: 133
Fairfield County: 25,31,38,41, 69,70,88,89,94,107,114,154,168, 180,215,222,227,237,246,250, 255,263,293,319,364,369,374, 375,419
Fairfield District, SC: 218
Fairfield Negro Baptist Church: 381
Fairfield, SC: 52,96,208
Fairforest Baptist Church: 23, 164,175,408,416
Fairforest National Baptist Boyd's Convention Church: 409
Fairforest Presbyterian Church: 23,412
Fairforest Village, SC: 409
Fairmont M.E. Church, South: 410
Fairmont Mills Village, SC: 410
Fairmont Southern Baptist Church: 410
Fairview Methodist Protestant Church: 383
Fairview Negro Baptist Church: 404
Fairview #1 Southern Baptist Church: 410
Fairview #2 Southern Baptist Church: 410
Fairview Southern Baptist Church: 412
Fairview Baptist Church: 139
Fairview Presbyterian Church: 139,416
Faith Bible Church: 139
Faison family: 210
Faith Chapel - Protestant Episcopal: 395
Faith Evangelical Lutheran Church: 402
Faith Tabernacle - Interdenominational: 409
Fair, Mildred C.: 238
Family Puzzlers: 7
Fannin family: 238, 240
Fanning family: 238
Fanning, Lawrence: 238
Fant, Alfred E.: 238
Fant, Christie Z.: 70
Fant family: 238, 246
Fant, Mrs. George C.: 140
Fant, Sandy: 23
Fare family: 282
Faries family: 238
Faris family: 206, 238
Faris, Thomas M.: 238
Faris, Thomas Murray: 238
Farish family: 234
Farly family: 235

Fraser, Benjamin Porter: 276
Fraser, Charles: 71
Fraser family: 266,276,282,283,
332
Fraser Memorial Presbyterian
Church: 411
Fraser, Walter J.: 71
Fraser, Walter J., Jr.: 317
Fraternal Cemetery Association,
Florence: 71
Frazer family: 254,282
Frazer's Temple A.M.E. Zion:399
Frazier, Evelyn M.: 200
Frazier family: 206
Frazier, Irvin: 240
Frech, Laura P.: 317
Frederick family: 210,249
Free Blacks: 195
Free family cemetery: 375
Free Light Independent Mission-
ary Baptist Church: 397
The Free Negro in Ante-Bellum
SC: 213
Free Persons of Color: 194
Free Vine Negro Baptist Church:
397
Free Will A.M.E. Independent
Church of God: 398
Free Will Baptist Church: 391,
398,407
Free Woods, SC: 397
Freedman's Bureau: 117,194,195,
309,346
Freeman family: 210,282
Freeman, James: 94
Freeman, J. Earle: 144
Freemasons: 89
Freemasons. Claremont Lodge
No. 64 A.F.M.: 111
Freemasons. Clinton Lodge No.
60: 72
Freemasons. Dalcho Lodge No.
160. Latta: 49
Freemasons. Grand Lodge of SC.,
Ancient York-Masons: 64
Freemasons. Kershaw Lodge No.
29: 72,116
Freemasons. Landmark Lodge,
Charleston: 84
Freemasons. Mackey Lodge No.
77, Dillon: 113
Freemasons. Orange Lodge No.
14: 95,117
Freemasons. Union Kilwinning
Lodge No. 4: 80
Freemasons. Supreme Council:
197
Freer family: 282,285
Freewill Baptist Church: 159,
403,413
French, Mrs. A.M.: 71
French forts: 359
French Hospital: 354
French Huguenots: 352
French Huguenot Church of St.
James, Goose Creek: 354
French Jamestown: 335,352
French, Janie P.: 241
French, Justus Clement: 71
French Protestant Church of
London: 351
French Protestants: (see also
Huguenots): 35,93,344,356
French Protestant (Huguenot)
Church: 84,144,145,150,176,180,
307,358,360,387
French Protestant (Huguenot)
churchyard: 374
French Quarter: 352
French Reformation: 361,362
French Santee: 351,356
Freneau, Phillip: 323
Freshley family: 368
Friend, Carter W.: 241

Friend, Captain Thomas: 241
Friendfield, SC: 392
Friendship A.M.E. Church: 395,
403,405,412
Friendship Baptist Church: 145,
364,399,402
Friendship Chapel Pentecostal
Holiness Church: 391
Friendship churchyard: 373
Friendship M.E. Church, South:
389,394
Friendship National Baptist
Church: 409
Friendship Negro Baptist
Church: 328,381,386,391,395,
401,402
Friendship Pentecostal Holiness
Church: 395
Friendship Presbyterian Church:
146,400
Friendship, SC: 381
Friendship Southern Baptist
Church: 383,410
Friendship United Methodist
Church: 134
Frierson burying ground: 376
Frierson, Rev. David Ethan: 241
Frierson family: 210,241,262,
287,289
Frierson, John: 262
Frierson, John L.: 145,241
Frierson, Robert E.: 241
Frink family: 206,253,273,282
Frink, Henry Farnsworth: 253
Frink, Wilbur Gustavus: 253
Fripp family: 236,241,282
Fripp, Nellie Hasell: 377
Fripp, William Edward: 317
Fritz, William R.: 2
Frizzell family: 271
Frogmore, SC: 64
Frost, Donald McKay: 71
Frost family: 282,283
Frost, Mary Pringle: 72
Frost, Susan P.: 72
Fry, Ron: 200
Fryer family: 282
Fugler, Madge Q.: 241
Fuller, Benjamin: 216,219
Fuller, Elizabeth B.: 72
Fuller family: 210,214,216,217,
219,241,249,282,285
Fuller, Theodore A.: 241
Fuller, William: 325
Fullerton family: 241,284
Fullerton, Gordon W.: 241
Fullingham family: 210
Fullingim family: 212
Fullinwider family: 263
Fullwood family: 210,241,263
Fulmer family: 240
Fulmer, Verley L.: 145,241
Fulton cemetery: 376
Funchess family: 255
Fundaburk, Emma L.: 191
Funderburk family: 241
Funderburk, Guy B.: 241
Funderburk, Harold W.: 72
Furchgott, Max: 300
Furman Baptist Church: 396
Furman family: 241,249
Furman family cemetery: 375
Furman, James D.: 241
Furman, James C.: 145
Furman M.E. Church, South: 396
Furman, Mary C.: 72
Furman, SC: 396
Furman University: 65,381
Furnas, Esther: 271
Furniss family: 206
Futch family: 281
Fuzzlebug, Fritz: 72

Gabeau, Antoine: 362
Gable A.M.E. Mission: 389
Gaddy family: 210
Gadsden, Christopher: 338,341,
347,350
Gadsden, Gen. Christopher: 324,
345
Gadsden family: 282
Gadsden, P.H.: 300
Gadsden, Mr.: 311
Gadsden, Reverend: 359
Gadsden, Sam: 72
Gaffney family: 241
Gaffney, Michael: 72,83
Gaffney, Captain Michael: 120
Gaffney Sesquicentennial: 72
Gaffney, SC: 31,137,141,148,
158,159,161,388
Gage, Robert J.: 72
Gaillard, _____: 354
Gaillard, Clermond LeClair: 253
Gaillard, David DuBose: 352
Gaillard, Lt. Col. David
DuBose: 356
Gaillard, Edward McCrady: 354
Gaillard, Esther Paparel: 260
Gaillard family: 206,241,253,
260,282,284,340,353,354,358
Gaillard, Joachim: 260
Gaillard, John: 317
Gaillard, Leize Palmer: 72
Gaillard, Peter Charles: 359
Gaillard, Pierre: 253
Gaillard, Samuel Gourdin: 329
Gaillard, Thomas: 354
Gaillard, W. Lucas: 354
Gaines family: 206,214,219,
241,288
Gaines, Francis: 241
Gaines, Henry: 241
Gaines Hill Negro Baptist
Church: 396
Gaines, Isabella Pendleton:288
Gaines, Lewis P.: 241
Gaines, Thomas R.: 241
Gaines, William: 288
Galbraith family: 210
Galbraith, J.E.H.: 317
Galilee Negro Baptist
Church: 382,388,411,412
Galivant's Ferry Baptist
Church: 396
Galivants Ferry, SC: 396,397
Gallagher family: 282
Gallardo, Jose Miguel: 317
Gallman cemetery: 40
Gallman family: 210
Galloway family: 210
Galloway Memorial M.E. Church,
South: 394
Galluchat family: 282
Galphin cemetery: 363
Galphin family: 363
Gamble family: 202,210,215,
241,272
Gambrell family: 206,233
Gambrell, Raymond D.: 212
Gambrell, Sarah E.: 241
Gamewell, J.A.: 24
Gamewell, Prof.: 120
Gammill family: 206
Gandee, Lee R.: 72
Gannaway, Mrs. T.A.: 212
Gantt family: 241,262
Gap Hill Baptist Church: 149
Gapway Baptist Church: 145,403
Gara, Larry: 319
Garber, Paul N.: 145
Garber, Virginia A.: 241
Garden, Alexander: 72,322,339
Garden, Maj. Alexander: 317
Garden family: 282

Gardner, Benjamin H.: 241
Gardner family: 241
Gardner, George W.: 145
Gardner, William L.: 241
Garlington family: 278
Garlington, J.C.: 197
Garlington, Thesta K.: 278
Garner cemetery: 40
Garner family: 241
Garner, Sam: 241
Garnett, SC: 395
Garnier, Elizabeth: 358,360
Garnier family: 285
Garretson family: 252
Garrett, Cynthia: 269
Garrett, Edward: 265
Garrett family: 206,241,242,
265,282
Garrett family cemetery: 36
Garrett, Hester E.: 241
Garrett, T.H.: 145
Garrison, Caleb, Jr.: 276
Garrison, Charles Cleveland:242
Garrison family: 206,207,236,
247
Garrison, Harry C.: 242
Garrison, Sarah Fleming: 276
Garrou, Hilda W.: 242
Garth, Charles: 309
Garth, Hon. Charles, M.P.: 310
Garvin, Mrs. Cora: 34
Garvin family: 282
Gary, Arthur: 222
Gary family: 206,222
Gary's brigade: 31
Gaskins family: 223
Gasper family: 206
Gasque, Lonnie M.: 72
Gassoway family: 210
Gaston, Amzi Williford II: 242
Gaston, David A.: 72
Gaston family: 206,208,232,242
250,263,280
Gaston, SC: 401
Gaston, Thelma: 242,280
Gatchell family: 242,282
Gate City Mission A.M.E.
Church: 392
Gatell, Frank Otto: 317
Gates family: 239
Gatewood, Williard B.: 317
Gaudelock family: 242
Gault, Charles B.: 242
Gault family: 242
Gault, Francis Beers: 242
Gault, Mrs. Francis Beers: 242
Gault, Pressly B.: 242
Gault, William: 242
Gause family: 206,219,282
Gauthier family: 215
Gauvain, Louise: 269
Gay family: 206,245,258,282
Gayden family: 206
Gayle, Charles Joseph: 347
Gazette of the State of
South Carolina: 321
Geauregard, General: 327
Geddings family: 291
Geddings, Friendly Swepson: 291
Geddings, Dr. J.F.M.: 300
Gee, Charles: 239
Gee, Christine S.: 242
Gee family: 239,242,282
Gee, Hannah: 240
Gee, Mary G.: 242
Gee, Wilson: 242
Geer, William M.: 347
Geiger, A.F.: 72
Geiger family: 206,242
Geiger, Florence Gambrill: 317
Geiger, Percey L.: 242
Geigleman family: 210
Geimer, Alfred F.: 2

Gelston, Arthur Lewis: 317
Gelzer family: 282
Gendron family: 354
Gendron, John: 355
Genealogical Institute: 200
Genealogy Exchange: 213
General Committee: 326
Generostee Negro Baptist
Church: 384
Generostes A.R.P. Church: 383
Gentry, David: 243
Gentry family: 206,242,252
Gentry Memorial Baptist
Church: 408
George, Annie L.: 145
George, Bernice A.: 33
George family: 206,282
George, King of England: 337
George Street, Charleston,
SC: 59
George, Virginia M.: 146
George, W. Williams & Company:
57
Georges Creek, SC: 221
Georgetown Baptist cemetery:
375
Georgetown County: 42,49,52,85,
100,107,148,214,289,330,375,
418
Georgetown County Memorial Lib-
rary: xiii
Georgetown District: 339
Georgetown Hebrew cemetery: 375
Georgetown Historic District:
121
Georgetown Library Society: 89,
317
Georgetown Methodist Church:342
Georgetown Post No. 114: 97
Georgetown Presbyterian Church:
24,35,416
Georgetown Rifle Guards: 69
Georgetown, SC: 6,21,22,24,26,
30,35,49,52,54,85,87,97,101,
107,109,114,119,134,136,141,
156,172,176,322,327,335,416
Georgia: 2,17,20,39,43,60,73,
77,81,82,84,89,93,95,111,115,
127,138,148,153,163,176,191,
202,203,207,209,213,224,225,
229,232,241,244,250,258,259,
260,266,272,280,281,287,312,
326,336,337,359
Georgia Genealogical Magazine:
7,379
Georgia Genealogist: 7
Gerezion M.E. Church, South:405
Gergel, Richard Mark: 347
German Artillery. Companies
A & B: 303
German Artillery Memorial
Association: 31,374
German cemetery: 374
German Colonization Society: 72
German Colony: 95
German Friendly Society: 72,74
German Fusiliers: 300
German Protestants: 111,329
German Reformed Church: 369
German Rifle Club: 66
German settlements: 125
German - Swiss: 115,350
Germany: 256,355
Gervais family: 282
Gervais, John Lewis: 336,355
Gethsemane Missionary Baptist
Church: 386
Gethsemane National Baptist
Church (Negro): 410
Gethsemane Negro Baptist
Church: 386,399
Gethsemane (Penn Swamp) M.E.
Church, South: 406

Getsinger, Boardman G.: 146
Gettys, Ebenezer: 146
Gettys, James W.: 72
Geupel, Mrs. Ruby T.: 212
Ghents Branch Southern Baptist
Church: 384
Ghirelli, Michael: 13
Gholston family: 219,267
Gibbes, Carolina Elizabeth
Guignard: 276
Gibbes, D.L.: 146
Gibbes family: 239,282,284,285,
320
Gibbes family cemetery: 311
Gibbes, James G.: 72
Gibbes, James S. Memorial
Art Gallery: 301
Gibbes, John E.: 354
Gibbes, Gov. Robert: 320
Gibbes, Robert W.: 72,243,321
Gibbes, Robert Wilson, M.D.:
276
Gibbes, William Hasell: 312
Gibbon family: 282
Gibbs family: 240,269,282
Giberson, Sallie G: 212
Gibert, Anne C.: 73,243,354,
355
Gibert family: 243,250
Gibert, Pierre: 73,250
Gibert, Pierre, Esq.: 243
Gibson, B.M.: 146
Gibson family: 206,237,243,282,
317
Gibson, J. Preston: 243
Gibson, Lewis: 146
Giessendanner, John: 34
Giessendanner, Rev. John: 329
Giessendanner, John Ulrich:309
Giessendanner register: 365
Gifford, SC: 396
Gignilliat, Captain: 357
Gignilliat family: 255,282,284,
285,354,355
Gilbert family: 206,282
Gilbert M.E. Church, South:401
Gilbert, SC: 154,401
Gilbert's Negro Baptist
Church: 406
Gilchrist family: 206
Gilchrist, Robert C.: 73
Gilchrist, Major Robert C.:300
Gildea, Michael M.: 317
Gilder family: 206
Gilead Free Will Baptist
Church: 392
Gilead Southern Baptist
Church: 412
Giles family: 208
Giles family cemetery: 375
Gilgal M.E. Church, South: 381
Gilgal, SC: 381
Gilkey family: 206,243
Gilkey, George L.: 243
Gilkey, John: 208
Gill family: 206
Gillam, Mrs. Eulalie S.: 73
Gillam family: 233
Gillams Chapel (M.E. Church,
South): 412
Gillas Baptist Church
cemetery: 40
Gillespie family graveyard: 312
Gilley family: 243
Gillham family: 210
Gilliam family: 261
Gillis family: 210
Gillisonville, SC: 377
Gillispie family: 206
Gillon, Commodore Alexander:
324,334
Gill's Creek A.R.P. Church: 399
Gilman, Arthur: 243

447

449

452

Hogue family: 237
Hogue, L. Lynn: 320
Hoke, Rachel H.: 250
Holcomb, Brent H.: 10,26,27,28,
31,200,251,368
Holcomb family: 283
Holcombe family: 206,263
Holcombe, Lena: 150
Holden, Pauline: 251
Holdren National Baptist
Chapel (Negro): 410
Holesonback family: 206
Holiday, Billy: 150
Holiness Church: 383
Holiness or Sanctified Church:
399
Holiness Tabernacle Christ's
Sanctified Holy Church: 409
Holiness Tabernacle Pentecostal
Holiness Church: 392
Holladay, Elizabeth D.: 251
Holland: 277,355
Holland family: 210,250,251
Holland, Janice: 78
Hollenman, Frances: 78
Holleman, Joseph T.: 28
Holley, Edward C.: 2
Holley, Gerald D.: 78
Holliday family: 214,283
Hollings, Marie F.: xiii,5
Hollingshead family: 210
Hollingsworth, Clyde D.: 212
Hollingsworth, Mrs. Clyde D.:
212
Hollingsworth, Dixon: 191
Hollingsworth family: 206,214,
283,287
Hollingsworth, Julia A.: 251
Hollingsworth, Leon: 212
Hollingsworth, Leon S.: 10,251
Hollingsworth, Valentine: 251
Hollingsworth, Valentine, Sr.:
251,287
Hollingsworth, William B.: 251
Hollinshed family: 210
Hollis, Daniel W.: 78,150,320
Hollis family: 206,251
Holloway family: 210
Holley Creek Negro Baptist
Church: 384
Holly Grove Baptist Church: 400
Holly Hill Baptist Church: 405
Holly Hill M.E. Church, South:
405
Holly Hill Negro Baptist
Church: 390
Holly Hill, SC: 73,405
Holly Springs Baptist Church:
150
Holly Springs Negro Baptist
Church: 384
Holly Springs Southern Baptist
Church: 410
Holman family: 206,227,246,283
Holman, Harriet R.: 320
Holmes, A.G.: 150
Holmes, Alester G.: 78
Holmes, Ann M.: 78
Holmes, Emma E.: 326
Holmes family: 206,237,283,285
Holmes, Francis Simmons: 301
Holmes, George S.: 150,301
Holmes, Henry Schultz: 320
Holmes Memorial Pentecostal
Holiness Church: 394
Holmgren, Virginia C.: 78
Holsombake family: 206
Holsonback, Mrs. J.C.: 212
Holston Creek Baptist Church:
148
Holston family: 206
Holt, Henry: 314
Holtzclaw family: 206

Holy Church Freewill Negro
Baptist Church: 403
Holy Comforter Reformed Epis-
copal Church: 385
Holy Communion Church
Institute: 98,150
Holy Communion Protestant
Episcopal Church: 382,386
Holy Cross Episcopal Church:
22,319,416
Holy Divine Tabernacle Holiness
Church: 408
Holy Road cemetery: 376
Holy Springs Negro Baptist
Church: 404
Holy Trinity Episcopal Church:
318
Holy Trinity Evangelical
Lutheran Church: 401,404
Holy Trinity Lutheran Church:
382
Holy Trinity Reformed Episcopal
Church: 387
Holy Trinity Roman Catholic
Church: 405,412
Home Branch Baptist Church: 389
Home Branch Baptist church-
yard: 374
Homewood M.E. Church, South:397
Homewood, SC: 396
Honea Path Baptist Church: 147
Honea Path Bicentennial
Committee: 78
Honea Path Presbyterian
Church: 28,150,383
Honea Path, SC: 28,77,78,383
Honea Path Southern Baptist
Church: 383
Honey Hill, SC: 378
Honilton: 361
Honour, John Henry: 301
Hood, Belle M.: 251
Hood, C.W.: 150
Hood family: 24,206
Hook, Captain James: 251
Hook, James W.: 251
Hook, John Martin 1st: 258
Hood, Kate W.: xiii
Hooker cemetery: 39
Hooker, Flora J.: 251
Hooks, Charles: 247
Hooks family: 247
Hooks, Margaret Monk Harris:247
Hooper family: 210
Hope family: 210
Hope M.E. Church, South: 409
Hope, Robert M.: 78
Hope, William C: 251
Hopewell (Pickens' family
home): 91
Hopewell A.R.P. Church: 28,155
Hopewell Baptist Church: 28,
150,161,175,390,396,416
Hopewell Baptist Church ceme-
tery: 36
Hopewell Baptist Church (Negro)
400
Hopewell Baptist churchyard:373
Hopewell C.M.E. Church: 396
Hopewell Church: 150
Hopewell M.E. Church, South:
391,400,403
Hopewell M.E.S. Church: 399
Hopewell Negro Baptist Church:
388,403,411
Hopewell Negro M.E. Church: 388
Hopewell Presbyterian Church:
28,124,150,167,216,382,394,
404,413
Hopke, J. G. August: 301
Hopkins family: 206,251,259,
268,283
Hopkins, Laura J.: 150,251
Hopkins, Margaret: 268

Hopkins Presbyterian Church:
28,407
Hopkins, SC: 407
Hopkins, Solomon: 268
Hopkins, Thomas F.: 301
Hoppin, Charles A.: 251
Hoppingrill family: 273
Horan family: 210
Hord, Arnold H.: 251
Hord family: 251
Horeb Baptist Church: 150,395
Horeb Presbyterian Church
cemetery: 375
Horeb Southern Baptist
Church: 411
Horlacher, Hans Michael: 251
Horlacher, Levi J.: 251
Horlacher, Maria Veronica: 251
Horlacher, Vaneta T.: 251
Horlbeck, Elizabeth Miles: 355
Horlbeck, Mrs. Frederick H.:28
Horlbeck, Dr. H.B.: 301,304
Horlbeck, Peter: 298
Horn, Rev. E.T.:301
Horn, Edward T.: 150
Horn, Edward Trail: 289
Horn family: 210,289
Horne, Erleen: 78
Horne family: 251
Horning family: 242
Horn's Creek Baptist Church:
28,161,183,417
Horn's Creek, SC: 45,415
Hornsby family: 210,314
Horry County Histroical
Society: 7,10,78
Horry County Library: 29
Horry County, SC: 10,12,28,29,
78,95,107,115,147,157,162,205,
206,208,213,214,219,244,273,
287,368,374,375,396,417
Horry, Daniel: 329,358,360
Horry, Elizabeth Garnier: 358,
360
Horry, Elias: 301
Horry family: 283,285,358
Horry, Col. Peter: 333
Horry, General Peter: 332
Horry, Harriott: 310,316
Horry house: 317
Horry, Independent Republic
of: 78
Horse Branch Free Will Baptist
Church (Negro): 389
Horse Creek Valley: 171
Horseshoe Robinson: 82
Horton family: 206,283
Horton, McDavid: 79
Hosannah Negro Baptist
Church: 404
Hosmer, James: 202
Hot & Hot Fish Club: 79,319
"Hotspur" [pseudonym for
Robert Barnwell Rhett]: 309
Hotten, John C.: 13
Hough, Mrs. Ben C.: 29
Hough family: 210
Hough, Franklin B.: 79
Hough, Perry B. Bennett: 320
Houlditch family: 206,207
House of God Pentecostal
Holiness (Negro): 402
House of Peace Orthodox
Hebrew: 407
House of Peace Synagogue: 155
House of Prayer for All: 393,
396
Houseal family: 278,369
Houser cemetery plot: 40
Houser, John: 251
Houser, Mary A.: 231
Houston family: 206,214,224,
226,251,252
Houston, Florence A.: 251

453

Media Research Bureau: 265
Medical Society of SC: 91
Medical University of SC: see
 SC. Medical University.
Medway: 332
Medway plantation: 86
Meek family: 207
Meeks family: 238
Meeting St., Charleston: 59,144
Megee family: 210
Meggett family: 284,285
Meggett, SC: 356,386,387
Meherin family: 265
Mehringer, Corinne P.: 265
Mehringer, Mrs. Ernest: 207,208,
 212
Mehringer family: 265
Merixner, J. Edward: 160
Melchers, Alderman Theodore:303
Melchers, Franz: 303
Melina Presbyterian Church (Ne-
 gro): 389
Mell family: 265
Mell, Patrick H.: 265
Mellard family: 282
Mellett family: 207,246
Mellichamp family: 265
Mellish family: 354
Mellon family: 210
Mellon, Knox Jr.: 326
Melnick, Ralph: 3,5
Melrose cemetery: 373
Melton family: 207
Melvin, Patrick: 326
Memminger High & Normal School:
 90
Memminger Normal School: 112
Memorial Baptist Church: 155,
 160,173,391
Memorial Presbyterian Church:
 395,400
Mendenhall family: 210,266
Mendenhall, Samuel B.: 90,266
Mendes, Lucia N.: 266
Mentzel, Laura W.: 266
Mercer family: 296
Merchant, Marie: 160
Merck family: 207
Meredith, Doyle C.: 266
Meredith family: 207,266
Meredith, Gertrude E.: 266
Meriwether, Colyer: 90
Meriwether family: 204
Meriwether, James B.: 3,91,198
Meriwether, R.L.: 212
Meriwether, Robert L.: 91,326
Meriwether, SC: 403
Merlat family: 284
Meroney, Geraldine M.: 326
Merrens, H. Roy: 91,326
Merrill, Eleanor B.: 266
Merrill family: 283
Merrill, John Leonard: 358
Merriwether family: 234
Mersereau, Warren: 118
Mesick, John: 266
Messer family: 207
Messiah Reformed Episcopal
 Church: 385
Messick, Hank: 91
Metheringham family: 218
Methodist cemetery: 374,375
Methodist Church: 163
Methodist Church. Charleston:
 308
Methodist Church. Darlington
 Circuit: 417
Methodist Church. Kingstree
 Circuit: 417
Methodist Church. Lynch's Creek
 Circuit: 417
Methodist Church. SC: 199,417
Methodist Church. SC. Black
 River Circuit: 417

Methodist Church. SC. Central
 Jurisdiction of the SC Confer-
 ence: 152
Methodist Church. Upper SC
 Conference: 417
Methodist Church. Waccamaw
 Circuit: 417
Methodist churchyard: 375
Methodist Episcopal Church
 (abbreviated M.E. Church): 145
M.E. Church. SC Conference.
 Charleston: 139
M.E. Church. SC Conference.
 Darlington: 183,194
M.E. Church. SC Conference.
 Dorchester Circuit: 130
M.E. Church. SC Conference.
 Historical Society: 182
M.E. Church. SC Conference.
 Laurens Circuit: 30
M.E. Church. SC Conference.
 Santee Circuit: 183
M.E. Church. SC Conference.
 Santee Circuit. Sumter Sta-
 tion: 183
M.E. Church. SC Conferences:
 96,160,182
M.E. Church, South: 145,177,307
M.E. Church, South. SC Confer-
 ence: 125,197
M.E. Church, South. SC Confer-
 ence. Chester District: 19
M.E. Church, South. SC Confer-
 ence. East Chester Circuit:35
M.E. Church, South. SC Confer-
 ence. Greenville Circuit: 147
M.E. Church, South. SC Confer-
 ence. Johnston Charge: 153
M.E. Church, South. SC Confer-
 ence. Richburg Circuit: 35,36
M.E. Church, South. Upper SC
 Conference: 153
M.E. Church, South. Upper SC
 Conference. Columbia District:
 153
M.E. Church, South. Upper SC
 Conference. Columbia District.
 Womens Missionary Society: 196
Methodist Protestant Church:145
Metropolitan A.M.E. Zion Church:
 127,408
Metropolitan Negro Baptist
 Church: 404
Metts, Ethel C.: 160
Mexican-American War: 68
Mexican War: 323,327
Mexican War Centennial: 68
Mexico: 323,348
Mexico, Valley of: 68
Meyer, Jack Allen: 91
Meyer, Leona: 266
Meyer, Mary K.: 200
Michael family: 207
Michau family: 213,355,362
Michaux, Andre: 91,103
Michaux family: 210
Michaw family: 207
Michel family: 207,283
Michel, Middleton: 91
Michigan: 311
Mickle family: 207
Mickler family: 218
Micou family: 243
Middendorf Baptist Church:
 388
Middle District: 369
Middle Tyger Southern Baptist
 Church: 410
Middlebrook, Louis F.: 91
Middleburg Baptist Church: 402
Middleburg M.E. Church, South:
 402
Middleton: 324
Middleton, Alicia H.: 91

Middleton, Hon. Arthur: 309
Middleton family: 210,237,283,
 284,326
Middleton, Henry A.: 303
Middleton, Margaret S.: 91
Middleton, Margaret Simons:
 266,303
Middleton, N.R.: 91
Middleton Place: 80,93,324
Midland Park M.E. Church,
 South: 386
Midway A.F.W. Baptist Church:
 413
Midway Baptist Church: 399
Midway Church: 153
Midway Congregational Church,
 Georgia: 176
Midway Meeting House: 153
Midway Presbyterian Church:
 32,127,158,161,382,389
Midway Presbyterian churchyard:
 373,376
Midway, SC: 32,381
Midway Southern Baptist Church:
 381,413
Mikell family: 266,283,333
Mikell, Isaac J.: 91
Mikell, Townsend: 266
Milam, Jane C.: 91,160
Milam family: 222
Milbank, Jeremiah: 91
Milby family: 242
Miles Brewton house: 72
Miles, Rev. Edward R.: 303
Miles family: 207,236,282,283,
 284,285,328
Miles, J.W.: 91
Miles, James F.: 91
Miles, James Warley: 315
Miles, Rev. James Warley: 1
Miles, William P.: 32
Miles, William Porcher:350
Miley Community Church - Unde-
 nominational: 395
Miley, SC: 395
Milford Baptist Church: 32,147,
 156,417
Milford, Charles P.: 266
Milford family: 207,266
Military Club of Charleston:
 91
Militia Act of 1792: 317
Mill Branch A.M.E. Church:
 393
Mill Creek cemetery: 32
Mill Creek M.E. Church, South:
 406
Mill Creek Negro Baptist
 Church: 398,403,407
Mill Creek Primitive Baptist
 Church: 395
Mill Prison: 309
Millar, Mrs. Ernie: 212
Millar family: 267
Millar, Frances: 212
Millbrook Baptist churchyard:
 373
Millen family: 210
Miller: 32
Miller, Alice Davis: 212
Miller, Allie E.: 266

465

Mt. Lebanon Southern Baptist
Church: 412
Mt. Lebanon United Methodist
Church: 162
Mt. Leon Baptist Church: 396
Mt. Level Negro Baptist Church:
388
Mt. Lisbon Presbyterian Church
(Negro): 401
Mt. Moriah, A.M.E. Church: 399,
404
Mt. Moriah Baptist Church: 122,
162,393,395,417
Mt. Moriah Baptist Church
cemetery: 33
Mt. Moriah Free Will Baptist
Church: 393
Mt. Moriah M.E. Church (Negro):
401
Mt. Moriah Missionary Baptist
Church: 397
Mt. Moriah National Baptist
Church (Negro): 408
Mt. Moriah Negro Baptist Church:
383,386,395,398,407,408,411
Mt. Moriah Union M.E. Church
(Negro): 390
Mt. Nebo Negro Presbyterian
Church: 386,390,407
Mt. Olive A.M.E. Church: 381,
397,401,404,405,411
Mt. Olive Baptist Church: 129,
162,391,397,399,407,409
Mt. Olive Evangelical Lutheran
Church: 401
Mt. Olive Holiness-Apostolic
Faith-Church of God & Christ:
391
Mt. Olive Holiness Church
(Negro): 403
Mt. Olive M.E. Church, South:
388
Mt. Olive Missionary Baptist
Church (Negro): 397
Mt. Olive Negro Baptist Church:
381,383,395,396,402,412
Mt. Olive Pentecostal Holiness
Church of God of America
(Negro): 393
Mt. Olive, SC: 397
Mt. Olivet A.M.E. Church: 405
Mt. Olivet Baptist Church: 388,
398
Mt. Olivet Evangelical Lutheran
Church: 404
Mt. Olivet Lutheran Church: 148
Mt. Olivet Missionary Baptist
Church: 385
Mt. Olivet Negro Baptist
Church: 386,387
Mt. Olivet Presbyterian Church:
33,162,176
Mt. Paran Baptist Church:161,162
Mt. Pilgrim Evangelical Lutheran
Church: 404
Mt. Pilgrim Negro Baptist
Church: 398,407,412
Mt. Pisgah A.M.E. Church: 385,
395,411
Mt. Pisgah Baptist Church: 147,
162,183,397
Mt. Pisgah Baptist Church
cemetery: 33
Mt. Pisgah community: 56,104
Mt. Pisgah Negro Baptist
Church: 395,402,405,411
Mt. Pisgah Presbyterian Church
(Negro): 390,400
Mt. Pisgah Southern Baptist
Church: 383
Mt. Pleasant Baptist Church: 417
Mt. Pleasant A.M.E. Church: 395,
396,401

Mt. Pleasant Baptist Church:
153,154,162,400,409
Mt. Pleasant Baptist Church
(Negro): 401
Mt. Pleasant Evangelical
Lutheran Church: 407
Mt. Pleasant Exchange Club: 33
Mt. Pleasant M.E. Church,
South: 404,407
Mt. Pleasant Negro Baptist
Church: 381,386,401
Mt. Pleasant Presbyterian
Church: 33
Mt. Pleasant Primitive Baptist
Church: 382,401
Mt. Pleasant R.U.M.E. Church
(Negro): 390
Mt. Pleasant, SC: xiii,33,69,85,
89,108,160,297,316,364,381
Mt. Pleasant Southern Baptist
Church: 382
Mt. Prospect M.E. Church: 398
Mt. Prospect Negro Baptist
Church: 413
Mt. Rouah Negro Baptist Church:
393
Mt. Seale Baptist Church: 393
Mt. Sinai A.M.E. Church: 384
Mt. Sinai Church: 395
Mt. Sinai Fire Baptized Holi-
ness Church (Negro): 389,410
Mt. Sinai Methodist Church
(Negro): 383
Mt. Sinai Negro Baptist Church:
382,409
Mt. Sinai Presbyterian Church
(Negro): 401
Mt. Sion Society: 304
Mt. Sion Society of Charleston:
91
Mt. Sion Society of Winnsboro:
91
Mt. Taber M.E. Church, South:
388
Mt. Tabor Baptist Church: 406
Mt. Tabor Evangelical Lutheran
Church: 162,404
Mt. Tabor Lutheran Church: 162
Mt. Tabor Lutheran Church
Committee: 160
Mt. Tabor M.E. Church, South:
390,392
Mt. Tabor Negro Baptist Church:
403
Mt. Tabor Presbyterian Church:
33,417
Mt. Tabor Presbyterian Church
cemetery: 40
Mt. Tabor Southern Baptist
Church: 382,383
Mt. Tabor United Evangelical
Lutheran Church: 401
Mt. Teman Negro Baptist Church:
391
Mt. Vernon M.E. Church, South:
404,413
Mt. Vernon Methodist cemetery:
376
Mt. Vernon Presbyterian Church:
412
Mt. Zero Baptist Church
(Negro): 389
Mt. Zion A.M.E. Church: 162,381,
385,386,389,392,395,396,397,
401,403,405,413
Mt. Zion A.M.E. Church (Negro):
399
Mt. Zion Baptist Church: 155,
162,167,391,393,403,404,410
Mt. Zion Baptist Church (Negro):
400
Mt. Zion C.M.E. Church: 388,393,
400,410
Mt. Zion Church: 138

Mt. Zion Holiness Church
(Negro): 397
Mt. Zion Methodist Church: 122
Mt. Zion M.E. Church: 406
Mt. Zion M.E. Church (Negro):
393,413
Mt. Zion M.E. Church, South:385
Mt. Zion Negro Baptist Church:
383,386,390,391,393,395,396,
398,402,407,411,413
Mt. Zion Presbyterian Church:
135,158,160,162,382,400
Mt. Zion Presbyterian Church
(Negro): 381
Mt. Zion Presbyterian church-
yard: 373
Mt. Zion Society: 53
Mt. Zion Tabernacle-Holiness
Church (Negro): 403
Mt. Zion United Pentecostal
Holiness-Church of God (Negro):
408
Mountain Creek Baptist Church:
395,417
Mountain Creek Baptist Church
cemetery: 33
Mountain Creek, SC: 416
Mountain Creek Southern Baptist
Church: 383
Mountain Grove cemetery: 42
Mountain Grove Southern Baptist
churchyard: 376
Mountain Springs Negro Baptist
Church: 383
Mountain View Baptist Church:409
Mountain View C.M.E. Church:383
Mountain View Southern Baptist
Church: 409,410
Mountville Baptist Church: 399
Mountville Presbyterian Church:
400
Mountville, SC: 134,399,400
Moursund, Mary: 268
Mouzon family: 354,355,360
Mouzon, Harold A.: 93,327,351
Mouzon, Henry: 354
Mouzon, Louis: 355,360
Mouzon Presbyterian Church: 413
Moye family: 222
Moze, Caesar: 362
Muckenfuss, Dr. B.A.: 304
Muddy Creek, SC: 137
Mueller, William A.: 162
Mulberry: 197
Mulberry Negro Baptist Church:
389,395,411
Muldrow family: 230
Mulford, Susan: 256
Mulford, Susan (Kitchell): 256
Mulkey family: 274
Mulkey, Floyd: 349
Mulkey, Rev. Philip:124,274,349
Mullen, Harris H.: 93
Muller family: 207
Mullins Centennial Commission,
Inc.: 93
Mullins First Baptist Church:158
Mullins Presbyterian Church: 402
Mullins, SC: 93,145,160,402,403
Munch, F.: 268
Munch, Professor F.: 268
Munford cemetery: 376
Munnerlyn, Annie: 162
Munnerlyn graveyard: 375
Munsell family: 252
Munsell, Joel: 252
Murchison cemetery: 376
Murchison family: 363
Murdock, Richard K.: 327
Murf family: 283
Murff family: 207
Murff, Paul B.: 268
Murff, Randolph S.: 268
Murff, Vaughan W.: 268

Murphee family: 283
Murphy, Anne J.: 268
Murphy family: 207
Murphy, Louise: 162
Murphy, Marion E.: 268
Murphy, Martin C.: 162
Murray, Andrew Buist: 304
Murray, Chalmers S.: 93,162
Murray family: 207,278,283,294
Murrell family: 210,249
Murrell's Inlet, SC: 51,125,183
Muse family: 262
Musgrove family: 259,283
Musgrove, Mary: 61
Musgrove's Mill, battle of: 61
Musselman family: 255
Mustard, Harry S.: 327
Mutual Aid Association No.1: 50
Myers, David: 162
Myers family: 210,226,255,283
Myers, Florence B.: 93
Myers, T. Bailey: 304
Mynatt family: 252
Myrtle Beach: 108
Myrtle Beach Presbyterian
Church: 33
Myrtle Beach, SC: 33,128,142,
396,397

- N -

Nabors family: 202
Nadelhaft, Jerome: 327
Nafe, Paul O.: 93
Nail cemetery: 363
Nail family: 207
Nairne family: 211
Nairne, Thomas: 93
Names in South Carolina: 8
Nance graveyard: 376
Napier, J.M.: 162
Napier, John M.: 93
Nash, Edward: 268
Nash family: 268
Nash, Lucinda Bell: 268
Nash, Sara M.: 33,163,268
Nash, Shepard K.: 268
Nates family: 370
Nathan's Temple-Fire Baptized
Holiness Church of God of
America (Negro): 391
National Endowment for the
Humanities: iii,387
National Genealogical Society:
201
Natchez Trace, Louisiana: 14
Nathan family: 283
Natlow family: 207
National Society, Colonial
Dames: 28,33,37,38,102
National Society, Daughters of
the American Revolution: 20
Nations, Cynthia Garrett: 269
Nations family: 268
Nations, Loye E.: 33,268,269
Nations, Mattison: 269
Nativity United Evangelical
Lutheran Church: 409
Naugher family: 207
Nazarene Church: 159
Nazarene Negro Baptist Church:
403
Nazarene Tabernacle-Holiness
Church: 407
Nazareth A.M.E. Church: 393,
405,412
Nazareth Church: 164
Nazareth Church cemetery: 15,
161,204,308
Nazareth Evangelical Lutheran
Church: 401
Nazareth M.E. Church, South:408
Nazareth Negro Baptist Church:
398

Nazareth Presbyterian Church:
33,409
Neagles, James: 201
Neagles, Lila: 201
Neal cemetery: 363
Neals Creek Baptist Church:
33,138,147
Neal's Creek Baptist church-
yard: 373
Neal's Creek Southern Baptist
Church: 383
Neal, Carl B.: 269
Neal, Diane: 349
Neal family: 207,245,269
Neal, John W.: 269
Neale family: 207
Nebo Baptist Church: 402
Nebo M.E. Church (Negro): 406
Nebo M.E. Church, South: 403
Needham, David C.: 349
Neel family: 207,219
Neel, Oliver: 212
Neely family: 207,222,248,269
Neely, Juanita H.: 269
Neely, Lucile B.: 93,163
Neely's Creek A.R.P. Church:
32,34,163,413
Neely's Creek, SC: 293
Neeses Baptist Church: 131,405
Neeses family: 219
Neeses M.E. Church, South: 405
Neeses, SC: 94,405,406
Neff family: 255
Negrin's Sociable Magazine &
Quarterly Intelligencer: 326
Negroes: 82
Negro Baptists: 194
Neighbors family: 269
Neil family: 207,248
Neill family: 254
Neilson family: 207
Neilson, Margaret: 262
Nell Townsend Memorial Chapel:
142
Nelson family: 207,269,283,284,
371
Nelson, Jack: 94
Nelson's Church-Holiness
(Negro): 402
Nepveux, Ethel T.: 94
Nesbit family: 283,284
Nesbit, Newton Alexander: 269
Nesbitt family: 283
Nesbitt Manufacturing Company:
348
Nesmith family: 207,289
Nesmith, SC: 413
Nesmith Southern Baptist
Church: 413
Nettles family: 207,264
Neuchatel: 145
Neufville family: 283
Neville, Thomas J.: 94
New Allendale Baptist Church:
34,417
New Bethany Negro Baptist
Church: 386
New Bethel A.M.E. Church: 163,
183
New Bethel Baptist Church: 399
New Bethel Negro Baptist
Church: 411,413
New Bethlehem Lutheran Church:
384
New Bethlehem M.E. Church,
South: 400
New Bethlehem Methodist Church:
383
New Bordeaux, SC: 73,93,243,
357,358,360
New Branch Union M.E. Church:
390
New Broadmouth Negro Baptist
Church: 383

New Brookland, SC: 162
New Brunswick: 227
New Castle Negro Baptist
Church: 395
New Chapel M.E. Church, South:
404
New China Negro Baptist Church:
395
New Deal era: 356
New England Historical & Gene-
alogical Register: 14
New England Society: 94,106,
117,198
New Grove Baptist Church
(Negro): 400
New Hampshire: 207,243,245,267
New Harley Negro Baptist
Church: 403
New Harmony Baptist Church:399
New Harmony Church of God: 168
New Harmony M.E. Church, South:
400
New Harmony Methodist Church
(Negro): 383
New Harmony Presbyterian Church:
34,138,163,389,400
New Heaven Church: 401
New Holland Baptist Church: 163
New Home No.1 Baptist Church:397
New Hope A.M.E. Church: 385,
389,397,399,400
New Hope Baptist Church: 139,
163,398,399,402
New Hope Baptist Church
cemetery: 34
New Hope Church of Our Lord
Jesus Christ-Apostolic Faith:
163
New Hope Free Will Baptist
Church: 393
New Hope Independent Baptist
Church: 397
New Hope M.E. Church: 392
New Hope M.E. Church, South:
382,404,405,412
New Hope Methodist Church: 417
New Hope Methodist Church
cemetery: 40
New Hope Missionary Baptist
Church (Negro): 383
New Hope Negro Baptist Church:
382,396,400,404
New Hope Presbyterian Church:
34,401
New Hope Reformed M.E. Church
(Negro): 389
New Hope Southern Baptist
Church: 384
New Hope Union M.E. Church
(Negro): 389
New Hopewell Negro Baptist
Church: 391
"New Ironsides" (frigate): 307
New Jersey: 242,290,334,353
New Jerusalem C.M.E. Church:412
New Jerusalem Free Will Baptist
Church: 390
New Jerusalem Negro Baptist
Church: 400,401
New Life Church: 402
New Life Freewill Mission Holi-
ness Church (Negro): 403
New Life Negro Baptist Church:
390
New Light Baptist Church: 396
New Light Negro Baptist Church:
384,398
New Light Negro Hardshell
Baptist Church: 390
New London, SC: 108,335
New Market cemetery: 376
New Market M.E. Church, South:
391
New Mt. Grove Baptist Church:394

South: 157
Reformed Society of Israelites: 130
Reformed Society of Israelites, Charleston: 138
Refuge Baptist Church: 398
Refuge Church of Our Lord Jesus Christ - Apostolic Faith: 386
Refuge Southern Baptist Church: 382
Register, C.S.: 167
Register family: 211
Register, Jeannie Heyward: 330
Regulators: 53
Rehobeth Baptist Church: 168, 397
Rehobeth Baptist Church cemetery: 40
Rehobeth cemetery: 370
Rehobeth Church cemetery: 375
Rehobeth M.E. Church, South: 385,389,395,397,407,408
Rehobeth Methodist cemetery: 28
Reichart, Walter A.: 330
Reid, Charles S.: 99
Reid family: 208,215,263,275, 284,289
Reid, Helen R.: 215
Reid, J.W.: 99
Reid, John S.: 275
Reid, Joseph: 197
Reid, Mary R.: 11,36,275
Reid, Nathan: 215
Reid, Nell P.: 275
Reid, Rev. R.H.: 167,184
Reidville Presbyterian Church: 410
Reidville, SC: 410
Reily family: 208,237,284
Rej, M.S.: 99
Rembert family: 213,254,255,275, 284,358,362
Rembert M.E. Church & cemetery: 24
Rembert M.E. Church, South: 401, 411
Rembert Negro Baptist Chapel: 411
Rembert, Sallie H.: 275
Rembert, SC: 167, 411
Remedy (newspaper): 25
Remount Baptist Church: 167
Renddick family: 211
Renfro family: 208,284
Rentz family: 250,284
Republican Baptist Church: 160
Republican M.E. Church, South: 404
Republican Party: 317,349
Republican Society of Charleston: 348.
Revill, Janie: 14,36,99,275
Revolutionary War (see also American Revolution, SC Military Units): 11,17,31,32,33,34, 35,36,41,43,61,72,102,107,117, 118,120,134,189,190,197,207, 214,238,299,300,304,330,361, 363,365,366,368,370,371,379
Reyersz, Adriaen: 277
Reyersz, Martin: 277
Reyes, Jenness R.: 275
Reynolds burying ground: 376
Reynolds Conference: 109,198
Reynolds, Emily B.: 198
Reynolds family: 208,223,259, 271,284,285,289
Reynolds, Harriet D.: 275
Reynolds, Julia R.: 122
Reynolds, Alderman Thomas H.: 305
Reznikoff, Charles: 99
Rhame family: 218,284
Rhame, Henry Wilton: 275

Rhame, Col. J.A.: 99
Rhame, Lee R.: 275
Rhea family: 214
Rhems, SC: 413
Rhett, Colonel: 327
Rhett family: 217,282,283,284, 285,319
Rhett, James M.: 100
Rhett, Dr. R.B.: 304,305
Rhett, Robert Barnwell: 309
Rhett, Robert G.: 100
Rhett, R. Goodwyn: 299,305
Rhett, Col. William: 319
Rhine River, Germany: 253
Rhinehardt family: 211
Rhoades family: 255
Rhoades family. Joseph Edwards Rhoades Family Association:255
Rhoades, Joseph Edwards: 255
Rhode Island: 215,311,328
Rhodes family: 208
Rhodes, George: 328
Rhodus family: 208
Rhyne family: 250
Ribault: 353
Ribault, Jean: 358
Ribault, John: 63
Ribault Quadricentennial: 51
Ribault's Fort: 353
Ribble, Hunt & Ribble: 36
Ricard family: 255
Ricards, Sherman L.: 330
Ricaud, Lulu C.: 275
Rice cemetery: 373
Rice Church cemetery: 36
Rice family: 262,275,284
Rice, James H.: 100
Rice, Janie C.: 167
Rice, Mr.: 100
Rich family: 208
Rich Hill Baptist Church: 399
Rich, Peggy B.: 36
Richard, Edridge Fortier: 212
Richards, J.P.: 100
Richardson, Carol: 167
Richardson cemetery: 312,374
Richardson, Capt. Edward: 273
Richardson, Eleanor: xiii
Richardson, Elizabeth B: 275
Richardson, Emma: 330
Richardson family: 208,228,273, 275,284
Richardson, James M.: 100
Richardson, Laurence: 167
Richardson, Mrs. M.B.: 167
Richardson, General Richard:354
Richardson, Robert: 167
Richardson, William: 330
Richbourg family: 237,284,354
Richbourg, John: 352
Richburg burying ground: 376
Richburg M.E. Church, South: 19
Richburg, SC: 154,155
Richey family: 205,208,275
Richey, Mattie Francis: 330
Richey, Norine B.: 167
Richland County: 6,44,45,69,74, 103,108,122,152,206,226,238, 286,376,406
Richland District: 76
Richland Presbyterian Church: 167,173,406,407
Richland School: 36
Richland, SC: 404
Richman family: 208
Richmond: 330
Richmond family: 211
Richmond Presbyterian Church: 36
Rickman family: 208
Riddel family: 208
Riddick family: 233
Riddle family: 208
Riddle, Hazel: 167

Riddlehoover, Wayne: 168,275
Riddock, Edward J.: 305
Ridge Branch Negro Baptist Church: 408
Ridge, Davy-Jo S.: 3
Ridge family: 192
Ridge Spring Baptist Church: 123,164,167,408
Ridge Spring M.E. Church, South: 408
Ridge Spring, SC: 408
Ridgefield Baptist Church: 396
Ridgeland Baptist Church: 398
Ridgeland, SC: 108,397
Ridgell, Mrs. E.C.: 167
Ridgell family: 208
Ridgeville Baptist Church: 392, 396
Ridgeville, SC: 108,134,392, 396
Ridgeway family: 208,238
Ridgeway, SC: 118,122,178,415
Ridgill family burying ground: 374
Ridgill Shed Negro Baptist Church: 389
Ridlehoover, Wayne: 168,275
Riggins family: 284
Righton family: 284
Riley, Andrew J.: 305
Riley, Edward M.: 330
Riley family: 208,284
Riley, John A.: 168
Riley, Mary R.: 36
Riley, SC: 386
Riley, Mrs. Willie: 168
Rimini, SC: 390,411
Ringold, May Spencer: 330
Rion family: 275
Ripley, General Roswell S.: 305
Rippon family: 284,285
Rippy family: 208
Riser family: 208
Rish family: 208,272
Risinger family: 291
Ritchey, Eliza: 228
Ritchey family: 228
Ritchey, James: 228
Ritchie, E.B.: 212
Ritchie family: 208,267
Ritchie, John: 208
Rittenburg, Sidney: 305
Rivelon Baptist Church: 135
River Falls, SC: 108
Rivers Chapel Negro Baptist Church: 388
Rivers, E.L.: 168
Rivers family: 284,285
Rivers, John: 327
Rivers, Thomas: 365
Rivers, William J.: 100,345
Riverside Baptist Church: 129, 133,394,406
Riverside cemetery: 40
Riverside Southern Baptist Church: 382
Rives family: 208,264
Roach family: 238,271,275,284
Roach, Henry A.: 275
Roach, William: 275
Robbins, David P.: 100
Robbins, Mrs. John C., Jr.: 212
Robbins, Mary Lee Donaghey: 212
Robbins, Walter L.: 330
Roberdeau, General Daniel: 354
Roberson family: 251
Robert family: 208,266,284,285, 356
Robert, Jean: 356
Robert, Pierre: 266
Roberts, Bruce: 100
Roberts, Charles Pressly: 278
Roberts family: 208,238,273, 278,284
Roberts, Owen: 212

Russell family: 208,262,284,285
Russell, George E.: 277
Russellville Christian Church
  (Disciples of Christ): 385
Russia: 310,330
Rust, Ellsworth M.: 277
Rust family: 211,277
Rust, William: 277
Rutherford family: 208,232,277
Rutherford, William K.: 277
Rutledge, Anna Wells: 305,331
Rutledge, Archibald: 101
Rutledge, Archibald H.: 195
Rutledge Avenue Baptist Church:
  169
Rutledge, Benjamin Huger: 352
Rutledge, Edward: 331,342
Rutledge family: 208,284,285,
  340
Rutledge, Harriott Horry: 320
Rutledge, J.: 298
Rutledge, John: 322,324,332
Rutledge, Chief Justice John:
  325
Rutledge, Dr. John: 340
Rutledge Street Southern
  Baptist Church: 386
Rutledge, Thomas Pinckney: 310
Rutt, Richard H.: 101
Rutter family: 257
Ryan, Frank W.: 349
Ryan, Frank W., Jr.: 331
Ryan, Harold W.: 331
Ryan, Capt. John: 368
Ryerse family: 277
Ryerson, Albert W.: 277
Ryerson family: 277
Ryerss family: 277
Rysn, Frank Winkler, Jr.: 305

- S -

Sabb family: 285
Sabin, Elizabeth: 3
Sabin family: 284
Sabine, Lorenzo: 198
Sacheveral family: 285
Sacred Heart of Jesus Roman
  Catholic Church: 388
Saddler family: 277
Sadler, Catherine Elizabeth:360
Sadler family: 208,248,271
Saffold, Ruth: 277
Sainsbury, W. Noel: 345
St. Alban's Protestant Episco-
  pal Church: 413
St. Andrew the Apostle Catholic
  Church: 177
St. Andrew's Catholic Church:
  136
St. Andrew's Chapel cemetery:
  40
St. Andrew's Chapel - Holiness
  Church of God: 401
St. Andrew's Episcopal Mission:
  387
St. Andrew's Evangelical Luth-
  eran Church: 402,418
St. Andrew's Lutheran Church:
  135,137,169,387
St. Andrew's Lutheran church-
  yard: 374
St. Andrew's M.E. Church,
  South: 409
St. Andrew's Parish: 59,176,330,
  335,341,387
St. Andrew's Parish Church: 22
St. Andrew's Parish Episcopal
  churchyard: 374
St. Andrew's Protestant Epis-
  copal Church: 381,394
St. Andrew's Roman Catholic
  Church: 384

St. Andrew's Society: 37,58,68,
  83,101,102,144,298
St. Andrews, SC: 78
St. Andrew's Town: 335
St. Andrew's United Evangelical
  Lutheran Church: 406
St. Anna Protestant Episcopal
  Church: 407
St. Anne's Protestant Episcopal
  Church: 401
St. Anne's Roman Catholic
  Church: 411,412
St. Anthony's Roman Catholic
  Church: 384,390,392
St. Asia Negro Baptist Church:
  413
St. Augustine Expedition: 189,
  345
St. Barnabas Evangelical Luth-
  eran Church: 387
St. Barnabas Lutheran Church:
  169
St. Barnabas' Mission: 169
St. Barnabas Protestant Episco-
  pal Church: 391,392
St. Bartholomew's Episcopal
  Church: 22
St. Bartholomew's Parish: 46,
  244,317
St. Bartholomew's Parish
  Episcopal Church: 418
St. Bartholomew's Protestant
  Episcopal Church: 390
St. Beulah Believers Holiness
  Church: 393
St. Charles, SC: 162
St. Coecelia Society: 102,331
St. Cyprian's Catholic Church
  & School: 169
St. Daniel's African Zion
  Church: 403
St. Darcus Negro Baptist Church:
  405
St. David's Episcopal cemetery:
  20
St. David's Episcopal Church:
  131,133,146,159,169,418
St. David's Episcopal Church,
  Cheraw. Women's Auxiliary.
  Chapter B: 131
St. David's Evangelical Luth-
  eran Church: 169,401
St. David's Parish: 27
St. David's Protestant Episco-
  pal Church: 388
St. Denis' Parish (see also St.
  Thomas' and St. Denis' Parish):
  19,22,45,232,351,352
St. Dennis Catholic Church: 159
St. Dennis Parish: see St.
  Denis' Parish.
St. Elizabeth Missionary Bap-
  tist Church: 397
St. Frances M.E. Church,
  South: 387
St. Francis de Sales Roman
  Catholic Church: 407
St. George Baptist Church: 174,
  392,405,406
St. George Greek Orthodox
  Church: 394
St. George M.E. Church, South:
  126,391
St. George, SC: 78,108,126,155,
  160,391
St. George's Club: 331
St. George's Episcopal Church,
  Dorchester: 334,392
St. George's Parish: 22,28,
  29,176
St. George's Society: 102
St. Helena's Chapel of Ease
  (Episcopal): 384

[continued on page 480]

481

Scott, Edwin J.: 103
Scott family: 208,237,284,285,
289,342
Scott, Florence Johnson: 349
Scott, Herschel K.: 172
Scott, Kenneth: 333
Scott, Mrs. B.K.: 212
Scott, Marie G.: 212
Scottish: 80
Scottish Highlanders: 226
Scott's Ferry: 75
Scranton Baptist Church: 393
Scranton Free Will Baptist
Church: 393
Scranton M.E. Church, South:392
Scranton Pentecostal Holiness
Tabernacle: 392
Scranton, SC: 392,393
Screven Baptist Church: 172
Screven family: 211,284,285,289
Scruggs, Martha: 253
Scurry family: 211,262,292
Scurry's Spring Hill Negro
Baptist Church: 404
Sea Island Relief Committee:307
Seaboard Air Line Railroad
Company: 96
Seaborn family: 208,235
Seaborn, Margaret M.: 103,172
Seabrook, E.M.: 172
Seabrook family: 282,284,285,
340
Seabrook, Henrietta: 103
Seabury, Bishop: 358
Seago family: 208
Seale family: 208
Sealey family: 208
Sealy family: 284
Sean Swamp Baptist Church: 406
Searcy, Margaret: 212
Searson, Louis A.: 104
Sease, Elberta: 278
Sease family: 278
Sease, Kate: 278
Sease, Rosalyn S.: 172
Seaver, Jesse M.: 278
Seawell family: 225
Seawright family: 208,278
Seay, Jamie: 203
Seay, Dr. W.M.: 377
Secessionville, SC: 108
Secona Baptist Church: 406
Secona Baptist churchyard:376
Secona cemetery: 42
Second Baptist Church: 38,133,
172,179,399
Second Calvary Baptist Church:
128
Second Calvary Negro Baptist
Church: 382,398,406
Second Independent Church: 297
Second Negro Baptist Church:
395,403
Second Point Savannah Negro
Baptist Church: 396
Second Presbyterian Church: 3,
38,127,138,158,172,174,297,
387,398,408,411,419
Second Presbyterian Church
(Negro): 388,398,403
Second Presbyterian Church,
Charleston. Education Society:
127
Second Presbyterian church-
yard: 374
Second Southern Baptist Church:
409
Second Thankful Negro Baptist
Church: 395
Secret Committee: 326
Sedalia, SC: 412
Seegars, Mary R.: 104
Seewee Barony: 335

Seewee Indians: 191
Sego family: 208
Seigler family: 211
Seigling C.M.E. Church: 382
Seigling, SC: 382
Seitler, George: 280
Seitzler family: 208
Selby, Julian A.: 104
Selden family: 211
Self family: 284
Sellers, Edwin J.: 278
Sellers family: 202,278
Sellers, Hazel C.: 172
Sellers, Leile: 104
Sellers M.E. Church, South:402
Sellers, SC: 402
Sellers, W.W.: 104
Sellneit, Minnie L.: 278
Seneca Baptist Church: 405
Seneca First Presbyterian
Church: 405
Seneca (Old) Pickens Presby-
terian Church: 405
Seneca Presbyterian Church: 157,
173
Seneca, SC: 70,78,104,136,161,
173,181,405
Senese, Donald J.: 333
Senf, Col.: 340
Sere family: 284
Serre family: 284
Sessions family: 278,284
Sessions, Frederick: 278
Sessoms family: 224
Sessoms, Patti: 224
Setzler family: 208
Seven Oaks Presbyterian Church:
173
Seventh Day Adventist Church:
388,407,408,411,412
Seventh Day Adventist (Negro):
392,402
Severance family: 208
Severans family: 284
Sevier family: 214
Seybolt, Robert Francis: 333
Shackelford family: 234,278,284
Shackelford, Richard: 337
Shackelford, Robert B.: 278
Shady Grove A.M.E. Church:
381,398
Shady Grove C.M.E. Church: 392
Shady Grove Free Will Baptist
Church (Negro): 393
Shady Grove M.E. Church, South:
386,407
Shady Grove Negro Baptist
Church: 391,395
Shady Grove Presbyterian
Church: 38,400
Shady Grove Southern Baptist
Church: 383
Shaffer, E.T.: 349
Shaffer, Edward T.: 104,173
Shaftesbury papers: 305,345
Shand, Peter J.: 173
Shand, Rev. Peter J.,: 179
Shandon Baptist Church: 406
Shandon M.E. Church, South:406
Shandon Presbyterian Church:
173,406
Shandon, SC: 161
Shankman, Arnold: 104,333
Shanks family: 202
Shannon-Cash Duel: 56,93
Shannon family: 279
Shannon, Sarah B.: 279
Shannon, William G.: 279
Shannon, William M.: 104
Sharon Associate Reformed
Presbyterian Church: 371
Sharon Baptist Church: 397
Sharon Baptist Church cemetery:
28

Sharon M.E. Church, South:
381,383,402
Sharon Methodist Church: 173
Sharon, SC: 17
Sharp, E.M.: 279
Sharp, Rev. E.M.: 212
Sharp, Eron M.: 279
Sharp family: 205,208
Sharples family: 284
Sharrer, G. Terry: 333
Shaw family: 211,219,220,254,
282,371
Shaw, Jessie O.: 279
Shaw, Rev. Murdock Wesley,
Sr.: 219,220
Shaw, Roderick Lodd: 220
Shaw's Mission A.M.E. Church:
400
Shealy family: 211,229,241,249,
279
Shealy, Sara B.: 279
Shearer family: 211,279
Shearer, James J.: 334
Shearer, James W.: 279
Shecut, Dr. J.L.E.W.: 362
Shecut, John L.: 104
Shedd family: 208,292
Shedd, Mary A.: 173
Shedland family: 284
Sheed family: 208
Sheffield, Eileen B.: 279
Sheffield family: 208
Shelburne family: 279,284
Shelburne, Robert C.: 279
Shelby family: 214,226
Sheldon, Christine: 279
Sheldon Episcopal Church
cemetery: 29,39
Sheldon Episcopal Church,
Prince William's Parish (see
also Burnt Church): 314,320,
385
Sheldon family: 226
Sheldon Township, SC: 385
Shell-Anderson Memorial M.E.
Church, South: 410
Shell family: 211
Shell, SC: 397
Shelton family: 242,249,284
Shelton family cemetery: 375
Shelor, John W.: 173
Shenk family: 255
Shepard, Charles U.: 104
Shepard, Dr. Charles Upham: 305
Shepard, Mrs. Coleman D.: 212
Shepard, Henry E.: 305
Shepard, Jack: 279
Shepherd A.M.E. Church: 411
Shepherd Baptist Church: 392
Shepherd family: 208,281
Sheppard family: 208,242,284
Sheppard family cemetery: 325
Shepperson family: 250
Sherard family: 232
Sherer family: 211,248
Sherer, Palmer G.: 104
Sheriff family: 208
Sherman, Nellie C.: 279
Sherman, General W.T.: 51,52,
54,63,74,87,319
Sherman, Wm. Tecumseh: 118
Sherman's Army: 114
Sherman's Raiders: 236
Sherrerd family: 208
Sherriff, Florence Jansen: 349
Sherrill, George R.: 349
Sherrill family: 208,217,232
Sherrod family: 211
Shetley family: 250
Shields family: 208,214,279
Shields, John E.: 279
Shields, William: 279
Shiloh A.M.E. Church: 388,389,
404,405,407

488

Thomas family: 208,223,248,264, 284,285,288,289
Thomas, Herman L.: 179
Thomas, J.A.W.: 42,112
Thomas, Rev. J.A.W.: 42
Thomas, Rev. John N.: 361
Thomas, John P.: 112,179
Thomas, Col. John Peyre: 288
Thomas, Jno. P., Jr.: 337
Thomas Memorial Baptist Church: 42,159,179,419
Thomas, Mrs. Samuel: 314
Thomas, Rev. Samuel: 179,314, 324
Thomas, Theodore G.: 112
Thomas, Velma M.: 289
Thomas, W.J.: 179
Thomasson family: 211
Thomasson, Nathaniel: 279
Thompson, _____: 187
Thompson A.M.E. Church: 396
Thompson, Alexander: 218
Thompson, Brooks: 341
Thompson Centennial Methodist Church (Negro): 384
Thompson, Mrs. Cleveland: 213
Thompson Creek Baptist Church: 388
Thompson, Edgar T.: 113
Thompson, Eileen Lanier: 213
Thompson, Elizabeth C.: 113
Thompson family: 207,208,223, 284,292,363
Thompson Family Magazine: 289
Thompson, Henry T.: 113
Thompson, J. Waddy: 42
Thompson, John R.: 330
Thompson, Lawrence S.: 337
Thompson Negro Baptist Chapel: 412
Thompson, Ruth M.: 289
Thompson St. National Baptist Church: 408
Thompson, Rev. W.T.: 307
Thompson, Gen. Waddy: 323
Thompson, William W.: 113
Thomson family: 208,285,332,338
Thomson, Col. Moses: 332
Thorn family: 208
Thorngood family: 285
Thornhill family: 208,217,243, 284
Thornwell family: 253
Thornwell, James H.: 42,348
Thornwell, James Henley: 311
Thornwell, Dr. James Henley:42
Thornwell Memorial Presbyterian Church: 400
Thornwell Orphanage: 87
Threadcraft family: 284
"Three Brothers" (ship): 327
Three Rivers Historical Society: 11,42,113,289
Thurman, Edward Moroni: 264
Thurman family: 234,253,284
Thurman, John: 253
Thurmond, Phillip: 234
Thurston family: 225
Tibwin A.M.E. Church: 387
Tibwin, SC: 387
Tidmore family: 208
Tidwell family: 208,222,254
Tiedeman, Mrs. John C.: 307
Tiernan, Charles B.: 289
Tiernan family: 289
"Tigertown": 87
Tigerville Baptist Church: 151
Tigersville, SC: 217
Tileston family: 292
Tilford family: 252
Tilghman family: 211,289
Tiller family: 289
Tiller, Lorena Lavender: 289

Tilley, John S.: 113
Tilley Swamp Baptist Church: 397
Tilley Swamp, SC: 397
Tillinghast family: 284
Tillman: 349,350
Tillman, Ben: 348,349
Tillman, Benjamin R.: 113
Tillman era: 95
Tillman family: 211,289
Tillman, Gov.: 196
Tillman, James D.: 289
Tillman, Mamie N.: 42,213
Tillman movement: 350
Tillman, Stephen: 289
Tillman, Stephen S.: 289
Tillotson family: 266
Tilly Swamp Baptist Church cemetery: 28
Times Dispatch, Richmond, VA: 275
Timmons family: 226
Timmons, John Morgan: 254
Timmonsville Baptist Church: 393
Timmonsville M.E. Church, South: 394
Timmonsville Negro Baptist Church: 388
Timmonsville Presbyterian Church: 393
Timmonsville, SC: 142,165,393, 394
Timms family: 284
Timothy, Peter: 313,325
Timrod, Henry: 330
Timrod Memorial Association: 307
Timrod, William Henry: 339
Tims, Eugene C.: 289
Tims family: 284,289
Tims, Nathan: 289
Tindall family: 208
Tindall, George B.: 195,337
Tippin, Ernest E.: 289
Tippin family: 289
Tippin, George Manton, Sr.:289
Tippin, James J.: 289
Tippin, Sanford Lathadeus: 289
Tipton family: 232
Tirzah A.R.P. Church: 35,42, 413
Tirzah cemetery: 40,42
Tirzah (Lower) Presbyterian Church: 399
Tirzah Presbyterian Church: 42, 411,414
Tirzah Presbyterian church-yard: 29
Tirzah, SC: 414
Tischendorf, Alfred P.: 337
Tisdal family burying ground: 374
Tisdale family: 208
Tison family: 208,262
Tison, John Laurens, Jr.: 337
Tison, Rebecca Mary Jane McKensie: 262
Tison, Reuben Henry: 262
Titshaw family: 208
Tobias, Thomas J.: 42,113,337
Tobin family: 245,246,284
Tobin, R.M.: 179
Toble family: 284
Tobler family: 208
Tobler, John: 330
Todd family: 289
Todd, John R.: 80,113,337
Todd, Joseph N.: 289
Todd Memorial Presbyterian Church: 400
Toddville, SC: 397

Togoodoo plantation: 360
Tolbert, Joseph W.: 113
Tolbert, Marguerite: 198
Toliver family: 211,279
Tollemache, Capt.: 188
Tomkins family: 289
Tomlinson family: 249,284
Tomlinson, Maude R.: 289
Tompkins family: 289
Tompkins, Daniel A.: 112,113
Tompkins, Robert A.: 289
Toms, Carolina Smith: 337
Toney family: 208,288
Toole, Casper L.: 113
Toomer family: 285
Toomer, Joshua W.: 113
Toomers family: 284
Toomey, Thomas N.: 289
Torbert family: 208
Tories (see also Loyalists):299
Torquet family: 284,285
Torrence, Clayton: 290
Torrence family: 290
Torrence, Robert M.: 290
Tory: 82
Touchstone family: 208
Tower family: 274
Tower of London: 344
Tower, Roderick: 113
Towles family: 208
Towne, Laura M.: 113
Townsend, Daniel: 220
Townsend family: 208,215,220, 222,236,284,285
Townsend, Leah: 179,337
Townsend, Leon: 179
Townsville Presbyterian Church: 42
Townsville, SC: 42
Townville, SC: 384
Townville Southern Baptist Church: 384
Toxaway, M.E. Church, South: 382
Tracy family: 290
Tracy, Sherman W.: 290
Tracy, Stephen: 290
Tracy, Lt. Thomas: 202
Tradd Street, Charleston: 144
Trail family: 284
Trairs family: 284
Trammell family: 208
Tranquil M.E. Church, South: 395,402
Tranquil United Methodist Church cemetery: 42
Transactions of the Huguenot Society of South Carolina: 8,351
Transactions of the McCormick County Historical Society: 8
Trapier family: 284,285
Trapier, Paul: 43,179,361
Trapier, Rev. Paul: 43,179, 321,361
Trapsman family: 290
Trask, John M., Jr.: 378
Travelers Rest National Baptist Church (Negro): 410
Traveler's Rest, SC: 39,74,100, 125,148,182
Travers family: 290
Travers, Rev. Marshall: 361
Travis family: 290
Travis, Robert J.: 290
Traylor family: 208
Traywick, Joseph B.: 179
Treadway family: 290
Treadway, Jonas Robert: 290
Treadway, Oswell G.: 290
Treadway Southern Baptist Church: 382
Treadway, William E.: 290

Vogt family: 209
Vogtle, Alvin W.: 290
Voight, Gilbert: 338
Voigt family: 209
Voigt, Gilbert P.: 115,180,350,
377
Voltaire: 357
VonDohlen, J. Albert: 307
VonKolnitz, Alfred H.: 115
VonKolnitz, Sarah C.: 115
VonMeister, Leila G.: 290
VonNessen, H.W.: 180
Vorhees: 62
Voss family: 211
Vox Memorial M.E. Church,
South: 413
Vurpillot, Rev. Florian: 362

- W -

Wacca Wache: 54
Waccamaw: 49,52,129,196,203,
320,329
Waccamaw Circuit: 397
Waccamaw Club: 115
Waccamaw Neck: 119,194
Waccamaw Presbyterian Church:
397
Waccamaw Presbyterian church-
yard: 375
Waccamaw Region: 115
Waccamaw Regional Planning &
Development Council: 115
Waccamaw River: 166
Wadboo Barony: 68,335
Waddell family: 211
Waddell, Gene: xiii,192,338
Waddell, Moses: 43,346
Waddill family: 225
Waddle family: 211,371
Wade, Earl W.: 5,185
Wade family: 218,234,295
Wade, Forest C.: 192
Wade, Lottie F.: 290
Wade, Mary Hatton: 218
Wade Ophelia R.: 290
Wade private burying ground:373
Wade, Zachary: 218
Wadlington family: 211
Wadmalaw Island: 30,81,108,125,
152,386,387,388
Wadmalaw Island Presbyteritan
Church: 30
Wadmalaw Island, SC: 417
Wagener, SC: 132
Waggoner family: 209,248,291
Waggoner, Hans: 291
Waggoner, John G.: 291
Wagner family: 209,284
Wagner, SC: 142,382
Wagner Southern Baptist
Church: 382
Wahee M.E. Church, South: 402
Waight family: 284,285
Wait, Jane: 291
Waites family: 284,311
Wakefield family: 222
Wakelyn, Jon L.: 338
Waldo family: 282
Waldrop family: 268
Wales: 237,238,253
Walhalla Centennial Committee:
115
Walhalla Chechee cemetery: 42
Walhalla M.E. Church, South:405
Walhalla Presbyterian Church:
172,180
Walhalla, SC: 16,56,81,99,115,
142,170,183,405
Walker, Alice A.: 291
Walker, Anne K.: 291
Walker, Cornelius I.: 43,115
Walker, Eloise Wingo: 213
Walker, Emmeline D.: 291

Walker, Evans & Cogswell: 4,
94,115
Walker family: 209,227,236,250,
252,261,262,284,291
Walker, George: 236
Walker, George E.: 115
Walker, Jon L.: 199
Walker, Joseph R.: 291
Walker, Joseph Rogers, D.D.:377
Walker, Mrs. L.W.: 213
Walker, Legare: 116,291
Walker, Lucile G.: 291
Walker Memorial C.M.E. Church:
408
Walker, O.K.: 116
Walker, William E.: 338
Walkins, Louise: 181
Wall family: 209,284,291
Wall, W.O.: 378
Wall, Mrs. W.O.: 378
Wallace, D.D.: 24,350
Wallace, David D.: 116,181
Wallace, David Duncan: 362
Wallace, Elizabeth Woods: 291
Wallace family: 211,271,291
Wallace, George S.: 291
Wallace, James A.: 181
Wallace, James B.: 72,116
Wallace, John S.: 116
Wallace, Nettie S.: 291
Wallace, Peter: 291
Wallace, Sarah Agnes: 338
Wallbank family: 285
Waller family: 209,234,291
Waller graveyard: 29
Wallingford Presbyterian Church:
386
Walloons: 361
Walls family: 264
Walls, William J.: 181
Walnut Grove Baptist Church:
150,168,181,395,406
Walnut Grove Baptist Church
cemetery: 43
Walnut Grove Negro Baptist
Church: 382
Walnut Grove Plantation
cemetery: 312
Walnut Hill: 287
Walnut Hill Baptist Church:409
Walnut Hill Farm: 111
Walpole family: 282,284
Walsh: 43
Walsh, Richard: 116,338,350
Walsh, Thomas T.: 181
Walsh, Walter Richard: 338
Walsh's Anderson City & County
Directory: 43
Walsh's Charleston City Direc-
tory: 43
Walter family: 283,284
Walter, Margaret C.: 181
Walter, Thomas: 229
Walterboro Baptist Church: 390
Walterboro Jewish Congregation:
390
Walterboro, SC: 16,108,390
Walters family: 211,284
Waltham family: 220
Walton, Mrs. E.M.: 213
Walton family: 209
Walton, L.: 213
Wambaw Church: 419
Wampee M.E. Church, South: 397
Wampee, SC: 397
Wands, Beatrice: 213
Wands, Mrs. Burton: 213
Wanger family: 239
Wannamaker Baptist Church: 397
Wannamaker cemetery: 373
Wannamaker, David: 373
Wannamaker family: 291
Wannamaker, John S.: 291
Wannamaker, W.W.: 116

Wannamaker, William J.: 116
Wansley, Reba: 116
Want, Leroy M.: 181
Wappetaw Independent or Con-
gregational Church: 175,320,
325
Wappoo: 74,335
War Between the States: see
Civil War
War of 1812 (see also SC Mili-
tary Units): 17,38,87,93,348,
366,371
War of Independence: 312
War of Northern Aggression:
see Civil War
War of Secession (see also
Civil War): 306,339
Ward Baptist Church: 408
Ward, Carolyn P.: 11
Ward, Ebin J.: 291
Ward family: 211,245,284,285,
291
Ward, Josiah: 291
Ward, SC: 164,408
Ward, William: 291
Wardlaw family: 209,268,291
Wardlaw, Frank H.: 199
Wardlaw, Joseph G.: 291
Ware, Charles C.: 181
Ware family: 288,293
Ware, Dr. Lowry P.: xiii,350
Ware Shoals Baptist Church:395
Ware Shoals M.E. Church,
South: 395
Ware Shoals, SC: 395,400
Warfield family: 215
Waring, Alice Noble: 338,362
Waring Chapel Negro Baptist:405
Waring family: 221,284,285,339
Waring, Joseph I.: 116,181
Waring, Joseph Ioor: 307,339,
362
Waring, T.R.: 307
Warley family: 209,284
Warlick, Hal C.: 181
Warnard family: 216
Warner family: 226
Warnock family: 211,218,285,
289
Warr, Mrs. O.L.: 181
Warr, Osta L.: 116
Warren Chapel C.M.E. Church:
400
Warren family: 211,285
Warren, J.L.: 117
Warren, Mary B.: 43
Warren, Mary Bondurant: 363
Warrenton Presbyterian Church:
382
Warrenville, SC: 142,152,382
Warrior Creek Baptist Church:
399
Warrior's Chapel A.M.E. Zion
Church: 399
Warrior's Creek Baptist Church:
43,419
Washburn family: 234
Washington Avenue Baptist
Church: 181,394
Washington Baptist Church:
149,173
Washington District: 380
Washington District. Court
of Equity: 369
Washington, D.C.: 64
Washington family: 211,231,
251,265
Washington, George: 338,351
Washington, President George:
102
Washington Light Infantry: 71,
73,96,117,322
Washington Light Infantry
Monument: 297,306

494

Wohltman, John: 308
Wolf Pond Baptist Church: 388
Wolfe family: 209,295
Wolfe, Frank W.: 295
Wolfe, James Russell Daniel,
  Sr.: 295
Wolfe, John Harold: 350
Wolfe, W.M.: 183
Wolfe, William C.: 295
Wolfton, SC: 406
Wolling family: 295
Womack family: 252
Womack, Helen R.: 295
Womack, Mildred C.: 295
Woman's Memorial Evangelical
  Lutheran Church: 408
Womeck family: 242
Women's Association for Improve-
  ment of Rural Schools in SC:
  119
Women's Christian Temperance
  Union: 92
Women's Missionary Society:
  196
Women's Missionary Union: 122,
  161
Wood, Christine: 295
Wood, E.J.: 119
Wood family: 203,209,215,216,
  258,295
Wood family cemetery: 33
Wood, J. Wilbert: 295
Wood, Marie S.: 295
Wood, Peter H.: 195
Wood, Rev. Raymond D.: 362
Wood, Robert C.: 183
Wood, William: 295
Wood, Willie M.: 295
Woodal family: 295
Woodard, Janet H.: 12
Woodberry family: 209,284
Woodbridge family: 224
Woodburn family: 295
Woodburn, James A.: 295
Woodbury family: 272,284
Woodfields Baptist Church: 153
Woodfin Baptist Church: 407
Woodford family: 219
Woodford, SC: 94,405
Woodham family: 284
Woodham, Martha A.: 4
Woodmason, Charles: 120,322
Woodrow Memorial Presbyterian
  Church: 44
Woodruff A.R.P. Church: 410
Woodruff, Caldwell: 295
Woodruff family: 209
Woodruff First M.E. Church,
  South: 410
Woodruff First Southern
  Baptist Church: 410
Woodruff Presbyterian Church:
  410
Woodruff, SC: 80,143,152,410
Woods, Elizabeth: 291
Woods family: 203,209,223,232,
  233,281
Woods, Gary D.: 295
Woods, W.D.: 183
Woodside Baptist Church: 394
Woodside M.E. Church, South:
  394
Woodson family: 209
Woodson, Hortense: 42,61,120,
  183,295
Woodson Thesis: 319
Woodward family: 209,283,285,
  291
Woodward family cemetery: 375
Woodward, Dr. Henry: 217,310
Woodward, J. Herbert: 184
Woody, Robert H.: 4,104,350
Woofter, Thomas J.: 195

Wooley family: 211
Wooley, James E.: 44
Woolfolk family: 223
Woolley, John B.: 295
Woolson, Constance Fenimore:
  218
Woolson family: 218
Wooster, Ralph: 342
Wootten, Bayard M.: 120
Workman M.E. Church, South:
  413
Workman, SC: 413
Workman family: 209,293
Workman, W.D., Jr.: 120
World War I (see also SC
  Military Units): 34,38,78,
  120,361
World War II (see also SC
  Military Units): 34,38,49
Worley family: 209,245
Wormeley family: 243
Worrty family: 211
Worthington family: 259
Worthy family: 209,221
Worthy, Pauline M.: 295
Work Projects Administration
  (abbreviated W.P.A.): 44,45,
  46,47,184,373
W.P.A. Federal Writers Project:
  120,199
W.P.A. Federal Writers Project.
  Spartanburg Unit: 120
W.P.A. Historical Records
  Survey: 4,6
W.P.A. Inventory of Church
  Archives: 381
Wragg family: 284,285,335
Wragg, Joseph: 331
Wragg, William T.: 308
Wren family: 209
Wrench family: 282
Wrens M.E. Church, South: 387
"Wrestlin Jacob": 132
Wright, Anne M.: 295
Wright, Cynthia Rebecca Jones:
  296
Wright, David McCord: 342
Wright, E. Baskin: 350
Wright family: 211,222,254,
  259,284,285,295,296
Wright, Florence E.: 255
Wright, James Wilson: 296
Wright, Louis B.: 121
Wright, Marion A.: 350
Wright, Nathalia: 342
Wright, Russell: 121
Wyatt Bible: 209
Wyatt coat-of-arms: 209
Wyatt, Dr. Ed: 209
Wyatt, Elijah: 209
Wyatt, Eugene: 209
Wyatt family: 208,209,242,284
Wyatt, James Foster: 209
Wyatt, Mrs. John W.: 209
Wyatt, Lillian R.: 296
Wyatt, Redmond G.: 209
Wyatt reunion: 204
Wyatt, Tula Townsend: 213
Wyatt, Mrs. W.A.: 213
Wyatt, Major William: 209
Wylie family: 246,271,293,296
Wylly family: 224,284
Wyman family: 271
Wynes, Charles E.: 342
Wynne, Edward W.: 308
Wyrich family: 209
Wyrick family: 209,296
Wyse family: 296
Wyse, Frederick C.: 296

- X -

XYZ Mission: 325

- Y -

Yancey, William L.: 350
Yarborough, Ann: 5
Yarborough, Charles D.: 213
Yarborough family: 209
Yarborough, Mattie J.: 184
Yarborough Methodist Protestant
  Chapel: 410
Yates, Adlai Robin: 213
Yates, Edward M.: 296
Yates family: 205,243,284,296
Yates, Gladys Collins: 213
Yates, William: 296
Yates, William B.: 121
Yeadon, Richard: 184,296,347,
  359
Yeamans family: 284,296
Yeamans Hall: 373,374
Yeamans Hall burying ground:318
Yeaman's Hall Club: 121
Yeldell families: 209
Yemassee, SC: 41,331,337,395
Yemassee Indians: 323
Yemassee War (see also Indian
  War of 1715): 83,298
Yeo, Cedric A.: 362
Yerkes family: 257
Yonce family: 209
Yonge, Francis: 121
Yongue family: 229,233,284
York A.R.P. Church: 413
York County: 22,29,30,33,40,43,
  57,69,71,76,90,104,108,118,124,
  125,126,130,136,146,165,174,
  196,216,219,223,236,247,248,
  252,266,268,275,289,290,291,
  293,371,376,380,413,415,416
York County. Clerk of Court:
  14,47
York County. Commissioner of
  Roads: 47
York County Multiethnic Heri-
  tage Project: 5
York District: 14,24,47,79,293,
  367
York District Bible Society:372
York family: 209
York First Baptist Church: 413
York, SC: 22,92,121,135,138,142,
  143,148,178,371,413,414
Yorkville Compiler: 25,341
Yorkville Enquirer: 25
Yorkville Female College: 18
Yorkville Miscellany: 25
Yorkville Pioneer: 25
Yorkville, SC: 10,143,166
Yorkville Weekly Advertiser:341
Youmans, LeRoy F.: 308
Youn family: 365
Young, Abram Hayne: 312
Young, Emory F.: 184
Young family: 209,251,252,254,
  284,296
Young, Marjorie W.: 199
Young Memorial Associate
  Reformed Presbyterian Church:
  166
Young Men's Christian Associa-
  tion: 120,121,409
Young Mt. Zion Negro Baptist
  Church: 408
Young, Pauline: 19,47,208,213,
  296
Young, Rogers W.: 342
Young, Major Thomas: 120,370
Young, Thomas J.: 184
Young, William Gourdin: 330
Young Women's Christian Asso-
  ciation, Greenville: 105
Youngblood family: 296
Youngblood, Georgia K.: 296

Younge family: 284
Young's Negro Baptist Chapel:
395
Yutzey family: 211

- Z -

Zahniser, Marvin R.: 342,343
Zamba (slave): 195
Zeigler family: 211
Zeigler, John A.: 121,296
Zimmerman family: 259
Zimmerman, Laura: 184
Zimmerman, Samuel C.: 195
Zink family: 296
Zink, Phillip: 296
Zink, Robert L.: 296
Zinn family: 209
Zion A.M.E. Church: 385,388
Zion Baptist Church: 390,409
Zion Benevolent Negro Baptist
  Church: 406
Zion Canaan Negro Baptist
  Church: 407
Zion - Carolina Holiness Church
  (Negro): 403
Zion Church: 287
Zion Fair Negro Baptist Church:
  395
Zion Fire Baptized Holiness
  Church of God of America (Ne-
  gro): 382
Zion Hill Apostolic Faith
  Church: 402
Zion Hill Baptist Church: 409
Zion Hill Baptist Church (Ne-
  gro): 400
Zion Hill Church: 398
Zion Hill Negro Baptist Church:
  382,388,409
Zion Holiness Church (Negro):
  401
Zion Hopewell Negro Baptist
  Church: 401
Zion Lutheran Church: 370,419
Zion M.E. Church, South: 383,
  391,392,397,399,403,404,407,
  410
Zion Methodist Church: 130
Zion Negro Baptist Church: 406,
  407
Zion Negro M.E. Church: 385
Zion-Olivet Presbyterian Church:
  184
Zion Pilgrim Baptist Church
  (Negro): 398,399,407
Zion Presbyterian Church: 47,
  180
Zion Presbyterian Church (Ne-
  gro): 386
Zion Protestant Episcopal
  Church: 407
Zion, SC: 403
Zion Temple Pentecostal Holi-
  ness Church: 393
Zion United Lutheran Church:
  401
Zoan Baptist Church: 397
Zoar M.E. Church, South: 388,
  408,411
Zoar Methodist Church: 388
Zorn family: 262
Zornow, William Frank: 343
Zubly cemetery: 363
Zubly family: 211

* * * * *

Addenda to Index

Baker, Pearl M.: xiii
Brandes, Diane M.: xiv
First Church of Christ (Discip-
  les of Christ): 394
Mapp family: 207
McKoy family: 210
New Home No. 2 Baptist Church:
  396
Pleasant Meadow Baptist
  Church: 396
Poplar Springs, SC: 416
Shiloh A.R.P. Church: 19,399
Shuler, Beverly S.: xiii
Stokes, Dr. Alan: xiii
Traut family: 290